ARNA BONTEMPS–
LANGSTON HUGHES
LETTERS

1925–1967

Arna Bontemps and Langston Hughes

ARNA BONTEMPS-
LANGSTON HUGHES
LETTERS

1925–1967

Selected and Edited by Charles H. Nichols

DODD, MEAD & COMPANY · NEW YORK

1   2   3   4   5   6   7   8   9   10

Library of Congress Cataloging in Publication Data

Bontemps, Arna Wendell, 1902–1973.
Arna Bontemps–Langston Hughes letters, 1925–1967.

Includes index.
1. Bontemps, Arna Wendell, 1902–1973—Correspondence.
2. Hughes, Langston, 1902–1967—Correspondence.
3. Afro-American authors—Correspondence. 4. Authors,
American—20th century—Correspondence. I. Hughes,
Langston, 1902–1967, joint author. II. Nichols, Charles Harold.
PS3503.0474Z486 1979   816'.5'208   79–17341
ISBN 0–396–07687–4

FOR MILDRED THOMPSON NICHOLS

ACKNOWLEDGMENTS

I am deeply indebted to Arna Bontemps, who preserved and assembled many of these letters after the death of Langston Hughes. I would like to thank Alex Bontemps; George Bass; Allen Klots of Dodd, Mead & Company; and George Cunningham of the James Weldon Johnson Collection at Yale University for invaluable assistance in the editing of these letters. Useful information and ideas came from R. Baxter Miller, Richard Barksdale and Therman O'Daniel, whose writings on Langston Hughes are among the most perceptive available. I am also grateful for the cooperation of the librarians of Brown University, Yale University and Syracuse University. I am indebted, too, for the secretarial assistance of Winifred Bell.

Charles H. Nichols
Brown University

PREFACE

Between 1925 and 1967 Langston Hughes and Arna Bontemps exchanged about 2300 letters. I have selected perhaps 500 of the most interesting and significant. The criteria used in choosing these letters for publication are discussed in more detail in the prologue. Briefly, those letters are selected which

(1) reveal interesting aspects of the personality of the writer;

(2) record significant literary activity or growth, e.g., stories, plays, poetry or novels planned;

(3) present literary criticism or estimates of their work and the works of contemporaries;

(4) show the breadth or depth of the writer's concept of the writer's responsibility to his readers, his audience or to society;

(5) record significant developments in race relations in the United States and abroad;

(6) give us fresh insights into literary, social or world events.

CONTENTS

PROLOGUE

"The past is prologue"

Reflecting on the recurrent struggles against oppression and toward self-realization in our history, Arna Bontemps wrote, "Time is not a river; it's a pendulum." To him the experience of the slave, Gabriel Prosser, in 1800 (of whom Bontemps wrote in *Black Thunder*) bore a striking resemblance to the fate of the Scottsboro boys in 1931. The documents here collected are concerned with the struggle for full freedom and equality of opportunity, the interaction of Afro-American culture and western history. The dialectic of the freedman's fight for his humanity is given concrete expression in the careers of Langston Hughes and Arna Bontemps. This book is a selection of the letters they exchanged over a period of about forty years—a few in the years 1925 and 1926, a large number from 1931 to 1967. What stands out in their correspondence is the firmness of their commitment to African and Afro-American culture throughout the world, the creation of a vital and productive art among Negroes, the effort to fulfill the splendid promise of an often-despised minority. This sense of mission obsessed them both and drew them into a lasting bond of mutual interests and deep affection. Like virtually all the middle-class Negroes of their time, both struggled with what Du Bois saw so clearly: "this double consciousness, this sense of always looking at one's self through the eyes of others, of measuring one's soul by the tape of a world that looks on in amused contempt and pity. . . ."[1] As Bontemps himself said, "In their opposing attitudes toward their roots . . . every educated American Negro must somehow take sides."[2] Both Hughes and Bontemps were the sons of ambitious, middle-class men, men disdainful of the Afro-American folk heritage—its music, literature and art. Arna Bontemps was dispatched to a white boarding school during his high school years. "Now don't go up there acting colored," his father admonished him (although, of course, as Bontemps observed sardonically, "white people have been enjoying acting like Negroes for more than a hundred years.") Langston Hughes's father, a lawyer, acquired property and status in Mexico and hoped his son would turn his back on the United States entirely.

The lives of Hughes and Bontemps were, of course, unique—yet they are representative. In speaking of this correspondence Arna Bontemps wrote his publisher in 1969: "All told I am convinced we have the fullest documentation of the Afro-American experience in the new world, artistic, intellectual, covering the mid-20th century, one is likely to find anywhere. The immediate response of two writers to events and conditions that touched their careers."[3]

1. *Souls of Black Folk*, pp. 16–17.
2. *The Old South*, p. 11.
3. To Allen Klots, 7/1/69.

1

What is the nature of that experience and how is it documented here in these voluminous letters? The selected letters are presented chronologically. The first section, covering essentially the years from 1925 to 1941, gives us insights into the identity of each writer, his effort to learn his craft, to experiment, to gain an audience. It is a vivid revelation of the struggle of the black writer for the essentials of his art and for the recognition and rewards which he needs to sustain him. The second section, including letters written from 1941 to 1959, makes us aware that they have achieved some degree of artistic success, for they are well-known authors, yet find themselves increasingly involved in the social and racial conflict of a turbulent world—a world of conflicting ideologies, a world at war. Between 1959 and 1967 they are reacting to the civil rights revolution of the 1960s and to the revival of interest in African-American culture. They are in touch with writers all over the world and strong in their support of a dynamic cultural heritage which they helped to create.

In dealing with the identity of Arna Bontemps and Langston Hughes we can learn something by examining their relations to their parents and the experiences of their youth. It would be a mistake, however, not to see the enormous influence of the socioeconomic and racial relations of the black population in America during their formative years. Both men were born in 1902. Arna Bontemps was born in Louisiana, the son of a strong-willed, austere man, a brick mason and later a lay minister in the Seventh Day Adventist Church. His mother died while he was rather young, and he lived for a time with his grandmother. The family moved to California and joined that group of fundamentalist Christians—with their Hebraic theology and otherworldly outlook—the Seventh Day Adventists. But young Arna was strongly affected, too, by the life of his grandmother's younger brother, Joe Ward ("Uncle Buddy"), about whose love of wine, women, song, money and horses, Bontemps wrote so vividly in *God Sends Sunday.* Indeed there is so much life in Uncle Buddy that his image went through numerous performances of *St. Louis Woman* and some of Bontemps' most moving short stories.

Having graduated from San Fernando Academy, an Adventist private high school, and Pacific Union College, Arna Bontemps found his personal dilemma in "the opposing attitudes toward my roots" of his father and his great uncle. The latter "embraced the riches of the folk heritage" with all its spontaneity, music, joy and original creative force. The former was dogged by the group's memory of their recent emancipation and the challenge to fulfill the moral and intellectual assumptions of western humanism. Arna Bontemps was ever somewhat ambivalent about the two worlds. Yet he well knew that his original contribution lay in what he was to make of the Afro-American experience, its ineffable sadness, its bursts of joy. He knew the creative power of generations of African folk expression. ". . . What did one do," he wrote, "after concluding that for him a break with the past and shedding of his Negroness were not only impossible but unthinkable? First, perhaps he went to New York in the twenties, met young Negro writers and intellectuals who were similarly searching, learned poems like Claude McKay's 'Harlem Dancer' and Jean Toomer's 'Song of the Son', started writing and publishing in this vein himself . . ."[4] So Arna Bontemps went to Harlem—the Mecca of the black world in 1924.

It was a heady atmosphere with all the vital currents of New York City

4. *The Old South,* p. 12.

bombarding his senses: the throngs jostling one in the streets, the theater, the universities, the clubs, the shops, the publishers and the literary coteries. As one European visitor put it: "To be in London is to confront London; to be in Paris is to meet Paris; but to be in *New York* is to confront the world!" In Harlem, Bontemps exclaimed: "We were heralds of a dawning day."[5] Carl Van Doren, addressing the black literati, expressed the striving of the American artist, poet and critic for a final end to our cultural colonialism, and the "lost generation" as well as the Harlem writers took it up: "Once they find a voice, they will bring a fresh and fierce sense of reality to their vision of human life on this continent, a vision seen from a novel angle by a part of the population which cannot be duped by the bland optimism of the majority. What American literature needs at the moment is color, music, gusto, the free expression of gay or desperate moods."[6] Other views of the meaning of the Harlem cultural scene abounded, as in Carl Van Vechten's *Nigger Heaven* or Wallace Thurman's satiric and bitter *Infants of the Spring.* Characteristically, Hughes in *The Big Sea* and Bontemps in the *Harlem Renaissance Remembered* present the Harlem of the 1920s with more restraint and objectivity. In any case, the visit to Harlem was the culmination of Bontemps's apprenticeship as a writer.

He had begun imaginative writing in school. After his graduation from college he worked nights in the post office (where he got to know Wallace Thurman) and read the current literature voraciously during the day. His first poems he sent to Jessie Fauset, the literary editor of *Crisis* magazine. When he got to New York, he quickly found his way among the literati and made lasting friendships with Langston Hughes, Countee Cullen, Claude McKay, Rudolph Fisher and others. Charles S. Johnson, editor of *Opportunity: A Journal of Negro Life,* gave a "coming out party" for such black authors and intellectuals as Walter White, Eric Walrond, Jessie Fauset, Gwendolyn Bennett, Alain Locke, W.E.B. Du Bois, James Weldon Johnson and others. In fact Charles S. Johnson, who presided over the "rebirth" like a midwife or an impressario, also brought young writers in contact with such literary pundits and editors as Carl Van Doren of *Century,* Frederick Allen of *Harper's,* William Bartlett of *Scribner's,* Freda Kirschwey of the *Nation* and Paul Kellogg of *Survey.* Later in 1925 Vachel Lindsay, whom Hughes met while working as a busboy in a Washington hotel, introduced Langston Hughes, the poet, to one of his larger audiences.

The vitality of the Harlem cultural scene drew people from all parts of the country as well as from the Caribbean, Africa and Europe. On Broadway the black musical comedy *Shuffle Along* was the talk of the town. Numerous clubs entertained enthusiastic audiences night after night with jazz music and poetry readings. Sympathetic patrons lent their support to struggling young authors. Langston Hughes's first published poem, "The Negro Speaks of Rivers "(1921) became the harbinger of what was to come.

Late in 1924 Bontemps met Hughes. They were together in 1925 and 1926 at gatherings of their friends and acquaintances. Bontemps recalls hearing Langston Hughes's reading of his poems at a tearoom near Columbia University in 1925. Bontemps was deeply impressed by Hughes's naturalness, ease and spontaneity and by his use of blues and jazz idiom. He found himself quoting Hughes's words from the *Nation* (1926)—words which expressed his own convictions so well:

5. Introduction to *Personals.*
6. *Harlem Renaissance Remembered,* pp. 13–14.

3

We younger Negro artists who write now intend to express our individual dark skinned selves without fear or shame. If white people are pleased, we are glad. If they are not, it doesn't matter. We know we are beautiful. And ugly too. The tom-tom cries and the tom-tom laughs. If colored people are pleased we are glad. If not, their displeasure doesn't matter either. We build our temples for tomorrow, strong as we know how, and we stand on top of the mountain free within ourselves.

Arna Bontemps was well aware of the contributions of the earlier generation of black writers—Paul Laurence Dunbar, Charles W. Chesnutt, James Weldon Johnson and that formidable group of teachers and social critics—Alain Locke, Charles S. Johnson, William S. Braithwaite, Carter Woodson and W.E.B. Du Bois. Bontemps was liberally educated in western literature and alert to the literary stirrings of postwar America. The extraordinary flowering of poetry, novel and even the drama from Whitman and Mark Twain and Emily Dickinson to the Imagists—Pound, Eliot, Vachel Lindsay, Sandburg, Frost, Faulkner, Hemingway, Fitzgerald and Eugene O'Neill—was a world Bontemps knew very well indeed. Bontemps had struggled with the hostility of the Seventh Day Adventists to fiction. For them, only the Second Coming mattered. Arna Bontemps's hunger for literature was the more intense because he had been denied it in Adventist schools. No Negro author of the Harlem Renaissance read the "little magazines"[7] more religiously than he. It is not surprising that he should have gone on to a degree in library science and to become the librarian of Fisk University in 1943. No doubt his learning enriched his creative work, but there is nothing derivative or "second hand" about his exquisite early poetry, the tough folk endurance, the militancy and power of his novels.

Like Langston Hughes, Claude McKay, Eric Walrond and Zora Neale Hurston, Arna Bontemps sought the source and shape of his creative work in his own roots—the deep South of Louisiana and Alabama. The stark, laconic, poignant stories he wrote in the early 1930s are in the realistic mode of American regionalism. Bontemps's method recalls not only Chesnutt and Dunbar, but also Stephen Crane, Willa Cather and Joseph Hergesheimer. Stories like "Lonesome Boy, Silver Trumpet" and "A Summer Tragedy" evoke with warmth and humanity the South that few writers were portraying in 1930. *God Sends Sunday* (1931) brings to life his Uncle Buddy in the jockey, Little Augie, and the world of sporting men and racehorses. Although Bontemps, like Hughes, never faltered in his devotion to the Negro peasant, the man in the street, the broad masses of the oppressed and despised poor, the fact is both, as I have pointed out, were products of the middle class, educated and self-conscious race leaders, of mixed and distinguished ancestry. It should be observed, however, that each of the men bore a special, marginal relation to the black middle class. Hughes's work sometimes met with their censure. And Arna Bontemps moved deftly among a three-layered society—the black masses, the Creole society of Louisiana and the larger white world. In spite of the joblessness and desperation they faced during the Great Depression, they nevertheless endured and produced.

No doubt financial exigency led Arna Bontemps (he was now married to Alberta Johnson, who had been his student at Harlem Academy, and the father of two children) to accept a job teaching at Oakwood School, a Seventh Day

---

7. *Poetry, The Smart Set,* etc.

Adventist junior college in Huntsville, Alabama. An all-black parochial institution . . . it smothered rather than broadened its students and faculty. It was the time of the Scottsboro boys: nine Negro teenagers had been arrested on a freight train and charged with the rape of two white women. The racial tensions of rural Alabama were heightened, for it was an era when the penalty for rape (where black men were involved) was death—by a mob or by the state. The case against the Scottsboro nine was flimsy indeed, and civil rights groups all over America made the case a *cause célèbre*. Langston Hughes himself came to Alabama to interview the Scottsboro defendants and stopped off to see Bontemps in Huntsville. The white principal of the school was alarmed. Black students became more intractable. Bontemps was interested in slave narratives and in the rebellions which later suggested his novels, *Drums at Dusk* and *Black Thunder*. His wide-ranging contacts and liberal spirit were regarded with suspicion. His association with Langston Hughes, Bontemps says, "was anathema to the institution which had with some admitted reluctance, given me employment."[8] He was accused by the administration of subverting Oakwood School with racial ideas and ordered to burn all his books. There was no alternative but to resign. Bontemps bought an old Ford and moved with his wife and children to his father's home in California where he finished his book in cramped quarters. From California they went to Chicago, still living a hand-to-mouth existence. "We had fled from the jungle of Alabama's Scottsboro area to the jungle of Chicago's crime-ridden South Side, and one was as terrifying as the other."[9] By 1932 the "Renaissance" was devoured by the Great Depression.

It is difficult for young people hastening toward the twenty-first century to visualize the life of men like Hughes and Bontemps in the 1930s. They survived by giving talks and readings to schools, clubs, fraternities (for as little as $25.00 each) all over the country, traveling in a dilapidated Ford. Everywhere they encountered segregation and discrimination, insult and rebuff. Meanwhile they wrote and published diligently—newspaper and magazine articles, lyrics for songs, musicals for the theater and what-not. They collaborated on a successful children's book about Haiti, *Popo and Fifina,* published in 1932. Their productivity is astonishing. The black writer's effort to learn his craft, to find an outlet, to gain recognition and understanding is a time-worn and familiar tale. The hostility of American society to Afro-Americans, the legal and extra-legal forms of racism, the denial of the most commonplace human rights can only fill an impartial observer with rage and dismay. They protested. They joined the civil rights efforts of the NAACP and other groups. They were accused of being communists. But in their lives and in their work they created new images of the realities of black life. Moreover they remained throughout their lives gentle men. They would not stoop to anger or recrimination, and nothing could deflect them from their larger purpose: to bring to fruition the promise of Afro-American art in a humane society. As Howard Thurman used to say, they knew "they had to affirm the SELF in an environment that would reduce them to zero." There were better times ahead. In 1932 Bontemps was appointed to the Illinois Writers Project. In 1933 Hughes was invited "to assist in the preparation of a Negro motion picture to be made in Moscow." Upon his arrival in Moscow, Hughes found the planned film a caricature and refused to make it.

8. *Black Thunder,* p. xiv.
9. *Old South,* p. 18.

The austerity and dedicated moral purpose of the parents of Bontemps and Hughes and of the generation which taught them is not difficult to explain. One generation removed from bondage, they felt the obligation to prove that Africans were not only educable but capable of high culture. In 1902 when Hughes and Bontemps were born, African-Americans were disfranchised in virtually all the southern states, subject to peonage and intimidation (often by officers of the law) and everywhere segregated, vilified and discriminated against. The idea of the innate and biological inferiority of the Negro race was rarely challenged even by "enlightened" liberals. The brave manifestoes of The Niagara Movement, The Amenia Conference and The National Association for the Advancement of Colored People set out to remove mountains of prejudice at a time when business and government leaders often boasted that they would keep the Negro in his place. Lynching was commonplace and condoned and rarely investigated. A president like Woodrow Wilson, who set out "to make the world safe for democracy" established by executive decision segregation in governmental agencies in Washington. Booker T. Washington felt there was little use in trying to achieve full citizenship rights, and Du Bois, who refused to ignore the moral issues and foresaw the coming conflict over color and democracy, was regarded as a visionary.

But the "young Turks" of the Harlem Renaissance, like Bontemps, Hughes, Claude McKay, Wallace Thurman and others, were not much inclined to conciliate the bigots and the vested interests of what Du Bois called "the land of the thief and the home of the slave." For after World War I the peoples of African descent achieved a new identity, a more militant social philosophy, a new dignity born of suffering and a sharp vision of their own possibilities. The Black Nationalism of Marcus Garvey, the Marxism of McKay, the militancy and intellectual power of W.E.B. Du Bois, the pan-African movement—indeed the *self-discovery* of blacks—created the extraordinary élan and productivity of the Harlem Renaissance. The renaissance was, perhaps, short lived, but its afterglow lingered in the west.

What manner of man, what sort of writer, then, was Arna Bontemps? He appears behind his imaginative work and in the forefront of these letters in several personae. As Kenneth Burke says, however, a writer may assume any number of disguises; but in the depths of his imagery he cannot lie. "It is my conviction that we are nearest to the center of the essential Bontemps in his poetry. We can grasp his longings for Afro-Americans in his most memorable characters: Gabriel Prosser, Frederick Douglass, Lil' Augie and the others. Arna Bontemps achieved an aesthetic distance, a mastery of form, an empathy for the disinherited which rested at bottom on an old-fashioned kind of *character,* a structured value system which could "see a world in a grain of sand" and "heaven in a wild flower." He can appreciate the natural beauty of rural Alabama even while he is threatened by the violence and barbarism of that cultural wasteland in which he had to function. The toughness, balance, unswerving purpose and gentle civility of the man rests on the security of his self-image and the stability of his early family life. It is not too much to say that Bontemps achieved the substance of that *noblesse,* that chivalric gentility of which southerners boasted but understood so little. Small wonder that he recaptures the eighteenth-century atmosphere so vividly in *Black Thunder.*

The facts seem to be that Arna Bontemps—though reared by a proud and demanding father after the early death of his mother—nevertheless found himself

6

among a larger family which loved and cherished him. He learned from his grandmother how to meet the inevitable "slings and arrows of outrageous fortune." There is, however, a certain nostalgia, a regretful backward glance at a lost youth, in many of his stories. His "Sad-Faced Boy," his "Lonesome Boy," his "Hopper-Grass Man" seem to reveal his own childhood longings. His poetry (gathered in the slender volume *Personals*) radiates an almost Wordsworthian sense of wonder—the freedom, joy and love of a beholden soul in the face of the awesome infinity of the universe. This quality informs his verse and gives substance to his stories. He sums it up with simplicity and profound insight in "Miracles":

> Doubt no longer miracles,
> This spring day makes it plain
> A man may crumble into dust
> And straightway live again.
> A jug of water in the sun
> Will easy turn to wine
> If love is stopping at the well
> And love's brown arms entwine.
> And you who think him only man,
> I tell you faithfully
> That I have seen Christ clothed in rain
> Walking on the sea.

There are other, better-known personae of Bontemps—the scholar, the teacher, the father and husband, the friend and counsellor, even the role of the stereotyped "cullud" man who uses bad grammar and phonetic spelling. He is a sensitive and perceptive literary critic—always judicious, sane and kind—yet objective and candid. He is not impressed by the power and prestige of the Southern Agrarians or the New Critics with their pretentious, formalistic, arcane learning and reactionary politics. He can see the tortured spirit of James Baldwin behind the bitch bravado and towering ego of his essays. When attacked by Walter White and others for allegedly perpetuating the demeaning stereotype of the peasant Negro in *St. Louis Woman,* he can refrain from responding to harsh remarks in the same spirit (in spite of the fact that he believed that the severity of these attacks had hastened the death of its lyricist, Countee Cullen). Bontemps has an eye, an ear, a feeling for what is vital in obscure persons and distant places, and he knows how to relate to white Americans, Frenchmen, Haitians, Africans and Japanese as well as he does to his own children. Perhaps more consistently than many better-known black leaders, he was the "keeper of the flame." He kept us aware of the valor of our past in *Drums at Dusk, Black Thunder* and *100 Years of Negro Freedom* (not to mention the monumental anthologies of poetry and folklore). He could recall for us the heartbreak of the uprooted in *They Seek a City.* He was active in carrying the Afro-American heritage to school children and in collecting documents, art and artifacts in libraries and museums not only at Fisk and Syracuse and Yale but throughout the land. Together with Langston Hughes and others, he contributed valuable books and art to the museums of African nations like Ghana.

Langston Hughes, an extraordinarily versatile author is better known throughout the world than Arna Bontemps. Yet the two men had a great deal in common. Bontemps tells of having visited the home of Countee Cullen's stepfather, who, upon seeing Bontemps, took him for Langston Hughes. For they strongly resembled each other in color, height, hair texture and in their invariably deferential manner. They were often mistaken for one another and each insisted jokingly he was slimmer than the other. As they collaborated in their books and appeared together on lecture platforms Bontemps seemed to the casual observer almost to be Hughes's alter ego. This impression is not consistent with the facts of their distinctive and separate personalities which emerge in their letters and other writings.

⊥ Langston Hughes is without rival as the most prolific and influential Afro-American writer in our history. Born in Joplin, Missouri on February 1, 1902, he grew up in Lawrence, Kansas and spent short periods in Topeka, Mexico City and Cleveland where he graduated from high school. His parents separated, and Hughes lived with his mother, his grandmother and an aunt except for a time in his adolescence when he lived with his father in Mexico. He was attracted by the wandering heroes of Afro-American folklore—the railroad men, jazz musicians and Pullman car porters. His father expected him to get a college education, but after one year at Columbia University he tossed his books into the sea and sailed as a common seaman on the *S.S. Malone* to Africa. He worked on other ships and at various odd jobs in Paris and other cities. Numerous trips across the continent, to Europe, the Soviet Union, Asia, Africa and the Caribbean followed. For throughout his life he was a frequent traveler. Yet during the 1920s he returned to finish his college education at Lincoln University and to settle in a Harlem townhouse, where he lived and wrote for the rest of his life. Hughes devoted himself to poetry, fiction, essays, song lyrics, plays, musicals, librettos for the theater, children's stories as well as histories, translations, anthologies and radio, television and Hollywood scripts.[10]

Both of Langston Hughes's parents were well educated, and his mother and grandmother introduced him to the wonderful world of books in his pre-school years. Elected the class poet in his Lincoln, Illinois grammar school class at 13, Langston was further encouraged by a sympathetic teacher in his high school class. He began to publish poems in the junior magazine of the NAACP, *The Brownie Book*. His best known poem, "The Negro Speaks of Rivers," appeared in the June 1921 issue of *Crisis* magazine, whose literary editor, Jessie Fauset, could recognize talent. The poem made Langston Hughes famous, and his first book of poems, *The Weary Blues* (1926), was hailed as evidence that the Harlem Renaissance had definitely arrived. With Countee Cullen and Claude McKay, Langston Hughes seemed to embody the independence, the challenge, the creative experimentation, the wider horizons of the new generation. Employing the rhythms, language and tone of the blues and jazz, the wild abandon, the hedonism, militancy and celebration of the common life made his work stirring and controversial. His social protest themes raised the cry of "communist sympathizer." The general tone and daring imagery of Hughes's next volume of poetry, *Fine Clothes to the Jew* (1927), "affronted and alienated an important segment of the black upper middle class."[11] For his vigorous attacks on injustice continued. Yet by the decade of the 1940s Langston Hughes had largely won over the black as well as the white reading public.

10. See Donald C. Dickinson's *Bio-Bibliography of Langston Hughes,* Twayne Series, 1967.
11. Barksdale, p. 4. In 1944 the University of North Carolina Press commissioned a book of essays by prominent Negroes entitled *What The Negro Wants* and then tried to withdraw from its contractual obligation to publish it. After some legal sparring, the University of North Carolina Press did issue the book (which its editor found too radical).

The emergence and development of Langston Hughes's identity as a man, a writer and an international personality is too complex for consideration in so limited a space as we have here. Suffice it to say his work continued with unflagging zeal and originality. In 1925 when he came to know Arna Bontemps he surely represented the vanguard of a cultural dynamic which could profit by the self-conscious art of his older contemporaries even while he broke new ground in poetry and fiction as well as drama. Hughes and Bontemps make clear their debt to Alain Locke, W.E.B. Du Bois, Paul Lawrence Dunbar, Charles S. Johnson and James Weldon Johnson even while they embrace the common life in forms which express the agony and longing of their people. In an interview with Walter Kerr, Langston Hughes referred to himself as "a documentary poet." "I kinda document the happenings of our time in relation to myself and my own people—and, of course, our democracy." His literary use of the spirituals, blues, and jazz was recognized early as a vital and original contribution. The experiences of Afro-Americans, Hughes observed, have produced the folklore—the language and feeling of black America. For Hughes the cultural isolation of Negroes even in urban areas produced the folk atmosphere. ". . . the people who are apart from the main stream of life develop certain ways of talking, certain social characteristics of their own, and in the case of the Negro, of course, although we have been free almost 100 years, we are not entirely, by any means, integrated into American democracy, and our big cities have their great Negro ghettoes and Harlem is one."[12] The French scholar Jean Wagner has summed up the achievement of Langston Hughes well in his study:

> Instinctively in perfect harmony with the temperament of the black masses in the huge cities of our day, and abetted by a lively sensibility that rarely overlooked the imponderables affecting the psychology of his fellows, he was uniquely successful in capturing every subtlety in the atavistic rhythms that characterized his race and marshalling them to express poetically some of the most significant moments of its life.[13]

No well-known personality of our time was more amiable than Langston Hughes. In his letters he expresses his concern for each sickness or death, each publication or performance of his friends. He wrote innumerable letters. Yet we find it difficult to know the inner life of the man. As a writer he adopted numerous personae. But who was *he* in essence? Caught in the hostility which separated his parents and forced to adjust to constantly changing households, Langston in childhood must have had his moments of anguish and uncertainty. There is something deeply personal in "Soul Gone Home": the conflict between the uncaring mother and her dead son. The loneliness of the character Sandy in his first novel, *Not Without Laughter,* is unmistakably autobiographical. A lifelong bachelor, Hughes's lyrics were inspired by a profound loneliness, a sense of the inevitable tragedy of human experience:

> Sometimes when I'm lonely,
> Don't know why
> Keep thinkin' I won't be lonely
> By and by.[14]

12. Telecast for Channel 2, 1963(?).
13. *Black Poets of the U.S.: from P.L. Dunbar to Langston Hughes,* p. 385.
14. "Hope," *Poems,* p. 35.

In writing Bontemps about his wayward god-child, Hughes sympathizes with the boy, admitting that as a child he, too, felt rejected. Even more poignant is the sense of long-suffering sadness which he evokes in "The Weary Blues." The isolation of spirit in the work of Langston Hughes has its source in the sad history of black Americans and creates the music, language and rhythm of ghetto life. But there is a deeply private sadness beyond that. Bontemps remarked on one occasion, "No one has enjoyed being a Negro as much as Langston Hughes." Of course there is joy in his songs, his gospel plays, his Simple stories, even in the blues. But the Hughes personality is, in spite of its joyful mask, alone in a hostile world. He can write with some bravado, yet with ambiguity:

> I play it cool
> And dig all jive
> That's the reason
> I stay alive. (1951)

The paradox of Hughes's sense of identity is that we fail to get really close to him precisely amid the sounds of music and the crowds of friends who throng him constantly. Even his autobiographies, *The Big Sea* and *I Wonder as I Wander*, though filled with events and details, are reticent about his genuine feelings, his experiences of love and sex, his candid estimate of his contemporaries. The personal revelation of the man, Langston Hughes, will not be found in these letters either. He rarely lowers the mask. There is no doubt that he and Bontemps loved and trusted each other completely, but they usually wrote (even to each other) with posterity in mind. As writers they were ever conscious of their audience. For the most part, they regard scandal and gossip as ungentlemanly and personal attacks as self-defeating.

The work of Langston Hughes and Arna Bontemps is a celebration of the triumphant creative spirit in Afro-American life. There is, however, an ambivalence, a kind of characteristic group self-doubt in the personae they sometimes adopt. Thus Hughes, who is fascinated by the theater and ever involved with it throughout his career in writing and producing his plays, vows in letter after letter that he will give up the theater and abandon the role of playwright. When he is hassled by black actors or inconsiderate neighbors he cannot resist the common put-down: "just like cullud." Both men refer to distinguished and Caucasian ancestry and comment on the color of their acquaintances. Hughes's god-son is as black as the night around him and a Senegalese is "dark, dark, DARK!" But the Bontemps children are "golden babies." The down-beat approach to race is often a part of their humor. Thus Hughes's dog runs away, and he comments in a letter to Bontemps: "That dog was last seen rounding the corner at 110th Street muttering: *'no more niggers'!*" Significantly Hughes was fascinated by the mulatto theme—a theme he treated in drama, poetry and fiction.

More characteristically, both receive and respect all kinds of people with sensitivity and appreciation. They stand firmly on principle and contribute mightily to the struggle for equality without ever losing the capacity for brotherhood or the ability to enlarge our understanding with grace and style. Langston Hughes got his world into clear focus at an early age: "Through my grandmother's stories always life moved, moved heroically toward an end. Nobody ever cried in my grandmother's stories . . . Something about my grandmother's stories . . . taught me the uselessness of crying about anything."[15] A facile writer, Hughes created characters and a world that seems at times obvious, natural and simplistic. But like Whitman, he enhances our love of humanity, our vision of a just society, with a spiritual transcendence and ever-widening horizons of joy and hope. In its spontaneity and race pride his poetry found a welcome among the West African poets of *négritude* like Senghor. "As I understand it," Hughes remarked at the Dakar Festival, "négritude has its roots deep in the beauty of the black people —in what younger American writers and musicians call *soul*."[16] Above all, Langston Hughes and Arna Bontemps, though steeped in the life and heritage of black folk, achieved an enduring kind of universality in the range and depth of the human experiences they depicted.

The first group of these letters, written between 1925 and 1941, recalls for us the unshakable determination of both men "to be a co-worker in the kingdom of culture, to escape both death and isolation, to husband and use his best powers and his latent genius."[17] In the earliest of his letters to Hughes (written about 1925), Bontemps praises Hughes's verse, and throughout their long friendship they share ideas, information and encouraging words. When Bontemps is isolated at Oakwood School in Alabama, Hughes sends him the Sunday newspapers. They alert each other to each new article, review or book on the American literary scene which they find significant. They sustain each other's morale by their mutual involvement not only in Negro affairs but also in the world of art and ideas. In collaborating on *Popo and Fifina,* and *The Boy of the Border,* the juvenile stories, they could agree not only on plot details, but in their capacity to create an atmosphere, tone and style unified throughout. Bontemps is impressed by the spontaneity, freshness and rapidity with which Hughes writes, describing himself as "plodding along." Hughes sees Bontemps as the scholar, a man of learning and sound judgment. Their modesty is touching. Yet they know their capacities and dare to produce original adult fiction and poetry as well as plays for the theater. Although Hughes is proud of his academic honors and produces some sound and solid research, he tends to think of this realm as Bontemps's metier. Thus in a letter written Arna on October 22, 1966, he says he has decided not to participate in a Virginia Conference "since Edmunds come writing here for me to send in advance a *paper*. Nobody told me it was going to be that academic and Ah has no paper and won't." The lapse into ungrammatical and dialectal speech is part of the act. (Earlier Langston Hughes had been a visiting professor at Atlanta University and had given informative lectures all over the country—with obvious relish.) Bontemps, though a man of great dignity and propriety, can use this semiliterate ghetto talk, too, as when he seizes upon the possibilities in their next project in 1939: "Hog dog, boy! I knowed they's a ace in that deck somewheres." Not the least interesting aspect of the letters is the range of style and feeling which they express. It is also true that as busy men they wrote with great haste—there are errors in spelling, grammar and factual detail. (An editor is tempted to correct such errors as "dinning" for "dining" or "Kessler" for "Koestler." In most instances obvious typographical errors have been corrected.)

These letters are most affecting in their good-humored and steady struggle to refine their work and gain a hearing in the world of letters. They are constantly

15. *Big Sea,* p. 17.
16. *New York Times,* April 24, 1966.
17. Du Bois, *Souls of Black Folk,* p. 17.

searching for and gleaning original material. They explore the literary possibilities of Baudelaire's Negro mistress and plan a book on Josephine Baker and *Famous Negro Athletes*. Hughes unearths a question with tantalizing possibilities: "Did you know that a Negro discovered Arizona? He was the first 'white' man in the territory." And Bontemps discovers a black Civil War veteran in Alabama who never got a pension. Think what such a man might reveal of our distorted history. Both Hughes and Bontemps work on numerous revisions and stalk their prey relentlessly. They devour relevant details of the publishing world with insatiable appetites. They will maintain themselves in the 1930s and early 1940s by traveling long distances in borrowed tuxedos rattling along in an old Ford car. They will endure the constant insult of being denied decent accommodations and given inedible food. Yet their morale is sustained by appreciative and generous audiences. When Bontemps has his overcoat stolen a group will buy him another. What drives and sustains them is the literary life, the joy of creation and communication, the enthusiasm of their audiences. Having produced *Boy of the Border, Drums at Dusk* and the ghosted biography of W.C. Handy, Bontemps can feel some just pride in his accomplishment. Hughes has turned out a long list of plays, poems, stories and articles, yet he is always "broke." The years before 1945 were very lean years. The help from the W.P.A. writers project (denied Hughes completely) and from the Rosenwald Foundation has been meager indeed. "This is the seventh month we have lived on 'literature,' " writes Arna Bontemps in 1939. "None of the brood has starved."

Furthermore, the 1930s are momentous years for these men as they were for many Americans. The background of this correspondence is the Great Depression, the Dust Bowl, the wretched poverty of the migrant worker and the unemployed on farms and in cities, the hysterical reaction to communism, the gathering storm of fascism in Europe, the Spanish Civil War, where Langston Hughes was a correspondent, and the rape of Ethiopia as well as the continuing deprivations of segregation and discrimination. It is a time, too, of extraordinary literary activity here and abroad. And these men are affected by the critical standards of the age which was reading Faulkner, Auden and Eliot as well as Steinbeck, Sandburg, Frost and William Carlos Williams.

The second period covered by these letters—1941 to 1959—is dominated, first of all, by World War II. Like all their black countrymen, they are constantly oppressed by a racist society, a segregated army, the displacement of Japanese-Americans, the cultural isolation of minorities in their native land even as the "free" world confronts an aggressive Hitlerian fascism. Yet the letters reveal a dauntless will to defend human rights wherever possible—as in their attack on discrimination in the armed forces and the Red Cross. ("The angel of mercy's got her wings in the mud/and all because of Negro blood.") They support the Negro Freedom Rallies and the pressure on government which makes possible President Roosevelt's Executive Order on Fair Employment Practices. The Nazi invasion of the Soviet Union is calmly noted by Langston Hughes, but what he has seen of Russia and Europe helps him create the broad humanity of *The Big Sea*. And *St. Louis Woman* finds its way to a fairly long, successful run on the New York stage (113 performances). Bontemps and Hughes perform an invaluable service, too, by producing the two definitive anthologies, *The Poetry of the Negro* (1949) and *The Book of Negro Folklore* (1958).

By 1950 they have arrived as recognized literary figures. In 1961 Langston Hughes was elected to the American Academy of Arts and Letters. Later he was

12

active in PEN and ASCAP He was the guest of the President of the United States on more than one occasion. Bontemps is a valued consultant to some of the best known cultural foundations. The two men have little money, but they are well known even in foreign lands. And the academic atmosphere of Fisk had its advantages for Bontemps. "If a refuge for the harassed Negro could be found anywhere in those days," wrote Bontemps later, "it was to be in such a setting."[18] Hughes continues to produce poetry, plays, fiction and essays. A regular columnist for the *Chicago Defender* and the *New York Post,* he creates his best-known character, Jesse B. Simple. Hughes, through Simple, found a way of transmitting the canny judgment and ironic insight of the man in the street. Both men embodied the expanded vision and wider democratic hopes of the post-war world—the world of nations "united," of nuclear energy and automation. They could witness with satisfaction the rise of Malcolm X and Martin Luther King, Jr., the Supreme Court's epoch-making decision of 1954 and the violent, yet inevitable desegregation of America.

It was an exciting time to be alive, and they lived with gusto the life of a world which saw most of America liberated and black America asserting itself as never before. The black writer, too, seemed to them to have seized freedom's plow by both handles: they hailed the successes of Richard Wright, Gwendolyn Brooks, Ralph Ellison and Le Roi Jones as well as a whole host of young authors— anthologized by Langston Hughes in *New Poets: U.S.A.* Although Hughes was shocked by Jones's plays, *The Toilet* and *The Slave,* he saw the substantial merit of *Dutchman* and of Jones's poetry and essays. They recognized that the Afro-American influence in American culture could no longer be denied or ignored. There is therefore a sense of fulfillment, a more authoritative voice in their letters of the 1950s and 1960s. For even Hollywood films and national television (not to speak of universities and professional organizations) provide the two men with a wider, more immediate audience for their work.

Nevertheless, they are never complacent or pontifical. Their last years—the 1960s—show an amazing readiness for the new black revolution. Bontemps becomes a member of the Nashville Library Committee and a guest at Peabody and Vanderbilt University. In 1966 he joins the faculty of the University of Illinois and in 1969 he goes to Yale. Langston Hughes declines academic appointments but is hailed around the world as a distinguished American author. Both men are frequently invited to world cultural conferences in Africa and in Europe. There is little doubt that the African diaspora fulfills itself in their utterances in Dakar and Nairobi where the rising power and influence of Africa reverberate around the world. There is poetic justice in the careers of Langston Hughes and Arna Bontemps, who live to see their hardy faith fulfilled as they view the fruits of the century from the top of Kilimanjaro—like Moses looking over into the promised land.

18. *The Old South,* p. 19.

LETTERS
1925-1940

Saturday

Dear Langston,

Thanks much for the group of fine poems. As usual, with your pieces, they intrigue my memory with their vivid rhythm and melody, like a swaying boat. Of this set I like best the Suicide and the Lover-Lass—the "dancers" too are nice. These first two I have added to my already lengthy list of favorites, including: Rivers, Sea Charm, Song, Variation, Banjo Dance, and Dream Keeper. To me Sea Charm is the most perfect of them all, the most unusual music. Which is your own favorite?

Another colored musical show is on Broadway, Lucky Sambo. I don't expect it to last long. The music and dancing are ordinary—the humor was to me unusually fresh. I laughed heartily.

I will be in D.C. for a week or two with Thurman in August. If you are there then, will look you up.

Are you in the Crisis Contest, or coming to their affair?

Next week end I am going up in New England—I have never been in those parts. Then I am thinking about camping on Long Island part of the summer.

Write soon. Adios,
Arna

Oakwood Junior College
Huntsville, Alabama
Friday,

Dear Langston;

This hurry-up note is begun while I am waiting for a car that is to take me to town for the afternoon. If it comes before I finish I'll have to break off suddenly. This is a warning.

Your letter came this morning. Sorry Harpers did not see the light but will continue to work and point for Macmillan. All suggestions have been carefully heeded. I will try to make a complete and finished copy of the book. Then will send it along. Meanwhile, will you send me the first copy—the one Harper's read? I'd like to send the whole thing to Macmillan as a unit.

I also hope that you will talk with Miss Fuller [Juvenile Editor, Macmillan]. I have written her but said that you would probably get in touch with her before leaving N.Y.

We'll call that Christmas arrangement a date. We have only about four or five days of vacation but I am sure I can arrange to be away for the Tuskegee run.

17

But, of course, I couldn't tell these folks that my main reason for going was a football game. I'll have to invent a more intellectual motive.

This is . . . one of the most picturesque locations. By the way, will you ask Walter if he ever hears of teaching opportunities in the better southern schools for an honest English 'professor'? I'd like to make a step up within the next year. But I like the South and would never care to *teach* elsewhere. I'll not likely be returning to the North until I can live without teaching, or until I get another chance to go to school.

Luck to you with your Musical Comedy. Undoubtedly something will come of the venture now that money has been spent.

Scottsboro is not far from here but I have not had a chance to go there yet (we came through the place on the train). If I get as much as two hundred dollars for my share of the advance on Popo and Fifina I'll get a car at once. From then on I'll be doing the South.

Have lots of good ideas for use when I get into real writing form again.

Thanks for sending my name to the Amsterdam. Did you also give it to the World-Telegram office?

Write on your way around the circuit if you have time. Will be glad to know how business is.

Thanks too for the Sunday newspapers. They are the only papers from N.Y. that I have seen since leaving. I am glad to learn that Paul Green's play is a success.

Will look forward to the visit and to the work on the next opus. And meanwhile I hope that what I have done will enable this one to ring the bell when it is whipped into final shape.

Sincerely,
Arna

Oakwood Junior College
Huntsville, Alabama
Sunday. . . . .

Dear Lang;

What has happened to you out there in California? I have been hearing reports of your triumphs and, of course, I am very anxious that you should love the place. How long will you be there? How did the tour turn out from a business angle? Etc? Etc?

I have just written to the GOLDEN STAIR PRESS for a copy of the *Scottsboro Limited*. Did you hear about Nancy Cunard's book of Scottsboro poems? It is a good idea. I had thought of it myself. Though, of course, I am no anthologist.

Did you see the dummy of *Popo and Fifina*? [Juvenile by Hughes & Bontemps] And how did you like it? I was pleasantly surprised. I like the style of the drawings—those that I have seen. But I will not be too joyful unless you are too. When will the *Dream Keeper* be off? and who is the illustrator?

I notice that Wallie has another novel, a collaboration entitled *The Intern*. He is writing books faster than I can afford to buy them, but I will try to get this one anyhow.

The boys here in school were successful in getting Tucker out. The board voted it last week, but they also voted to send the leaders in the strike home. So Herman Murphy, Allan Anderson, Earnest Moseley and Rashford and Fordham are gone (you may remember some) and the place is dreary as a result. I was also pointed out as being favorable to the revolution and, as a result, may not be rehired. I am not really bumped, but the faculty is to be cut in half (due to depression) and I may not be on the new slate. If not, I shall come to California and go to U.S.C. next winter—that is really what I want to do. Then I could spend time in Mexico, write more children's books, finish a long delayed novel, etc. etc.

Made the long trip through Mississippi last week. They talked about you at Tougaloo, Le Moyne, Greenville, etc. It was a great trip.

So long,

Arna

Monday
Oakwood Junior College
Huntsville, Alabama

Dear Langston;

This is less a letter than a burst of excitement.

I received your card and the word from Knopf. But just ahead of it came two letters from Miss Fuller of Macmillan in rapid succession. Both were forwarded to me down here. Evidently she does not know that I have left town. So please get in touch with her and do what you can to pacify her mind. Evidently we have caused a tempest in the famous old house of Macmillan. But let me quote from the letters themselves.

The first said in part: "I asked Miss Seaman [editor of Juveniles at Macmillan] how she felt about your ms. and she was really enthusiastic. She liked the authors too. I wish I might see you and know exactly what she told you. At any rate I know she is definitely interested in the material but feels that there should be a little more action to hold the child's attention. She told me she was afraid you were going to take it to another publisher.

"It seems to me this is entirely different from the matter of your novel 'God Sends Sunday'. In the first place our novels here at Macmillan are not outstanding so it was probably just as well that you took it to Harcourt, Brace. But the Children's Book Department at Macmillan is rather famous. It is the largest in the world and has been developed entirely under Miss Seaman who started it about twelve years ago. We do excellent book making and our books sell. During the depression all the other departments here have fallen down except ours. For the past three years a Macmillan book has taken the Newbery Medal which is awarded the best piece of writing for boys and girls during the year. (Wouldn't it be great if your book would take that Medal and of course it stands a chance no matter who the publisher though of course I wish it were Macmillan). Etc."

And the second letter contained the following gems: "Of course I know my note of the other day did not need an answer unless you had wished to see me further about the ms. And naturally there wasn't much I could say.

"However, I thought you might be interested to know that the matter came up again last night when Miss Seaman and I were working late on the "list".

19

She again expressed her willingness to see the completed ms. and said she felt you had good stuff there and would probably not have any trouble placing it. As you may know, it is really harder to get a book on the Macmillan Children's list than any other for the reason we have more known and famous authors who are writing for us. I honestly believe it means a little more to have a book on our list than anywhere else, and that isn't just loyalty to the department for which I work.

"We talked further about the things you and Mr. Hughes had done, and Miss Seaman became so interested in God Sends Sunday that she told me to order a copy for her which I have just done. I also ordered a copy of Not Without Laughter.

"Of course you are very busy getting ready to leave for the South. I am wishing you all kinds of luck, and can't help hoping the Haiti manuscript will come back. Etc."

So you see what is going on. At least, I glean, the Macmillan company would like to see the thing again. When they write so many long letters to authors without provocation or answer there must be something cooking. But you will have to *wrassle* with that problem. I will finish my draft of the ms. as quickly as possible (a week or ten days more—you see I am just getting settled here and am only now getting down to my writing) and pass it along to you. First of all I think you should not be embarrassed in your relationship to Knopf. But if we can get to Macmillan's gracefully and without loosing anything elsewhere it might not be bad to let them have the things we do in collaboration. And by the way, How about our doing the child's life of John Brown next? But on second thought, maybe the research could make that harder than the modern fairy tale. And with our limited time for collaboration, the second might be best. In fact, I am already quite sure of it. At any rate you must plan to come here and spend a few weeks while we do the job this winter. And the sooner you are able to let me know about when you will be able to come the better for my plans—you know I intend to make many trips to nearby cities and country sections.

Now for another subject. This is a sublime place for the delight of the eye. The school is tiny and unimportant but it is a good place to work and I like it. I even like the white folks I have seen in the neighborhood. They are as simple and deferential as the Negroes.

We live in the house that was formerly (a hundred years ago) the Old Mansion. It looks across the campus with quiet and ruined dignity. From our up-stairs porch (like the one from which the broken-hearted mistress fell in your story) we can almost touch the branches of trees. Further away there are magnolias and beyond these a fountain under a rose arbor in the center of an almost park-like campus.

I have a good bit of work to do but I think I sh..l manage to write.

Will tell you more about things—the trip, the place, the new routine—next week, after I have finished with Popo and Fifina. I must have a little money to make a payment on a car.

Meanwhile, take it easy. And write me. Tell me what progress you have made with the tour. And most important of all, about when you will hit Alabama.

Incidentally, What did Harper's say?

Sincerely,
Arna

Post Office Drawer 853
Huntsville, Alabama
February 3rd

Dear Lang;

I have just received the congratulations of Margaret Fuller. She says that the O. K. on our book has come down from the president of the Macmillan Company and that I should receive Miss Seaman's departmental letter of acceptance tomorrow or the day after. She sent that second report along too, and it was enthusiastic to say the least. Miss Seaman, M. F. says, will want only very minor revisions. I am now eager to know their terms. She says that they are already planning to give the book good publicity, and they have already written Doug [Aaron Douglass, artist, Fisk] to see if he would be interested in doing the illustrations—of course, they are not at all sure he will want to try anything of this particular type, but his letter, she says, has gone out.

Not much time to write now. . . . mail going out in about a minute. . . . . but I think you ought to write Miss Fiery and set her mind at rest. . . . Too bad we are in such demand for our literary efforts. And incidentally, I may have time to enclose that report. Will you make a copy and return since I will have no time to make one and also make this mail. . . . A letter will be at Tuskegee for you, giving all new developments and details.

Write me. Tell me the whole story about N. O. and the Mardi Gras along with the account of the flood.

And since the publication of the opus is assured, you might start advertising it. And thinking about the next one.

Sincerely,
Arna

Tougaloo,
(Swell Place),
Sunday night.

Dear Arna,

Thanks for all the letters. If I don't write Miss Seaman and Miss Fuller (as I probably won't) you'll express my agreement and appreciation, etc. to them—since I've never had more on hand at once to do in my life. Dozens of letters. And a wire from Knopf to rush revisions on my other kid's book which they want at once with a dozen more poems added to it. And a letter from Miss Gynt saying Robeson is interested in the play for London in the spring, but it, too, must be revised at once. So you see! And a series of heavy dates for the next ten days. So I'm glad our Haitian kids have another father besides myself. . . . With me the terms are O.K. (Sorry the advance was no larger, but glad we have such a fine firm.) And I like the sliding scale. . . . About pictures: you can say that I'd be happy to add details or suggestions, if I can, to help the artist. Or to send more snapshots. . . . I agree entirely with the need for editing the first 3 chapters, and think the last two could well be made one—so let's do it. For humor, maybe something like this: In Haiti there are millions of goats. (It seems we left them out.) In the last chapter why not have Popo see a beautiful little brown goat standing out in the rain, as they go home. Popo thinks the little goat ought to be sheltered and attempts to run it into a shed or under a tree, when the goat turns around and butts Popo down into the mud much to the amusement of everyone else. That would make a nice funny picture for the illustrator. . . . I think we can do our own revisions ourselves. Why not edit at once the first three chapters, and add whatever you think may furnish "more colorful detail" as Miss Seaman suggests. Why not put in a rum shop near the sea where sailors come and Santo Domingan revolutionaries with long curling mustaches and Spanish mouths. And a parrot on a ring over the door who speaks only Spanish, and the old crone who runs the place who is reputed to be a voodoo priestess, but nobody knows; and who keeps a piece of bread on a nail beside the door for the Gods when they pass. . . . Etc., etc., etc. . . . . if they want color. . . . And the ringing of many church bells in the morning which is new to Popo and Fifina. And the fine gentlemen with high colors and linen suits who work in the offices and shops; brown skin gentlemen with bushy heads and watch chains of gold and shiney pointed shoes; and the automobiles bouncing and swaying over the few cobblestone streets of the towns; and the radios: that hidden music that floated out from some of the bars and cafes and big houses of the place. . . . I'll read over the parts in question in the car some day this week, mark passages, etc, and send you the pages. And on the 17th, the day after Birmingham, I can come by for an hour or so on our way to Arkansas, if necessary. But let's get this off our hands as soon as possible so we can do something else: the Mexican play particularly, as I'm sure we'd have luck with it, if we do it soon enough, before the market gets flooded with cosas Mexicanas.

Que le vaya con Dios,
Langston

The Oakwood Junior College
Huntsville, Alabama
March 9th

Dear Lang;
    Here is the contract. Please insert your permanent address beneath your name. And by all means rush it to the headquarters so that they can send us the berries.
    Entranced by the news of 'daddy' Handy [W. C. Handy]. I have written him already (mailing the letter along with this one) proposing to visit him for a week-end within the next month.
    I am going to Chicago—leaving here the 22nd of March, stopping one night in Nashville, one in Louisville, one in South Bend, and spending three days in Chicago before starting back. Will leave there the 28th or 29th. Is there any place that our paths might cross? If so, don't fail to tell me.
    Of course, I envy you the New York trip, and somehow I have a premonition that you might do *real* business in connection with your play [*Mulatto,* 1935]. The more I think about the parts I read of it, the more I feel that it is the goods.
    I have discovered an interesting old Negro who fought in the civil war but who has never received a pension. I may work on it for him. He should have 15 or 20 thousand coming by now, but it will require some red tape to get it. Will you give any suggestions you can for the procedure?

22

Don't forget to send more mail stops after the 19th. There will always be need for them. And remember to RUSH the contract home to Fifth Avenue.

So long,
Arna

Post Office Drawer 853
Huntsville, Alabama
Friday. . . . .

Dear Lang;

Just received your letter this morning, so am not at all sure this letter will reach you at LeMoyne College.

There is no news from Macmillan's. The corrected manuscript is by now in their hands but they have not sent the contract nor written me concerning the revisions. Perhaps I shall have some word tomorrow.

In their last letter they were eager to have us say that they could save the book for the spring list of 1933. I told them that I would turn that over to you, for I have no strong reason for insisting on a fall date. You, I said, might have one, since you plan another tour that will begin in the fall. Will you, therefore, write them, giving some point of view on the matter? I, personally, think fall is a better time for children's books, but maybe spring has certain advantages.

From now till the closing of school I shall be working a bit on a draft of a new adult novel [*Black Thunder*]. I'll suspend work during summer so as to better enjoy my home state and to do our other juvenile, our Mexican play, etc. etc. But I think it well, considering my California project, to have something on hand that I can finish between September and the end of the year. By then, I may be in desperate need of a few dollars.

Everything is set for the long jaunt in June. I should arrive between the fifteenth and twentieth. Till then, keep me posted on western news.

Was in Nashville last week-end. Am going to Chicago with the school male chorus March 22nd. Where will you be then? How about the N. Y. trip? I may get there too—last of April or first of May.

Please send me another mail schedule. The contract will undoubtedly be ready the next week.

Luck to you. . . . Hello to Raddy.

Sincerely,
Arna

The Article for the Am. Lib. Children's Year seems to me top. Nice the way you insinuated the Haitian theme by mentioning Black Majesty.

Wednesday
Hotel Theresa
Seventh Avenue
    at 125th Street
New York

Dear Lang,

Dorothy Schwartz told me before I left Chicago that there was a good chance that we might give our performance (you, Frederick and me) several times if it

23

comes off well. What would you suggest for music? She thinks we should have some, but there is only the $150 to play with. If we cut it 3 ways, there will be 50 each. If we pay a musician, we'll get less. How do you feel? She thought the added attraction of music might help us line up the other dates. Have some suggestions for me when I get home Monday.

Had dinner with Dick and Ellen today, Countee and Claude yesterday, Doug and Alta and Savain before that, etc., etc. So you see I'm raising hell with the knives and forks. . . . Dick and Ellen expect a bundle from heaven. . . . Remember what I said about religious novels? Well, *Dick has written one!* He is all heat up about it.

Will make arrangements for you with Horace and Irina on your stated terms. . . . Lots of news when I get to a typewriter—or else when I see you. . . . I'm spending my morning at the Schomburg collection—researching down.

Here are some reviews!

Ever,
Arna

Oakwood
April 25th

Dear Lang;

Unless the Ford breaks down, I'll be in L. A. about the 5th or 6th of June. Within a very few days no more than one week (allowing me to salute my relatives) we can leave for the ranch. When we shall return to L. A. we can decide later. We are free to stay there as long as we choose. If I should go to summer school, I'd have to come up after the 4th of July, but I will not go unless I get more money than I now see, and if I get *enough* more I will not go either. The bets are ten to one against summer school therefore. I have now just my transportation in sight—the price of this Ford is killing me—but I read in a paper that you and I are going to write for the movies, and if that is the case, I'll soon be jingling money. But the book will make a little; I'll get there with a fully outlined story, a story that we can finish in two or three weeks. And I have been studying over the play. I do think that outline was inspired. But we should call it *The Peon* or something like that instead of *The Soldiers Pass.* I can hardly wait to get started on it. I believe we'll make a stirring play and that we'll find a stirring title for it. And by the way, this may be my chance to go to Russia—that possible Moscow production you mentioned.

I have a black and white novel that is trying to sour on my hands. I'm going to put it by till fall. At one time I hoped to finish it this spring. No luck.

The dramatic version of *God Sends Sunday* is being held by some producers who say they will start a Negro Repertory theatre in Harlem. But there is a catch: they have not put down the option money, though they promise to do so in the summer. I'm smiling too. I've learned from others to take nothing for granted in the theatre. But with *The Peon* or *The Soldiers Pass* or *Lamp in the West* or whatever it may be, the case will be different. They'll be glad enough to lay the money on the line.

Do you remember any good stopping places in Arizona or in western Texas? Anything in Phoenix or El Paso? And what is the best route from here to the coast? I have never driven it, you know.

24

If we can borrow a shotgun and if I can regain my eye, we'll have grouse for breakfast frequently.

Ever,
Arna

If you get there before I do look up my cousin Ben Albons. Wilbe or Fay will know his address.

8 November '36
731 East 50th Place
Chi. . . .

Dear Lang:

A day or two ago I received a telephone call from Mr. Shaw of the Federal Theater and an invitation to come down and talk about the *Jack* with him and Miss Glaspell, his associate down there. The upshot of it all was that they like the play better than any other they have read for their Negro unit. They'd like to put it on. They definitely want some re-writing, however, based on the enclosed comments of their readers. I asked them to forward a copy of these to me so that I might study them and also get your reactions to them. So if you'll give me your reactions to them, I'll be glad to work on the play ["When the Jack Hollers"] and try to make it acceptable. Don't forget to return the comments when you've digested them. . . . The Negro unit has just had the misfortune to have their production of *Hymn to the Rising Sun* by Paul Green banned by the authorities on grounds similar to those that halted *Tobacco Road.* They now have a revue under way. So now they are turning to the *Jack.* Mr. Shaw says that he believes our play will land in a commercial theater if done well by the unit here, for all the Broadway scouts cover the WPA productions here. Incidentally, he is from Carmel and says he knows you fairly well. He wonders if you will come over in the event they put the thing on. I hope you will not say *no,* even though you might be uncertain, because I think such an interest by you will help to speed things along. Shaw, whose first name I don't have, is at the Midwest Play Bureau, Federal Theatre Project, 433 E. Erie Street, Chicago, Ill. He would love to have a note from you. He seemed to think you had gone back to Carmel.

The revisions on my *Sad-Faced Boy* evidently took. The book will be published by Houghton, Mifflin about first of March. No advance this time, however. So I'm scratching my head for other means of making money.

Drums of Haiti is thrilling. The ending of the first act is masterful in my estimation. Most of the play, of course, presents Negroes in a mood unfamiliar to usual stage productions, but I imagine the production of such opuses as *Macbeth* has partly cleared the way. Personally, I would allow Desallines to speak about as any other peasant speaks, while trying at the same time to put a poetic quality into his words. I don't see any reason for making a marked difference in his speech and the speech of the others. On the other hand I don't see that there be any incorrect grammar at all—only a sort of naive simplicity, like the speech of children. . . . The version you sent me flows along very fine, I think.

So *Buddy and Domino,* tired of waiting on *Sad-Faced Boy,* must be patient a little longer while the *Jack* is being fed and watered to do a little plowing. But patience will be rewarded.

It's raining here; how about there? I think I mentioned Hardwick Moseley, who knows, likes, and would like to be in touch with you.

Ever,
Arna

P.S. I'm to see them again soon, so let me have your slant right away.
How about dusting off our Mexican story for Houghton, Mifflin? Have you read it recently? I have not.

28 March '37

Dear Lang,

Are you home yet? Hardwick Moseley, the Houghton, Mifflin representative here tried to reach you while in Cleveland, but you seemed to be still away. He said he'd try again. They are having the best of luck with *Sad-Faced Boy*. (Not out yet.) On the basis of advance sales they say they anticipate a royalty for me of $1,200 by the end of this year. They have offered (H.M. Co.) to give me an advance on a new one before I put paper in the typewriter. So you see it's worth while to write for the Rosenwald libraries. Why don't you talk with H. Moseley and get something in mind—between the H.M. Co. and the Rosenwald Fund. By the same ratio yours should sell a million through the same channels. And they still want you terribly, and they keep hinting as much to me. As a tip-off, if you can use it, they want a plantation story—with lots of plot and many share-cropping problems, wicked enemies, etc.—for the teen age readers—say about sixteen. Better if it had a mystery like a lost deed to property or something like that.

Trounstine says the New York W.P.A. is interested in the *Jack*. Ronald Hammond is especially enthusiastic about it and is recommending it to Hiram Motherwell and Mrs. Flanagan. If they put it on during the summer, I'll be in a position to see it.

I hope your lectures came off well. That radio skit—now there's a real break. . . . I see your friend Myron Brinig has a big best-seller on his hands. . . . The Guggenheims said no to me: I never felt I could muster a strong enough record, so I wasn't disappointed. Besides I suppose I'm cut out to write under persecution, if I write at all. . . . I loved the poems. You have recaptured the mood and the form that give you your personality, for which you were born—short, fragrant, breath-taking expressions of feeling.

Arna

Your best poetry, I think, is in this manner—and this is of it.

731 E. 50th Place
Chicago
11 April '37

Dear Lang:

I envy you your trip to California, but since it's you going, I hope you're carrying along the complete notes for that autobiography which you owe me personally—along with a great many other people. When do you leave? Be sure

26

to leave a forwarding address, because a copy of *Sad-Faced Boy* is coming to you there within the next week. And when you come through Chicago, how about keeping a copy of *Joy to My Soul* in your brief case, so I can read it—since I have no hope of going to Cleveland or Detroit or any other place soon. Except Alabama—I'm going down there for a week-end, April 28–May 2nd. Power to the opera, nevertheless, and may you land in the movies while you're in the West.

Even though you don't take on a juvenile till fall, what's to hinder your seeing the folks concerned while here and getting something on the docket? Will you be back in time for the tour in July?

The relatives you saw were probably Owen's aunt and cousin. . . . One a principal, the other a teacher in Cincinnati public schools.

Concerning *Poetry.* I was not able to get anyone there by phone yesterday but will try again tomorrow. Frank Marshall Davis (*Black Man's Verse*) told me last week that the future of the magazine was uncertain. Chicago U. has assured its publication till one year after H. Monroe's death, but no longer. Recently a large dinner was given here to raise money for the brave little journal, but nothing seems to be as it was—even now. Still I will promise to talk to someone directly tomorrow and try to have them write you before you leave.

Will send Robert Magidoff something at once.

The Children's page for the *Courier* went phft! If that's the way you say it. My guess is that the editor proposed to use too many of her own stories and that consequently they lost interest. Why are niggers like that? Like Roscoe Bruce who had found backers for a publishing house he was going to establish. He asked me to be on the honorary editorial staff. Come to find out he was going to publish his own writings almost entirely. So I imagine his backers lost interest too. He was going to call it the Harriet Tubman Publishing Company, I think.

> See you in Chi. Hunh?
> Arna

> January 17.
> 1938.

Dear Arna,

We are doing lots of research into the St. Louis period of the '90's and finding some swell stuff to put into your play [*St. Louis Woman*]. We have also found several old gentlemen who lived there at that time. One of them is full of priceless anecdotes and stories of the characters of the time. We have also worked out a tremendous opening for the play that ought to be terrific "box-office" and good, too.

Are you and Countee going to get together on that agreement for a sharing of all rights outside Federal Theatre with Muse and I, or do you want us [Muse and Hughes] to draw up a tentative agreement out here and submit it to you-all? Let me know about this soon, as we're now going full speed ahead on preparing the script. And it looks as though you'll surely have a California production, at least. (But don't believe it until the curtain rises!)

San Pedro High School at nine! in the morning finishes my lectures for a couple of weeks so as to leave time for writing. After that I may have some with a professional lecture bureau out here, besides the schools again February after exams and graduations are over.

It is marvellous July weather out here.

Write soon,
Langston

1379 E. Washington Blvd.,
Los Angeles, California,
March 7, 1939.

Dear Arna,

Your play [*St. Louis Woman*] is coming along fine, and the Federal Board likes our revisions very much. Clarence is working along with me on it, so as to have it in producing shape by the end of the month. They now expect to put it into rehearsal in April so as to be able to open it at the same time as the Hollywood track opening in the late spring, as they feel that would be a good tie, since it is a racing play. . . . . We are putting in a scene at the paddock with real horses in it. . . . . Boy, you ought to see your first act now! St. Louis reborn through HOLLYWOOD, the new set including not only the interior of the bar-room, but the street outside as well, which adds greatly to the scope of your action. And Little Augie now makes his entrance, a la Carmen, in an open hack of the period drawn by two milk-white bobbed-tail horses. I thought that might amuse you. . . . . Mr. W. C. Handy has given us permission to use the "St. Louis Blues," weaving it into the play. And in your cake-walk scene, we've inserted Black Patti and her Troubadours, who graciously contribute several numbers at the ball, including her famous rendition of "Last Rose of Summer." It ought to be grand entertainment, and I think both you and Countee will like it. . . . . Please try to get this agreement through as soon as possible, as I'd like to have it all settled before the end of the month, when I leave for the East. (Has been sent to Lieber from Salisbury.) In fact, it must be settled, since it won't be O.K.ed for production until it is! ! ! . . . . . Where is that lecture engagement for us between the 4th and the 9th? Huh? Since I may have to come right back out here, I at least want to make my fare to-and-from from the lectures—outwise, why lecture?

Sincerely,
Langston

Perhaps you'd better sign this, too, and shoot it on to Leah Salisbury, since you're not in New York, either.

703 East 50th Place
Chicago
17 March [39?]

Dear Lang:

Let's just have a quiet little funeral for Lil Augie. Nothing like the one Biglow Brown had. No fancy gals, etc. Let's just bury him in a box in a potter's field.

Leah Salisbury has at last written me. The letter just came, and it sounded like a knell for our easy-rider. The hope of getting Salisbury, Lieber, Harcourt-Brace, Countee, Clarence, you and me together on a sort of Munich accord with the play as the pawn now seems to me almost too much to hope for. I can't see much hope for Czechoslovakia, under the circumstances.

But re: Miss Salisbury. She should have been your agent on *Mulatto.* I bet you'd never been *one* day behind in royalties! All of which bodes no good for Augie. She hinted that she tore her hair when Lieber applied the pressure, telling her that no cut meant no production. She has seen Harcourt-Brace, who turn out to be her close friends, and they are working in harmony with her. I doubt that she will budge ½ inch now. Lieber should have sounded the lady out and led with his left instead of his right.

Another thing that has contributed to her willfulness, I think, is the fact that she has (or hopes she has) a taker on Broadway at last (or again). After Jed Harris and Orson Welles, I don't know what to expect. But with Broadway Negro-minded again she feels optimistic about the present proposal. Well, ho-hum! I ain't never expected nothing nohow!

Toledo Lecture changed to April 23rd. Indianapolis maybe the night before. Just heard from Jenkins in Buffalo (who seems to know you from Lincoln). He sent addresses. Do you think it's too late now to try to get those spots for the 24th & 25th? Let me know post haste.

Mikado is a hit in N.Y.—the Chi company. Nothing whatever doing here in these diggings but a lot of noise and five pages of *Tom-Tom Treasure* per day. A lecture at Du Sable yesterday. The April Atlantic is supposed to have a letter from me in Contributor's Column, talking about you and others. *To Make A Poet Black,* published at Chapel Hill, praises you to the skies in page after page. It's a book for schools—$1.50. (out this week).

Ever,
Arna

Dear Arna:

What time and what night *exactly* is the Kansas City date? I'm under the impression it is the 5th? Is that right? Must know at once to coincide with Oklahoma City.

Then leave Clarence's [Muse] name out of it from now on. And make the agreement solely with me, if you wish. Or not at all, as you *darkies* choose. The play [St. Louis Woman] is just about done. A conference yesterday with the production director and the scene designer—both of whom like it immensely—also Clarence—means that they are going ahead full force with production plans. At least, I hope you-all [Bontemps & Cullen] let that go through—since I think a good show out here would be a great help to any future productions anywhere at all. . . . . . WHO COULD HAVE POSSIBLY GIVEN ANYONE THE IDEA OF A THREAT ON CLARENCE'S PART? Not at all! ⚔⚔⚔ But as co-writer with me, he has been a great help on the script, being an old theatre man and knowing all the angles of building lines for sure-fire theatre reactions. Should you cut me in on it, of course I would divide with Clarence. (Which you need not mention further.) It's 75% a new show now, and I hope you-all like it. I'm sending it to you to read and pass on to the rest of them as soon as revisions are made. Or maybe I'll send the first draft up to Act 3 now (just for you to read to see how it is going. Keep up. But send on any suggestions.) When the full script is ready next week, I'll send the final version to be passed on to New York.

Looks like I'll be working in Hollywood right up to the day to leave. We're engaged for an extra week now. The picture goes into production at once, as soon as cast.

We have done *two tons* of writing! Never take a Hollywood job—slow as you work. They vary from nothing to do at all, to rush! rush! rush! No nice in-between kinds.

The Negroes who want OPERA have begun to oppose *St. Louis Woman* already. But unless the present production board is ousted entirely, including Clarence, it will surely go through—as they're sold on it. The scene-drawings look swell. Smooth out that New York thing, will you, so you can have a show to look at next time the Pollia folks bring us out for a return engagement—cause it'll probably run a year.

Langston

P.S. Advise Lieber [B & H's agent] as to how best approach Miss Salisbury—in case you take the matter up again. Maxim Lieber, 545 Fifth Avenue, New York. (Leave music rights and billing out of it, if you wish, if that will simplify matters. Four names on the thing would be three too many anyway. Let's bill it as being by LIL AUGIE.)

Monday the 22nd

Dear Lang,

. . . Your "Simple Minded Friend" seems to me a very happy creation, especially as a device for treating topics which would otherwise seem high-flown or academic. You can use him to show the application of theoretical questions to his life. International events might thus be related to his affairs. The GOOD-MORNING, STALINGRAD technique. I would not advise a) using the "Friend" *every* week or b) wasting him on the kind of material which needs no pointing up. It would be ideal, I'd think, to do an occasional "Friend" piece about the perplexity that comes to the common colored citizen when he tries to apply certain current statements of American ideals and war aims to life as he knows it. It might, in other words, be a way of commenting on current events and pronouncements.

Thanks for bringing order out of chaos: OWI vs IWO. In any case things seem to be happening where you are concerned. The sociology magazine came—or so I am told over the phone. Thanks, I look forward to reading the whole series of articles, including yours.

Dubois takes some of the steam out of my plan to do a Negro press article by making my main point in his first *Defender* article: namely, that the black press is a symptom, not a disease; a result of the Negro's lack of participation in American life, not a cause of anything. The thing to treat is the condition which makes the daily press insufficient for the needs of Negroes. The justification of the Negro press, according to my argument, is that it fights for goals which if attained would liquidate itself. Thus it proves its essential integrity. Its essential patriotism and Americanism. In sum, we shouldn't ask why this or that is printed by Negro papers, but what it is that causes Negroes to want to read such and such.

30

Well, *maybe* I'll write it up, but the Du Bois article certainly dampens my zeal. . . . . Will look out for the records for Poppy. I know she will be excited.

Ever,

Hear about Zora winning that $1,000? Apparently the reactionaries still pay off. Did you-all give her the Spingarn medal, too?

Remember what I said about wanting to see the Arthur Spingarn Negro collection?

703 East 50th Place
Chicago, Illinois
1 May 1939

Memorandum to Langston Hughes
AGREEMENT
Between Arna Bontemps and Langston Hughes

It is at present understood between Countee Cullen and me that you are to receive a division of royalty on the play *St. Louis Woman* in the event of a professional production of that play employing your revision or growing out of the Federal Theatre production in Los Angeles in which your version is to be used. I have on file our correspondence guaranteeing this, and I understand it to extend to a possible movie or radio production as well. No specific percentage has yet been agreed upon. If, however, the amount agreed upon by Cullen and Leah Salisbury, agent, turns out to be less than the special consideration (above that provided in my original contract with his firm) which Mr. Alfred Harcourt promised me in letter to Leah Salisbury on April 4th, I hereby agree to exchange this amount (the difference between ⅔ and ⁹/₁₀ of income from dramatic rights on the book *God Sends Sunday*) for such percentage as the aforementioned agree upon.

This agreement to remain confidential till Leah Salisbury and Countee Cullen have arrived at a decision as to what they will offer you in consideration for your acceptable revisions.

Signed
Arna Bontemps

703 E. 50th Place
Chicago, Illinois
Wednesday

Dear Lang:

Way Down South by now has been shown in about a dozen neighborhood theatres in Chicago proper, but not once in the black belt. Maybe later. It's doing somewhat better houses at present. Alberta and I saw it last night and enjoyed it far better than did the critic you mentioned. I definitely see no grounds for a panning on any score, but I suspect that the criticism was based on somewhat the same grounds as those in which we criticised *Run Little Chillun.* And I would imagine they came from would-be liberals who thought it

31

their duty to take a fling at the old good darky types. But I hold that all of such criticism would have to be leveled at the direction and acting. I saw nothing in text or incident or situation to give such grounds. I will grant that some of the spades of the ensemble tended to over act and sometimes drew twitters when they were playing for heart throbs. Like the girl who says, "What are we poor slaves going to do?" Nothing wrong with the line, but she fails to make it ring true. . . . . Altogether a respectable effort, I'd say, considering the fact that it was perhaps done on a "B" budget. We saw it as a part of a double feature, and we as well as the rest of the audience found it far ahead of its running mate— which had Jackie Coogan in it. . . . . The songs, especially *Good Ground,* were very good. The way they gave you credit was handsome. I was flattered to see that you had named a very good man Bouton.

Have just written Tommie McKnight to see how many "Y" engagements she can help us line up, as per our conversation there last spring. What do you say to the Salt Lake and Denver suggestion, as a starting point? I've written to find out who one should contact in Gary. I've received a few "Y" addresses myself, well two to be exact, but will wait till I hear what Tommie is doing before I write them myself.

The check from the Rosenwald Fund has not come yet. I'll call on Mrs. Simon if tomorrow fails to bring any word. Meanwhile I've just mailed another batch of manuscript to Trounstine on the Handy book and am at the same time trying to work out details of the Mexican story.

There is really no news, but *Way Down South* was worth far more than just a note of gratitude.

Hasta Luego,
Arna

Friday, 19 June
703 E. 50th Place
Chicago, Illinois

Dear Lang,
I weep to think of what I missed when I missed the rally in the Garden. But one has to be philosophical. It's just one of the prices of not living in New York.

Just called Horace to ask about your royalty check. He says he sent it. Then he wanted to know what we could do to get you out here to direct *God Sends Sunday*, no *St. Louis Woman*. We'll lunch together and see what can be cooked up. Would a few pay lectures help you to make up your mind? And how much coin would you require? I ought to have a general impression in the back of my head as the talks progress—whether or not I advance it.

Now I know how you feel with a bale of mail on your conscience. Everybody in the world wrote me while I was away. More, it seems, than had written in the past six months. And here I am trying to do a hurry-up book and getting registered for my course at the University!

Mrs. Florence Crannell Means (*Shuttered Windows, Tangled Waters,* etc.) was luncheon guest today. She's on her way to be main speaker at the A. L. A. convention at Milwaukee. Also getting ready to write about Negroes again. . . .

What is the full name of the juvenile editor at Knopf? Will want to write her in a couple of weeks. At present the chances of my doing the book she wants seem somewhat dim—what with two or three other things already in mind. . . .

Tell CVV I'm still remembering a most pleasant evening—and still talking about my first birds' nest soup. Yum-yum. . . . . Also, I'm still worrying about "Think-a-drink" Hoffman. Boy, was he terriffic!

Hello to Toy and Emerson et al.

> Ever,
> Arna

> c/o Mrs. Rebecca Sehley
> 108 South Street
> Philadelphia, Penna.
> 19 July '39

Dear Lang,

Of course, we're not in Philadelphia yet, but Alberta and the kids—except Paul—intend to leave tomorrow, and Paul and I intend to follow about the 22nd. So —if you hear any good news about St. Louis Woman, Jack, etc., write me there about it. That is a temporary address, I hope, but we should be there nearly a month at least. The money is running short, so I thought Philadelphia would be a good place in which to starve; it's not good for anything else, so far as I know. They also say rent is cheaper in the slums there. Moreover, we'll be nearer N.Y. in case good luck (I've heard of such a thing) should overtake us.

Maybe you'd better mention to the Rosenwalds that I'm moved—if you're corresponding about the book. Incidentally, I called there the day after you left and found that Mrs. Margaret Simon is away for a month—which may delay our project. But don't let it fall. I stand ready to do my draft on the drop of a hat.

Trounstine [agent] saw Handy. He's negotiating. If it works out, I'll go up to N.Y. and talk it over. . . . Trounstine also sent a copy of *Hack* to McClintic, but reports that the boss is away till Sept. 1st, play reading department closed till then also.

Houghton Mifflins say they have not reported on my manuscript in these two months because the juvenile editor, Kent, is in England till sometime in August. So you see how things are during the summer. Isn't it a curse to be broke this time of the year?

The snaps came out fairly well—most, at least. We'll send you some as soon as we can have reprints made. . . . What are prospects out that way now?

> Ever,
> Arna

> 703 E. 50th Place
> Chicago, Illinois
> 31 July 1939

Hey Lang!

I ain't gone nowheres yet. Alberta and the females of the brood got away, but before Paul and I could catch our train, I received a little glint of hope from the writers' project. I then turned the tickets in and stayed—still hoping. Now Alberta and the others are on the way back.

Nothing ever happens around here at this season, but I don't suppose this will last forever. I've completely revised my "Frizzly Chick" story, and it's on the market again. Nothing on *Tom-Tom* yet, due to Kent's absence—he's the monarch in the children's book dept. at Houghtons. Not accomplishing much these days as a result of a) hot, sticky weather and b) unsettled mind, etc. . . . Mr. Handy has offered to advance me $50 if I come to N.Y. to talk over the rewrite job. Trounstine now has the mss. I'll go as soon as I see what's going to happen on the job line for me. . . . Is anything going to happen to any of our plays out there? Or are we going to get jobs in the movies?

If you gave the Rosenwalds the Philadelphia address, will you change it—in the event of another letter to them from you. . . . How is the *Big Sea* turning out?

I see we got $28.64 apiece from Macmillans on the 29th of November. Also, another letter from Mrs. Quereau offers another Denver lecture—in event of a passing through stop.

So long,
Arna

703 E. 50th Place
Chicago
21 August '39

Dear Lang:

Just back from New York where I talked with Handy about his biography (auto). He sent for me. I think perhaps I'll undertake it, but the agreement is not yet reached. I hope to do a couple of chapters this week; if an advance comes out of these, I'll go ahead. . . . . Saw everybody in N. Y. and was photographed by Van Vechten. He, by the way, is very high on *The Hack*—thinks it a sure thing for eventual production.

I had hoped to have a job by the time I returned, but no soap. Perhaps by October. It seems unusually hard to turn a trick along through here, but I hope you are getting things under control. *Way Down South* suffered a small kick from one of the metropolitan brutes on the grounds that it was in the traditional vein. I left too soon to see the picture or to read the other criticisms.

IMPORTANT: Leah Salisbury wants (and needs) a copy or so of your version of *St. Louis Woman*. She said she was writing you, but that I too should impress it. You see, Evelyn Ellis is to do the play for Broadway critics and producers in the near future. Someone, seeing it on the stage, might be impressed to take it over. L. S. is cooperating to get everybody who is anybody there. You might through her arrange for any you'd like to have present to get bids. But if it is at all possible, a copy of your version (or several of them) might serve a good purpose along through now.

McClintic is reading *The Hack*, I'm told. Cross your fingers.

Dorothy Peterson gave a birthday supper for your Aunt Toy. Very nice.

Shall I get in and book up a flock of lectures for spring? It would be well to write in the next week or two if we wanted to get the Southern schools. What did the Rosenwalds say? Be sure to finish the biography!

Ever,
Arna

703 E. 50th Place
Chicago, Illinois
Monday

Dear Lang:

Ah, I think you're going to change our luck for us. I'm not sure whether it's an authentic hunch or just the good feeling that your letter produced—anyhow, I'm looking upwards most mightily for a change. And we'll be sure to see *Way Down South* sure's it hits Chicago. Meanwhile, "I eat well and grow strong", thanks to your intuition plus upsurge of fortune. You're a genius and a scholar —honestly.

Well, we should worry about how to write for children. I just had a letter from Miriam Blanton Huber saying that she has arranged with Macmillans to use a portion of our *Popo* in her forthcoming college textbook on the subject. It is to be published by Macmillan soon, but she did not give the title. The purpose of her letter to me was to ask how to pronounce my name. Anyhow, seems like we're going to be models for future generations of writers for children and students of that literature. *Still,* I'd like very much to borrow your copy of *Writing the Juvenile Story* soon's you're through going over it.

I'll do the first draft of the Miguel story whether we hear from the Rosenwalds or not. In that case, however, it might have to wait till after the first of the year. But I'm sure the story has a chance, and I want to do it, come what may.

Meanwhile, I think I told you Trounstine says he's reached an understanding with Handy, but it's not signed yet. I like doing the job, and hope much I can bring it off in a lively style. He does have sparkling material—if he'll only let it stand in the new dress. According to the terms, he'll give me small checks to keep the pot boiling—up to a couple of hundred dollars above the trip he has already stood. Then when the book gets a publisher, I'll get a hundred or so more out of the advance—providing there is one. All of which will be a help, if it comes off as per plan, and if I can do my end of the work a bit more swiftly than I usually work. Matter of fact, it may yet prove to be the life-saver, thanks to you. Now, if Miguel would just come along, I'd begin to think that life is almost good again.

I hesitate to call Mrs. Simon because the only danger to the project now is that I may have benefited too much, in their opinion, from the Fund recently, and I'm afraid she'll guess I'm pushing the Miguel project too much for modesty. But if I get the least excuse for contacting her again, I won't hesitate to do so.

Maybe you're right about devoting yourself to books for a while. In fact, I'm quite sure you are—as witness the advance on your biography. Smaller rewards, but more likely. Anyhow, all told, we've got enough plays out to fill a Broadway season. I don't suppose we help ourselves by becoming a drug on the market. Too much is sometimes enough. You get to the place where you compete against yourself.

Meanwhile, I hope you take all the time necessary on *The Big Sea,* leave nothing out, make it a real titan's book. It will probably be a log that you can keep rolling as long as you live. Here is my bet that it will not only be an artistic success, but that it will buy an awful lot of fried chicken in the years ahead. Matter of fact, I'm betting that it will be a best seller.

You mentioned *Popo* going into a new edition. Is that a fact? I haven't seen a new copy in ages. I know the price was raised. Is that the evidence.

Of the two copies of *St. Louis Woman* to be returned to you after Carl V. V. and Watkins read them, I'd like to see one for a while to refresh my mind, but I think the other should go to Leah as soon as possible, and I'll hurry mine along pronto, too. She complains that she's never had as many copies as she would have liked. . . . . Do you suppose she has the first two by now? I have written Leah, urging her to send your copy of that contract. Hope she does it. I gave her your present address, too.

I'm now sending out first feelers Re: lectures for January. It may be a couple of weeks before I even get to negotiating, but will try Gary, Milwaukee, Chicago and all other possible points of the vicinity.

This regiment is all on its feet again. And a mighty proud feeling it is, too.

Last week the temperature was 100 here; this week it's 50. That's why people go to Monterey!

> Ever,
> Arna

Hollow Hills Farm
(Carmel Valley) Jamesburg
Route
Monterey, California
September 9, 1939.

Dear Arna,

AT LAST! The letter to Mrs. Simon. I hope it meets with your approval— and does the work! I would suggest you follow it up with a personal interview. And if we don't get three hundred, (I mean four) take three. I have never been broker in my whole life. Will soon be back in eternal debt again, I reckon, if something does not come to pass. . . . . At any rate I'm settled here to finish my book, and our book, too, if the letter produces results. I have a charming little Mexican style house on a hillside above a pear orchard, quiet and all my own for work—one little room, a fireplace, and a patio—built by Mario Ramirez before he died. A dog and some pigeons to keep me company. At the big house there is a wonderful library, and an equally large record library, so I play music and read books all night—since there are only candles in my own place and I no longer work at night—which means I'm about down to four pages a day since it's usually sundown by the time I get started. But I don't care, since I never had much by working all night, and don't suppose would be working all day, either. I am now doing like the Y.M.C.A. and leaving it all to Jesus! . . . . . I hope something will come of the Handy biography for you. I can think of no better person to write it! . . . . Carl said he liked you immensely and will send me some photos when they're done. He usually takes weeks. . . . Did you say *Way Down South* suffered a small kick? How kind of you to put it so mildly. I saw two N.Y. write-ups myself that left it not a leg to stand on. But the bad things I do are the only things that ever make me any money. . . . . However your beautiful *St. Louis Woman* ought to make some money for somebody. I have been working on it again, and like it better and better. I've recently sent it off to be typed in N.Y. and asked the typist to send copies to your estimable agent. Please tell her so and ask her to send me the agreement we signed, as I have not received it yet. I've met a producer summering here who is dying to see it, and will, as soon as I get a script back. He's put on several important shows here on the coast. When is Ellis doing the show? And where? . . . . Mary lost her job. Dick married Deema. The ladies of the race, I presume, are raising hell! Equality, where is thy sting? . . . . . Get us some Chicago, Gary, Peoria, Springfield church and college lectures for late January when (if I have an overcoat by then) I'll be coming through—as I expect to have Grinnell College and Antioch about that time, early February I think. Could do Chicago region before or after. Get lots of little ones and let's spread culture. Let's wait until we get a car to do the South. By train, too expensive. . . . . Is Countee back, or in the war? . . . . . Did you visit the Suitcase Theatre? Have you got on the writer's project yet? . . . . . How is Alberta. Tell her art is long—but lasting! Posterity usually loves it! . . . . . I'm sending a copy of *St. Louis Woman* to Carl V.V. and also to Rowena Jelliffe. From the Gilpins at least you'll have $60—and maybe the Rockefeller's'll get interested. Imagine Lil Augie in the Centre Theatre at Radio City! Wouldn't that be swell? And I don't see why not, do you.

> Sincerely,
> Langston

> 703 E. 50th Place
> Chicago
> 12 Sept. '39

Dear Lang:

I feel ten points better now that I know you are safe in a cottage on the side of a hill. I can also stop worrying about the progress of the book, now that I know you have a grove in sight, not to mention pigeons, dogs and a patio. These will keep you going. Your letter to Mrs. Simon was persuasive, too. Unless she feels that they have done enough for me already, it ought to accomplish its purpose. I'm *sure* it will make an attractive book. . . . The material, as you outlined it.

In New York I failed to attend the Suitcase Theatre, but spent much time with most of its leaders, heard all the plans and the news and attended the reading of *Bright and Morning Star.* Ted put on a good one-man performance on a sweltering night. Then there was the buffet supper by Dorothy Peterson for your Aunt Toy, on her birthday.

The Handy book is still in the discussion stage. I have done three chapters plus an outline for the new *whole* and plus all groundwork for the new version, but that's where it stands and will stand till Trounstine and Handy can get together. Handy will take no steps without his lawyer's guidance, and the lawyer is a rather difficult substitute for a literary agent. Personally, all I want is *assurance* that I'll be paid for my work. That has not been forthcoming as yet, though I have had a two-week trip to New York at his expense and have gone over the details of the story with him at great length.

Lots of cards are still being played, but still nary a trick is being turned. Not on the Writers' Project yet, though a slender hope is held out for October. *Tom-Tom* turned down! They thought that maybe I'd worked on it too much and hence lost the easy, spontaneous quality they'd expected (and they are right!). At any rate, I won't send the mss. around to other publishers, but will trunk-it at Houghton's suggestion and stay in their fold. Which means that as soon as I've done Miguel a draft, I'll try another for the Boston folks. . . . Provided I'm eating again by then.

To top off this marvelous epoch, all our brood had "flu" last week, me the worst of all, Constance cut two new teeth and Alberta had a couple extracted—all in school-opening week, and Poppy going for the first time, and Paul and Joan changing to public school. But I say, "Let the old bad luck happen—we can't stop it. I wouldn't care now if it should cloud up and rain cobblestones. I'm toughened." But if I ever got to California again, by George, I bet I wouldn't leave without a round-trip ticket. You can be more contented out there on nothing than any place I know.

Did I tell you that contracts were signed for an English edition of *Drums* just two or three days, perhaps a week, before war broke out. That is a symbol of my present off-stride operations. At the present, however, my hopes are all set on Miguel, the boy of Mexico. Your letter will do the business if anything can.

Will there be a copy of *St. Louis Woman* for me, too? If not, never mind. I'll read yours when you come to town. I failed to see Ellis in N.Y. She has no phone. Salisbury didn't tell me when or where the performance would be given, but I'll ask again. Carl V.V. and others might want to attend as well as the producers and critics Salisbury has promised to have on hand. Lieber and Trounstine might like to look in. You write Salisbury, too, because she seldom answers me. . . . Have not heard whether Countee came back or not, but I'd guess he returned on the Normandie. He left on it, writing me a note while aboard, and seemed to have definite arrangements to return by the 1st of Sept.

Say, wish you and I could take a couple of weeks out and dramatize *Black Thunder,* building up at the center of it a love triangle between the yellow gal Melody and the Planter's son Robbin and the young Jacobin Biddenhurst from Philadelphia, and making Melody betray the insurrection because of her love for young Robbin—during a moment of wavering. It might be just faintly possible to weave in enough standard American history (The Sedition Law, the jailing of Callander Jefferson, friend, etc.) to interest some producer, while the doings of the slaves would remain a most dramatic and different background. It keeps coming to me. Yellow gals are always popular on the stage. Also slaves—as background.

I did not see *Way Down South* nor the write-ups, but someone gave me the tenor of one. I happened to leave the morning after it opened. Hope I didn't get a wrong impression of the criticism. But I'd gladly take an occasional razz while I'm making the pot boil—no harm in that.

I'll cast my eyes about for some lecture spots near here for January, and will report findings promptly.

Best wishes to Noel Sullivan—when you see him. And don't forget to take time out and brighten these dismal diggings with a letter now and again.

Ever,
Arna

Dear Arna,

The era of trials and tribulations is indeed upon the world. The only good thing about suffering is that it gives you something to write about afterwards. The compensation, of course, for those who aren't writers, is that they have something to read. (The only difficulty about all that is that, alas, both reader and writer would often prefer something to eat!). . . . . Well, my reversal of fortune is that nowadays I am eating too much, rather than not enough, and so have gained 12 pounds here on the farm, and will have to get up early and take exercise, or shortly I will look more like you than ever before. Or maybe you are getting thin now, and will look more like me. In which case we can substitute for each other whenever there's a lecture date one or the other of us don't want to fill. This coming season I think we had better take all dates from Five up! (How wonderful a Five in days of drought!). . . . . Kindly take a small portion of this one and take Alberta to see my *Way Down South* now making its way across the screens of the nation. Since you would not go see *Mulatto,* I will never forgive you if you don't see this one, and hear "Louisiana". . . . . Sight unseen, I got an advance on my book. Naturally, it is vanishing like the snows of May, since I owed everybody, was on the verge of eviction in New York, and had my nice grey suit in pawn. But for the nonce, all is well again. Is there any way of keeping all well????? If there is, please let me know, and I will share with you accordingly. With no peace of mind, I couldn't even create a letter to Mrs. Simon.

Re MRS. SIMON:

Hadn't you better follow up with a casual call? So far I've had no answer.

Re MR. HANDY:

He'll probably have no money until he gets his ASCAP check in October. He's always broke, too. Do you like working on it? His verbal anecdotes are wonderful.

Re ST. LOUIS WOMAN:

2 to Leah. 1 to Perry Watkins who reads for producers. 1 to Carl who can drop a good word here and there. 1 to Gilpins who have money. 1 to me for the man out here. Watkins & Carl to be returned to me, so you can have one—unless you'd prefer to keep them active, in which case better Leah have it. I refuse to write the lady, so please write her yourself and urge sending of my contract, also find out when and where the play is to be done—or ask Countee to do so.

Re BLACK THUNDER:

I wouldn't dramatize *Hamlet* if it were lying around loose, until some one of the various dramatizations we now have going around get done. If starve I must, let it be on books from now on and not the theatre! Carajo! Me caigo en la puta madre del teatro!

Have you read *Writing the Juvenile Story* by May Emery Hall? I am ordering it today and will lend it to you if you haven't seen it.

I'm sending you a swell poem a guy in New Orleans sent me to read months ago and I just now read. Also a Vern Durham had sent me some poems in 1938 that I just read, too, and found some of them very good. Said Vern Durham (male or female, I don't know) lives in Chicago. Do you know the person? I've just sent the poems back. Still have about three feet of (thick) outside manuscripts to go through, but the pleasure of finding some real talent among them makes me hope to read the rest before 1942.

BOTH my theatres are in a grand state of upheaval and bust up! How about that one in Chicago? (Which isn't mine, thank God!) Do you ever hear anything of it?

If Shakespeare and Ibsen were my collaborators, me, I would not start another one! (I will only start another one someday when I have something of my own I want to put on! If you have anything of your own you want to put on, you start your own!)

I would love to see Constance with her new teeth, and all the rest of you-all, flu or no flu.

I will try to write a beautiful book so that next winter you will have it to read. I hope, also, that we get to write *Miguel* so we will have something to eat while we are reading. Too bad the soul depends so on the belly!

Maybe we should put in our time achieving Nirvana instead of worrying about working and eating. Several quite wealthy people I know out here don't care at all about eating and are spending great portions of their time squatting in the Buddhist position. Once achieved, it is said to take a great load off your mind.

> Avec mes sentiments les plus
> sinceres,
> Langston

> Hollow Hills Farm,
> September 21, 1939,
> Monterey, California.

Dear Arna,

Just at this moment, as I'm about to leave for Frisco for a day or two to get my monthly haircut, comes a joyful letter from Mrs. Simon saying that they're delighted to have us do the book and inquiring whether they should send us each a Two Hundred Dollar check at once or not. I am inclined to say AT ONCE and get it over with. *That* bird in the hand, one can then proceed to catch others. So I am writing her to that effect. . . . . Would you immediately start a draft of the book? [*Boy of the Border*] Create a family for Miguel to leave behind and get back to— Mother, little sister, a little brother he wants to impress, or a big brother he wants to live up to and top in adventure—perhaps this latter is preferable. Bring in a nice American boy in trouble somewhere on the road that Miguel helps, or that helps Miguel—perhaps this last also better; a couple of flaming sunsets and a dust storm; a Los Angeles cloud burst that washes out roads and carries off a colt that is rescued, etc., etc., etc., plus plenty of simplicity and a few near tear drops, and something heroic once to keep the faith with the possibilities of the human race and buoy up the Mexicans. . . . . . Also go see the lady and discuss it with her.

Tell Alberta time is fleeting but ART eventually catches up!! Just keep your hand on the plow and make a good meat stew once in while!

> Sincerely,
> Langston

P.S. If *St. Louis Woman* has all the possibilities (and I think it has) that Salisbury feels it has—why don't you-all get a typist to make you six more scripts? $15.00 is the price. Do you want me to order them for you?

703 E. 50th Place
Chicago, Illinois
23 September '39

Hot dog, boy! I knowed they's a ace in that deck somewheres. I'm starting a draft of the book immediately. Now if that two hundred will roll in tomorrow or the next day, so that I can pay the rent, all will be peaches in Georgia for a while.

Way Down South is in town, so we're going to see it tomorrow if it's still at the Hyde Park Theatre then. This is the first I've seen of the notice, and I'm hoping that today is just the opening day.

I'm writing Countee, offering to join him in ordering more copies of *St. Louis Woman*. If he's in for it, I'll let you know so that you can order them through the same individual who did the last batch.

You were inspired, literally inspired, when you decided to ask for the money from Mrs. Simon *immediately*. This is the time when it will do the most good. . . . I'll send you an outline draft within the week; so you may rest assured the book is making. Also, I feel inclined to take whatever time it demands, to make it somewhat larger than *Popo,* to make a serious bid for real sales. Meanwhile, if a dream I've been having comes true, I may be in L.A. by the time you finish your book. That is provided I *don't* get the Writer's Project editorial job. My father has his head set on a new car and has suggested that I drive it from the factory for him. I'll know for sure within a month perhaps. Meanwhile, too, I'm dreaming of a month of *lectures* for late January and February. More of that anon.

Well, the stew is boiling again.

Ever,
Arna

703 E. 50th Place
Chicago
14 November '39

Dear Lang,

It is ripe good news to know that *The Big Sea* is safely dispatched. Also that you are going to get TWO books instead of one from the work. Sales may be helped, too, by the fact that the Russian adventure will wait for the second volume —this being, as I'd imagine, almost the poorest possible time to issue anything on that theme to the American market. In the second book—well, all who read the first will want that ir-regardless. Let me know as soon as Knopf definitely schedules it. I want to start a campaign to have Gabriel Heater summon you as a guest of his popular "We the People" broadcast, just as he has had several other authors with interesting lives, about the time of publication. They bear the expenses of those invited to and from N.Y., and the plug is terrific. The boy who wrote *Christ in Concrete* was on a few weeks ago. Between a letter from me and one from the Knopf publicity department about the same time, I think it should work.

Tomorrow morning I'm off to Raleigh, N.C. to talk about three or four times under the Aegis of the Richard B. Harrison Public Library. There's a hundred dollars in it, but I'll count myself lucky if I get home with a month's rent after paying traveling expenses. Anyhow, I expect to be on my way back by the time you get this. I think the library folks intend to pay the freight by subletting me to some of the schools around, like Shaw, St. Augustine, etc. . . . Also, I think I have return engagement for you in Evanston—different place. It is under consideration now, but don't know that they can pay for two of us, so I'm working on it for a solo for you—particularly since I'm selling my birthright locally by taking two or three free things.

Bronco Herd, né *Boy of the Border,* is coming along. About thirty-five or forty pages completed (circa ⅓ of total) and I would have sent a copy on to you today had I not been groggy most of the past week with a miserable head cold, plus the agony of writing two or three speeches for my engagement down South, before getting one that I can stomach. I'll try to learn it en route. . . . The Handy book is a headache. He jumps on my neck when I jazz it up; Trounstine screams when I fail to. I'm afraid it'll come to no good end. I'm going to take a long rest from it, perhaps a month, and finish up my draft of our juvenile. Incidentally, I've departed from that outline somewhat. The little hero is not a peon, but the son of a Mexican artist of some standing. He is nephew of a wealthy owner of an hacienda. The house in which the boy lives is the twin of the one your father owned when you visited him. I got the details from the Big Sea!

The latest on *St. Louis Woman* is that Lew Leslie is still trying his best to uncover an angel with golden wings. It would be good if he could get in touch with those men Clarence knew out there on the coast . . . Leah Salisbury must feel up-stage these days, with her *Sky Lark* such a hit. But she's had many of those. . . . I enjoyed your proclamation. It shows remarkable restraint. . . .

I'm reading a lot about South America these days. Brazil in particular. You and I must go there soon's we've both scored a big hit!

A batch of manuscript will accompany my next. Meanwhile,

Ever,
Arna

November 20, 1939

Dear Arna,

Under separate cover the book on children's story writing goes off to you today.

LECTURES: Having an extremely one-track mind, I can only work on one thing at a time, so for the last three days I've been working out my much delayed lecture tour for the months of February and March which Miss Wills in New York is booking for me—but it being her first time at such a job, I sort of have to outline it and all. I have about five or six dates already booked and they now run from Downington Prep School on February 19th through to the Book Fair at West Virginia State College on March 29th. Area to be covered meanwhile (and now being booked) is New York, Pennsylvania, Maryland, Washington, D.C., West Virginia, Southern Ohio, and Kentucky, all of which I'm trying to fit into a consecutive trip of six weeks duration. Then in April I'll be in Chicago for the whole month, so any lectures which we can get jointly (or for me alone) will be most welcome. So as things now stand, I'd suggest you limit our joint appearances to April and May (if they run that far). Or if you've already got us for February, week of Feb. 5–10 ought to be alright as I'd be passing through on my way East about that time as plans now stand—and if God sends me the fare.

We ought to be able to get a lot of YM & YWCA engagements together (also YMHA (Jewish)—I'm speaking for them in New York) in the Spring in Illinois, Michigan, Indiana, etc. around about Chicago. Also try Urban League & NAACP, sororities and fraternities, clubs and churches. For churches take a 60–40 percentage. The 60% of gross to go to us with a minimum of $25.00.

I'd be delighted to take Evanston again. There must be some Negro frats at the Illinois State and the other colleges round about that could present us. What about white literary clubs in Chicago area? What about Federation of Colored Women's Clubs? I have got to lecture me up three or four hundred bucks this spring to write that novel on while I'm in Chi. Such is IMPERATIVE. So we might as well hustle it up together.

Also the trade unions are beginning to be culturally inclined. Try Hank Johnson's and Ishmael's and Dining Car folks.

One more day on this and I shall take up our kid's book. So look for a letter shortly.

C.V.V. says *Big Sea* is my best so far. Couldn't put it down. I hope Knopf's can't either. Haven't heard from them yet.

How was Raleigh?

Sincerely,
Lang

P.S. Oh, yes. The Adult Education Council in Chicago uses speakers. Pays a small fee. Contact their Speakers' Bureau—a Miss Saunders—if she's still there.

And ask Miss Harsh about the Libraries. But PAY groups!!! Can Rosenwald's help on lectures?

Should we get out a printed penny post card announcing our availability for lectures in Middle West?

703 E. 50th Place
Chicago
24 November '39

Dear Lang:

The hosannas are all for Dick Wright, I imagine, from now till *The Big Sea* comes out. His new novel has just been announced as the Book-of-the-Month for January. I tried to get in touch with him in New York, but he's already living out of town, perhaps partly on the strength of this latest jack-pot. If the usual signs hold, Dick's financial problems should be solved from now on. I'm sure he deserves it abundantly.

Raleigh and Durham were grand. I stayed with the James Sumner Lees. He was your classmate at Lincoln, I believe. And if you want to swing that far South in the spring you can perhaps have all the 25 dollar shots you want. They mentioned (Mollie Lee, the Raleigh librarian) wanting you for next year if you were near enough to be secured when book week rolls around. But spring might not be out of the question, if you'd care to have the girl write Mollie. Also Shepherd, the president of North Carolina College, one of the lecture spots, mentioned you pleasantly, remembering your last turn down there. They have all new buildings now—a beautiful campus.

To top it all, Zora [Neale Hurston] was there. She lectured there a year ago and got her hooks in so good she is now on the faculty, teaching dramatics. She gave me a wonderful time. Zora is really a changed woman, still her old humorous self, but more level and poised. She told me that the cross of her life is the fact that there has been a gulf between you and her. She said she wakes up at night crying about it even yet. I told her not to be ridiculous, that you have never ceased to insist that she is wonderful. After that she could not do too much for me. When I told her that I was going to tell you what she said, she even promised to try to get me a job in the South someplace. So, in order that she won't change her mind, I hope you'll write her a sweet letter, or at least send a nice Christmas card. She also said another thing that sounds reasonable to me. She said her hysterics, etc. were not provoked by you at all, and I believe it. She said, or intimated, that the whole thing could be traced to old-fashioned female jealousy between her and Louise, jealousy over the matter of influence over you. When you look at it this way, it is hard to blame poor Zora. She can't help it if she's a woman. Anyhow, she's sure she's never been so well despite her sins of the past, and if I had a bigger sheet of paper, I could give a lot of reasons why it would be grand if you'll recognize her flag of truce. . . . To show how she's improved, she has only had one really big fuss since she came to the school in September, and she came off rather well in that, since it was with a sharp-tongued man whom everyone wanted to see set down. And I'm here to tell you Zora really set him down with a bang. I have just barrels of details for you when you come to town.

Carl Van Vechten sent my pictures—lots of them—and all are good. His note praised the *Big Sea*. . . . Things are so uncertain for me that I can't do much about lectures for a week or so, but I'll work along on lines you laid down and will turn on the pressure soon's I find out definitely whether or not I'm to have a job and whether or not I'm to stay here . . . Meanwhile, as security for the writing of the new novel, I'd suggest that you add Virginia and North Carolina. Things are popping down there now. I'm sure you could line up three hundred dollars worth with no trouble. I took an even hundred out of just Raleigh and Durham. Not far away are Bennet, A. & T., Petersburgh, etc. etc. . . . There'd still be enough of the South left if you wanted to make a strictly southern tour later. . . . Anything I can get in the mid-west, I'll put down for April. Why don't you get Denver and Salt Lake on your way East. And I'm told that Morgan College is now a good spot. Also, Zora just spoke at Hampton last week; maybe that's good again. Why don't you let her help book some, incidentally? She'd love it!

I just got home yesterday so have not seen anyone or written anything. But I'm getting down to *Bronco Herd* presently. . . . Lew Leslie has given up on *St. Louis Woman*. Todd now interested, it seems. Lots of sepia on Broadway now, but I saw none, my quick turn through N.Y. lasting only a couple of days. Had to get home for Thanksgiving dinner—and glad indeed to have one!

Ever,
Arna

Dear Arna,

This, I hope, is the last day I shall be working on lectures. All this week, I've been outlining my spring tour, digging up addresses, and so on. . . . . A few more ideas occur to me about joint engagements: Thinking in terms of something we can sell easily, why not get up a program called something like: *Negro Literature from Then to Now* as discussed by Arna Bontemps and illustrated by Langston Hughes, both in person! And you would give a talk on everybody's books including yours and mine, some personal anecdotes about writers you know, something about how to write, and then introduce me (or whoever happens to be with you) as a living and modern example of Negro literature. . . . . . It seems to me to have endless possibilities for colleges, Book Fairs (both Negro and white) women's clubs, etc. And when I wasn't along, (Once the lecture got sort of standardized and known) you could take any writer who happened to be available like Frank Marshall Davis or Bob Davis in Chicago, Dick Wright or Claude McKay in New York, and let them serve for the living example or Exhibit A of your talk. . . .

In fact, somebody ought to take the place of the late James Weldon in spreading culture, and it might as well be you, going James Weldon one better by taking a real live writer along with you to show that we have more than one in the race. In other words (like the movies) a double feature, *you* plus! How does that idea strike you?

Let's try it out at Bloomington, Peoria, Springfield, Terre Haute, Ann Arbor, etc. this spring. It ought to be swell for inter-racial conferences, etc.

Where is *Boy of the Border?* I hope he is riding a fast horse with a flying mane.

I'm having a penny post card printed to announce my own tour in East, Maryland, West Virginia, and Kentucky, and southern Ohio, and southern Indiana. If you've got negotiations on for joint lectures anywhere, let me know, so I won't cut in on it. Also whenever you have an engagement for us (or me) please let Miss Frances Wills, 370 Manhattan Avenue, New York, know about it so she can put it on her schedule and thus not book that date somewhere else. As I told you, (I believe) I can take dates in Chicago area between February 11 and 16, or after April 1, and any time in spring from then on.

I'm going to try to do first drafts of several things I have in mind, just *first* drafts while I'm here. Then on tour I can do the polishing up. I've got about seven things I still want to write this winter before I start East. I think I shall start doing short stories again, too, as I seem to have some ideas coming up.

How are Camille, Poppy, Paul, Joan, and Constance? Ask Alberta what she would do if they all grew up to be writers?

HEY! Did you get a *Popo* check? I didn't yet, and my need is growing greater day by day, because I intended to pay December's rent with it!

Langston

703 E. 50th Place
Chicago
3 December

Dear Lang:

You are certainly leaving no stone unturned in getting the lecture tour under control. Your ability to do things all in a heap makes me feel like the slouch I am. But don't worry, I'm trying to do my tiny little bit more like an ant would do it. At the moment I don't know a soul in Ann Arbor, Bloomington, Peoria, etc. to whom I can write for engagements. I've got to try to hustle up some addresses first. Then the salesmanship! Also I'm slowed down to a walk by my efforts to get a job. Haven't given up yet. Anyhow, any dates I make in these parts will be made according to the date schedule you gave me—most likely after April 1st. Provided I get some! The program arrangement you suggest sounds good. I'm in for trying it. And I'm determined to turn up a *little* business some way or other.

I'm on the last half of Miguel, despite interruptions, etc., but I'm wondering if I hadn't better finish the draft before sending it. Even with the Handy thing going along at the same time, I should be able to get it to you around Xmas. Let me know just how long you will be at the Farm. In my opinion you are wise to remain as long as possible, getting as much work done as possible. There should be a good short story market for your stuff by now, since you haven't offered anything to speak of for a couple of years.

Did I tell you Lew Leslie had finally returned *St. Louis Woman?* L.S. says she's working on Todd now.

Evidently I did a bit better with my talks in N.C. than in the past. At least, they're writing me some kind letters. What somebody should do, of course, is offer me a job. One talked about it a little—don't know how seriously.

My coming to California in my father's new car grows less likely daily. Of course, nothing certain yet.

The *Popo* check came. I'm sure you have yours by now. . . . The chapters of *Boy of the Border,* as completed, are: 1. The Bronco Herd 2. Bandits 3. A Story Beneath the Stars 4. Cactus Country 5. A Mistake 6. (No title yet). I've departed rather far from outline. Better this way, though.

The kids and Alberta all muy robusto—and noisy!

Ever,
Arna

Sunday,
6 December

Dear Lang,

Just had another telephone conversation with Shaw of the WPA theater here. Nothing further has been done about the *Jack* from their angle but to have six copies typed. They have, he said, re-read it and come to the conclusion that it needs less changing than their first impression gave them to think. A new colored woman—whom I don't know—working on the project gave them the report that she considered the play vulgar. He, however, is willing to dismiss this as merely a case of high-mindedness. Yet they have been delayed in their work by reorganization and the business of cutting their forces here and there. I'm supposed to

46

hear from him again in a day or two and something should start cooking right away. He was delighted—as am I—to know that he may have a chance of seeing you after New Years. I rather feel that Chicago will see our *Jack* within a month or two.

Had a talk with Dick Wright also. Have you read his long story in the *New Caravan?* It has been singled out for special notice in some of the reviews, especially the *Daily News* here. The book costs 3.90, or I'd have read it by now. No library copies on hand yet.

You have never mentioned your novel, but I'm sure you must have a reindeer concealed in your silk hat. . . . I mentioned the Seattle company to Trounstine. . . . February 27th—Sad-Faced Boy: I hope it's the first Harlem story for children. I'll leave you to guess from whom I got the idea of having the colored kids kidnap a little Jew and having the little Jew hesitate to go home after he was released, albeit that's only one chapter of the story—the debt is obvious.

I'm overworked as usual, but the Xmas holidays are near. Hurry on over and plan to stay a long time.

Ever,
Arna

703 E. 50th Place
Chicago
14 December

Dear Lang:

The best thing about the poetic mood is that you are in top form. The Blues are certainly as good (and perhaps a little better in the case of the first three) as you ever wrote. They go deeper. The over-tones echo longer. Meanwhile, none of the old wit and freshness is lost. Are these among the poems you sold to the New Yorker? And I liked just about as well, in their way, the kid's poems. Now why not a "child's garden of verses?" If you could do fifty of these on this level of quality, you might find you had written your most successful volume of poetry.

Please let me know when *Big Sea* will be published. And have the Knopf publicity man call the attention of Gabriel Heater of "We The People" to you about that time. This should put you right in the groove for that program and a good send-off. I intend to write him, too, when the date approaches. The fact that you have an autobiography at this age should be arresting immediately. A few details should do the rest. With or without this, of course, I'm ready to bet a Stetson the book becomes a best seller. That'll make two of you on the list in '40. (Dick's, I now learn, is part of a Dual choice.)

Trounstine just heard from the English publisher of *Drums.* He is bringing it out early in '40, and he sent along a modest advance which, trimmed of 7 shillings on the pound as my contribution to the War, reached me just in time to buy some Christmas candy. Also Macmillan wrote that they have been urged by the state department (along with other publishers) to make South America, Central America and the West Indies an open field and to sell American editions down there to help the pan-American good-will along. So Macmillans have put *Drums* on the list of books their representative will try to sell in those countries, beginning almost immediately. It required a new agreement with the publishers and authors.

I hope it works out, especially since so many educated Latins read English anyhow. Besides, anything that extends the book market is good.

Handy was here a few days. Look what he's been up to. This clipping is from the N.Y. Times.

About 35 pages remain to be written on the first draft of *Boy of the Border* and about the same number on the portion of the Handy book that Trounstine will peddle. I have determined to finish this 70 page stint and do the copying before the year ends. I think I can make it. That will give you all of January to doctor up Miguel, add homey detail about foods, etc., speed up the narrative where I've let it bog, and make the last copy. Hunh? It's a pretty good story, I think, but there may still be plenty of work for you. It's got to be as good as we can make it.

I still don't know whether or not I'm coming out that way, but I'm pretty sure it won't be in January. There are 3 big IF's. If I get a job as editorial supervisor on the Writer's Project, I won't cut out till times get better, and it's still 50-50 whether or not I'll get it. I figure it should certainly be settled by early in new year. Then I can do more about lining myself up for lectures, too. In the case of the trip, there are also a couple of minor considerations. I'm working hard and waiting for things to hatch.

This is the seventh month we have lived on "literature," and I can hardly believe my eyes when I look around and see that not one of the brood has starved. Let's hope the first seven are the worst! I hope to get back on my novel Jan. 1st. If I can keep meal in the barrel till that's finished, I'll feel like shouting and hallelujah.

Are you going to celebrate Christmas on the Farm, in Carmel or in Frisco? Everything's the same round here. Everybody well and far too hopeful.

Ever,
Arna

P.S. Say, want one of the Van Vechten photos? Or is he sending you some? I think you said he was, but I'm not sure.

703 E. 50th Place
Chicago
20 December '39

Dear Lang:

It's a bright idea: *The Blues* of Langston Hughes.

You could make the introduction a substantial essay like the one by Day in *A Time To Dance* and sell it to a magazine like Harpers or the Atlantic first. And since the poems will be pleasant and humorous, the book should indeed do well —better perhaps than any of the other books of poetry.

I told you about the first batch of poems. These last ones are even better. *Dustbowl* is perfect. It belongs beside your very best in this pattern. I have memorized it as well as *Southern Mammy Sings* on two or three readings, without intending to do so. Both are spanking good. The latter goes down beside *Cross* and *Way Down South In Dixie.* I don't know, however, that the little refrains help it much. Surely it would be fully as good without them, but I might not think so after I've slept on the poems a little longer. *A Cabaret Girl* comes next. Very good. Then *West Texas,* medium. I liked *Daybreak in Alabama* least. Individually I liked the lines and parts, but it didn't seem to add up so well. I'd like to see the punch line "When I get to be etc." used in another setting and the descriptive parts (all good) used in another poem perhaps. But *Dustbowl* and *Southern Mammy,* each in its way, show you still to be in excellent voice. I'm crazy about them.

Owen and Ruby [B's sister & brother-in-law] are tickled pink because Owen has just been appointed to a neat, newly built church in Pasadena. They say they're in California to stay now.

You'll be able to tell Mrs. Simon [editor at Knopf] by the first of the year that *Boy of the Border* is finished (first draft) and wanting only revisions and improvements, etc.

Gonna shoot any Roman candles Xmas?

Ever,
Arna

703 E. 50th Place
Chicago
Thursday A.M.

Dear Lang,

Most of what I said in the letter I wrote last night turned out to be imaginary when I finally got in touch with Truman Gibson. First, your telegram *did* come —it came at a particularly hectic moment and, largely through accident, was unintentionally snowed under till it was too late to get it. In the meantime the picture of things here has been somewhat altered by theatrical people and groups who, since I wrote you first, have heard what's going on and are making energetic bids to work in their own pet productions. Leading the scuffle is Mintern (I think that's the name who did the first Swing Mikado.) He wants to bring in the same group for a repertoire of Gilbert & Sullivans in Brown skin. I'm swinging from my heels against it. He has held the company intact. My opposition to that line is so outspoken that my collaboration on a black Cavalcade (should it win out) might possibly have to be a silent one between you and me. In the meantime I shall get out today and try to take up other opposition to the G. & S. fanatics. Your help right here would be valuable, particularly if it came through an agent or producer who would step up and make an offer to sell the sort of thing you suggest (which is obviously the best one). Wouldn't Lieber, for example, want to put Todd or Leslie or somebody in touch with the Exposition? (or Salisbury?)

In view of the above I think it would be better for you to wait till this is ironed out before coming. You will thus remain in a better position to actually do the show—not having injected yourself into the discussion of whether it shall be this or that. But I'm assured that something will be worked out before your lectures in W. Va. are finished, and I will wire you further at this same address unless you give me another one. . . . The Rosenwalds are behind the Expo to the tune of 10,000, and I'm on my way over there to get Mrs. Simon against the G.S. forces, if possible. So sit tight a few days, jot down ideas for a black Cavalcade by us and write a letter or two if you have time and feel inclined. Truman has already tentatively approved commissioning such a show. He is boss, but not exactly dictator, of course. So the war helps. Could there be a production in the theatre without it???!!!! See where your poems in Esquire, illustrated by E. Simms Campbell, have been announced by the magazine publicity dept.

Ever,
Arna

703 E. 50th Place
Chicago
3 January '40

Dear Lang:

Guess what! I'm employed. Editor on the Writer's Project. Santa brought it two days before Xmas. Now if I can only make it till the first pay day, things should bear down with less pressure for a time. The new job means that I haven't been able to work on my own writing for more than a week and may not get back to it for another ten days. By then, however, I should be well adjusted here and in a position to do even more and better work than was possible during the past month or two.

Several good writers are down here, serving as editors. One is Stuart David Engstrand* whose first novel *The Invaders* was published by Knopf. His latest, *They Sought For Paradise,* was brought out by Harpers. I think he was a runner up to Dick in the Story Contest for WPA writers. I was fortunate enough to get in down here without being certified, which is much better, but harder, since only one tenth can belong in that category and the tenth is generally overfilled. I'm in the office all day at the moment, but I hope to get a field assignment that will enable me to work at home later. To begin next week!

Maybe, in view of all the above developments, I better hold the *Boy of the Border* manuscript till you arrive. What do you say? And why don't you pack up and come along almost immediately. A snow is promised for tomorrow night. The meals should be substantial in our quarters by the time you arrive—substantial by past standards. There are a number of shows here. A whiff of holiday cheer is still in the air. Why delay? Button up your overcoat and hit the chilly.

Just had an invitation to speak in West Virginia this coming spring. Don't know that I can make it, however. I won't be able to go just for the trip, under present circumstances, and I doubt that they could pay much more than just expenses. . . . Don't know why Tommie McKnight never answered me about those "Y" lectures for us. But maybe the dirt I heard in N.Y. has something to do with it. Aaron and Alta were telling some sort of anecdote that put the girl we met there—remember?—in a different light. So maybe Maggie and Jiggs have been going round and round. Maybe, too, this is just evil-minded.

Christmas was a fine day—thanks to you and ME and the gods of the Writer's Project, not to mention the ZOO! Thanks multiplied.

We'll be expecting you on every train now, so hurry along. I know you've sated yourself with the serenity of the hills and dales by now. So come along.

Ever,
Arna

*Also Jack Conroy

50

703 E. 50th Place
Chicago
4 January '40

Dear Lang,

Piquion [Haitian writer] is on my conscience, too; let's hope, however, that times get better—for his sake, if no other. I just about went broke myself, buying the kids things for Xmas that I had been forced to deny them last year and on still earlier years. But thank God I still had this fin in my sock, and there's a pay day coming next Sat'dy. So let me know if nothing breaks 'tween now and then, and there'll be another one coming up.

The real winter weather that you take such good and wise pains to miss hit us today. It's twelve above now but headed for zero tonight.

As nifty a piece of writing as you ever did is that statement on *Good-bye, Christ.* It seems to me to put the stopper in the bottle most neatly. I'll read it to Embree and others come Monday—this being a Saturday. I hope it will be reprinted widely. I take it that you are sending it to the S. E. P. as well as to all other rags that mentioned the episode one way or another. The net effect, I'm sure, will be favorable to you. It would be good if *Time* could get a copy of the S.E.P. page plus newspaper clippings plus your statement. A sweet story might be hatched for the wider reading public. Who is that fellow who wrote the Joe Louis story for Life?

I gave you a bum steer on that reprint plan. It is not Modern Age, but Pocket Books that are entertaining the notion. Yours seems to be still on the griddle, but last Embree mentioned it he was debating whether to suggest *Laughter* or *Sea* as his preference for the purpose. If you have already called Knopf's attention to it, maybe you'd better put him straight: *Pocket Books.*

One of the things I gave the kids for Xmas was a copy of *Story and Verse for Children.* It's a grand anthology published by Macmillan. Included are a poem of yours, a generous section from *Popo,* biographical sketches of us both. We are in the best of company there—only topnotchers among current crop included. It will perhaps become a standard for libraries, colleges, etc., being designed also for use in classes for librarians and others studying the whole range of children's literature.

I'm working hard (as I have time) but progressing slowly on my novel. My New Year's resolve is to perk up. At best, though, I don't hope to see it in print before '42. Like you, I mean to write literature or bust! Yes, suh!

Arna

Remember me to the Hollow Hills family. Speaking of coming to year's end broke—that's nothing if you've been everywhere and done everything! A socially conscious artist wouldn't want a *surplus,* would he?

Hollow Hills Farm,
Monterey, California,
January 18, 1940.

Dear Arna:

Congratulations on the job. I think that is swell! I wish I had one, too. Even a little regular income takes a lot of worry off the mind. . . . . I've been broke as a mujick lately, but yesterday *Esquire* delighted my heart with the nicest kind of a nice check for "Seven Moments of Love." God bless the art of poetry! If it wasn't for poetry I wouldn't have had any Xmas money, either. Gee, if I could just write poetry at will I'd keep *The New Yorker* and my other markets *semi*-glutted. In the hope that they would keep me semi-filled.

Now, about *Boy of the Border.* Wish you'd make a report of some sort to Miss Simon, because I was sort of holding off writing her until I got your draft. I'll be through Chicago about the 10th or 12th of February, if all permits, as I have to lecture at Downingtown the 19th. But that wouldn't give us much time on *Boy of the Border.* If you get it to me before then, I can work on it on the train, providing I'm not dead of exhaustion. In any case, tell the lady something and let me know WHAT so we can keep our wires straight. I think I'd better drop her a note and say that I've been delayed a bit out here and will be in Chi in Feb. and get together with you on it? Is that O.K.? Lemme know right away.

Can't come to Chicago right now because the book ain't done. And when I pay my honest debts I won't have the fare, so have to wait for another poetic windfall. Besides, I have no overcoat! Nor ear-muffs! . . . . But I got some pretty nice Christmas presents that will help me dazzle my public when I get on that tour.

Luther Green, leading coast producer, took MY manuscript copy of *St. Louis Woman* with him to New York the other day. Wrote back he liked the beginning greatly and would soon report on the rest. I've dropped Salisbury a line about him and where to reach him. One of his backers got all excited about the play here at Carmel and had me send it to him the day he was flying East. (quiet about this!) So I hope something comes of it for you-all, as the gentleman plans to produce in New York shortly also, as well as in L.A. & Frisco.

RIGHT AWAY LET ME KNOW ABOUT SIMON, et al.

> Sincerely,
> Lang

P.S. Detroit lecture for me in May. All April open. So lets go!
At the moment literature has about got me down.

> Hollow Hills Farm,
> Monterey, California,
> January 26, 1940.

Dear Arna,

Last go-round on *Big Sea.* Finished final corrections today and am having a hundred or so of revised pages typed. Have a couple of short chapters yet to do and insert, but that is all. Cut the Harlem part 25 pages as it was part publishers liked least and thought had least of me in it, which is right, as it is not very anecdotal. . . . . . I am tired of that book now. . . . . But eager to write the second volume for which I have even better material. So maybe that is what I shall do in Chicago in April if I can find a good hide-out. That is the speakingest town! Who told everybody I was coming through there in February. Have three or four letters already asking for FREE talks. Don't they know I'm a writer not a speaker —except to speak for my supper money—which does not seem to occur to them to offer? Huh? Or have you spoilt them? Great big town like Chicago with half the Negroes in America in it and two-thirds of the white folks—and still wanting to hear somebody talk FREEEEEEEEEEEEEE! ! . . . . . Anyhow, speaking of lectures, Miss Wills in New York has done swell by me, and has practically filled up latter half of February and all of March. I'm speaking at West Virginia on the 29th. Still trying to get Bluefield. I recommended you for the BOOK FAIR at W.V. State—since my date, I believe is later and they wanted somebody for it, too, but could only pay expenses to and from New York. Maybe to and from Chicago would leave something over. I wrote them about the impossibility of anybody lecturing for NOTHING since writers don't live on air and lectures out of town take three days out of one's life and works. Certainly State schools of that sort ought to get used to paying speakers. The white ones pay—and pay well. And God knows cullud authors need it worse than the white best-seller folks. . . . . Haven't heard any more from Luther Green, but his angel lives here—so I will call him up shortly and see if he has had a reaction. Failure of *Dream* and *John Henry* both have probably killed colored shows on Broadway for another ten years. Me—I'm through with commercial theatre. May do a play now and then for the Gilpins who at least pay $60–80 dollars—short story rates. Which helps out when other things are low. . . . . I'm dropping Mrs. Simon a little note, too. Will be there between 10th and 15th. If I get me some fare. That, at the moment is missing. *Esquire* check all checked out already, owed and due before hand. . . . I loved the kid's letter and Paul's poem. Kiss all the babies for me. And don't let them freeze in that sub-zero weather I'm reading about in the East. . . . . I shall be looking for that draft of boy of border as I mail off *Big Sea* Monday so can take up the next most urgent thing.

Sincerely,
Lang

703 E. 50th Place
Chicago, Illinois
26 January '40

Dear Lang,

Good news is scarce right along through here, but hopes are abundant. So I'm also hoping that being in the hospital has its compensations—just what they could be, I'm not sure. Likewise I could wish that something good would come from eviction.

We've had a bit of sickness here, too. Poppy measles. Constance flu. Me a cold. All pretty well shaken off today, thank God.

If Knopfs do not decide favorably on the young English artist they have in mind for your new collection of poems, I can suggest one whose work Hardwick Moseley just showed me. Of course, the specimens I saw were on the juvenile level, but the gal really draws Negroes as well as anyone I know. Her name is Sharon, and she's southern white, and she can be reached in care of Houghton Mifflin.

Hank Johnson was over last night. Seems that he followed his boss John L. Lewis in the support of Willkie, with dire results: (a) lost job with the packing house workers—though he is still employed in another capacity by C.I.O. (b) won the antagonism of the C.P. He hopes eventually to get back his previous work, however, but toward the C.P. he's pretty bitter.

Hints for recuperation: (a) Don't worry about shortage of funds: you're going to get a fellowship in a couple of months or so (b) Give up ideas of mass production writing: its puts too heavy a burden on your mind. Concentrate on two or three things that really interest you. If you can boil it down to one, so much the better. In other words, don't get frantic about making some money right away. It will only delay work on whatever serious project you may be planning. Don't get excited: wait for the worm to turn! . . . . These, if followed tacitly, will restore health. Honest-to-God!

Just read in a Publishers' Weekly, summarizing 1940 in the book marts, that one of the sensations of the year was the sudden boom and abrupt decline of *Native Son* as a best seller. It concluded that the boom was due to novelty of such a book being chosen by Book-of-the-Month and the fade-out followed discovery on part of readers (who thought they were getting a murder thriller) that the book contained a "political argument." The piece was contributed by Harry Hansen. Interesting afterthought, I thought. . . . Have not heard any more about the dramatization—have you?

I'm most involved in *The Negro in Illinois,* but trying to get a little of my own work done. The Handy book should go to press soon—vastly diluted since I last saw it, no doubt. I take no credit or blame for its final shape. . . . More anon. Meanwhile—put on your clothes and walk out of that joint!

Ever,
Arna

Sunday,
Jan. 28, 1940.

Dear Arna,

I am on my last go-round, trying to get everything out of the way, ESPECIALLY THE BOOK, so I can have a few days clear for packing up and getting off. Tried my darndest to get the old book all done today, but there was big dinner party tonight that just let me get back upstairs by 10:30, although I've got a kid still typing the too-much-re-corrected pages that have to be inserted in the manuscript. How tedious the last go-round on a book is! Not to speak of three full chapters yet to write—but they can always be inserted later, if I just get this much off—since the manuscript is due in the Knopf office February 1st. . . . . . When I get to be a big rich famous author, I will have not even the faintest intimation of a dead-line.

Enclosed please find my carbon to Mrs. Simon. I hope it meets your approval. Luncheon date is dated. Let me know if (and which day) is O.K. by you both. I have to be in New York on Saturday. First lecture is following Monday in Penn. Did I tell you Miss Wills has booked me up a swell lot of lectures. If you ever want to book a tour let her do it—since I have now taught her how.

I wondered how come the last half of our book arrived first! I thought maybe your new job had gone to your haid. But your card explained all. . . . . I think it is good, but wish (and maybe this is the Hollywood influence) we had more suspense elements to make our readers hang on breathlessly from chapter to chapter. Couldn't there be one suspense element running from

54

Miguel's home all the way through to the return. Maybe not a time element, but will some thing be OK. when he gets back? Or will the money be enough to save the family honor, or something like that demanding a solution in the final chapter. See what I mean? Can you think of such an element, since you created the story and know the people—and I haven't seen the first part yet anyhow? . . . . . Do you want me to send this part I have now back ahead of me, or bring it? Will bring it unless you say other wise. . . . . . Don't like MECCA as a name for its Oriental associations. And Colima, I think, is a girl's name so better get another one for him. But this is very minor. . . . . . *What age are we doing this story for?* I've forgotten, or else never knew. . . . . SUSPENSE AGAIN: Couldn't someone get lost perhaps only for a hot minute in the sand storm, or the herd stampede or something to ad excitement and suspense as to WHAT WILL HAPPEN? OH, will Miguel lose his good friend Juan?!! Or will the whole trip come to naught because the herd thunders into the deep ravine? Or something like that to make you read a long time after Mama has done said, "Put out that light and go to sleep." Get me. Kids (and people full grown) like to feel like, "Oh, Lord, don't let that happen!" And then sigh with relief when it doesn't, quite. N'est-ce pas?

Sincerely,
Langston

Post Office Drawer 853
Huntsville, Alabama
February 3rd

Dear Lang;

I have just received the congratulations of Margaret Fuller. She says that the O. K. on our book has come down from the president of the Macmillan Company and that I should receive Miss Seaman's departmental letter of acceptance tomorrow or the day after. She sent that second report along too, and it was enthusiastic to say the least. Miss Seaman, M.F. says, will want only very minor revisions. I am now eager to know their terms. She says that they are already planning to give the book good publicity, and they have already written Doug to see if he would be interested in doing the illustrations—of course, they are not at all sure he will want to try anything of this particular type, but his letter, she says, has gone out.

Not much time to write now. . . . mail going out in about a minute. . . . . but I think you ought to write Miss Fiery and set her mind at rest. . . . Too bad we are in such demand for our literary efforts. And incidentally, I may have time to enclose that report. Will you make a copy and return since I will have no time to make one and also make this mail. . . . A letter will be at Tuskegee for you, giving all new developments and details.

Write me. Tell me the whole story about N. O. and the Mardi Gras along with the account of the flood.

And since the publication of the opus is assured, you might start advertising it. And thinking about the next one.

Sincerely,
Arna

Dear Lang:

Let's see if I can knock out a letter in two or three minutes without missing any of the essential points. . . . Just returned from a meeting of the Committee on the American Negro Exposition. I'm doing a bit of work for them (creative), and they are *paying*. Now, I've not forgotten you, and if you want it, you can come in on things. I'll write you tomorrow on their stationery and from their office, but here's just an inkling. There is a large auditorium connected with the Coliseum (4 or 5 thousand capacity) and into this they would like to bring shows and other attractions during the exposition (July 4th to Labor Day). I said that you had contracts, etc. just what they would need to further the program. There was talk about the *Aquacade* or the *Hot Mikado* at the N. Y. fair. (We might use the occasion to work in on the lyric-writing or book-writing end or something, but that would be up to you to negotiate.) Anyhow, they would like you to come to Chicago between lectures *(on Exposition expense)* if possible. If not, they would like to know where you will be so that somebody from here—perhaps Horace Cayton or Truman K. Gibson (the swell young lawyer who is head of the thing)—can come down and sign you up. Then when you come in April, if you wish, you might be put on salary for a few months for making such contacts as you might in connection with filling the auditorium with shows. Of course, I don't know how that would exact much work from you, but your advice would be valuable to them—then you might, as I said, bring about the production of a show in which you, and maybe even I, might be lined up for a writing assignment of some sort. If it sounds a bit dim, don't worry. The state has appropriated 75,000. Ford, Rosenwald, Swift, Nat. Tuber. Assn., Gen. Education Board, Harmon Foundation, and many others are already in as exhibitors. I'm research man in art dept., giving historical material for mural painters, diarama makers, etc. Lots of fun. So let me know in a hurry when you can come up for a conference or where someone from here can go down! My letter tomorrow may not add much to this. It will only be for their files. I'm also trying to get Doug and Barthé in on the work. Think both efforts will succeed.

If you'd come this week-end you would have eaten turkey. You would also have run into Dick who was here with a *Life* photographer guiding him around to South-Side scenes.

Folks think about same concerning Dick's book up here. Algren: "Might defeat its purpose by causing anti-Negro sentiment." Simon: "No-like. Strong writing. Not wholly convinced." Etc. All on bandwagon in one sense (powerful work), but all fear bad re-action from middle-class white readers, etc.

What do you think on paragraph *one?*

Ever,
Arna

703 E. 50th Place
Chicago
14 April '40

Dear Lang,

I hope you come out of it unscarred. Two and three and four a day is really trooping. Don't let it get you down. But thank God for little things and particularly for *Boy of the Border* now that he's out of the bag. Do you want the final typing to be done here or in New York? I think we should rush that phase of it —since the other has taken a bit of time—don't you? We'll also have to rush to get it on the fall schedule—if that is yet possible.

The play business is still dangling. Truman Gibson has not (yesterday) returned yet, due to many negotiations in D.C. He should arrive at any minute, however. Meanwhile, I've suggested that Lieber scrape up a Negro musical aready prepared, if the time seems short, and let you and me revise it for Exposition purposes —should he and Gibson fail to land the producer they want for the Cavalcade type of show, or should they find the time too pressing. We really should NOT lose out completely on this proposition. It's our own fault if we do. Somebody MUST have a Negro show up his sleeve that could be twisted to our purpose. Any musical comedy or review of first class entertainment value could be adapted— especially in view of the fact that it would have to be shortened to three-a-day proportions, or something like that. You put the pressure under Lieber too. (In case no producer wants to start from scratch at this date.) All he needs to do is find the show and talk it up to Gibson. These folks are still very susceptible to salesmanship. He shouldn't ask them too many questions. He should offer them something definite on behalf of a producer and then see what happens. I could even help urge acceptance. See the point?

Missed Dorothy Maynor last Sunday to hear your play on Columbia. A fair exchange indeed. I liked it much, but it didn't sound militant—maybe they left that part out, or played it down. Also thrilled to Roland Hayes singing of your song on the Tuskegee program.

Aren't the Librarians paying you? I thought they were. They are now talking about getting you for their convention at Cincinnati. This SHOULD be for pay. . . . Three letters here for you: I'm holding them—huh?

Alberta says we'll expect you here in time for dinner on Monday the 22nd. . . . If anything further develops meanwhile, I'll flash the news. Keys's address: 612 East 51st Street. Sent him your message.

Ever,
Arna

New York,
May 1, 1940.
66 St. Nicholas Pl.,

Dear Arna,

Just a few points to take up with you quickly:

CAVALCADE: Just had a long conference with Lieber. All theatre people to whom he has shown our outline think it excellent, but wish to see the book and some music before giving answers of a very definite nature—as they seem largely

57

unfamiliar with Negro material—except for Leslie who has no money and feels he cannot raise any himself. Leslie delighted to stage show if money is raised. Or to incoporate some of our material into his show (which had lousy reviews when tried out in Boston some months ago) and which he needs 15 thousand to get out of storehouse and recast and rehearse. (But it does not seem to me a very good idea, since I don't believe it is a good show and much of the music is by whites.) So, I've gone to work on

THE BOOK in order to be able to show something more than the outline to producers like Max Gordon, etc., that Lieber is trying to contact. As well as to Leslie who then will be better able to give an accurate estimate on cost of production. I have a girl today locating for me the sources of the old song material and minstrel stuff. Florence Mills' niece who has theatre knowledge and contacts is doing this. Got from ASCAP full list of Negro hit songs past. And from my Aunt names of several living old performers who can help us if we get to that point.

IN CHICAGO, if you would locate Abbie Mitchell [actress], who was in the Pekin stock, or Glover and Nettie Lewis, kindly get from them at once as much source material as you can. What songs and actors came up in that company. What books, plays, sketches did they use. Can you get hold of any of these sketches and songs that we might have them in hand to show producer and to have played for him to hear? If so, do so, or find out where they can be gotten. Also from Abbie get information concerning other early musicals she was in, as her career spans two generations.

COST of show seems to depend largely on SETS, number to be painted and handled, as each new set requires additional union stage hands to handle, union truckers to move, etc. and causes costs to mount up swiftly. So as many scenes as possible should be done with drop curtains to cut down cost greatly. So I am cutting some of the scene requirements. Even then about the lowest estimate seems to be $20 to $30 thousand to mount and cover Equity bonds and secure orchestrations, etc. So if you-all see any way of raising that amount in Chicago, go to it. Lieber suggests 6 investors at % thousand each. He has also written the *Afro American* suggesting they sponsor such a show as publicity and profit for themselves. Most of the Broadway angels seem to be still in Florida (due to cold here) and many do not back musicals which are considered a high risk—especially colored. Lieber says Columbia Broadcasting was thrilled with the air possibilities of our outline, but will not back stage productions, but thought Hammond might be interested if we could reach him. So far that has not been possible, but shall keep trying.

TIME: I have promised to have a tentative book to show on Monday. So am working hard on that. Any help you give, send by air-mail. If you send one, put special on it.

LIEBER has spent the entire afternoon on the phone talking to prospective backers about it and practically all wish to see book and music—to that end I shall try to rent or buy some of the old hits from the big Whitmark library here who are looking up what they have on hand for me. Also am contacting Handy, Johnson, etc.

TIME again. Miss Wills had three lectures for me that I was not aware of as her air-mail to me just came back here. One is on the 8th, next Wednesday, in Chicago. The American Student Union on your university campus. Wish you'd inquire of them how it is coming on and if they're expecting me—as, we heard nothing of it when I was there, but Miss Wills says they've just confirmed the date. Please let me know what you can discover about it, since I'd have to leave here Tuesday to make that. Another at Wisconsin on the 13th, and the final one on the 15th at Northwestern—all ASU's at $25.00—which would ad a little to the pot. Therefore, I'll work all this week on our show and see what I can do. Will also contact the TROPICS people for you so that you-all can write them direct. Do Do Green would be a good comedian.

ARTIS. You recall Gibson spoke of having William Artis come out to make the big statues for the large hall. Artis says he can get a leave of absence from his work here to do so. He has just had a very successful participation in a show at the Barbizon Plaza where all his heads got 4 stars and some were sold.

I looked through *Othello* last night and couldn't find anything that seemed to fit in, so think will cut that in favor of a Creole belles pretty girl number of some sort—unless you've found something there.

The Harlem Library Negro collection are making photostats of theatre pictures and material for the Detroit Fair. Why not write them and have them do it for you-all, too. I mentioned it to them. They have a swell collection of pictures of old actors, etc.

If push comes to shove, we could very nearly reduce our show to props and back drops, could we not, with effective lighting and costumes. With good singing and dancing, it should not have to depend on the backgrounds—in which case 15 thousand ought to put it on—and it should be possible to raise that—even in Chicago. It's a mere skimption as shows go. Have somebody try Joe or Roxborough. Or the owners of the Regal Theatre.

Let me know reactions to all this at once. Particularly Artis, as he says he did not see Barnett this past week-end.

Sincerely,
Lang

COLLABORATION CONTRACT

Memorandum of Agreement made this 10th day of July, 1940 between Langston Hughes and Arna Bontemps, care of Maxim Lieber, 545 Fifth Avenue, New York City.

WHEREAS the parties hereto are mutually desirous of collaborating in the writing of a work entitled CAVALCADE:

Now, therefore, in consideration of the mutual covenants herein contained it is agreed as follows:

1. That the parties hereto shall undertake jointly to write the said work entitled as aforesaid.

2. That copyright in said work shall be secured and held jointly in the names of Langston Hughes and Arna Bontemps and that all receipts and returns from said work, or from any rights therein, and any dramatic, literary, photographic or any and every form thereof, whether specifically herein enumerated or not, shall be divided as follows:

to Langston Hughes—50%
to Arna Bontemps—50%

3. Each party agrees to keep the other party fully informed of the progress of all

negotiations held in connection with the lease of the work, or leading to the disposition of any rights therein. No contract for the production, presentation or publication of the work, or the disposition of any right therewith connected, shall be valid without the signature thereto of both parties to this agreement.

4. Signed contracts concerning the initial production of the work shall be given each author and shall contain a special provision stating that all monies as and when due shall be paid by the manager direct to the agent as herein subsequently provided for.

5. In making contracts for the production or presentation of said work the parties hereto shall use their best efforts to secure the insertion in said contracts of clauses providing that on programs, billings, posters, advertisements, or other printed matter used in connection with any production thereof, in any manner, the names of Langston Hughes and Arna Bontemps shall be equally announced.

6. No change or alteration shall be made in the script of the work after its completion by any of the parties without the written consent of the other; but such written consent shall not be unreasonably withheld. Such written consent shall be deemed to be for a specific revision unless it shall state that permission is given for general revision.

7. All expenses which may reasonably be incurred under this agreement shall be mutually agreed upon in advance, and shall be shared according to the percentage of interest of the parties hereto.

8. It is expressly understood that the parties hereto in no wise form, nor shall this agreement be construed to constitute, a partnership between them.

9. The term of this agreement shall be co-extensive with the life of the copyright, and any renewals of said copyright in and to the said play. In the event of the death of any of the parties hereto during the existence of this agreement, then the surviving parties shall have the sole right to change the said play, negotiate and contract with regard to the disposition thereof, and act generally with regard thereto as though they were the sole authors thereof, except that the name of the decedent shall, where possible, always appear as co-writer thereof; and the said survivors further shall cause to be paid to the heirs or legal representatives of the deceased party hereto the agreed upon per centum of the net receipts from the said work, and furnish true copies of all agreements to the personal representatives of the deceased.

10. In the event of any dispute arising under this agreement or concerning the work, or should any difference arise between the parties concerning any dealings between them or as to any of their rights hereunder (whether the same is between the parties hereto or between one of the parties and any third party arising under this contract) such dispute or difference shall be submitted to arbitration under the laws of the American Arbitration Association. Any decision made by the said arbitrators shall be binding upon the parties.

11. The terms and conditions of this agreement shall be binding upon and inure to the benefit of the executors, administrators and assigns of the parties hereto.

12. Langston Hughes and Arna Bontemps do hereby designate Maxim Lieber, 545 Fifth Avenue, New York City as their sole agent with respect to the said work, as well as with respect to the sale, lease or other disposition of any other right or rights thereto. All sums payable to Langston Hughes and Arna Bontemps hereunder shall be made by check drawn to the order of Maxim Lieber as agent, and shall be sent to said Maxim Lieber, 545 Fifth Avenue, New York City, and the receipt of said Maxim Lieber shall be full evidence and satisfaction of any

payments made. All statements required to be furnished to Langston Hughes and Arna Bontemps shall likewise be sent to Maxim Lieber. Said Maxim Lieber shall be entitled to receive and deduct a commission of ten (10) per cent of all sums so received as agent. It is understood and agreed that the designation of the said Maxim Lieber as agent for the said work, as herein-above provided, shall be a continuing employment and interest, and shall not be revocable at the will of any of the parties hereto so long as said Maxim Lieber performs his services honestly. IN WITNESS WHEREOF, we have hereunto set our hands and seals this 10th day of July, 1940

> Langston Hughes
> Arna Bontemps
> Maxim Lieber

> Hotel Grand,
> 5044 South Parkway,
> Chicago, Ill.,
> July 21, 1940.

Hon. James W. Washington,
American Negro Exposition,
3632 South Parkway,
Chicago, Ill.

My Dear Mr. Washington:

For the past eight weeks we have been engaged in the writing of a *Cavalcade of the Negro Theatre* at the request of Mr. Truman Gibson for the American Negro Exposition Authority. This production has been given wide national and local publicity through your official press and publicity department. We have given various interviews to newspaper men, been photographed, spoken over the air, and otherwise aided in the publicity of the proposed production at the request of the Exposition Authority. We have attended numerous conferences with Mr. Gibson, Mr. Bishop, Miss Moten, and Mr. Mintern attendant upon the preparation of the script. Aside from the writing of the libretto, we devoted a great deal of time to the gathering of copies of old Negro music and the hit tunes of the past for the show, and to the securing of clearance of copyright so that the Exposition might use this material. (All of this music is at present in the hands of Mr. Minturn, ready and available for use.) We have done extensive research with the aid of the Schomburg collection in New York, the Chicago Public Library here, and personal letters to and conversations with old Negro actors and theatre people, so that the details of the production might be authentic and correct. The finished manuscript of a *Cavalcade of the Negro Theatre* has been for some weeks now in the hands of Mr. Gibson, and fifty copies in the hands of Mr. Harry Minturn, who is to direct the production.

Our contracts have likewise for some time been in the possession of Mr. Gibson. These contracts have not as yet been signed, nor have they been returned to us or our agent. Apparently no attention whatsoever has been paid them. A letter of inquiry to Mr. Gibson from our agent (Maxim Lieber, 545 Fifth Avenue, New York) has so far gone unanswered. Since the opening of the Exposition, personal conversations with Mr. Gibson have been hurried, interrupted, vague and unsatisfactory regarding the production or compensation for our time and labor. Since this seems to us a highly irregular and unbusinesslike procedure, we wish to call this matter to the attention of the entire Exposition Authority, and to respectfully request your prompt consideration and immediate action thereon. We would appreciate an answer at once both to Mr. Lieber and ourselves.

With sincere regards and great admiration for the excellent Exposition which you have prepared, we beg to remain

Very truly yours,
Langston Hughes
Arna Bontemps

703 E. 50th Place
Chicago
Birthday '40 [Oct. 13]

Dear Lang:

Nothing has happened here since you left except—

Today I corrected the final chapter of the Handy book. But I'm not through with it yet. He's asked me to do a chapter which he had at first expected his lawyer to do. Evidently Macmillan is going to push the book. They are making up dummies right away to aid the salesmen, though publication is not before next March. Title: *Memphis Blues,* An Autobiography of W. C. Handy.

What did you find in L. A.? I'll bet they killed the fatted calf for you at Hollow Hills. I ate surprisingly well myself today—beingst it was my birthday, I reckon.

Anyhow, hello to your fellow dirt farmers and gentlemen farmers and others!

Ever,
Arna

703 E. 50th Place
Chicago, Illinois
11 November '40

Dear Lang,

The only reviews of *Big White Fog* I have seen were the ones in the *Times* and the *Herald Trib*—which you sent. There is a picture in *New Directions,* however, which I'll enclose here if I can remember it. I was on WBEM the day before yesterday with Miss Agatha Shea, of the Chicago Public Library system, and two others in a program launching Children's book week in this area. After the broadcast I stopped by Ben Abrahamson's. He says *The Big Sea* is still selling well. He has put out more than 175 copies to date and expects to sell more. . . . Dick's [Wright] piece hasn't yet appeared in the *News,* for some reason. Ever it does, I'll see that you get copies pronto. I'll have a chance to give your book as well as Countee's a bit of a plug on December 11th when I'm to be guest at a luncheon at Mandell's store, in their blue room, or cream room or something of the sort. Only people in the book trade belong to the group. I'm there, it seems, as a result of the broadcast of *Sad-Faced Boy,* which seems to be reviving interest in the book from the trade angle. The station is KNX in L.A., and the date

62

November 28th—should any of the folks there be interested. Librarians or teachers, I mean.

I think I'd like *Hamlet in Harlem,* better than *Shakespeare in Harlem.* More suggestive of the tragic note in the blues and more easily understood from that point of view. But this is just a guess. . . . Concerning the BALLADS: There is a sameness about them which, I should think, would make you hesitate to use too many of this group. You see, they lack the continuity and progression and unity of the Unsonnet Sequence of Blues. In other words, I think they read better—for me—as single units than as a group. But I may be wrong. Anyhow, my favorites are "The Girl Whose Name Is Mud," "The Black Sheep," "The Sinner" (except for the last line), "The Killer Boy," and "The Clown." Perhaps "Pawnshop" and "Man Who's Gone" are just as good. It will be great if you can persuade Knopf to do the book in classy format with Covarrubias illustrations. And it ought to come out about November of next year—for the Xmas trade. . . . Bring me up to date on the revue and other L.A. doings. Where is Loren and Juanita's new house located?

Ever,
Arna

Clark Hotel,
Wash. & Central,
Los Angeles, Cal.,
December 6, 1940.

Dear Arna,

Read "Young Black Joe" to the Rosenwald folks and see if they think it is the kind of song colored kids ought to have to sing in school—if so we'll see that they get copies when it is published. You'll notice your *walking proud* phrase therein. So I'll send you a present out of the first royalties! What do you want? . . . . . The song has swell music to it, with a series of bugle calls on the end. . . . . I'm trying to wind up the rush work of the show this week, and get back to Carmel on the 16th as I have an NAACP appearance here on the 15th. I find that *Boy of the Border* got left up there, so can't do anything about it until then. But will ere the New Year. . . . . It is my full intention to fill out that Rosenwald blank for a Fellowship to write a series of historical one-act plays and radio skits for Negro schools and radio programs. Would you be kind enough to permit me to use your name thereon and thus help me to forward the education of our youth?

Sincerely,
Langston

December 30, 1940.

Dear Arna,

I'm halfway through the *Pilgrim Hawk* and am inclined to agree with the review in this week's *Nation* in that the book is a little too over-written and full of digressions, interesting to be sure, but hold up the story so—if story it turns out to be. So far the hawk is still sitting on the lady's wrist and everybody is waiting for dinner. But I am glad to have read my first book of Wescott's and to thus, to some extent, be aquainted with his work. . . . . Been terrifically busy this week trying to get all the undone things done before New Year's. It catches me broke and remorseful as usual.

My sky is sometimes cloudy,
But it won't stay that way!
I'm comin', I'm comin'—
But my head *AIN'T* bending low!

Except that Aimee is still hitting at it with a vengeance. So I have issued to the press the enclosed statement. Lord help me! Better show it to the Rosenwald folks so they'll be clarified, too, since without their first fellowship I would have never gotten down South to see all those things that so riled me! . . . . . I re-did and shortened most of the ballads and cut them down to seven in the book, which has now gotten revised and gone off. In due time *Boy of the Border* will get off, too. Everything does in time if you just hold on long enough. There sure are a lot of rocks in the field, though, for any old cullud plow to get over. But I mean to turn out some literature this year or die! Also to pay Mr. Piquion, and write him, too. . . . . At the moment I am broke and ruint and would sell my rights to my next book for $5.00 cash having invested my final cent on earth in postage on "Young Black Joe" this afternoon sending out publicity copies.

Langston

LETTERS
1941-1959

731 East 50th Place
Chicago, Ill.
Sunday

Dear Lang:

The days have been terrible thus far in the new year—all work and no play, not even any writing on the new play. I have just naturally quit fooling myself. There is just no chance of my doing any writing while tied up as at present. So I have decided not to let it worry my mind any more. Of course, I get up an hour early each morning and do a few paragraphs on a nebulous and legendary novel just to keep my hand in, but I have no hope of finishing anything worth while till one of three things comes to pass: 1. I get a new job with more hours of leisure, 2. I lose my present job and go on relief, or 3. Pennies fall from heaven. Meanwhile I console myself with the assurance that I shall have your new biography to comfort me, come fall. If that fails me, then woe indeed. All joking apart, more than to the Louis-Braddock fight I look forward to your long, full-bodied, meaty, gossipy, anecdotal, wistful and evocative tale. Incidentally, how is it coming along?

I notice that Angelo Herndon has a biography coming up next month. Lyle Saxon has a mulatto novel of Louisiana. A Negro named Turpin, I think, has a novel on the Harper list; it's called *These Low Grounds*.

A young ex-librarian here, Consuelo Young Megae (?), is trying to cook up a child's page in the *Courier*. I promised to suggest some possible young illustrators. So who is that fellow in Cleveland, and what is his address? And who else should I offer? This ought to be a chance for the talented beginners.

Katherine Dunham gave two most successful programs with her dancers—Haitian dances, carnival stuff, etc. Excellent houses at 75 cents a head.

Today I'm on my way to hear Marian Anderson for the first time.

The Rosenwald people threw a fit when they saw the pictures for *Sad-Faced Boy*. So back to the artist they went—though cuts or plates had already been made. Hence publication is delayed a month, till March. The book will be one of those nearly square things, which phase I like.

When are you coming back? Ho-hum, Negro History week is on, but I have evaded free speeches.

Adios,
Arna

Dear Lang,

You were grand on CBS Saturday! You have never read better, and the selection of poems was just right. Too bad *Shakespeare in Harlem* is not in the book stores so that it can profit by the plug that this would surely give, but maybe there will be others.

Incidentally, my anthology was finally accepted. Now I've got to get it together. Will you help? I mean give suggestions. It is to be an anthology of Negro poetry for children. Oh, yes, Harper is the publisher. Houghton Mifflin turned it down, but they felt such an interest in it that they placed it for me with Harper. Their own list seemed to be a bit heavy with such backlogs as anthologies. I plan to use about ten or a dozen of your things. With this in mind, I'd like to get a complete copy of *S. in H.* as soon as possible, perhaps manuscript or proof, so that I can be as up-to-date as possible in my selections. I plan to use a good bit of folk stuff like John Henry, Water Boy, Po' Ol' Lazerous, etc. If you think of any interesting items that might fit, please pass the tips along. The book will be on the age level of *The Dream Keeper,* the difference being that it will include all the poets.

You seem to be right about this being the anthology season. Don't know yet when mine will appear.

Your broadcast seems to have been widely listened to around here. Several people have already mentioned it to me. One did not like the preliminary chat between Frederick and Dillon, but I personally found it quite interesting.

Did I tell you that Arnold Gingrich asked about you the night we were at the Grand Terrace. Wanted to know where you were and what you were doing. I told him you had been trying your hand at radio. . . . Later I saw Katherine buttonhole him and heard her putting him on the spot for not taking a piece she had submitted to the magazine.

Nelson Algren has a story in the current Louisiana Review. . . . . Stewart Engstrand has a new novel about nazis in Norway, *Spring 1940*—you met Engstrand while here. He just lost his job with the Writers' Project. Hope he makes something on the book.

Ever,
Arna

Dear Lang:

Nice send-off Marvel gave the Suitcase Theatre in the Amsterdam News. How is the play standing up? I hope it is still on when I get there in August.

You know I got the Rosenwald Fellowship, but on second thought have about decided not to move the headquarters this year. But I'm supposed to be off for Haiti in August, so why don't you get ready and go with me? I'm so un-traveled I sort of hate to go alone.

Say, you'd better get down and write a child's book. An adventure for older kids, perhaps. *Sad-Faced Boy* had given me quite a surprise—still going more than a thousand copies to the 6 month period, and publishers think it should hold this. Me for another one *soon!*

School closes for me tomorrow. I'm hoping to get some writing in then.

What do you think of this AFRICAN under the editorship of Claude McKay? And wasn't that lead article of this past week's Saturday Evening Post interesting —*Black Omens!* Looks kinda like a revival of the New Negro.

Write me the happenings. Hello to Louise.

Ever,
Arna

The *Horn Book* has article of mine and is supposed to get me by Jane M. Rider —remember her in the Watts library—about my kid books. I suppose, Miss Gladys English—we had breakfast with her—suggested this lady to the editors, it seems.

PERSONAL AND FRIENDLY
MEMORANDUM NOT TO BE
FORWARDED TO NOBODY

Dear Arna:

Re ST. LOUIS WOMAN:
1. A bird in the hand is worth 20,000 in the Broadway bush.
2. The Federal Theatre production out here has at least reached the stage of preliminary designs for the sets; and research is being done on the costumes of the '90's; a tentative date has been set for the opening to coincide with the summer racing season.
3. A Los Angeles (HOLLYWOOD) production would perhaps mean more financially than BROADWAY for the simple reason that any *new success* out here is bound to get a Broadway production, too—and probably backed by movie money, since there are two producers of film now in the mood for something Negro, if it is sure-fire.
4. Clarence Muse has a backer for a Broadway show, an owner of a big chain of theatres out here, who has great faith in Clarence as a director who can make commercial (nee money-making) shows. The man is already excited about the possibilities of *St. Louis Woman.*
5. Since RUN LITTLE CHILLUN has been such a box-office draw, the Federals out here now are in the mood for spending a lot of money for a bang-up good production of their next Negro unit show. And you will have the advantage of the Hall Johnson choir and his arrangements automatically.
6. As to the music: I believe I already wrote you that we have in writing from Mr. Handy permission to weave the "St. Louis Blues" into the show, free of payment, since he wishes to contribute that to the good work of the Federal Theatre in giving employment to our people. As to the other music, it is through the musical arrangements that the writers get their royalty payments —not through the music itself—which may or may not be in open domain. And the arrangement would be made to suit the mood and dramatic action of the play. The money-end of it, of course, would be quite aside from author's royalties, and not come out of you-all's part at all, so it should make

no difference to either you or your publishers, or Leah Salisbury.

7. Mr. Ulmman has resigned out here. He did *not* bring the play with him from New York. He brought Theodore Browne's Harriett Tubman play—and Clarence Muse had to show him wherein your play would suit the needs of the project much better, before he changed his mind and called a meeting of the board to O.K. *St. Louis Woman.*

8. Agents are much more difficult to get together on things than authors. It was an agent of Kaj Gynt's who prevented us from having a Duke Ellington score for *Cock O' the World.* Now my collaborator is sorry she paid her any mind, and is running after Duke again to re-consider, the agent having retired to the desert with consumption meanwhile, leaving us with still no production. After all, agents are secondary to authors, and *have* to do what you request —or give up your work.

9. So are you really going to give up as easily as your letter indicates? If so, then kindly send me one more *air-mail* and let me know. In which case I won't use a lot of the material from my own files that I've picked out to heighten the folk quality of the dialogue. I wouldn't want to lose it on a script that might see the ash-can.

10. Now, as to the minor details (and as a personal explanation to you): Any theatre is bad enough, but the F. is worse, judging from both New York and here, what with all the fighting and inner intrigue that goes on. Hallie Flanagan was just out here to try and straighten out things once again, since they ran Ulmman to hell and gone, and the political gangsters are trying to upset the works. Yesterday's paper carried a story on the front page concerning some of the excitement—which included one man beaten up, another given a bottle of poison milk which killed his dog, and put him in the hospital, and is seemingly going to cause his faction of the Democratic party to lose their charter—all over F. Theatre. So under the existing circumstances, the fact that Muse has been able to maintain the Negro unit as a sort of little island apart—especially since it is the only unit really making any money for the cast set-up—he really has the say there, so far. And since this is your first play—and you at least have your finger now a pretty good ways into a production pie, (which in no way would hurt your Broadway chances anyhow) whatever you choose to do about that, my personal advice would be to juggle things around someway (including Miss Salisbury and Countee) so that you won't miss out on this West Coast chance. Get them to offer some counter-proposals—which I will do my best to get Clarence to accept—if you hurry as I have only ten more days here—and am about to go with Clarence to the ranch for the final polishing up of the script. Clarence has been working with me on this version—which is a great help—as he certainly is a good showman, knowing how to heighten and improve a scene theatrically. So I am not speaking to him about your letter until I hear from you again, as I'd rather not have him fly up in the air right now, and withdraw his help. (Which is quite aside from his job, as he's not being paid to write with me. But he does like the show, and wants to make a big splurge with it—and has so far managed to keep all factions concerned out here in a good humor toward it—in spite of some Negro opposition who want to do an OPERA next. . . . . To me a cut in and all that business doesn't matter. I'm getting my bi-monthly check direct from the theatre and will do the best job I can on it anyway (minus my own material which I see no need of using if it will do

you no good, and if the show is likely not to go through on account of your agent's attitude.) But since your agent hasn't gotten you a production of any importance in all these years, my advice would be to take the bull by the horns yourself—since getting a start in the theatre is the important thing. Once there, then get as high-hat as you wish.) . . . . . A note from Lieber tells me that Miss Salisbury refuses to discuss the matter further. (Which agents have a way of doing with other agents.) Also that Countee agrees with her. (Which collaborators have a way of doing also—a la Zora.) But since the final word is up to you—it's *your* Lil Augie—and a swell character he is, too— I await your *wire* (preferably) since time is short—as to what tactics you'd like me to employ on this end.

As to lectures, leave Buffalo out of it. But if you get anything between K.C. and the 9th, take it. . . . . I spoke on Spain at the Main Library night before last, and Mrs. Rider, Miss English, Mrs. Spect and all send their best to you. Miss Mathews mentions you practically every week in her library column in the Eagle.

Don't You Want to Be Free opened here last night to society!! We finish our movie scenario this week. Before the camera the 1st of April. I got all my debts paid!

Do something about AUGIE, please, sir! I hate to think about those nights I worked until five A.M. on him and Della going to waste. Did I tell you we brought Black Patti and her Troubadours into the ball? Also that we've devised a new and much more dramatic ending, mounting to a great big song climax? And also, since this is a church town, we've put in a couple of nice moral elements by using the preacher more, and bringing back Mr. Woody, as a man who wants to keep racing clean? . . . . Tell Leah and Countee to let us turn out a nice show for you, all three—and we will. After all ART is ART—and a cut is merely a cut.

Langston

Lieber just collected a sizeable *Mulatto* check for me—which puts him in Salisbury's class, almost.

Hollow Hills Farm,
Monterey, California
January 6, 1941.

Dear Arna,

Did I ever tell you I finally got the magazine with the biography in it? . . . . Also that I wrote the Knopf's again about the Fund's interest in *Not Without Laughter*. . . . . . They're busy at the moment with *Shakespeare in Harlem*, which title they all like and want to retain, but nobody else here likes it. They tried Zell Ingram on illustrations but did not feel his things were suitable, now they're trying an English artist named Kauffer whom they feel is excellent. We shall see. . . . . I'm just getting over my flu, with complications—largely due to brokenness which always aggravates an otherwise bad condition. . . . . This time I swear by all that is holy I will NEVER fool with shows any more. NEVER! NEVER! NEVER No! . . . . IMPORTANT: A note from Claude Barnett this morning contains the following:

"The legislature has not met. Have you a definite bill for services in the hands of Secretary-Treasurer Williams? If not, I would get one to him immediately if I were you, because all outstanding bills have been turned in—the hope being that we will get a deficiency appropriation."

SO: Will you kindly confer with Mollison about this, also with Lieber by mail, and between you-all decide upon what amount and SEND THE BILL IN AT ONCE, either by way of Mollison or Lieber, as they think wise? Please take care of this since you're right there on the grounds and can check on it. I presume you have, or can get Williams' address.

Finished *Pilgrim Hawk*. Hope to tackle Hemingway soon. But better start writing something of my own.

Sincerely,
Langston

Feel awful!

Dear Arna—

Shall be in hospital week tomorrow. Kind of acute—rather arthritis. Too many playhouses fell down. Last straw N.Y. eviction. Guys let their rent get behind—way behind—without my knowing it. And put out. Well, anyhow, here I am moaning and groaning. Fever is down, so can write with effort. Thanks for favor. More news when able to write. Love to Alberta and kids. I'm weak and groggy.

Langston

Hollow Hills Farm
(Carmel Valley) Jamesburg
Route
Monterey, California
Wednesday

Dear Arna,

Thanks for your cheerful letter and the generous enclosure. How swell of you! I'm still in the hospital, but much better, out of bed a while today, and expect to go back to the farm this week. Acute arthritis is really something! Had me groggy with pain and pills!

I have to miss a recital with Browning (Negro Songs and Poetry) at the Los Angeles Biltmore Sunday. That makes me sicker! But no more lectures this spring. Knopf came through with a check, (Small but helpful. My book bill was $450.00.) and my new book of poems, *Shakespeare in Harlem,* comes out in May. They like and insist on the title. Are having the English artist.

"Young Black Joe," our song is catching on all over the South. Fisk has asked to use it for commencement. And Negro History Week requests it several places. I'll send you the music for Paul and Joan soon as I get up.

Give my love to my beloved Poppy and Constance and tell them so sorry they have been sick. Tell Alberta I think one of her meals would make me well. Best to all, more when better.

Lang

P.S. Give my best to Hank and his wife. Do you ever see Louise?

72

Friday.

Dear Arna,

How do you like this new blues? Influenced by the Spanish, it would seem.
. . . . . Well, I am up and at the typewriter again for a bit. But am enjoying
convalesing so much, little danger I'll over work. Have a brand new album of
Louis Armstrong to play, and a new Carmen Miranda, also several good
books to read—which seem to put me to sleep. Shame for a literary man, but
I don't seem to be much of a reader. Although I find Isak Dinesen's *Out of
Africa* charming. . . . . . But best news of all is I started my new book the
other night, by accident—which is the best way to start. So the second autobiography is off to a first draft. I bought a big note book and write long
hand in bed. Determined to follow your example and do FOUR pages a day,
rain, sun, or landslide. . . . . Murky bad weather here, can't sit on porch, so
am inside with the records and books. A lot of old mail came back—and
wonders of wonders, two checks therein. ASCAP and another little one. So I
shall make token payments on most pressing of the debts. I have been waiting for some music copies of "Young Black Joe" but they haven't come yet.
Want to send you one, also several who've requested it for Negro History
Week. But soon will be too late for that. . . . . I have withdrawn from the
board of the revue. Letters report too much arguing for me. They're free to
use my material but for so little money I can't fight and cuss, too. Although
I hope they finally get a good show out of it all. Did I tell you Still resigned,
too, to devote his time to a WPA concert version of our opera to be done in
April, which he will conduct? I'll be there for that. Until then, will sit tight
here and write. Want to do a special article for the *Crisis* since this is the
20th anniversary of the publication of my first poem, the Negro Speaks Of
Rivers, June 1921. . . . . Tell Poppy, Constance, Camille and all my beloved
little ones, hy! Give Paul and Joan my best regards, and to you and Alberta
all the good wishes in the world for a bright and fruitful spring. (Any signs
of it yet in Chicago? The mimosa is blooming here.)

Sincerely,
Lang

703 E. 50th Place
Chicago, Illinois
7 February '41

Dear Lang,

You sound like yourself again, so I'm sure you're feeling better. I do envy
you the sunshine of your porch. It's snowing here again today, and it seems
ages since we saw the sun. I'm hoping to absorb a little of it around the end
of this month, however. Tolson lined up a trip to Wiley for me, with two
other lectures en route (Texas College and Pine Bluffs), so I'm planning to go
during Mardi Gras and to run down to New Orleans on the same ticket—
since I found out it won't cost any more. . . . This is not an outgrowth of the
new Frances Wills folder, Tolson having mentioned it when he was here to

the Exposition but just now finished up plans. I hope however that the folder will bring some business from other directions. It's a good folder.

A one-day wonder around here was an episode that occurred in a U. of Chicago class conducted by Napier Wilt. The *Big Sea* was being read, it seems, and one of the wives of one of the professors came across your mention of Quarles as an ancestor. She became astonished. This could not be. *She* is a grand (or great) daughter of said Quarles, and she knew the facts you mention are wrong. So off she goes, writes letters and commences to check up. Result: she found you are right. She is a remote cousin of yours. She said she was sending you documents to substantiate what she has learned. There are a good many details that I can't remember, but I suppose you have heard from her by now. If not, ask Bob Davis. Here at the Fund they thought it a good story.

The Rosenwald folks are off to Mexico next week, about forty of them to study rural education down there, trustees and everybody. Not me, of course. . . . We MUST attend the Hampton folk festival. I'd love it. Wonder, however, if you could use your influence to secure me an official invitation. No participation or pay or anything, just a personal invitation. Maybe my editorship of Handy's book will gain consideration for me in the field of folk music. If not, I'll assemble an anthology between now and then. Which reminds me that an agent writes a client here that Sterling Brown is now at work on an anthology of all types of Negro literature for some publisher or other. Re: the Handy book (page from Macmillan catalogue enclosed): Frederick has invited us both to be on his program "Of Men and Books" when he reviews it late in March. Hope we can get together. If not, I may have to speak for both.

I see where Dick is one of Carson McCullers' sponsors in her application for a Rosenwald Fellowship *(The Heart Is a Lonely Hunter)*. . . . Also that he's doing 30,000 words of text for a non-fiction book about Negroes—one of these photographic books to be published by Alliance. . . . New *Anvil* seems to have folded: printer out of business, taking a job in Colorado. Jack plans to turn over the thousand or two subs to *Direction*. . . . Olives are my dish. I can't visualize Cocteauish sketches of Negroes, but I'm prepared to like them. The one-family epidemic of measles has finally gone the rounds. Hope we're seeing the last of it this week. . . . Have not seen Louise in Chicago at any time. . . . See that new movie star from the Dominican Republic (colored, of course) in *Life* alongside Carmen Miranda and the Argentina find? Marie Mendoz, I think. Too bad about Playrights, but they started out wrong; it was easy to see their fall coming. Good piece on Gilpins, Sell, etc. in *Time* this week. Next time you take a house, why not let it be in L.A., Pasadena or some such place? Cheaper and less danger of eviction and more room to stretch your feet.

Ever,
Arna

Hollow Hills Farm,
Monterey, California,
February 14, 1941.

r Arna,

)elighted to have your long letter. Yes, I am much better and up and even out
thinking about going to San Francisco next week, if I can get a free ride, to
the Lunts in *There Shall Be No Night* and to the dentist—but nevertheless
dying of chagrin and envy at the thought of you in New Orleans at Mardi
s and Mr. Sullivan in New York (leaving Sunday) and me nowhere but here.
all probably relapse. . . . . . You will enjoy Texas. Swell folks down there. Why
take a couple more engagements while thereabouts? Prairie View, High
ɔol in Houston, that other college in Austin? Going all that ways might as
speak up a breeze. . . . . . I just had a letter from Tolson, too, saying
ıerica's Young Black Joe" is to be sung all over down there. . . . . . Be sure
ok up a cute little twin at Texas College, (Tyler) named Ina Quarrels—sister
ıe Ura who had a Rosenwald, I believe, and teaches at Fisk. Ina used to be
and freckled faced—and I reckon she still is. Also do you remember that
dark girl who used to live at Louise's in New York, Martilla Womack? She
Texas, too, just had a little from her before I fell ill. Has a wonderful job
as only colored social worker in State Hospital for the Insane, and seemed
bubbling over with hospitality. Seems to me its Austin she is, but I'll look up her
letter if you are interested in looking her up, as I'm under impression you'd know
her from New York. . . . . Anyhow, I am desolate at the thought of all that
travelling, and me stationary here! . . . . . Nice announcement about the Handy
book. Mine, the poems, are in the new Knopf catalogue, too. . . . . Didn't see that
Time with Gilpin's write-up. We seem to have them all here, but couldn't find
it. What issue? Or could you lend it to me? Will return promptly. . . . . . If you
see or call up Jack, ask him to send me back my story, "One Friday Morning,"
if he hasn't already returned it to Lieber. I want to give it to the *Crisis* for I owe
them some material. Did I tell you this was my 20th year of creative writing—
1921 Negro Speaks Of Rivers first appeared in *Crisis*. . . . . . Still tells me
rehearsals for *Troubled Island* have begun in Los Angeles, mixed cast, chorus of
one hundred, orchestra of seventy which he will conduct. . . . . . Duke Ellington
is signed for the revue, so they say. Me, I believe nothing till it comes off. Its all
beginning to sound like Chicago and the Expo now. (Which you won't even
mention any more!!!! Did Mollison, YOU, Lieber, get that bill in to the treasurer
—as Barnett advised?????? . . . . . Or don't you-all want the money, should the
good legislature by some off chance vote it to them?). . . . . Me, I have retired
from the show business and shall devote the rest of my creative life exclusively
to words on paper not on the stage. . . . . . Hey, take some of our skits from
Cavalcade with you and leave with the drama teachers at the various colleges to
which you go, Dillard in New Orleans (Get a lecture there!) ought to put on the
whole *Cavalcade*. We must also submit it to Hampton for the Folk Festival
they're talking about in '42. . . . . Talk it up down South and see if we can't get
some of those cullud colleges to stage it as a starter. . . . . Did Locke have his
annual revue of books in *Opportunity* this last month? Never see it or the *Crisis*
out here. Must subscribe. What did he say about *Big Sea* if he did? I remember
the *Crisis* revue in December (?) said I knew first class colored and second class

75

white folks! . . . . . Colored have had a big military wedding in Monterey with all Fort Ord's darker artillery out. The bride, a young lady whose mama breathed a sigh of relief because, these past months she could hardly do her work for the white folks for worrying about what the soldiers were doing to her daughter while she was on the job. Now she is safely wed and walked out of the church through an arch of former admirers on the arm of the one that mama said was responsible. Anyhow, the bugles blew and colored society turned out. It was on a Thursday when most everybody was off. My great regret was to be still convalescent.

Drop me a card from the balmy South. It is cold as blazes here. Dark and rainy. . . . . . Best to family,

Sincerely,
Langston

703 E. 50th Place
Chicago
18 March '41

Dear Lang,

The trip was lots of fun. My lectures were far from hot, but no one had the bad manners to complain, thank God. I arrived in New Orleans during the Comus parade of the final day of Mardi Gras. And what a time to arrive! No street cars were running. It took me half an hour to get into the phone booth —thanks to a dozen or more excursion trains all leaving at the same time in the midst of the biggest of the parades. When I got the number, I found that all the people I knew were out enjoying the fun. Even Flint-Goodridge hospital seemed lonesome. After another half hour I managed to land a taxi. I persuaded the guy to take me to the parade before taking me to the house where I stopped. Later I went out for a dinner at a new place just opened on Louisiana Avenue. The joint was hopping. Took hours to get served. Finally my hostess—who turned out to be Walter White's cousin—took me to a blue-vein shindig. By that time I was groggy from want of sleep. Fortunately Mardi Gras ends at midnight, when lent begins. . . . Next year I would like to arrive a week or two earlier and try to get into the spirit of things better. The rest of the week was thrilling, however. Visits with Lyle Saxon and others, a day in the old French graveyard (the name intrigues me, also the stories of the grave keepers). Altogether I picked up lots of the kind of history that interests me in New Orleans. The visits to the schools were good too, but I was amazed by the poverty of the places. Some of the top teachers were in patches, and the food in the dining room at Arkansas A.M.&E was so plain I could scarce believe it. Nice young teachers everyplace, however. Tolson and Edmonds both promised me to attempt to do the *Cavalcade*. Which reminds me—

I was in to see Claude Barnett today. He had your letter before him at the moment I arrived. Said the deficiency has yet to be presented to the state legislature, but that the president of the senate was a member of the commission and that he feels sure it will be presented and that it has a fine chance to pass. So if you will keep writing to refresh his mind, I'll keep telephoning and visiting.

Du Bois came here last week to explore (at my suggestion) the possibility of having several of the writers' projects cooperate on the Encyclopedia of the

Negro. Some progress was made, but the big getting together (involving several funds, etc.) remains to be done.

We mustn't forget to make that trip to Brazil. Reckon you and me would be o'fays down there—no? Did Handy stop? How's the book coming? And the lumbago? (or rather arthritis—it was Bousfield who had the lumbago at the time you were having your misery). All as usual here.

Ever,
Arna

P.S. Did Mr. Sullivan get back from his trip? And how did you make out as host to royalty?

The Rosenwald trustees are going to meet at Tuskegee this time—I won't get to meet Mrs. Roosevelt.

"The Big Sea" is still widely discussed. The latest: Certain Washington officials are giving blacks a mild going over as a result of your story. So reports Dr. Will Alexander of *Farm Security*. . . . Saw copies all over South.

Did your *Anvil* story reach the *Crisis* okay? The *Anvil* had set it up when things happened.

John T. Frederick had Irving S. Cobb as his *guest this week*.

Librarians are calling on me heavily for Library Week here.

Hollow Hills Farm
Monterey, California,
March 22, 1941

Dear Arna,

Enjoyed your letter greatly, especially about your arrival in New Orleans, which must have been exciting. Mr. Sullivan got back from New York, too, full of news of Harlem, *Cabin in the Sky*, Barthé's new work, etc. While there he donated a pint of blood to the British. . . . I'm quite O.K. again and just returned from San Francisco with a new brown suit! At last, that suit, even-much shoes and ties to match. Now if the Lord will bless me with just a little more cash I'll be ready to stand on a corner and sun myself all summer. What with the legislature about to take up our bill, another *Mulatto* arbitration on, and the revue still "about" to go into rehearsal, maybe, quien sabe, some ship or other might accidently get washed up on my beach. . . . I told you, did I not, to be *sure* to read *Lanterns on the Levee*. About cullud, it's terrific! . . . . I've also just read *Sapphira and the Slave Girl*. Much of your quiet style there. I liked it very much. . . . You didn't, by any chance, hear "Young Black Joe" sung anywhere down South, did you? Letters tell me it is getting around. And Robbins is now interested in publishing it. Hope that goes through. . . . The Anvil story got to the *Crisis* O.K. Thanks. I've also done an article for them, "The Need for Heroes." I believe I sent you a copy, did I not? . . . . This June marks my twentieth year of creative activity. *The Negro Speaks of Rivers* appeared in June, 1921. . . . Today a skunk got under my house. All the dachshunds got after it, six of them, and the poor little skunk ran out while a fellow went for the farm man to shoot it. Nobody saw it come out, but when we did see, all the dogs had it and had torn it up and were covered with skunk smell, so it took all afternoon to wash them off and spray them with toilet water—but they still smell. And they are house dogs! . . . . Wonder how *Native Son* really went in New York? I've seen no reviews of it but Carl Van Vechten writes that it is very effective melodrama with the same faults as the book. . . . I hope to get to Chi in time to see *Cabin in the Sky*. But I won't leave here until I finish a draft of the book. And lately I haven't had a chance to work on it. But have only one other little promised job to write up before I get back to it: the thing for the James Weldon Johnson Memorial Fund. Just can't seem to get to that. . . . Had a nice letter from the Johannesburg Library about *The Big Sea* which seems to be going big in South Africa! What do you know about that?!!!!! . . . I sold a poem to *Poetry* and another to *New Yorker,* the last that can be sold before the book comes out. I hope colored folks will like that man's drawings. I wrote to him to be sure and put some hair on their heads because nobody was nappy-headed any more! If he don't, I am ruint. . . . Dorothy Maynor was a triumph with the San Francisco Orchestra the other day. And she is such an intelligent girl she ought to go a long ways. Besides she has prima donna busts. I also saw *Fantasia* in the city, but there is too much of it. Like reading the funnies all day. . . . If you ever get a chance, please show "Young Black Joe" to Spencer and ask him if he has any ideas for promoting such a song, or knows any night club entertainers who might sing it. ("Young Black Joe" is my favorite work after 20 years of creating! So I want to see it get launched in the world.) . . . . Did I tell you the Still opera is off? WPA appropriations cut out half the cast when they were reduced. So it goes in the theatre! . . . . Ay, Lord! . . . . It is Lent.

Sincerely,
Langston

P.S. Thanks no end for the $10.00. Herein enclosed. Next thing: Piquion. How much were those books. How many did I get?

Did you see Selma Gordon's razz of the Expo in *The Crisis* and Frank M. Davis' answer month later?

I would love to see your babies. Tell Alberta to kiss them all for me. (And spare the rod. Try sweet reason!) (and ice cream)

703 E. 50th Place
Chicago, Illinois
28 March '41

Dear Lang,
Native Son seems to have been a complete success. Here are a couple of items from the *Times.*

Also enclosed is a form letter which I think will interest you much. Claude Barnett passed it along to me. Thereupon I went to work as follows: a) showed the letter to Embree and influenced him to write Studebaker suggesting that you be called in on the plans for writing the scripts, b) helped Miss Waxman word the letter for Embree's signature, c) asked Barnett to write to Caliver, d) wrote the letter for Barnett's signature (copy enclosed). NOW the rest is in your hands and in the lap of the gods. I'd suggest that you have Lieber, working independently, inquire of Caliver as to what plans are being made for the writing of the stories—provided you do not hear from headquarters yourself within the next week or two. And if you get the job and happen to need any help, remember I am available.

The first meeting of the fellowship committee has been held—sh! Keep this under the hat! They made out a tentative list which will have to be revised downward at the next and final meeting. *You* are on the tentative list, but the committee did NOT warm up to the project you outlined. The next meeting will check the list and seek to reduce it to the size of the budget. One or two additional people—including Moe—will be present. So—fast and pray on that day. You'll be surprised to hear that Carson McCullers was *not* placed on the tentative list. Reynolds thinks that Moe may insist on putting her back on, but the committee left her off without qualm. Thought, no doubt, like Clifton Fadiman in his recommendation (favorable on the whole) that she is . . . unpredictable.

Sapphira and the Slave Girl is quite good. I reviewed it at the Hall Branch book club. Alberta, too, thought it was the kind of thing I might have written. But I'm gonna surprise you. Action—bang, bang! That's me now. You should also read *Raleigh's Eden,* another best seller of the past season in which a colored girl is the foil for the plot. This one is set in Revolutionary Carolina. Interesting as a specimen of the new treatment of the femme de colour in fiction—particularly historical. But wait till you see Ginette Rochon, my sugar pie and heroine. I'm adding a mite to her story each week. . . . Miss Waxman just called up to say they had ordered *Lanterns on the Levee.* It will be here in a couple of days. Will Percy, the author, seems to be a friend of Mr. Embree. I'm taking home *Delilah* and *Let My People Go* today. Next I'll try *The Mind of the South,* but I don't promise to finish it.

You and me musta shopped simultaneously—you for a brown outfit, me for a gray, including sweet hat (but it's dirty already). . . . Jack just frightened me about the EXPO. Said he saw in the paper that the state legislature, now strongly republican, was kicking about footing the EXPO shortage which they said was entered into by a democratic majority and used for the advantage of that party. Let's hope it ain't so. I have not talked to Barnett since I heard that. . . . The ten spot goes back where it came from to wait for the rainy day. You had 15 books from Piquion at $1.50 a throw. I had ten, and I hope to pay him by summer. If you pay him before I do, please apologize for me, and reassure him of my good intentions. . . . Handy has his proofs. When will I see a complete manuscript or copy of *Shakespeare in Harlem?* I have a "different" kind of anthology in mind, if I can sell the idea. Will make some inquiries.

Hello to Noel Sullivan et al. All are rugged and robust hereabouts.

Ever,
Arna

703 E. 50th Place
Chicago, Illinois
21 April '41

Dear Lang,

If you hear nothing officially about the tendency of the committee to be lukewarm about your proposed project (while being red-hot about *you*), there'll be no point in thinking about it again. When I was spoken to, they were debating whether or not they would write you a second letter calling it to your attention.

The sum of all their thoughts is perhaps that they will be pleased with whatever you do—such being their esteem and confidence. By all means do that reading. My main reasons for mentioning the above was to indicate that a certain leeway exists—by virtue of the question raised—which you might wish to exploit to your own purpose. Nothing more.

Did you see Locke's book on *The Negro in Art?* Pretty good. Wish it had been done in color, however. . . . Incidentally, I'm not acquainted with the two N.Y. artists who got Rosenwald Fellowships. The white Texan, Tom Lea, I know from his work in *The Longhorns.* Swell performer. Lots of stuff on the ball—if you like his *kind* of stuff. . . . Clyde Winkfield got a Fellowship in music. That about covers all those I know. Evidently Zell did not make it. I didn't know he had applied. They tell me, however, that a few came through this time after as many as three unsuccessful attempts in the past. Zell might like to hear that.

Things seem to be slow in publishers' row. No news on the publication date of the Handy book either.

Dick had his wife with him this trip. But it was not Deema. Ellen Poplar seems to enjoy that honor at the moment. What happened to Deema? Wasn't it you who told me he was married to her? Well, anyhow, Ellen is a pretty little trick and perhaps the best bet—if one is to judge by looks. She told me at a party given by Horace that the Playwright's Company ended 12 grand in the hole. That Dick had been forced to cut from them quite cleanly to keep himself from becoming responsible for their bills. That he felt he had done his duty by them when he appeared with Paul in their behalf. To all of which I'm sure you would say "amen."

Let's hope that writing for radio turns out to be a little more solid business than the theatre sometimes is. I suspect it will. . . . Saw the letter that Studebaker wrote Embree concerning you and that program they are planning. Seems that the Rosenwald put up $5,000 for the venture—covering all expenses except time, which will be donated. He said the writing has already been arranged for, but that they would use some of your poems and *consult* with you over some special matters in connection with the broadcasts. Ho-hum, wonder who got the money for the *writing?*

Du Bois is here. Spoke last night to an overflow crowd—at 50¢ a head—on "This War and the Darker Races." Very deep, scholarly and enlightening. He goes again tonight at Northwestern. His views are pro-Russian and strongly Marxist, but he opposes violence, a la Gandhi.

Will you come by and help me with my anthology—if it comes through? The publishers have said, "Yes in principle." No contract has been signed yet, however. Still something should happen soon, one way or the other. . . . The trees outside my window are really something to write about now. The palest of green —tinged with gold. The sort of color that lasts only a couple of days. Makes you feel like going around to your friends and distributing bouquets of cherry blossoms.

Ever,
Arna

P.S. Sing—leaving for S.F.—called to get your number.

Hollow Hills Farm,
Monterey, California,
May 12, 1941.

Dear Arna,

Did I tell you I'm to be on the "Of Men and Books" program this coming Saturday? When will your program about the Handy book come off? Mr. Handy wrote that he intended to come out for it. . . . . . I am deep in mail DETERMINED to get it all caught up before June 1st when I start on my Fellowship. I'll do a month's reading here as Douglass and some of the other older books are available out here, then come East. I hope to bring the first draft of the new book along, too. . . . . The rumor out here is that Hess killed Hitler. Although that isn't in the papers yet. . . . . Did I tell you I had a nice note from Willa Cather to whom I wrote about her book? . . . . . And that the Brown Sisters turned over in a car a month or so ago—but are O.K. now and working in Vancouver? . . . . . And that Margaret Bonds had a song on the Kate Smith Hour: "Spring Will Be So Sad." . . . . And I'm telling you all this because I'm trying to think of some news I had in mind to relay to you and I seem to have forgotten it. Reckon I am sleepy as it is now 2 A.M. So I will just go on to bed. . . . . It is raining again! Mon dieu! . . . . . Just had word that one of my dear old ladies in Mexico City died May 3rd, Fela, the oldest. . . . . . I hope to get down to L.A. before I come East. . . . . My Uncle John surprised me with a visit the other day for a hot minute. Drove up with his doctor who came to the medical convention at Del Monte—the only Negro there. Why don't more Negroes attend such things, I wonder. . . . . . Have you heard from Sterling Brown who is getting out a big new Negro anthology of prose, poetry, and everything, with Lee and Davis also as editors? Also the folks who put out the FRED DOUGLASS autobiography plan an anthology of short stories. Must be anthology year in 1942. Especially if you come up with one of poetry. . . . . Have you seen the Jelliffe's Art Exhibit at the Art Center in Chicago? Zell has some things there. . . . . Please let me know the names of the various librarians at Hall Branch, also address of said Branch. I want to send them a card —since they're always so nice to me when I'm in town. . . . . And be careful because it looks like they're going to raise and lower the draft age, both, so as to catch you, and Paul as well! . . . . . If you will tell me how to write a book that will sell, I will tell you how to write one the critics love. I will also throw in a copy of my latest poem autographed by my own hand. . . . . When is Mrs. Joe Louis going to have that baby? . . . . . Well, I will now close. As ever,

Sincerely,
Lang

May 26, 1941

Dear Arna,

Thank you very much for sending me the list of Hall Branch librarians. It was my intention to send them all *Negro Speaks of Rivers* cards, but I only had 250, mostly for my intimate friends, and I ran out before I even got that list covered. So I just sent one to Miss Harsh. . . . I am delighted about your having placed your anthology with Harpers, and I will do my best to aid you howsoever I can.

Right off the bat I give you permission to use any of mine, and will shortly look up for you the newer poems that might be suitable for children that so far haven't appeared in book form. For proofs of *Shakespeare in Harlem* write Mrs. Blanche Knopf, 501 Madison Avenue. Galleys are ready, but the continued illness of the artist is delaying page proofs. I hope he recovers in time to get some hair on his colored folks heads. . . . Marie Joe Browne is giving her readings with great success in Los Angeles, I hear. . . . Also hear that Zora is in Pasadena and has laid me out to the dogs therein. But made the localities mad by not appearing at a dinner given in her honor. . . . Lieber informs me that the Cafe Society management is planning a Negro revue in New York for the stage. I've asked him to see that they get our *Cavalcade* script. . . . By the way, did the Legislature ever do anything about our money? . . . . Singh and Mr. Sullivan have gone down South to visit the Chester Arthur's. . . . It seems I have some poems in *Poetry* this month as I've just received a check. . . . Charles Holland, the new radio singer with voice not unlike Hayes was here for the weekend. The poor fellow just had lots of trouble about a white lady in L.A. and they put his carcass in jail and now his wife is suing him for divorce. Why do all leading colored singers get involved with white ladies so early in their careers? Voice teachers ought to throw in a few with their scales so they could get used to them early and thus not get excited later on when their names are beginning to be known and the newspapers are looking for copy and the colored ladies get jealous because they are making money and spending it on the white ladies who have so many other chances to have money spent on them without taking it from colored. . . . Eulah says they should have put his carcass in jail. I wonder if that is a Christian attitude? . . . . Mr. Handy heard me way off in New York the other day when I was on the air and wrote me a nice note about it. . . . Give my love to Alberta and the children.

Sincerely,
Langston

June 5.

Dear Arna,

Mr. Edward Lawson, Opportunity, 1133 Broadway, New York, writes me that the colored actors and actresses there have organized themselves into The Negro Radio Workshop whose purpose is to put on professionally a series of pieces illustrating the Negro's part in American life, the sketches to be paid for at the regular radio rates by the broadcasters. They want material. As something of immediate value I suggested an adaptation of our *Cavalcade* to suit their needs, since it well illustrates the Negro contribution to the theatre. Why not send Mr. Lawson a script, at the same time referring him to Maxim Lieber for the business end, in case they would wish us to cut and adapt the script to the requirements of the air. Or we could let some one else do this, if they give us the proper cut in on the cash—since we are not there with the group, and the adaptation, I imagine, would have to suit the talent on hand, etc. In any case you might drop Mr. Lawson a line about our material, and any other that you yourself might be able to do for him, if you feel in the mood to try a dramalet yourself. Me—time is of the essence! There's much too little. It's almost as scarce as money.

I see where Josephine Baker is a big hit in Madrid. Can't keep a good gal down!

My Rosenwald check came. Thank the good Lord! I had $1.20 left in the bank.
    And my brother writing that he is being sent to the hospital with pleurisy and a temperature of 102. Is that high or not? Anyhow, he needs money.
    Jesus, lover of my soul, let me to thy bosom fly!
    How blissful then to be a sheep with nothing to do but graze and sleep.

Sincerely,
Lang

703 E. 50th Place
Chicago, Illinois
Sunday, June 22, 1941
The day the Nazis marched
against U.S.S.R.

Dear Lang,
    The last time there was big radio news from central Europe it fell on a day when I was writing you. Now here it is again, proving that history repeats itself. Being one who has never retrenched in his anti-fascist sentiments—with regard to the U.S.A. as well as other countries—I hope the big boy will fare no better than did Napoleon on the road to Moscow. . . . This, incidentally, should set the stage beautifully for volume II of your autobiography, since Russia is sure to come into better favor in this country. I say that because Macmillan has just asked me to take into consideration the lessened esteem for France in writing my next novel—if I hope it to reach a better audience than did the last one. And I have agreed to leave out an extended prologue in the French colonies and to concentrate on the doings around Savannah. Here's hoping we both hit the jackpot in 1942! As things look today, I at least will need to: The order went out yesterday for a 60% cut of the cultural projects in this area. I have heard nothing more definite than that, but I don't see how I can survive (or how my job can survive) so drastic a cut as that. If it were only about 40%, I would continue to hope. So there is gloom along the literary front here. Jack, Nelson [Conroy and Algren], etc. all trembling in their boots. . . . If the worst happens, we'll know it in a couple of days. As I see it, however, things may not be badly dislocated for us this summer, since I have writing jobs to which I can address myself for that long. . . . Wouldn't mind falling into the kind of spot you have landed for the winter. That sounds great. Maybe I'll get a chance to visit you there. I like Horace Mann Bond, and I've heard only good about his school. So you are in luck.
    BUT. . . . This is the point of this letter: rush the complete poems to me if you will. I'd love to check my selections for *Golden Slippers* against the total output. Several of the last group you sent will definitely go in. Hope you get here in time to look over my manuscript before I send it—but that will have to be very early in July. Do you plan so early an arrival?
    We saw *The Lady Eve.* It *was* amusing. . . . Thyra's complaints against Onah resulted in his being psychoanalyzed by WPA physicians. He claims that *she's* the one who needs her head examined. It's terrific. He tells a story of how she fainted on meeting him on the street. . . . Long ago I sent a copy of *Cavalcade* to Ed Lawson, also wrote him two notes, one in reply to an air mail from him.

. . . Whew! Didn't Joe Louis have a close call. Boy, he just pulled that one out of the fire in time. Several good shows still running here.

Ever,
Arna

P.S. The Handy book seems to be having the same delay—trouble your collection of poems is having. Set back again. But I hear from Macmillan that they are having a cocktail party for him. Maybe you'll be there for it, if the delays continue.

703 East 50th Place
Chicago, Illinois
2 July '41

Dear Lang,
The box of poems came yesterday. Thanks heaps. I have arranged with Knopf for ten poems from *The Dream Keeper*. They urge me not to use "If-ing," in view of the postponement of *Shakespeare in Harlem*. In which I'm only too glad to cooperate, especially since I want to use about eight or ten of the poems not yet included in books. Among them "Song to a Negro Washer Woman," "Florida Road Builders," "In Time Of Silver Rain," "Trip," etc.

The Handy book is out and well reviewed on day of publication in the daily book column of the N.Y. Times—and presumably other dailies. Handy mashed it up a lot in the interest of dignity, etc., but I hope the story still holds interest.

I seem to have survived the 61% cuts on the cultural projects in this area, but Jack got liquidated, along with 20 other supervisors. Nelson Algren [novelist] is still working, but fearing a later trim or purge, for we are promised that from 2 to 6 more may go within a couple of months. Meanwhile Jack and I are to have a conference with Hardwick Moseley tomorrow about a juvenile that I may make out of a folk tale originally transcribed by him. The job can be done in a week if the publishers like the plan.

Ever,
Arna

P.S. Miss Hadley came in and took my picture.
Irma says she's hoping you will stay with them at the center when you come through. You know they have fine guest rooms. Dick [Wright] and Ellen stayed in one of them on their last trip. The rooms are designed especially for visiting celebs. May be free—like the quarters for guests at Tuskegee—far as I know.

July 4, 1941.

Dear Arna,
I am glad the Handy book got off to a good start in the *Times*. Could we in some way work our sketch on *The Birth of the Blues* into the current exploitation of the book, possibly on the air or via the Apollo stage shows or something? Would you propose the idea to Lieber as I'm rushing off to San Francisco to see Katherine Dunham about some movie shorts and won't have a chance to write

him now. Also has Mr. Handy seen the sketch and does he approve? If so, he might help place it somewhere. . . . Lawson writes that Davidson Taylor of CBS (the same fellow who arranged for my Booker T. sketch last year) is interested in our *Cavalcade* and that he (Lawson) is making a condensation of it. (Lawson says he has quit *Opportunity* as they were way behind on his pay.) If you write to him point out to him the value of exploiting the Handy sketch at this moment. . . . Piquion writes that any N.Y. draft is accepted in Haiti so I reckon we will have to pay him after all. . . . Be sure to *check with Lieber* on *all* my poems not taken from Knopf books as he will have to clear the magazine copyrights for you. . . . Hope you could use something of Effie Lee Newsome's. Also Anne Spencer whose "At the Carnival" in the Johnson anthology I think is one of the *BEST* of Negro poems. . . . *Common Ground* has taken an article of mine. . . . And the Guild has awarded me the *Mulatto* money due, but—like the colored expo—now try and get it—as the producer ignores their ruling! Folks like that are the kind who are waiting for Hitler. That's why we could start housecleaning here with the better effect than using Dakar for a springboard, I should think.

Besides the folks in Dakar are bad enough off now without sending any of the kind of Texas crackers—army officers—who are now invading Carmel and bringing their color prejudice along with them—over to Africa to defend democracy.

> It's a mystery to me
> How we can send folks from Texas
> To defend democracy
> When they don't know
> What it is at home.

You look so intelligent and executive behind that beautiful desk in Miss Hadley's picture that I reckon you could clarify me! . . . . Last Sunday I went to hear some colored gospel singers at the colored church and you should have heard the shouting when they sang:

> I am looking for that stone
> That rolled down the mountain!

The stone was the Bible which they marched down the aisle carrying. Praise God!

Sincerely,
Langston

Hollow Hills Farm,
Monterey, California,
July 24, 1941.

Dear Arna,

Mail is piling sky high again. I get entirely too much not to be in a profitable business—with an office. The Junior College kid who typed for me has a full time summer job, and Mr. Sullivan's secretary, who is a Naval Reserve, has gone to work in the Navy Yards (and regular Carmel typists charge Park Avenue prices). And to make life a bit more complex, just went to the doctor today about an aching arm and he says I have another -itis of some kind. Need heat. And have a time typing mostly with one hand. I think I've probably caught my death of dampness, as warm dry weather has been a rarity out here this season and folks all up and down the Carmel Valley have been or are sick. Sen Fearnely the English writer on the next farm is down in bed with arthritis or something or other aching all over. And Eulah can hardly bend her knees. And last week Mr. Sullivan was limping around. So if the Lord just sends me an extra shilling, I think I'll head for the desert where it is HOT, although I wanted to wait until I was ready to start East and probably stop off a week or so in Arizona or New Mexico. But I have had so many interruptions on the book that I have at least a month's work yet to do to finish a first draft. I'm trying to work on schedule these days which is probably why I have an arm ache. I reckon the Lord did not intend for me to be that kind of a writer—that is why He ought to send me an endowment! Also Edna Ferber was right when she says it looks like there ain't no place where a writer can write in peace uninterrupted and unbothered. To tell the truth, Carmel might as well be 42nd Street and Fifth Avenue—so many white folks and Negroes are always passing through.

> Selah!
> Langston

> 703 East 50th Place
> Chicago, Illinois
> 19 August '41

Dear Lang,

Ho-hum, I reckon that anthology is off my chest at last. The final acts, I hope, were correction of proofs (mailed yesterday) and the letter to Mrs. Spingarn. Now all I have to do is write a letter to about a dozen of the poets, returning poems, thanks, etc. Publication date is now set for October 1st.

Handy was here for a week, along with Andy Razaf, Eubie Blake and others. There was a round of doings.

Lawson wrote me about the change of date (now Sept. 1st) on the "Jubilee" broadcast. Hope it comes off. He says they hope that an ASCAP settlement will be effective by then. Which would help a lot, in my opinion. . . . Mrs. Schwartz also tells me about a broadcast for the same week in which John T. Fredericks will be narrator. Seems that this will contain some Negro stuff, but I don't know just what. Better keep an ear bent.

Have you gone to the desert yet? I have been reading Louis Fischer's autobiography *Man and Politics,* a very interesting job which I imagine is something like your second volume will be—like it in length, area covered, people met, etc., if not in mood and style. Anyhow, the Fischer book is a best seller—as I am counting on yours to be. You might enjoy reading it. Much of the ground covered will be familiar to you, as will many of the people mentioned. I also found *Berlin Diary* interesting, though I am annoyed by the way Shirer always has himself predicting the exact outcome of events of the early thirties at a time when no one else seems to have such a prophetic gift. I wonder if he realized how omniscient he makes himself appear. . . . My advice is that you get yours out as soon as possible, for Russia is coming into increasing favor, and you might catch the tide at the full about this time next year—seeingst that you'll have a good section on that country. I look for a number of books designed to correct all the bitter feelings caused by the Finland business and the Hitler pact—a re-examination of the Soviet Republics, as it were. Also Spain.

This week I'm trying to decide whether to go back to my juvenile, my novel or what. . . . Trounstine (Turner) tells me he is withdrawing from literary agency. . . . See where Attaway and Dick both have books coming up, entitled "Blood on the Forge" and "12 Million Black Voices Speak" respectively. Looks like this will be a heavy fall for our crowd. . . . What's this about Orson Welles doing a movie about life of Louis Armstrong? Sterling Brown is doing for Doubleday, Doran that book on the South that they wanted you for. . . . Jack Conroy just sent Lieber a short story and a brief for a novel. . . . Follett book company is still trying to collect a balance of a hundred or two from Horace who signed the order for the Exposition. The books were SOLD, so there is no excuse there. . . . . . Dorothy Maynor has Marion Anderson's spot on the Northwestern series this year. . . . Hear about all those Negroes tromping each other in Harlem last Sunday? Those excursions are terrific. Too crowded.

Ever,
Arna

1229 East Washington Street
c/o Mrs. Emma Gardner
Phoenix, Arizona
August 27, 1941

Dear Arna,

What ya know, Joe? I am over here for a couple of weeks catching some sunshine. And believe me, it is really shining, too. Incidentally, I brought our *Boy of the Border* along and, being right here in the desert, I see lots of places where we can improve it as to color and atmosphere. I came across a wonderful old book, too, in the farm library on Arizona and its history with amazing chapters about Indians and cowboys. (Did you know that a Negro discovered Arizona? In fact, was the first "white" man to enter the territory—but never got out because the Indians put him to death before Fray Marcos, for whom he was a runner, could catch up to him, three days ahead.) Anyhow, I am going to take a bus trip across the desert in the interest of *Boy*'s authenticity. . . . I also brought along three other books to read, including *Father of the Blues* and *For Whom the Bell Tolls*. Also my notes through Russia for my book. So, intending to stay three weeks, I have enough work for about a year—considering really how long it takes to do things well. So far I've been here almost two weeks and haven't touched most of it. It has been too nice and hot to stay in at all, and too nice and hot to work out of doors. But I have got some reading done on my Rosenwald material —Douglass—and I marvel that no one has made a novel out of his life? . . . . Also was it you who once told me something should be done with Baudelaire and his lifelong Negro mistress? Most dramatic material there, too. . . . Only question is would any of this stuff sell? Or would we have to be endowed the rest of our lives to do it? Or else get a bell-boy's job and write on the side. . . . Have you heard any more about our broadcast? I've been watching the papers, but see nothing. Airmail me, if you have heard when it is coming off. (Airmail me anyhow, since I haven't been getting any mail over here anyhow and so would like to know who still lives.) But address it: *JAMES* Hughes, above address, as I am rooming with the State President of the Colored Women's Clubs who, I am afraid, would tea me to death if she knew I was a poet-writer. As it is, so far, my time has been delightfully my own. There has been so much company, white and colored, at the farm this summer, I am delighted to NOT have to dress for dinner. (Three separate race visitations were about to descend upon us when I left, and half the East was in L.A. for the Boule and I reckon several probably drove by Carmel on the way back—which is another reason I took to the desert. Phoenix is really a charming place where almost everybody—at least of the Race (and Mexican) seem to live in little houses with no windows at all—just screens—and rent is only six and eight dollars a month. Good old home cooked meals are only 25¢ and 30¢. And WHOLE watermelons on ice are only a dime! If I ever go to war and get a pension I think I will settle down right here. The fare to LA is only $5.00. . . . Right after Labor Day I'm going back to Monterey as my money will have run out, and my R check is due the first there. And my suntan is almost as good as Aaron's. . . . Best to all,

Sincerely,
Lang

P.S. If you have occasion to visit the Hall Library, just kindly say real loud around Miss Hadley that you heard I've gone to the desert for months. As she wrote me a second time about doing an introduction for a booklet of her photographs about the library that I already told her once I'd rather not do—as it seems to me it should be done by a Chicagoan—and anyhow I have no facts at hand about the Hall Branch—(and have enough lined up to work on for the next two years as it is)—but she seemingly won't take no for an answer, so I haven't answered her letter—and probably won't for the next ten weeks. So kindly give her the impression that her letter is in California and I am in the desert—and *can't be reached.* I never do forewords anyhow—have turned down about six this year. And politely declined the honor of hers sometime ago once.

703 E. 50th Place
Chicago, Illinois
29 August '41

Dear Lang,

Last night when I went home I read your letter. Before that I had been told about it in general terms by Alberta over the phone. I wonder now if I made it straight about the broadcast. It is set for the evening of Labor Day as indicated by Lawson in his last letter. Also, be assured about money, if your pocket change is short. There is a check waiting for you at Hollow Hills. If you do as I did last night after cashing mine, you will go to town and buy yourself a mellow new tweed—looking just like it came from the Isle of Man. You will then turn over the balance to five urchins with instructions to get themselves something for school, which opens next week. But, boy, that tweed—gimme some skin! That makes me have two gray suits—and no other kind.

Douglass would, in my opinion, make a warmly admired novel, somewhat on the level of *Black Thunder* perhaps, but without much hope of great sales. The best that one could hope for with him as a hero would be something like *God's Angry Man* (John Brown). BUT I *am* cooking up a juvenile based on some few

88

episodes from his life. In the kid's field, I calculate, such a book might become a steady seller. So that's my next aim—unless someone does it before I get around to it.

Baudelaire's Negro mistress is still, as I see it, a natural. It should interest both blacks and whites as the subject for a novel. I would have been working on it for the past two years had I (as you have) greater facility in reading French, plus an experience in France to help me with the background. You really ought to do that job. Do it somewhat as Stone did Van Gogh in *Lust for Life*. Tell the story from the mistress's point of view, but let it be equally the story of the poet. I believe readers will consider it an ideal story situation for you. If anything will get one off fellowships and pensions, etc., that should. Moreover, it should be the kind of thing that will interest a publisher right off the bat—perhaps on the basis of a chapter or two, plus a synopsis.

Reviews of Handy this week in Courier, Harper's Magazine. A picture in Publisher's Weekly—one Miss Hadley took at the Argus Book Shop. . . . It rained here for the Spiritual Festival, so the crowd was just middling. Jackie Robinson did all right by himself in the All-Star game, however. And Booker T. Beckwith, the new twenty year old flash from Gary, did a fine job in beating Red Burman. He's the boy I'd like to see take Joe Louis' crown. Sort of like Armstrong. Preacher's son, plays several instruments, comes from a family of ten. A picture fighter, like Chocolate used to be.

The desert always appealed to me! I'll try to get this to you before you leave it.

Ever,
Arna

Los Angeles,
Sunday, Sept. 28, '41.

Man,

It looks like I can't get away from this town, but I am POSITIVELY leaving tomorrow! . . . . . Have been having some conferences with movie producers, but no results. I think only a subsidized Negro Film Institute, or the revolution, will cause any really good Negro pictures to be made in America. And right now, we need them badly to underscore our democratic aims and help change the American mass mind away from its Hitlerian attitude toward us. In a single day more people see a picture at the Paramount than read any one of our Negro writers' books in a year. . . . . Did I tell you Zora is living in Los Angeles proper now? . . . . . And that Fay Jackson is the public relations lady for the Gold Furniture and Clothing Company and just sold your father a new carpet for his new church and she says he looks fine. . . . . And that Eulah is in town on her vacation and her sister, Juanita Williams had a party for her last night. . . . . Dorothy Johnson said she received a nice note from you. Her thesis on influencing race attitudes in children is very good. She mentions our *Popo* in it. . . . . The Dramatist Guild finally collected for me from the Ellington show so I bought a new suit, grey tweed, like the one I used to have. . . . . Loren's [Miller] new house is beautiful, modern, with circular staircase and terraced garden. . . . . Just read *So It Doesn't Whistle*, a very badly put together novel, but with amusing passages—New York bohemia a la *Infants of the Spring* among whites—but not so good as Tess Slessinger used to do it. She gets 20 to 50 thousand for movie scripts nowadays, so doesn't bother with novels any more. Can you blame her? While buying the book (BUYING mind you! I must be crazy) I glanced through half the others in the shop. One was a vicious tome about the Virgin Islands praising the scenery and all, but damning the natives as being exceedingly impudent and not at all like the sweet southern darkies "we have in America." . . . . . I wonder what makes us so sweet? . . . . He says they don't have spirituals down there either. . . . . Which maybe accounts for it. . . . . Kiss my beloved Poppy for me, also Camille, and all others not in high school! Give *them* some spending change.

Best to Alberta whom I hope to see soon,
                                        Sincerely,
                                        Langston

Louis Sharp is in *Mamba's Daughters* and was at Eulah's party.

                                        3 October '41
                                        703 E. 50th Place
                                        Chicago, Illinois

Dear Lang,
    Anyone who sees us on the street now, in our new tweeds, will sure think he is seeing double—especially since Louise says you are now my size! . . . . You are about to convince me that there is simply no resisting the lure of the movies. Somehow, however, I'm not quite sure that you are any the worse off by not coming to terms with them: people will be reading your poems and novels (see where *Not Without Laughter* is being reissued) and autobiographical books after new forms of entertainment have displaced talkies. Moreover, if make-believe is bound to win you, I still think Negro material has a better chance on radio and the stage—as American Democracy stands. Why not take another throw at Broadway?
    Handy and I go on Frederick's "Of Men and Books" on the 18th of November. Don't know what days it will be rebroadcast on. Frederick says we are also going to talk about *Golden Slippers*. . . . . I may have to make a trip in connection with my work—a trip that will take me away from here for the two weeks following October 19th. This is not at all certain, but I hope anyhow (to be sure) that you will not let your stay here fall entirely during that two-week period. It would be nice if you were going to stay at *least* a month or two in Chi this time! It would also be nice to go to N. Y. and see the shows, etc. as you go, but I'm inclined to guess that my trip (if it comes off as above) will be too early.
    Nelson Algren has a short story in the forthcoming O. Henry Collection. It seems to be a part of his new novel—which Harpers has accepted. . . . . How is Zora living? I mean is literature her staff? I think I put her up to going to the Coast when I was in Durham. I drew the usual Chamber of Commerce picture of the place.
    Where does Loren [Miller] live? I've often wondered where in L. A. he built his new house. . . . . The fixing up of that new church in Watts is sort of in celebration of his retirement at the end of this year. He has bought a little place near San Bernadino where he and my step mother will presently move. . . . . The novel that is getting the talk round here is *The Sun Is My Undoing*, a huge

romance about the slave trade and mixing blood. . . . . Changed my mind about Eros stealing Katherine's [Dunham] thunder since seeing *Carnival of Rhythm*. Beautiful picture. Please pass my compliments to Katherine et al.

We are enjoying our third straight day of rain. Think about that!

Ever,
Arna

October 23, 1941

My dear Mr. Bontemps,

Whoever says I am as stout as you is a prevaricator of the first water. I am certain I weigh several ounces less. Especially since I have begun to lecture again. I have just come back from Sacramento where a colored high school club had a program for an audience of three hundred in a school auditorium that seats three thousand and the stage was as far from the audience as you are from the Grand Hotel. But otherwise it was most pleasant. I took occasion to speak about *Golden Slippers.* . . . [Richmond] Barthé is just rounding out his two weeks here. He's in San Francisco at the moment. . . . I will speak in Los Angeles on the 16th of November and come on East from there for the engagement with you and Fredericks on the 21st. Tell Horace [Cayton] and Irma [wife] I'll be delighted to stay with them if they don't make me attend teas. . . . How about us together or separately getting an engagement at Good Shepherd Church? Also anywhere else in the Chicago area during November or early December? Christmas is coming and a little extra change wouldn't hurt. . . . I haven't seen the new *Not Without Laughter.* But *The Democratic Spirit* in which I and seven other Negroes are included looks swell. . . . Loren's new house is just beyond the West Temple district around Hoover, Virgil, etc. . . . . I sent six short stories off to Lieber recently, including "Banquet in Honor" that I sent you. . . . The poem "Merry-Go-Round" will be in the next issue of *Common Ground.* And *Harper's Bazaar* wants some, but I haven't any very good new ones. . . . How's your trip?

Langston

P.S. Donnan Jeffers got married last night in Ohio. His parents flew East for the wedding—were grounded in Salt Lake—so flew back and celebrated the mating here last night at the farm with cake, champagne and all. I was near high.

October 29, 1941.

Dear Arna,

I haven't any tuxedo. But if *absolute* necessity dictates one, I'll either have to buy it or rent it—according to how my funds are. . . . . And they ain't much. . . . . I'm glad you had what sounds like a nice trip East. . . . . I always did want to stay at the Theresa once . . . . . Man, I have written seven short stories! Just to keep from writing any letters—or working on my book as I should. My subconscious is full of Old Ned. Also Christmas and New Years are coming and if I am broke this time!?&%$#"*! . . . . . At long last it seems that *Shakespeare in Harlem* has gone to press with the drawings. But not to appear until early in

91

the New Year. If the Negroes therein come out *with no hair on their heads,* I shall retire to Arizona and remain. . . . . Tell Horace I'll take him up on that bed, Alberta on board (you know, once in a while) and the Rosenwalds on that office from November 24 on. . . . . But who has an overcoat and some earmuffs to lend me? . . . . And who will be my secretary? I really can't create and type, too. Truly, 'tis difficult. . . . . If it were not for you I never would have known *Not Without Laughter* was out again. And *Golden Slippers* I haven't seen either, but save me a copy. . . . . . But *The Democratic Spirit* looks swell and has seven Negroes in it. . . . Do you hear two typewriters going as I write this? I'm fortunate to have a typist this week. I've used up Five Dollars worth of paper the last fortnight— such a writing as is going on here. A prospective trans-continental journey is always conducive to work in me. . . . . A grand colored cutting was held in Monterey Sunday night. A kind of free for all, ending with two in the hospital, two in jail, and one in a sling. Besides assorted unaccounted-fors. A lady named Fannie attacked a lady named Virgil in the phone booth and cut her from here to yonder before she could get out. Whereupon various men became involved. And one poor innocent soldier just looking on was also stabbed. All of the race. But it happened in a Japanese pool hall. It was all over love. . . . . . Barthé has been here and gone. We enjoyed his visit. He will be in Chicago shortly—if he survives Los Angeles. . . . . Eulah has a cold so I am about to go and help her drink a hot toddy. . . . . We are planning to have a colored party here for all our friends next week, a lawn fete—so if fighting is done there will be plenty of room. . . . . Carl Van Vechten wants manuscripts, first drafts, etc., for the Yale James Weldon Collection. So if you have any of yours, send them to him. . . . . The second annual Negro Twenty Four Piano Concert will be held in Oakland next week. They say it is terrific! Maybe I might go. . . . . Poor dear Miss Hadley! I just haven't been able to answer letters—especially when they involve doing something else, too. It is always so hard to do the something else. Even a writer has to have time to do his own something elses, too. And time is of the essence! It evaporates before you can bat your eye. This whole day has gone already—and when I think of the fun I could have had if I hadn't been working, I cannot bear to sit down and attend to somebody else's something else tonight when by not working I can catch up on what I miss by working. . . . . . Come and in the fires of spring your winter garment, etc., fling! But when you have no winter garment (nee overcoat)—?,,,?,,,,?,,,,?. . . .

As ever,
Langston

Hollow Hills Farm,
Monterey, California,
October 30, 1941.

Dear Arna,
    For $150 I do not think they should have music and tuxedos both—not if the music has to come out of the speakers' fees. . . . But if they are going to pay for it themselves, I'd suggest Etta Moten singing "Little Gal," "The Negro Speaks of Rivers," and a spiritual. And looking pretty. Which would guarantee any

number of engagements more. . . . . (But SLAY her if she sings the "Carioca" again.) . . . . . Or in seven languages.

If you-all cut my $50.00 I will appear in a sport coat. And tell all about how much prejudice there is in Hollywood under Israel. Also about Bobby Breen.

I have been lecturing all these years and got along right well without any music —except a member of the club singing "Trees" just before the chairman introduces me.

Of what racial strain is Ellen [Mrs. R. Wright]? And how do Claude [McKay] and C.L.R. James [West Indian writer] get on? They're both colored, West Indian, literary, and in mourning for Trotsky.

Hey! You didn't say anything about making arrangements with Alberta! . . . . . . I want some good old navy beans.

What are you researching on? If you'll do mine for me, I'll give you half interest in all the forthcoming non-royalty high school plays, no jive.

Thanks for the reviews. Dutton said they were sending me *Mr. George's Joint* but it hasn't arrived yet. . . . . . That lady ought to go to Phoenix and write about Sammy Moore's, where the cotton pickers hang out. . . . . Or Togo's Pool Room right here in Monterey where Fannie cut Virgil in the phone booth the other day. And Bernie cut a soldier, another man and Argyle. They put Argyle's arm in a sling where he was cut at. But when he got home he also found that he been cut in *the side!* . . . . I'll bet the Negroes in *George's Joint* don't holler any louder than they did in *Mamba's Daughters* as produced here on the coast. The women always stand straddle-legged too on the stage. How primitive, child-like, immoral, amoral, and simple!

I will now write you a poetry:

Uncle Sam
With Old Jim Crow
Right behind you
Everywhere you go.

Uncle Sam,
Why don't you turn around—
Before you tackle Hitler—
And shoot Jim down?

After which I will now close. As ever,

Sincerely,
Langston

703 E. 50th Place
Chicago
5 November '41

Dear Lang,

This is Wednesday; I have been here since Sunday. This is also the day on which a *Tribune* headline reads, "Red Votes Elect La Guardia to Third Term." But mainly the excitement I find in Chicago is due to the rattling of plates and the sweeping of floors, looking toward your arrival. I have called Horace's secretary, and they are expecting you anytime after the 15th of November. When you have an exact date, I suggest that you let them have a line direct. Desk space is awaiting you here in these diggings. And Alberta has just bought new table and chairs. To make the welcome complete, "Native Son" will commence a run at the STUDEBAKER on November 10th (with original cast) and Etta Moten told me yesterday that she would love to appear with us at the Standard Club, singing

Negro Speaks, etc. She will take what she can get in money, understanding that it will be modest—due to the fact that this is an afterthought. And Mrs. Schwartz assures me that Tuxedos can be rented for three or four dollars. Maybe if you and I get ours at the same time we can drive a bargain. So I'll wait and see what you are going to do before I decide. Etta was thrilled when she learned the character of this affair. Evidently it's just her dish.

I liked much "Harlem Sweeties" and "Domestic Happenings". Each seems to me to have two or three lines that are less smooth than the rest of the poem, but in general I'm whistling them both. Too bad "Sweeties" wasn't ready in time for my *Slippers*. It's just the type. While "Happenings" is ironic enough to interest the *New Yorker*. . . . I also like the after dinner speech in "Banquet in Honor." Let's hope it gets read and reread by the talented tenth of our group. Where are you going to send it? I think the *Courier* has the audience that would be helped by it—but maybe a magazine will do. . . . Be sure to bring your copy of *The Democratic Spring* along (if it's not too big to tote). I don't seem able to stumble upon a copy. Dick Wright didn't even have one—perhaps his had been lifted. It will be my pleasure to review "Shakespeare in Harlem" at the book club when it comes out. . . . Won't you write Van Vechten and tell him that you will bring one of my manuscripts with you to New York? John B. Turner is contributing a copy of our "When the Jack Hollers." And I have sent Tolson one of my copies of the same for consideration by his LOG CABIN THEATRE. No reply.

Had a grand time in New York. Ell and Dick have a charming, secluded place in Brooklyn, 11 Revere Place, with an unlisted phone. Ellen is cute. Her mother dropped in while I was there—to my surprise. Maybe I shouldn't have been surprised. Dick has a new dictaphone and all the trimmings, and is he going to town? Knocked out his new novel about religious life among Negroes in a couple of months. Written at white heat, as they say, "The Man Who Lived Underground." His "12 Million Black Voices" is going around—advance copies. I got one yesterday. Yours must be on its way. It's a beautiful creation: pictures and text both lyrical. Embree just commented that he thought it was too much on the "wailing wall" side and that it neglects to suggest a way out, but as a "wailing" performance, he says, not even Du Bois has ever wept so beautifully.

I met Claude McKay and took him to dinner. This was our first meeting. He was all charm—the gentle, wistful poet. So I did not see his profile, or the side of his personality which had been most widely publicized. He did, in an aside, take occasion to blast Stalin, but C.L.R. James was not mentioned. Claude is living at 33 West 125th Street on the top floor of an old store building. He has what looks like a typical Greenwich Village artist's roost of the more musty variety. Across the hall young Bearden has a studio. There is a genuine bohemian note up there—like the old days. Even the international note of the Latin Quarter is struck. Claude has a Japanese friend who hangs around—a gray-haired oriental who wears corduroy slacks and talks "art" very fluently. The place is warmed by an oil heater that smokes a bit. Claude looks well-fed and reasonably well-clothed, but he says he is terribly broke.

Harold said he heard that James is sick. . . . Petion Suvain, the Haitian artist, is in N.Y. studying, and doing quite well—an etching of his having appeared recently in the *N.Y. Times* Sunday graphic section. His brother is also there. He's a dentist. You'll like them both. Petion also writes well, you remember. . . . Dorothy Peterson has collected gobs of Puerto Rican poetry for you. She is better looking than she has been in twelve years. Her father showed me his old scrap books—when he was a young editor of the *N.Y. Age,* more than fifty years ago. This, I hope, will help me do my juvenile on Fred Douglass. Douglass used to drop into their offices, as did Ida B. Wells and others of interest. . . . Countee's wife Ida is quite lovely: petite, dainty, very friendly, very devoted to Countee. As a result Countee is writing as of old. Another book about a cat (this one in prose) is due in the spring, and he is actively planning his next. They have a large apartment from the windows of which you can look into the Polo Grounds, as we did with glasses to see the football score. . . . At Harold's I met Christian Belle, a French consul at Puerto Rico. He made a strong case—though it didn't quite fully convince me—for Petain, to whom he is loyal. He is a poet and novelist as well as diplomat. . . . Doug and Alta are unchanged. . . . And the Theresa is a good place to stay.

See you soon, hunh?

Ever,
Arna

P.S. Give a parting greeting to Mr. Sullivan and to Eulah for me. See Rochester in this week's *Look*? Boy!

Hollow Hills Farm,
Monterey, California,
November 8, 1941.

Dear Arna,

Do you, by any chance, happen to know Miss Florence B. Price, 647 East 50th Place, just below you? It's she who set to music my *Songs to the Dark Virgin* that Schirmer's have just published.

Well, we had an enormous big party the other day, Eulah and I, cocktails from 3–6, but practically nobody went home until 3 in the morning. It just went on and on and on, and the joint jumped. About 50 came. Nobody fought, but one girl got mad at a former boy friend and pulled all the wires out of his car so it wouldn't budge when she heard he intended to take another girl home. Budge it did not, until the garage man came to fix it next day. It belonged to a soldier from Fort Ort. Result: about six other soldeirs were also stranded out here, and Eulah had to drive them all home. Then when she got back we were washing dishes until 6 A.M. Hundreds of glasses seem to have been drunk from. Thus went the $18.00 from *Golden Slippers.*

If we are going to have more than one lecture possibly, it would be better to buy a cheap tuxedo, $22.50 or something like that, than to rent one three or four times. That is what I think I will do, but I would have to get it out here, as I wouldn't have time in Chi.

A note from Mr. Frederick says we ought to get together the day before and line out the program. He says he'll set the time with you, so do that, and any time Thursday afternoon would be all right with me. I can read as many or as few poems as desired, so whatever you-all plan is O.K. anyhow even if I'm snowbound and not there. I'm glad Etta is going to sing.

But it's quite clear, isn't it, that said fifty shan't be cut? Only for Jackie Mabley would I split mine. Or possibly Lil Green.

Thanks for so much news of New York and all my friends there.

I'll send you *The Democratic Spirit* on ahead probably, and maybe a couple of more trunks full of things—providing I can get packed up in time. It is my full intention to start tomorrow, so I won't be over rushed.

Mr. Van Vechten wants to know (for his Yale collection) if Henrietta Bruce Sharon is white or colored. I'm sure she must be white, but since I couldn't swear it, would you mind dropping him a card as to who she is and what? . . . . It seems he doesn't like the drawings very much. I can't say that I do either. White artists illustrating Negro books still seem to think we're living in Uncle Remus days. I reckon they've never been to Harlem and seen all that pretty straight hair up there, and beautiful children. Or to Georgia where the girls out-do the peaches in golden loveliness. . . . . Not that I have any right to yowl because I'm practically sure every Negro in *Shakespeare in Harlem* will come out nappy-headed in spite of the fact that I wrote long ago to the publishers and objected. They keep writing me how beautiful the drawings are and that an artist's conception must be his own emanating from what he sees in the text, etc. If such reasoning be true, then one just can't trust the average white artist to illustrate a Negro book, unless they are known to know Negroes in life—not Uncle Remus—and be sympathetic to the poetry of Negro life—and not to it's (to them) humorous and grotesque, amusing and "quaint" aspects.

Barthé should be in Chicago by now.

The radio says it's cold there.

I shall be delighted to see you-all again and will let Horace know the day and hour of my arrival, as well as yourself. I shall try to make it the morning of the 20th.

Delighted at the prospect of seeing all the Bontemps once more. Maybe I can finish my book in Chicago. So I'll pack and ship my trunk full of notes.

Sincerely,
Langston

634 St. Nicholas Ave.
Apt. 1-D, c/o Harper
New York, New York
January 27, 1942

Dear Arna and Alberta,

New York has me going around in circles. I haven't seen a single play except the opening of *Porgy and Bess* to which I was invited. Met Schiaparelli thereat. . . . It is now 4 A.M. and I am very sleepy but thought I had better write and tell you what to do with the pine knot to make it grow green and beautiful. You simply put it in a shallow bowl with an inch or two or three of water around it, enough to cover the base, and in a week or so nice green sprouts will come out and in a couple of months they'll be almost a bush. . . . Have seen quite a little of Doug, and Dorothy Maynor, and Dorothy Peterson, but that's about all— except Carl V.V. who's house is full of things for the Weldon Johnson Collection that he now works on all day, listing, annotating. . . . It took me two full days to sign and explain my stuff. And over a week to dig out more from my trunks in the basement. It's a good thing he got me started on that because I discovered a lot of things had gotten all mouldy from having sat under the pipes in the basement that seemingly drip moisture all summer long. Some of my favorite autographed books—God's Trombones, first edition of Saroyan's first book he gave me, etc. ruined and all stuck together. Also the Josephine Baker Folies Bergere programs, etc. . . . Which only further confirms my opinion that it's very little use for cullud to try to have anything. I was kinder sick for a couple of days. But have recovered now. Luckily pictures and manuscripts were not spoiled—only a few. . . . The janitor said very calmly, Oh, water just drips down all summer! —as though people didn't have their belongings stored underneath the water! . . . So it goes in Harlem.

Well, OPM called me up from Washington five times and Will Alexander flew over here to talk with me about a radio script for Rex Ingram and Canada Lee for the Lincoln's Birthday "Keep 'Em Rolling" program on February 15th. I thought they meant paid, but it turned out they didn't—since Norman Corwin and all those highly paid commercial guys so nobly donate free scripts. I told Mr. Alexander I didn't think they ought to ask Negro writers who never get any commercial work in radio (or anywhere else hardly) to do the same—since a well-done 15 minute script takes at least a full week out of your life—but he said it was to help win the war and lift civilian morale—so I did it. Sent it to you the other day. What do you think of it?

Delighted about your Houghton Mifflin contract! Swell!

I'll be out your way around the 12th. Will save all the news till then. Too sleepy now. And have to get up early. Dined with Walter Saturday, Maynor Sunday. But am not taking any social engagements at all this week and have gone to a hotel to work.

Knopf, added to my other troubles, have put a wishbone and a dice on my book jacket! They think it's charming.

I hope the Red Army marches right straight through (to) the Channel.*

Sincerely,
Langston

*and helps England

703 E. 50th Place
Chicago, Illinois
8 May '42

Dear Lang,

Alberta just read your letter over the phone. I'm still waiting to hear from H-M about that career book. Unless the contract is forthcoming presently, I'll get started on something else. Plans for the trip are therefore in abeyance.

Last night Paul went to help backstage, and Joan and I picked him up—or rather called for him along toward the time of Rock's homecoming. What made the evening more exciting than usual was that after the show Mrs. Lewis made a brief talk. She said that once in a while amateurs like themselves get word that greatness is in the audience. On such occasions the thrills behind the footlights are greater than those in front. Last night, she said, was such a night. In the audience was Irene Castle. Whereupon that marvelous lady went forward, congratulated the cast, had herself photographed with the leads, and said pleasant words to the audience. Thereafter she and her party of four stopped in Horace's place for coffee and cake, where I engaged her in conversation anent the reference to her in *Father of the Blues*. She and her group all had good words for the show. One of them observed that you had, by making the play easy to mount, made it uncommonly hard to direct. By requiring less in the way of scenery and curtains, you had required more in the way of acting ability and general performance by all concerned—including the directors.

Horace had indicated that he wanted to talk about *St. Louis Woman* and his plans for having you to come out to produce it, but we never got around to it. Perhaps later. I'm to call him this morning.

Lieber just sent *Common Ground*'s check for "Rock, Church, Rock!" Either the June or September issue, according to Margaret Anderson. Dorsey, who gave permission to reproduce some of his music, was here to lunch last week. He asked about you. I'm quoting part of "Rock Me" and part of Roberta Martin's "Didn't it Rain", the song that Cobb's choir made famous. The music along with the words.

Tonight we go to the Civil Liberty's special showing of Steinbeck's *Forgotten Village*. Yesterday, between a conference with Hubbell of the *Sun* and Joan's music lesson, I dropped into the Chicago Theatre and saw Gene Krupa's band feature their Negro Trumpet player. He is beautifully integrated into the organization and the program—a blow for democracy. The night before, the kids and I saw, for the first time, the Nicholas Brothers in *Down Argentine Way*. I had the same re-action that night, too.

I'll let you know if and when the N. Y. business gets arranged.

Ever,
Arna

Yale University
May 17, 1942

Dear Arna,

I'm stopping with the Knollenberg's (the Librarian) and Norman Pearson, one of the editors of the Oxford Book of Am. Lit was here for the evening. He admires your work very much, asked for news of you, and says he expects to be in Chicago shortly and hopes to see you and Jack. Yesterday at the Lafarge's, I met Thornton Wilder who's about to go to Hollywood to work with Hitchcock on a movie, then to the intelligence division of the army. Saturday I read [the play] "Merry-Go-Round" acted out by two very cute colored kids, at Westport, for Common Ground. Miss Anderson was delighted with your article, scheduled now for issue after next. This issue has a long Tolson poem to lead off, and an Ottley article on housing.

The Yale Library is the biggest campus library in the world—really enormous, almost the size of Radio City. Bessie Smith is now singing therein!

Sincerely,
Langston

P.S. I would just as leave you did *not* give my letters away. How about yours? Do you want them to go to Yale? The ones of mine to Wallie look very juvenile now. I do not like the idea of writing to one's friends—for posterity and the world. Everybody seems so rich up here! (Harlem is worlds away! Maybe isn't at all.)

634 St. Nicholas Avenue,
c/o Harper, Apt. 1-D,
New York, May 23, 1942.

Dear Arna,

I shall be delighted to see you on June first, will even come to meet you if you let me know what time—especially if you would be so kind as to bring that big bundle of Spain material (so marked) up on the shelf in the guest room closet at Horace's. . . . . Anyhow, I have several things to talk over with you, briefly herein listed as follows:

1. JOB AT YALE: The librarian there, who is a splendid fellow, wants to add a Negro or two to the permanent staff of the University Library. (There is one colored undergraduate boy working there now.) Of course, I immediately mentioned you, since they must have a trained person, and wish a bang up good one, so that it might lead to further entrance of the race into things thereabouts. However, after I told him your various distinctions, he felt that the job would be too minor a one, for you. It is in the card cataloguing department, and pays to start, $1200 a year. However, by the time you finish Library School you ought to write him anyhow. Maybe you could become Curator of the James Weldon Johnson Collection—since they hope someone will endow it so that they may have such a curator. (So keep these things under your hat and ruminate thereon.)

2. Piquion writes from Haiti that he is now a director of rural education or something of the sort there, and feels that *Popo and Fifina* would make an excellent text book for Haitian children. He wishes to translate it himself, and wants the permission of you and me to do so. Would you kindly write him granting that permission, also write Macmillan's and ask them to work out the business arrangements with him, explaining to them that Haiti is not a rich country. (I should think, however, that if the book could be printed in French by them here—in his translation—they might sell it throughout the French speaking colonial world. Perhaps that might be even better than permitting it to be printed in Haiti where the distribution would be limited, no doubt, to that island.) Anyway write your personal permission for him to begin work on the translation.

3. The lady in charge of the children's department at Knopf wants very much to have a good simple well-written history of the Negro in America for their list. I told her nobody in America could do the job as well as you. She asks that I bring you to see her when you arrive. So think on that, too.

4. Origenes Lessa, distinguished Brazilian writer and member of the cultural mission here plans a series of articles on Negroes for Brazilian publications, also a series of radio programs on writers over the air from here on the big new net-work just opened up. Wishes to meet you. Save a moment for that.

5. Mr. Carl Van Vechten was delighted to hear about your proposed book and

feels that he would have some helpful suggestions to make. He also wants to photograph you in color. So save a cocktail hour for that.

6. Also would you work out *St. Louis Woman* details while here to assure the use of *our* script, etc. if Horace puts it on in Chi next fall?

7. And would you tell Alberta and the kids, HY! And that I love them and hope to get back to see them soon.

8. Bring me some programs of the show, etc. if you have a chance to.

Sincerely,
Lang

June 18, 1942

Dear Arna,

Too bad, really TOO BAD, you could not have stayed over for the big meeting at the Garden. It was TERRIFIC!!!! The enormous Garden, all but one end at the very top, packed solid with Negroes. And they went to town! Randolph marched in between a great guard of Pullman porters in uniform, behind the Ethiopian flag! The orators got off BIG. Best were Adam Powell, who announced his candidacy for Congress, Walter White, who made a sound factual speech, and Bethune. But topping them all was a hard hitting very effective and moving play by Dick Campbell in the manner of my *Don't You Want to Be Free,* with Canada Lee, Mercedes Gilbert and others showing short scenes of refusal at the factories, in the Navy, etc., that had the audience cheering. Canada played a Native Son before his draft board, laying out fake democracy and saying, yes, he would fight, but would start fighting at the Grand Central Station and fight the crackers right on straight through Georgia. Whereupon folks cheered for five minutes! There was also a wonderful song about Dorie Miller. And things went on so long and so late that Randolph, who organized the thing, and was billed last, didn't get to speak at all. Just had about three minutes before twelve when the Garden had to be cleared, or overtime rent paid. So he didn't get his chance after all, and Adam Powell had run off with the honors! Downtown looked like Harlem that night. You should have been here. . . . Ran into a colored sailor just off a raft, torpedoed. Still jittery. Interesting story. . . . How was the trip home, and everybody? Best to all, and write soon.

As ever,
Sincerely,
Langston

Also just wrote a new song, "The Waitress with the Dimples."

STILL HERE
by *Langston Hughes*

I been
Scarred and battered.
My hopes
The wind done scattered.
Snow has frize me.
Sun is baked me.
Looks like, between 'em,
They done tried to make me
Stop living,
Stop laughing
Stop singing—
But I don't care
Folks I'm
Still here!

100

634 St. Nicholas Avenue,
New York, New York,
July 4th, 1942.

Dear Arna,

No check from Horace yet, so I'd appreciate immensely your making another call for me, because now I *really* need it, and NOW. (plays never vary when it comes to paying royalties.)

I'll be at Saratoga until September 15th, after that, say October 1st, could come to Chi for six or eight weeks. I'd suggest some arrangement, lectures or otherwise, to net $200 in return for staging the play—supervising the production with a director as assistant and a technical man. Is Harvey Cogbill still around? He works well.

Louise was in town, and attended the premier of *Freedom Road* at Cafe Society. The song is going over well down there, but my family and I have an even better one now—*That Eagle of the U.S.A.* (He really flies—and in boogie woogie tempo!) I'll send Paul and Joan copies of both shortly to sing and play for you-all.

Speaking of songs, Jimmy Davis, the fellow who was helping us on the piano copies, talented Juilliard School student, went to jail yesterday rather than go into a Jim Crow army after his appeals to be allowed to enlist in Canada were denied. Three to five years, probably. At the request of his draft board he gave himself up voluntarily to the F.B.I. A swell boy, so we all feel sad today.

It looks like to me the British better give up a little of their Jim Crow in North Africa or they'll be backed right on up into the Red Sea, and it probably won't open to let them pass, either.

New verse for *That Eagle:*

> I don't feel like fighting
> For the *status quo*—
> Cause it ain't nothing
> But old Jim Crow!
> That eagle said,
> You told that right.
> It's a new world for which
> We've got to fight.
> That eagle! That eagle!
> That eagle's got his wings over me.
> That eagle! That eagle!
> That eagle of the free. . . . .

PLEASE send me that little Quaker book for the man at Yale!!!!!!!! And write and let me know how you-all are. . . . . . Mr. Handy is publishing our *Negro Speaks of Rivers.* I've been in the office often of late. He's fine, and still able to lift his voice.

Sincerely,
Langston

The Lunts are appearing soon in a new show now casting with Negro chorus and background, West Indies in 1820. The music by Herbert Kingsley who set my blues.

101

Dear Lang,

Just came in from the U., and I have about five minutes before running to the shindig described in the enclosed clipping. Meanwhile, here is a request that can't wait. Will you take a few minutes from your week-end activities to write down (however crudely and swiftly) what you saw and knew of Arthur Koestler in Russia or Spain or wherever? Any small details will help. Do you remember anything he said, anything he did, any impressions of the way he looked or behaved? Anything whatever that you can say about him. If it comes off well, I'll try to sell it to a magazine. I want to bring you into the story if possible—thinking that that might add to the interest. I have reviewed his latest book for the *Sun* and become quite interested in his work. How did he rate himself when you saw him? Did he seem to you to be a definite comer? You know, he's about to join such company as Hemingway, Steinbeck, etc.

Well, here I go to Evanston! Let me hear from you.

Ever,
Arna

Two reviews on tap for next week. The H. T. "Books" is sending another one, so maybe they were satisfied with the first. Quien sabe?

Yaddo,
Sunday.

Arna, ole man,

Your review in the *Herald Tribune* is *swell!* Everybody up here has read it. . . . . Did I tell you *The Seventh Cross* is a Lieber book? Half the authors up here this summer were his, including McCullers, who don't get on with him, , , , , Leonard Ehrlich got his call for a physical. Those who've read parts of his new novel say it is swell. He's been working on it for years, and says he just needs two more months. That's what he said when I first came two months ago, but he still needs two *more* now. (Which I understand so well.) . . . . . Zell Ingram writes from Camp way down in West Texas where he has been sent to train to fight Paratroopers. And a dismal prairie it must be, too. My next door neighbor in New York and college mate was sent to Mississippi. Soon as I get my call I'm going to write all the commanders and boards there are howling about *lack* of respect for the uniform in the South—and that I don't approve! Thought I would just howl about general army segregation on the first paper, and take up segments on later communications. Also probably do a couple of articles in between. . . . . *Common Ground* took my article on "What to Do About the South." Seems like most of the next issue is devoted to the subject. . . . . According to this poem enclosed, Jim Crow is on his last legs. But I neglect to say those legs are STRONG. Well, you can't put everything in a poem! That is why I also write prose books once in awhile. I would be writing one now if I did not stop so often to write poems and songs and letters, etc. . . . . Say, can I get a Chicago lecture around

November 20–21? I have one in St. Louis just preceeding. But need a couple more out that way to make it really pay. *HELP ME!* . . . . . . Your friend and admirerer,
L. Hughes

IMPORTANT P.S. *(Kindly read)* Never did hear from Bush at Good Shepherd about the play, but with my questionnaire and all, and everybody going in the army making a play very hard to cast, probably better not consider our trying to stage (or at least *my* trying to stage) *St. Louis Woman* this fall in Chicago. It would need a lot of people, besides Harvey isn't around to help on the technical end. Heard from him at some Mo. camp way down by Arkansas. Dismal, too, from all I could gather, but I imagine Hitler would put us all in sorrier camps than that if he ever got over here. And all the guards would be crackers!

Yaddo,
Saratoga Springs, N. Y.,
August 9, 1942.

Dear Arna,

This is really a delightful place to work, 700 acres, with rose gardens, rock gardens, fountains, lakes for boating, tennis courts, croquet, a game room, a Mansion House where most sleep and all eat, and a couple of dozen studios scattered about in the woods where nobody can bother you all day long. Mine is so far back in the woods I can't see a thing inside except by electric light. They must have known I like to work at night and so were trying to supply me with the correct atmosphere even in the day time. . . . . . Carson McCullers is here, also Kenneth Fearing, Newton Arvin, Nathan Asch, Nathaniel Dett, and a dozen more artists and writers and composers. A very congenial group and we have fun. . . . . The race track is only a quarter of a mile away. I'm going down there some day and see if I see Little Augie. There seem to be lots of Negroes working around the stables. . . . . . Bricktop is in town and Chick McKenny who was in *Mulatto* and several other New York folks I know. Brick is having a birthday party on the 14th to which I am invited. . . . . My boy, Jimmy Davis, went off to the army a couple of weeks ago and had the good fortune to be put in an Aviation unit in Maine, so he writes me, with a bunch of fellows who all passed a very high I.Q. test. Which is certainly better for him and the cullud race than the Atlanta Federal Jail. With a million or so folks behind you like Gandhi, it's a different matter. When he sits in jail, the world shakes. Yaddo is shaking right now. . . . . . Man, I wish you would:

SEND ME THAT LITTLE QUAKER BOOK FOR THE MAN AT YALE! ! ! !

Also send me the names of the folks at the Rosenwald Fund to whom I should send cards (first names, etc) like Miss Utley, the nice little secretary with the desk next to hers, the guy who used to show us the movies, etc. PLEASE! And I will do a favor for you some day. . . . . ; Two or three people want you to rewrite their books for them. Georgette Harvey, among others, whose draft, C.V.V., says is full of interesting material on the many years she's spent in the theatre. Also a lady named Sweetwine, also of the theatre that Harold referred to me and I referred to you—and Lieber. (You could become a re-write artist, if you wanted to.). . . . . Me, I am determined to be a song writer. Dett and I are trying a couple,

103

one pop tune and one for Dorothy Maynor. If I can turn out a hit and ASCAP keeps going, I'd have a small but steady income all the time to live and write on. . . . "Freedom Road" is moving along. Might even make some money. Copies and orchestrations will be out this week, and the 372nd Band in Harlem is doing a 70 piece band orchestration for the soldiers to march by! Hey! Hey! . . . . . That radio script of mine was finally accepted by the *War Scripts of the Month* for transcription all over the country, to be produced by Erik Barnouw. . . . . I'm invited back to the Montreal Forum this season. If I go, I'll try to get Boston on the way up or back. . . . . Could you send me the name and address of Rev. Cobb's church so I can send him the religious version of "Freedom Road?" They could sing it down to the bricks. . . . . Well, I got so thin in New York I could pull my belt in four notches more. But up here I shall probably get fat all over again, sitting down at a typewriter all day. We have a wonderful Norwegian cook and three great big meals. I actually get up at 8 for breakfast. Ashamed to let the rest of them think the Race is sleepy headed. . . . . Carson McCullers is fun. She wants to take a gun and go after Talmadge . . . . . Are the Skylofters doing anything this summer? . . . . . And how is your book coming along? . . . . . And what is Horace doing without Irma? Is his mother still there? And what are you & Alberta doing without Joan and Paul? I reckon Poppy and the others can hold the fort though. Give them a kiss for me and tell them they are adorable. . . . . . .

Best to you-all

Langston

Would you like to come here some summer? If so, I'll have them put you down.

703 E. 50th Place

Chicago

12 August '42

Dear Lang,

You make Yaddo sound terribly alluring. Of course, I'd love to spend a summer there. Just invite me and see! I'd like to come NEXT JUNE! By then I'll need the trees and the cabins and the fellowship of writers—if this school work continues to be as tough as it is now. Incidentally, you can ease my load a mite by sitting down immediately and writing me a paragraph about Arthur Koestler, recording any impression he left with you or telling me anything you knew or heard about his background. PLEASE! I must do the paper within 10 days. Just a paragraph will help.

I have just addressed the sticker for the package which will contain *Stories of the Underground Railroad,* the book you mentioned. Sorry I kept forgetting it when you asked before. You know how it is, "Out of sight, out of mind."

And, of course, we'll be looking for the printed version of the song here!

I am still doing my writing at the office on the third floor of the Fund. At lunch today we talked about Yaddo, and everybody was anxious to know what the folks there are like. I see now that I led them to believe Sholem Asch was there, rather than Nathan. . . . Good for Jimmy, up there with the I.Q.'s; sure, it's better than rotting in Atlanta.

I read the Georgette Harvey manuscript about a year ago, when I was in N.Y. Also talked to her about it. If you want to pass the word along, here is what I would consider doing about it: If she can (through Carl or otherwise) get a publisher interested in the book, I will a) make a blue-print for the re-writing; then, if they will give the job to Bob Lucas for the actual re-writing, I will b) edit his completed work. In all (for a reasonable stipend) I will give about one month to it. I would NOT want to undertake the total re-writing and thereby tie myself down for a half-year or more. My own program is too large. Bob, on the other hand, writes well, given an outline (he used to work under me on *The Negro in Illinois*), and he would gladly do a version for about $300; and for a like amount I would function as indicated above. The same goes for Sweetwine and whomever else. To re-write a whole book in my own hand, I'd require a year's rations, and I doubt that any of these folks are in a position to foot the bill. . . . I see where Rackham Holt, the lady who is doing Carver's biography, is having the project underwritten by Henry Ford. That is why she has been able to spend nearly a year at Tuskegee already, has run around the country no end, and is now returning to work some more with the old man. That, too, is why she can turn out fine jobs, like the one she did on *Odyssey of an American Doctor*. If I lend my name to another one, I will do it right, or not at all.

You know I adore Carson McCullers; it must be nice to have her around. And Fearing is topnotch, too, but I don't place Newton Arvin. What did he write? Nathan Asch is a fellow Macmillan author. . . . Which reminds me, how did you like that *Popo* statement? Nearly a thousand copies last year, but unfortunately we got less full royalty on the ones that the Fund bought. Morrow has put my *Possum* back in this fall's catalogue (it is a steady seller) and they are talking about another juvenile by me to put beside it. Don't see when I'll get around to that, however. *The Fast Sooner Hound* was postponed till Sept. 15th.

Horace has been running hither and yon since his return from the coast. The C.I.O. convention (U.A.W.) was taking all his time last week. He says he still looks forward to the Skyloft production, but actually he has done little if anything about it. His mother is with him, but the work of the Center is at a low ebb at this season. He was here to lunch last week and asked Embree about underwriting a Negro Newsletter, like the Kiplinger Washington Letter; was mentioning you to work on the thing, perhaps tying in with your production activities. Don't know how far he got. Today I hear that Charlotte Carr was trying to reach Mr. Embree (who is now away on vacation till after Labor Day) about giving you a fellowship to come and live at Hull House and write plays that would tend to create better relations between the Negroes and the Italians of the community. Don't know how she fared either. If either get anywhere, you will of course hear.

I am counting on finishing me little book between the summer and the fall sessions at the University. That will be about six weeks. Then, at long last, God willing, something *creative!* . . . . Alberta has gone to Riverview today with the three stay-at-homes of our crowd. Joan seemed surprised to find Mexico so "primitive." Don't know what they expected.

Why don't you and Dett make a race track musical comedy of Little Augie, seeing you are so near the track. You could toss aside the play and get your script right out of the book, plus lyrics and trimmings by you. I'd even give you some new episodes that I didn't use in the novel.

Ever,
Arna

Yaddo, Sunday,
Saratoga Springs,
New York, August 16, 1942

Dear Arna,

We had a big party in my barn last night, Saturday, so this afternoon I am just getting cleaned up, throwing out bottles and cigarette stumps. I missed breakfast today so went down the road to the Racing stable restaurant and had breakfast with the jockeys and stable boys. Yesterday I went to the *Travers,* the oldest racing event in America, held every year at the Saratoga track. Packed and jammed. Leonard Ehrlich and I bet together on six or seven races and didn't pick a winner in the whole lot, so I am broker than usual today, in fact suffering of brokenness. A couple of colored jockeys rode in the first race, a jumping race. The one we bet on came in last but the other one won. The colored boys say they only let them ride in the kind of races where they are likely to break their necks. . . . . Thanks for the clippings, particularly on "Freedom Road." I didn't hear that broadcast, but I guess I can hear a recording of it when I get back to town. I'm delighted if it sounded good. . . . . Did I tell you Dett and I are doing a couple of songs? He's finished one, but I haven't heard it yet, as he says he's still working out the harmonies. . . . . Mr. Handy and I have done a blues, too, that is a killer —"Go-and-Get-the-Enemy Blues." It jumps, Jack. . . . . . It looks like I am becoming a song writer at last! I shall have four, possibly six numbers published this fall. Professional copies of "Freedom Road" are already out. Let's hope some one of them makes some MONEY$$$$$$$. I need it as I am just as overcoatless as I can be and winter is on the way. . . . . . One of the nicest people here is Katherine Anne Porter. (She and Carson don't speak, though, for some reason or other.) . . . . . Here is:

Koestler: Hungarian birth, former Berlin reporter, only one to accompany the Graf Zeppelin to the North Pole, was in Soviet Union a year or so in 1932–33 when I was there. Wrote a book in German about Soviet Asia. I met him in Askhabad and we went to Bukhara and Merv together, later saw quite a little of him in Tashkent, too. He had begun to dislike Russia then, the dirt disturbed him and the lack of order from a German point of view. He was always saying if only the revolution had come in Germany how much better they would do things there. But when Hitler came in that year, he couldn't go back, being Jewish and left-liberal, so he finally got to Paris, they say, then London. I last saw him in Paris in 1938, looked pretty beat as he had been in Franco's concentration camp or prison in Spain. He has evidently had some hard going of late. But his books should put him in the clear now. I haven't read his books, but judging from reviews, he's another confused intellectual, more capable of recognizing and deploring mankind's faults on all sides than their few virtues on the less faulty side—which, God knows, is faulty enough, too. But you have to join hands with somebody, and you can't with Hitler, nor very well with the "too little and too laters" who are afraid of India, Negroes, and the Second Front. So what is left but the folks with their backs against the wall—and it seems to me wrong for Koestler or anybody else to throw literary brickbats at them at the moment. Am I right or not?

Now, WHERE IS THE QUAKER BOOK FOR THE MAN AT YALE?????????????????????

There is an excellent editorial in *The New Republic* on India this week. And a Newton Arvin review of a Whitman book.

106

Tell me, is Lonnie Johnson still at Squares on 51st and Michigan? I want to send him the Handy blues and "That Eagle."

Langston

> I've got those so bad,
> Evil and most mad,
> Go-and-get-the-enemy blues!
> W.C. & me.

Erhlich says he likes your books very much.

Hazel Scott has gone to Hollywood. . . . . I want a fellowship to write songs on! . . . . I sure do.

703 E. 50th Place
Chicago, Illinois
19 August '42

Dear Lang,

The *Popo* statement came: about $58, as I recall, royalty on nearly a thousand copies sold. 500 of these were sales to the Rosenwald Fund, and on these the discount was so great we got only ten percent of the sale price (according to our contract) rather than ten percent of the retail price. But your $58 is waiting for you, payable in November normally.

Did you, by design, save two of the most exciting names of your fellow Yaddo guests for later mention? Katherine Anne Porter! Leonard Ehrlich! Porter's forthcoming novel, according to the Harcourt, Brace catalogue is to be one of the big books of the fall. They are evidently getting set to make it a best seller. I shall, of course, read it as soon as it appears. You and she should have something in common, considering her Latin American background. . . . As for Ehrlich—well, I can almost quote *God's Angry Man*. It belongs with a few novels like *Of Human Bondage, My Antonia, The Grandmothers* and *The Sun Also Rises* that I go back to now and again. But I have always wondered why he produced nothing else. Has he written himself out in one terrific bolt? Or is something very big coming up?

Which reminds me that Dorothy Farrell (ex-wife of James T. Farrell) says she was once at Yaddo for a spell. She seems to have been, according to her own slightly unreliable account, the amanuensis of the lady who ran the place at that time. Of course, knowing Dorothy, I wouldn't be surprised if she dreamed it all. In any case she professes to know Leonard Ehrlich. She, with a group of others, including Rackham Holt (the biographer of Carver), was at Jack Conroy's Saturday night. Two or three gallons of beer absorbed by the small group in jig time. And by the way, Harvey Curtis Webster (reviewer for the New Republic and other magazines and English prof. at U. of Louisville) was there with his wife Lucille. She was one of four white people conspicuously and uncomfortably seated in the front seat when you spoke to that large church crowd in Louisville a year or two ago. Remember? Well, she was greatly impressed. In fact, she was 'sent', for she compared the thrill of your performance with that of Louis Armstrong's. They are, incidentally, a very good lot—she and Harvey. And he is projecting a serious book on Negro writing in this century. He has just done a biography of Hardy which Macmillan had expected to publish before the war caused them to change their plans. One of the University presses will likely bring it out now.

Thanks for the dope on Koestler, all of which makes good sense in the light of his books except your evident impression that he is anti-Marxist. His *Dialogue with Death,* the Spain book, is bitterly anti-fascist and contains the strongest kind of condemnation of the western democracies which left loyalist Spain to its fate. So strong indeed that I suspect it kept the book from being published here till history had sort of justified his values. I'll now study him more closely. He actually writes like nobody's business. Political views aside—or not, as you will —he is a spellbinder.

Nothing on Lonnie Johnson yet; maybe next time. Keep writing song! But do a book, too!

And invite me to Yaddo!

Ever,
Arna

Could I do a review for the *New Republic* now and then? Who around that office would throw an occasional book my way? Could I be recommended? This sort of thing is my vice—like song-writing is yours! So I must plug.

Yaddo

Dear Arna,

Looks like things are shaping up pretty good for a Mid-West lecture series. I had a letter recently from Horace White asking if I could appear in Detroit, so have written him suggesting early December. I've also written Jefferson City and Kansas City to follow St. Louis. In any case I should be in Chicago about the 25th in time for Thanksgiving, and could work out from there for whatever else came up, so the Chicago dates could run from Thanksgiving through December 15th, as I'd like to start back East about then.

Thanks for all the interesting clippings and things. Too bad I won't be out there early enough for the Sun or Porgy parties, but I want to stay here at Yaddo as long as I can since it is an ideal place for work, and I want to clear up all the odds and ends in case I get a draft call.

Leonard Ehrlich was placed in 1-A today, and is applying for a deferment— that last two months to finish that book that still needs two months!

Suggested lecture topic this season: POETRY, NEGROES, AND WAR.

The New Masses has a pretty good all-Negro issue out this past week.

Enclosed a recent Kenneth Fearing poem signed. I ran off a couple of copies, one to send Mrs. Robinson Jeffers who was intently listening to celestial trumpets and things when I left Carmel, conjured up by a fashionable medium lady out there.

Wish I could send you-all some of these good apples lying all over the ground here at Yaddo.

Met a boy in Albany the other night who looks like Walter White and who was marked down as "white" at his first registration and so went on through with it and was home on furlough from four months in a white regiment in the South, with many amusing tales to tell.

108

You will like Jo Herbst if you meet her, I think. And you would love Carson McCullers who is about the most anti-cracker cracker you ever saw, and with a Southern drawl that beats Billie's in melodic slurs and softness.

I am going to put all my lyrics together for a book while I'm here that maybe can be published at some future time. Leaving out the "social" poems, I have enough pure lyrics for a book alone. But typed as I am as a "Negro" poet, I imagine it will be difficult getting them published.

Katherine Anne's novel is postponed again. She has moved to her farm and is evidently working hard on it, as we haven't seen her for weeks. Last news was she'd opened up one of her South American barrels and a tarantula walked out after years in storage.

Lang

Yaddo,
Saratoga,
August 22, '42

Dear Arna,

You wouldn't, by any chance, have a 5 spot you could airmail me, would you? (I'm transferring my account from California, so can't cash a check at the moment. My typewriter is in the shop—from too much song-writing—and I have to get it out. Also I would like to see the night races—over in one more week. I will make *one* bet. And if I win, will cut *you* in on the odds.

Carson just read to me from her new story in her Georgia drawl. Quite "Southern," and wonderful amusing touches like a girl who kept a motor running in her room for no good reason. Cowley will be here Monday. Will ask him about N.R. reviews.

Katherine Anne is delightful, lived in Mexico a long time, knows lots of people I know. She and Carson bring George up *200%* in my eyes and Texas. . . . There will be a Spanish version of "Freedom Road" for Latin America. And looks like the Ink Spots might sing it, so the publishers write. . . . I am well pleased with *Popo.* If I knew where Fifina was, I'd send her a present. She is a real baby, you know. I must go back to Haiti sometime and look for her.

Ehrlich was happy over what you said about his book. He's been working on a new one for several years, he says. He spends the winters here, too, alone in a farm house.

Dett's and my song turned out nicely. Met Will Vodery last night. Dett wants to set the Cullen poem you sent me.

Langston

P.S. It looks like I can't get any work done for the Latins. Delightful—but it's all free. (And they are getting paid for being up here representing their countries.)

I am going to Westport and Yale Saturday. May also stop off and see the Robesons.

I am moving to a room to write. In fact am half moved. My pen is there.

Dett wants to set the Cullen poem you sent me.

Koestler is anti-Soviet, no? Did you see Cowley on him in *N.R.* couple of weeks ago? Agrees with you as to his literary value.

Friday,
No-good day except for (that)

Dear Arna,

Thanks immensely for that (Five!) It came at a most needed moment. Funny how invariably all one's toothpaste, shaving creams, and things like that run out simultaneously, just when one is also broke. Also, I usually get stiff neck, or bursitus somewhere, and have been suffering from such a neck all week due as much to brokenness, I'm sure, as to the dark and unpleasant weather we've been having here. (Like Californians are wont to say, this has been "a most unusual season of rain" at Saratoga this year.) . . . . I have come to the conclusion that I can collect more honor and less cash than anyone else not putting words on paper. Fine letters about "Freedom Road" are coming in from all over—Gilbert Allen's Chorus is singing it in Los Angeles, a glee club is doing it for the Governor of Connecticut Sunday, and the 372nd Band in New York is also playing it that day, with Lawrence Whisonant as soloist. All this—and not the first penny so far. Maybe in due time! But the time has been due so long. . . . And I do not feel good this morning! . . . . They say a girl named Rosetta Lenoire is due to sing "That Eagle" in the Canteen show opening on Labor Day. At the moment I do not care who sings what when nor where. . . . Say, Newton Arvin was telling me a swell story he said he saw in the *New Yorker*. (Maybe you did, too, as, next to Carson McCullers, you are about the reading-est person I know.) Anyhow it seems somebody stopped to have breakfast at an Inn in the general vicinity of, but yet some miles away from, the site of the Battle of Gettysburg. While at coffee, glancing over the gloomy news in the morning paper, the person looked up at the waitress and said, "My! If things keep up like this, the battle will be here shortly." . . . . The waitress said, "Oh, no, sir! Not here! The battlefield is ten miles away." . . . Arvin says Alfred Kazin is more or less in charge of book reviews for the *New Republic,* but Cowley says the man to write to is Bruce Bliven. You would, I think, be an ideal reviewer for them. . . . The *New Directions* poetry series is being suspended for the duration I hear. I think the head guy is in the army. It would have been a nice outlet for your poems. . . . . Folks stay at Yaddo until about mid-September. A few may be asked to linger on a couple of weeks or so, it seems, in smaller living quarters than the Mansion which, already, is far from cozy with its vast halls, interior fountains, and marble bathrooms—*cold* as ICE at this moment. It takes a ton of coal to heat the joint a day—like Horace's center —and the endowers evidently didn't leave enough money for that. (The usual trouble with philanthropy—never quite enough. And the way I feel this morning, to hell with it all!) . . . . As Zero Mostel says, "Get away, you bore me!". . . . Personally, I think the Grand Hotel on South Parkway is a wonderful place to write a book. I bet they've started their furnace already. Where big-shot number barons live, there's bound to be comfort. Top-flight writers aren't looked after nearly so well—behold the distinguished gang now shivering at Yaddo! . . . . Tell Alberta I wish I had some of her good hot soup.

Langston

P.S. Sent off rush requested article on "Negro Writers And The War" for Chicago Defender Victory edition. Probably not very good, but best I could do with a cold—and in a hurry—in answer to Lochard's wire. . . . Blaine, the steeplechase colored boy we bet on other day, was thrown at a jump yesterday and rather badly injured. "They only let us ride in races where we can break our necks."

110

703 E. 50th Place
Chicago, Illinois
8 September '42

Dear Lang,

Doris Patee of Macmillan has just written to ask me if I favor their plan to offer *Popo and Fifina* to the Haitian publisher for an outright fee of fifty dollars (half to go to the Macmillan Company), since her experience with Latin America makes her believe (in view of their cheap editions) that a larger fee would not be accepted. She says she will direct the same question to you after she receives my answer. Well, my approval goes out with the mail that takes this letter. I'd let them have it for nothing, if that were necessary, and I suspect too that fifty will be as much as they can pay. I did, however, ask her to require them to give each of us ten or a dozen copies of their edition. I also told her to write you at Yaddo if she wants a prompt reply, since I feared you might leave mail at 734 till your return. Is all this Okey by you?

Yeah, Zora is in this week's SEP, and she has done herself pink and brown, a really good job of reporting. It has a flavor; it creates a good character, and it moves right along. Of course, she had to go out of her way to take a concealed swipe at the leftists (though I'm told that the left-wing press has always been very kind to her), but maybe she thought this was necessary to put the job across. The statements I have in mind were not very strong, and not terribly objectionable to anyone, no matter what his position, but they seemed dragged in, and I couldn't help feeling that (ever so slightly) she had touched her thumb to her nose in the direction of some of her personal antagonists. Well, anyhow, I praise her for rising to the occasion and (generally speaking) out-doing herself when the chips were down. And it was a forward step by the Post to let her have a chance. They did, however, spit in the food after serving it up, so to speak, by putting the word *Negro* under her name in the by-line. Like saying John Jones, colored! They just couldn't resist that gesture of contempt—or so it seemed to me, but perhaps I'm being hard on them. Maybe the next writer who sells them something can escape even this stigma. Zora's article, incidentally, was right in line with a suggestion I wrote the new *Post* editor on the day he gave out his statement of new policy. I'll show you the letter when you come this way. Such letters bear fruit; we should all write them more often—particularly when we can be objective and not seem to be talking up a sale for ourselves. It just happened that I had nothing to show the Post and nothing in mind for the immediate future, so I let go with a couple of pages, naming some of the other Negro writers. I received a nice letter from Ben Hiben, and I now believe he was influenced by what I wrote.

Thanks for the pictures. Say, is Katherine Ann Porter striking?!! She is one literary lady who more than looks the part. She will go down in history if she allows herself to be photographed enough. . . . I didn't hear the "Midwest Mobilizes" program on which they used "Freedom Road," but Horace says it was the best Negro show yet—connected with the war effort. Franklin sang your song (Miss Utley helped me line him up—he was her suggestion) as the program signed off. . . . Most exciting of all the news, however, is that you are working on your book . . . Make it read—like *Big Sea* in style. . . . Joan and Paul home and back at Du Sable today. . . . *Common Ground* is out with "Rock, Church, Rock!" Most of the Fund folks are back from vacation. . . . We're all gonna dress up and go to the Chicago opening of *Porgy and Bess* in a party. . . . Ruth Hobbs has taken

111

a six-weeks leave of absence to work with Col. Bousfield and his outfit. If she likes it there, she may stay; she was uncertain when she left. Barbara Golddammer has gone home to marry a flying officer stationed in Alaska. She may return in a week or so. Vandy just this minute came in, looked at the pictures, admired KAP's looks and wanted you to know the town's expecting you presently.

Ever,
Arna

P.S. I'm sending you a copy of Nelson's book—in case you haven't read it. Don't bother to return it. Pass it on to somebody else.

Yaddo,
Saratoga Springs, N.Y.,
September 10, 1942.

Dear Arna,

I missed not hearing from you for a long time. . . . . Say, listen, since you like to write letters uplifting the race, why not write one to Mr. Sol Lesser, Producer, Hollywood, California, who is producing the forthcoming film, *Stage Door Canteen,* and point out to him *now* in advance, that Negroes take part voluntarily and without pay in all the activities of the Canteen—the best entertainers appear there, the big colored bands play there, Negro actors and others are hostesses and bus boys along with famous white actors and actresses—and best of all, the Canteen is open to ALL alike, white and colored soldiers and sailors eat, dance, and amuse themselves there without any trouble whatsoever, not an unpleasant incident so far in all these months. It is a real example of democracy in action —and certainly should be a part of the screen portrayal of the Canteen. At the moment, also, a charming Negro girl, Rosetta Lenoire, is singing my song, "That Eagle," in the new Canteen show, *The Canteen's Show.* So Mr. Lesser and his producing company should be made aware of these things—in advance. Maybe somebody else at the Fund would write a letter, too. And I've relayed the request to Walter White. But the more the better. Instead of squawking after a film appears, it is better to be active ahead of time. Lesser produced *Our Town,* you know, and is an intelligent fellow on whom letters might have some effect.

Well, thanks for all the news. Sure, let *Popo* go for Fifty. We owe the man that much for books, anyhow!

Yes, Katherine Anne Porter is really delightful. She's had many husbands, mostly diplomats, and lived all over Europe and Latin America. She has done various charming translations, helped edit the forthcoming anthology of Latin American short stories—which she says is woefully incomplete, though, as she only came in near the end. And she has a delightful Paris printed book of translations with music of old French 14th, 15th, 16th century songs. We've cooked up the idea of getting Maxine Sullivan to sing some of them—as they'd be down her alley—sentimentally folk-sy and impudent.

Song writing, unfortunately, seems to have stopped book writing again. If no slip occurs (but I know full well they ALWAYS occur) I'll have six published this fall. And already they've had more performances than all the rest of my former songs put together. So that is something. (The union *would* stop all making of records, though, just when I have a chance to have some good recordings! It is my fate to be defeated in the amusement field, through one slip or another, all the time! But my *determination* is to keep on! Just like dice, you have to pass *sometime*—if your bank roll will just hold out till "sometime" comes!)

I'm invited to stay on at Yaddo through October if I wish. Now that they've heated the house, I might.

When *Porgy* arrives, send ETTA a BIG bouquet! She deserves it! . . . . Eddie Matthews is singing "Freedom Road" in Spencer's place at Cafe Society. Get him to sing it for you-all when he comes with *Porgy*.

I put your name on Yaddo's invite list. They also want Sterling Brown next season—if the war permits them to open.

Langston

703 E. 50th Place
Chicago, Illinois
22 September '42

Dear Lang,

Did you hear about yesterday? Well, cullud folks made headlines in all local papers. In the Hearst press and the *Times* they got streamers six inches tall. Seems that the various cult groups have been talking pro-Japan. You know about the groups: Nation of Islam, Abyssinians, etc., none ever taken as more than clowns by Negroes at large. Last week a junk man told Alberta that he was surprised to learn that "people could talk against the government during war-time." He was referring to their meetings in Washington Park. Anyhow, the climax came Sunday night when the FBI arrested 81 of them, including ten leaders. Among the latter was Robb, the so-called African who did a bit of work for the Exposition as adviser on African lore.

I must say you are up to your ears in songs—all exciting. I'll keep my eyes open for copies of them in stores here.

The best description of Handy's retinue is to be found in *The Constant Nymph;* his is a colored "Sanger's Circus." If you have never read the book, you should immediately. Otherwise, you won't really know what makes Mr. Handy tick.

Mr. Embree has just done an article for the special number of the *Survey Graphic* (Dr. Locke, editor) in which he recommends that another million Negroes leave the South during this war, as a million others did during the last. Don't you think that will be a bomb-shell? Actually, I think it's pretty smart. If all the Negro leaders and the press harped on the same point, it might force the status-quo crowd to defend their position and maybe do something to make Negroes *want* to remain. On the other hand another million scattered over the North would do no real harm: maybe some small irritation, but no harm. Besides, the new pro-democratic attitude is much stronger here than down home. Here you can put up a fight with an even chance of winning at least a partial victory. Down yonder they should be forced into the position of trying to peacefully restrain the Negroes from another Exodus.

Who else is remaining at YADDO for the first snow? My hope is not that you will do fewer songs during the remainder of your stay but that you will soon pile up so many that you will be compelled to return to the book just for the change —if no other reason compels you. A great many of us (lovers of music and song

113

though we are) are simply panting for the second installment of that autobiography! The times demand it!

Be sure to have your song publishers circularize some of the leading Negro schools, etc. Handy can tell you something about that. Seems that he had done it to advantage. . . . . See that M. L. Becker in *Books* this week says what I say about *All-American*. Also, note what I say in a short note about *American Negroes: A Handbook*—next to the last page. I read the report they are forwarding to Mrs. BIG in D.C. . . . . Sent some stuff for Yale last week. . . . Oh, yes, nearly forgot the big news: Hubbell has just been fired by the *Sun*. Don't know why, nor how that will affect your article for the literary page.

Ever,
Arna

703 E. 50th Place
Chicago, Illinois
15 October '42

Dear Lang,

You know I caught up with you day before yesterday: I was forty the 13th!

Yesterday Ruby and Owen came. En route they had had their car stolen in Kansas City, but recovered the next day. They will leave Sunday for some kind of ministers' meeting in Cincinnati. Thence to D.C. and then back to L.A., stopping over again with us. While they recovered their car, they did not recover about $100 worth of clothes that were missing when the Ford was returned.

On the eve of my birthday something interesting happened. I had reviewed a book called *Green Grass Grows All Around* for the *Sun* a week earlier. The following day the author, an ex-Chicago woman, called me. She was elated by the review. Then on the afternoon of the 12th I received a case of jellies and jams made from wild Ozark plum, strawberry, dewberry, etc. You see, she and her husband had fled the depression. In the Ozarks, where they settled, they had first tried to commercialize native patch-work quilts. This failing, they had tried jellies and jams made from wild berries and fruit. All of this adventure is part of her book. Imagine our current debauch in jelly, jam, etc.!

In the *Sun* office a day or two ago I saw a wire from Marshall Field to A.C. Spectorsky, literary editor, telling him to be sure to invite you to the party they are planning (on a big scale) for the new *Book Week* Sunday supplement, beginning November 1. You will hear from them. It would be grand if you could arrange to be here for it.

Which brings me to the main business: I have set out to contact (directly or indirectly) Miss Carr of Hull House, Rabbi Weinstein, Duffy Schwartz, Marcella Ricks and perhaps a few others in regard to lecture dates. We shall see what we shall see, and I will report to you next week. I'll see Marcella Monday night when I speak to her book club at the Oakland branch. By that time I hope to have all the preliminary answers in. . . . Tomorrow Spectorsky and Rackham Holt, the biographer of Carver, will be luncheon guests at the Fund, along with Dorothy Farrell (for color). In the afternoon I am scheduled to work on the book week broadcast with Mr. John T. . . . Meanwhile, I have a stack of six or eight books to review. Boy, do they pile up? Never thought they would swamp me this way.

I was excited over your *Common Ground* article, but neglected to say so in my last. It is really down the right land: positive, constructive suggestion. We should do more of that at every opportunity. So many reviewers of Herbert Agar's new book, for example, lament the fact that he does not tell them just how to right their ways. There are many people who want to do something now—having been moved by Pearl Buck's admonitions—but they don't know just what steps can be taken. Those you suggest are very fine. I hope you will do the same thing (slightly recast) in various articles. Alberta just called to say that there is a song and some poems from you in the mail this morning. I'll see them when I get there. Meanwhile, Joan sends thanks for *The Negro Speaks of Rivers* and I for the *madame* sequence. It is not at hand so I can't guess the ones you sent out.

Horace has his notice to report for his physical examination. Very excited, as you can imagine, with his board (Good Shepherd Board) trying to get a delay—all this having broken so suddnly. Irma is back at Dem Moins in some more important capacity.

The party for the *Porgy and Bess* is all set: November 2nd. They open here at the Studebaker. The FUND really means to put on the dog for them. You should attend that, too. So if you were here for the *Sun* party, you could wear your starched front twice in a single week and wouldn't have to search for studs but once.

If I get around to an extended Report, a requirement for the M.A. in Library Science, maybe I could do it on the JWJ collection at YALE. What do you think? I could ask the Fund—or maybe Yale—to pay for my trip, and perhaps the thing could be shortened into a monograph which Yale could publish and sell or distribute to visitors to the collection. Would this please anybody, in your opinion? It will require many okeys and some encouragement. Yale and Carl, for example, should express interest if I am to have a good chance to make it acceptable to the U. of C. faculty committee. You know how it goes. Would you mind reacting to the project? And mentioning it, if you have occasion.

Your chance of getting drafted seem slighter—what with developments of the last two days. More youngsters, fewer men of our age.

Katherine Ann Porter will review for the new *Sun* section, she writes. Poor Ehrlich, I hope he gets that novel finished before he goes to the army. And you that autobiography!

Ever,
Arna

703 E. 50th Place
Chicago, Illinois
19 October '42

Dear Lang,

This is just a hurry-up affair to put your mind at ease with regard to the lectures in this area. Horace will give you $50 for a lecture at the Center. Mr. Embree plans to line-up the Quadrangles Club (U. of C.) for another at $50. Mr. Embree has still another one in mind, but doubts that this second one will bring more than $25. Billy Haygood plans to arrange one in a Hinsdale church (the pastor is on Horace's board) for still another $50. More may result from present negotiations.

Horace, with whom I just spoke on the phone, feels that at least a hundred is as good as in the bag—so much so that he will personally guarantee $100 on the strength of what has thus far been done. You understand that most of these dates require confirmation by local boards, etc. and hence take time. The ball just started rolling last week, and I rather think the outlook is favorable. Horace suggests, and I agree, that you definitely arrange to come out, on the basis of present assurances. Your entertainment will be provided by the Center, and there will undoubtedly be various other gainful pick-ups once you are on the spot. Moreover, with these various Fund people working actively on the plan, I think you can afford to take your courage in your hands.

Let me make a correction about that *Sun* party for *Book Week*. The date is October 26th.

The luncheon Friday was quite a success: Rackham Holt, Spectorsky, Hardwick Moseley, Dorothy Farrell, etc. Very bookish.

Ruby and Owen left at five o'clock this A. M. Jo Herbst has found a job here and is now living in town, though I have not met her.

You have done some good poems at Yaddo. Several of them belong in the collection I have always thought should be built around non-Negro themes like "House in Taos," "Stalingrad," "Barcelona Air Raid," "Havana Dreams," etc. I mean poems not done in the folk manner, though some of them like "Let America Be America Again" may touch the Negro and his problems. I have in mind a question of rhythms and mood, and I think such a volume will emphasize a facet of your work that may well be obscured by the bolder humor and stronger rhythms of your vernacular writing. Both should survive, in my opinion.

More anon.

Ever,
Arna

703 E. 50th Place
Chicago, Illinois
25 October '42

Dear Lang,

"Brothers" is very interesting, but I notice a couple of points that seem to me worth working on a bit. First, page 5 and the first half of page 6 could be compressed into a dozen or so lines, omitting all the discussion of the "problem," for all this is covered again later. Moreover, it seems to me that the same sort of thing is spread on a little thick in the last 5 pages of the script. If you could extend the little humorous, homey banter, while letting your remarks about Jim Crow drop into the conversation like a touch of acid, it would cut more deeply than does the more extended discussion of the battle on the "home front." The mother's prayer at the end is swell and swell for pulling the thing together. It should not, in my view, be tampered with. Also, I think that all your other points should be retained, though more concisely stated, if possible. To sum up: I think the points on Jim Crow at home should be stated more briefly and the air-minutes thus saved devoted to more of the home-tie stuff. You bring the latter off very effectively throughout.

116

Dr. Camille Lherisson, the Haitian notable, is here lecturing for the Pan-American group. He is guest of the state department.

Charles Johnson is due to lunch today.

Lieber has instructed Mr. Buster to send me his manuscript. My idea is to turn the job Bob's way, if that can be arranged.

They are selling tickets for your lecture at $1.00 a throw.

You are invited to be present at Hall Branch on the night I review *Shakespeare in Harlem,* February 18th. Reckon I'll have a book by then? Ulysses Lee will be there, and I will comment on that fine *Caravan* he helped edit.

This sounds like a bulletin board—which, I daresay, it is. My best to your aunt, etc.

Ever,
Arna

703 E. 50th Place
Chicago, Illinois
31 October '42

Dear Lang,

Boy, have things been happening. I've been trying for nearly a week to get a chance to write a letter—just one—but no go. Since the *Sun* party (Horace got drunk and couldn't drive his car home) last Monday night the whirl has been on. And what a party that was! More swank than I've ever seen before. The Buttery of the Ambassador was so jammed you couldn't walk from end to end till the night wore on and the weaker guests gave up the ghost. Only two Negroes— Horace and me (yes, and Lucille went with Horace)—and behind that lies a drama that I'll have to tell you about. We didn't get our invitations till nearly the last day. S. Evans, top man under Marshall Field, struck the colored names off the list and had to be high pressured by the head man to replace them. So I'm told by the grapevine. Lots more to this that will interest you. Yes, Jack, the party was epochal. Writers, publishers, critics, and their ilk were there from the whole mid-west.

The first issue of *Book Week* comes out Sunday. I'm doing the "Rare and Fine" book column under the name of "Bibliophilus" as well as reviews under my own name. The Herald Tribune sent me Roland Hayes' biography to review. The publishers are pushing me like all get-out for the manuscript of my book. The university classes continue to meet and pass out assignments. Where that leaves yours truly you can easily guess. When they drop in these occasional parties and speaking assignments, the confusion becomes complete. That is the current situation.

Miss Utley tells me you are about to leave YADDO, so I'm rushing this to try to catch you before you leave.

Plans for your lectures are still in the making, so far as I can gather, with the exception of the one Billy was working on in Hinsdale. The group there would like you on their platform, but they have no money for same.

Dr. Du Bois was here to lunch (at the Fund) yesterday. In Chicago to speak at the meeting of land grant colleges. Horace Mann Bond was present a day earlier. Jones of Fisk dropped in a day or two earlier than that to ask how I'm coming along with the school work and what-not. At last I've met Jo Herbst. She was at the Sun party, and she clapped her hands in glee when I told her you would be in town within the month. I received your letter asking me to sign the call for the writer's meeting in N.Y. on December 6th. I signed promptly and returned to headquarters. Walter White was in town for lectures. He was as full of energy as ever. Horace's draft board refused to re-classify him. Seems that only General Hershey can keep him from being called in the near future.

What do you think (as an afterthought—since I do not have enough girls) of my including Zora in the career book. Lord knows she is a career gal!

More anon. Meanwhile,

Ever,
Arna

Yaddo,
Saratoga Springs,
New York,
November 2, 1942.

Dear Arna,

Well, sir, wait till I see you and I will tell you one of the funniest stories you ever heard about something that happened here at Yaddo a year or two ago that Carson told me last night—apropo of something not so funny that just happened while I was in New York (I would miss it) and that I think probably involves one of the colored persons working on the place, too, as so far everyone carefully conceals the name of one of the main participants, although hastening to tell me all the other details. Anyhow, the person departed leaving a trail of complications reaching all the way to Hollywood even, and the little Chinese girl who was here, now under contract out there. Life on the battle front is terrific but it is also something on the art front!

Time is too *much* for me. There just isn't enough, as you indicate in your letter, and if the army gets me, I don't care. I will just go to camp and sit down and rest and relax myself. Man, I had no sooner written you last time than I got a wire from New York that the draft board had sent me a card to report for my first physical, which I did, and which resulted in the expected 1-A. So I am now 1-A! Which causes me to leave Yaddo about a week sooner than I had expected —tomorrow, in fact—because I want to consult the draft board concerning my lectures, how far I can book ahead, etc., as I am now booked up to January 11th, and don't want to be called back in mid-tour. The first week of my coming November tour is now booked solid—in fact, I'm puzzled as to how to fit in Fort Leonard Wood USO and Jefferson City, since I haven't any train times here for those places and don't know how long it takes to get from one to another. Anyhow, I'll be in Chi around Thanksgiving. If you see or talk to Horace, tell him to let me know about his date at once, as I still have to possibly fit in Milwaukee and Detroit and so on in that region, in and out of Chicago.

Never rains but pours. Just when I get this tour lined up, Irving Mills sends for me to work with him and his song writers on lyrics for the big all colored picture he is producing for Fox in January, a musical with lots of big names. I start to work on a couple of numbers with Jimmy Johnson on Wednesday. Spent

118

two afternoons last week in New York listening to proposed tunes with Mills and Jimmy and the dance director, with half of Harlem in the offices being interviewed, looked at, tried out, etc. At the Handy office there was equally great confusion, with old man Handy laying them all out and explaining to me between blows that his family once took eleven years to copyright two songs, and it cost him thousands of dollars to fix things up due to that bit of procrastination—but that they were still procrastinating. Just about that time one of the stenographers who had gone out to lunch at one and was just returning at four, walked in—and you should have heard the fireworks! I gathered that the old man lays much of it to race. He says such things don't go on in an o'fay office. I wonder if they do? Or have white folks somehow got time licked?

See my letter in *Time* this week? And the cracker one following it.

Write me to New York, 634 St. Nicholas Ave, Apt. 1-D, please. Do you think I ought to enlist? They tell me you have then a better chance to get in the Morale Division, or special services, maybe get sent to Latin America as a translator, etc???? Has the Fund any dope on that?

Lang

P.S. Tea in my honor at Skidmore college this afternoon to sign some 30 books ordered as result of my appearance the other day. Who says I can't sell books, huh?

My invite to the *Sun* party just arrived today!

703 E. 50th Place
Chicago, Illinois
4 November '42

Dear Lang,

Alberta read your letter to me over the phone, whereupon I immediately made two other calls a) to see what date—if any—has thus far been set for your evening recital at the Center and b) to see what the Fund can suggest about your entrance into the army. Maybe I can add a post script on one or both of these later, but at present no answers are in, both parties having been tied-up in one way or another. Meanwhile, let me make a suggestion. Telephone Walter White immediately. He has a very fine contact with General Hershey and told me last week that he stood ready to help in a situation such as yours. I further suggest that you have him ask General Osborn of the morale branch about that job with *Yank*, the overseas paper. A while back they offered Horace a commission to become a member of the staff. This was turned down by Horace [Cayton]. One is left to presume that at the time Horace had his eyes on other things. And now, I am told, that commissions of this sort have ceased (the giving of them has ceased). At any rate the need for a Negro on the paper's staff remains, and they may be only too glad to get you, though they may not be able to offer more than top non-commissioned rank—this latter is all guess-work, understand. At any rate, no matter what else Mr. Embree suggests, I will ask him to write a letter to Mr. Dollard and General Osborn calling your name to their attention so that it will be on their desk to add weight to anything else that may come in from Walter, General Hershey, etc. (See later paragraph)

Billy says that now (he has been trying his damnedest to line up something for himself—something that would make use of his training and experience) one has to be asked for by the Army itself to get very far in such an attempt. He has had no luck, but, of course, his case is not like yours. My guess is that the question of whether or not you should enlist will come out of the above inquiries. More about them in my P.S. if Mr. Embree has anything to offer.

Say, boy, there's another non-such party to report. The Tavern Club, at which it was held, is on the 25th floor of a skyscraper across the river from the Tribune building. It includes an entire floor, and there are windows all around, beautiful big ones. Flossy? Will, I reckon! The party was the one for the *Porgy and Bess* cast. It was a wonderful success—positively wonderful. Champagne was served, along with all the lesser drinks. All in abundance. The barmen were worked to death. Irma was there in uniform—and tight as a tick. George Gershwin's mother was there. Likewise June Province and all the top newspaper people of the city —including the editor of the *Sun.* All the Rosenwald trustees. The director, producer, etc. of the play. Too many others to name. And everybody happy. I mean HAPPY. Home at 3:30. Now the social season can end successfully. The two fanciest parties I've ever attended, and both within eight days. . . . The play opened to the largest advance sale (so it is reported) in twenty years in Chicago. Fine notices from the papers. Though, I suspect, the critics are commencing to question (as I do) the little ghetto world of Catfish Row. . . . Avon Long, . . . scored his usual success. Knocked the critics off their feet. He was better even than when you and I saw him in N.Y. Folks who tried to talk sense to him at the party were—as usual—greatly let down.

I agree with you that it never rains but it pours. Hope the work for the Negro movie comes off as you'd like it to. And hurry out here and tell me that story Carson told you. A party I missed was one given at the home of the "Mad Buslers" for Hayakawa, Jo Herbst, etc. It conflicted with the *Porgy* doings. Friday there is to be a luncheon at Marshall Fields' (the store) for literary folk, to which the Macmillan representative (a Frenchman named Rousseau Vorhees, who thinks he and I may be related through distant branches. . . .

Three copies of Zora's autobiography "Dust Tracks on a Road" have arrived: one to be reviewed for *Books,* one for *Book Week,* and the other to be used in case I write a piece on her in my career book for kids. I'll save one of them for you in case you don't get one directly.

The telephone calls have now come in, so I can report on the two items. Miss Mitchell says she will take up the matter of an exact date with Horace and write you forthwith. I'll call again and make sure this has been done—tomorrow, perhaps. Mr. Embree says that his letters to Captain Charles Dollard, who is connected with the staff or office of General Frederick Osborn, Division of Special Services, U.S. Army, Washington, D.C. have not been fruitful in the past, though they have called on him for suggestions. Mr. Embree, however, leaves today for the trustees' meeting in Chapel Hill Saturday. En route, tomorrow, he will be in Washington and will attempt to see Dollard and/or the General in regard to you. This, he thinks, may be better than a letter, especially since he's not satisfied with the results of his letters in behalf of Billy and Horace. He secretly hopes, notwithstanding, that his third try (your case) will carry further than did the other two. So by the time you read this, God willing, you will have been the subject for discussion in the above mentioned quarters. Mr. Embree is of the opinion that you *should* enlist. He feels that a definite advantage will result therefrom, so far as choosing your branch of service is concerned. I think you should weigh this

120

against the opinions of Walter and others in N.Y. in making your decision. But I observe that those who have put off enlisting (vide Billy and Horace again) in the hope of being missed by the draft entirely or of waiting for something better than they could see at the moment have all been disappointed. That, too, you can put on the scales for whatever it may be worth. . . . Horace is taking his expected call rather hard, it seems to me. Drunk more than usual. And at unaccustomed hours of the day. He says it is because Irma is in the WAACs. I think his own military prospects figure in it. Now he says he will go in as a private, accept no commission. I wouldn't be bitter or too gloomy if it were me—but maybe that's because I have 5 kids and could do with a little of the quiet and peace one has a right to expect in an army.

Last week I had a chance to write a letter of recommendation for Nathan Banks, who used to teach in the private school where I worked here. He is in the army, stationed at Tuskegee, but hopes to be assigned to officer training in meteorology at U. of Chicago. You met him, I believe. Came from Pasadena. Good in math.

Please call Carl [Van Vechten] today, and tell him that I'm trying to get an autograph from my co-author before sending the book in question. That goes for yours, too. But the rush of things has kept me from seeing Jack.

Here is a suggestion of another sort. Eat Thanksgiving dinner with us at about 3 o'clock. This will leave you fit for another by 8:30, should you find yourself in a spot where *two* are required of you. What do you say? If no other is on tap, then we can both raid the ice box on the second round.

Ever,
Arna

P.S. Wonderful—but rather simple—idea for a play about Negroes, the army and the question of being patriotic amid bad conditions and lack of democracy. Beautiful little *object lesson in our block.* Can't you write it up?

Monday the 22nd

Dear Lang,

Your wire came Saturday. I immediately telephoned Louise and wired Dorothy. From Louise I got this post script: a) Loren Miller is in town attending a lawyer's meeting of some sort and b) the big date for the Patterson family promises to fall next month. I have not seen Loren personally, thanks to his very tight schedule and to a cold which I spent the week-end trying to get rid of.

Your stenographic suggestions most welcome. I have turned them over to the Fund, and already they have gone to work on them. Let's hope one or the other works out. The information about Mrs. Celia Siegler was also joyously received by Scudder McKeel, the new man who has been designated to head the research phase of the race relations program. He said he would write her promptly. His office, incidentally, is across the hall from me.

The first draft of my birth control pamphlet got a favorable reaction. If it can now get by all the committees and advisers, you will have another paragraph for your book—one more of those ironies of which the world seems to be made.

Your "Simple Minded Friend" seems to me a very happy creation, especially as a device for treating topics which would otherwise seem high-flown or academic. You can use him to show the application of theoretical questions to his life. International events might thus be related to his affairs. The *Good-Morning, Stalingrad* technique. I would not advise a)using the "Friends" *every* week or b) wasting him on the kind of material which needs no pointing up. It would be ideal, I'd think, to do an occasional "Friend" piece about the perplexity that comes to the common colored citizen when he tries to apply certain current statements of American ideals and war aims to life as he knows it. It might, in other words, be a way of commenting on current events and pronouncements.

Thanks for bringing order out of chaos: OWI vs IWO. In any case things seem to be happening where you are concerned. The sociology magazine came—or so I am told over the phone. Thanks, I look forward to reading the whole series of articles, including yours.

Du Bois takes some of the steam out of my plan to do a Negro press article by making my main point in his first *Defender* article: namely, that the black press is a symptom, not a disease; a result of the Negro's lack of participation in American life, not a cause of anything. The thing to treat is the condition which makes the daily press insufficient for the needs of Negroes. The justification of the Negro press, according to my argument, is that it fights for goals which if attained would liquidate itself. Thus it proves its essential integrity. Its essential patriotism and Americanism. In sum, we shouldn't ask why this or that is printed by Negro papers, but what it is that causes Negroes to want to read such and such. Well, *maybe* I'll write it up, but the Du Bois article certainly dampens my zeal. . . . Will look out for the records for Poppy. I know she will be excited.

Ever,
Arna

Hear about Zora winning that $1,000? Apparently the reactionaries still pay off. Did you-all give her the Spingarn medal, too?

Remember what I said about wanting to see the Arthur Spingarn Negro collection?

25 January '43

Dear Lang,

Can you do me an urgent and important favor right now while you are at Toy's reading your mail?

Here 'tis: The head librarian at the U. of Chicago has commissioned me to make a little survey of Negro newspapers for him. The motive, which I'll tell you anon, is a good one, though not yet public. I wonder if you will help me out by making a couple of telephone calls and writing me the results post haste. What I want from that end is the following information: How long has *The Amsterdam News* been running? Has this been continuous? Do complete files exist? If not, what portion of the file? Where are these located? Check! Now, can you get the same information or any part of it, concerning *The New York Age? The Afro?* The Norfolk *Journal Guide?*

Tips: Raddick should be able to supply much of this. The papers themselves, or their local representatives, some. Mr. Jerome Peterson knows the early history of the N.Y. *AGE.* Roi Ottley knows about the local files, having used them extensively in connection with the N.Y. Writers' Project. Don't let any of them feel that anything too ambitious is being planned. Actually, however, the survey is connected with post-war government planning. And the proposal WHICH IS STRICTLY BETWEEN THE TWO OF US has to do with microphotography. It can't be told because various universities are scouting for post-war projects, and the folks here don't want this one grabbed off by a rival. Neither do they want to arouse false hopes in the papers—in the event that there should be a slip *entre* cup and lip. At any rate, if the plan should work, whole files of these papers could be made available to various Negro collections, research libraries, etc.

Enough of that for now. I've had flu. Wrote a pamphlet—the one for PLANNED PARENTHOOD—in bed. And I fear the conditions of the composition are only too evident. . . . As you may have guessed, the University is demanding a pound or two of flesh. . . . "Good Morning, Stalingrad" is nice going; I like it very much. . . . I suggested Horace's name to Alliance for the Father Divine book. . . . They are considering same. . . . Mr. Embree is back, after a jaunt to N. Orleans. Will go to L.A., so the report goes, next month. . . . Miss Mitchell left Horace's employ to work for one of the government agencies. Secretaries, says H., are all blowing their tops. A guy who has a secretary, he adds, is like one who has an apartment of his own in Moscow. He can go in business, almost. . . . Any answer from your letter to the *Atlantic Monthly*? Any re-actions from your 'hotels' piece in the *Defender*? . . . . Are you still planning the Southern tour? If so, when? If you go soon enough, I'll want you to carry two notes for me (one to the librarian at Duke, one to the librarian at Hampton), make certain observations (which I can ask you about after the tour), and thereby contribute materially to my dissertation on the Yale collection and kindred collections. The thing is taking somewhat broader scope as I go along. . . . That is a grand picture of you that Carl has made into a post card. Is there a larger edition of the same available?

What's happened since I left town? Love to Toy, Dorothy, et al.

Ever,
Arna

Wednesday,
Feb. 10, 1943.

Dear Arna,

What a week! Looks like after I got some information for you, I'm not in long enough to write it to. Charlie Leonard showed up from Hollywood via Virginia where he has been doing movie scripts for the army—showed up with an idea for a colored musical and interested Columbia's Eastern Story Editor in it, so we went to work on a synopsis. Then Tommy Webster of the Urban League showed up from Kansas City. And then it was time to have this radio script ready for the Urban League so Dean Dixon could start to work on the score. Meanwhile the I.WOC. [sic] wanted to stage *De Sun Do Move* and I had to dig up the script for them to mimeograph. Etc., Etc., all of which takes TIME. I haven't got up to Yaddo for that week-end yet, but when I do go, shall probably stay a couple of weeks.

Here is what I gleaned from the Amsterdam: It started on December 4, 1909. The New York Age started 25 years before that, by T. Thomas Fortune. The Amsterdam put out a special 30th Anniversary Issue, June 29, 1940. They have some extra copies available, containing various articles on its history, and a resume of its career by Thelma Berlack. Back numbers of the Amsterdam cost $1.00, adding a dollar for each year it goes back, which makes this issue cost $3.00. I didn't know if you wanted it that badly (I started to buy it for you but hesitated when I learned the cost) so I told them to write and ask you if you wanted it.

No dope on the AGE yet other than its age. Why don't you drop Dorothy a line and ask her to ask her father about it.

No, the Amsterdam files are not complete. Several years are missing. Which ones, they could not tell off hand, as they are all stored somewhere. It has been running continuously, however, since it started.

You'd have to get other than New York paper's information from their home offices.

Did I tell you the government is going to make a poster out of "Freedom Road"? . . . . . Carson was to have come over for dinner the other day, but is sick in bed . . . . . This Urban League script is going to be revised. Do you see any places to cut? I think it drags a bit.

Hey! I am going to be a Dr.! Lincoln is conferring a degree on me this commencement! I shall use my title on my next book.

They tell me white folks are still ahead down South, way OUT ahead!

Sincerely,
Langston

February 17, 1943

Dear Arna,

Re a stenographer for the office, you remember the girl who used to work for Charles S. at *Opportunity* from Minneapolis? Ethel Ray, I believe her name was. Well, anyhow, I had a letter from her some time ago that I cannot now find—having more than likely given it to Yale—asking me about job opportunities on the coast. Since we knew her she has been married, has two kids, I believe, and is now Secretary to the Dean of Education at Hampton, but wants to change in order to get the kids out of the South. It might very well be that she would consider an offer in Chicago, so why not have the office drop her a line, at Hampton, as it has not been more than a month or so that she wrote me about that very thing, expressing a desire to change positions. From all I know about her, she would be quite competent.

Re your article on the Negro press, why not write Katherine Woods directly at *Tomorrow?* We spoke of you at length, as I told you, at the *Common Ground* tea the other day, and she is familiar with your work and expressed a desire then to have you as a contributor to the magazine. They pay, I understand, about the same rates as *Common Ground.* Write her NOW while the subject of the Negro press is hot.

How do you like "My Simple Minded Friend" columns?

I've been up to my neck in song plugging. Good results due, too, it seems, as a couple of the better Negro bands are now interested in some of my numbers and looks as though they'll shortly be playing and broadcasting them. Tomorrow we're going after Louis Jordan with *King Kong.*

I ordered some records for Poppy from Musette. Don't tell her till they come, but let me know if they do come. Musette is so Jewish they're colored, and take a long time to do things.

Will you dine with us in April? Delighted!

Did a short wave for OWI to Sweden the other day. It's the OWI NOT IWO making the poster (like the Joe Louis one) from "Freedom Road." And it's the IWO–NOT OWI–interested in producing *De Sun Do Move*. . . . . . You better stop getting those initials mixed. One is the government!

Inez Cavanaugh, 25 Hamilton Terrace, New York, is also said to be an excellent steno, one of the best in New York according to Marvell Cook. She was due to start work with the NAACP recently, but fell ill, so perhaps that is off. Since her husband is going to Hollywood, she may be willing to come to Chi. Have them write her if you like. Nice looking brownskin girl, formerly an entertainer, but nice, and good mixer, used to associating with white folks.

Langston

Tuesday
April 13, '43

Dear Lang,

Thanks for tipping me off to "Mr. and Mrs. Massa." It is grand, better than 100 grand's worth of surveys of tension points, etc. My copy of the New Yorker is now being passed around. Results: good!

Dick is in town. He was at the Fund to lunch last week. He has since wowed the folks at the institute of psycho-analysis and at Fisk, where he lectured on *fear* as the dominant Negro emotion. He is hurrying back to N. Y. in time to celebrate his daughter's first birthday.

I have been too busy to call Brunetta Muzon about the dramatic version of *Popo,* but I hope it is prospering and progressing. . . . . A bid has just come from the "American Scholar" for an article suitable to their heavy-thinking readers. Maybe I'll try, but at the moment I'm wondering what to say to the English teachers of Chicago high schools this coming Saturday at luncheon. . . . . The Association for Childhood Education (they publish those Macmillan anthologies known as the *Umbrella* series—*under the blue umbrella, under the silver umbrella,* etc.) is asking for a story for their fifth and final volume—a story which will bring tolerance to the kids of elementary grade. That I will definitely try to provide. . . . . Then *Highroad,* the Methodist magazine which wants the piece on Handy, says they have arranged to use some of Doug's murals at Fisk as decoration for my article—if and when it arrives. They don't seem to know that I'm scheduled to hold forth under those very murals come fall.

All in all, this is a busy time for me, and I might have procrastinated this letter (as I am doing most things) were it not that I need relaxation and counting my more agreeable burdens is my idea of breaking the tension.

We had a party for Billy Haygood (a 4:30 affair after work) last Friday, celebrating his departure for the army. Another affair, this one quite big and glamorous, is scheduled for Saturday afternoon. It is in honor of Lillian Smith and Paula Snelling. They are holding it at the Fund, following the meeting of trustees.

The Fund is still losing personnel, and Miss Howland has been given an office job—in charge of files.

We are having another big snow here. Imagine it! When will you be here? And what is our Oberlin date? . . . . Paul wanted me to thank you for the stamps and the map. . . . .

Ever,
Arna

4/17/43

Dear Arna,

Fate has overtaken me with a heavy foot again. I added up my bank book the other day and found out I had mighty near minus zero. And then when the income tax man told me that, not being married and having no dependents, I would have to pay $126.00 tax, I mighty nigh fainted. However, I recovered enough to go home and figure that thing all up again, percentages and all by myself, and got it down to a more sensible figure. But still one that left me ruined and broke in both spirit and finance. So I reckon I can't buy any show tickets for us in advance. And I also reckon I'd better write myself half a hundred lecture letters AT ONCE and prepare to hit the road heavy this spring. (Always something to keep a writer from writing!) Chicago was cancelled. Said they recently had Horace. (One Negro a season being enough, I guess. See how the color line hits the lecture business!) But I had already booked Wayne University at Detroit, so have to come out that way anyhow now. Know of any contacts in Evanston or round abouts?

Did you hear the Muni broadcast? I didn't, at least not very well, being right there in the studio. Sound and singers being on different mikes, you couldn't tell how it sounded as a whole. But it got some good notices in the press next day, so I guess it was O.K. Muni, I thought, read it beautifully.

Did I tell you ALL my plays, a whole suitcase full, disappeared out of the basement? No use for poor folks to try to keep anything! Well, they are all up at Yale, anyhow, for posterity to worry about producing. Personally, I don't much care. And certainly I've written my last free bit of entertainment. Turned down two chances to do free scripts since the broadcasts. Folk know what I can do now. If they want ME to write for them, dig up some dough. Nobody else connected with radio or theatre works for nothing. Why should they expect the author to do so? Huh? The technicians don't, nor the directors, nor the studio executives. I WON'T NEITHER. Hell with 'em!

One more free lecture appearance in the offing—and that is ALL there. With Rackham Holt at a Carver Memorial on April 6th at Columbia University. You'll probably be here at that time.

Did I tell you met Wendell Willkie at Walter's the other night? Swell guy.

Sincerely,
Lang

Saw Saroyan's *Human Comedy* last night and liked it very much.

Call up and see if Lou's baby is here yet. Tell her my brother's wife (no. 2) is also expectant. Send them both your pamphlet, please!

126

Mr. Arna Bontemps
703 East 50th Pl.
Chicago, Illinois

Dear Arna:

Thanks for all your letters and clippings. I have been so busy with that pageant which has now turned into a dramatic spectacle that I haven't had time to do much about anything else. However, I did manage to get a couple of hours with Emerson at the piano, last night, and worked out some of the lyrics for the Mouzon production in Chicago, and I have just written her a note telling her that they will be along shortly. I am just about through with my work on the Garden show, having now to do only one very short scene in monologue form for Canada Lee, who has reopened in Native Son and so, unable to rehearse with the rest of the cast.

Man, since you-all are moving away from Chicago, and it is so cold and windy out there, anyhow, why in the world would I want to be working on the Sun?

I was at the Kenneth Spencer's night before last and saw Doug, who gave me news of you. It was a party for Dr. Price-Mars. Paul Robeson and Lawrence Brown were also there.

I hope you will be able to go to Yaddo because I think you will enjoy it. Margaret Walker has also been invited and I might be there myself for a while.

I saw Gordon Parks the other night and he tells me he is making the photographs for the Embree book. Tell Mr. Embree that I shall send him some up-to-date material on my latest activities, such as the Writers' War Board work, etc., which he might wish to include.

"I Wonder As I Wander" might even now be published, if I did not wander even more than I wonder. But I expect to sit down and finish it this summer.

You should see my degree, which is all in Latin. The University also gave me a hood of velvet and satin and silk and what-not, which I can now wear in academic processions, should I ever appear in another. Carl Sandburg gave the commencement address, which was good, but like almost all other addresses, including my own, too long. I was sitting on the platform for more than three hours and got both hungry and sleepy. Many mothers in the audience also dozed occasionally, but naturally woke up when their son's names were called to get their degrees and at such point, applauded very loudly.

Between you and Elmer Campbell That "Planned Parenthood" booklet ought to be a killer. Mrs. Elmer, according to the colored papers, has just gone to Reno.

Kindly tell the Rosenwald Fund people—whoever is in charge of buying books for the school library—that "Freedom's Plow" has just been published (at 10¢ per copy) by—(booklet form)

Musette Publishers
Steinway Hall
113 West 57th Street
New York City

I am sure they can secure it at regular wholesale rates. It should be in every Negro school and home; also in every white home and school. It is Musette's intention to give it wide publicity and distribution.

The theme song of the Negro Freedom Rally, which I have written also, is called "For This We Fight" and is being published by the Committee with Capt.

Mulzac's picture on the cover and will also sell for 10¢ per copy. Tell all Chicago singers to put in their orders NOW! The song will shortly be ready for advance singing. It's range is not very wide and it is suitable for any and all voices. It is so simple that I can almost sing it myself.

If you really want to hear some bad singing, listen to Leigh Whipper in the "Ox-Bow Incident", which is a good movie except for his spirituals.

Anxiously awaiting the appearance of your "Planned Parenthood," I am

Sincerely yours,

Lang

703 E. 50th Place
Thursday

Dear Lang,

Zora [Neale Hurston] won the Anisfield Prize, given jointly by the *Saturday Review of Literature* and some association of sociologists for books contributing to better race relations. It may be possible to discover a link between the SRL selection of Zora's book for this recognition and their publication of Warren Brown's piece on the Negro press. In any case, both were the products of reactionary thinking: Zora the muse of black-face comedy; WB the shade of Uncle Tom. . . . . Fortunately, for the dignity of the Prize committee, the other award was given to Donald Pierson for *Negroes in Brazil,* a book which I believe *would* influence race relations here if it were widely read, and influence them favorably!

Just received a request for an article about Handy from a high school level magazine. They had seen and approved the piece I did for *Common Ground* on Dorsey. Well, there goes a week-end and another of those small-change jobs that blight my career. My fees are always too little to do me any real good but tempting enough to keep me from turning them down. In this case I think it worth while to plow a bit in another field, especially since this is a group I hope to reach with my career stories.

April 13th will be a good time to be in Chicago. I'll be back from the East by then. In fact, we may be able to travel together—unless you plan other stops. At the moment I expect to make the jaunt about the 26th of March. Plans are still vague, but I'll have to work them out within two or three days. Rutland, Vermont, Washington, D.C., and another trip to Yale all hang on the same thread. I will also have plenty to do in N. Y. So run on up to Yaddo and get back in time to see some shows on Broadway. I'd like to see Harriet by all means and *The Patriots, Something for the Boys,* and *The Skin of Our Teeth,* if possible. I rather think I'll come to N. Y. first and then make side trips to these other points, so the week-ends of March 27th, April 3rd and April 10 (?) can be safely depended on—particularly the first two should you be inclined to pick up a few tickets with the understanding that you will hawk them to me.

We saw *Lady in the Dark* here, and last Saturday night I went to see the Goodman Theatre semi-pro production of John Van Druten's *Old Acquaintance*—a cozy theatre and a good production—with the kids. . . . . Mr. Embree, back from the coast, is excited about the Walt Disney films aimed at good neighborliness and about the studio's promise to let their activities lap over into the field of race relations here—as discreetly as possible. Apparently he made no notable headway with Walter's contacts. Of course, he seems to have had in the back of his head an idea for a script based on something he is now doing, and whether or not that very fact (innocent though it is) awakened the subtle defense mechanisms of the producers I can't say, but Hollywood goes in for crystal balls.

I'd suggest the new Abraham Lincoln school (Pat is asst. director—Kenneth Spencer sang at the opening last week) as a lecture possibility. Shall I speak to them or will you broach the subject?

Ever.
Arna

703 E. 50th Place
Chicago, Illinois
7 June '43

Dear Lang,

The lyrics are fine, particularly the one about the kite and the one which repeats the words "load up." They sing beautifully, these two. The same is perhaps true of some of the others which I have not had opportunity to check on. However, a dress rehearsal is scheduled for Thursday evening—the day on which you should receive this—and I should find out then. . . . . Brunetta Mouzon was here today. She picked up those other lyrics, concerning which you wired me. . . . . I am getting one of the girls here to make a few copies of the play. The little narration of which you spoke is being written by me. There was a note about the production in the *Sun* last Sunday. All in all, the outlook is hopeful. We can look forward to more productions come fall, maybe. My hope is that interest in POPO as a book will be promoted at the same time. A published version would be a great help.

This is the day for the huzzahs and bonzanas and bravos, is it not? I am itching for a report on the Madison Square Garden affair. The fact that the Garden was sold out ahead of time is in itself impressive. I saw some of the publicity in P. V., etc.

Things have been popping here, what with a lawn party at the Fund for the Chas. S. Johnsons, a conference of Negro leaders (Powell, Bethune, Townsend, etc. & etc.), and one thing and another. . . . . Owen Dodson, Chas. Sebree and others of the naval contingent have been around occasionally. Also Rackham Holt and John T. Frederick. The latter says there is a flying field near his farm in Michigan at which two squadrons of Negro fliers are stationed. These are in addition to the ones at Selfridge Field. At any rate, he has invited me to spend a few days at his farm and visit the boys at the field with him as co-missionaries of culture. Books directed to them through him are gratefully received. Also the same through Owen at Camp Robert Small, Great Lakes Training Station, Ill. Owen says they have only two Negro books in the library there: my *Drums at Dusk* and JWJ's biography, I believe. Maybe it is his *Trombones*. Anyhow, this for your information and the information of those you meet. I'll try to contribute to both groups. John T.'s address is c:o Northwestern's Chicago campus.

Jack [Conroy] and I have finished a draft of our play. Maxim speaks highly of it, though he suggested plenty of revisions. We shall now try to get it ready for official typing. It is a loud, bawdy, macabre farce. Maxim, to my considerable pleasure, went so far as to call the idea "hilarious" and the dialogue (at least in parts) "deliriously funny." This in spite of substantial criticisms. Strong words, they seem to me! I hope the final version can merit part of them.

The columns have been uniformly interesting!!

Ever,
Arna

18 June '43

Dear Lang,

Just came from an afternoon party at the Fund for Katherine Dunham, her husband and others. Earlier today the presidents of Dillard, Spelman, Tuskegee, Fisk, etc. had a session with Mr. Embree. After the conference Dr. Jones (Fisk—my new boss) asked me to make suggestions for two posts which are open at Fisk. I could think of no one for either, but I now hasten to ask you to nominate if you can. The first is the drama director. You know, they have one of the top little theatres, and the former director is being snatched away for some reason or other. Well, who should have the job? Dick Campbell? Who, then? I would be in a position to help steer some of YOUR work into try-outs if we could influence the selection of a person of real vision where Negro theatre is concerned. But you must move fast. Jones left here for the East. If you have a likely candidate, a wire to his office at Fisk would be doubled back, no doubt, in time to reach him in New England (Maine), and he would perhaps investigate the prospect on his return next week via N.Y. City. Please do what you can with this opening. How about the boy at Morgan? Wouldn't this be a step up for him—if he is still out of the army? Any first rate girl? Of course, my first thought runs to Dick Campbell, if he is available. He might still do things for radio and on the big time once in a while. Fisk would give him a solid base.

The poet post is publicity director (public relations) for combined Fisk-Meharry arrangement. Colored or white. But must be first string. Somebody like Milton Mayer (who used to do the job for the U. of Chicago). Somebody who can get stuff in SEP, *Colliers,* etc. If you have suggestions in this department, I suggest that you shoot me the names (with qualifications) and let me pass them along. WORK THE DRAMA ANGLE DIRECT, however!

Saw a few stories on the big Madison Square Garden show. All praised your drama-pageant highly. BRAVO!

In much haste,
Ever,
Arna

P.S. Do I take my typewriter to Yaddo?

130

29 June '43
703 E. 50th Place
Chicago

Dear Lang,

My present aim is to make Yaddo by the first of August. The original date was July 5th, but the University clings to me and Fisk beckons. In other words, I am off to Fisk tonight for a week of orientation and taking over of my new work. When I return to Chicago, after the 4th, I'll have a couple of weeks more of work on my dissertation before I can take my comprehensive exams and get shed of the slavery under which I have been laboring. I'm sure it will be better this way than to interrupt my work and thereby keep to the original Yaddo schedule. Mrs. Imes hasn't yet told me that I will still be welcome come August, but I have written her and hope she will.

At Fisk I will say a word, if I get the chance, in the interest of the two prospects nominated by you for the drama department. It would be grand to have a first rate person in that little theatre—especially since at this very moment I have a new play which they could try out. *The Great Speckled Bird.* And what a bird! Revisions are being completed today, and I am leaving the copy to be typed while I'm away. The job is so completely satisfactory to me that I don't care whether Broadway likes it or not. Maybe this isn't a very practical mood to be in, but this is the first job on which I've worked recently that didn't get stale on my hands.

The great success of Rackham's book, plus Roi's $2,600 prize from Houghton Mifflin and the Latin American Prize to the Haitians for *Canape Vert,* all tend to reinforce my old contention that the time is more than ripe for that second volume of autobiography by you—with stress on the Russian, Spanish and Mexican years. Not to mention the Southern journey and the interludes at Hollow Hills.

Will you tell Hazel Scott for me, before you go to Yaddo, if you find yourself in Cafe Society, that I enjoyed her in *Something to Shout About,* that I have long ago finished my chapter about her, that the book should be out by spring—if I can get to Yaddo!

Meanwhile, Mr. Embree is about to finish his book of biographies, including you. It may be out by Thanksgiving, if he can get what he needs from you.

Paul has a summer job with the Follett Book Company—stock clerk in out-of-print department. What would I have given for such a job in my high school days! With me it was pitching hay, truck gardening or mowing lawns. Never once a desk nor a typewriter. And he has both! And much more money, too!

Hurry up and get down to letters again. They're missed.

Ever,
Arna

Thursday, the 8th
Back at 703

Dear Lang,

The first thing I noticed on my return from Fisk yesterday was that Knopf had started sending your mail here again. There are three letters (Larkin, Roosevelt & Larkin, Mrs. Maxwell Nurnberg of Brooklyn and S. Agnes Eugenia of the St.

Mary College at Xavier, Kansas) and a book which I do not have at hand. Must I hold them with the expectation of your coming out this way in the near future, forward them to 634 in N. Y., or send them to Yaddo?

Meanwhile, Yaddo is washed off the schedule for me. August was not within their plans there, since they expect to take children during that month and plan to keep only a very small number of guests beyond the end of July. Well, maybe there will be another summer.

My librarianship began officially the first of July. I spent a week on the Fisk campus and promptly availed myself of a month's vacation. Our house will not be ready before the latter part of August, so we are not planning to move till about the first of September. I will not really be needed during August, for the library will be closed, following the termination of summer school on July 17th. Two or three assistants will be there to receive periodicals, etc., and I have arranged to handle the correspondence from this base. . . . Such of it as they can't manage without me. . . . . I still hope the work is going to be down my alley and that I can do lots of writing—since I am being hired partly as a writer, and of what use is a writer who isn't writing?

Saw your poems in PV. One of them I had previously read and reacted to, you remember. The other, "Beaumont to Detroit," very timely!

Several people, including Louis Zara, asked about you at the party last night —given by the World publishing company for David Apell, new literary editor of the *Chicago Daily News,* formerly on one of the Cleveland papers. He takes the place of Sterling North who has gone to N. Y. to the *Post,* while he takes over a page of the *Sun's* Book Week each Sunday. The party was at the Palmer House. I was the only Negro present, and the waiters (several of them) brought me napkins, etc. to autograph. . . . The A. L. A. is having a display of children's authors this coming Sunday at Ida Noyes Hall.

I have clipped your column on Pearl Primus and shouting and dancing and jim crow trains. Wonderful! The best of the columns to date by a good margin. It worked up marvelously, and the last paragraphs were truly exciting. And moving. I hope it gets the reactions it merits. . . . . The same week Horace did unusually well, I thought, with his piece in the *Nation,* and Thomas Sancton did his best piece to date on race relations in the *New Republic.* The one on the riots. All together, they made quite a satisfying week.

Ever,
Arna

With Yaddo out, it may not be easy to get East at all this summer, but I sha'n't give up trying. Or hoping!

Yaddo,
Saratoga Springs,
New York,
July 9, 1943.

Arna,

Dog plague your soul! Just when it is the nicest of summers here, not too hot, not too cold—as it was last year—you don't arrive! Carson is here again, and

132

Margaret Walker, and Agnes Smedley with marvellous tales of China, and Karen Michailis from Denmark, a wonderful old lady, and a dozen others. No races this season so it is quiet. . . . . I hope you can come in August. . . . I've spent all this first week on Mr. Embree's material. His letter went to California and I didn't get it for weeks later. Both he and Horace evidently keep that old address in their files, and how can secretaries know? The Japanese probably have their minds on the Coast anyhow. . . . . Where will your family be this summer, Fisk or Chicago? I'll bet it's a job moving. I never again in life intend to leave New York permanently. I never again will move another book or trunk of manuscripts. If I get evicted again I will just let the landlord have them all, including tons of still unsorted Yale stuff. . . . . Nobody ever told me how *Popo* went over! Also please send me Mrs. Mouzon's address so I can return that Haitian song book. . . . . I am about to give up song writing forever, too. Now that the musician's union says they never again will make records, what's the use? They *would* start that stuff just when I was getting published good. The Lord must have it in for colored! Or else He works in a mysterious way his wonders to perform!

Sincerely,
Lang

Yaddo, 7/30/43

Dear Arna,

I seem to have my mind set on being a song writer. It must be my father. There is no sense in it otherwise—with not a record being made in the land!

For This We Fight, the Garden pageant, was produced with great eclat at Bennett College—outdoors before 2000 people. (It's paid better so far than *both* those shows we did for the Chicago Exposition.)

Did I tell you Jimmy Davis graduated as a Warrant Officer from the Army Music School? And now has a band of his own in Virginia. Three colored. He was top of cullud list—98. They even segregate the grades—so he doesn't know how he stood in reference to the whole class. (WACS and colored last.)

Next week all we Yaddoites are going over to Katherine Ann Porter's farm for a wiener roast. The refugees here are overjoyed at the fall of Mussolini. Me joyed, too! (But not over.)

Say, you promised to send me a final script of *Popo.* Where is it?

I'm booked for Detroit again in the spring. Columbia U. and Montreal Forum this winter.

Lang

P.S. Claude McKay is ill in Harlem Hospital. Stroke. Write him. Tell *Fauset.* Delighted your play is done and good!

I'm getting wonderful fan letters thru my column. Three today, one from two house servants in darkest Mississippi; another from the colored sailors on a Pacific battleship.

3 August '43
703 E. 50th Place
Chicago, Illinois

Dear Lang,

It is now time for you to begin checking on your mail. The *Popo* script was sent to you ages ago. I have no more, but you might get one now from Brunetta Mouzon to whom I gave all extra ones for purposes of rehearsal. Last night someone brought me a copy of the book to autograph for the kid who played Popo in the play. So at least the production earned us 17½ cents in royalty. Which reminds me that the new Macmillan statement on the book shows 407 copies sold during its *eleventh* year! Which means a little better than $35 each for us come November—or sooner if you need it.

The article on the JWJ Collection for the *Yale Library Gazette* appears to have been approved. Which relieves my mind a lot, since I'm not too pleased with it and felt a little nervous about its acceptability. Anyhow, there's considerable mention of your things in the collection, and the issue is due to be published in October. Mine, I believe, is to be the lead article.

The column "On Missing a Train" interested me very much—and almost as much for what I thought it could be as for what it is. When you get around to a book of short essays, bringing together your *Common Ground* articles, the best of your columns, etc., (as you surely will eventually) you may decide to revise some of the pieces for one reason or another. Well, in such a case, I suggest that you change the above to "On Catching Trains," that you begin with a series of memorable train-catchings in your experience (some of them are already in the article), that you thereby work up gradually to the *one* train you *failed* to catch. Your story of the missed train would remain essentially as is, but the whole article would gain in climax—a shortcoming which, I felt, was the difference between a gem of a column and just a good one.

The party the Fund gave for me last Friday was grand. All out on the lawn and everything. . . . . Bob Davis was here, as were Owen Dodson, Charles Sebree, Frank Silvera and Jackson from Great Lakes. A host of others, including many who asked about you.

Do you count yourself lucky or unlucky to miss the Harlem riots?

You heard that Horace's [Cayton] mother died? Horace was in N. Y. at the time, trying to line up a contract for a book. Revels came from the coast. . . . Last night I spoke to Jack's class in creative writing at the Abraham Lincoln school, and tonight begins the round of going-away dinners to which we have been invited. Something like a half dozen definite and as many hanging fire. No new ones can be scheduled!

I'm still reading *Between the Thunder and the Sun* and thinking about *I Wonder As I Wander*.

Ever,
Arna

8/5/43

Dear Arna,

There is nothing like farewells to bring forth parties and dinners. If you and Alberta were in New York I would give one for you myself. . . . . . You know

I am sorry I missed the riots. It has always been my fate never to be in one. I think I will go down to New York this week end maybe though and survey the damage. The better class Negroes are all mad at the low class ones for disturbing their peace. I gather the mob was most uncouth—and Sugar Hill is shamed!

Thanks for all the interesting clippings. There's an article of mine in the current Canadian magazine *The New World* with a big picutre spread of colored celebs.

Rain, rain, rain here at Yaddo. I got to read poetry to the kids on vacation here tonight. Agnes Smedley "organized" it. She's been working out classes and programs for them. She didn't use up all her energy in China.

I am so sorry to hear about Horace's mother. I hadn't heard before.

You got a good point about the train column. What do you think of this one enclosed?

I reckon I lost my watch in the riots. I left it at Herbert's opposite the Theresa to be cleaned—and they tell me the place was cleaned out!

Lots of Harlem glamour girls up here vacationing say they had their fur coats in "storage" (nee pawn shops) for the summer. And they were all cleaned out, too. So they reckon they will be cold next winter. I expect that is one of the reasons Sugar Hill is so mad. Laundries and pawn shops looted, they suffered almost as much as the white folks.

I do not know why that tickles me, and I am sorry in my soul.

Dear sweet *Popo!* I will certainly need that $35.00.

NEW DAY A-COMIN' says Mr. Roi Ottley. NEW NIGHT would probably be better. (How sweetly optimistic is the cullud race!)

Kappo Phelan, cousin of Noel Sullivan's, is here. She writes *New Yorker* style stories and humorous poetry. Morton Zawbel arrives today.

I've picked out all my lyrics for the Cullen-McKay-Hughes book they've proposed. Nothing of race, just beauty. Has not that been known to sooth the savage breast? (Did I tell you, Claude is in Harlem Hospital—stroke?)

Lang

WRITERS DINE OUT: Carson McCullers and I were entertained at dinner Sunday by Mr. Jimmy Elliott, leading colored barman here. He had champagne and chicken for us. Good, too!

> Till August '30th
> 703 E. 50th Place
> Chicago, Illinois
> 16 August '43

Dear Lang,

Mark this down as the day on which I wrote the last page of my M.A. dissertation. NOT as the last day on which I worked at the job. I expect to be polishing and revising and taking exams till the day we leave for Nashville. That would be, if I can believe the tickets we have already bought, the 30th and 31st. I'm to leave on a night train on the 30th so as to be on hand next morning when the truck (let it be hoped) arrives with the stuff. That afternoon, according to the schedule, the rest of the family arrives to find (let it be hoped again) a chair on which to rest and a bed on which to sleep and a table on which to eat. It's all quite involved and all dependent on a chain of events which must hang together or cause no end of confusion. What time I'm not polishing aforementioned dissertation I reckon I'll be packing my books and saying goodbyes for the next two weeks.

You, I hope, will be giving your book no rest! I could do with a book called *I Wonder As I Wander* about now. And I believe, judging by the reviews which *New World A-coming* is getting, that the country as a whole would lap it up, too.

Yesterday it was a cocktail on the northside for Alberta and me in the early afternoon, followed by an auto trip to Ravinia with Mr. Embree and the Gruensfeld family to hear the final concert of the season (the Budapest string Quartet) in that leafy out-door chamber, followed by a trip to Great Lakes (having picked up another car load of friends and trustees of the Fund) to hear Owen Dodson and Charles Sebree's production of Owen's *Dorie Miller,* followed by a drive to the beautiful tree-shaded home of the Reisers (this time the number of cars was three) for supper, etc. and then by a return to our own diggings perhaps two hours before sunrise. Well, I got enough sleep to enable me to do the last page of the above mentioned dissertation.

Here is a copy of the *Yale Gazette* article. I'm glad they were able to use it, for I'm plowing a new field and feel none too confident.

Your columns go off like good cannon crackers these days. You have really got them times, etc. just right. . . . I have an advance copy of *Battle Hymn of China.* Will read soon as possible.

> Ever,
> Arna

> Yaddo,
> Saratoga Springs,
> New York,
> August 19, 1943.

Dear Arna:

You write indeed with a great deal of charm. Your article on the Yale Collection is like a cinnamon doughnut sprinkled with sugar and spice with a hole through it whereby one might see this warring world. It was good of you to send it to me. In retaliation I am sending you a couple of this week's radio scripts of mine which, if produced will at least be historically important, as never before so far as I know has Jim Crow in the Army or on the railroads been treated dramatically on the air. KINDLY SEND THESE BACK as copies are short. . . . . .
You are indeed so good a writer that I regret seeing you with a job. Although I do not know why I should regret—lest it be out of envy—because I am again as usual at one of my brokest periods, and my brother's wife is in Hospital bearing child and he has written me for money and I have none to send him—my Canadian check having just bounced back since *New World* didn't make proper arrangements for money to be paid across the border. . . . . Miss Walker departs today having written a children's book and some good poems while here. She's not returning to teaching, having gotten so many lectures this coming season, she don't have to. She has a very good agency—Columbia Concert Bureau. . . . . .
Did I tell you the William Morris Agency wants me to work on a musical for one of their biggest stars? Exciting idea they have, too, that appeals to me. . . .

136

The ladies of the DAR have discovered "Goodbye Christ" and no doubt should I speak in Washington would picket me with their lorgnettes. To hell with the Aryan hussies! . . . . . Soon as I get time, I am liable to write a poem about them! . . . . . Reaction grows apace. I give all cullud—except Bill Robinson—five years to stay out of jail. Better stock up your library with cook books and agricultural manuals because Fisk will shortly be a trade school. God knows, Negroes are getting too smart—even for the liberals to cope with. So what to do, but put 'em in jail and keep 'em from coming up North? Huh?

Sincerely,

Lang

Scripts follow under separate cover . . . . . . C.V.V. has written me twice how pleased he is with your Yale article. . . . . Smedley's book has had three printings before publication! Are you reviewing it anywhere? . . . . . Bricktop, Mercedes Gilbert, and Blanche Calloway are in town, among others. Congress Street, cullud, is jumping. . . . . A bunch of us went down there the other night and did the rounds of the cafes. An emotional triangle was in progress among three of the white writers who couldn't bear to see one dancing with another. Kappo Phelan, (Mr. Sullivan's cousin) who is something of a wit, said, "The situation is Freud with possibilities." But not being primitive, they did not fight. . . . . Jimmy, the bar owner who had Carson and I to dinner, had a quarrel with his girl friend the other night, got mad, and left his bar with her sitting thereat. She thought she saw him coming back, and threw a beer bottle with marvellous aim. But it was not him at all. Merely a luckless customer who got it dead over the left eye, and was knocked prone! He is still in a fog. . . . . Too bad you are not here this year because this is an exciting season. You could have more fun and go further than you did that night at the Vanguard! . . . . . Here there are seven hundred acres!

703 E. 50th Place
Chicago (15), Illinois
Sunday, Aug. 22, '43

Dear Lang,

Here is some V-Mail for you. You had better start notifying Knopf and others that we move from this address on August 30th, 1943, and that thereafter they may safely write you in care of us PROVIDED they direct the mail to FISK UNIVERSITY, Nashville (8), Tennessee. I can't be sure how dependable the forwarding will be from Chicago, for the postal service has been hard hit by the draft and whatnot and has gradually deteriorated in its regular activities.

You do leave me wistful about my failure to make Yaddo this summer. *Please beg all the interesting and attractive people to return next year and at the same time urge Miss Lady (the one in charge) to invite me again!* Something tells me I'll be more than anxious to breathe a breath of free air after nine months in the slave-South. And I herewith promise you that I will take on NO graduate study in the University. This summer has been my cup. Now, thank the good Lord, I'm on the home stretch. My thesis (of which the article on the Yale Collection constitutes one chapter out of eleven) has been approved by the pagan gods of the department, and my final comprehensive examinations have been officially scheduled for Thursday and Friday of this week. I must then take an oral on the thesis on Monday the 30th—the very day on which we leave Chicago. If I pass, I'll come back in December to march with a class in a convocation. That part isn't essential, but I'll take it in stride if nothing hinders.

The radio scripts have not arrived, of course, but I'll expect them tomorrow. Your columns to the white shopkeepers were both most interesting and to the point. I hope they touch off a campaign on the part of Negroes to MAKE these business men join the struggle for Negro citizenship: they are boys on whom compulsion can be exerted. . . . I am not reviewing the Smedley book but am reading it for a bibliography. . . . Luck to you with the musical show, but don't completely neglect that book called *I Wonder As I* ETC. Ted Poston was here again, talking about the Russian adventure. More and more I'm sure you have an important story to tell—important for *these times!* I hope you do it while the time is ripe.

Ever,
Arna

Fisk University Library
Nashville, Tennessee
23 August 1943

Dear Lang,

I'm walking on air: the assurance that *I Wonder* is under way is the news I've been waiting for these past months! The above address seems to me from this distance to be the best one to use in sending the installments. You might mark the letters *personal* in large letters underlined with red to make sure they don't get mixed up with library mail, but I expect to have a box at the University post office ere long and hope there'll be no mix ups. Our house number is 930 Eighteenth Avenue North, but I've noticed that all the other Fisk folk use the school as a mailing address. So start with that, and if I should discover any reason to change, I'll let you know. Also remember that we'll have a house big enough (though somewhat run down at the heels) to bed a guest from time to time, so you need have no anxiety about getting stranded in those parts from now on.

Most hilarious story on the Harlem riots was delivered last night by Gladys Johnson (Mrs. Hank), who is here for just a day or two. She saw the whole mess from her window, 144th & Seventh. Said a gentle fairy later, recalling the events of that chaotic night: "All my life I've been inhibited, people telling me 'don't touch this! and don't touch that!' So when the rioting started, I went out and just stole, and stole, and *stole!*" All this delivered with proper inflections and falsetto. I believe this originated with Dan Burley.

The radio scripts came today, also your letter. I'll return the former sometime this week with my comments. . . . Saw Owen Dodson last night. He is being moved to Hampton the middle of September. He's been having too much fun in Chicago recently: it couldn't last. . . . Already my Fisk worries have commenced with the problem of getting people to work. People are being drawn out of the lower branches of teaching and librarianship by the lure of higher wages, and those who remain are being drawn upwards into higher brackets, and as a result

138

there are at least two gaps in the staff of our library at present. And where to turn to find people is a question I can't answer.

Horace is in the West making a grand tour. Restlessness, I'd guess, though he proposes to write something about the condition of the country *vis a vis* the brother in black. . . . And do you know that an important, highly promoted full novel will be called "The Darker Brother"—a title obviously derived from your poem? (Doubleday, Doran). . . . And Giggy (Gilbert) is learning "Freedom's Plow." You remember how well he did "Song of Spain." Also he is heading for N.Y. to try and get a part in a play on Broadway. He is plenty good enough for a character role. I hope he lands one.

Ever,
Arna

Yaddo, 8/23/43/Hey, now!

Dear Arna,

Please leave a forwarding address for me, too, when you leave Chicago just in case any more mail comes there for me. PEOPLE HAVE A WAY OF NEVER STOPPING USING OLD ADDRESSES. I do not know what makes them like that!

The War Board lady says *In The Service of My Country* is the best script ever heard tell of on the cullud soldier and they are going to try to get network time for it. The local is assured. As yet they have said nary word on *Pvt. Jim Crow.*

Send them back, please, with your estimable comments—if you have time for comment with all your other rush activities. Otherwise, just send them back.

I am afraid you will be broke down before you reach Fisk!

Six of the cutest little kids were vacationing here from the New York slums. One little brown Porto Rican looked like a cherub. They invited me to a camp fire supper they had and fed me so many toasted marshmallows I still feel sweet inside. They left yesterday loaded down with enormous squashes, ears of corn, tomatoes, and bags of string beans from the farm gardens for their mamas. Also Mrs. Ames gave them all a box of vitamin pills to take this winter.

I have been typing the *Madam to You* series all out—18 of them now. *Poetry* will have three in next issue. It takes all day everyday to do something like that. But next week, I swear, I shall devote each morning to *I Wonder.* (It's always next week.)

Katherine Anne Porter paid us a pleasant visit the other day. And gave me her French songs in translation for Maxine Sullivan who lives right around the corner from me in New York in a big new house with hard wood floors.

Tell Alberta I am distressed at the thought of you-all going so far away. I am sure nobody will bring me to lecture in Nashville as often as folks do in Chicago. And I probably won't see Poppy any more until she is as big as you.

I am addressing the Saratoga Historical Society next month. Got any dope on colored jockeys I can bring back to their minds?

I hope you get packed up and off O.K.

How is the *Great Speckled Bird* doing? . . . . . I am sorry I was not in New York during the rehearsals of *Run Little Chillun.* I hear the air was rent asunder! . . . . Clarence has gone back to the coast, they say. . . . . All the Broadway producers are now colored-show minded. I hope somebody does one of mine, but

I will go as far away as I can during the doing and let lawyers and agents look after the affairs. Might as get gypped in distant peace as in strife and turmoil. Rain today.

Sincerely,
Langston

Yaddo,
Saratoga Springs,
New York,
August 31, 1943.

Dear Arna,

Greetings to you in your new home! I hope everything turned out O.K., that the furniture and the family arrived safely and you-all will like it very much! Tell Alberta I still love her even if she is far far away. Tell her I will try to lecture myself in that direction just to pay you-all a visit. . . . . Carson McCullers has a wonderful story in the August *Harper's Baazar* which I am sure your library, being that of a fashionable school whose young ladies have style, carries on its shelves. So do read it. . . . . Our Yaddo family grows smaller and autumn comes apace. I'll be here till October 1 when ALL go as the establishment will not carry on later than this this year. . . . . *New Republic* carries a piece of mine shortly —one I think you saw when you were in New York, "Down Under in Harlem," brought up to date now to cover comment on the riots. . . . . *Poetry* has poems in next issue, and also *Contemporary Poetry*. Lieber still has selling powers! Gracias a dios, because as usual I am broke and ruined, and will await those little checks with pleasure. . . . . I have used up three reams of paper here so you know I have been writing SOME. . . . . I am getting wonderful fan letters from my column. When the year is up—November—I am going to ask those Negroes to raise my salary so I can better take care of my postage. . . . . Thanks for returning the radio scripts. They wrote that *The Alcan Highway* one is the best ever seen on cullud soldiers and that it *will* be PUT on, maybe national hookup, in which case I'll let you know. Nary a comment on *Pvt. Jim Crow* so far, altho it followed by a few days. I reckon that gave them pause! Although, I repeat, it was a request job. I wouldn't just go writing such a script out of thin air. . . . . My brother's wife has a baby girl.

Sincerely,
Lang

AFTER SUPPER: Agnes Smedley is back from New York. We're having a party for her Monday, the day her book, *Battle Hymn of China,* comes out. Already in its 3rd printing. . . . . . Willa Mitchell of Oklahoma, Paris, and Harlem, comes up for a week in town this week-end. Just phoned me to find her a place. . . . . I believe I have just written THE lyric for THE war song! It's got all the boys of all the branches, mama, papa, love, tears, and prayers in it! So that ought to be it! . . . . It has almost made me cry. Also feel noble. Also buy War Bonds! So I shall take it to New York with me for a couple of days next week and see if I can't find a big name composer to set it. I am bent, bound, and determined to be a song writer yet!

Dear Lang,

Your letter was actually NEEDED. You see, our house was not ready when we arrived (won't, in fact, be ready for another week), as we had expected; our truck load of everything we owned in Chicago, promised to us for the day after we gave it to the trucking company up North, has still not arrived; we are put up in the faculty club here, comfortably enough insofar as beds are concerned, but lacking sufficient clothes and kitchen ware with which to prepare meals in the club's kitchen. Add to this the fact that the weather, up to yesterday, has been beastly hot and Camille and Constance have summer colds, and you may get a picture of the conditions under which this Nashville landing was made by our commandos. We are looking forward to establishing a strong beachhead, but up to now it hasn't been easy. So, as I said, your letter was needed for morale, and happily it arrived!

Most of the personnel of the University faculty is still away on vacation and whatnot, and our early arrival (designed for getting set) is being largely wasted. We could have stayed in Chicago two weeks or a month more. I'll know better next time. Meanwhile, please, don't let me spend next summer down here. They tell me the temperature has been over a hundred every day for as much as a week at a time. Please impress it upon Mrs. Imes that if small youngsters need evacuation from N.Y. during the summer, how much more so does a small writer who must for the rest of the year shoulder the weight of this rather large library!

I like this environment of books. They intoxicate me, and that is quite fortunate, too, considering everything, for I suspect there will be little other intoxication during the sojourn. Unless there are jaunts to the big shining cities. . . . I can now give you our house number:

923 - 18th Avenue North
Nashville 8, Tennessee

Use it in case of telegrams and specials to be delivered outside of library hours. I think I gave this number to you once before, but I gave it wrong! The above is official. Whether or not the house number will be better for ALL mail I have not discovered yet. If and when I do, I will let you know. Till then, use the library (marking each item *personal*) for ordinary mail.

I am excited over the Alcan Highway radio play, too. "Pvt. Jim Crow" is just as good, if not better, but I fear it is too strong. You were in excellent form when you knocked out those two jobs. Poetic in conception, neat in craftsmanship. When you have more copies, send me some. Eventually, as with other manuscript material of yours that I have, I'll put them in the Negro collection of this library. So henceforth make sure name is on everything. Noticed one or two without any when I was packing to move.

You should touch the *Defender* for more money. You have taken your columns seriously, mastered a technique, made them progressively more interesting, tossed off at least half a dozen memorable jobs: the two letters to white shop keepers (people in Chicago were running off copies and sending them to such whites), the one on Pearl Primus leaping to heaven, the one about missing trains, etc. Moreover, you have created in "Simple" a fresh and delightful imaginary character. All of which is good going for a year's work, and you may quote me on that.

Incidentally, why don't you, just for fun, meet Simple on a train sometime when you are taking a trip. Meet him at the races in Saratoga. Meet him up in Canada when you go there to lecture. Meet him in a variety of unexpected places. Now that he is identified with Harlem, this should be amusing. Always, of course, he should continue to speak for the Harlem man-on-the-street. I am not, I hasten to add, recommending that you use Simple any more often than in the past. You have been working that about right for my taste.

Agnes Smedley certainly got a fine page-one spread in *Books*. Also a very funny review (favorable) in *Newsweek*. Did you see it? She must be interesting to know.

I don't know about the lecture prospects hereabouts yet. Depend on me to study them, however. . . . Knoxville ought to be gettable, with Imes there as president now. . . . In fact, I think this is the season for you to make a Southern tour. There is much money in most of the schools. And Mollie Lee wants you for that area. Any such tour should include a rest period at 923 Eighteenth North, no matter what the pickings happen to be at Fisk and Tennessee State (which just last week bounced Hale). It would be wonderful if you could tell all your audiences to get set for the forthcoming *I Wonder* etc.

Ever,
Arna

Yaddo, 9/14/43.

Dear Arna,

Sorry about your furniture and your house! It doesn't pay to rush and worry in this world. It will wear you down. Also Camille and Constance. . . . . *The Alcan Highway* script was done on a local New York station last week. Not too good a production. . . . . I saw my brother's new baby, a very cute little girl. . . . . I've gotten a nice fan letter from the white principal of schools at Lula, Georgia, (of all places) who likes my *Defender* column. He happens to be a writer, Don West. Says he has succeeded in getting nine months for the cullud school. Sent me a good piece of his from the *Westminster Magazine*. Maybe he'd be a good one for the Rosenwalds to consider for a Fellowship, if they have not already done so. . . . . I'm back at work trying to get things cleared up to leave at end of month when season closes. It is already quite cold here, 24 above last night. . . . . Bessie Beardon is quite ill in Harlem Hospital so Willa Mitchell who is here vacationing tells me. . . . . . Agnes did not know about her review in *Newsweek* so was pleased to hear. She's to be the speaker for Women's Day at the colored CME church here. . . . . I see another Dodson masque in the current *Theatre Arts*. Also see Collier's on "Race Riots Coming." Also me in *Poetry*. Also this week's *Amsterdam News* swell spread with laws that inter-state passengers DO NOT and NEED NOT change to Jim Crow cars when going South as Supreme Court has ruled that such state laws do not apply to interstate travellers and they can sit anywhere they wish all over the train!!! Hey! Hey! Here's hoping they do. The Jim Crow car seems to me the most antiquated and barbarous thing on this continent. And should be broken up RIGHT NOW!

Sincerely,
Langston

Yaddo,
9/23/43.

Dear Arna,

Have you any information about the P.E.N. Club and their attitude toward Negroes? Do they admit Negroes? Agnes Smedley and Malcolm Cowley want to know. I said they didn't and that I have never heard of any American Negro who belonged or had been invited to belong. Agnes has just been invited to join, and intends to refuse (with publicity) if that is true. So send me whatever information you have on the subject, please, sir, by *air right now.* . . . . Poem enclosed by one of my *Defender* fans in Camp Stewart, Georgia. I'm making a column out of it, "On the Positive Side". . . . . It is so cold here I cannot stay much longer as this big old Mansion does not have any heat, and I am about friz.

Sincerely,
Lang

P.S. I am going to do an article on "Jim Crow and Humor" citing various absurdities of the color line that make us laugh. May I quote you about that, "Why don't you step back?" the whole length of the train corridor instance? It's for *Common Ground.*

Fisk
23 September '43
The day the freshmen descended
upon us.

Dear Lang,

Sorry I can make no suggestion on that income tax problem. The idea of deducting the expenses of writing a book sounds good and worth investigating —next time! This time I had to rush to get under the wire, having forgotten to take care of my royalty accounting, thinking that the deductions from salary here would cover everything. But I caught the boat (with the aid of one of the fellows in the business office) on the last day.

Just a few moments ago saw Charles S. Johnson for the first time since we've been here. I've been *that* busy—and he's been away that much. We have seen Marie, however. A few times. . . . I've written one review for the *Sun* on this typewriter. . . . nothing else. I now have Mercer Cook's new book to do for the *N.Y. Herald Tribune* "Books." When that's done, I swear to get back to my career book and knock it off.

This time I can fully share your emotions re: being broke. Moving has whittled me down, too. I'm trying by every means to round up little outstanding checks. Don't know what luck I'll have. Between the railroad man, the truck man, the furniture man (we've had to buy many new things), the clothes man (it is fall again, you know, and all the kids feel that they must look their best in their new schools), the grocery man (food is not cheap down here), and the man who put down the linoleum and the men who turn on the gas and lights and the men who provide packing barrels and boxes and the men who repair bicycles and the men who press clothes, etc. & etc., I'm near about to the ground. My desk is full of writing assignments, but getting them done is something else again.

143

Did you see Zora in this month's *American Mercury* ("High John de Conquer"), Bob Weaver in the *Atlantic,* Nelson Algren in last month's *Mercury* (very interesting story)? I saw you in *Poetry.* Also I approve of the final version of "Margie's Day."

You certainly see to it that I suffer for my failure to make Yaddo this year. Has Katherine Anne Porter finished her novel? I greatly admire her work, and I certainly hope there will be another year and that Yaddo will think of me again and that KAP and the other interesting and *attractive* guests you have mentioned will be returning! Please recommend me by saying (promising, if you wish) that I will be wonderfully good company—after a year in exile.

If you go to California, you will go by Cincinnati, won't you? So you can come down and visit us awhile en route. . . . This is going to be Fisk's biggest year.

Ever,
Arna

Fisk
24 September '43

Dear Lang,
Yeah, man. You may quote me in *Jim Crow and Humor* with respect to the porter and the southerner who said, "Why don't *you* step back?"

Re: the P.E.N. Club, you are right: no Negroes are members. I know of two attempts. It was rumored in Chicago that Dick was suggested for membership in N.Y. shortly after *Native Son* became a best seller, but *something* came up and the idea was dropped. Mr. Embree broached the subject of Negro members in Chicago last year when he was admitted. The answer he got was that there was no particular reason why none should be in the Club, but it just happened none were! He had meant, at the time of joining, to press for positive action and intended, I believe, to suggest me for the Chicago chapter. Perhaps he has been too busy to follow through. Leastwise, I've heard no more. . . . Many Jews are in the Chicago outfit, and many of them are liberal. I'd think that a strong stand by Smedley and Cowley would blast the business open. Also many refugees from Hitler are members. Wouldn't it be an irony if THEY turned out to be luke-warm on the subject of admitting Negroes? The simple fact is that you and Dick and two or three others should be in the N.Y. group, and I (to name but one) should be in the Chicago bunch (to which a number of my friends there belong). I'd suggest that you tip off S. and C. that they can get immediate support from Embree and perhaps Louis Zara and others in the mid-west, if they want to attack from both directions.

Nice idea, "Something for Hitler." And good subject for a column.

Bob Lucas says he is putting the finishing touches on his version of Georgette Harvey's autobiography.

There is steam heat in the Fisk Library today. Draw your own conclusions. . . . I hope you draw the right conclusion (incidentally) about the success of Roi's new book: the market for such material is just naturally good now. Your new one will do even better. The tide must be taken at its full. That's Shakespeare, you know!

Ever,
Arna

144

P.S. You oughta dig these freshmen—near 'bout 200 of them. Sophs and Juniors (still a sprinkling around) are giving the boys (of whom there are quite a few) a hard way to travel. But they're a wonderful crowd of kids. They may win the battle vs. Jim Crow, given some luck. . . . Meharry fellows (about 300, mostly in army uniform) are back today from 11-day furlough. The place is commencing to jump. Rest of Fiskites due next week.

Yaddo,
Monday.

Dear Arna,

Thanks for the information about P.E.N. . . . . Agnes had already written some days ago proposing me and Roi Ottley. No answer as yet. Cowley is writing Carl Carmer, the new president. I move that you yourself write Embree, if you want to do so. I am personally not interested in the least in belonging to it, but I suppose since the American branch poses as a liberal organization, it should be faced with the Problem! . . . . . I'm speaking at Hampton on November 29th and can then go on down to N. C. if Mrs. Lee wishes me. . . . . Better write me to New York from now on as I'm leaving here toward end of week. . . . . Did I tell you the Song Writers Protective Association has started collecting for Muse, Bemis, and I for the use of our song, "African Dance" in the picture, *Stormy Weather,* the one to which Bill Robinson dances on the drums? The publishers, Mills, had made no move to report or pay up to now. Thus it goes in the entertainment sphere! They just NEVER want to pay! How fantastic! . . . . . Column on Pvt. Barrett's poem will appear week October 2. . . . . I sent you the new "Simple Minded Friend" ones for your collection.

Sincerely,
Langston

Dear Arna,

Bessie Beardon died today in Harlem Hospital, so Willa Mitchell just phoned me. In case you'd want to send condolences, they should go to her husband, Mr. Howard Beardon, 351 West 114th Street.

Willa spent a week up here. Did I tell you? Brought me Roi Ottley's book, a carton of cigarettes, and bottle of Carioca rum. I thought it was Christmas.

Got a wire today from Marc Connelly inviting me to the Writers War Conference at the University of California in Los Angeles October 1. But can't make it. I may go out later in the winter, though. Looks like travel is too tough for much of a lecture tour, and I haven't done a thing about booking this summer.

Used up 3 boxes of writing paper working though. I'm 8 columns ahead at the moment. Some of my best, I think. Three amusing "Simple" ones concerning the dark nuances in his thinking, his landlady, and his girl friend. The idea has occurred to me that he might make an interesting comic strip. I shall investigate the possibilities.

Agnes has been picking tomatoes all day. The vines are loaded. So we called up the colored preacher tonight and gave him a big box full for his parishioners.

Cowley helped me with my income tax and I have to pay more than I possess, so am paying nothing at the moment. Several others here aren't either. Agnes says in the case of a book like her's, a writer can legally deduct all the expenses of the eight or ten years it took her to gather the material! That being so, I didn't deduct anywhere near enough on *Big Sea* income in my last statements. Wish I had known. Do you think that is true?

Ernestine Evans dropped in tonight. Katherine Anne Porter is coming for dinner tomorrow. You would really find her charming.

Miss Maynor, no doubt, would like to come out to Fisk. Why not drop her a note when she gets to town? Did I tell you her husband has the Imes church just across the street from us?

Well, I believe I have finally got "The Ballad of Margie Polite" [poem or song] in the final form I wish it. I sent you one version, didn't I?

It is really getting too cold for comfort up here! I think I will have to go to bed to keep warm.

Common Ground is full of cullud articles this issue!

Please send any clippings on the Smedley book you might come across. She hasn't even seen *Newsweek* yet.

Sincerely,
Lang

634 St. Nicholas Avenue,
New York, 30, New York,
October 4, 1943.

Dear Arna,

They are low-down dogs, that's what they are, when they do not pay off for songs! . . . . . Just ran into Tony Hill on 125th Street in for a few days from California. He says yes Archie took her money, $10,000, and $23,000 worth of jewelry and told her yes he took it. Because she had brought another man back with her from New York and put him out. However, she will not appear in court against him. . . . . Last week she married the other man, so rumor saith. . . . . Ralph says it must have been the same big roll of money she showed Dick Wright and Ted Ward when they went to ask for a contribution for their theatre that time and she said you communists will never get none of this! . . . . . Ran into Dr. Locke today down at Gwennie's school. I do not like the name of the school, otherwise I think it will be O.K. . . . . . The P.E.N. Club has invited me to a tea tomorrow!!!! At the home of the former President of Chile for visiting Latins. Colored and Latins, I reckon, they figure are somewhat in the same dark boat. . . . . . Better send that ch. on here anyhow if you want seats to Oklahoma because they are sold out TWO months ahead. Even if I got to N.C. I will be back by the 7th or 8th providing they are letting Negroes get on trains. Seems like they just pass us right on by if they want to these days! I trust you are Spanish.

Sincerely,
Lang

146

Dear Lang,

By now I hope you have good news from the *Reader's Digest*. That little article is certainly a gem. It'll give the old hard-back jimcrowers a lump in the throat —if they've got any humanity left at all. You'll have no trouble placing it elsewhere if the *Digest* turns it down, but I would like to see it go to the large audience which that magazine reaches.

Bob Davis writes to say that his commission came through, without warning and apparently without reason—perhaps somebody covering up with anonymity the stupidity which caused it to be withheld the first time. I hope he gets his wish to go overseas and see some of the more exciting experiences which army life can offer.

Now that I have your word that you'll be in N.Y. by the 7th of December, I'll go to work on the idea of curving round that way en route to Chicago. A couple of letters must be written and answered. When that is done, I'll be able to do something definite about the shows: Othello and Oklahoma. Something in the form of a check for seats!

I'm getting in the groove and starting to write. Which is perhaps a sign that things are settling down to normal. Think I'm going to like living here quite well. I certainly will if I can carry on a good program of writing. . . . Fisk has everything in the way of students this year: there is even a white girl (better not put this in the paper) living in the dormitory. I give her two hours of work per day in the library, so maybe they could say she *works* at Fisk if the legal angle comes up in question. Also a Japanese girl and a young white couple attending here under similar conditions. All hope for careers in one line or another of interracial endeavour. . . . Three teachers who just beat Hitler in the race to the border. One was in a concentration camp. And the president of the Royal Anthropological Society of London is conducting courses here. Yesterday (Sunday) he wore a cutaway coat and striped walking trousers to church. Also cane. Very, very correct! In the music department they now have one of the great harpsicord artists of the world, so I'm told. A Dr. Parrish (Ph.D. Harvard), formerly in the music faculty of Welles College.

I agree with Charlie Cherokee: yours is the best column in Negro journalism! Give me an assist for being quite a severe critic! . . . . Your poem about Ethel: very amusing. She is poetry, and poetry is happening to her, too. Poetic justice.

Ever,
Arna

Dear Lang,

Yesterday was a mild sort of a killer. First, the enclosed, involving a Fisk student who works for me here in the Library. Her trial was this morning, but she, being the shyest of people, had lost her sudden and rather surprising nerve. She did not appear, hence forfeited her $25.00 bond. The . . . Nashville lawyer who won equal pay for the Negro teachers of the city wanted to make this a test case and fight it to the highest courts, but money would be involved, and the nice but timid little girl didn't have the courage to go ahead with the business. I think she mainly lacked time. One needs to think a thing like this through in advance —a thing which may involve months in jail and perhaps years of waiting, etc. A youngster away from home needs to think long before signing up for the balance of one's youth perhaps. It's kind of like Christ leaving heaven to die on the cross. So the excitement ended abruptly this morning at 9:30.

Also yesterday a preacher friend of Owen's, originally from California, came by and said that he and his wife had just seen a Negro take his courage in his hands on the main street of Nashville—Church Street. Being slapped by a white, he promptly whipped out a switch blade and was about to put it to work, despite a crowd which gathered before you could say Cordell Hull. He was completely unafraid and was the last person in the picture to be restrained from his first intention.

I am collecting many stories like the above—stories which show the Negro braver than he has ever been before. At Pearl High, Paul tells me, the kids are fully as race-conscious and ready to walk hard and talk loud as those at Du Sable. Nearly every day they bless out some white folks on the bus which many of them ride down Joe Johnson street. They groan aloud in school when the Red Cross is mentioned—or anything else identified with discrimination and Jim Crow and indignity. They are constantly nipping at the color line—asking for service at 5 & 10 soda counters, etc. & etc. . . . . It's quite a place, this Dixie.

Harold Preece has been working in the library here of late. Miss Ovington is coming down for the same purpose. Preece is doing an interesting book for Dutton on Holy Rollers, Harpo & Hoe Handle Primitive Baptists, etc. Don't know Miss Ovington's project yet. . . . . . I'm doing a little writing myself. . . . . I have papers like the one about the Yale collection on both the Schomburg collection and Mr. Spingarn's private one—do you know any learned journal that might like to use one or the other? Ask Mr. Spingarn and Raddick, if you see either, will you? I don't have the energy left to shop around on my own.

Ever,
Arna

11/1/43

DE-lighted that I shall be able to come down to Fisk for a couple of days. The Omegas have confirmed the engagement! So reckon I will be pulling in on the 18th. Quiet! So I can have that evening to visit with you-all. . . . . . Man, the *Reader's Digest* article came back so long I had forgotten about it! Lieber is trying it elsewhere. . . . . . . Looks like I shall have a chance to see War time Washington at last. Writers War Board wants me to go down on the 11th to a Pledge For Peace meeting in the Cabinet Room of the Hotel Willard where Chief Justice Roberts is to start the ball rolling for a decent world after the war. (It's not quite clear to me why nobody seems to want a decent world NOW—but maybe after the war would be better than never.) . . . . . Killer, Jack, that letter to the Red Cross man! . . . . . Did I tell you, they finally PAID for the song in the picture, so better let me know before the 12th what show tickets you want, if you're coming North, as I have MONEY! But it won't be long. . . . . . Mr. Handy is somewhat better, but not yet out of danger, Bill tells me. Too bad, he was planning his 70th birthday celebration when he fell. He had sent Miss Logan after his horn, promising to sit on a bench in the sub station until she returned. No one knows why he got up. . . . . No one knows why I keep fooling around with show business, either. Only the Lord, and he won't even tell *me*.

Sincerely,

Lang

Wednesday

Dear Arna,

Johnny Hammond invited me over for the opening of *Carmen Jones* in Philly. It's a beautiful show sung straight—except for an interpolated jazz ballet with Cozy Coles at the drums—and mounted and costumed in the most gorgeous of Ziegfield Follies manner—probably the handsomest show ever with a Negro cast —excellently sung and with a Carmen who is really a great acting discovery! One thing that *spoils* it and strikes a jarring note is the too heavily-laid on "White folks" idea of Negro dialect. Just wrote John Hammond to this effect. And shall tell Oscar Hammerstein when I see him at our next Music War Board meeting, or ASCAP. Otherwise it is really swell and probably will be a great hit in New York and is certainly a big step ahead for the Negro in music and theatre. Novel production idea—each scene is done entirely (from sets to costumes) in varying shades of a single color: The opening all yellows, saffrons, ambers, beige. The Cafe Scene all violet lights, purple clothes, mauve sets. The third act all blues with Carmen in dark blue sequins and everybody all dressed up—girls in gorgeous evening gowns—that certainly ought to please colored. Except that when they open their mouths they're given this outlandish *dis-and-dat* dialect to speak and sing—which doesn't go with the beauty of the sets or the people at all. And Carmen has to sing—in a Parisian gown and a gorgeous voice—things like, "You's a drip, you is, sho you is!" Which simply sounds stupid and not the least quaint or funny. As well done as the show is, full of splendid dancing, singing, and entertainment, I think even a Washington audience would take it without dialect. . . . Believe I'll do a column to that effect.

Yours,

Lang

Fisk

3 January '44

Dear Lang,

You are still perhaps buried under Xmas, but something tells me it's time to wriggle out and hit the chilly. At least, that's what I've had to do. What with all the librarians back from New York and Oberlin and such like places and me getting up at six o'clock in the A.M. to do some writing before coming to work (part of my New Year resolve) and work of all kinds piling up!

Dr. C.S. Johnson of the Methodist publications called to read me your poem

"Song," which I already know and like, and to rave over it and say how much they are all walking on air since it came to their office. He also wanted to borrow my picture of you, the one by Gordon Parks which was on exhibit when he visited the campus at the time of your lecture-reading. I have sent it to him. Hope that's okey with you.

Your little poem in the current *Crisis* has that old Crisis-touch of yours. Like the poems you wrote for them in the early days. Nostalgic.

The trip to N.Y. was just what I needed to charge all my batteries. One can keep going even down here if occasionally he gets a chance to breathe the free air. A refreshing interlude. Chicago was pleasant, too, except that the graduation bored me, once I got on the spot and had to go through with it. I received my announcements too late to use them so I sent them out as Christmas cards!

Did you hear Fisk on the air last Sunday? The campus may be said to be back to normal now, for John Hudson is back from Fort Worth, wearing a diamond ring he got for a gift and telling about a cream-colored *silk* suit of clothes he also received.

The *Fast Sooner Hound* was on the air (American School of the Air), and I knew nothing about it till the royalty check came through. . . . Tell me about Canada's new play . . . Does it say any of the things you had in mind for your new novel? Incidentally, why not enter said novel in the new Doubleday-Doran $2,500 competition for a book on the Negro?

Hello to Toy and Emerson and Happy New Year!

Ever,
Arna

New York, 1-6-44.

Mr. Arna Bontemps, Esq.,

My dear sir,
Did you get lost in the holiday rush, never get home, are down with the flu or Fiskitis, or just don't write any more, or what? Anyhow, this is to let you know that I mailed your books off today, and spent the rest of the day in the ticket offices trying to get reservations for Camp Sill, Oklahoma, where I am going next week for the 2nd Anniversary of their USO. They had Joe last year, but claim the soldiers are clamoring for me now! Well, sir! I am flying back as I have to be here to hear that all-star jazz band, 20 of whose 26 members are colored—winners of the Esquire poll—with Miss Billie Holiday as chief vocalist invading the Met, no less, on the 18th. . . . . Also have to do a script for the big British Broadcasting Company's Negro Salute to the English at War program across seas first week in February. Pays, Jack, sure enough money! . . . . . Saw the opening of Canada's play with Dorothy. He did a fine job with a poor play that raised the question we contemplated for our play, but didn't attempt to solve it, save on a mechanical basis. Only lasted four days. . . . . I had a wonderful holiday time, so am snowed under, naturally, now with mail all over the floor. . . . . Flu came back on me after you left, so if you-all didn't get a Christmas card, that is why. I only got half of them sent out. The others are still on the table, so guess I will wait until next year now. . . . . . Mollie had a *fine* New Year's Eve party! . . . . . Have some

frightful correspondance with University of North Carolina Press over the cancelled anthology, *What the Negro Wants.* Their opinion is that if what me, Du Bois, Bethune, et al, say is what the Negro wants, then he had sure better revise his wants—because he ain't gonna get it! . . . . . Write!

Langston

Get *War Poems of the United Nations* for your library. It's good—has me and Guillen in it! Also various Brazilians. . . . See article in this week's AMSTERDAM on Brazil.

Fisk
10 January '44

Dear Lang,
  You'll be in Fort Sill when this reaches your mail box, but I must tell you about that silent gap of half a month. The Christmas tree fell on me, that's what. It fell on me directly after I returned from Chicago and Convocation and whatnot, and I'm just now pulling out from under its branches. You see, I big-heartedly let nearly all the librarians go during the holidays (since I'd been away quite a long time) with the result that I had to work unusually hard during those days (the library being open on all but the holidays and the ones just preceding each). Add to this the nightly festivities of this gay little community, eggnog with practically everybody on the campus at least once, and you begin to get the picture. However, I writ you a time or two recently, as you have discovered, and I hasten to post script what went yesterday with this detail: Dr. Du Bois, writing on another matter, remarks on the Chapel Hill publication of *What the Negro Wants* as follows: "I think the North Carolina University people are scared to publish it." So scared or mad, it all works out the same.
  Read a perfectly KKK article by David H. Cohn (Jewish?) in the new *Atlantic Monthly.* I would have written them a letter, but I was too full. Would take ten pages to express myself fully. . . . I'm now enjoying something like your mail problem, my own plus the library's. Lord help us! Also a sudden deluge of requests for articles of the 25-dollar size and dimension. Why doesn't anybody solicit anything with big money involved. . . . Told you 'bout our idea for a play. Now get that first draft (novel) done, and quick, so we can give them what most of the critics begged for in their reviews.

Ever,
Arna

Fisk
15 Jan. '44
Nashville 8

Dear Lang,
  This is mainly to get the Roumaine poem in the mail before it gets buried under an avalanche of detail—and before the book goes back to the stacks. . . . Now that the typewriter is cranked up and running, however, let me suggest that you

151

ask Carlo to tell you a most wonderful secret!!! Also, PLEASE send me programs and other materials relating to the historic jam session at the Met! Our Negro collection requires them—urgently. We can't, of course, hope to catch up with theatre programs and such like, but this we MUST HAVE.

Snow has been falling all day, and I hope that it will not ground your plane either coming or going, for obviously time is of the essence, considering all the items you have put on your calendar. You will manage them all, I'm sure—but I'd thank you for a copy of that BBC script. . . . Also any other radio scripts, both typed versions and mimeographed and printed ones, you find occasion to deflect this way in the course of your *normal rounds.*

Evidently the next big best seller in the Negro field will be Lillian Smith's novel *Strange Fruit,* coming in February, which Reynal and Hitchcock are launching with a four-page spread in the *Publishers Weekly*—January 8th. They promise to promote it with big money. . . . It could just as well be you! The whole idea is to come up with a timely and sincere problem novel about the Negro while the excitement is still high. Nothing to it.

Do send the letters!

If *What the Negro Wants* made the Chapel Hill people mad, I don't know what my *Arch Above the Road* will do to the conservative Boston house of Houghton Mifflin, for one of my stories centers around social equality, too. This for youngsters of the junior high age! It has to do with an episode dealing with mixed dancing at a Freshman Frolic, and the whole chapter turns on that incident. Am I bold? Well, we'll see whether or not I can get away with it. . . . That chapter was just written last week. I'm trying to make good on a New Year's promise to Grace Hogarth to deliver by the end of February. If some necessary dental work doesn't take up too much time, I hope to make good.

Spoke in Chapel yesterday. . . . On RATS!

Alberta read your letter and learned for the first time about the candy. She understands both flu and the complications that often attend it. Yet and still it was a nice thought, that candy—for candy is hard to get down here (the good kind!)!

You should get a copy of *The Poets of Haiti.* It is a charming little book.

Ever,
Arna

New York
1/21/44

Dear Arna,

Here is an *Esquire* Concert program for you. Also a copy of my LAST book review. Never will I take another, having broken a long standing rule for this one, and having carried the book to Fisk, to Hampton, to Fort Sill, and all around without being able to read it. When I did, except for two poems, it was by the hardest! Bookreviewing—tain't worth it! . . . . At the moment I am struggling with that BBC script. Hope to finish it before leaving for Montreal on the 29th. . . . Looks like I shall do a cross country tour in March, stage by stage to California for a month. . . . Greta, my beautiful police dog, died last week. Fourteen years old. . . . Doug is preparing to leave for Fisk. . . . Thanks for the

Roumain poem. See *Defender* this week on light Haitian diplomats. Ask Price Mars about it. New York Haitians in past have said it to be true? .... Trust you've told C.V.V. about *Poets of Haiti* for the Yale Collection? .... Guess I told you I was taken off the plane on account of priorities at Buffalo, so got to New York at midnight, too late for the concert. Had wonderful luck with flight otherwise. Hope to always fly from now on. Imagine having breakfast with Horace in Chicago and luncheon in Oklahoma City! Flying right over Jim Crow, too, without having to change cars! For long trips, cost is the same. .... I am snowed under, my stenog is moving to the Village, her husband, Baron Timme Rosencrantz, having suddenly come up in the world, what with a radio program and all.

Sincerely,
Langston

P.S. Did you get your books I mailed O.K.???

Saw the new Embree book. Looks good. Flatters me, at any rate! Moving sketch of Joe, the other I read. He gave me copy for soldiers at Sill. So I left it there.

Fisk
6 Feb. '44

Dear Lang,

Alberta was delighted with the valentine—and, I blush to confess it, *we* shared the pleasure! It was delicious. And welcome back to Earth, after your flight from Montreal. I take it that your card was written just prior to take-off. I know a French-Canadian editor and author in Ste Hyacinthe who is interested enough in your work to have come over for the lectures had he been reached in time, but there wasn't time after I learned your definite schedule.

The *Sun* has sent me the Latin American prize novel by the Haitian fellows for review: *Canape Vert,* by Pierre Marcelin and Philippe Thoby-Marcelin. Starts out well. I think you'd like it. You'd also like Gene Fowler's book on *the* Barrymore: *Good-Night, Sweet Prince.* Lordy, how that guy can write! It's been a long time since I've been so carried along.

The girls at the Rosenwald Fund tell me that you will be in Chicago again about February 22nd. Does that mean you will continue westward from that date? And if so, when will you be in the East again? .... I'm committed to a couple of errands, maybe three or four, which will take me hither and yon in the interests of the library, the new Gershwin Collection, an AMA committee and the Rosenwald fellowships, but there is some danger that I may not be able to catch you at home till after your return from the Coast. Have you any information about Yaddo? If there are any chances that an invitation will be extended to me again, it would help to know about it fairly soon. Otherwise I'll have to cook up some other form of vacation. So many people and so many duties and activities are involved that I have to go to work on such things farther in advance than would be required in the cases of many creative spirits.

A peach of a letter you wrote to Dr. Imes of Baltimore. I hope he feels adequately answered. One great problem in the field of race relations is that when conditions are bad at a certain point, they are likely to be so shockingly bad that people in general (colored and white) will not believe the reports. Therefore they

153

will remain unexcited when they should be yelling their lungs out.

Dr. Robert Park, the great sociologist, you know, was expected to die last night. He had failed to bounce back after a stroke and seemed to be sinking fast. I have not heard what happened, though I have seen a steady stream of cars going to his house today.

Doug is here, and Fisk seems more like familiar ground. He has been hanging curtains and otherwise putting his apartment in order. He seems pretty happy over finishing his work at Columbia. I know that feeling. Graduate study is a chore at our ages.

Ever,
Arna

Wednesday,
2/8/44

Dear Arna,

So I don't get any sympathy for being near-mugged, heh? O.K. . . . . . Anyhow, next time, having successfully taken the razor, I think I will mugg the mugger and take whatever else he has got. . . . . . I'll be in Chicago Feb. 2–March 8, Junction City USO, March 12; Sam Houston College, Austin, Texas, March 19; Hollow Hills Farm, Monterey, California, for four weeks, then back via Detroit for dates there in early May, and on to New York to put in shape the 2nd NEGRO FREEDOM RALLY for the Polo Grounds June 18th. . . . . Other lectures pending on way out and back. . . . . . And of course in between I might just maybe perhaps write a play and a book. You never can tell! . . . . . Listen to "Town Hall Forum of the Air" next Thursday. I might be arguing thereon.

Sincerely,
Lang

P.S. I am sending you that fabulous Chapel Hill Correspondence to show Charles S. *Return it to me next week* c/o Horace Cayton, Parkway Community House, 5120 South Parkway, Chicago, Illinois.

Fisk
9 February '44

Dear Lang,

You break such interesting news! That on-again, off-again Chapel Hill book, *What the Negro Wants;* that Town Hall date; your latest mugging, etc. I like very much the final paragraph of "My America." Something tells me it will do the work. . . . In your column this week, however, you sounded just like rich white —Mrs. Roosevelt, to be specific. How you went to Fort Sill and who you saw, etc. It was not without interest, of course, and I suspect a secondary purpose: to show folks how to relate themselves to the military personnel of a Negro establishment.

Will show Charles S. your script on Jim Crow if and when he stops here long enough to read it through. He will be in Chicago all this month assisting with

154

Mayor Kelley's kindergarden of race relations for employees of the city of Chicago. Quite an important development, I'm told. See first page story in last Saturday's *Christian Science Monitor.*

You *loved* Cohn's *Atlantic* article! You mean as a medicine?

I don't blame Margaret Walker for being dazed by too many lectures. Lecturing requires a special kind of steel, which you and a few others have, but not all of us. A steel that will bend without breaking. For myself I would consider four to six jobs a year par. Better still, two. And one of mine for '44 I have just done: the annual meeting of the Nashville YMCA. Charles S. introduced me. No more down here, I hope, before fall. One is pending with the librarians of the Chicago system at their monthly down-town meeting in March. Then no more, I promise you, till the snow flies.

Nelson Algren is in Texas, whence he was transferred just before his outfit sailed for Armageddon. He is a cannoneer, but he is also in God's pocket and doesn't seem headed for immediate action. . . . See where Harper has announced a new book by Dick Wright for June: *American Hunger.*

Have you seen *Decision?* Doug has not told me about your mugging, but I must now ask him for details. He and I are improving our French with the assistance of a Haitian tutor. We, in turn, help him with his English.

The first boxes of Carlo's music collection have arrived. Five of them. The rest, he assures me, will follow in a steady stream. This is going to be fun!

Alberta's candy came and went. It was grand, and I think I conveyed her approval, indeed ecstasy, in my last. Or at least she asked me to.

Best ever,
Arna

Fisk University Library
Nashville 8, Tennessee
15 February '44

Dear Lang,

We have ordered *War Poems of the United Nations.* Two copies, in fact. And the letters between Logan and the U. of N. C. Press are being sent to you in care of the Center in Chicago. Also a copy of a letter I wrote to Logan. Will you help me get that total correspondence, notes, first drafts, etc. for Fisk. If I'm the first to see its value as a library property, we should have it, don't you think? Anyhow, we'd make good use of it—keeping the whole as a commentary on our time as well as a footnote on the book.

Have seen one good review of the new Embree book *(N. Y. Times)* and one bad one *(Post,* sent by you). The next will tell the tale. . . . You are wise to let Lieber handle future lectures. You may be able to do more of them if you don't have to worry with the planning, etc.

UNLIKELY THAT WE'LL HEAR YOU OVER THE TOWN HALL FORUM THURSDAY NIGHT, but count on me to try. NOBODY SEEMS TO THINK THERE IS A LOCAL OUTLET. B-U-T PLEASE SEE THAT WE GET PRINTED VERSIONS. I'll be pulling for you. You can take Graves. His argument is that social equality for the Negro is not a matter of argument in the South but a major premise. I take this to mean that he rejects reason as a basis for settlement.

And if you rule out both reason (as he does) and justice (as others do), then where are you? The South is then saying, "Either like what we do, or lump it." In such a case the Negro can only study ways and means to lump it— one of which is to join hands with all other liberal and progressive forces working for the betterment of ALL the people.

I'll have more to say about W. T. Couch [editor, *What the Negro Wants*] anon. For now, I think he is just an old traditionalist who has made some effort to rationalize his position. Not, as he would perhaps say, a liberal at all. There is hope, however, in his intimation that perhaps fifty or one hundred years will see the end of segregation in the South. All the other die-hards talk about periods running from 500 to 10,000 years. Maybe they are just whistling. Maybe they suspect it may be even less than 50 years.

Some colored spoke well of Graves' book *The Fighting South.* I did not like it at all. They are all just about the same: Couch, Graves, Ethridge, etc. They are NOT Southern Liberals. They are old-line Southerners who have made certain minor concessions just for the sake of argument, for they are educated men who must somehow justify their way of life if they are to keep their own self-respect. This pseudo-liberalism is the result. . . . Couch thought he had cut the ground under many arguments when he hadn't damaged them at all. Like when he suggests that Negroes should keep their Jim Crow trains, stations, etc. clean and like white's. As if Negroes could force the RR's to hire more janitors, kick the conductors out of the JC cars, etc. He is not really a seeker after truth.

Just be yourself at Town Hall. No more, no less than in your humblest lecture, and you'll do yourself brown! You need not try to argue. Just take your usual cut at the questions. I, personally, am full of confidence—for you.

Ever,
Arna

Fisk
16 February '44

Dear Lang,
When you go to work on John Temple Graves, please ask him this easy question:

IN WHAT ESSENTIALS DOES THE POSITION OF ATLANTIC MONTHLY COHEN, HIMSELF, ETHRIDGE AND SOME OTHER SOUTHERN "LIBERALS" DIFFER FROM THAT OF THE KKK WHICH HAS LONG BEEN RECOGNIZED AS FASCIST IN TENDENCY?

I grant that the edges have been rounded, but what FUNDAMENTAL objective has the KKK which these men do not share?

The enclosed, taken from today's paper, would seem to indicate that nothing has been modified. I send it as extra amunition to you, should you have a chance to fire it.

You DO have my sympathy in connection with your late near-mugging. But if you got the razor, I'm not sure but that you won that bout. Congratulations are in order, rather than sympathy.

Bob Lucas has dramatized *Black Thunder* very well, I think. Would the Gilpin Players be in a position to do it now? Once they were interested. Fisk will not be ready for it till we have more men students.

Ever,
Arna

Fisk University Library
Nashville 8, Tennessee
21 February '44

Dear Lang,

When you open that envelope containing the Chapel Hill correspondence, be sure to remove a letter to you and a copy of one to Logan, plus a copy of a news release. I just had the sneaking feeling that you might be passing the correspondence along to somebody else to read and *could*, if I didn't warn you, leave the enclosures with the rest. I'd rather you kept them with your more private papers.

I didn't say in my wire all I wanted lest Western Union regard it as a congratulation and refuse to send it—as they frequently do, you know. It was just right (the broadcast), and I suspect Graves and all like him were given something to think about. The audience helped you, too. Their questions went to the heart of the reactionary position. . . . Poor Shepherd. Uncle Tom was the only one on the platform to frankly state that the Negro does not want "social equality" without any definition or qualification. And he said it when he didn't have to. He seemed anxious to make the statement. Maybe he will ask for an increased appropriation from his legislature next week or next month.

All Graves said was that people must understand not the logic of the Southern position but the passion with which they (the South) intend to defend it. Whether our allies like it or not, it is a matter of such determination to the South that the support of other colored nations will have to go if they can't accept the South's color-complex. Ho-hum! But I must say M.G. is a fluent guy and makes a clear statement of the bad position he holds.

Our copy of *PM* did not carry the picture of the broadcast you mentioned. Could you send it to us? Also the *Post* write-up. We've just this week subscribed to the latter, and copies are not yet coming through. . . . Thanks for BBC script —when it comes. We'll be waiting. . . . Harold Preece says the *Defender* just *doubled* his pay for column. . . . From 10 to 20, I believe. . . . Now don't go flirting with Hollywood! Here is a better idea: that new Haitian novel *Canape-Vert* is grand. See *Time* this week. I just reviewed it for the *Sun*. The book contains wonderful material for a Katherine Dunham play. Why not ask Max Lieber to investigate—for us? All kinds of ceremonies involved in the plot. Would be pie to arrange it for stage. Or screen. With Katherine, lots of music and color, it would be sensational.

I'll be in Chicago mid-March, but you'll be gone. Good flying weather to you. . . . I've done my story on Hazel Scott. Also all others but one. Now for the revisions. Morrow has just written to ask for a book. I could do nothing but write juveniles! Take it easy, man.

Ever,
Arna

157

P.S. Twenty or so boxes of the Geo. Gershwin Collection have now arrived! If you make an honest man of a Southern "liberal," you'll deserve a medal. By all means take Graves up on that Birmingham business!

Fisk University Library
Nashville 8, Tennessee
29 February '44

Dear Lang,

Please let me have your revised itinerary if and when you stop long enough to scribble your name again. Meanwhile, I'm glad to know your first Chicago lecture was to a capacity house. No doubt a result of the success of the Town Meeting of the Air which many of them heard. We even get letters about that event here! How was the response from the point of view of the Radio station. Big, little, favorable, unfavorable or mixed? We have ordered ten copies of the broadcast for the library. Perhaps that speaks for itself. . . . I like to dropped in on you at the Grand, but not quite. My ticket now takes me first to New York, March 9–15, Chicago, 16–20, and then home. An AMA committee on race-relations film (documentary) in N. Y., a Rosenwald Fellowship meeting in Chi, and some library business in each place. Also a hop to Yale perhaps, to see their music. . . . *Time* and the *N. Y. Times* have both sent reporters to see CVV about the Gershwin Collection. Maybe some stories. Who knows? We need good promotion. . . . Just had nice letters from Handy, Still, Bob Lucas, etc. Bob is in Chicago now, briefly maybe, maybe longer. . . . Just mailed my long paper (50 pages) to the *Library Quarterly*. . . . . Bringing my juvenile *Arch Above the Road* to a close. Driving hard. Hope to have most of it to take to N. Y. with me. . . . Did you see my review of *Canape-Vert* in the *Sun*. I'm telling you, fella, that is the basis of a play for Katherine. Just what she needs. We should dramatize it—*providing* Maxim can get the permission from F & R and the idea can then be sold to Katherine's manager and an interested producer. . . . . Spoke to Dr. Louis Price-Mars about the *Defender*'s articles vs Lescot. Mars doesn't doubt that some Haitians prefer pinks, perhaps to the extent that American Negro Md's do, but he distrusts this attack. Thinks he knows the source and suggests that it is a dissident element of the Haitian government. Maybe clerical—since Lescot has been more liberal than his predecessors and had given the clergy less rope. Maybe an ordinary opponent. In any case, the danger (Mars says) is that a) present plans to have Robeson and other American Negroes down as guests of Haitian government may be spoiled and b) that a persecuted minority will be made of the high browns of Haiti on the same grounds that Hitler made same of Jews: too many high offices, professional jobs, etc. . . . Moreover, there are some silly things in the *Defender* articles: like the statement that d'Artigue, minister of education, is *light*. I know that guy well, and he is about as light as Lochard! You can't kill him for having a Jewish wife unless you want to kill Dick, Roi, etc. If I were invited to do so, I wouldn't hesitate to say these things in print. I don't like having Negroes raise the color question—in reverse. We should be joining up with Haitians, if anything, and congratulating Lescot for taking Jacques Roumaine and others out of the dog-house into which Vincent had put them—he and the

158

Catholic clergy. Remember, these are pro-Vincent elements who are dropping these hints to the *Defender*.

Your letter was just brought in, answering some of the questions on the other side of this page. . . . Glad you've written Maxim re: play. I join you in not intending to work without cash. And I salute you on getting a contract with the D. . . . . New mail also included package of material from Still for music collection. . . . . I do not think you are a SIMPLE MINDED FRIEND, but I don't expect you to look for letters in parcels—not too closely anyhow, if you are as much like me as I have been led to believe. . . . Logan has not answered, incidentally. A nudge from you, when you write him, might help. I'll miss you in N. Y. No tickets or anything!

Arna

Fisk University Library
Nashville 8, Tennessee
23 March '44

Dear Lang,

I've been back about a day. What a trip! No doubt, you are letting out a similar sigh as you arrive at Hollow Hills. My schedule calls for another jaunt to Chicago on the 15th of April and another to New York the 12th of May or thereabouts. Incidentally, this N. Y. business has implications for *you:* it is a committee working with the American Film Center and planning educational movies dealing with Negro life and race relations. I have given your address to Donald Slesinger and also suggested that one of the films be that documentary you once mentioned dealing with "The Negro Speaks of Rivers." I asked them to include you among the script writers approached on the general themes, too. This means that Donald, who is the brother of Tess, will call on you as he calls on his sister and her writing friends in Hollywood. Ten percent, please!! Read the enclosed clipping and then tell me whether or not I know play material when I see it. Do we do it or don't we?

N. Y. and Chicago are both jumping. In N. Y. I had lunch with Bucklin Moon of Doubleday, and he talked me into signing for a book on Negro migrations in the U.S. in collaboration with Jack—a reworking of the material Jack and I had done for the Rosenwald Fund and the Writer's set-up. In the same sense that Roi's book was based on the Harlem material. But ours will have to depart from the original, cover additional ground, etc. So it is not all peaches in Georgia. They liked the idea well enough to advance us a grand, however. Which ain't bad. Hope to finish it up by the early summer.

In N. Y. I also delivered the manuscript of *Arch Above the Road,* the juvenile book of careers. I learn to my disappointment, however, that it can't be published till early '45, thanks to the paper shortage and that run-away best seller *The Robe* which is eating Houghton Mifflin out of house and home. . . . There wasn't time for much else in N. Y. and I only saw two plays *(Early to Bed* and *Decision)* and two movies. And only two parties, no three: Mollie's, Ed and Helen Solomon (those white friends of Billy and Vandy, remember? now living at the Royalton), and Roi Ottley's. Saw along the way Carlo, Harold, Canada, Alta, Grace N.

Johnson, Countee and Ida, etc. Tried to call your house, but learned that Toy was out of town. . . . . Shall we see *The Voice of the Turtle* and *Winged Victory* and *One Touch of Venus* in May? If so, who will get us tickets?

In Chicago the fellowship program took up a lot of time. Guess who got them? Or at least stayed in the running for the next meeting? Dick and Ellen and the young one came to the city as I was leaving. I spent a couple of hours with them at Horace's. Dick's new book is his autobiography. Look what you started among the young colored writers—you, Zora, Dick, and I don't know who else. Saw Bob Lucas and many more. And went to an interesting party at Dorothy Farrell's beautiful new home—given to her by her chain store uncle.

I don't think a tour provides the material for your most arresting column style, but I won't quibble. You do your best when you're sitting around Harlem or in the Grand in Chicago, not when you are being entertained by sweet people in small towns. For better or for worst, I fear Harlem's got you.

Had dinner with Louise and Pat in Chicago. Agnes Smedley was in town, and I should have gone to her party, but I was beat to my heels and fell asleep in a rocking chair.

Tell me how it feels to be in the lap of luxury!

Ever,
Arna

Fisk University Library
Nashville 8, Tennessee
30 March '44

Dear Lang,

Are you there? [Monterey, Calif.] You must be, considering that you were on a plane in the vicinity of El Paso about a week ago. Of course, as my last indicated, I did get home, though thoroughly exhausted. I don't stand up so well as you do under the strain of travel. I sleep poorly on trains, and on a short trip I always find myself swamped with things I never in this world intended to have on my program.

This time, to make matters worst, I came home with that contract for a book with Jack (partly written, of course) and now I have editorial reactions to my new juvenile, *Arch Above the Road*—no, we're going to call it *We Have Tomorrow*. I don't suppose you'll mind the change, since each suggestion is taken from the same poem by you. Anyhow, I must add three new chapters. Imagine publishers asking such a thing in these days of paper shortage! Well, they think it's odd themselves, but they say they are high on this book. Let's hope they're not fooling. Who shall I add? Drew? He of the Spingarn Medal? Or is he young enough—under forty? Margaret Walker? Or could she be found for an interview? Emmett May the merchant seaman who was torpedoed and is now a radio man and a commissioned ensign in the merchant marine? Who?

I dug your piece in the *New Republic*—which I had read before in manuscript —but did not dig either you or Walter in this week's national edition of the *Defender*. How come? We also have the printed version of the "Town Meeting of the Air," which is good reading.

Owen is expected here tonight or tomorrow. He came East for a churchman's meeting in Chicago and is supposed to come down to spend the week-end with us. Alta is to come next weekend for a stay with Doug.

Mr. Handy has just written to say that he is mailing us autographed copies of his total output, including 27 versions or arrangements of the "St. Louis Blues"!

Hello to Noel Sullivan [H's friend, owner of Hollow Hills Farm] and to Eulah [housekeeper]. I bet you're ready to settle down for a couple of weeks . . . The *Chicago Sun* is running a wonderful series (enlightening, I mean) on the Negro in the Army. Reckon you could add something to their findings. And Bousfield has sent us an interesting paper he read before the American Medical Association on Negro doctors—we helped him with the research. . . . Where can one see the film *The Negro Soldier?* And did you hear from Donald Slesinger? Well, maybe not yet, since I just sent in yesterday a memo I was asked to prepare.

Well, sunshine and all the trimmings to you.

Ever,
Arna

On tour,
Phoenix, Arizona,
April 9, Easter, 1944.

Dear Arna,

If you've recovered from the Chicago Conference, drop me a line at Hollow Hills Farm, Monterey, California, where I'll be shortly for ten days.

Eastward trek starts again at Salt Lake on April 24th. I think I might maybe do it by air, since it is just as cheap, faster by days, and less crowded, and you can stop off anywhere as by train. I took a plane from Dallas to the Coast and have been stopping off all along the line. Flying on to Los Angeles Tuesday.

This is a grand book year, everything from *Popo* to *Jim Crow's Last Stand* going like hot cakes. Entire edition of *Freedom's Plow* is sold out. Which makes me mad, as Detroit has built their entire program around it, with a big chorus singing the background music—and now no copies to sell!! I am chagrined!

Had a most interesting week as house guest of Col. Bousefield at Fort Huachuca. Cullud call it the Country Club of the Army. Reminds me slightly of *Carmen Jones. (Do not quote.)* Fun and frustration are all mixed up.

I sent you various things for your Gershwin Collection, etc., from Tucson. . . . Did you see my piece in last week's *New Republic?* They had kept it almost a year. Somewhat dated.

Hey, now! My classification has gone up a notch in ASCAP. After awhile I can live off of it entirely. I told you you ought to be a song writer—and let the drama alone!

Sweet and Hot in L.A. has my song "Hollywood Mammy" in it. Haven't heard of any money from it yet, so shall call on them in a few days. The show has been running two months now and is a hit, I understand.

Wonderful roses in this Phoenix backyard!

Hello to Alberta. Hy to Constance.

Sincerely,
Lang

P.S. Lt. Bob Davis, at Fort Huachuca, has charge of some portion of the M.P.'s, looks fine, and is getting married in July to Dorothy Coleman. Margaret Walker was so excited at the news that she called me up from Dallas to get the details. She is thinking of Mexico for the summer.

> Hollow Hills Farm
> (Carmel Valley) Jamesburg
> Route
> Monterey, California
> April 19, 1944

Delighted to find your letters here. An absolute ton of mail and wires otherwise awaited arrival. Which appalled me, as I have only 4 days to stay. . . . Our plane fell into an air pocket on the way up that I thought would relieve me all mail forever!

Never get on a plane with a hang-over! They had a big party for me in L.A. the night before.

I'd be most pleased to work on a "Rivers" film. If you're in New York the 12th, stay till I get there the 15th. My aunt is back so phone her.

Malvina Hoffman was here for luncheon, also the Jeffers. Martin Flavin for dinner yesterday. He said Canada Lee wanted to revive his play about the elephant keeper that Walter Hampden did some years ago.

Well, I am sleepy! So

> Sincerely,
> Lang

P.S. Loren is up for nomination for Congress . . . Democrat . . . Saw Foy. Looks O.K. . . . Fred Miller, former student at Oakwood, now waiter at "The Last Word" cullud America's swankiest drinking place, sends regards to you. Says you were a most wonderful teacher—will never forget your discussions of Poe and the Brontes.

> Fisk University Library
> Nashville 8, Tennessee
> 19 April '44

Dear Lang,

The assumption is that you are still at Hollow Hills Farm and that this will reach you before you fly to Salt Lake City. Anyhow, we'll try! . . . Rockwell Kent was here today and he told me that he had greatly enjoyed your broadcast with Cary McWilliams, that you and he had often shared platforms, etc. Very likable fellow.

The Festival is on, of course, and we also have spring frenzies. I have just returned from four days in Chicago, during which time we gave Margaret Walker a fellowship—among others—dined with Lillian Smith and her new best-selling glory, went around with Earl Brown in connection with a forthcoming *Life* story on Chicago (pre-Convention), checked with Horace on his story in my new book,

162

worked with Jack on the migration book we have contracted to do, shopped, saw movies and whatnot.

NOW I want to know where I can reach la Walker. Please tell her that I want to put her in a book and ask her if she's going to be near enough to Nashville to come here for an interview. Or, will she be in N. Y. about the middle of May —or rather, during the 2nd week? I need more girls in my collection and I believe poetry should be represented, if it can be represented by one who has found a way to make a living at it. I can't add any trips to my slate and still get any work done here, so I'll either have to do her by one of the above mentioned contacts or by having her write her story up and then mailing it to me.

All your items for the Gershwin Collection have been received with pleasure and interest. They will be formally itemized for you when my secretary gets well. I came home to a loaded desk and an absent typist!

Alberta, too, has been somewhat ill—not seriously, but enough to keep her in bed several days.

Saw Clarence Muse in Chicago. He said for you to get in touch with him re: a writing job in connection with a proposed film, on Carver, I believe. Well, use your own discretion.

Roland Hayes is here for a concert tonight. . . . I agree, this IS a year for books. Everything is selling. The publishers can scarcely keep my juveniles in print. Oh, if we only had a novel apiece or an autobiography or something in the works. This would be the time to make a killing. *Strange Fruit* has 100,000 copies in print!

Buy up some theatre tickets for the week following May 10th!

Ever,
Arna

On tour
San Francisco
April 22, 1944

Arna,

For your book, why not add Sengstacke of the *Defender*, Young of the *Guide* (Jr.) or one of the younger newspaper publishers. Possibly Leon Washington of the L.A. Sentinel? It would give you a good chance to defend the cullud press.

Also add a progressive young minister—Clayton Russell of L.A. (Plus Washington—good excuse for trip to Coast!!) Rev. Russell has a very modern church —with social services, a large co-op store, etc. (Is Adam Powell too old?)

I don't know Drew's age.

I am swamped with mail. But have a secretary all day today. Leave for Salt Lake tonight. Capacity audience—standing even—last night at Interracial Community Church in Oakland. Heartbroken because books ran out much too quickly. Sold 6 *Popo*'s—all I had!

Yours for unity—

Sincerely,
Langston

P.S. Have you a labor leader in the book? Ask Lou or Pat who. There are several good ones. Revels Cayton on Coast. (Trip to L.A. again—3 birds.)

On tour,
Hotel Monroe,
Grinnell, Iowa
April 29, '44

Dear Arna,

Well, it seems that this here hotel refused to house Marian Anderson a year or so ago—but here it is housing me! So I reckon the war has done some good. . . . Just left Stuart Brown who wrote "We Hold These Truths"—on faculty here. . . . Sold 4 copies tonight at Chapel! ! ! ! . . . . Why don't you lecture and sell books, too? Huh? I have gained 12 lbs. on this trip!

Sincerely,
Langston

[Detroit, Michigan]
May 8, 1944.

Dear Arna,

Your letters reached me in Chicago but I didn't have a minute to catch my breath. Saw Charles S., as usual, in the Grand, and told him about *Rivers* as I was rushing to the train. I have to leave for Flint in about a half hour, but will try to put an outline, very tentative, in this letter, if I can.

I saw Margaret in Chicago. She was just leaving for New York. She says she'd be glad to see you. Better drop her a note before hand as she may be out in Jersey and would have to come in town.

I still think Leon Washington or John Sengstacke would be good for your book. Many whites, I discover, now read the Negro press. The whole sociology class at Grinnell take the Pittsburgh Courier!

Sure, let's have dinner on the 15th. I am not officially in New York until end of month (so do not tell everybody) as it will take me that long to read my mail.

Earl Brown was arrested in Chi and *Tribune* accused *Life* of abetting race riots, and I think he went on back to New York.

Is Radio Patrolman Jake Goldberg Jewish? Please let me know as I want to do a column on those six kids.

Man, I will have to pack for Flint AT ONCE! The RIVERS poem should serve for a historical continuity from Africa right up to now. (We can always add the Harlem River or the Chicago.) Spoken continuity like "Negro Soldier." Birth of various black arts and cultures along banks of Nile—mathematics—Congo—smelting of iron—Niger—weaving, ivory carving, dancing, syncopation—up to Mississippi and Abe Lincoln sailing down on raft to see the New Orleans slave markets, up to cotton up to St. Louis and the "St. Louis Blues" up to Ohio and the steel mills along its banks turning out war materials for 1945 and the INVASION. See?

Margaret is de-LIGH-ted with her Fellowship. . . . I have sold out the whole edition of *Jim Crow*. A new one of *Freedom's Plow* has just been printed. . . . . .
The affair last night at the Art Institute here was very swanky, ushers in evening gowns, etc.

164

I
   do
      not
         know
            why
               cullud
                  like
                     to
                        usher
                           in
                               evening
                                 gowns!

They are long and they trip up their feet and things!
                          Sincerely,
                          Lang

                          923 - 18th Ave. No.
                          25 May '44

Dear Lang,

It has taken a few days to get myself together, following the N.Y. trip, and it was made more complicated by simultaneous preparations for today's jaunt to Chicago for the "Of Men and Books" broadcast Saturday. I must turn right around and rush back here for the graduation ceremonies which begin Sunday morning, so I don't expect to get around much in Chicago.

Today the library received a $1,000 check from one of its local friends for the purpose of decking the room which is to house the George Gershwin Memorial Collection of Music and Musical Literature. We ought to be able to put it in fine shape with that—considering that the room is not bad off *now*. We will buy cases and things and build special little compartments, etc.

Hey, man, hurry up and write that book! I get at least one letter a day from people who are starting little shelves or collections of books on the Negro's contribution to American life. Most of them are going into the libraries of small colleges throughout the South. Of course, I give you many a plug as things stand, but the newer books come in most handy because all the stores have them in stock. . . . I'm hurrying with both of mine! Unfortunately, Margaret will be left out of the juvenile, but I can't wait longer for her material, and I'm determined to make this deadline, since I've missed a couple already. . . . Imagine what Alberta said when I told her the story—just about what Toy said! That does not influence my decision; it's just that Margaret's material has not reached me.

Amusing column you had this week—about the fly.

I enjoyed N. Y. Also the trip back. Met several nice folks coming to Nashville. Next time we must see *The Voice of the Turtle*, plus some more musicals.

REMEMBER: the treatment for *The Negro Speaks of Rivers* is promised for the middle of July. Copies will then be made, and the idea will be acted on definitely at the September meeting of the Committee on Mass Education.

I have proofs on Watkins' *Anthology of American Negro Literature*. Looks pretty good. You are well represented.

Think I'll stay in Nashville till about the end of Summer School, July 21, and then go to Chicago for the lake breezes—and incidentally to complete the migration book with Jack. I'm too fed up with travel to go all the way to California just now. Besides, the book must be finished while the demand is hot. Why don't you come out to the Grand and work if things become too hectic in Harlem? I understand Claude McKay is in Chicago now—working for the Catholics!

Luck to you with that mountain of mail!

> Ever,
> Arna

> Fisk University Library
> Nashville 8, Tennessee
> 8 June '44

Dear Lang,

Thanks (the Library says) for the most useful list of your songs, and thanks (I say) for at least two carbons of columns by you—which the Library will eventually get. . . . All of which reminds me of a letter I have just received from a white admirer of Scott Joplin, including the white gentleman's memories of the latter. Most interesting for purposes of the migration book. And a gentle reminder to thee, from whom I expect presently to receive a copy of an English magazine devoted to the equally great Jelly Roll Morton, whom I'd like to say something about. Now if I could only learn more about Tom Turpin and his brother and Otis Saunders and Gussie L. Davis! The former three from the same old St. Louis era, the latter from Cincinnati of a decade earlier, the '80's. Know any leads?

Didn't know about the Negro Music Collection in the Detroit Public Library, but glad to learn.

You are absolutely right: I am already gray-headed, nearabouts, but I don't aim to get more so over worrying with the theatre. I'm afraid I have given up on *St. Louis Woman* in its present incarnation. If I had the whole say, I would have contributed it to the paper drive. . . . Your informant was right, I fear, about the songs Lucky wrote for the play. I listened to them one night last fall, saying as I listened, "Surely they can't be as bad as they sound to me." To spare the feelings of all concerned, I said nothing, but *St. Louis Woman* has been in my thoughts much less frequently since then. . . . . Someday I'm going to do that job over completely, from scratch.

I can think of nothing more attractive than an NBC program featuring the Hall Johnson Choir and narrated by you. Hold your thumbs, man. That's *it!*

How about the *Christening* of which you spoke? Doug left here on the run, hoping to be present in time.

Shame on Yaddo for getting persnicketty about new faces just at a time when I might have been able to pay it a pop call! Might at least have invited me up for Labor Day week-end. Just for that I hope a DOZEN old world couples violate the fishing rule and that every one catches no less than a dozen silver trout and deposits each in a separate bright red pocketbook!

166

While that's going on, no doubt, I'll be attending meetings of librarians—and feeling *glad,* in the manner of your unsonnet sequence. There'll also be a race relations conference down here in July.

Ever,
Arna

6/20/44

Still working on that NBC show—third script! This one is about WORK so it ought to suit them—cullud and work.

Did I tell you (well again!) that Decca took 12 of my blues for an album?

Common Ground wants me to do a month's tour of nearby white high schools next season.

I'm trying to buy my book rights back from Knopf's. If I were not part Jewish myself. . . . .

So—Atlanta! You better stay out of that *deep* South!

Como me llamo?

Me llamo

Langston

P.S. Lightening struck the Hotel Theresa yesterday—knocking various unmarried folks out of bed. It did not, unfortunately, strike the switchboard!

Fisk University Library
Nashville 8, Tennessee
23 June 1944

Dear Lang,

It's a hundred in the shade today, as usual, with me down here trying to keep digging without suffering sun-stroke—and you up there in Harlem enjoying thunder, lightning and various other refreshers! No fair!

Anyhow, I'm tickled about your Decca album, your third version of the radio script and your recent column about Simple and the girls who *drink* you up. And I'm enjoying the issue of *Jazz* devoted to Jelly Roll Morton, which I found waiting for me on my return from 102-degree Atlanta. It will be returned to you in the fullness of time, to put it eloquently. I'd like to keep it a couple of months. You must see to it that we get one of the Decca albums for the Collection here —and for posterity. . . . Which reminds me to say that I'll get around to the formal thank-you note to you presently.

Knopf is still pushing me to do that history of cullud folks for children. If you go to reminding them of your Jewish blood, they may wish to drop the idea. Which won't make me cry, for I'm sure I can't get to the job unless they can see their way clear to dangle some attractive incentive money.

How about Tuskegee for you this summer? And Yaddo? And the movie treatment for *The Negro Speaks of Rivers?* Oh yes, will you telephone Elmer

Campbell for me and beg him to reply to my request for pictures of himself for *Classmate? Most important!*

> Meanwhile, adios.
> Arna

St. Louis
July 10, 1944.

Dear Arna,

This place is hot as hell, but not so crowded with white and colored as, I presume, is Hades! . . . . . I am sending Gershwin Collection all programs, etc. of the Festival. W.C. Handy is here with me, also Madame Evanti (of I speak *all* European languages fame—"All but Spanish!"). . . . . Muriel Smith, also Don Ameche, Bonelli, Southernaires, Noble Sissle, etc. etc., really an ALL STAR million dollar show! Poured down rain in Chicago, but still drew 15000. Expect 35000 here tonight. At any rate, the Negroes are paying and I am getting mine after *each* performance. Flying to Detroit tomorrow where Rochester will be the big star. . . . . Golly, is that *Rivers* treatment due NOW???????. . . . . No, have not got yet. . . . Better air-mail me c/o Horace in Chicago as I think I'll be back there for a few days following Detroit. . . . . Cullud are wonderful—if you don't believe it you ought to see how they are running this Festival. The Lo-d must be with them! It is sometimes very difficult for a human to be.

> Avec mes sentiments les plus
> sinceres,
> Lang

Tuesday

Arna,

Hot here, too! . . . . . We had a cocktail party Sunday for LaVilla, 5–7, but it went on till three! Dean Dixon, Nora Holt, Dan Burley, mostly musical people, from classics to boogie were there. Had fun! . . . . . . NBC show still hanging fire. But me collecting money. . . . . . Aunt Toy probably knows about some of those old time musicians, if you were here to ask her. . . . . Knopf *gave* me the book rights back! . . . . . Lieber has poison ivy so he can hardly walk. . . . . I go to Chi on the 5th, I think. Contract came but no ticket money yet. Shall fly. . . . . Ralph Ellison has a story in current *Tomorrow*. He has done a fine piece on Dick Wright, too, for them. . . . . . Ted Ward's baby was born. Margaret's is on its way. Dorothy's sailor boy Frankie's in-laws send a wedding announcement. Bob Davis writes that even military weddings are costly.

> In spite of wars and race
> Still propagates the human race!

My secretary is about to work me to death, so I gave her two days off! . . . . .
Got a fine letter concerning my Chicago high school speeches, too. . . . .

168

Last night made my debut on the stage at the Garden. Scared!v/8x/vnto death! . . . . Assistant Attorney General Littel almost got booed off! Sensible enough to stop in time. Implications of his speech was since we're only one tenth population, a one tenth democracy ought to do us! . . . . . . I'm telling you white folks amaze me! They can't be right bright! . . . . . . Quintanilla wants to paint me. But to pose amuses me not. . . . . . A wonderful dog followed me home last night but I could not take him in so I told him to follow some other people and he did! . . . . . You-all should have a dog for the kids now that you have all that yard-room.

My best to Constance,
Poppy,
Camille
Joan
Paul
And their mama,
Sincerely,
Lang

923 - 18th Avenue North
Nashville—8, Tenn.
July 27, '44

Dear Lang,

Are you home yet?

Simple-Minded-Friend was swell this week, he of the dark glasses. I think you'll break up the fad if you spread the suspicion that the wearing of them at night is for one of the reasons Simple indicated.

I should be on vacation now, like all the folks who have good sense. Instead, I'm here in my pajama pants (no shirt) working six hours a day on my next book and going to the library in the late afternoon to bother my head with the business there. Maybe I can earn a week's idleness when I come to N. Y. for the September 9th meeting. If you are going to be around then, how about some more shows?

Meanwhile, what's holding the treatment of *The Negro Speaks of Rivers?* It has a good chance to be the first movie on the Committee's schedule, but you really ought to write up the treatment you have in mind. I think they intend to let the contracts for the actual scripts at the time of the September meeting. They are to decide which on the basis of the memos or treatments they have sent out in advance.

This to OFFICIALLY release you from the rather absurd request to call Elmer on the telephone. I have dreamed about the idea and decided it was a weird request to make of a gentle soul, himself pursued by scores of similar furies. Anyhow, I have given the magazine the great man's address and asked them to do the worrying.

See your picture all around—in evening clothes, narrating and smiling and generally making life pleasant to the folks at the big musicals. . . . Had the NBC show incubated during your absence?

169

Summer school and the Race Relations Institute and all related activities, plus the writing I was trying to do on the migration material, plus the hops to library conferences had me beat by the end of the sessions, last week, and a little ill. Back at normal speed now, however. . . . . Have failed up to now to learn anything personal or interesting about either Scott Joplin or Gussie L. Davis, one of whom I wanted to include in the St. Louis story, the other in the Cincinnati. Nor have I learned anything about Mrs. Jelliff's or her husband's backgrounds or the lady's stage interests. I was about to ask you to inquire of your readers in the Defender if any had recollections of Joplin or Davis, but I am off bothersome requests, for today, at least. I can't even learn from people who knew Davis in Cincinnati where he was born or when, where or when he died or where he was buried, what relatives or survivors he had, etc. Joplin's widow I've located, but she won't answer a letter. Cullud will never have much history! They are too scared somebody will find out what they had to do for a living, etc. Too anxious to live up to (or appear to) middle-class morality. I'm afraid there will not be as much fondness in the book as I wanted there.

Rum-colas and rondeaus to you for being cullud, but different!

Arna

634 St. Nicholas Avenue
New York 30, New York
August 11, 1944

Dear Arna,

I have inquired from my Aunt Toy and two or three other older people of the theatre if they knew anything about Davis or Scott Joplin. Aunt Toy has an early edition of his "Maple Leaf Rag" which I am sure she will be willing to give your collection in case you do not have a copy of it there. However, she has no information about the man, and she never heard of Gussie Davis. I imagine when you come to New York the Negro Actor's Guild can probably put you on the trail of somebody who may have some information.

Between a summer cold and summer visitors, (of whom there are legion) I think I shall retire to Philadelphia or some place like that. I had thought I would go up to Yaddo for a couple of weeks, but Mrs. Waite is desperately ill, and the activities there are quite curtailed. Also Carson McCuller's father has just died in Georgia and she has gone South again.

Tell me what shows you would like to see and I will get some tickets for the second week in September. Give my best regards to Alberta and all of the children.

Sincerely yours,
Lang

P.S. Sold another song for children's records. Copy enclosed. Also about to publish Powell's campaign song, "Let My People Go—Now."

170

Dear Lang,

Add *Anna Lucasta* and *Follow the Girls* to the plays to be seen, if possible, between September 8 and 18—remembering my meetings on the 9th & 10th.

Another note has come from the *American Film Center,* and I have replied that the treatment of *The Negro Speaks of Rivers* will be forthcoming (with your mercy) presently. They give instructions for arranging this material, etc. I'll have my secretary re-type what you send according to the plan they cooked up.

I'm ready for a trip or something NOW. Have worked too hard at writing during this infernal weather. A little stimulation would help about now. But the book with Jack is far from finished, so I'm still at my oar, pulling as best I can.

Looks like I'll be your fellow Borzoi author—for one book. They're offering a nice contract for that juvenile on the history of the Negro. A good "little" book of that sort should be able to help race relations quite a lot. Hope I can do it right.

Good column this week, man!

Ever,
Arna

923 - 18th Avenue North
Nashville 8, Tenn.
Jubilee Day, '44
[Oct 6]

Dear Lang,

On October 6th, 1871, the first Jubilee singers left this hilltop to introduce the Negro spirituals to the musical world. By '73 they had sung them from one end of this continent to the other and in most of Europe, had had themselves painted by Victoria's favorite portrait painter and raised enough money to build Jubilee Hall. So today we are celebrating. There will be no classes at Fisk. Instead, memorial services in chapel, football in the early afternoon, games later and a big dance tonight. Did you know all this?

Whether you did or did not, you are certainly hep on the subject of combing hair. Everybody to whom I've shown the piece has been completely devastated by it. I consider it your funniest and *best* column. When you tied combing of cullud hair up with the united nations and the hopes for victory in the war, I thought I'd expire. Classic, man! Let me know what comes in your mail as a result.

Yep, I'm back home—by the hardest—greatly refreshed and hitting the ball every morning in an effort to deliver the manuscript of *They Seek a City* by October 20th. Looks like Doubleday will push it if we make the deadline. Meanwhile, Max has placed another of those sketches from *We Have Tomorrow* with the Young People's Magazine and is still working on the rest. And Houghton Mifflin have commissioned Marion Palfi to photograph the subjects of the chapters—or as many of them as she can contact in New York. They saw and liked her photographs and thought that her zeal to do something of this sort made her a good choice. A deep bow to YOU! For this as well as the title of the book.

Fisk student body is bigger than ever. Most attractive bunch. How about some theatre tickets for the week following December 9th? *Sadie Thompson,* etc.? More about this in a day or two—including details.

Ever,
Arna

923 - 18th Avenue North
Nashville—8, Tennessee
19 October '44

Dear Lang,

The excitement has begun—re: the combing of the cullud haids. Every now and then somebody falls out in the library. Investigation reveals in each case a copy of this week's *Defender.* I fear you've done something!

Yeah, man, get us tickets for *Bloomer Girl.* Also, *Sadie Thompson* and *Men at Sea* and *Voice of the Turtle* and anything else good. I'll stay several days, beginning the 7th or 8th of December, if I can finish the Doubleday book by then. I'll figure I deserve a few more days of recreation.

What you are doing in Philly has my double blessing. I hope you'll feel like doing it on a bigger scale next year, using (ahem!) *We Have Tomorrow* as recommended reading for the young people who hear you. But no fooling, it will fit excellently in any good-will or inter-racial program with the young, for it was written specially for such. . . . I hope Palfi can get all the temperamental geniuses to sit still for her. I'm sure some of them will cooperate, maybe all, but it may take coaxing to get Hazel, for example. I do think the book will be better if we have exclusives of all concerned, rather than publicity photos they have already used.

I will promise to sing "Let My People Go" if you send me a copy!

Reckon you'll be home by the time this arrives?

This is one of those days on which I want to swear to leave the South behind, forever. While I see improvements almost every day in some quarters, I can't help getting mad when travel is involved. It is so easy for the cracker ticket agents to lie when they don't want to accommodate you. I'm having trouble getting train reservations to my Greensboro engagement. Will try to get a plane. If none is available, will be tempted to cancel—though I do hate to put the folks on a spot. What I hate most about such an experience is the feeling of depression it induces. I could take the discomforts if they weren't compounded with insults and fabrications and whutnots. . . . I oughta hear you lecture. I need the lift. . . . I who have just written the last correction on the manuscript of the most optimistic and encouraging book ever written for young American Negroes!!

Ever,
Arna

Paul starts at tackle vs. Manassas High of Memphis tomorrow!

Hey, Jack,

Tell Charles S. to stop changing his dates—because it is harder to get theatre tickets these days than it is to change meeting dates! (I had *Mama, Sadie Thompson, Harvey,* and *Bloomer Girl* for you. Nothing for *Turtle* till March!) Practically everything is sold out until February or March, and even the bad plays are weeks ahead.) Dorothy had planned a buffet supper for you and Alberta on Sunday, the 10th! I will let her know. . . . . Wonderful birthday dinner for Mr. Handy last night, Sunday. . . . . Man there said he had a million dollar angel at his disposal to produce a dramatic version of *Father of the Blues.* Asked me to work on it. Wants to see you when you come to town. . . . . Met Stokowski tonight. Casting for *Troubled Island* begins after the holidays. . . . . After five weeks of early morning high school assemblies, I now wake up daily before dawn. (But turn over and go back to sleep!) *Common Ground* wants me to do 40 weeks next season!!! They have gotten wonderful letters from the various principals. Some make me blush for modesty's sake! . . . . . . The Adam-Hazel story finally broke in the papers today. Harlem has a dozen variations. I am glad he is safe in Congress. . . . . Almost as sensational are two other tales going around about two other cullud leaders and their marital affairs. I think it must be the war! It shakes loose many old ties.

Sincerely,
Lang

Loren and Juanita due in town shortly.

Send me a copy of that Phi Beta Harlem article of yours and I will send you a libretto of *Troubled Island* for the Gershwin Col.

Lucky says he has a backer for *St. Louis Woman.*

Frances has joined the WAVES. Also Harriett Pickens.

923 - 18th Ave. No.
Nashville 8, Tenn.
1 November '44

Dear Lang,

Swell column again today—"My Brother's Keeper." Hope it gets around among the Mexicans and Jews as well as among cullud and ofay. Home from Bennett, I'm trying to catch up mail, campus duties and stints on my books in process. Must also get around to the Blessed Martin soon, for he must be frocked by the 30th of November.

Bennett was grand, and I think that I finally have a fool-proof lecture outline, one that can be twisted and revised to fit any kind of occasion. You must hear it sometime. I'm even of a mind to book some lectures for next year! With two new books out and two kids in college, maybe I could make one pay for the other. But what makes me happiest is the working out of a pat speech idea. . . . At Bennett I gave 4 talks, including one on the air, one on a platform with the mayor of Greensboro and the city manager (anniversary of the local colored public library—20 yrs.), one before student body and faculty (about 500 in all), and one at the Library Association banquet (which paid my way there). Charlotte Hawkins Brown was present, as were many college presidents and lower officials as well as ALL the library people. Some of the latter also came from Virginia, South Carolina and Florida. Could have sold a whole edition of books, had I had one!

Think I told you Alberta has decided to accept a trip to N.Y. with me as an Xmas present. So if you can fix us up with some show tickets, I'll not only name you "the Blessed Lang" but will also repay in coin all expenditures. Count on our spending a solid week there beginning December 8th, but *don't* get tickets involving Alberta for the night of the 8th or the afternoon of the 9th. She may be tuckered out on the 8th, and on Saturday she plans to go to church (while we are in our meeting) and see some folks not seeable at any other time.

Got fair accommodations on my Greensboro trip. Not too good, however.

Have you made democratic citizens of the high school kids of New Jersey? And their teachers!

Did you know that Walter White has a book with Doubleday, Doran? It will come out before ours, because it is described as "topical." And WHAT THE NEGRO WANTS is on display in Nashville Book Stores. We have not received our copies yet. I'm burning to see it.

Ever,
Arna

You heard, of course, that Hank Johnson died last week and was buried in Texas yesterday. A wire was here when I returned, but I have no other details.

Election Day '44

Dear Arna,

Just what you said don't do is what I had already gone and done: bought tickets for *Bloomer Girl* for the afternoon of December 9th, Saturday, evidently forgetting the meeting! Well, I will try and change them for the following Wednesday. It is a delightful show, with a very pro-Negro theme in it, so you ought to see it. I just left the guy who wrote the book, Dan James, who was a watcher at the polls up here today. He's a friend of mine from Carmel. . . . There are no tickets for anything but matinees until February, and then only gallery seats. . . . I've been out of town all week long the past four weeks doing these high school assemblies, and have ten days yet to go. W.C. was with me yesterday at White Plains and played his "St. Louis Blues" on the trumpet and *broke it up!* We hadn't appeared together for ten years, since St. Louis. Wish you were going to be here for his big birthday dinner on the 19th. I had dinner with him last night. First time I'd seen his house. . . . Remind me to tell you about Hoboken's wonderful and amusing high school when I see you. . . . A Southern kid from Virginia presented me at assembly yesterday, and his name is Langston Randolph Harrison, white, but I reckon we must be cousins, certainly of the same family that birthed my grandpa. He seemed a little flabbergasted at the idea, but took it like a gentleman! I told him about Chester Arthur discovering that Angelo was his cousin. He said, "What did he do about it?" I said, "He gave a party!"

Sincerely,
Lang

174

P.S. I might even do a children's book myself for Knopf! I have a cute little idea that they like.

Friday

Dear Arna,

Your check came just as I was going downtown for the Association of English Teachers Luncheon, so I went from there right to the box offices, and stood in numerous lines with fairly agreeable results. My feeling that hotel Negroes and Broadway box office people are the rudest in the world was doubly reinforced. There are two old ladies in the box office at *Othello* who have been bad and mad each time I've been there to everybody in the line, insisting that they have nothing before next Jewvember—but on minute inquiry, they always have two for February 14 or three at 2.75 for December 27, or scattered dates. I don't know why they add to the confusion in that manner, but they do. Anyhow, Carrol Thomas, who was in front of me, and Frances Wills who was behind me, all managed to get some kind of seats before doomsday. And in the case of *Oklahoma,* believe it or not, I was lucky enough to secure two matinees for us! In spite of the fact that the lobby attendant said there wasn't a thing until February except boxes at 4.40. Maybe these were turned back. Anyhow, there they were. Net result of battling six lines:

Wed. Mat. Dec.	8	*Harriet*	2 seats
Thurs. Eve.	9	*Oklahoma*	2 seats
Sat. Mat.	11	*Othello*	1 seat

I tried *Winged Victory,* the Air Force show, which is a big hit and for which Leonard DePaur, they tell me, directed the chorus, but nothing before December 28th, which I got for myself. Tomorrow, I will try the rest on your list that I didn't cover today. If you haven't seen *Tomorrow the World,* I think you'd like that and probably can get in after you come, as it has been running a long time. I saw it last year and liked it very much. At any rate, I'll probably have one or two more by the time you get here, perhaps CARMEN JONES which opens the 2nd. . . . . . I will see about your railroad ticket tomorrow. The advance windows had closed when I got through with theatres.

So sorry about Constance! I hope she's getting on O.K. . . . . . Tell Alberta I certainly enjoyed my visit with you-all, and that I think she is a perfect hostess, plus all the other charms she possesses.

I'll be back in town the 5th for an engagement at Dorothy Maynor's husband's church. Will look for you on the 7th.

Yours,
Lang

P.S. Head New York Librarian tells me he is on board of Fisk and is one of your admirers. Better plan to drop in on him when you're here......Don't forget the campus postcards for CVV. Also anything else hanging round loose for Yale.

923 - 18th Avenue North
Election Day plus two
(Your vote helping!)

Dear Lang,

We must not forget the 9th of December, because that is the day on which each of us collects $$$ from the American Film Center—providing we do our home work. So I DO hope you can exchange the *Bloomer Girl* tickets for the following Wednesday afternoon. Also: Why not try the not-yet-arrived *Sadie Thompson* musical? I hear it has grand music, and it should be in town before we get there. *Angel Street, I Remember Mama, Jacobowsky,* and *Harvey* are also of interest to Alberta and me, if any of them are easier to enter than *Turtle,* etc. A total of THREE shows would be ideal, but we'll take what we get. Here's some change toward the project. $15.00

Your columns have hit a high level in the past weeks. You must be getting a great kick out of writing them. . . . By all means do that juvenile for Knopf, for juveniles are selling *down* now. *Sad-Faced Boy,* more than 1100 copies in 6 months ending September! Don't know what it would do if they could or would keep it in print. *Hound* doing even better, in fact much better, though I share in the returns very modestly. Want to do a cullud child story for a church group? I just turned it down, hands being full. Of course, you don't. . . . Looks like *What the Negro Wants* will do right well, too. Pub. Weekly says first printing was 7,500. . . . At this minute I'm writing a chapter on Karamu for "They Seek a City." Almost the wind-up for that volume!!

Keep on spreading Democracy 'mongst the kids. About the time you wind up your tour my pieces will start appearing in *Classmate.* Between us we oughta put the new generation on a new track. . . . Chas. Drew speaks here tonight. A formal reception (not connected with him) is also on tap. The Little Theatre put on *Cry Havoc* last night.

Ever,
Arna

This has been written a week—near 'bout. Waiting in my letter box!!

634 St. Nicholas Avenue
New York 30, New York
December 8, 1944

Dear Arna,

Too bad you-all aren't here this week-end—Loren and Juanita are, also Jose Antonio Fernandez de Castro and his wife of Havana (THE authority on Negro literature down there) just back from an air-plane trip around the world in Cuban diplomatic service, also Mrs. Browning of *Story Magazine,* and Charlie Leonard of Hollywood—so I am having a cocktail party Sunday for all and sundry. Dorothy is also going ahead with her buffet supper tomorrow night. But no doubt things will be jumping equally but differently when you do arrive! I've sold some of your theatre tickets to Ralph Ellison and Fanny. But will try to get you some more.

I've been head over heels in things to do—opera libretto to revise, some urgent articles to get done, etc. etc. so haven't been able to rummage through all my stuff to look for that statement for Crates, but will send him copies of all the wonderful letters that came in from the various high schools I've been lately, several in response to a troubled principal in Bridgeport who wrote everyone after the Sokolsky attack to see what I had said, also had the FBI in attendance, who evidently gave me a clearance, as his assembly was held. The whole business made me a bit sore at folks who strain at a gnat and daily swallow all the camels of discrimination we have to put up with year in and year out. My personal feeling is TO HELL WITH THEM! I do not care whether they like me or my poems or not. They certainly do us as a race very little good—Christian though they may be.

Your article on the two Harlems is very very good indeed! I think it is just about your most beautiful and effective piece of writing and, if widely read, should provoke a lot of discussion. I just about bet it will choke all these people with moral fishbones stuck in their throats!

Harlem writers have been invited to a press conference with Sec. of State Stettinius tonight. Shall go see what it is all about.

Congratulations on the show contract! Hope it comes off and makes a big hit so you can make some BIG money. . . . . Barney Josephson sent for me again to work on the proposed Cafe Society Revue. Says they definitely will start on it after New Years with money up and all. Seems Oscar Hammerstein II is interested.

So, I leave you now to consider the stack of mail on top of mail piled on the bed. I cannot take my rest until I unpile some of it.

Sincerely,
Langston

Thursday.

Dear Arna,

So glad you like my current columns on the movies. I'm getting quite a few complimentary letters from the columns lately. . . . . Did I tell you a guy tried to mug me the other night? But I retreated too fast for action on his part. Giving nothing away, neither to muggers nor the Red Cross, as you can see from the enclosed. . . . . Negro Victory Committee wants me to work on a pagent for Madison Square Garden. I've put them in touch with Lieber and am asking for a substantial advance before touching pen to paper. Don't wish to repeat the Hollywood and Chicago experiences. Also consulted with NBC today about a Carver Memorial show with Ethel Waters, but nothing happened yet. All white boys working on it so far. Always is, when there's money concerned. Cullud got the freebies to do. Me, FINI on that score from now on. Plus a few bad words added! . . . . . Yeah, man, would love to speak for the People's Institute of Applied Religion. Fee, $50.00. Any date after April 15th through to Easter open at the moment. . . . . Do you like our choice of Hastie for the Spingarn Medal? Unanimous, it was!. . . . Lou has a baby girl!. . . . Pan-American Inter-Racial folks got hot because I wouldn't be on a Conference Committee they're planning. Said they *had* to have a Negro. I told them I certainly wasn't the *only* one. 14 million more around.

Lang

P.S. Please put "Merry Go Round" in that Calverton Anthology, please, sir. Ladies weep thereat.

Dear Lang:

Thanks heaps for the address of Scott Joplin's sister and the tip which came from Ida Forsythe. I have followed through, inviting Miss Joplin to deposit Scott's mementos, etc., in the George Gershwin Collection. I hope she will be feeling generous on the morning she receives my note. We would love to have something unique on Joplin.

I imagine you are back from the nether regions by now. Nearly everybody had seen you in Chicago, and two or three people have written from the hinterland to say that you passed by. All exhilarated as usual.

Put the *Glass Menagerie* on your schedule. I saw it in Chicago and am trying to tell the whole world about it now. Beautiful! The young man who wrote it, Tennessee Williams, is included with you among the *Five Poets in Search of an Answer*. He is also an old friend of Jack's.

Lots of things to tell you presently. Meanwhile, some of the *Defender* people told me to tip you off to the fact that this is a good time for you to ask for a raise! Your stock, they say is very high, and the paper is well able to pay you more. All that is needed, this particular assistant editor says, is for you to make your request known.

Hello to Toy, Emerson, Frances, etc.

Ever,
Arna

3/2/45

Dear Arna,

There is *not* any Tennessee Williams in "Five Poets In Search of an Answer." But I want to see his play anyhow!

I'll be in Huntsville April 4—almost near enough to holler at you! Then Atlanta, La., Tex., & Oklahoma.

Palfi called up to report a swell trip.

Aunt Toy says to tell Alberta there is open stock on kids' shoes now in New York.

Emerson was at the Apollo for a week. Left for points South today.

When is your play coming off? The opera—when they raise 29 thousand more! (and from cullud! They are simple minded—but optimistic!)

You will notice I spared *you* any columns on my trip this time. I wonder if the rest of my public realize who spared them that infliction?

I always go on 1st call and sit dead in the middle of the diners now. One steward in Alabama asked me if I was Puerto-Rican. I said, "No, hungry!" and he handed me a menu. The waiters recognized me, and were most courteous. A Navy man who sat in front of me asked if I was Cuban. I said, "No, American. Are you Cuban?"

Southerners puzzle me no end, as if only Cubans or Puerto Ricans of color got hungry on trains!

178

Wonderful reviews of Dick's book! See Orson Welles column. ("Negroes don't need to be studied any more. They need to be saved.") Good, huh?

Lang

Sunday

Dear Arna,

I pull out for the South April 3. Have spent my life buying tickets all month. Five minutes for 3 plane tickets. 5 weeks for 3 or 4 Pullman reservations. (And they mark "Colored" on the orders even here in New York! May the Lord smite them down!)

Lang

Fisk University Library
Nashville 8, Tennessee
March 7, 1945

Dear Lang:

I have just put the Milwaukee letters on the desk of Charles S. When he is finished with them, they will go into the Negro Collection of the library. And this suggests to me that we do not have copies of that larger batch of letters, plus the statement which you wrote for people like Crates Johnson. Can't we put these on file for posterity too?

If you have time to telephone Katherine Dunham at the Roosevelt Hotel, I am sure she would welcome a conversation with you on the subject of Negro colleges, etc. She is considering the possibility of doing a short tour with her entire company. I am writing her today. You could give more up-to-date advice.

I see that Doctor Du Bois gave a dissenting opinion of *Black Boy* in his review for BOOKS of the *New York Herald Tribune*.

Still no news about the play, though I have begun to get letters from people who saw the notice in the papers and who would like to appear in the production. Carlo tells me he hopes we will not have the bad luck to get EITHER Lena Horne or Katherine Dunham for the lead! He has some reservations about the dramatic ability of both the ladies. Me, I am indifferent.

Ever,
Arna

30 March '45

Dear Lang,

Just got through reading about you (and looking at you) in the new *Publishers' Weekly*, March 24. Still clasping that graven image, I see! I also saw you with the group of Marion's photographees in the Courier of the same date and read about you in the April *Negro Digest*. You are getting around, man! The poem for

Jacques Roumaine is strong and moving, and the columns have been in the groove, too. . . . Owen Dodson has his best poem to date (to me) in the current issue of *Tomorrow*. Don't miss it. . . . And my piece that you read, "The Two Harlems", is out in *The American Scholar*. . . . . . And an excerpt from *They Seek a City* is scheduled for a later issue of *Tomorrow*, due just two days before book publication.

When you settle down for the summer, I'll send you the news in fuller detail, but nowadays I keep wondering whether you'll get my dispatches while they are still news or when they're history. . . . . Travel is certainly a good device for inducing a bad mood. Which is one of the reasons why I shun it as far as possible. Ticket agents would seem to be selected (often) on the basis of their pledge to make things hard for cullud. But I can't say that my last trip to Chicago (last week) was bad. In fact, things went very well—including the Fellowship meetings and the dinner Mr. Embree gave for the Committee at the Shoreland. And I'm quite ready to come to N. Y. at the first opportunity, despite the efforts of ticket sellers to discourage us.

No news from the play whatever, but I am certainly losing no sleep over the silence.

Joan has just been selected by the Pearl High faculty as valedictorian of this year's class of two or three hundred graduates. It involves a speech in War Memorial auditorium (the city municipal auditorium) before nearly every Negro in the city, and that is the part she does not like—having never given a speech before. Paul should have had the job, but he was too busy with football, and she (like the steady plodding turtle) passed him up. He, however, is vice president of the class and has a lead in the class play—not to mention a certain following among the bobby sox element of the school. So both of them are pretty steamed up for college.

Me, I've got spring fever!

Ever,
Arna

Monday,
Returning to
light, 1945.

Dear Arna,

I was about to die with a stye in my eye that I'd just had lanced when, purely by chance, I ran into Countee at a newsstand with the new PV in his hand, and he had just read what Fredi said, and he was trembling like a leaf more from anger than grief—mad not sad! And he grabbed me and cried for me to take heed to a letter that he pulled from his pocket to read. It was three months old and in it Fredi told how since she could not sing but Isabel could sing, being free from Adam the lead for her now in a play would be the thing, and Fredi closed by saying how *fine* the script was—like wine! And Countee cried, "It's a disgrace!" And shook the letter in my face, and said, "Sure's you're born, it's because Lena Horne has the lead in the play, and not Isabel, and I say, Fredi can go to hell!" He was in a state, but I said, "Man, I can't wait to discuss this with you because I'm in a state, too, with a stye in my eye that's giving me hell, and I can't see

180

very well, but in *this* or any other *nation,* theatre is nothing but *worriation!"* Whereupon I grabbed a subway train and went on home with my eye in pain. . . . . Today I called up to see where on earth your records could be, to learn they are still piled high all wrapped but waiting for the express man to come by! So all I could say was, "Oh, my!". . . . . A wire from Owen to me says our meeting will be September first and second, so you'll be here, I reckon, huh? . . . . . . I still cannot see clearly, but beg to remain

Yours sincerely,
Lang

Saturday

Hy, Arna,

Is this article O.K. as first of series for *Negro Digest?* Next one, "Fooling Our White Folks" on passing, and another on "So Near and Yet So Far" concerning the intimacies and gulfs between the races.

Any truth in the *Amsterdam*'s report from Winchell that Lena has withdrawn from your show? . . . . . As I reckon you know, Mr. Cullen read the script last night at Walter White's before a censorial cullud group of about twenty (A BIG MISTAKE TO DO, I THINK) and was soundly trounced by Walter, Roy, Dr. Louis Wright, etc. Mollie, Doug, Dr. Peyton Anderson stood up for the play. Me, I wasn't invited (neither there) but heard about it later in the evening at a party at Alta's for her sister who is in town. Doug will tell you all about it when he gets to Fisk. . . . . If I were you-all, I'd go on with the production and pay all this prejudgement *no mind.* It do not make sense. Frank Wilson, Dooley, and all show folks I've run into are behind the play and mad at the prejudgement.

By the way, the soldier-hero of *So Deep Are the Roots* is a Fisk graduate in the play. So when Nonnie shows up (PORTRAYED BY JANE WHITE!!) as a Spelman grad, both our better colleges will be represented on the Broadway stage. The race is rising. Maybe all you need to do to your play is have Della a graduate of Tuskegee or some such place before she went to St. Louis. That might even shush Mr. Hardwick.

I TOLD you about the theatre! . . . . . Hey, now!

Lang

See current *Esquire.* George Jean Nathan has a piece on Negroes in theatre. 8 to 2 is, by the way, the *official* Washington figure for continental U.S.A. But since it was not given to me officially, I simply say as "one source reported."

Friday,

Dear Arna,

Yep, he is writing (or will) that Negro novel. (Secret!) Johnny Silvera will be his assistant. Laid in North, but heading South soon to look it over. I had one of those *giant* pancakes at the Algonquin. Saw Rackham Holt there. . . . Saw the enormous lot of wonderful material Grace gave the J.W.S. collection of his stuff, manuscripts, etc. today at Carl's. . . . I am going to Walter's movie com. luncheon

181

to say my say, but *not* be on committee. Censorship is without my ken. . . . Man, I am making a wonderful Whitman Anthology. . . . also making a music drama of *Street Scene*. No secret now. Was in *Times*. And I *have* my check and agreement (20% of movie rights!!!!). Hey, now!. . . . Will be in Chi. until Nov. 10. Come on up. (In and out, me.). . . . Sgt. Waring Cuney back. . . . Dorothy's moved again. . . . How is Poppy?

Lang

P.S. Saw your pic. in *Ebony*. As haint git "Careless Love" read! Kin you?

c/o O. A. Troy
735 Winona Avenue
Pasadena 3, Calif.

Dear Lang,

Wherever you may be. Maxim [Lieber] tells me that he thought you would be in Chicago about now for a couple of weeks. If so, maybe we can arrange to cross paths there. Tomorrow I'm going to work on the train reservation problem. I'd like to leave here the 3rd of June. Whether or not I can do it is an open question. But I plan to return home via Chicago.

The *St. Louis Woman* business is moving along quite actively. Several people from Metro (the songwriting team of Johnny Mercer and Harold Arlen, the young director Lemuel Ayres, the producer Arthur Freed) are involved in the proposed production in one way or another, so I have been in and out of half a dozen of those fantastic Hollywood houses which, heretofore, I'd only seen from the outside. I've also had a little talk with Lena Horne. There still seems to be a possibility that she may want to do the leading role. Of course you know that the present plan is to make a musical of the job. Which explains my presence out here. I came in response to a wire—which also included expense money. Countee was unable to take time off from his teaching. Newest plans call for rehearsals by September.

Your Simple Minded Friend was good again this week. I've been reading about your lectures, too.

California is beautiful now. You should see it. I drove up to San Bernardino over the weekend to see my Pa and Ma. Passed Santa Anita en route. Thousands of people were at the races. The roadsides were all in bloom. Likewise the orange trees. Wish I could stay here the whole summer—which has always been the season which I like best in California.

Have made no move to see people yet. In fact, I've been much too busy with the work, but maybe I can get around to a little pleasure next week.

Hello to the bunch at the Center, if you're there. We must hurry up and get together and tell our experiences and whatnot. I have some very interesting news for you, but it's under the hat for a couple of weeks more.

Till then,

Ever,
Arna

Sunday
923 - 18th Ave. N.
Nashville 8

Dear Lang,
Here is the story:
Item: I have NOT received the album of records you spoke of sending. Neither the one for Miss Boswell, but there hasn't been time for that one.
Item: I'd like to leave here for N. Y. about August 5—if I can get train space.
Item: Paul has received, bragged about, worn, displayed and sported in your present, but being cullud (unlike Joan) has convinced himself that he hasn't yet had them long enough to write the letter.
Item: Simple was wonderful this week. All the Race Relations Institute folk were giggling about him.
Item: I've now seen Owen's "Journey to Paradise," also Charles S' extended comments on it. . . . I get the impression there isn't enough money in the cash register to call Committee meetings any more.
Item: AAB [Alex Bontemps] is a mighty man at one month!
Item: CITY is first book by me to really make the South mad. From V. Dabney on down they don't believe Negroes leave because they don't like the way they're treated. Imagine it! But book is selling quite well. I'll bring yours to N. Y.
Item: 30.

Ever,
Arna

V-J Day,
New York.

Dear Arna,
I TOLD you theatre is a worriation! A double worriation when it has to do with RACE! And no limits on worriation when it gets mixed up with the LEFT. (Now the viewpoint.) Put all three together and you:

Did you see Dick Campbell's article, or interview, in *Variety* a few weeks ago? I didn't either, but evidently that was what started Negroes to worrying about the cullud shows listed for the coming season. See Abe Hill's column in last week's *Amsterdam* where he casts slight doubt on your opus, too. And everybody seems against *Strange Fruit.* Also the proposed Octavus Roy Cohen musical.

Thanks a million for the book and its inscription. . . . . Did you ever get YOUR records? I signed an album for you specially a couple weeks ago, since the original list I left when I went on tour didn't get completely filled, evidently. For instance, Arthur Spingarn got his, Amy evidently not yet. Asch's business is getting too big for his small set-up and limited office force, so I guess they got kind of mixed up. . . . . WHEN are you coming to town? Aunt Toy is back, roasting chickens! . . . . . Harlem really hollered last night! And poured downtown! TIMES SQUARE was good-naturedly interracial. A summertime New Year's Eve!

Lang

Story bought that story once it was colored-up.

634 St. Nicholas Avenue
New York 30, New York
July 21, 1945

Dear Arna:

I am afraid the lady will probably be having her first child by the time the records arrive, judging by the time your own album and others have taken to reach their destination. I ordered all my complimentary ones sent at once just after I got back from my tour, but it was ten days before Carl Van Vechten received his right here in New York City. At any rate, you will get one in due time I am sure, as I just had a letter from Dorothy Johnson in California that hers had arrived. Current *Esquire* has it on their Best Sellers.

Aunt Toy is going to Chicago this weekend for a vacation with Emerson, but I trust she will be back to cook us a good dinner by the time you get here. She has been securing some very large ducks recently from her butcher, and so we have duck quite often, instead of meat.

I imagine those documentary movies of ours are going to turn out just about like everything else in the theatre—indefinite delay. I'll believe we have created one when I see it on the screen. As I suppose you see by the papers, Owen is now busy producing "Hamlet" and "Outward Bound" at Hampton—white productions in color.

Someone sent me one of the southern reviews of your book. I think the fact that white southerners disagree with it will help its sale possibilities no end. I am glad to hear that it is going well.

I just had a nice note from Paul today and am happy to know that he is going to Oberlin after all. Is Joan going there as well? And where does Alexander intend to attend college? It is my intention very soon to send him a silver spoon, unless you advise me that he was born with one in his mouth.

All my best to Alberta.

Sincerely,
Langston

Dear Lang,

Your letter to Owen is very interesting and to the point. Have you sent a copy to Charles S., or should I show him mine?

I also applaud the question you raise re: the summer dramas at Hampton. Why no Negro themes? I have been expressing the same feeling down here, with the result that last night Miss Voorhees, our drama director, came by to say she wants to get a new Negro play to give next spring as the high event of the Stagecrafter's Twentieth Year Celebration. She wondered whether you or Owen or even I had something in mind or on a shelf that could be made ready by the end of the fall to go into production during the second semester. I gave her your address, and she will no doubt write. What immediately takes me out of the picture is that she must have a play tailored to fit a student body that is made up mostly of girls —hence one with few male roles. None of the things I have in mind at present fit that specification. I hope, however, that you will think of something. They will probably make a very big noise about whatever they do.

You and Simple beat the snaggle-tooth world! Folks down here say y'all get better and better the more you carry on.

My business errand to N. Y. is not developing as fast as I expected it would. If I must come on my own, I'll hold off a few weeks and give the heat wave a chance to lift. In any case, my arrival should be in August—which gives me a fairly wide margin of time—and I'll let you know at least a week in advance so that you and Toy can do something about the duck situation! I have an important regional meeting of Graduate Deans to address (white and colored) on August 2. After that I'll concentrate on writing—and the N. Y. errands involved.

Nevil Shute, the popular British novelist, is about to do a novel about an American Negro soldier in England. His publishers have written me to help him collect background data on Negro thinking in U.S. today, Negro soldiers in this war, etc. I recommended Walter's book, copies of *Negro Digest,* etc. If you have any thoughts, send them to Miss Frances Philips at William Morrow & Co. How about sending copies of those radio shows you did for OWI? The Alcan highway, for example. Shute has had about three or more book club selections, as many movies, and is widely read. He may do good if he puts his heart in this job—as Miss P. seems to think he is doing.

More later.

Ever,
Arna

July 27, 1945

Dear Arna:

This bit of correspondence might interest you. You probably remember a story of mine which I think you read in manuscript called "A Bottle of Wine." The title was since then changed to "On the Way Home," and Lieber submitted it to *Story* Magazine, that seems to like it, but as you can see by these letters, Whit Burnett seemed worried that the characters were not definitely described as colored. I don't necessarily see why they should have been since the story doesn't deal with a racial situation. It just seems to me to illustrate the curious psychology that our white folks have that everything written by a Negro has to be definitely colored colored. Is that the way you would explain it?

Please return the letters next time you write.

Sincerely yours,
Langston

634 St. Nicholas Avenue
New York 30, New York
July 30, 1945

Dear Arna:

Delighted to have both your cards. I gather from the brief information which they contain that you are just about as busy as I am, but I hope not, because I don't believe that authors should have to work so hard.

I have been revising my Lorca poems, which, I believe, I told you Covarrubias is interested in illustrating for a book. Also, I have been getting all my Guillen poems together, as Ben C., who has done a number of excellent translations of him, wishes to combine them with mine for a book. Besides that, I have a dozen other little jobs which all need to be done this very week. However, I am bent, bound and determined to take time out to attend THE wedding reception on August 1 at Cafe Society.

When are you coming to New York? Aunt Toy is now in Chicago, but Dorothy says she will cook us a dinner.

I have recently had a letter from Mrs. Paul Wakefield, 603 So. Fifth St., Springfield, Illinois, Vachel Lindsay's sister, who tells me she is taking over his old home in Springfield and will always have a guest room there for wandering writers who might wish to stop over. She says that she once met you in Chicago and would like to hear from you. She has since become, apparently as the result of your talk, deeply interested in the Negro problem and has read many books about it, and sends me a long letter and a lot of carbons she has written to folks about it. If she had sent them to you, I know you would have read them by now, since you seem to be able to manage to work and read too, but that is not one of my gifts. I am enclosing simply the P. S. to her letter which concerns you. Would you kindly return it to me.

Say hello to Alberta and Alexander for me.

Sincerely,
Langston

Dear Arna,

Your letter just came. 1st in years! Didn't send Charles S. a copy of Owen's letter. Show him yours.

Somebody else called me *you* (of all things!) at the N.A.A.C.P. free party for the Negro newspaper men yesterday at Downtown Cafe Society.

Since Fisk is noted for its music, tell that lady to do my "De Sun Do Move" with the Choir. I am mailing her a copy.

Had breakfast with K. Dunham yesterday. She asked about you. Her new show

186

"Carib Song" went into rehearsal today. She is getting very fat where she sits down at.

Langston

Monday the 6th of August
923 - 18th Avenue North
Nashville 8, Tenn.

Dear Lang,

Miss Voorhees, drama director at Fisk, is away for the rest of the summer, but your copy of "De Sun Do Move" is sure to catch up with her. The idea of having the drama department collaborate with the music department in doing it is a very logical one—almost too logical—but it might work anyhow. The music folks will be doing an opera during the same festival, no doubt, and they might want to think twice before taking on a double assignment. Even so, it's a swell idea, and I'll say what I can in its behalf as I have opportunity.

I'll try to remember to write to Mrs. Paul Wakefield. I don't remember her too distinctly but do recall meeting someone who was said to be Vachel Lindsay's sister.

Speaking of being mistaken for me—I have even been mistaken for *you* over the TELEPHONE.

According to Charles S. a meeting of the Film Committee will soon be called. This may not be for publication but Marshall Field and the Rosenwald Fund are about ready to back a picture in a big way as a sort of experiment. But they will want to give the whole idea of education in race relations via this medium a good try in this one attempt, so a great deal of thought and meditation will have to go into the plans. Charles talks of a two-day meeting this time. The backers have already rejected the theme advanced in Owen's script, I understand. Considerable collaboration from the film industry is expected. Don't think I'll set the time for my N. Y. trip till the time of this meeting is set. Otherwise I'd spend too much energy jumping back and forth on trains.

If I can remember it, I'll put your copy of *They Seek a City* in the mail tomorrow—since I seem to be so slow getting to N. Y. To make it easy on you, I'll check chapters for you to read. Which reminds me, we have quite a lot about W. P. Dabney in the book, not to mention quite a bit about you and your kin. . . . I can't figure why they selected that Garvey passage for the *Negro Digest.* . . . Do you see the book in the Harlem bookshops? . . . . It is listed as a best seller at Krock's in Chicago. Other Chicago stores have also done well with it. . . . . Publishers keep saying it is going very nicely and "completely satisfactory" but they don't say how many.

I am now neck deep in the juvenile history of the Negro for Knopf. Quite an interesting job. Hope I can finish it in time for their spring list. . . . I guess I told you that Jack and I have another of those tall stories—like "The Fast Sooner Hound"—with Houghton Mifflin. It's called "Slappy Hooper." Slappy is a wonderful true-life sign painter. Even fools the birds and the tramps.

Ever,
Arna

Ever hear of the time of silver rain? This is it—this one afternoon!

VJ plus 1

Dear Lang,

Your VJ-Special has just been delivered. Ho-hum, let the woman rave. A little bad-mouth shouldn't hurt a good play. But this attack by Fredi Washington is a little surprising in one way, for Countee tells me that she had hoped to play Della in *St. Louis Woman herself!* And as for Abe Hill, he wrote me about a year ago that he was considering the play for his Harlem Theatre. I now suspect that he is building fences to justify himself for not doing it—in case the thing succeeds. In fact, when people become too suddenly moral about such matters, you can generally find a little malice or jealousy lying around somewhere. Perhaps the word is sour grapes.

But I say, Let the old bad luck happen. I wouldn't care if it clouded up and rained cobblestones.

The serious fact is that neither Fredi nor Abe has read *Woman.* They read a play by that title that was written 14 years ago. Since then it has been completely re-written more than twice, and they know it darn well. Why then this prejudgment on the basis of an ancient script? Especially when you remember that they raised no such objections back in the days when they expected to have a hand in doing the story on the stage. The theatre is indeed a worriation, but I'll be dog if I let it worry me.

I also recall that the highly moral Fredi once acted in a thing called *Black Boy* (and Lordy what a cheap tart she played!) and that Abe had a hand in *Anna Lucasta* whose heroine was less pure than Della (who is a one-man woman in our newest version). So let 'em keep on talkin'. Somebody'll answer 'em sooner or later, I reckon.

I don't know what Dick Campbell's article said, but I do know that they (he and Muriel) sought the Della role—and I mean SOUGHT. Or maybe it was the "other woman" role, but up to the time I left California, it was almost assumed that Muriel would be Lila. But maybe Dick is not one of the rock-throwers. I hope not.

Maybe I can get away from here on the 26th. That's my aim. . . . Include me with Amy Spingarn among those who did NOT hear from Mr. Asch re: a record album. But I know how that is. Doubleday messed me all up by not telling me which of those on my list they had sent books to. I hope Houghton Mifflin will do better with *We Have Tomorrow*—due early September.

Two magazine articles have just been ordered. Hope I can get them written. . . . Glad you colored up the story for *Story.* You should do more fiction. Also autobiography! . . . . . Please let me have anything more that breaks in the anti-ST. L W campaign. . . . . . Did I tell you that Marshall Field and the Rosenwald Fund are about ready to back a movie in a big way?

Ever,
Arna

Rainy Wednesday
22 Aug. '45

Dear Lang,

My sympathies to you in your sty misery—I used to have lots of 'em, and Poppy has one now (or something like it, her eye is giving her fits)—and I know

188

they are a botheration, but nothing like the Theatre! This theatre business is the stuff you gotta watch. But I am really tickled about Fredi's attack now that I've had time to think over it. If there is to be opposition to SLW on the grounds indicated by her article, I'm happy to have her as the spearhead. Countee's letter from her (a copy of which I have now received) will blunt that spear allright. And the others who may take their tip from her and follow in her wake will have to explain why they did not go to war against *Porgy*, etc. Actually, this new version of SLW, while still a folk tale, is certainly not to be classed with the anti-Negro stuff. Neither, in my opinion, is the book. It is all rhythm and color, of course, but nothing to low-rate a heads-up brown-skin on the Avenue. I even find that I have some strong favorable comments on it from people who are (or have recently been) most active in the left—this to take care of Fredi's brick about "Social" understanding.

If I can pick up a reservation this afternoon, I should be leaving here for N.Y. on the morning of the 27th, arriving at the Theresa (if they received my note) the following A.M. See you then, hunh? May stay around a week or more.

Carl Parrish, head of the music department here, wants to meet Negro musicians, critics, etc., in the hope of getting leads on talented younger people he can bring down here for the Annual Festival. He is especially anxious to meet Kenneth Spencer. And, of course, he will see Carlo. Maybe he should also meet Nora. If you run into any of these, will you drop the word—don't make a special effort to do so, of course.

I have a good story about the atom bomb that I think Simple would like to hear. Remind me.

See you directly.

> Ever,
> Arna

What shows shall we see?

> Fisk University Library
> Nashville 8, Tennessee
> 14 Sept. '45

Dear Lang,

Thanks for the clippings. . . . And did you see that Jane White has been signed for the role of Nonnie in *Strange Fruit?* I'm wondering what attitude Walter [White] will now take toward our Della in ST. L. W. He has written me a long letter (or sent me a copy of one he wrote to Countee) which is completely bewildering in the light of this new development. A poor yellow girl can't take an occasional present from a gentleman, but a Spelman girl can be a Nonnie. It's all quite wonderful. But the *Courier* spoke up for us in the Sept. 15 issue. Bless their hearts.

And Houghton Mifflin is talking about making a textbook of *We Have Tomorrow*—and soon. Which means, I suppose, that 8th grade kids will be using it as a reader or something in such schools as adopt it. I'm quite tickled about this idea. It is certainly an advance step for a big publisher of textbooks. Now if the white schools will use it as well as colored, we might get somewhere.

How many new lyrics did you do at the beach? And what changes did you make in our *Careless Love?* And what is the typing bill? . . . . Leslie Collins is here to take a post on the English faculty.

Everything under control on the homefront. But I'm finding it hard to get down to writing—too many library duties. And too few staff members on the job. . . . More anon. . . . . Thanks for all the gifts to the library.

Ever,
Arna

Tuesday

Dear Lang,

"Eight to Two" is certainly warm stuff. It should do much for the self-esteem of the returning GI. You do have great capacity for selecting arresting journalistic themes. Also subjects which will not make the senator from Mississippi happy. The two projected titles sound equally good.

Now what about "Careless Love"—or don't you think Walter [White] and Roy [Wilkins] would let us have it produced? Otherwise, this seems to be the time to get going on it.

Not only does Walter's opposition to *St. Louis Woman* seem strange in view of the Nonnie role for Jane, but the claque which you describe would seem to suggest that he and Roy have wearied of the fight against the Negro's enemies and turned their guns on their comrades. Maybe there is less peril in this.

Re: the Amsterdam story quoting Winchell (which I have not seen), I can now whisper to you that Lena has never at any time been signed up for the role of Della. Neither has she ever said that she would do the part. At least not to Gross. She may have discussed it with Metro, but I know nothing about that. When I was in California, Arlen was much opposed to building any show too much around any one star. My own attitude is that I like Lena as much or more than any star I have met and I recognize her great drawing power, but I don't think our show needs her now. We can find another pretty girl, and this controversy should take care of the box office for a while. In other words, if Lena rejects the role, that fact will cause almost as much curiosity as her presence in it. (This may not be the reasoning of Gross or Countee or the others.)

Did I tell you about the textbook edition of WHT? . . . . Getting big mail on this SLW mess.

Ever,
Arna

Tuesday

Dear Lang,

Here are some left-over clippings which I'm sure you have seen. Use these as you wish. Yale might want them if you can think of nobody else.

Did I tell you that my cousin Leslie Collins is here on the English faculty this year? Meant to. Publishers are asking for his doctor's dissertation which got so much attention (on Katherine, Paul and Marian), but he is waiting for a copy to come from the Western Reserve librarian (who is having it bound).

190

And a publication called *Plays: A Drama Magazine for Young People,* whose address is the same as the *Atlantic,* wants some one-act plays based on the stories in *We Have Tomorrow.* (Have you received your copy?) I can't do them. Would you like to oblige with a couple? Wide distribution assured. Everything from Scouts to Schools, dramatic clubs to camp groups. Don't tell this *unless* you feel like doing one or more because they may have other ideas in case I fail to arouse the interest of a sufficiently capable person.

Me, I'm gonna write a novel—dog if I ain't. All signed up. So if I can get the New Orleans play and the juvenile for Knopf out of the way, the way should be clear. In view of the above I have had to wire the Defender that I certainly can't start writing for them for a number of months at least.

I have no secretary at the moment. That's why you have not been thanked in rich and eloquent English for your most interesting contributions to the library. All received and treasured. The freshmen are here, the "crabs."

Ever,
Arna

634 St. Nicholas Avenue
New York 30, New York
September 29, 1945

Dear Arna:

I never did get my copy of "We Have Tomorrow." And even if I had it I do not believe that I could dramatize any of the stories this winter, since I shall have my hands full with the other show and with the lectures which have already been booked. The agreements for the show came through and I am supposed to have the first act finished by the end of October so that the composer can go to work on the music. Since it is really to be an opera (although they are calling it a music drama) that means that almost every line has to be put into libretto form, so it is quite a job. I have just been working on the opening chorus and I have just about got it finished. . . . . I greatly regret that you are not joining the estimable ensemble on the *Defender* this year. I am trying to find my contract now to see when it runs out. . . . . I am telling everybody that the heroine of your "St. Louis Woman" is not a prostitute at all but merely a good girl trying to get along in this world, even if she did not go to college like Nonnie in "Strange Fruit" and Lieutenant Brett Charles in "Deep Are the Roots." By the way Mr. and Mrs. Walter White were in the front row *center* at the opening of the latter the other night. Walter is forming a film committee to advise Hollywood and has asked me to be on it. I told him I would have to come to the *luncheon** they are having first.

Sincerely,
Lang

*Marshall Field

Saturday night

Dear Lang,

Here are the clippings back. Very interesting. Especially the wringing and twisting of the Southerners (Robert Garland and Burton Rascoe). They have certainly made me anxious to see *Deep Are the Roots,* and I hope they've put the same desire in all their readers. . . . Did you know that Sono Osato and her husband own a piece of the show?

Watts tells me he has signed Paul Bowles for the music of the New Orleans musical. Don't yet know what will finally be done about the lyrics. I was offered an opportunity to "try" my hand at some, but I can't work on speculation right now, so I passed it up. There will be only 4 lyrics in the show (it's mostly a dancing affair), and Watts will try to get a Guild dispensation to cut the share of the lyricist to something less than 1% of the gross. Don't know how he'll come out. . . . No hitch thus far in the plans for this opus, but L'Affaire de Dame St. Louis makes me think that all you have ever said about the theater is understatement. Maybe it isn't that the theater is evil but only that it brings out the evil in people.

But never no bad luck without some good: my new contract (novel) with Houghton Mifflin is killer, Jackson! I'll save the details till I see you. . . . Which reminds me that Miss Gladys English (in charge of branches in the L. A. Public Library system) wrote to praise *We Have Tomorrow** but ended up by wanting to know where and how *you* are, etc. I told her you're being booked now through this large bureau and that you might get as far west as the coast this winter. You ought to write her a card sometime. Perhaps this is a lead for your lecture agent.

"Simple" is better than ever in his remarks about his "Indian Blood". This one will make the Creoles love you. You know they think they don't have to talk about *their* Indian strain; they think it's too obvious to mention. Kinda like yours. More obvious than Simple's, but possibly less amusing.

See review of G. Brooks' poems in this month's *Phylon* and comparison with your work. Will make you feel good.

Any news from the Film Committee? I can't pump any out of Charles S.

> Ever,
> Arna

*Your copy arrive?

Tuesday night

Dear Lang,

The sin of St. Louis Woman was not that its Della did not get to Spelman or Fisk or Tuskegee so much as that Gross neglected to sign Walter White Jr. for the role of Lil Augie. Why didn't somebody think of that? I just thought of it after reading the piece in *Variety,* Sept. 19.

Didn't really think you'd have time to write the little one-acters for *Plays.* The suggestion represented a wish more than an expectation. Incidentally, the new fall announcement number of the Publishers' Weekly carries your lecture schedule along with others under the aegis of the same bureau. It leaves me puzzled as to where you will be at Xmas time. Do you know?

"Books" of the N. Y. Herald Trib has just sent me the 1,000 page book by Horace and Drake for review. So if I had nothing else to do, I could still keep busy for the next two weeks.

I have a copy of "Careless Love" but will have to dig for it. Will gladly suggest cuts if and when I come upon it. Meanwhile, I hope you will go ahead with the typing and send me my share of the charges. . . . What is Abe Hill thinking about when he tells the N. Y. Times (Sunday) that he's looking for a "different" folk play? Hasn't he seen ours? But maybe the Morton Gould lead is better. Let's try it anyhow.

Ever,
Arna

Friday

Dear Lang:

Your poem about united nations over the back fences is the kind of effortless, spontaneous, and stimulating thing on which your reputation rests. I have passed it on to the new class in creative writing (advanced composition) for class-room comment and discussion. It is so "different" it ought to provoke much talk. I liked it very, *very* much. But I thought the last line, the "you", should have been something like "yee-oo." Like a call to a neighbor to come to the fence. Maybe *you-hoo!*

All excited about Grace Johnson's gift to Yale: the total literary remains of JWJ. I'm burning to go up and plow through them.

I hope Walter is feeling exhilarated over his campaign to protect the American public from Della Green. He will HAVE to succeed because he will look awful foolish if the innocent little play ever actually opens. Theater-goers would then be able to analyze the motives behind the attacks.

Miss English says she is looking forward to hearing you on the coast.

Ever,
Arna

October 18
923 - 18th Avenue North

Dear Lang:

Thanks for the tip about the items by Dan Burley. I've just written to thank him, but I had to confess I have missed all three of the pieces you mention. Do you have them? Could you send me clips? We take the *Amsterdam,* but I didn't seem to latch onto the references. Maybe we get the wrong edition. Which reminds me, could you get me *copies* of the two (especially the most recent one) articles which *Variety* ran on the subject of Negro roles, etc., with special attention to the *St. Louis Woman* storm? The Courier quotes the most recent one this week, but I'd like very much to get copies (one or more) of the original pieces.

Did you see the *Afro*'s interview with Jane White? Whew! I wonder if Walter can swing the support of Negroes as a whole behind his personal scheme to censor the stage and screen now. How did the luncheon turn out?

Which down-town Cleveland hotel is courteous to Negroes? I believe you said you had stayed at one or another of them with success. I might be running up to see Paul in a few weeks or curving around that way while en route elsewhere, and I'd like to get a reservation in early.

Magnificent piece about the soldier in the south who needed a gun to go to the toilet! I get worried about your columns. They're so good that I fear they will give you so much satisfaction you won't care whether you get down to your novel or your autobiography or not. Other than that they're too good to be true.

Ever,
Arna

634 St. Nicholas Avenue
New York 30, New York
October 19, 1945.

Dear Arna,

The movie luncheon was interesting, everybody very strong for a bureau of *information* not censorship—and sure that the latter would only make the movie magnates mad and curtail what little Negro work there is now in Hollywood. No committee was formed there, only discussion.

I rode downtown with Walter and told him what I thought about their jumping on *St. Louis Woman.* The more I talked, the more I resented it, and when I looked at Walter he was red as a beet. Since there were other people in the cab, I perhaps should not have yowled so loud. He and Roy both seemed like they had rather not been in it now. I said *Porgy*'s interminable crap game ran for years and I never heard a word out of them. Roy said he did denounce it, but he was unknown in those days and nobody paid him any mind.

The other day after a conference at the Playwrights, I stopped by the movie committee office and—wonder of wonders!!—Owen was there for once—expecting Charlie Johnson. He showed me a couple of swell letters he had written, one to Lena Horne, the other to Gross. I asked him to give me carbons for you. I notice now that his secretary gave me two of Lena's and neglected to enclose the Gross one, but I am sure he'd send it to you if you want to see it. I enclose the Lena one.

Me, I am nowhere near ready to leave on tour next week, but I got to go. Still have the first main aria of SS to do, but have done about a dozen of the other lyrics so far and they like them. Weill is a swell guy to work with.

No, I'll be gone by the time you get to Chi, back in New York by then, in fact. Sorry. Look, I go to Dallas again in February! (Don't know why they want me back so soon.) Then up through Arkansas. Do you reckon Fisk or State would like to hear some poetries long about then, too? I will be fresh out of the West!

Harvey is wonderful! Be sure to see it next time you're here.

Owen showed me a new play by Robert Ardrey which Herman Shumlin is now casting. He says it's as good as *Roots,* also about a returned soldier. Gee, I wish some Negroes could cash in just a little bit on this Broadway vogue! *Amsterdam* reports Pearl Bailey for lead in your play. True? Anyhow, I HOPE it gets on soon. Montreal paper I saw gave *Strange Fruit* a good review, spite of fact it ran FOUR hours opening night! And Walter told me the preview was before an audience of wounded soldiers, many of whom must have been psychos because they hollered and laughed and threw spit-balls at the actors! (Nuts—or not?) Huh?

Lang

October 21, '45

Dear Lang,

I knew that sooner or later you'd get a chance to say your piece to the gentlemen who have undertaken to protect Broadway from Della Green. My thanks to you—and to Owen! Let's hope I get as good a chance to help you-all fight the wolves sometimes.

Jones is leaving Fisk at the end of this year. The news just broke. He will become president of Earlham College, Richmond, Indiana, beginning July 1, 1946. Complete surprise to everybody here.

Fisk and State should, as usual, be soft touches for your poetries. Of course, neither has a regular lyceum series or budget, but here is one tip: contact Dr. Harvey Curtis Webster, chairman of the program committee of the Humanities Institute (of which I'm leader this year) and let him know of your availability. My hand must NOT be seen in the operation. Dr. Poag might be a good one to write at State. And why not try Scarritt College (white) here, at which I have spoken once. Very liberal over there. Write Webster *soon!* He's working up his programs NOW. Maybe you could come back for Omegas if the other didn't work.

I'm now invited to D.C. the 24th. May dash there from Minneapolis (unless Owen comes to visit us from Pasadena). In such case might run up to N.Y. to see *Harvey* on your recommendation. All very vague and unsettled though.

More anon.

Ever,
Arna

En route to Marquette
October 27, 1945

Dear Arna,

Just passed Green Bay—home of the Packers. I have "Black Boy" with me and it is my determination to start it this time. . . . Seems like you asked me about a good hotel in Cleveland. It is the Hotel Cleveland—biggest and best—right next to Union Station. Don't even have to go outdoors. . . . What you going to do in Minneapolis? and in Washington—picket Bilbo? . . . . Pearl Bailey is a good-looker—chocolate brown—and very droll. I saw her at the Apollo. I think she would be good as S.L.W., if she also can emote a bit. . . . When did you say you'd be in New York? Write me to the Grand, Chi. . . . Phylon I told to get either you or Ralph Ellison to do a really serious article on Simple. Mine I sent you is purely subjective. I forgot a couple of things I shouldn't put in, too. . . . The trains are still running late, so give yourself plenty of leeway if you are travelling to an audience thirsting for your wisdom. . . . I forgot my fountain pen! . . . . Next weekend I shall spend with Vachel Lindsay's sister in Springfield. . . . Carlo is all excited about Mrs. J.W.J's gift. I have to do a column on it! . . . . Here is my

195

Xmas book column. Please note I give you a plug ((2)—NOT FREE!) You gimme one to the Def. as my contract is run out and I have writ for that raise! (It had been run out since July!!! I just found it by accident—looking for something else.)

Lang

P.S. Wait till you hear *Street Scene.* They are going to sing from low to high C!

Marquette—Sunday—Am having supper with Caroline Stone, who has a new kid's book just out. Going to the penitentiary now to see my life-termer.

923 - 18th Avenue North
Nashville 8, Tenn.
Halloween Eve '45

Dear Lang:

A band of ghosts has already been here, rattling bones and enjoying themselves in their devilish costumes, and the Nashville fire department seems to be going hogwild. The latter has been racing around with its siren open since night-fall. Me, I got to put the final touches on the first complete draft of the New Orleans musical show before morning, for I'm determined to get the thing in the mail tomorrow (November 1st). I'm tired of working on it now, and I want a change. Of course, I'm quite prepared for extensive revising before any curtain ever rises on the opus. . . . Did I tell you that Watts decided to follow his own hunch rather than mine about a lyricist and accordingly signed La Touch (Sp. ?), who has done several shows you know about. He says he had three reasons: 1) the fact that Touche is signed to do lyrics for the Duke Ellington show, which also has a Gulf-coast setting (pirates), and Watts thought this was a sure way to make certain the two did not lap over one another and come into competition; 2) the fact that our show uses only 4 lyrics and Watts wanted to get someone who would take less than the normal 2% under the circumstances, and he thought Touche would; 3) in addition to the above he thought Touche would have a strong feeling for the material and at least do a satisfactory job. That was his last to me. I expect to hear no more news of any kind till he receives my work. It is most interesting to see these producers "handling" their writers, etc., using psychology to keep the artists going. But it is a new experience to me to be the object consideration, as I have now been twice in a year. Well, by the time you receive this, I hope to be deep in that history of the Negro for Knopf's juvenile department.

The American Council of Teachers of English meets in Minneapolis the week of November 19. I'm invited as a member of their special committee on intercultural education. I'm wavering now in my intention, since there was something in their last letter that puzzles me; on their answer to my question will depend my final decision to go or not. The Washington invitation was from some "Co-Ordinating Committee for Building Better Race Relations." I'm thinking of backing water on this one too. I'm a little weary of these things. It would be a lot more fun to go to N. Y. and see some shows—or to Chicago. And more stimulating too.

Thanks, man, for the plugs in your Xmas book column. Right this minute I can't gracefully write the Defender in the interest of your raise (since I'm negotiating with them myself and they have used *you* as the main reason for wanting me to accept $25 per week), but I'll bide my time. When they raise *you*, then the stipend I'm asking will no longer be out of line with what they regard as their "rate." Of course, I'm told by others that Walter and Du Bois pull down $45 and $38 respectively—the littlest getting the mostest.

I don't think Pearl Bailey is under consideration for Della. In fact, I heard Gross had sent some Ruby Hill to Hollywood to be tested for the role, or rather inspected by the men who carry the money bag—Freed and Katz. They tell me almost nothing, but I am informed that Lem Ayres, the director, has arrived in New York and that Johnny Mercer and Harold Arlen were expected momentarily several days ago—and may be there now.

Will try the Hotel Cleveland first time I get up there.

Did you have your lecture bureau follow through on my suggestions for Nashville lectures? Why don't you just come here and rest between engagements anyhow—and lecture if anything develops between now and then?

Paul says his first impressions of Oberlin are all very fine.

Ever,
Arna

923 - 18th Avenue North
11 November '45
The day of the coronation of
Miss Fisk!

Dear Lang:

Back? How did they go, the lectures?

You certainly did your duty towards Simple in your absence. That piece on shouting was in the very best Simple-manner. Clap hands, church!

And what is the play by you that Abe's group is doing? Seems that the theatre has reached out and drawn you back—you who seemed for a time kind of fed up on its fantastic ways. My advice: don't give it all your heart. Play with it a little, even do a little work for it upon occasion, but regard it as a poker game, and invest no more in it than you can afford to lose—whether of time, money, or affection. Neither let it come between you and your more important work. On these terms it and I can get along. No others. 'Cause I'm told it broke the heart of many a po' boy, and I'm resolved it'll never break this'n o' mine.

The weather reports have about changed my mind for me about going to that Minneapolis meeting. I hear it's near-about zero up there. Unless I'm subjected to great persuasion, I intend to call it off in the next day or two. The D. C. jaunt is already off. Instead, I think I'll go up to Cleveland and Chicago if and as I feel like it, without responsibilities or committee work.

You'll like "Gumbo Ya-ya," the book I'm currently reviewing, "a collection of Louisiana folk tales." By Lyle Saxon et al. And do you know that Frank Yerby's forthcoming novel, "The Foxes of Harrow", is said to be under serious consideration by one of the book clubs? His sister-in-law works for us here in the library. He's another product of the Chicago writers' project. Seems like everybody *else* can find rainbow gold nowadays! Marion's AMA assignment has taken her as far as Florida, she says, and she'll eventually make a stop at Fisk.

Pearl Bailey will be Butterfly (a part I wrote in last summer when I was in the

197

West) in *St. Loo*. The Nicholas boys will be Lil Augie and Barney. Ruby Hill is signed for Della and June Hawkins for Lila (the other woman.). But Broadway won't see the show too soon. Rehearsals are now set for late December, with several months of the road to come before the N. Y. opening. This due to theatre shortage. For the same reason Watts is talking about a Chicago run of *Creole Square before* Broadway. And I don't see how that could happen before spring at the earliest.

This is the third day of continuous rain—gray and drippy, not silver and slanting.

Ever,
Arna

634 St. Nicholas Avenue
New York 30, New York
November 14, 1945.

Dear Arna:

I never was so glad to get back to New York before in my life! The Middle West raw, cold, and prejudiced, trains crowded and smoky and travel the worst I've seen it so far, soldiers going home and mad, and an air like pre-cyclone weather in Kansas used to feel, with open and under-cover gust of fascism blowing through forlorn streets in towns where desperate little groups of interracial Negroes and whites are struggling to keep things half way decent. . . . . Charles S. was at the Grand as usual (he ought to buy the joint) but seemed as sleepy and tired as I was, although we had a good visit. . . . . Me, I caught a bad cold mid way the tour, and only pulled through because I know the old routine by heart. Cold seemed to disappear the minute I got back to Penn Station! . . . . . Your *Herald Tribune* piece looked swell. . . . . Horace was in New York so I didn't see him. . . . . Had dinner with the *Negro Digest* Johnsons who have a big Packard, FINE apartment in house they have bought, over-crowded office so they're looking for a new and better one, business booming! . . . . . Got a ten dollar raise from my paper. Under threat of retiring altogether. They want you and Mrs. Bethune. . . . . Thanks for *Tomorrow*. Reckon I forgot to tell you Marion gave me a copy just before I left. . . . Did you EVER get your records? They swear they were finally sent! . . . . . Wish I had known where Paul was since I was nearby in Massillon. (Got your letter after I got back here yesterday.) I certainly would have called him. . . . . I guess *Phylon* is using the piece as they had wired *Defender* for permission to reprint some column or other with it. . . . . Do you not recall that Simple did go to Chicago once and spoke of how dark the bars are there? . . . . . Stop spelling Dr. Du Bois with an *e,* BOISE it is not! Did you see all the mistakes in name-spelling in Ben Richardson's note preceeding his piece on me in his new book? How can cullud be so careless? . . . . . A darling old lady of eighty tottered up to me at the Oak Park 20th Century Woman's Club and told me all about how her family had been active in the Underground Railway in Ohio in the old days, and how she remembered one slave they had saved at the risk of their lives by holding off the slavers with rifles. "But," she said, "don't you know, he wasn't worth saving! He had the nicest little wife, and he just beat her all the time!" . . . . Which probably is what helped to give me the cold. I never had thought

before that escaped slaves were other than heroic and noble! Had you? . . . . . .
Had a nice note from Marion in Ocala, Florida—Zora's country. . . . . . YOU are
telling *me* about the theatre!?!? . . . . HUH? . . . . . I have bought two fine suits
with the *Street Scene* check and intend to see some fine shows, and it do not worry
my mind! I have wished Mr. Stokowski well on his South American honeymoon,
and the American Negro Theatre which was to have opened with my *Joy to My
Soul* but have now put it last for spring, do not worry my mind neither. Cullud,
white, amateur, professional—all samee—nothing ever as is swore will be! SKY-
LOFT in Chi split in two groups—each with big posters out all over town about
their coming season. Bob Lucas won their contest with a very good war play in
one act that I helped judge. . . . . Front of Theresa is all scorched like top of
Empire State Building. Beautiful lady who jumped out window nude was well
known matron from up Yonkers way in bed with playboy when their mattress
caught on fire. They say she could have escaped in hall but couldn't find her
clothes, so she jumped to her death instead. Too much modesty does not make
sense in cases of emergency like that! The playboy just walked on down the hall
as he was! . . . . . I gave *They Seek a City* a plug in several of my talks when I
speak of urban conditions and trials and tribulations. . . . . Josh White is using
my "Crazy Hat" song at Cafe Society. Golden Gates plan to record it soon, I hear.
. . . . . You had better stop reviewing all those books and get down to your WORK.
(I am just mad because I can't even read anything, let alone review it.) I had to
turn down doing a piece for the Christmas issue *Chicago Sun*. . . . . I am getting
a new said-to-be-very-good-secretary (half day every day till I go to Coast in
January) starting this week—fellow who is studying for MA at NYU. . . . . My
agreement for Atlanta for next fall, half year, came through at rate I told you.
. . . . I find a whole basket full of books here on my return—including *two* of
Horaces big volumes which looks most imposing. . . . . . *Carmen* and *Anna* both
are making a mint of money in Chicago, so the road is not a bad idea for both
your shows long about now. Another road company of *Anna* as well as a London
one are said to be casting. Looks like all actors will work for a while, which is
good. . . . . Now if Negro playwrights can just get started! . . . . . Give my best
to Alberta and tell her maybe I will get by that way sometime during the winter.
I'm booked for Mississippi in mid-February. I don't know yet which college that
December War Bond rally will take Mark Van Doren and I to. Wish it would
be yours.

                              Sincerely,
                              Langston

                              923 - 18th Avenue North
                              Nashville, Tenn.
                              11-19-45

Dear Lang,
    It goes without saying that when I run off to you about the theatre, I'm just
talking to hear myself talk, and thereby lecturing myself. Can't afford to start
taking that mess seriously, you know. The sheer hysteria of it is beyond all belief.
Everything is either wildly wonderful or so bad it's an insult. Everybody connected with the business lives by waves of high enthusiasm, going up and coming

down with clock-like regularity. If a scene is a shade off, needing only a few revisions, it is "pure phony." If it rings a bell, as any normal scene should, it is the best thing since Ibsen. . . . Maybe that's why Mencken said that the theatre rots the brains. Me, I got no business fooling with it, and I'm aiming to quit soon's I can get my hand out of the bear's mouth. I'm tired of *Creole* already, and the struggle has only begun, with fall or winter of '46 suggested as an opening date to aim at. Think I'll put my foot down and tell the guy that if he wants to pull and tug over the comas and semi-colons, he can do it himself. Meanwhile I'll try to write a sure-'nough novel.

Don't you remember I told you that the record album came ages ago addressed to 5th University, etc.? Also the one of which I made a gift and for which I paid when I was in N. Y.

Start dusting off a chair for me at ASCAP. My first song just came through, a poem called "Idolatry," set by Still. A very impressive job for the more profound music lovers. I hear there are some more to come, by him as well as a few others, but none will be recorded or make the hit parade, I assure you. Writing songs is something I'd like to do more often—could I but find the words.

Congratulations to you for signing up with Atlanta. That ought to be a good arrangement—teach a semester, write and lecture one, then vacation during the summer! And you still won't have to stay in one place long enough, as you have said, for things to begin to get complicated.

Your getting a raise at the Defender sort of clears the way for them to give me what I asked—which, I take it, is about $5 less. Of course, it will be quite all right if they decide otherwise, for I have enough to do as things stand. Almost too much, counting the book reviews.

Irma Cayton—was here yesterday, drove through in a fine new Buick, she and another Wac. The other girl plans to attend Fisk after she gets out of the army, and Irma says *she's* already out, though she still wears the uniform and is now en route back to Huachuca (?). Frank Yerby's mother was here too, saying that her boy's novel has been bought by the Dollar Book Club. And Leslie's aunt and foster mother (she was my mother's girlhood chum and cousin) is also here, spending a few weeks. And Owen is expected before you receive this—a quick stop. And Paul says he likes Oberlin, but you frighten me off visiting him with your tales of travel discomforts, etc.

Ever,
Arna

Dear Arna,
It'll be about February 19th now as the last Mississippi date is February 18th in the town where Hugh Gloster got his haid beat. . . . I shall see the preview of *Strange Fruit* tomorrow night and inform you thereon. . . . . I just finished another ARIA. And they are getting a guy from the Met for the lead! . . . . . If travel you must this year, do it by plane. Jimmy Davis, out of the army, is flying to Hollywood tomorrow—just for fun. . . . . Frances had her farewell party in the Bronx last night. WAVES have to move out to make way for soldier-civilian families. . . . . I bet you have not read nary word of *Jack* yet! Me, neither! So I just better have it typed as is. . . . . My brother is sick in the hospital. Run DOWN! Young folks have so little stamina these

200

days. Suppose they had to make their living out of LITERATURE! . . . . . I have sold a picture idea to *Ebony* for a series. . . . And I do believe my eight columns have run out! Must do a few more.

Sincerely,
Lang

NOVEMBER 26, The day Miss Scott appeared in Carnegie Hall—her last prenatal concert, 'tis said. (An heir or -ess is coming.)

Arna,

Well, they are practically all morons in SF [Strange Fruit], so instead of being a moving tragedy, it affects me like *Of Mice and Men* did—about a hero and heroine both without much sense. Nobody makes any real effort to solve anything, get away from trouble, or DO anything. *Tobacco Road* they at least had fun being morons, but these folks don't, so it makes for too long an evening, and I felt like I did in Marion, Indiana, recently when I went to read some poems at a military hospital for the pathologically off. But there it didn't cost me $4.40, and I didn't have to stay all night. Nonnie is an inane little dolt played with so much restraint that she ain't. I think the hero is suffering from battle fatigue—although it is not said whether he was in this war or not. When Ed shot him, he should also have slapped Nonnie down! It's sad, man. *Roots* much better racially and theatrically, I think. . . . . I saw Izzy Rowe there and congratulated her on SLW columns.

Lang

923 - 18th Avenue North
Twelve-four-forty-five

Dear Lang,

Here is what:

The dean of the chapel, Mr. Faulkner, is working on the project to bring you to Fisk. He is in touch with your lecture bureau and may have completed negotiations by now. According to the tentative plan, you will arrive in Nashville at 2 o'clock P.M. on the 20th of February. You will speak to the chapel audience (same one you addressed before) at 4 P.M. At about 6 you will be dined by the Humanities Institute group—of which I'm the chairman. At 8 o'clock (if this part is worked out) you may address the A & I State College student body and faculty in their auditorium. From then on your time will be your own—and ours, no doubt.

But that's months away. In the meantime I'm likely to see you in Harlem (you and Simple) next week, about the 13th or 14th of December, if all goes according to plan. Our sub-committee on Owen's documentary is called to meet on the 16th and 17th, and I'll try to get there somewhat early. Back to the Theresa as usual for me—but don't announce it. I won't have time for getting around much.

Rehearsals for *St. Loo* are called for January. You be there then?

Thanks for the reports on *Fruit,* yours and P. M.'s, which were about the same estimate in each case. Perhaps the wide popularity of the book will carry the show at the box office not-withstanding.

My other show, *Creole,* is in the agony stage, the this and that stage, the more here and less there stage, the bubble blowing and bubble bursting stage, the merry-go-round (without jim crow) stage. Of course I'm not worrying—gray hair just runs in our family.

You look good in Ben Richardson's book—which just arrived and which I haven't yet read (though I will soon, of course). Also in The Fireside Book of Christmas Stories, you look good. That one I do not promise to read in full. . . . Have you seen how I look in Under the Stars and Stripes? . . . . I missed getting my piece to Book Week (Chicago Sun) in time for the Xmas number too. Also the one requested by the Chicago Tribune. A good New Year's resolution for us both: no peanuts during 1946—shoot at the big stuff. In other words, one or two major jobs; resist all else.

Ever,
Arna

634 St. Nicholas Avenue
New York 30, New York
January 2, 1946

Dear Arna,

Please do me a favor and tell Charles S. [Johnson] (or whoever is in charge of his inaugural invites) that Lynchburg College, Lynchburg, Virginia, will surely send a representative if they receive an invite. The sociologist there, Dr. Gordon Lovejoy, who is a great admirer of Dr. Johnson's, told me this, and says he hopes they are invited. . . . . . I was the first colored assembly speaker down there, as I reckon I wrote you—and talk about southern white folks being POLITE and Mister-ing me all over the place, and luncheoning me in the campus dining room, etc! Perfect ladies and gentlemen! . . . . . . Well, the show is making its last changes tomorrow, Thursday, before New York. Still slow in spots, and needs further cutting to my mind, but neither book nor music will give in another notch. Moss Hart, Marc Connelly and Arthur Hammerstein have all had their say—former two feeling that there was too much "musical comedy" in it—which caused Juanita to lose her most effective moment when the "Wrapped in a Ribbon" number had all the dancers and extra people cut out today. (Plus ANOTHER new lyric!). . . . . New leading man, Joe Sullivan, out of *Show Boat* is swell, and gives whole show a big lift. Leading lady (a North Carolina Hollywood glamour gal) still looks like a junior Mae West instead of ROSE of the tenements—but I reckon that can't be helped. She talks like Mae, too—and says bad words in the middle of rehearsal—which so shocked Mr. Wiman that he refused to give her the curtain call a leading lady feels entitled to—so she comes on with FOUR others now! White folks is something! . . . . . . Me, I've had very little work to do here, so I have rather enjoyed Philly—and the Chesterfield. . . . . Loved your kids book! Merci! . . . . . Also delighted at the cullud history's dedication. . . . . I'm struggling with tour tickets. Have to leave Manhattan the 13th for the Mid-West. . . . . . Show biz is falling off by the hour here and in New York. *Dream Girl* is probably cancelling its road tour on that account. Worst holiday week ever in Philly, so they say. I guess the price of meat don't leave much for shows in folks' pockets. Or else the new depression is here. Just MY luck, huh! . . . . . The Lord does not intend for me ever to roll in even pocket change! . . . . . Snow and slush here for New Year's—looks a little like winter at last! . . . . . Saw Louis a couple of times. His show is all set for New York, too.

Sincerely,
Langston

In Flight
On the mainliner
L.A. to Del Monte
January 14, 1946

Dear Arna,

What happened to Countee [Cullen]? Everyone in L.A. was shocked at the news. No details have reached here as yet. I just learned it Sunday morning. I read a memorial poem for him on the air, and spoke of him at my program in the afternoon. I'm headed back to Hollow Hills Farm, Monterey, to be there until the 21st. If you don't get this in time, airmail me to the Urban League, c/o Berry, Portland, Oregon, where I'll be on the 24th.

Vivian had a FINE party for me at the Temple's, so I had a chance to see Dr. Ruth. All send regards to you, especially the grandmother. Very sweet people!

All in L.A. are fine. Loren and Juanita have a new baby boy. Bowen Memorial turned a hundred or two away at my program yesterday. Allied Arts cleared almost a thousand on theirs. Think I'll *raise* my fees next season.

Write!

Langston

On tour,
Cedar City, Utah
January 28, 1946

Dear Arna,

I'm way down here in the Southwest corner of Utah! Not a Negro in town! And it seems I am the first Negro (and the first poet) to grace the Branch Agricultural College Lyceum Series here. This is the fantastically colorful Brice Canyon region where lots of the Western movies are made. Wonderful dry clear weather.

Thanks for writing me all about the funeral.

And I'm delighted rehearsals are going so well. When and where does it open?

Wonder if you'll be in Nashville when I come? Due to arrive *about 3:30 or 4 Tuesday afternoon, Feb. 14, on American Air Lines—the flight that leaves Memphis at 2:48 P.M.* Unless someone meets me at the airport will take airport bus or taxi into town. Flying really is the nicest way to get around. And easier to get tickets. *I'll have to leave you all at 1:28 P.M. Thursday, the 21, same airline to New York.* Kurt Weill writes me the movies probably will back our show, and to hurry back as he is composing up a breeze and has over half the first act done.

Write (if you've time) to any of the stops underlined in red.

                                                                    Lang

                                                    New York,
                                                    4/23/46

My dear fellow,
   There is always something to keep people from getting their money from shows. But re the Street Scene contract, Max told me ALL travelling expenses regarding work on a show were to be paid by the producer, and not deductible from royalties—according to the Dramatist Guild agreement. . . . . . The show must be doing O.K. I keep seeing nice big ads in the papers, and "Come Rain Come Shine" is frequently heard over the air. All cullud I have seen LIKE the show, our press not withstanding. . . . . Marion has been after me about another book idea she has—but with Aunt Toy gone and nary phone ring answered I am safely secluded in the "country" just up the street at my studio and can't nary human reach me a-tall! With Paramount about to buy SS I cannot be worried with anything else. (At least it looks so. Mamoulian told them it was the finest musical score and lyrics since *Show Boat.*). . . . . I haven't been able to get anear the Martin Beck to see your folks, being deep in my second act. Got to go to Springfield this week-end, then Cleveland in early May, after which I hope trust and pray my travelling will be over for the season! I will not lecture another lecture till 1947. . . . . Aunt Toy is at the Vincennes with Emerson. Give her a ring. She's Cal. bound for a vacation. . . . . Tell Horace HELLO . . . . . Reynal and Hitchcock, who took that Haitian novel I'm to polish up, tell me the chapters they've seen of Ralph Ellison's novel in progress are FINE—if that will help him get a Rosenwald renewal which I believe he has applied for. . . . . . If you are in New York May 17th, drop around to the American Academy and see me and Ethel Barrymore get our blue ribbons. I've put you on the invite list. (Not for public announcement yet—till press releases are out—so don't tell nobody.). . . . . . I HAVE GOT TO WRITE MY COLUMN *RIGHT NOW*! . . . . . . Do not lean your haid on Horace's walls, says Simple. (See current issue—if it got there on time. I forgot I had run out last week.). . . . . . If you are writing that piece on me for *Ebony* you can mention Street Scene, also by that time, American Academy, too, would be O.K. Also that I have lectured more lectures this season than any other living Negro of mixed blood. (*One* great grandpa was Jewish.)

                                                    Sincerely,
                                                    Langston

                                                    April 30, 1946

Dear Lang:
   Just a quickie to raise two or three small questions in connection with the article I am writing this week about you for *Ebony.*
   1. Which is the exact title and description of the citation and honor which you

are about to receive from the American Academy—also the full and exact name of the Academy?

2. Can you estimate the number of lectures you have made this year? The number in your whole career? The number of people to whom you lecture in a big year and in an average year? The total number to whom you have given your lecture readings in your life-time as a poet? I would just like to play with these figures in some sort of way. Any other estimates involving dramatic numbers would come in handy. I still don't know what I'll do with them, but I have a vague impression that something interesting might be possible.

3. Will you jot down a quick list of novelties and interesting and important items which might otherwise be neglected or forgotten by me. You know I am doing this strictly off the top of my head—no notes, no nothing.

Please rush this data to my house number via airmail special.

More anon.

> Ever,
> Arna
> 923 - 18th Avenue, North

> 634 St. Nicholas Avenue
> New York 30, New York
> May 2, 1946.

Dear Arna,

How was Chicago and did you get my letter there? Glad Palfi got a Rosenwald. She has run me down to the ground about that book she wants to do with me! She intends going to California so will be there when YOU get there. (Like Marion Oswald whom I thought I had escaped a few years ago when I went Westward —but no sooner had I got to Hollywood than she too called up from one of them hilltops and said, "C'est Marianne!")

Dick Wright and wife and also child have gone to Paris.

Now as to your piece on me. You should have an invite by now. It is an "Arts and Letters Grant" from The American Academy of Arts and Letters—One Thousand Dollars. (Cash.)

2. 15 lectures in fall, and 40 since New Years, not counting freebies—I'd say about 75 all told this season including the schools they drug me by against my will sleepy and just off the train. My first was in Washington in 1924, so in 22 years I'd estimate from Mississippi to Moscow and Chicago to Shanghai well over a thousand public appearances reading my poems. There are seldom less than a hundred people in an audience, average I'd say five hundred, often a thousand, and high school or college assemblies frequently 2 to 3 thousand, so I'd say at least 500,000 or a half million folks have heard me read *Rivers* myself in person. (Although I doubt if the Chinese understood it.)

Six cross country tours, and up and down and back between times, so probably have travelled at least 100,000 miles in this country alone. Recent cross country tour as you know entirely by air.

More Negro audiences and sponsors in America than white, but white sponsors growing all the time. This season from Town Hall, New York, to Parent-Teachers Association (colored) Tupelo, Mississippi, fashionable Oak Park Nineteenth Century Women's Club to Colored Community Center, Anderson, Indiana, the University of Colorado to Lanier High School, Jackson, Mississippi, the sixth grades assembly of Kalamazoo, Michigan to the Brooklyn Academy of Arts and Sciences—all within a year. And reading the *same* poems from kids on up to whoever goes to Town Hall or Brooklyn at 11 A.M., same poems in Mississippi as in Boston, to colored or white or mixed—which proves something or other!

3. Translated into Uzbek among other languages. . . . . . Singers of my songs range from Lawrence Tibbett to Josh White, Marian Anderson to Marion Oswald. . . . . I get two sets of fan letters, some to me, some to Simple. . . . . Hobbies: Collecting House Rent Party cards and attending Gospel Song Battles. . . . . . In only one railroad wreck in all my travels. Got an overcoat out of that, and nary a scratch. . . . . Sometimes sleep 15 hours at a time. . . . Lately (more and more) am invited to deliver the Sunday morning message at churches (Paid). Recently Community Church of Boston and Unity Church, Unitarian, of Montclair, N. J. . . . . Did Tour USO's and army camps during war. . . . . Enormous fan mail from soldiers overseas re Defender column and Bedside Esquire story, "A Good Job Gone" which by the way brought Esquire its largest mail in pre-publication controversy. . . . . . Have only received one threatening communication—about ten years ago from Ku Klux Klan. . . . . As you know, have no mechanical sense. Took me eight years to learn to close vegetable bin in Aunt Toy's kitchen. Never turn on right burner on a gas stove. Still can't close a folding table (much). . . . . . Have a long head, but just recently learned I should always buy an oval shaped hat. Even then they get out of shape quick. . . . . Give away as many books as I sell. All of my books (except *Fine Clothes*) still in print. *Weary Blues* never out of print in twenty years. . . . . . . Try to answer every letter I receive at least once, but in recent years unable to keep up steady correspondences. (Haven't yet read all the mail that accumulated during my recent winter tour—a suitcase full still unread. Have only *part time* secretary—but two portable typewriters—one of which has been around the world with me and is over twenty years old. . . . Like to eat. Gain weight on tour from the good dinners folks fix. . . . . Get sick if get mad. . . . Have several hundred unpublished poems as far as book form goes. . . . . Read slowly. . . . . Read books I like over and over, but don't read many new ones. . . . . Never had a thousand dollars all at once until I was forty. Haven't had two thousand dollars all at once yet. . . . . . Pay bills promptly. . . . . Arrested once in Cuba for defying Jim Crow at Havana Beach. Put out of Japan for visiting Madame Sun Yat Sen in China . . . . . Picketed by Gerald L. K. Smith's Mothers of America at Wayne College in Detroit . . . . . By Aimee Semple McPherson in Pasadena. Never sued. . . . . Never married, but once reported engaged to Elsie Roxborough in public press (niece Joe's manager) . . . . . . Friends include Mrs. Bethune and Bricktop, Diego Rivera and Bootsie's creator, Ollie Harrington, Paul Robeson and Willie Bryant, Still and Duke, Margot and Butterbeans and Susie, Hemingway and Roy Wilkins! . . . . Hey, now! . . . . . Love kids. . . . . . Love dogs. . . . . Hate parsnips, narrative poems, bridge, breakfast invitations, Jim Crow cars, and people who recite poetry in a far-away voice . . . . . Also "Trees" sung just before I am introduced. . . . . Chain smoker. . . . . Height of ambition to live in Arizona. Love that there sun. . . . . Also to have plenty time to just stand on the street and loaf like street corner colored do. . . . . Also to have enough wall space to

hang all the pictures and paintings friends give me. . . . . . And shelves to pile the records I own. . . . And time to write another novel.

C'est tout.

Josh Logan (Director *Annie Get Your Gun*) told Kurt Weill your show is wonderful. (I told him, too.)

Sincerely,
Langston

923 - 18th Avenue North
6 May '46

Dear Lang:

Thanks for all that data for the biographical article. Now I am loaded, and my aim is to have the manuscript in the mail this coming week. A copy will, of course, go to you at the same time.

You might telephone Leah Salisbury's office if you get a chance. She has just asked me for your number, so if you don't hear from her, it may be because nobody was home when she called.

Don't you think you and I are the ones to write book and lyrics for that Latin American show Gross is planning for Carmen Miranda? Leah might be in a position to propose it—if you are interested, and if Gross hasn't already made other arrangements.

I don't believe I told you why that girl you recommended for a Rosenwald Fellowship didn't come through—the one who planned a book about Mme Walker & the tribe of beauty preparations women which she headed. Well, the gal did not send in a single specimen of her writing. Since neither you nor I nor Dick nor Buck Moon nor Tom Sancton could get one without at least making that gesture, they probably thought that neither should she. Of course, I can't guarantee that everyone would have been moved by her writing had they seen it, but I'm inclined to think that they would at least have given her more serious consideration. As it was, Willard Motley and Myron O'Higgins got the creative writing awards. Both very promising fellows, I think.

Lucky Dick. Is it now easy to get passports to visit Europe, or is Dick's mission important?

Why don't you talk up another meeting of the Film Committee with Owen so that I'll have an excuse to get back to New York?

On second thought, I'm not so sure I'll try to go to California for the summer. Perhaps the fact that I've been unable to get promise of a car has something to do with the decision, but I'm now wondering how it will be to take a bridge table and my typewriter to the basement here, come the hot days, and see if I can't knock out a writing job of some kind between June and September. . . . Horace will be at Yaddo, you know.

Chicago was fine, but I was much too busy during my stay. No time to get around much, but I did run into Marcella and her new husband, and I also saw George Martin (Our Vines Have Tender Grapes) and Jack Conroy and Bob Davis and the Rosenwald bunch and a few others of the same crowd. All by accident,

207

or mostly so. . . . Alta is here for a couple of weeks to recover from her operation. . . . Patricia Johnson-Clifford has a young son (last night), so Chas. S. is now a grandpa. More anon.

Ever,
Arna

Expect to get my *first* royalty check this week!

Dear Lang:

Tell me more about your conversation with Leah. . . . . If she has a good deal on tap, of course, we need not let it fall because you are involved with SS till August. Just say that I can get going but that you won't be able to give FULL time to it till August at least as a result of the other work. Of course, I have at least two jobs pending: the creole play and the novel. I'm driving to finish the former early in June. On the latter I have no deadline, but I'll aim to cut a big dent in it between June and the end of September—unless Leah comes up with something very, very attractive for us to do in collaboration. Say, for example, a script for Carmen Miranda! In which case I'm sure I'd be induced to put the novel on the shelf for a few more weeks. Remember in talking with her that what we'd like best to do would be to get a contract to collaborate on *both* book *and* lyrics. More money, of course, but more important still, I think it would give us a chance to integrate words of story and song—which is the best feature of *Carousel.*

First post-production check for *St. Loo* came through at last. Looks like they will average between four and five centuries a week for me—after all the cuts, divisions and subdivisions—provided we continue, as now, to do better than thirty grand per week at the box office. A good chunk of the first month's royalties however is being held pending arbitration of the question of taking my and Countee's traveling expenses out of royalty. Then, too, our advances, $100 a month for six months, then later $150 per month, had amounted to just under two grand. So I am not yet rich, though everybody seems to imagine that I am. All the *de ducks* are clear now, thank God, and if the show will only keep up as heretofore, we may gradually collect our wages.

Did you see Richard Watts vs critics and pro us in GO? Also a spread in *Stage Pictorial,* which I heard about but have not seen. Of course you've heard that the Rahn vs Ingram and Nicholas case was settled before Equity with love and kisses. But Handy is still trying to get somebody to pay off for calling the show *St. Louis Woman.*

My piece on you is nearly done. I'd have had it to you by now except that our house is torn up by paper hangers, etc., which always upsets my work as well as my mind. Soon though! Meanwhile, I'm fixing a place in the basement for summer writing—a cool spot—and I'm making it big enough to accommodate you too if you feel inclined to come down for a spell or if we get into a collaboration.

Have you been around to say howdy to the cast for me yet? Horace will be there for the show the night of May 18th. I've asked Gwen Clare Hale to greet him and introduce him to the members of the cast who interest him. If you go back stage that night, you'll see him and his five guests.

What has developed with SS? Any more data on production plans? How far along is your work?

Ever,
Arna

Fourth of July '46

Dear Lang:

The report I get is that Gross has suddenly decided to close the show. If true, the reason may be traced in part to the old feud between himself and his backers, for box office business is still adequate, I believe, for the season. But I promised you long ago that I wouldn't let the theatre worry my head, and it ain't! If the thing should close Saturday, there would remain the possibilities of a road tour and a movie deal. If neither of these should materialize, the earnings to date will put a couple of kids through college, so me—I'm not giving it a second thought. I'm writing a NOVEL, and Paul's helping me do that juvenile history of the Negro for Knopf. And with my left hand I'm putting the finishing touches on that New Orleans play.

The Third Annual Institute of Race Relations is roaring down in the Social Science Department with important new speakers being trotted out nearly every day and the Nashville papers giving their shocking statements front-page attention on some days. Embree twisted the tiger's tail as usual. . . . Between 150 and 200 people from all over the U. S. are here, representing race relations programs of churches, labor unions, school systems, civic committees, etc. . . . Since I can neither abandon the library nor discontinue my little writing program, I get to only the open sessions at night to which the whole public is invited.

Joan is enjoying McGill and the French House there very much, and Paul seems just as happy to be home again. In fact, he is listening without hostility to his old friends now at Fisk who have been trying to influence him to stay here this year. I think he's about convinced that the kids here have more fun.

Ben Burns compliments the article about you for *Ebony* but doesn't say when it will run. . . . The Record Album, mailed by Nate with such care, arrived—with every record broken to smithereens. I was especially sorry to see Nate's good work brought to naught like that, but all I can figure is that somewhere along the way the parcel must have been dropped out of a high window by the postal authorities, for it must have taken a real effort to accomplish what they did—with a package so well-packed.

It's been at least ten degrees hotter than hell down here for the past week, but there's been a beautiful rain all day today, and I've written a string of about six typed pages—a very good day for me. . . . Be sure to read interesting piece about Robert Morse Lovett in this month's (July) *Harper's* Magazine.

Ever,
Arna

634 St. Nicholas Avenue
New York 30, New York
July 20, 1946

Dear Arna:

I was certainly sorry to hear that your records were broken when they arrived, but I will order another album to be sent to you directly from the shop, in case you cannot get another one there. They still have beautiful displays of them in several of the downtown windows, and one Harlem shop has an enormous poster about five feet tall with pictures from the show on it.

I would be happy to get some theatre tickets for Joan if you will indicate to me what shows she might like and what price seats to secure, and also the date. During this hot weather it seems as if you can get tickets to almost any show without difficulty, although I haven't seen any myself since we have been having production conferences almost every day on *Street Scene*, Rice, Weill, Friedman and I whipping the script into final shape. Practically every line in every lyric has been changed since you were here, several brand new songs have been inserted, and the poor Negro has been cut down to one song, which is not any of the three which he had before, this one being somewhat more in the tradition of Broadway shows. The only way for colored to do much down on that street without outside influences diluting their product will be for the race to open a theatre of its own. (Then, being colored, I reckon they would put on things like *Juno and the Paycock, Angel Street,* and *You Can't Take It With You* which make up the American Negro Theatre's summer bill—not a single play by or about the race! No wonder the Lord made their haids nappy.)

Please kiss Poppy for me and tell her not to run into any poison ivy the next time she goes out with the Girl Scouts, because that is worse than too much sunshine.

Read about Simple and the snake in next week's *Defender*. Part of it really happened to me up at Kurt Weill's place last week-end. And across the road from him they killed two copperheads. (I am sending you a copy of the column in case you cannot wait for it to come out.). . . . I can hardly wait for the October *Ebony*. Tell them to send us proofs. . . . . If I wrote six pages a day I would have a book in no time. You are one of the most solid authors. How much do you weigh? 200 —and what?

Sincerely,
Lang

923 - 18th Avenue, North
Nashville 8, Tenn.
8-9-'46

Dear Lang:

An hour or two ago I wired you for the Dean of the college to learn, if possible, more about the qualifications, personal and academic and literary, of one Robert Hayden, currently being considered for one of the one-year vacancies now open in the English Department at Fisk. Hope you had some information to contribute —since you may have met the fellow on your travels through Michigan. Anyhow, muchas gracias.

And muchas gracias for the beautiful job you did on tickets for Joan and party. I'm sure they'll be delighted.

Now about us—are we going to see Ray Robinson fight for that championship early in September? If you'll get a ticket for me, I'll be most obliged, and I'll square with you for same upon my arrival at the Theresa about September 3rd. I've never seen Sugar Ray inside a ring. And me here talking about writing a prizefight novel!

Don't tell me you have re-written your play again, because if you do, you will have approached the record we made on *St. Loo*. That's what I don't like about the theatre. . . . the squirrel-in-a-cage stuff. Too much round and round. So I'm pulling for you to come through that phase. Of course, where it provides you with a chance to get up to the region of Bear Mountain when Manhattan is sweltering, perhaps there is compensation enough.

Leslie Collins is at the Theresa currently, for a stay of a week or two. Call him if you get a chance. I think he would like a chance to Meet Carl VV if possible.

We (the proprietors of *St. Loo*) are now being sued by Lucky Roberts AND Handy. Excitement is always lurking behind the hedges. Somebody always ready to take your lollypop.

Just got around to reading Carson McCullers *Ballad of the Sad Cafe*. What a mad genius that gal is! I never quite knew whether to laugh or cry about that hunchback. I intend to call the attention of all the budding campus writers to the story.

One of the three writing jobs on my agenda is complete: the doubtful one— the play. Now I'm well into the second: the juvenile for Knopf. When I reduce my jobs to one, I'll feel like a youth again—not an old man bowed with care. . . . *Ebony* paid $40 for that article about you. Colored are improving. Or maybe it's just you whose value is increasing!

I weighed 188 today—which means I've worked off exactly 12 pounds at the typewriter this summer. Meanwhile Paul's come up to 192, an increase of exactly 12 since he returned home. Which only goes to show how much more strenuous typewriting is than swimming and tennis and touch football—his chief occupations. This is the first time he ever weighed more than me!

Ever,
Arna

923 - 18th Avenue, North
Nashville 8, Tenn.
8-26-'46

Dear Lang:

Didn't realize I hadn't told you: Joan and Jo-jo arrived with high spirits and neither one air-sick. In fact, we notice only two immediate results of Joan's [B's Daughter] trip: 1) Montreal is good for her complexion and 2) Her summer travels have left her with a strong urge for more adventures of the same sort. Mexico, Cuba or France. Mostly places to which I have NOT been.

Owen's [Dodson] book is very good—his poems as a whole make a stronger impression than did the isolated ones I had seen in magazines. In fact, I think his work is more in the mood of "the awakening" than is any by the other poets that have appeared since. With Owen, Margaret [Walker], Gwendolyn [Brooks] and [Melvin] Tolson published and [Robert] Hayden, [M. Carl] Holman [poets] and [Myron] O'Higgins on the verge, it would seem to be time for another big anthology of Negro poetry. Why don't you (or one of your associates) ask Viking Press to have ME collect one for their PORTABLE series of books. I'd like to do it, but I'd rather not raise the question. The Portable series already has an Irish anthology. I believe that a Negro poetry (there has recently been a prose anthology or two) collection would do better in this series than published by another publisher as an independent item, but I may be wrong.

I'm leaving here tomorrow night (Tuesday) for a few days in Detroit's Gotham Hotel—till Sept. 2nd. Then on to the Theresa, arriving the 3rd. Speaking in Detroit on 29th at a little church affair in honor of its returned vets. . . . Thanks for the dope on Hayden, who may be coming this way for a year at least. . . . I'll have to tell you about the Great Defalcation when I see you.

Ever,
Arna

Just saw the review of the selected Whitman in *Books.* You didn't tell me about this—unless it's the same one you showed to Doubleday. Anyhow, we'll have to order for Library.

634 St. Nicholas Avenue
New York 30, New York
November 26, 1946

Dear Arna:

I go as far West as St. Joseph, Missouri, on lecture tour beginning January 14, so I won't be here unless you come sooner, as I shall have to go directly from the tour down to Atlanta, as I am due there on January 25. However, if the show is still running I see no reason why you couldn't see it, and I am sure that Hugh Smythe will get tickets for any shows you wish, since he is a very amiable young man and gets me any tickets I want—not only show tickets but also railroad tickets with the greatest efficiency and dispatch.

I will be delighted to come over to Fisk for the opening of the Gershwin Collection.

I will ask Hugh to try and get some copies of the *Chicago Tribune's* Christmas book issue.

Blanche has asked me to come in and talk over the anthology with her, so as soon as I do so I shall let you know what she says.

The first act of the show goes through very smoothly now, and we started on the second act yesterday. There are some headaches, but not enough to be normal yet.

I go away for a week's lectures next week, so I trust that all the *Street Scene* explosions will occur while I am gone.

Ann Jeffreys, the leading lady, looks just like Mae West must of looked when she was twenty-two. She is a far cry from Rose of the tenements, but she no doubt will be very good box office, and she has a beautiful singing voice. Also intelligent, since she grew up on the campus of Chapel Hill.

Best wishes, write soon.

Sincerely,
Langston

P.S. I'm sending you a complete copy of the S.S. lyrics for the G. Collection.

Shubert Theatre, (with *Street Scene*)
Philadelphia, Penna.,
December 22, 1946.

Dear Arna,

Well, here we are in Philadelphia going through just about what you-all went through, changing and re-changing, yowling and howling. Temperaments and tempers are developing, and the other night Kurt [Weill] and Elmer [Rice] both got sick and had to go to bed. But they bounded up again the next day and back into the fray! . . . . . . Me, I am resolved NOT to die of theateritis—nor even to have a stiff knee! . . . . . . The leading man is being replaced by "Ravenal" from *Show Boat*. . . . . . I'm in the same wing as you at the Chesterfield—Juanita has your room. I am just above. And Eulah [Pharr (Noel Sullivan's servant)], visiting, is just over me. . . . . . . Blanche Knopf wrote again asking me to come in to see her about the anthology, which I will do as soon as I get back to New York. . . . . When I saw who was editing that Book Section, no wonder your piece was cut out. Remember that lady? . . . . . I just this minute stopped writing to go down to Juanita's to see Louis Sharp (2 A.M.) who plays Bilbo-Turned-Black in *Finian's Rainbow* which, by the way, is a very amusing show, and a smash hit here, taking all OUR business. . . . . . No wonder Jack Conroy was let out of the *Defender!* See who is doing the Book Reviews now? The new editor's wife, who used to do them on the Detroit paper. Also they let out Bruce Reynolds and some others —so I don't think it was politics—at least not on a national scale. . . . . . Martin is an all right guy, I think. Margaret Anderson loves him, and he will probably make a very good editor. . . . . . Britannica wrote me for a picture to go with your article, so I reckon it must be O.K. . . . . . I didn't get a chance to do one bit of Christmas shopping—so just give the kids a hug for me, and tell Moe HY! There is nothing like a show to take up time! Only the Lord knows how I got my column out last week—in my sleep practically. And I haven't been able to write Atlanta a mumbling word—and supposed to send them a book list and stuff for the last month. I will be lucky to get there a-live! . . . . . . The show is good, but lacks pace, so far, and an over-all style. If it was me, I would do it all stylized. Now, it is weakly half and half as to style and lighting—neither natural nor sufficiently unnatural to have flavor. And as yet nobody is big and bad and bold enough to put a foot down flat and say it will be this or that OR ELSE. I wish I were running it. It would be one thing or another in a week. As it is now it sways back and forth between musical comedy, drama, and opera. (Which only a Meyerhold could make a unity—or ME!) (Maybe!) I'd do it like I did *Don't You Want to Be Free* in New York and L.A. (Except that out there Clarence Muse put his Muse to work, which gave it somewhat another flavor.). . . . . Anyhow, I got bids to confer about two more shows, which I will look into gingerly when I get back to town.

HAPPY HOLIDAYS!
Langston

Xmas plus 2, '46

Dear Lang:
I think I know very well that mixture of exhilaration, suspense, weariness, excitement, hope, misgiving and the rest of the moods that disturb one's sleep as his show heads for home. One must have a poker player's casualness about his fortunes if he wants to come through it without any marks. I think you got it. So give howdy for me to Juanity and Louis. I'm glad Louis caught on with a promising show. Tell him I was wondering what had come of him since he left the employ of Biglow's Bar. Also that I will see him backstage one night toward the end of January (the last week of the month) and would admire to have me a seat or two for his charade. As I would to your own during the same week. My present plan is to be in New York for about ten days beginning the '24th.

One of these days we must try to do a show OUR way. But the only way to do that is to write it on spec and then try to sell it. Once you contract in advance, I've found, you're in slavery. They'll press you to the limit for the few hundred dollars they've baited you with. I've had my taste of that and I'm sure I don't want any more. My next dramatic effort will be done without pressure. The producer will see a finished script only, and I'll let him change it or I won't—depending on how I feel.

Ruby Hill says she opens a week at Loews on Broadway the 30th of January and can go to London and Paris in February if she wants to.

I have sent about a third of my juvenile history to Mrs. Bragdon, dedicated to The Negro Who Speaks of Rivers, perhaps on the birthday of that poem. I plan to bring more of the manuscript with me to New York next month. Perhaps a month after that it will be finished. Hanging over my head at the same time are articles for The Saturday Review of Literature (Harlem Poets), the new S. W. Watkins book (a symposium to be published by Henry Holt) chapter which was assigned to me (Entertainment), an introductory essay for the brochure we are publishing here in connection with the opening of the Gershwin collection, a piece or two for the Negro Digest (which may or may not get written), a few book reviews, etc. I trust that all of this will be through the mill by the time you come to visit us here from Atlanta. Seems that God's aiming to make some changes and improvements in Georgia for your arrival.

Chas. S. is back on the campus, but I haven't seen him yet. . . . Your column on your activities with the show was very interesting. I think most folks want to know the inside of show business. . . . . Did you see where Shirley Graham's *There Was Once a Slave,* biography of Fred Douglass, won the Julian Messner tolerance book prize of $6,500? Why don't you or I compete for prizes any more? Last time I saw Buck Moon he was doing a book for that contest, too. They even extended the contest to allow him to finish it. It must not have won. And Miss Ovington writes that Harcourt, Brace have accepted her autobiography, much of which she

214

wrote in this library about a year or two ago. Buck Moon sends an advance copy of the new Kenneth Roberts heavy historical novel, much of which is set in colonial Haiti. And me, I'm worrying about where I can retreat next summer to work on my novel.

More directly.

Ever,
Arna

Fisk University Library
Nashville 8, Tennessee
February 5, 1947

Dear Lang:

Billy Haygood [of Rosenwald Fund] is anxious to spend part of the coming summer at Yaddo working on the book which Doubleday, Doran and Company commissioned: a novel reflecting some aspects of his own experience. I cannot sponsor him very gracefully, since he has written a beautiful note in my behalf and it would almost look as if we were scratching each others back. However, he wondered if I would ask you to say a word in his behalf. I assured him that I would and that I thought you would be only too happy. If so, will you tell him that you have written.

I am still singing the praises of *Street Scene.* You are in clover for life. Now that you are rich, but of course not haughty, perhaps we can think a little more about the poor man's profession of poetry. I mentioned the anthology to Buck Moon in New York, and he sprang at the idea. Of course, I did not commit us in any way, but unless Knopf comes through to our satisfaction, we can be sure that Doubleday is willing. Buck talked about a large volume, perhaps selling for $5 in the original edition and being reissued later in a more modest-priced reprint if that is desired. He is supposed to write me further about his idea. I suggest that if he wants the item on the Doubleday list that he simply make us an offer out of the clear, unrelated to any conversations which he and I may have had.

How does it feel to be a Professor of English?

Ever,
Arna

On tour,
Greensboro, N.C.
Negro History Week,
February 11, 1947

Dear Arna,

Lull between assemblies—waiting for Charlotte Hawkins Brown to transport me to her school this afternoon.

Sure, I'll write a Yaddo letter for Billie. . . . I'll be over for the Gershwin opening. Do I stay with you-all? If not please make proper reservations at Faculty Club or elsewhere for Fri., Sat. (maybe Thur. night, too, if I can get off early).

215

Did you see spread on S.S. in Sunday's P.M.? ($42,000 last week!)
Richmond tomorrow, then back to Atlanta.
Here come the folks now!

So long,
Langston

2-12-47

Dear Lang:

Of course you are to stay with us when you come to the Festival, and if you can get here as early as Thursday of that week, so much the better. It is on Thursday night that Phillipa Schuyler is to give her concert, and we would like to have her at lunch that same day. So the earlier you arrive the better.

I'm just back from Memphis where I spoke for the group that had you last year and stayed in the same room of the Watson home in which you stayed. I still don't do that sort of thing to my satisfaction—the lecture business—and consequently it wears me out. Nevertheless I'm booked for the U. of Minnesota for March 7th. Think I'll let them hear me read a paper, considering the conditions.

Here are a couple of recent Hayden poems which might interest you.* Did I tell you about the Paris production of *St. Louis Woman?* At least the contracts have been drawn. And Lemuel Ayers wants to be involved in the production of my *Domino Masque*—particularly if you do the lyrics—but he wants me to change the location from early New Orleans to colonial Haiti. I agree, but I can't afford to work on it anymore till a production contract is drawn with someone or other.

You have said nothing about your seminars. Like 'em?

More anon.

Ever,
Arna

*He also has one in the current *Atlantic.*

Atlanta University
Atlanta, Georgia
March 8, 1947

Dear Arna:

Your excellent article for the poetry issue of the Saturday Review of Literature just came. I like it very much and, of course, I greatly appreciate the kind things which you say about my work.

Yesterday I sent to you and Alberta the number-one copy of my new book of poems—which is your and her book, too. I know you will find it on your return from your horrendous engagements in the North. I do not know why anyone as calm, as placid, and as solidly built as you are would wish to go into public speaking. It is designed to break down and ruin anybody's health but such hearty souls as myself, Adam Powell, and Mrs. Bethune. I also do not understand why you should worry about what you are going to say, since none of us I have just

216

mentioned ever say anything except the same thing. However, we get by on our nerve and if you are going in for such a career just about all you need is the brass, gall, and determination to stand up in front of an audience and talk loud. After that, the rest is clear sailing, as an audience will always let you stay in front of them once you get up there. However, I would not worry about it beforehand, and also I would not READ a speech. Ten words spoken naturally are worth a thousand words read off paper, at least in my humble estimation As you probably know, I have been speaking now for a dozen years or more and have never never yet gotten around to preparing my speech, but I mean to do so some day as soon as I get time. I really would like to be prepared once before I get up before the public.

Anyhow, Please let me know how you came out on your triple speaking engagements. I hope well. Also please let me know when you are coming over to stand in front of my classes as a living example of a portly and successful writer. I assure you you do not need to prepare any speech to be given here. As I am continually told, "All they want to do is just *see* you." (I have told them that you are a sight to behold.)

Please let me know how the negotiations are coming on for the Anthology. I have written Blanche Knopf that another publisher is interested and has made a splendid offer which I feel should be accepted. I do not think she will mind, because she had a chance to make a splendid offer herself and made no such a thing.

I have just turned down the contract for the "Simple-minded Friend" book, because "Current Books" did not seem to me to understand what the character was all about and wanted many more changes and extensions than I am prepared to make. They offered a splendid advance, in fact, more than I have ever gotten on any book before, but even at that I do not see why a firm that does not understand Simple should be publishing him. He does not understand it either and he told me not to bother with them, and I do not blame him. Call me up or write when you get back.

I shall be flying to New York on the 19th for the publishing of the book and a Mary Margaret MacBride radio program.

With all good wishes to you and Alberta.

Sincerely yours,
Lang

Benny Goodman & Freddy Martin records of "Moon-Face" are out.

No flights yesterday so I couldn't make my Mobile date. Have to go on the 14th.

11 March '47

Dear Lang:

Fields of Wonder was here to greet me on my return from Minnesota. It's an honor and a pleasure—also a beautiful book filled with the riches of beauty. It contains a good handful of your very top-shelf poems, and the general level is way up there. I'll read it the *second* time tonight.

The lectures came off quite well, I suppose. I wrote a couple of addresses, but used neither. Instead, I stuffed my hands in my pockets and went tramping through the woods as usual. The banquet affair, concluding the Conference of English Teachers and Librarians at the University was about the shiniest event on which I've been presented. Looked more like the Waldorf-Astoria than a university. All tickets were sold much in advance, so after the eating about fifty standees were admitted to listen to the talk. They lined themselves against one wall. The five long (about 200 feet each) tables were ornamented with copies of my juveniles, arranged in clusters or singly every yard or two. I like to blush when they showed me in.

In Chicago, going up, Embree invited me to the dinner he gave for Charles S. at the Shoreland, and afterwards I went to the reception by the Fisk alumni at the Parkway Ball Room. Between the two I think I saw everybody. Coming back, I dined with Horace and his very delightful intended, Ruby Wright. Also with Jack Conroy, Nelson Algren, Mary Guggenheim, Willard Motley, etc., and ended up at a party at Metz and Julie Lochard's. That went on till 4 A.M. . . . See the March 8 *Publisher's Weekly* in your library there for a two-page spread on Willard's new novel. The publisher's campaign is to be a killer. Horace and Ruby will be down for the Festival. . . . Susane Torre, Horace's Japanese secretary, is getting married in a week.

Re: Anthology—I have told Buck Moon that I'll be ready to talk turkey with him by the time of the first Rosenwald Fellowship meeting, the first week of March. So if Mrs. K. advises otherwise, please check me in time. Buck wanted an estimate of size. Do you think we could safely limit ourselves to 500 pages? I told him I thought ours should be the most complete job anywhere, so that no competitor would be inclined to challenge it soon, and that our deal should provide somehow for keeping it in print as long as the demand for copies continues. Not to mention the reprint understanding.

That picture of you at your typewriter is a good action shot., also the one in the rocker—in the Morehouse magazine. Have you been seeing the Fisk *Herald?* If not, I'll send you a few.

More anon,

Ever,
Arna

Paul's been pledged Omega. Joan made AKA last year.
That dedication—Whew! Of course, we're overjoyed and proud all over.

923 - 18th Avenue, North
Nashville 8, Tenn.
31 March '47

Dear Lang:

I believe I told you that I'd finally received the long-awaited Royal quiet de luxe portable. Well, to show you how little I've accomplished since I returned home, this is the first time I've had the box open. You get the first letter.

Tomorrow I'm off to Chicago again, this time for the first of the Fellowship Committee meetings. In glancing over the application forms I notice that your candidate for a career in movies neglected one important step in his campaign: he presented no evidence that he could be admitted to the school and the courses he has in mind. That point always comes up, because they have had so many sour experiences with youngsters who take it for granted that all doors will fly open once they get their fellowships. Of course, I'll be for him on general principles, but I wish he'd fortified himself at that point. I'll let you know how the wind blows.

Didn't you say you might be coming to Chicago to check on the Freudian adventures of your friends? [Reference to Horace Cayton, who was being "psyched." Note by C.V.V.] This time I have a reservation at the Pershing. Never stayed there before. Thought I'd give it a try.

Spring arrived today, a week behind schedule, but right in the midst of house-cleaning. I was much too busy—and too indolent—to help. But I did steal a look at a charming picture book called *Paris,* photographs by Fritz Henle and text by Elliot Paul. You'd love it. . . . . And I noticed that the Saturday Review had sent sample copies of last week's issue to the English department and invited them to buy a lot of extra copies at a reduced price. Wonder if they've made a campaign among ALL the cullud schools using our piece as bait. Of course, I'd be delighted. Their letter looked like a general thing perhaps run off in quantity. . . . . And the new issue of Kiplinger's Magazine (April) contains a most unusual piece about the opportunity which the 14 million Negroes offer the business men of America. Most flattering to us—and all based on a careful survey by cold-hearted money-makers. It might give you an idea for a column. . . . And a copy of Sinclair Lewis' *Kingsblood Royal* arrived in the morning mail from Random House for comment —the first time I've been asked by a publisher to comment on the work of so important an author. . . . And from the *N. Y. Times* came, for review, a copy of a delightful juvenile by one Margaret Taylor (whom I suspect of being Margaret Goss) about Chicago's south side: Jasper, The Drummin' Boy. Sorry they're limiting me to 200 words. It's that good. . . . For some reason or other, the *Saturday Review* came back this week with an ugly review of Du Bois' new book. By Linton Wells—who doesn't seem to like us too well.

OUR play is building in my mind. Now I have a working title to offer: *Doctor Washington,* though I'm not sure we mightn't find reasons to take Booker T. out of it and make the thing fictional. Anyhow, and either way, I also thought the young white girl, the niece or secretary or something to the wealthy Northern philanthropist, might be southern—a southern girl who has been to Vienna and studied under Freud. She might have met the Du Bois-like young man over there, while he was studying in Germany, and she may almost have had a crush on him there. So she may have reason to accuse the older woman of being motivated by sub-conscious drives too delicate to mention. The possibilities are great. Only the exact story line, with some dramatic doings, remains to be constructed—hunh? I don't think we should get too heavy on this end. Psychoanalysis could easily bog us down. But a few little darts might be just the thing.

More anon.

Ever,

Arna

Sunday A.M.

Dear Lang,

I'm clearing my desk a little in preparation for YADDO, and one of the first things I come across is the title *North American Negro Poets* by Dorothy B.

Porter, published by The Book Farm, Hattiesburg, Mississippi, 1945. It is a bibliographical checklist of the writings of all Negro poets of North America, 1760 to 1944. It had been sent to me for review by the Library Quarterly, but I had never gotten around to it apparently. But the point here is that it saves us completely the task of making a new bibliography—for the years prior to 1944. It is complete and workmanlike and even includes a code indicating where the volumes may be examined. So call off your research assistant and instead write either to Mrs. James Porter at Howard or to the Book Farm and get a copy. If each of us carries a copy of this list, we can communicate by referring to page and item, etc. We can check from it as we go along.

Now that the contracts are signed, I feel the need of our having a conference to block out the work. When? I'm scheduled to hit Yaddo on the 4th, remaining till July 29th. After that a day or two in N. Y. C., perhaps, then home to Nashville.

Meanwhile everything is awhirl again as I try to get things in order for a short absence. Meanwhile too I'm still beating my brains out against that young history of the Negro for Knopf. The effort to work against campus and household distractions has worn me down, and I'm getting very little done on it now.

Nevil Shute, the British author of *The Chequer Board* (a recent Literary Guild selection, dealing with a colored American G. I. in England—with happy intermarriage, etc.) and other book club selections, was here last week. Delightful individual.

More presently. But now. . . .

Arna

Sunday, May 25, 1947,
Atlanta University.

Dear Arna,

I've been meaning to write you for sometime, but some time to do so has been lacking. . . . . Watkins called me from Chicago to do what you promised on Negro Theatre, but didn't. I have a file full of stuff (and our *Cavalcade of the Negro Theatre*) so will do it when I get to N.Y. . . . . . *Masters of the Dew* is due out June 16th. . . . . *Christian Science Monitor* gave *Fields of Wonder* a swell review, and I understand it is selling pretty well. . . . . I sold a pile at the Public Librarians Conference Banquet here the other night where I spoke. Mollie Lee, Sadie Delaney send regards to you. . . . . New Orleans I loved. Sunny and warm. I think I am going back. Cullud have just about taken over the French Quarter and are living all over the place, having a ball in those old houses. . . . . . Margaret Walker's father was here the other day and had luncheon with me. . . . . . See by the clippings that the Columbia album of *Street Scene* records is out. Not on sale here yet, though.

My amanuensis has been working all week on Slaughter Collection cards with Miss Bentley's guidance. But they (nor I) know which poets are colored and which are white all the time. Who can tell us that? He has fifty more books to catalogue, then I will mail them all to you, tomorrow or Tuesday. You have them checked and added to there, then send them on up to New York to me and I will have Nate check with the Schomburg Collection and the Spingarn. . . . . Shall we do the library of Congress, too? . . . . I'm due to make some records of my poems for them whenever I want to go down there.

Did you get the contracts and sign and return one to Lieber? You keep one, I suppose, and one comes back to me, no?

Sure, I like *"O Daedalus"* for our book. . . . . . Shall we include unpublished poets, or not? Couple of folks here write GOOD poetry, but unpublished as yet. At any rate, I'm filing their addresses.

Ben Carruthers is in Venezuela, so I'll write him to look out for Negro poets there—which he can translate for us.

Knopf man said he was trying to place a review of F.O.W. for us.

Ted Ward got a large advance on his play for Broadway for next season, he writes, *Our Lan'*. Reconstruction times. So our B.T.W. one would follow well.

I go to Chicago from here for a Skyloft Autograph Party May 8, then to New York about the 15th or so. Will run up to see you-all at Yaddo. And maybe later to Mexico, or somewhere nice and warm. Yaddo is *not* warm, so be sure to take sweaters, etc.

Did you give that music to the Omega fellow we met on the church steps?

Got a review copy of *Albert Sears* by Millen Brand, another Negro-white novel yesterday. They are surely coming out fast.

I go to Miami for a speech Decoration Day. Then back to Commencement. Hope to leave here the 3rd also for Chicago.

W. G. Still card for GMC.

Langston

July 4th, 1947

Dear Arna,

Still trying to get my ducks in a row. Have to do that *Negro in Theatre* piece for Watkins right away soon, also one for *Phylon* left hanging over from Atlanta, and eight columns for the *Defender,* then I will be free for the summer.

Dorothy and I saw *Brigadoon* yesterday. She had tickets and invited me. It's a mildly entertaining ballet-pretty chorus-boys-in-kilts show, but nothing to worry about not seeing. Not up to *Oklahoma, Porgy and Bess, On the Town,* or even *Carousel.* And it is over-loaded with tiresome DeMille skip-and-pose ballets, not related much to the story.

Variety says the lecture business did Two Million last season, and my agency got half of that! Leigh is the biggest.

Paul called yesterday while I was out. Seems he is staying with Doug and Alta. Dorothy is taking him to see *Happy Birthday* on Saturday. He had dinner with us last Sunday and we went to an old time blues jam session at the Ziegfield. It was fun!

Well, I have all my cullud poetry sorted out so I can put my hands on it, and have selected a few of my choices to include. Blanche was apparently kinder mad because Knopf did not get the Anthology, but I DO NOT CARE about that. They wouldn't have given nearly as good a contract, and she started off making counter proposals, and saying they could not undertake to help on permissions, etc. So let her be kinder mad.

Sincerely
Lang

Yaddo
Sunday, 7-5-'47

Dear Lang,
That review of *Masters of the Dew* in the daily *Times* a couple of days ago was fine. I hope the publishers have enough stock to keep up with this growing interest in the book. Since I didn't get it for review, it doesn't look as if I'd get around to reading it now till I get home. Instead I'm trying to write one of my own.

That piece from the *Commonweal* about the U. S. Hotel here is the best evocation of the old Saratoga days I've seen. I'll show it around.

A few of us talked nearly all night last night, so I'm having to fight hard to get my stint today.

Do you still think you'll get here before I leave. I'm now considering the 28th as a date of departure and planning to curve through Chicago on the way home. In such a case I'd stay in New York City till about the 31st. Guess I won't bother with *Brigadoon* under the circumstances.

I approve your plan of putting together a new collection of your brown-skin poems right away. That will be a nice forerunner for the ANTHOLOGY. While I'm sorry Blanche K doesn't like the idea of our taking the latter to Doubleday, I don't think anybody would have given us a better contract than we got. I hope she will be pleased with the book I'm sending to Lieber for her as I mail this letter. It is the final half of the juvenile history of the Negro (your book), all typed, corrected, etc. As soon as I hear from them about the manuscript, I'm going to ask if they will (or can) plan to publish it on the anniversary of the publication of "The Negro Speaks of Rivers." What is the exact date?

A little seed or berry fell from a tree into Constance's ear while she was playing in the shade. Two doctors failed to get it out. The third at the hospital had to put her to sleep before he succeeded. But I talked to her on the phone, and she says she is now all right. . . . . Leslie took off for Havana last week. That's where he'll vacation. More anon.

Best,
Arna

7-17-'47
Yaddo

Dear Lang,
Since you are still in N.Y.C. with work on your hands, and since I have little more than a week left here, I see no reason why you should not remain there at least till I make my next visit. I expect to come down on the night of the 27th (Sunday) and sleep in the apartment of Doug and Alta—they will probably be out of town. The next day I'll be around, but on the 29th I'm to go up to Sally Alexander's Green Pastures to talk library matters with her and Spingarn. Back to town on the 30th and out again via Pacemaker to Chicago on the 31st—afternoon. There I'd like to meet Poppy and Camille and give them a little holiday in the city, three or four days of parks, museums, movies, etc., and then back to Fisk toward the end of the first week of August.

Your article for *Phylon* is most interesting. Among other things, it answers the question of why some of us are so impatient for the second installment of the Autobiography. Robert Lowell is now reading it. He is very sincere in his views, but he and I have argued a bit on the question of the social uses of literature, so I await with interest his comments. He begins, of course, with a favorable attitude toward your poetry. . . . There is no change that I would want to see in the article at present, but I will ponder it even longer and let you know if I arrive at anything after the discussions I expect. Owen read it with approval and said he would write you about it. Horace and Buck will see it later.

Did you see Carlo's wonderful picture of you holding Alex? No word from Paul re: sweater, but am trying to reach him. Leslie writes a long letter from Havana —his feelings about the island are mixed. Main unfavorable item: prices.

I'm glad Mercer Cook will help with the book—by way of suggestion. Don't forget to mail any biographical data you can about any and all non-USA poets. That will be hard to get generally, I fear. We must block this work out more definitely, as soon as you complete present chores. I'd like us to deliver the manuscript before you start your winter lectures.

Ever,

Arna

PS. Would you care to make a date for you and me to talk with Du Bois (if he's in town) either the evening of the 27th (late) or the 30th? Or to lunch with us either the 28th, the 30th or the 31st? He might talk of his memories of Booker-T and his times. I'd also like to mention the juvenile history—in which both are treated at length—to him.

August 25, 1947

Dear Arna,

This is my paper. Yours is about the same, I think. Anyhow, near enough.

Did you get the envelope of poems I sent you for the ANTHOLOGY? Mine, and a couple of white poets—Miles and Bynner? Days ago now. Is the format O.K. to follow through on the rest?

Under separate cover I'm sending the James Weldon Johnson ones we choose, except for "My City" which is not in any book I have, so have it copied down there. I'm making five copies of all, keeping four here in files.

"The Ballad of the Freedom Train" 's double-page center spread in *Our World* for next month looks swell in proofs. Sammy Heyward has set it to music. Handy will publish it simultaneously with magazine. So it will be all ready to ride that train when it starts out at Philadelphia on September 17, along with Irving Berlin's official number.

Delighted Knopf likes your book. The Franklin one is ready now, they tell me. . . . . . . Chester's book sure does mean by Mollie Moon and company. Carl says it is great because it is like Dostoyevsky. But I swear his Russians had a little more sense, didn't they? I never read about a more unsympathic bunch of humans, I do not believe. Send me a carbon of your review.

I sent you a tentative arrangement of my cullud book of poems—which has

223

been weeded out and re-arranged since. It can still stand some more cutting down, so lemme know which poems seem to you least good. Blanche is back and I want to turn it in to her soon.

Also PLEASE tell me in which issue of the *American Mercury* was the Nathan piece so I can get it for my scrap-book?

Sincerely,
Lang

26 August '47

Dear Lang,

Still no move by us to across the campus, but I'il keep you posted. Till then, write us same as usual.

Your *Projection of a Day* came. I'm half through it and reading slowly. Looks like it's going to be another fine collection. Am keeping my eyes open for possible additions to our anthology selections. Up to now no substitutions have suggested themselves.

Chester Himes' new novel is going to start fights. He has narrative power, and he treats explosive situations. But does he hate leftists, blindly and without any reference to doctrine! Rankin doesn't hate them any more. He must have had some run-ins. My review of it is for BOOK, N. Y. Herald Trib.

Nothing here but steam and sun. Hot weather won't do.

Miss Ovington says some nice things about you in her autobiography. Which reminds me that now the way should be clear for that second volume of yours. It would pave the way for that first collected edition of your poems, which in turn might make a combined edition of the two biographical volumes possible. So drop everything except the anthology and start writing! Hear?

I'm still revising and adding paragraphs and notes of one kind or another to the history of the Negro. Sorry they rejected my suggestion to use Doug for illustrations.

Best ever,
Arna

1611 Meharry Blvd.
Nashville 8,
Tenn.
29 August '47

Dear Lang,

Well we've moved, man. Lot of trouble and lot of expense, so I hope it's worth while. Awfully tired now, also disorganized, dirty and low. Not to mention sleepy.

Your JWJ poems came, as did all the earlier ones mentioned by you earlier. I am filing all together. Will look for the Manhattan sonnet and copy, sending you a carbon, as soon as I get a new secretary—or make-believe secretary. . . . When that happens, we'll follow the format you are using, which looks very good to me.

224

My papers are all buried for the nonce, so I can't get that carbon to my review of the Himes novel (*Lonely Crusade*), but what I said was that as a piece of fiction writing it holds—it has power. That the key to much of it is the hero's confession that nobody had ever really liked him. I said this was easy to understand. Then I talked about the plot and subject matter and called attention to Lee Gordon's hatred of communists and his involvement with some of them. I quoted passages to show his bitter hostility to all humans. My tag line was that this book is more provocative than IHHLHG [*If He Hollers Let Him Go*], Himes' first.

I do agree with you, underneath, that it is a book filled with unlovely folk— almost exclusively. But in his mad way the guy can really handle narrative material.

More anon. Meanwhile,

Best ever,
Arna

P.S. That American Mercury piece by GJ Nathan: *July!!!*

634 St. Nicholas Avenue
New York 30, New York
September 16, 1947

Dear Arna:

It looks as though I might get off for a vacation at long last. At any rate I have been down to the airlines and got all kinds of folders and prices to go every which way. My plan is to pass by Fisk on the way back from wherever I go and attend the inauguration and make final plans for our anthology.

Griff Davis is photographing an interracial nudist colony out in the Midwest that has fifty-four members, and he says when he joins it will be fifty-five.

Aunt Toy says instead of ending your review of Chester Himes novel with the word "provocative," you should have ended it with the word "provoking." (Maybe I told you this before.) At any rate Carl Van Vechten asks if leading characters just have to have sense? It is his claim that Hamlet and Don Quixote do not have sense. I do not agree with this, but if it be true, at least they had an aim and objective, also character.

See current *Theatre Arts* for an article by Will Marion Cooke. And of course, you have seen last week's *Life* with the cullud picture of the cullud boy who married the richest girl in the world. Simple is very excited about all of this and will probably comment upon it at length in the *Chicago Defender.* By the way, I am *eight* columns, yes I mean *8,* ahead, so I will not have to write any until I come back from overseas. I have now gotten to the point where I now write a column like you write a book, without batting an eye or revising a line. And I have the help of such amiable and efficient people of the race as Hugh Smythe [Sociologist Ass't to Hughes], who is here at this moment, Marjorie Greene, who was here this afternoon, and Nathaniel B. White [Sec'y to Hughes], who is here off and on.

225

Tell Alberta that we have just been speaking about her, what a swell person she is and Hugh, along with Mabel too, sends her his best regards. Write soon.

Sincerely,

Lang

Myrtle Bank Hotel
Kingston, Jamaica, B.W.I.
October 18, 1947

Dear Arna,

This is a wonderful island—where everybody talks Ja-MAI-can! This hotel is right on the sea where all the big boats come into harbour. (And all the local and British big-shots dine and dance. Bustamente is sitting on the terrace right now —1 A.M.—with his entourage.)

I've just left Claude McKay's son-in-law who is helping me on our Anthology —and who's a very good poet himself. Today is the first day I've looked up anyone. And no sooner than I got back to the hotel, the phone started ringing, reporters and photographers arriving. But I've been here three weeks *in peace,* so it won't be so bad. Last week I took a delightful trip by car all around the island with three days at Montego Bay on the white sands of one of earth's loveliest beaches, living in a very cullud Jamaican inn—quite the opposite of the Myrtle Bank which is entirely international. I had planned to stop a week in Havana on the way back, but don't believe I will. Think I'll spend all the time here instead —and just look at Cuba from the air—since I been there before. And I'll see you on the 5th or 6th or so. Will wire from Miami probably—if the hurricanes let me by.

Sincerely,

Lang

3 A.M.
N.Y. Nov. 19, 1947

Dear Arna,

Well, I got back O.K. to find mail skyhigh—but pretty well acknowledged by Nate—and 50—!! little things needing immediate attention—like the Street Scene proofs and the African film narration. And before I could turn around off to Cleveland for a lecture at the Pub. Library—that Gerald L.K. tried to stop— without success—to a packed house on a dismal day. Now a few days in town then to Chi. to address the opening of the American Educational Fellowship on Thanksgiving at the Stevens. (Don't know where my lecture bureau got the idea I was either an addresser or an educator—but after the 27th I reckon I will be. . . . In Cleveland I got some good poetry from Helen Johnson. Also Russell Atkins (who publishes in "Verve" etc. and is "more so" even than O'Higgins) promises some soon. Looks like we are in for a set of Negroes who will out-do the most *avant-garde* whites! Which delights me! And if we don't have them in our Antho. we'll be behind the times by 1950 . . . New York is kinder chilly. Also kinder sad looking. Harlem looks quiet as Sunday everyday. . . . Mr. Handy was 74 Sunday.

Toy & Emerson went to his Tuckahoo party. I was in Ohio. . . . Elmer compromised on S.S., so it's settled. Next time I'll have 2 lawyers as well as an agent.

Lang

1611 Meharry Blvd.
Nashville 8, Tenn.
5 December '47

Dear Lang,

Here is the Seymore book. The clipped pages will indicate the racy portion of his fine poem that I thought should be omitted from our anthology in consideration for the youth of the country and their more tender instructors. I have had it copied as indicated, so I hope you will keep this book safe. If you should ever see your way clear (or gain the consent of the owner) to present it to the Negro Collection at Fisk—the ERA collection of Negroana—it would be most highly appreciated, of course. Meanwhile I want to see it in the hands to which it was entrusted.

It has now become a question of whether my trip to N. Y. should be right after Xmas, during the vacation, or mid-January. An official trip seems to be in the making for one time or the other but it may take two or three days to bring a decision. Will both find you near home base?

CSJ is just back from the UNESCO meeting in Mexico City and much in love with the place and talking about setting up, if possible, a conference or institute of some kind down there. He is also in a mood for a Southern Writers Conference here during the Festival week. Horace [Cayton] and Ira Reid [Sociologist] have both talked about such an idea in the past. Do you think it would be a good inter-racial project? Maybe a lot of young white southerners could be drawn in and thereby learn to know the well-dressed Negroes a little better. They would then go home, we hope, dedicated to writing poems and books that would foster understanding. I hope you will keep your lectures far enough apart so that you could fly in for a minute if necessary.

Got your card from Chicago. But how did you enjoy the Stevens? Would you recommend it to me on my next trip up there? Going now to look up that Fisk piece in the Chicago Tribune and the one about your lecture in the N. Y. Times. . . . We're making good headway with the poetry copying. Anything you want us to do? We'll have about everything by end of next week. Even The Congo and those long things. Only odds and ends after that. Very fine secretary! The shirt and shorts came—they needn't have, but thanks.

Best,
Arna

12/15/47

Arna,

Lord, have mercy! Here it is practically 1948! Also Xmas and not card 1 sent! Horace and Ruby are in town. Also Loren & Juanita. Went to parties for both. Much confusion in my life as usual! Like to froze in Chicago Thanksgiving.

Have to go back for Woodlawn Forum this week-end. In and out, Anthology has suffered, but have 5 clear weeks after 21st. Any time you come O.K. by me. Will be around till Montreal on January 27, Springfield 28.

All your material came and will get at it sold on my return from Chicago. Am clearing up everything else, (I hope) this week. Had only $4.83 in bank on return from Jamaica, so had to hustle a little bit.

We compromised on S.S. record deal, so I'll get that money soon, I reckon. Low dogs haunt the theatre, great art though it be. Shaw, Duse, etc. must be (or were) made of iron to live so long. Also Miss Waters (who prays and cusses equally well). . . . Hugh is here giving style to my mail (writing most of it. I give up).

Lang

17 February '48

Dear Lang,

You asked me, as I recall, what should be the theme of our next anthology, didn't you? Well, here it is: How about a prose anthology on Harlem? It could contain essays or articles, portraits in prose, and stories, and right off I think of Bud Fisher's piece in the old Mercury on the night spots as one of the essay-articles. Others in this category might be one of Eric Waldron's pieces on Harlem from the Smart Set, I believe; my piece called "The Two Harlems" from the American Scholar, a piece or two from the Renaissance days on the literary and artistic awakening, perhaps by CVV from the old Vanity Fair, or SJ's piece on blues as poetry from the Carolina Magazine, excerpts from the writings of Wally, James Weldon, Zora, etc. Also Chestnutt's essay on the Harlem writers in the Colophon. Some white, some colored.

Under the portraits in prose we could use things like the one on Duke Ellington in the New Yorker, Esquire's article on Dan Burley, CVV's piece on Blues singers in Vanity Fair, Roi's chapter on Adam Power in his book, the Hall Johnson portrait in the New Yorker, that piece on Florence Mills' funeral—where did it appear?—possibly one from Embree's *Thirteen,* etc. You will think of many more.

With the stories we can go to town. Your New Yorker tale comes to mind first, the guy who was kidnapped by Negroes and didn't want to go home. Then the Bud Fisher things: "City of Refuge," "Ringtail," etc. To these add something by Claude, Eric, and—half a dozen more noirs, and in between intersperse such things as we find by Tess Slesinger, Dorothy Parker, Buck Moon and such like.

If you like the idea, why don't you add a few more (like one of those stories in Paul Moran's *Black Magic*), write it up in the form of a short memo or statement of purposes, shoot it to Maxim and ask him to sell the idea either to Doubleday (when he finds the time ripe) or to Knopf. Perhaps the former, though both are rather good on anthologies. We might get a book club distribution on this kind of job—possibly as a dividend—if we made it entertaining enough.

With a prose anthology, we would have to be satisfied to pocket half the royalty while the other half was being divided among the authors included—like your experience with the Bedside Esquire, I believe. Even so, the income should be satisfactory.

By the way, among the essay-articles could be included that remarkable piece by the 24-year-old colored kid in the current issue of Commentary. Be sure to read it. Called, I believe, The Harlem Ghetto. What a kid! He has zoomed high among our writers with his first effort. His name is Baldwin. And among the stories we could use that O. Henry prize story called "No More Trouble for Judwick," about the southern Negro who escapes his tormentors and gets lost in Harlem at last.

I found notes for such an anthology among my collections of ideas. How do you like it?

Let me know when you plan to leave N.Y. and generally where you'll be and when and where you can be expected to pick up mail. . . . I'm scheduled to be in Chicago from March 11th through the 13th—perhaps I'll get there on the 10th. This is the first Fellowship meeting. Will either stop with Horace or at the Grand.

All is activity here as usual. Me trying to get up every morning at 6 A.M. and write for four hours on my novel before going to the library—but not always attaining my goal, especially after nights when I stay up too late or eat too much. It's a dog's life. . . . Paul surprised me with quite a good story last week, and I begin to think he may be a writer after all. He still doesn't know what he's in for. I'll try to get Alex ready to pitch for the Dodgers. . . . Hello to Nate, Hugh, Toy, Emerson, and all.

Ever,
Arna

On train,
Harrisburg bound
February 23, 1948

Dear Arna,

Saw Doug last night on my return from Wilmington with Grace Goens. Otto had a BIG party.

That Harlem Anthology is a SWELL idea. I'm starting a file immediately, and will work out an outline next week. Dan Burley's riot, etc., sketches from his column *must* go in it for jive talk and humor. It's *Commercial,* Jack, and will *sell!*

I'll be in Chicago the morning of the 11th of March—Springfield that night —and back all day on 12th—so we can get a couple hours more together on Poetry Anthology. Stay at the *Grand* so we can work.

Charles S. sent a nice blurb on Simple, too. (One of his Dialogues might also go in our Harlem book.)

Good for Paul! I hope he turns out to be a 1. Dumas—2. Motley—3. Yerby. In other words makes some money, *too.* Fame is lovely—but hard to eat.

These underwater pens are no good a-tall.

Lang

Grand, Chicago,
March 16, 1948.

Dear Arna,

Griff's pictures of us came out fine and he is sending you some, he says. He's going to Mexico next week to cover the King Cole honeymoon at Acapulco for *Ebony.*

I slept 12 hours Sunday night and 10 last night, so I am back to normal again.

Ordered your shirt and tie sent yesterday and bought one myself. Bee-ou-ti-
FUL!

Talked to Beulah Whitby in Detroit yesterday by phone and she says the Catholics have started it there. Rich Central Methodist Church for whom I read poems Wednesday evening refused to back down. But Council of Social Workers I am due to address at noon is about to be wrecked and ruined over the issue, calling meetings every day—Catholics insisting they don't hear me. Jews and Negroes insisting they do. Which is about to bust the organization up. They will probably all have high blood pressure by the time I arrive prepared to read such controversial poems as:

> I wish the rent
> Was heaven sent.

Anyhow, I see where I shall have ample time for writing next season—which is the Lord's way of getting me back to my main work.

Hope you had a pleasant trip home and found everybody O.K.

My best to all at your house,

Sincerely,
Lang

En route to
California,
March 29, 1948

Still snow this morning in Northern California—never saw the like of such a winter! If there is snow in L.A. when I get there tomorrow I will give up!

Next week I go to Arizona State and intend to spend the whole week in Phoenix if the sun is shining.

I will now do a column on "Game Preserves For Cullud" as well as for elk and deer. We need protection from the hunters, too.

Sincerely,
Lang

1611 Meharry Blvd.
Nashville 8, Tenn.
11 April '48

Dear Lang,

What a meeting with Koestler that must have been! Too bad he seems to wander in such confusion and fear. He happens to be one of my favorite prose writers, at his best, and I hope he isn't getting ready to tumble into Mr. Hearst's bag.

13 April.

This is something new for me: leaving a letter unfinished, but things do grow more complicated as time passes. Since the above was written, M. B. Tolson has been here, enroute from Langston U. (where he now teaches) to the Drama and Speech meeting at Florida A. & M. where Shep Edmonds is now operating. And

230

a card has come from Griff Davis with a wonderful picture of the Hotel Casa Blanca at Acapulco.

Norman Cousins will be here about the time you get this, and it has fallen to me to introduce him to the students. The next morning (Friday) I'll go through with my speaking engagement at the Hermitage Hotel (downtown Nashville), unless somebody takes a notion to bait me or the group that has invited me— can't find any cullud who've ever set foot in there. And the same evening off to Chicago for the second Fellowship meeting. Since I've promised on a heap of Bibles to deliver the first draft of the new juvenile yarn to Jack at that time, I don't anticipate leisure between now and then.

Cedric is in N. Y. (New School) and Washington (Howard) on lectures, hobbling on a cane but leaving quite a sick wife at home. . . . . A wonderful exhibit of Haitian paintings (Primitives) has arrived for the Festival. . . . Doug has come up with a genius child in one of his classes: Patricia Goldsbury of Worcester, Mass. Fisk has been rich in musical and literary talents for the past couple of years, but Doug is about to steal the show. He's terribly excited. . . . . Found out that Jessie Redmond Fauset graduated from Cornell in 1905. How old were you then? I'll put this date in her biography but will *not* mention her age! Hugh has just sent us some of Du Bois' manuscripts—don't tell. I think his whole book, manuscript and letter collection should come to Fisk, his alma mater. It would be treasured here as nowhere else.

See the Hastie story in the new SEP. . . . Also the picture of Jackie Robinson in the same issue. And Joe Louis (in Paris—with ofay gals) on the back of last Sunday's P. M. (April 11).

Much talk everywhere about your lecture troubles. All agree that the Lord is with you—trying to make you write the second installment of your personal history. Trust you will not rebell.

If those lovely West Indians will just acknowledge the books I sent them, I may be able to arrange to send them more from time to time. Right now we are receiving the Rosenwald Library and a number of duplicates are showing up. But I'll be darned if I'll mail a single one before I hear something from that covey of poets.

Any small ideas you may wish to send Miss Ruth Shair at Knopf's for promoting *Story of the Negro* will be most gratefully received by both her and me, I'm sure. Would especially welcome contacts with school people and board of education folk who might help push it into their school systems.

Shall we begin now to get tickets for *A Streetcar Named Desire, Mr. Roberts* and *The Respectful Prostitute?* I expect to arrive in N. Y. about June 20th and to remain about a week, but of course the 23rd is the night of the big fight, I believe. (Seats ordered May 6, '48 also *Manhattan*) To whom should I send my check and in what amount?

Ever,
Arna

28 April '48

Dear Lang,

I take it for granted that you are still at Hollow Hills. Since I wrote you last week, however, I have been to the Librarians' conference at Orangeburg, flying both ways and stopping off in Atlanta to spend a day with the folks there and to interview half a dozen prospects for employment in the Library here. The art show was still going on and Reddick was established in his new job. . . . . I did a Hughes at Orangeburg and autographed 30 books *(Story of the Negro)* for the librarians and others. . . . . Which reminds me of the fine review in last Sunday's *PM,* April 25—the first review of the book, I believe. Treated it as if the book were of equal interest to old and young. And I'm happy to see Knopf's adds in the *Atlantic, Saturday Review of Lit.,* etc. Also that they put my book at the top of the page in their juvenile adds in *Horn Book, Library Journal, Publisher's Weekly,* etc. . . . . Mrs. Rollins writes that all Chicago branch libraries have purchased the book—which I hope will serve as example to other systems.

Yeah, man, we'll see you in Chicago. Alberta and I both plan to come up for the goings-on. We'll be at the Stevens, too. We'll try to arrive Thursday, May 27th. Then in June you and I will attend the battle of the Joe's in N. Y. and see *Streetcar, Roberts, Prostitute,* etc. Hunh?

Did I tell you that Bob Lucas, James Baldwin and Yvonne Gregory were the cullud writers blessed by the Fellowships Committee? Accent on youth—and beauty, in the case of at least one. And Yvonne's brother Tom just had a bad accident at Meharry and may not recover his sight—hot acid during an experiment. And a pretty Fisk freshman drowned at a picnic last Sunday when her canoe turned over. And Miss Gibbs (our cataloguer) was slugged and lost her purse last week, while I was away—she is recovering at Meharry (about 15 stitches). And as a result of the crime and disaster wave Fisk has hired two special plain-clothesmen.

Festival starts tomorrow, and Eddie Matthews sings one of your songs on his program—of which I'll eventually send you a copy. And I have Dorothy West's novel for review (N. Y. Herald Trib). And the R. Torrence biography of John Hope (whose son lives next door) is about ready—Macmillan.

Best ever,
Arna

1611 Meharry Blvd.
Nashville 8, Tenn.
8 May '48

Dear Lang,

The post-Festival functions have been harder on the nerves and the constitution than the Festival. Some of the guests, including Sterling Brown, remained for nearly a week, which gave occasion for many all-night sessions, sometimes with refreshments. Sterling tottered away just yesterday, and since this is the first post-season week-end, the campus is asleep. It needs all of the same it can get.

Pearl Primus [Dancer] was the real knock-out of the affair. So much so that Embree called a special meeting of the Fellowship group and called for another vote on her Fellowship application. She got it this time! She'll go to Africa to study the background of the dances she has been doing. So let's you and me take bows: you for introducing me at that N. Y. pre-view, me for bringing about her invitation to the Festival. She will now disband her company and start a new phase of her career as a scholarly anthropologist of the dance—as well as the

232

world's highest and handsomest jumper, not to mention interpreter of blues, etc.

Reviews of *Story of the Negro* and letters of commendation reach me in a slow but steady trickle. All very favorable—some beyond the call of duty—and a few quite lengthy. One of the first by-products is an invitation to speak at the Columbia University summer session (to the whole bunch) as third speaker in the series that opens with Mrs. Roosevelt. I've got cold feet, but will try to go through with it. The subject they asked for is the title of one of my chapters: "Freedom Is a Powerful Word."

Doug wants to see the Joe Louis fight with us so would like to have his ticket bought at the same time. . . . . Where shall I send copies of the festival program, etc.? . . . . . Nice column by you this week on the 10,000 beds in which you have slept. In your best manner. That fascinating autobiographical touch which, I hope, means that you are pondering the second volume of *The Big Sea!*

See you in Chicago. . . . At the Stevens, hunh?

Ever,
Arna

Clark Hotel
1820–24 South Central Avenue
Los Angeles 21, California
Just in, 3:45 A. M.,
May 11, 1948

Dear Arna,

Delighted to have your letter with all that news.

. . . . . I sent Nate check to get show seats for *Street Car, Roberts,* etc., also *Make Mine Manhattan.* And asked him to let you know price of fight tickets and you can write him direct as what we should pay: Mr. Nate White, c/o Hughes, Apt. 1-D, 634 St Nicholas Avenue, New York 30, N. Y., as he goes down every day to take care of my mail, so anything you want him to do in New York, let him know. If you send a check for fight tickets, make it payable to him. . . . . Ivan has the TENNY REPORT (California's little Dies Committee) for 1948, and it even has Dr. Ruth Temple in it! Half a page is devoted to Loren. Mrs. Bethune is called "a notorious Communist" as am I (several times.) Curious thing about it is most of the actual party members are not mentioned at all or only in passing. Which is what makes me think much of this sound and fury is to scare the liberals and interracialists. It is certainly having that effect out this way, too.

. . . . . I've sold at least two copies of your book here and several teachers are ordering it. Eulah loved it and is getting a copy for her nieces.

. . . . . Laura Fowler (nee ?) former classmate of yours where Allied Arts had meeting Sunday sends regards to you. Fay has been married again and divorced since I was here last. There's a FINE new cullud hotel on West Side, the Watkins, where I don't intend to stay since they are so nice to me here at the Clark and it is too far from everywhere.

. . . . . Will be in Chi the 27th.

Lang

P.S. Juanita Miller can't swallow ever so often, but the doctors say it is all mind. (The Negroes say it is Loren! [her husband]). . . . . Bob Weaver wrote about the Dinner. He wants Simple there, too.

Nice spread on "The American Race Track" in current *Vogue*. Jockey's rigs in color, etc.

Clark Hotel

Dear Arna,

The West Indians got all your books and were highly pleased. (Did I tell you?). . . . I found a nice note from Motley at Pullman. He's 8 miles from the sea. I was 4 miles from the Idaho border. Whole state between! . . . . Saw Owen in Pasadena at my program. Miss Warren introduced me. Miss English and Miss Britton were there. All send Greetings to you (with a big G.) As do various others out here. . . . I'm just back from Beverly Hills and a couple of hours with Arthur Koestler who spoke at Philharmonic last night. Loren and I went and I, to my amazement, heard in the midst of his speech (part where he declares USSR has betrayed the Negroes of the world) this, "That great Negro poet I met in Russia, a member of the Party as was I, Langston Hughes, *who is now dead,* was stranded in Soviet Asia. . . . . etc."

When he saw me backstage afterward, you should have seen him! The best laugh this year! Shades of Countee Cullen! Do all cullud poets look alike even to European whites? . . . . He sent a wire to 7 newspapers correcting both misstatements—Party and funeral. And we drank Scotch together this afternoon. I told him his whole speech sounded just like the Chi. Trib. & the Hearst Herald-Ex. Which it did! He's a poor scared "half-Jew"—(his definition of nationality) altho he was a whole Jew when I first met him! Well, maybe he will get only "half"-baked when the next Hitler comes. I hope not entirely.

Lang

P.S. He looked when I walked in not unlike you, at Margaret Walker's dinner. He claims Robert Montgomery told him I was dead!

July 9, 1948

Dear Arna,

I've put in three days with Moe Gale, Noble Sissle and NBC trying to save the colored show that was to have been the National Minstrels till cullud started pouring letters of protest in and scared the white folks and made the Negro actors (to have been employed) MAD! Looks kinder hopeless though—and is now at the usual nobody-knows-what-they-want stage. All I want is my CASH which Ah intends to git. They're not doing anything with the racial taboos surrounding either Hollywood or the radio. (And the show as recorded *was* AWFUL originally.)

I found one good poem of the guy in *Les Cenelles;* short clever little love lyric, but only one long poem about Napoleon for Laneuse, not very good and very long in classical rhymes—so no can do! But the other one, yes.

234

BRUCE McM. WRIGHT came by today at my invitation and brought some new poems—on racial themes—and the one enclosed I like very much. Maybe we could include it, too, as I think the guy is going places and will surely have another book soon. He brought me the one published abroad, also a poem published in France translated. We would sort of be introducing him to America as he has had practically nothing published here.

I'll be looking for you night of the 13th—which is Tuesday. Looking forward to seeing you and hearing all the news of Yaddo.

Langston

20 East 127th Street,
New York 35, New York,
August 21, 1948.

Dear Arna:

Some thoughts for the PREFACE: It should be made clear (for the sake of the critics and also for the comfort of the West Indians—whom one drop of white blood makes white, and not the other way around as it is here) that we have drawn no color line in our anthology, using the work of all poets who write even obliquly on Negro themes, peoples, or lands. (Also since in Haiti our title word NEGRO means *jet black* to them—they must be comforted, too.)

From their viewpoint a better title would be, The Poetry of Color.

Also maybe you should mention LES CENELLES poets a bit more than they are in the two biographies. It's rather amusing how concerned they were with love while the rest of the poor Negroes like Horton and Mrs. Harper were writing about slavery and freedom.

It should also be made clear that the "Caribbean" is only a token representation, not intended to be comprehensive.

Possibly, too, it should be mentioned that although the main section is arranged chronologically, the other two sections are arranged—particularly the NON-NEGRO—in a historical-dramatic sequence for reading purposes.

All these are merely suggestions for you to use or not. I know the piece has to be brief.

Please insert the new enclosed copy of "The Caribbean" in your copy. 5th line was just backward. This correction came from Jamaica, as it had been misprinted originally.

Sincerely,
Lang

N.Y.C., September 14, 1948

Dear Arna,

The permissions department sent quite a long list to me of missing permissions, folks who haven't answered, etc. Most of them I am able to do something about. (For instance, just prodded Waring Cuney personally, wrote Guillen, Jamaicans (4), etc.)

But they are still worried about Fenton Johnson and Aquah Laluah. They also

235

wish the next of kin of Benjamin Brawley and James David Corruthers (or wish to know what to do about them). So since I don't know (and already relayed once what you said about the first two to them) would you kindly take up the matter of these four from here on in, and write Buck what you find out, or what decisions to make, PLEASE.

I DO NOT BELIEVE THIS HERE ANTHOLOGY WILL EVER END.

And last night Cedric Dover up at Doug's come telling me he had discovered a poet of color BEFORE Horton that we should by all means include and that he had told you about her! Well, should we???? (It would take just about one more poet to make me as dead as she is!) But maybe I could stand just one more.

A MOST BEAUTIFUL Italian edition of *The Big Sea* arrived today with, of all things, a Pablo Picasso jacket! Also Griff Davis arrived from Chicago. And Zell started our mural, and the plumber to install a shower on my floor. And the contract for a new musical came through with advance. And I have completed a new book I wrote last week! We will NOT put no parts of this in the Anthology. One more listing—and I expire! No kidding—a full book-length poem in five sections called *Montage of a Dream Deferred*. Want to see it? Or do you have time to read, being a writer your own self?

Langston

P.S. The new poem is what you might call a precedent shattering opus—also could be known as a *tour de force*. . . . Profiles of Walter White in last two issues of New Yorker. . . . He and Dr. W.E.B. feuding. So W.E.B. is fired again! (See today's *Times*.)

20 East 127th Street
New York 35, New York,
October 4, 1948.

Dear Arna,

Well, it is cold enough to turn on the furnace in the house today for the first time! . . . . . . Thanks a lot for your encouraging comments on *Montage of a Dream Deferred*. (It is *vraiment* a *tour de force*, but seems to come off somewhatly.) I guess I failed to tell you Jake Lawrence is doing drawings for it. And I am having parts of it set to music—song suites, no less. Also intend to make a ballet from what is left after that! . . . . Also, just for fun, I think I shall add "Ain't There Any Dialectics for the Heart" to it—in the light of Rex, Kenneth, and Paul's downtown carryings-on. Which would just about make it required reading for Harlem! . . . . . Margaret Walker was in town with a book of poems and part of a novel and talking as rapidly as usual. . . . . . From Thyra Edwards in Italy comes a long letter saying as how she is convalescing on Lake Como. . . . . Opportunity is doing a double page spread of our Jamaican poets with pictures. The *Crisis* ditto with Guillen. Virtue and Piquion sent quite a few photos we can use for publicity when the book comes out. Those guys have really been swell, so if you have any duplicate books around send them some. I will do the same on this end. . . . . . The Poetry League of Jamaica just celebrated its 25th Silver Anniversary. I sent a cable. . . . . . Nate and I are writing West Indian letters tonight. It is my determination to PUT that box out of sight after this evening. Not much more to do now. Except to entertain those who come to New York. George Campbell is back in town now. Hope to meet him. And

236

Louis Simpson consents to be in our book, but says he ain't cullud. (I don't blame him much!)......

Sincerely,
Lang

Tell Paul I'd appreciate his reaction—as a member of the be-bop generation —and an Omega brother.

L.

20 East 127th Street
New York 35, New York
October 11, 1948

Dear Arna:

No sooner said than done, my friend. Your letter arrived this morning and ere nightfall I have prepared the outline for our Harlem anthology and am dropping it in the mail for Max this evening. A copy is enclosed for you. Any additions or corrections which you wish to add may be sent to me and they will go on the next typing. I have urged Max to immediate action, due to your foresight in calling to my attention the rapid approach of Xmas. Also, I asked him to find out which publishers (if not Farrar, Straus) are bringing out the states and cities series, and to approach them. A letter from you to Max, further enlarging upon the possibilities and charms of the Harlem anthology, might put additional words in his mouth to entice the publishers. So kindly write him immediately.

Since the Spingarn Collection has moved to Washington and Antonio Jarvis of the Virgin Islands has perhaps come to fame since the death of Mr. Schomburg (and that Collection happens to be closed now for painting until October 13, anyhow) I do not know where to lay hands on any of the poems of Mr. Jarvis. Do you? His omission is, however, an indication of some negligence on our part. It might look as though we were discriminating against the American colonies, as we have no Puerto Ricans either. (I told Hugh to write EYE-THER).

The Doubleday office answers NO mail whatsoever, and Buck being in the country on Mondays, I could not phone him today. But I will let you know about the publication date as soon as I can. Both it and *One-Way Ticket* were not definite a couple of weeks ago, but more or less scheduled for mid-winter—that is, *some* time after the holidays.

If you have some extra books to send Piquion, I do think it would be a nice thing to do.

Concerning the *Ebony* article, I shall write Ben Burns shortly, and since Griff Davis is living here with us now, it would be no problem to get some new action shots of the colored poets around Harlem, such as Waring Cuney in his cups, myself in my new shower, and Mr. Braithwaite descending the steps at 409. These pictures, plus your prose, should make a very interesting piece, and as a sample of the poetry, we could include, "Upstaffed, upstood, upstanding" or Damas' on "Most doggishly dog," which ought to intrigue almost anybody—except conservative librarians!

My dear fellow, I do not see why you do not come to New York for a little

237

trip before the anthology comes out, and then you can make another one when it does appear. The Harpers always have bed and board.

Sincerely,
Lang

1611 Meharry Blvd.
Nashville 8, Tenn.
13 (Birthday of A. B.) Oct. '48

Dear Lang,

So This is Harlem is right. It will do as the working outline. I have added two items under the magazine section of my copy: the James Weldon Johnson profile in the *New Yorker* and the one on Dan Burley in *Esquire* called "Now I Stash Me Down To Nod", I believe. Others will come to mind all along the line, so this will grow rapidly like the "Montage" as it's worked on. Luck to us, and may the best publisher get the job! Or at least one who will advance us no less than $250 apiece by the first of December.

Flournoy Miller was here last night, en route to N. Y. C. You know, Nashville is his native town, and Fisk his school. Marie Johnson brought him here to a little club gathering, and Doug (between times) read part of your *Montage* and said it was like a re-flowering of the Renaissance. Like the silver tree, the shining rivers, the sobbing jazz band, the long-headed dancers and the shameless gals. He was quite moved. Miller mentioned working with you on the radio show.

"Early Bright" is a sharp section title, and the poems will fit too. After you have added and added, however, you may find yourself going back and cutting a little. But that's no trouble. Did I ever mention "Night Funeral"? Solid!

I've just reviewed *Booker T. Washington: A Biography* for the N. Y. Herald Trib. And I see where Walter *(A Man Called White)* still has *St. Louis Woman* on his mind enough to renew his attack and make his defense of his attack in his autobiography. He also speaks of being attacked in return, a fact I didn't know about. It wasn't none of me because all I did was to keep my mouth shut. But it amuses me to see that the episode stays on the conscience of even so busy a gladiator as he.

Said and agreed: I'll make up a box of books for Piquion. It will be in the mail to him this week, and if you are writing him you may mention it, since the regular mails may take a month to carry it.

Invitations still coming in for Book Week, but I haven't settled on ANY of them definitely yet. Would you throw the book at Mr. Moe for me if I was to ask for a Guggenheim—to tie-in with my forthcoming sabbatical?

Best,
Arna

17 Oct. '48 The day
Indian Summer ended.

Dear Lang,

That wonderful weather lasted through the football game and the Homecoming parade and dance, but toward midnight we realized it was finished. A

238

letter from Erick Berry saying they're heading for Jamaica presently, via Haiti, for the winter should have been a tip-off, but it took wind and rain to convince us.

So today I'm trying to gather into barns, and I have just about cleared up my desk, what with no visitors on this Sunday and no temptation to go out and get soaked and chilled to the marrow. Among the things done was a rather full letter to Era Bell Thompson at *Ebony* giving ideas for the picture story on poets. I suggested that the pictures center around the group of new voices which were not yet chirping when Countee and JWJ issued their anthologies: O'Higgins, Hayden, Dodson, Frank M. Davis, G. Brooks, M. Walker, M. B. Tolson, Bette D. Latimore, the infant of the lot. I mentioned the pictures Griff has already taken of the editors at work and suggested points of interest on these oldsters: Braithwaite (his selected poems coming out this fall), Anne Spencer, Clarissa Scott-Delany (early promise and death), Donald Jeffrey Hayes (his poems in popular mags., like Yerby in that he's had some non-racial vogue in H. Bazaar, etc.) and Sterling Brown who's interesting in his own way. I said that Wheatley is the only ante-bellum singer whose photo I'd seen and suggested using pictures of Dunbar, JWJ and Countee. I gave addresses where needed—except in case of O'Higgins who's in N. Y. now where perhaps you will run into him. Maybe I should have included Frank Horne, but I didn't—oversight. And I told her I'd write the piece when she lets me know she's ready for it.

One of the BWI fellows here has let me see his copy of the article that resulted in Roger Mais' jailing. I'm having it copied and will send you a carbon. . . . I thought we could leave all pictures of these out of the *Ebony* spread (not out of the article), since they'll get treatment in *Crisis* and *Opportunity* and maybe elsewhere. The more articles the better for the anthology. How about one in *Our World* on the non-U. S. bunch?

In a letter to Maxim I added what I could to your very adequate outline for the Harlem anthology. Just to show I was interested and punching.

You may find the piece on the Bronx melting pot in the SEPost (Oct. 23) interesting. Much oblique comment on Harlem. Profiting by experience.

And Charles Neider's *Short Novels of the Masters* is an excellent job. You'll like the introductory material. Not to mention the ten top novellas. Me, I'm deep in *The Young Lions,* most readable war novel (to me) since *A Farewell to Arms.*

Did I tell you that the secretarial situation has been saved by Magdelain Crawford, who was Horace's secretary until last week? She says Horace is not at all well and that he will take a year off—at least. So she will work for us in the hope of later getting into school to complete work for her unfinished degree and re-orient herself. My former aide is nearing the time of confinement and Alberta is this minute attending a shower the campus women are having for her.

C. S. J. rolled out in a new 1949 Lincoln last week—the biggest and best of the brand! Must have cost a million dollars.

If you see Hugh, will you ask whether or not he received the book I sent a month or so ago?

That package of books to Piquion is costing $2.40 postage, but now that it's all tied up (14 books) I'll try to raise the money and let it go. He's worth it.

Ever,
Arna

20 East 127th Street,
New York 35, New York,
October 25, 1948.

Dear Arna,
I reckon you got the proofs of the Biographies O.K. and that they are half-way back here by now.

Schomburg still closed for painting so no Virgin Islands Jarvis. Too bad to leave him out. Some critic will be sure to miss him—just like some will swear they do not see why we did not include "Sonnet" by J. Fillmore Yaffner or "When Dusk Breaks" by Sadie Maxwell Jenkins-Bailey. And I will say, "Why Mister Bontemps was in charge of that section."

Another little job for you: YOU do a short piece right now—5–6 pages—to submit to the *Negro Digest* on the "Adventures of An Anthologist", work and excitement of assembling, etc., as you've done several, jobs of getting birth dates out of folks, etc. humorous; thrill of discovering new talent, Upstaffed, upstanding", etc. As it WILL FURTHER HELP PUBLICIZE OUR ANTHOLOGY. And I will do one on translating and reconverting from one language to another—which will help publicize both anthology and Guillen book. And neither piece will take more than an hour or so to write. *So Write Yours This Evening!*

Look here: that address you sent here for Myron O'Higgins is the Manufacturers Trust Company bank! Does he get his mail there? WHERE does he live????????
We want to get his picture. . . . . . Griff has gone to Jersey to photograph Jessie this evening. Has Cuney, Braithwaite, Wright, already, and will send the lot off this week-end so check on Myron's address again, will you, and lemme know?

Hayden's poetry reads beautifully in Anthology proofs. *Fine!*

Lang

22 November '48

Dear Lang,
Texas was nice enough and paid well, but the New Orleans interlude is the thing I remember. Some of my remote kin showed up—though I had not told them I was coming—and later there was a fresh oyster place, and I ate 14 on the half shell while drinking a bottle of beer. But it was at Alabama State in Montgomery that they put on the show for me. I was there jointly in celebration of Book Week and in honor of the first anniversary of their new Library. The Library staff presented me in co-operation with the English department. Big audience despite rain, followed by one of those Negro college receptions! I'm still trying to catch up sleep.

You have taken more time with your tour, I see—which I should have done. Anyhow, I'm eager to see Hampton, and I'll go there for Negro History week if they invite me. Maybe it could be tied in with that D.C. thing I'm trying to promote—of which you received notice. Which reminds me, when do you go to Chicago?

A letter was here from Knopf (juvenile dept.) saying that they had reprinted *Story of the Negro.* I can scarcely believe it, considering the size of first. They told me it was 10,000, but that must have been wrong. I don't suppose there'll be an actual report before January. Half of the above will make me happy at this date.

But they did say that one dealer (McClurg) had sold 500 copies. So we'd better not give up the Negro theme yet. Maybe Negroes themselves are buying a few books now. . . . I trust *Poetry of the Negro* will fare as well. If the pattern is the same, it will have a modest pre-publication sale but pick up immediately afterwards and increase as the reviews and recommended lists begin to approve it. I plugged it all along the way on my trip. Half a dozen teachers told me they plan to use it.

Also in my absence, Paul was selected for inclusion in *Who's Who in American Colleges* (I think that's the title) for this year. Which puzzles me, since he never appears to "try" for anything. Just seems to let the tide carry him along.

Doug is having a showing of the water colors he did this summer, and the campus is anticipating Dorothy Maynor's concert next week, and I'm trying to get out of a half-promise to show up at the meeting of the National Council of English in Chicago the Thanksgiving weekend. On top of everything the need to get some writing done becomes pressing. Of course, I may just sit down and do nothing till the pressure's off. Particularly since I'm deep in a stack of huge new novels *(The Young Lions, The Naked and The Dead, Guard of Honor),* among other books, and would enjoy just reading for a while. I think you would enjoy these novels too.

The letter came from Jane Hudson of P.E.N. Thanks for putting her in touch. She said I had been invited *years* ago. I can't imagine which of my publishers misaddressed the letter in forwarding.

Have you started work on your musical? And what is the date on *One Way Ticket?* And do you suppose we'll get some personal copies of the Anthology by mid-December, so that we could use them for Xmas, ahead of publication?

Ever,
Arna

20 East 127th Street
New York 35, New York
December 2, 1948

Mr. Arna Bontemps
1611 Meharry Boulevard
Nashville 8, Tennessee

Dear Arna:

I have just talked to Buck Moon's secretary. She said that since we were both off on lecture tours when the page proofs were received, that they did not send them to either of us in order not to hold up the publication date which remains January 6th. The proofs were read in the office.

She says that the first copies of the book will be available between December 17th and 20th, so I am ordering a few for Christmas gifts to Hugh, Nathaniel, Cedric Dover, and perhaps one or two others of the folks who helped us so faithfully on the work involved.

Buck Moon (as frequently happens) was not in and so I could not discuss with him any of the promotion plans that you have written about. However, I do hope that programs can be arranged in New York, Washington, and Chicago. As to my time, I expect to be in South Carolina and possibly Virginia during Negro

History Week—that is from about February 6th to February 14th. Other than that, I shall be here in New York until February 28th when I go to Chicago for two months at the University there, having just put that commitment off from the 1st of the year to the Spring Quarter, since I have this musical show on my hands at the moment and have to work out my advance, having become a kind of literary sharecropper.

I have just looked through, personally, with my own hands, all of the anthology material which I have here, and I do not see any clippings of poems by Charles Enoch Wheeler. Neither do I recall seeing any in the anthology material which I sent to Yale after I finished reading the galleys, since I looked through that material very carefully to see if we have omitted returning anything to anyone. I gather that Mr. Wheeler must have sent us material of which he did not retain any copies. I should think at his age he would know better—because apparently we did not retain any copies of it either! To tell the truth, I do not recall having ever seen it. The only thing I know to do is to extend our sincere regrets and send him a free copy of the anthology, and tell him that with his genius, he could easily make up some other poems. (Or couldn't he get back copies of the papers they appeared in?). . . . In any case, poets are hardly likely to be as difficult as composers. Both of my opera people are behaving as though they smoked reefers between every note. Since I do not indulge in any such habits myself, I am not given to displaying temperament. I just sit calmly and let them blow their tops. I have never been one to take art too hard, nor to send off to anybody the *one and only* copies of my poetries.

May the Lord bless and keep you,

Sincerely,
Lang

P.S. My congratulations to your son Paul for achieving *Who's Who in American Colleges!* And to you for the splendid sale of *The Story of the Negro!* Let's hope your novel sells ten times that much.

Try writing Buck Moon another letter and see if you can get just *one* answer out of Doubleday before the anthology appears. It is the most non-letter-writing firm I have ever dealt with in my natural life.

12/8/48

Hey, you—

Thought I told you *not* to mention U. of C. deal! Folks writing from Chi already about free talks—said it was you! And in the cullud papers this week!

Did you get your "One-Way Ticket" yet? Jake Lawrence just brought 5 wonderful drawings for the be-bop poems.

Swanson is writing music for some of them. But wanted a new (longer line semi-dirge) "Night Funeral." So I did one for him.

Lang

P.S. Aunt Toy gave me a dog! (For Xmas) Wirehair.

242

Dear Lang,

I hope the enclosed, which I have just sent to W. Rose Benét, does not keep me from getting One-Way Ticket for review from the Sat. Rev. Of Lit., but I felt it was necessary in view of the approaching publication of The Poetry of the Negro for me to give them a chance to back out in face of the facts if they want to. As you'll see, I also used that as an opportunity to try to get them to have Jay Saunders review our anthology. Anyhow, the poetic pot is boiling, and you're in that pot.

It was also my pleasure yesterday to toot the horn for Hugh and support his application for Dorothy's job at the Schomburg. I really think he'll be very good for that work of curatorship. Tell him that if he thinks it will help him in the early stages, it could probably be easily arranged for me to come up and assist in the orientation, etc. I'll always be available for a week or two in the ideas department.

Since we are so slow getting our copies of *Cuba Libre* (through McClurg), I'm constrained to beg you to hold on to at least 3 of your copies for us *till it is determined* whether or not McClurg will actually come in on any of the 500 copies of the edition.

I'm an innocent victim on that news leak re: your going to Chicago for the spring quarter. It must have come from my efforts to line up the poetry festival there. I spoke to Era Bell, indicating that you might be available as a result of U of C work—vague, no more than that—and M. Crawford wrote M. Peters of the writers' group in the same connection. Well, maybe we're guilty. Alas, I'm most abject. Especially since nothing has come of the anthology idea which was behind it.

It will be exciting to hear the songs that are being written around parts of the *Montage.* "Night Funeral in Harlem" looks good for music. . . . Now that you have a dog to walk, you and Simple can have yourselves a time, up and down the avenue, through the park, etc.

Best ever,
Arna

Suggested names for dog: Thomas Mann, Marcel Proust, T. S. Eliot, or Josephine Baker, if it's a she.

December 16, 1948.

Dear Arna:

I was delighted to have both of your letters but have been so busy this week I have not had a chance to answer until now. I certainly appreciated your wonderful remarks about *One-Way Ticket,* and am showing your letter to Bill Cole of Knopf's publicity department, although, of course, I will ask him not to quote from it without your permission.

I phoned Doubleday but advance copies of the anthology have not come in as yet, although they think I may be able to see one before this week is out. Buck is at home with the Grippe, as is Maxim Lieber. But I am mailing Buck the enclosed memo for a proposed poetry festival. When you write him, also add a little persuasion regarding this.

Of course we would be delighted to have you stay with us when you come to town on January 6th. There is even a vacant room at the moment which can be all your own. Please send your check for theatre tickets soon and your selection of plays listed in order of preference.

Our brothers, the Omegas, possibly plan to arrange a book review evening at the Schomburg while you are here, as they did recently for Henry Moon's book.

You should have your personal copy of *Cuba Libre* by now as I signed one of the very first copies for you from my author's allotment. The ones I ordered have not come yet either, nevertheless I have written them to be sure your library order through McClurg is filled.

We do not need a name for the dog as somebody opened the front door the other day and the little hound lit out, turned the corner at a thousand miles an hour, headed straight downtown, and was heard to bark as he crossed 110th street, "No More Niggers!" (He had been raised and trained by whites.)

Sincerely,
Langston

20 East 127th Street
New York 35, New York
December 17, 1948

Dear Arna:

I have just come from Doubleday's and am in possession of one of the first copies of our anthology. It is a very fine looking book with a stunning jacket that will show up wonderfully in bookshop windows. Everyone is very pleased with its appearance. Six copies have been mailed to you, so they tell me, and five more to me directly from the printers. I hope that we both receive them before Christmas, but the mails are very slow these days. Buck was out so I did not see him.

I had luncheon with the Knopf publicity people and they are intending to propose to Doubleday some joint publicity activities since our Anthology and my own book of poems come out only four days apart.

A couple of people here in New York tell me that they have received their orders of the Guillen book, so I imagine yours is on the way for the library. Certainly you should have the copy I personally mailed to you by now. Perhaps you can review that book for some publication. It ought to be in the running for a citation as one of the handsomest books of the year.

I am enclosing an additional reviewer's list which I just sent to Buck Moon. I suggest that you send him a list also if any other persons come to mind. I've already submitted a list of Negro publications to him.

On Monday I have to pay a Three Hundred Dollar option to hold my interest in the Movie rights for *Street Scene*. I am still about Forty Dollars short of the amount, and it is a surprise assessment (I had forgotten those terms in the contract) that has wiped out all of my Christmas money. It is a good thing I did not do my Christmas shopping early or my movie rights might have been gone with the wind. I WARN YOU ONE MORE TIME ABOUT FOOLING AROUND WITH THE THEATRE. It does more than cripple your legs. It cripples your soul.

Sincerely,
Lang

12-19-'48

Dear Lang,

If one can believe the radio, you now have 19 inches of snow in N. Y. and no air service, so I suppose regular mail is best for this. But I'm no less excited about your two specials—in the space of eight hours. And I can scarcely wait to see the early copies of *The Poetry of the Negro*. I've seen one notice already. It appeared in the current issue of the Library Journal (perhaps January, since it just came Friday) and is slightly snide, though it does say the book will be a standard work, or words to that effect.

The roadblocks have not yet been rolled back to make the January trip definite, for I'll have to find a way to tie it in with Library or University errands to bring it off, but I hope to clear this—one way or the other in a day or two. Meanwhile, I see no reason why the plans for promotion should not move ahead, and if I fail to show, you can carry the banner. The Omega book review evening at the Schomburg, the Poetry festival—sure book them all and count on me to get there if I can, but be ready to stand alone if necessary.

Sorry about your race-prejudiced pup. I had already begun to see you in a new role: gentleman poet with slippers, pipe and dog.

If I think of any other possible reviewers of the Anthology, I'll send them in, but you seem to have covered the ground. No other thoughts come to mind at once.

Paul went with a bunch of Fisk boys to try and get Xmas runs on the Santa Fe as waiters during the holiday season when so many regular men take off. He is in Chicago now and hoping to ship out tomorrow (Monday). A year or two ago few Fisk boys would have considered working during their vacation, but times are getting back to normal—and this seems more real to me.

The theatre will do you in alright, but maybe it's worth it. I wouldn't know. Just the same I'm nursing a couple of ideas for plays, including the one about Mr. Jelly, and hoping to get around to them in '49 perhaps.

Meanwhile,

Ever,
Arna

12-27-'48

Dear Lang,

I just this minute got my first look at the Anthology. For some mysterious reason Doubleday sent my author's copies to Maxim, and he equally mysteriously took out one and sent it to me while holding the rest for me to pick up—he must have guessed that I'd be in N.Y. at some future time. Anyhow, I like the looks of the job very much and hope there are no boners between the covers like the one in the top line of the back page of the jacket: Richard Hayden! So hurrah for us and would that I might come to N.Y. right away to help celebrate our coming out. On this I still have nothing to report—no good or adequate justification has been found for asking Fisk to send me, and Xmas has left me totally unable to consider paying the freight myself. My only comfort is that you are right there and can speak for us both in case Doubleday arranges any interviews or radio appearances as Buck said. (Please tell Miss Blackwell at the Schomburg that

245

I'm delaying my answer to her letter in the hope of having something definite before the end of this week. I see no reason why she should not go ahead with her plans as set and apologize for my failure to show up if necessary.)

Now to another beautiful book: *Cuba Libre.* My copy did finally get here despite the Xmas log jam, and it is a delight to the eye, for which I'm most grateful. . . . And at almost the same time the Library received its copies via McClurg. So *Cuba Libres* are all over the place now, and come the second semester they're sure to be discussed frequently along with *One-Way Ticket* and The *Poetry of the Negro,* not to mention Braithwaite's *Selected Poems.*

Of real moment is a letter just received from Dorothy Porter in D.C. She says that her writing group will consider the plan I proposed in my letter very soon now (toward the end of this month) and let us know what has been arranged. She thinks the idea is grand and is hopeful of its success. So stand-by. At least one of our proposed poetry festivals may come off yet.

As soon as I can nail something down definitely I'll send the money for the theatre tickets, but I just seem to stay in a crack and hence no action. The only confirmed date is the Negro History thing in Indianapolis. And I hope to keep that flexible as long as possible in case something else comes through.

You know, of course, about Doug's exhibition at the Chabot Art Gallery in L.A. But have you read the poems in your honor in Pilar E. Barrios' *Piel Negra?* The Library has just received a copy, inscribed by the Uruguayan poet.

Let me recommend a book after your own heart, *The Saroyan Special,* containing more than 90 short stories in a handsome and exciting package—snappy, be-bop reading, and a great jacket.

Hayden is in N.Y. for the holidays. Myron is in touch with him, I believe. And Myron tells folks down here that he is melancholy in N.Y. and plans to pull out presently.

Have you finished your work on the show? I've managed to do about a dozen pages of creative writing since school closed, and maybe I can do that much more before it opens again, which doesn't seem like enough, but I suppose I should be satisfied, considering the total confusion Santa Claus has left in his wake.

You heard about *Opportunity* folding. Well here's a SECRET: C.S.J. is pondering the idea of taking it over and bringing it to Fisk. I'm trying to push him into it. I suppose it will depend in part on the money he can line up for it. If successful, I'll also propose an all-Southern writers' conference to launch its new phase—including, of course, some non-Southern writers closely identified with Negro and southern subjects. Your ideas will be thrown into the pot, if you offer them, but remember this is a SECRET.

Best ever,
Arna

January 8, 1949

Dear Lang,

Your wire just came, and the reports of the Schomburg meeting and the N.Y. Times review are thrilling. I'm terribly sorry I can't be there for the drum beating. But with the second semester tuition bills due February first (About $400, including Joan, Paul and Alex's nursery school) and the bills for the pre-Xmas buying

246

just coming in from the department stores, etc., I don't feel up to a New York journey on my own resources. Nothing could be arranged through the school because Buck wrote me so late there wasn't enough time to set up any legitimate errands. I begged for a word from him earlier so that I might plan other work to coincide with publication, but nothing came—not even a reply. As a result, I'm stuck. So please carry on for us both and make apologies for me where necessary.

Not to be completely pessimistic, however, it has occurred to me that maybe I could come up to N.Y. for a few days following the D.C. Festival. (If the second floor front is still empty!) Dorothy Porter's air mail special yesterday seemed to indicate strong likelihood of an event at Howard, prompted by the Library, on February 11th. So I'm trying to push my Indianapolis date ahead a day, and I've told her that she may schedule us so far as I'm concerned.

My authors copies came from Lieber a day ago, weakly packed and badly battered—to continue the dismal report—and I'll start paying debts to local helpers. And I'll ultimately adjust with you the difference in the number distributed to the folks to whom we're mutually obligated—as indicated by your underscored list.

Thanks for that warm send-off to the Guggenheim folks. It occurs to me that age may now be a factor against my request for grant, but your sponsorship could not have been stated better. I'm delighted with it.

In Nashville we have been carrying on our own promotional campaign for the Anthology through Mills Book Store. I've autographed 15 copies for them and given them names of local people who might be prospects. The Times review should help even at this distance. (I hope you have clipped an extra copy for me. And that you will do the same with others that may appear in New York papers.). . . . Please tell Mr. Cole and Buck that if there are any of those assignments that can wait till after Feb. 11th, I'll be happy to do what I can when I get there: you mentioned some for me alone, I believe.

You had a big day in the Fisk Memorial Auditorium yesterday. Miss Rhoda Jordan, now an assistant in the department of Speech, gave nearly an hour's performance of monologues and readings before the student convocation, winding it up with two of yours most effectively done, "Freedom Train" (as she did it on the Wallace campaign programs) and "I Dream a World," which was her l'envoy. Big response. And she was pleased afterward when I told her I'd report on it to you.

So let the poetry ring, and more anon.

Ever,
Arna

20 East 127th Street
New York 35, New York
Sunday, January 9, 1949

Dear Arna,

Just got your special. Too bad you'll miss the party tomorrow as Carl, Spingarns, Dorothy, and lots of folks we know are coming, plus book review people, etc. It's joint Doubleday-Knopf so ought to be quite something.

If I'd known for sure you're not coming, would've air-mailed this *Times* clipping at once and you'd have had it by now. You and Buck Moon are about equally bad about definite news, Ah regrets to say. Been around cullud too long, I reckon, the two of you.

Schomburg evening looked like a flashback to the twenties—all the old timers there, even Mirian Minus whom I hadn't seen for years—Arthur Spingarn, Ridgely Torrence, Braithewaite, Harold—etc.etc.etc.etc. Only you and Charles S. Johnson missing. And for so momentous an occasion as the appearance of the VERY FIRST ANTHOLOGY OF ITS KIND IN AMERICAN LITERARY HISTORY, looks like you all could have flown up for the evening and been back in time for breakfast (grits) the next morning. Anyhow, there was an empty chair on the platform in your honor!

> I been scared and battered.
> My proofs the wind done scattered.
> Sun has baked me,
> Snow has friz me—
> And didn't nobody come to help me
> Launch this here old antho-LO-gy.

Only thing we might miss out on due to your absence is AUTHORS ROUND TABLE as they need more than one person on it, and have been unable to get Louis Untermeyer or Benet as yet to fill in.

I am going right now to hear Mahalia Jackson at the Golden Gate and renew my soul. Also getting material for an article on Gospel Singers for *Ebony.* So, two birds with one event.

Do not speak of money! We are all so broke here it is a cullud shame. I am looking diligently for my two War Bonds that I hid from myself so they could mature. But almost nothing matures in Harlem soil. (And if I can find these, they will never mature in my hands.) (In fact, they will not even approach fruition.)

I air-mailed Dorothy Porter February 11 is fine for me enroute from North Carolina to Boston where I close Negro History Week. . . . . . . And sure you can come on up to New York. Always bed and board here for you here, be it ever so humble. At least we have plenty room now, and you are Mrs. Harper's favorite guest. So come on.

Sincerely,
Lang

Charged me 1¢ for your letter. AIRMAIL is now SIX cents. Did you know? A new Jamaican just came up the steps from Kingston.

L.

January 17, 1949

Dear Arna:

I am again sending Dorothy Porter a list of the poets living in Washington who might take part in our program to be held there on February 11th. Would you kindly write her urging her to make it a real Poet's Festival, utilizing the talents of these various people—because I gather from her note to me today that she seems to think you and I will just about constitute the whole program—and I'll be damned if I want to give Howard University a $200.00 evening for $20.00

248

expense money. My original idea was that this would be a poet's festival, not a Hughes-Bontemps program.

Mrs. Porter writes that the University will provide rooms for us in Cook Hall and that a small dinner will probably be arranged with faculty members and poets prior to the lectures. She asks that we arrange to have books on sale there, and I've already gotten in touch with Doubleday concerning this.

Today I have received a copy of KYK-OVER-AL, Published by the British Guiana Writers' Association in conjunction with the D.F.P. Advertising Service and the B.G. Union of Cultural Clubs. Edited by A. J. Seymour. Price, One Shilling Net. Vol 2, No. 7, December, 1948 (Contributions and letters should be sent to the Editor "KYK-OVER-AL" 120 Fourth Street, Georgetown, British Guiana. Business communications should be addressed to J.E. Humphrey, Esq, Manager, D.F.P. Advertising Service, 4A Hope Street, Georgetown, British Guiana. P.O. Box 267. I thought perhaps you might like to have this for your library.

But the main purpose of this letter is to ask you to write Dorothy Porter about our Washington program.

Sincerely yours,
Langston

Fisk University Library
Nashville 8, Tennessee
January 25, 1949

Dear Lang:

We are today placing orders for all the translations of your books except the ones marked in red to indicate that they could be obtained from you. We want these, too, and will look forward to receiving them in the Library. Meanwhile I hope there will be no delays for the others in Argentina, Brazil, Chile, and Venezuela. Your list of translations is impressive, to say the least! I am sure librarians will be grateful to you for this list, and I suggest that you send it rather widely to those who have shown an interest in Negro writing.

And while I'm writing I might mention that column Mrs. FDR wrote about our Anthology. Many people mentioned it to me at the Midwinter Meeting of the ALA but I have not yet seen it. Do you have a copy you could share?

I was very pleased with the circular letter Doubleday sent out on the Anthology. I would not have seen that either if Paul had not been on the mailing list by some chance. It is indeed a very good letter for the purpose.

The Chicago meeting was fine, and I stayed at the Edgewater Beach Hotel in more luxury than I've ever before experienced—even at Atlantic City. And all for only $4.90 a day. Even less than it would cost to stay at the Theresa and not much more than at the Grand.

I have accepted the engagement offered by the St. James Literary Forum in Cleveland for May 8. I am also booking several day-time engagements in New York during my sojourn. The man who wrote me about the Harlem Radio Broadcast has not replied to my question as to the hour of the broadcast. I would not want to miss the theater to talk on the air but would not object to saying a few words in the afternoon or morning of February 14. He mentioned you in his letter.

More anon.

Ever,
Arna

January 28, 1949

Dear Arna:

So far the two reviews that I have seen of our Anthology have been fine toward the Negro poetry, but, like this one in the *Times,* sort of lukewarm toward the white poets in our anthology, and the lady in St. Louis seemed a bit confused that they should be in there at all. My feeling is that they are still for strict segregation when it comes to poetry—as most of the "white" anthologies attest—since they leave us out entirely.

Sincerely,
Langston

3 February '49

Dear Lang,

The AUTHOR'S ROUNDTABLE suits me. I'll plan to stay for it. Which means a little more time for shows, doesn't it?

I have my fingers crossed for all concerned during the period of storm and stress in connection with rehearsals of the opera. If opera rehearsals are like those of plays only more so, they must indeed be something to behold. Wish I could find a way to drop in on one.

Maybe Mrs. FDR's column on the anthology didn't appear in N. Y. C., but it must have come out elsewhere. People even told me what it said: Countee had always been a favorite of hers, for example. She also said, speaking sociologically, that the book wasn't too pleasant to read, its implications of injustices, etc., but that all should have and read it. I'm sure several people couldn't all have had the same dream. That's what they told me. So we must continue to search.

Best ever,
Arna

Three favorable Chicago reviews this weekend: *Tribune, Sun-Times, Defender* —all of which you may have seen.

20 East 127th Street
New York 35, New York
February 26, 1949

Dear Arna:

I am sending you today four of my books in translation for the Fisk University Library:

250

Les Grandes Profondeurs (The Big Sea)
Histoires de Blancs (The Ways of White Folks)
El Inmenso Mar (The Big Sea)
Pero Con Risas (Not Without Laughter)

Yesterday, I turned into Maxim Lieber a large but tentative selection and, of course, incomplete, of folk verses and poems for our *Humourous Negro Verse*. Mr. Lieber was flabbergasted and amazed at the richness and extent of this material, and immediately began to puzzle whether or not it should be offered first to a regular publisher as a big book, or to a pocketbook publisher. He finally came to the conclusion, however, that the greater profit would lie in a pocketbook, although the initial advance would not be as much. Also, we felt that it would be unfair to Doubleday and in competition with the *Poetry of the Negro* if this book were offered as a large book to any other regular book publisher, except Doubleday.

Now, my dear collaborator, since I have exhausted the sources of folk material in my own library and my own files—except for additional old Negro humorous popular song lyrics which Miss Ida Forsythe, of the Negro Actors Guild, is collecting for me—I would suggest that sometime within the next two or three weeks you busy yourself with the resources at your command and do the following:

TALLEY—Go through this book for additional folk rhymes, and also any other books of folk verses that you have in the Fisk Library

BERT WILLIAMS' SONGS—If you have a folio of these in the Gershwin Collection, please select some for the anthology and see if you can ascertain which ones are written by Negroes. However, I do not think they have to be of racial origin since their fame depended upon their recreation in the theater by Bert Williams

Southern Road—I do not have a copy of this Sterling Brown book, so kindly have copied from it "Sporting Beasley," and any other humorous poem from there that you think we should use, except for the one which I have already included in the anthology, *Slim in Hell*

Rolling Along in Song—Please see if there are not some lyrics from this James Weldon Johnson collection that we might use

JOHN WORK—See what lyrics he has that we might use

ALSO—Check any other sources and Negro authors that you think have humorous material

BOOKS OF AMERICAN NEGRO SPIRITUALS—Please get from this a copy of "Scandalize My Name," and any other humorous spirituals that would be suitable to our collection. Also, check the Leadbelly and Lomax books and any other collections of Negro folk songs

And do not be like that goat in the Sheep and Goat poem in our anthology and come telling me that, "Your foot ahm sore," because I have a feeling that this manuscript will shortly be accepted and we might as well get this little bit of work done quickly, so I trust that you will soon be sending this material on to me. I find this job highly amusing, and am anxious to peruse further material myself immediately—because it tickles me and I have never heard our literary representative, Maxim Lieber, laugh so loudly before as he did at some of the things in our book. If everybody else laughs that way our fortune is made, and Joan can go abroad for future study, while Paul continues to gather folk material on the railroad.

The City Center is humming with preparations for *Troubled Island*. (Premiere

March 31.) I was down there yesterday to have photographs taken with some of the singers and heard some of the music which sounds very lovely indeed. It has a lot of melody and so should prove to be a popular opera with the public. And maybe even in due time I will get $9.17 back in royalties.

I am off tomorrow for Chicago, so kindly write me at International House, University of Chicago, and come on up for our anthology program at the Hall Branch Library, March 28.

May God be with you until we meet again. Sincerely

As ever, very truly yours,
Langston Hughes
Litt. D. (Lore)

Thursday 3-3-'49

Dear Lang,

Walk easy round my alma mammy! And if you want a sure-fire story for small fry, open up the treasured volume known as *The Fast Sooner Hound.*

Yesterday's note, written at the library, was not directed to your room number, but it went to the International House at the right number, so ask at the desk if it's not delivered. The essence: acknowledgements, thanks, etc., plus the report that I'm on the job with the humor material. Count on a full report within a week or ten days. This looks like a cheerful project—if we can get a publisher to encourage it.

Knopf just wired to congratulate me on the fact that *Story of the Negro* was mentioned as runner-up for the Newbery Medal (the Pulitzer of the juveniles), but near misses don't make me happy. I'd like a jackpot, a bullseye, or something —*sometime.*

Paul is not going to graduate this year: course changes, credit troubles. Another semester. Joan will, of course.

More anon.
Arna

The Laboratory School
The University of Chicago
Chicago, Illinois
March 28, 1949
Between Classes

Dear Arna,

Yours to the SRL is a very good letter. Like the mama of Kenneth Bright's unwilling draftee, I think Jean Starr "has done lost her mind!"

Only trouble about me getting folks to write the SRL is, I don't know anybody who reads it—it being found only on selected downtown newstands in both N.Y. and Chi. Nary a human last week in Harlem even knew they had reviewed our book. But I'll try to rouse up somebody to protest.

Carlo gave the Lab School a set of his pictures of poets of the Race—you among them. First thing the Librarian said this morning when she saw *your* picture was

—to *me,* "What a fine photograph of you."
I said, "That's not me! That's Arna Bontemps. Here is me."
She looked at my photo and said, "Why, I'd hardly know you."
So I guess you look more like me than I do myself.
"I sees *Lawd* Jesus a-comin'. . . . . Halleloooo-o-!

Lang

International House
1414 East Fifty-Ninth Street
Chicago
March 30, 1949
3:30 P.M.

Dear Arna,

Just through with school and flying to New York at 5 for the opera premiere tomorrow—non-stop DC-6—the kind that fall down most frequently—but get there in one fine swoop!

Hall Branch evening was most delightful, Dedman of the *Sun* a good chairman, and the proper tributes paid to you in your absence. Overflow crowd filling two rooms, Gwendolyn Brooks well received and encored to read a second poem, Wheeler ill and not able to come, O'Higgins gone. Couldn't sell books publicly, so only dispensed with Thirty Dollars worth in the Coffee Room—all I had in my brief case anyhow! Lots of photos taken, one to be in *Defender* this week. Margaret Goss had party afterwards.

Sengstacke kids, Allison Davis kids, Dailey kids, in fact, all the "leading" Negroes' kids seem to go to the Lab School, so I am always running into some parent I know in the hall. Joe and Marva's baby was in the nursery school until departure for Mexico. The nursery school (or rather kindergarten, I mean) is my favorite spot, but I didn't have time to visit them for two weeks until this morning when we wrote another story.

(Read to them from "Golden Slippers.") Enclosed.

The lady who evaluates books for the Dept. of Ed. just told me she, Alice Brooks, and all her Chicago colleagues—Frances Hanne, Mary K. Eakon—all voted for your book for first place. And it came very *very* near getting it, she says. Only fact that some thought it slightly on the adult or too teen-age side, held it back. . . . . . So do a history for babies next time and I bet it will win.

Just got my order of *Poetry of Negro* after a month's wait. First printing was exhausted so they wrote me, so I guess that bodes good. Some folks here who've ordered haven't received copies yet. That Doubleday is SLOW.

How is Buck's novel? Tell me so I can have an opinion as I probably won't get a chance to read the copy he inscribed for me.

They tell me I am writ up in this month's *Harper's*. . . . . . . Either deep like the rivers or a troubled island, Lawd, ma soul! I sees King Jesus a-comin' wid a rainbow! A la Jean Starr!

Yours very truly,
Lang

Kindergarten—4 year olds. Miss
Adams' class, March 30, 1949.
A story made up by Betsy,
Joan, David, John, Dev,
Joanna, Cynthia, and Eric,
also Janet, with Langston
Hughes. Also practice in
rhyming after hearing poems.

THE BAD LION

A LION LIVED IN A CAVE. HE RAN AWAY FROM THE ZOO. HE TOOK HIS TEETH AND BROKE THE BARS AND RAN DOWN THE STREET. HE ATE EVERY PERSON UP.

HE DECIDED TO GET IN A BUS AND EAT THE DRIVER AND THEN DRIVE AWAY, AND DIDN'T STOP AT A SINGLE STOP, AND DIDN'T LET THE PEOPLE OFF.

THEN HE DECIDED TO DRIVE A CAR, BUT THERE WASN'T ANY STEERING WHEEL, SO HE DROVE IT WITH HIS NOSE.

HE FOUND A TOY SHOP AND SAID, "I'M GOING IN."

HE ATE ALL THE TOYS UP. HE BROKE HIS TEETH ON AN IRON FIRE ENGINE.

HE GOES TO THE JUNGLE NOW. HE TOLD ALL THE OTHER ANIMALS IN THE JUNGLE A LIE ABOUT HIS ADVENTURES.

THE END

NOTE: of the three titles suggested, THE LION THAT WENT AWAY FROM THE ZOO, THE BAD LION, and THE LION THAT TOLD A LIE, we decided to use THE BAD LION because it was suggested by Betsy who started the story.

RHYMES:

A DOG	A DOG	A COP
KILLED A HOG.	SAW A FROG.	SAW A TOP.
Wally	Tony	John

A BEE	A BEE	A BEE	A BEE AND A FLEE (L.H.)
SAW	SAW	SAW	WENT UPTOWN. "
ANOTHER BEE.	A HE.	A FLEE.	THEY DIDN'T
Wally	Charlie	John	SEE ANYTHING (John)
			BUT A HOUND "

April Fools' Day '49

Dear Lang,

This goes to your home base on the assumption that you will remain in N. Y. over the weekend—after flying non-stop, DC-6, to the premier of the opera. Please remember to send programs, notices, etc. here for the library collections. Especially those things we won't see. (We get N. Y. Times, Time, Newsweek).

All the news from up your way is good. Nate knocking off those pyramids, Doubleday running out of copies of the anthology, Lieber getting an encouraging turn-down from Grosset on the humor, the shindig at the Hall Branch in Chi— all solid. Indeed it made me feel so good I went out and placed an order for an automobile in which to joyride my big family come summer.

Milton Mayer's piece in Harper's is fine, fine, fine. He really does a job on the Chicago Tribune, and for the first time in this controversy (you vs the native fascist element) an attempt is made to consider the merits of your side. That is in these big circulation media.

Thanks to Nate for his letter. I note what he says about the typing of poems and will instruct my secretary accordingly. Those received by him were as requested by you from the Talley book.

The Bad Lion is nice indeed for 4 year olds. By the time that bunch is 6, they'll be ready for my supplementary reader (biography)—which is now fully accepted, additions and all. So now to a few more licks on *Chariot in the Sky!*

Did I tell you that Wm. Gardener Smith, Willard Savoy and Herschel Brickell will be here for the festival. Lillian Smith dropped out—ill. We are still trying to reach Yerby and Sinclair Lewis. You will come down and hear "Golgotha", won't you?

Haven't had time to read Buck's novel. Hope to soon. Meanwhile,

Best,
Arna

5 April '49

Dear Lang,

My pleasant duty today is to write eight letters, beginning with yours, which delight me more than I can say. You see, the Guggenheim came through. Announcement of the awards will be made Monday, April 11th, and the secrecy will then be off, but I can't wait that long to thank my helpers—those who sold my stock to the Foundation. Now I can start dreaming again about that sabbatical, perhaps to begin about January '50. And if that car I ordered arrives, I might even drive around a little. So thanks again and more about that anon.

One thing I've decided already: to take a two-year truce on little chicken-feed assignments, to concentrate on clearing up outstanding commitments by the end of the year so as to concentrate on the dynasty of Negro leadership during the period of the leave and the fellowship. Since notification of the award reached me on April 1st, perhaps this can be taken as an April Fool's Resolution.

Best ever,
Arna

The University of Chicago
The Laboratory School
Chicago 37 • Illinois
April 10, 1949

Dear Arna,

CONGRATULATIONS on the Guggenheim! Was talking to Jack Conroy on the phone and he told me he'd heard from you, too. I was sure you would get it. HOO-RAY!

I'm giving two lectures at Monumental Church this week and shall place my

255

five recently arrived copies of our Anthology on display and sale. Friday a bookshop talk. In May a Parkway Community House program. So sales and selling will continue.

Horace, I hear, will not be coming back to the Center. Faith Jones, is as you know, acting director now.

Some of my kids are turning in some BEAUTIFUL creative work. (Better, I regret to say, than my Southern college kids did, freeer and more original stuff.)

Did you see the New Yorker having fun with our opery?. . . . . Dick Durham thought the review of our anthology in SRL outrageous. By the way, he wants to do radio sketch of you on his current CBS program, "Destination Freedom." Needs a dramatic incident or two in your life to build it around. Could you send him (or me) one or two such. Dark days, but ever going on, etc. His Ida B. Wells [Journalist, Women's Rights] sketch this morning was very good. (I was up at ten EVEN on Sunday, so in the habit now!)

Langston

Regret can't come to Fisk Festival. Can't go to Calcutta Writers Congress this month either. But had a nice invite from India.

International House, 755,
1414 East 59th Street,
Chicago 37, Illinois,
April 17, 1949.

Mon cher ami,

At an autographing party last night at Florida Sanford's Lending Library (at which I sold Forty Dollars worth of books) what should turn up in the hands of a fan but that illusive clipping of Mrs. Roosevelt's comments on our anthology! Upon being told that you had not seen it, nor I, the fan very kindly let me keep it. So I hereby send it to you for your perusal *AND RETURN* to me, kindly, please. . . . . . . Man, I am beat to my feet! Besides my nine-hour day at school this week I've had three public appearances, one tea, dinner with Miss Harsh and Mrs. Rollins, a party or two, and no sleep. I do not see how I will roll the stone of sleep away to go to church Easter Sunday as I have promised! . . . . . . My two lectures at Monumental Forum were based largely on our book—and are good for future forums. I read from the book and held it up real high so all may see. Also in my Lab School seminars this week I read from your *Story of the Negro* and held it up real high before each of my seven sections so all upper classmen might see, and possibly procure. . . . . . This week we take up be-bop in our Basic Jazz Hour.

Sincerely,
Comme toujours,
Yours truly,
Lang
(Simple)

"Ere sleep comes down to sooth the weary eyes. . . . . . . "

256

Dear Lang,

The poems from Talley's book are being copied at this minute, and it may be possible to get them in the mail today so that they will reach N. Y. before you leave. We'll try.

I'm just back from Birmingham where I did a lecture at Miles Memorial College. I suppose you've been there. Nice faculty of young people—nine of them Fiskites of recent vintage. Saw many copies of Anthol.

Have I told you about John Work's cantata setting of "Golgotha is a Mountain," now being billed as the highlight of this year's Festival? Let's hope it gets published and works its way East eventually. The music people here seem to think it's important. . . . A short poem of mine, "Dark Girl," has also been set to music. This one by Schoetle, and it is programmed for two performances within the next month. So dust off a place for me in ASCAP.

And that little supplementery reader I've prepared appears to have made the grade with the editors and publishers who ordered it. The ms. has gone to the illustrator—though I'm still being asked for a few additional pages. And the whole project keeps getting in the way of my *Land of the Free* series book.

You better plan on coming down for the weekend of April 22 and 23. In addition to the choir's singing of "Golgotha" you will hear an evening of Josh White, a seminar discussion of writing in which Lillian Smith will be supported by the two youngest Negro novelists: Willard Savoy of D. C., whose *Alien Land* is now being launched with a bang by Dutton, and William Gardener Smith of Philadelphia, whose *Last of the Conquerors* has just been issued in a 25¢ edition. You could make the round trip for about $25 via streamlined train. And you could sell that many books if you brought them! But you'd need to plan to arrive on the 21st—or *early* the 22nd.

I'm trying *not* to see the Sat. Rev. raze of the anthology, but I received a copy of the good review in the Fraternal Outlook. Can you help me get the N. Y. U. notice? . . . . . Pyramids have covered Nashville too. Paul was paid off.

Best ever,
Arna

4/28/49

Dear Arna,

How did "Golgotha" go????? You don't tell nobody any news at all! What went on down yonder during the Festival?

My 6th and 7th grade writers are the most wonderful! Thornton Wilder's niece is in the 6th and has written a most charming little poem. I have another week until the short vacation the Lab School has, then I'll be finished, although they want me to stay until June, but I have to get back to work on the musical in New York. And I need ten days rest and catch-up around here. Haven't even seen the first cousin yet. So will be in Chicago until the 15th of May—several lectures and book-selling dates until then to fill, too.

Durham says thanks for the information and if he needs more he will write you. It's biography dramatized with a very good cast, so he needs a dramatic incident or two to hang it on. Has good listening audience. Lots of Lab School kids listen, for instance.

Come on up to Louisville for the Derby! I'm going down for the day, the 7th, it is. There are special overnight trains. Might win my fortune.

By the way current *Tiger's Eye* REVIEWS OUR ANTHOLOGY, and my other two books. All quite brief, but good. I just got Redding's *American Scholar* piece, too. . . . . . My kids loved Gwendolyn Brooks. She visited the 10th grade.

Hello to Alberta (Madam Bontemps),

Lang

Aunt Toy had a nightmare. Emerson thought she was having a stroke, picked her up and knocked her head against the dresser in his excitement, and knocked her dead out! When she came to, she was far from paralyzed! (So I hear.)

May Day '49

Dear Lang,

I've been trying to figure how I could stop in Kentucky for the Derby next Saturday. Alas, the train schedules won't let me. You see, I'll be on my way to Cleveland to speak at the St. James Forum the following day, May 8th, and I'll have a connection to make at Cincinnati at 9:30 P.M. The train from Louisville, I fear, will leave too early to make it possible for me to see the important race. So there I am. I'll study some more timetables, but I'm not too hopeful. Would admission tickets be a problem at this date?

The Festival was more exciting than usual, thanks to such extras as a band parade, two balls (gym and Livingston Hall), Josh White, etc. The Nashville papers attacked Josh for using such numbers as "One Meat Ball" in the famous and dignified Fisk Chapel. But they gave happy cheers for John Work's cantata *Golgotha is a Mountain.* I liked the piece too. It was wonderfully sung, with Coleman (from cast of *Annie Get Your Gun*) flying in from the touring company to sing the baritone solo part. Oscar Henry, the Omega tenor you met here, also had a part. I'm eager to see what its further reception will be and what will happen when Broadway music critics get a chance to comment.

The writing seminar was good too. Very lively. Ben Burns substituted for Herschel Brickell (who had an operation) at the last minute, and the two new novelists both had lots of enthusiasm. Both still highly stimulated by their first adventures into literature. Students responded very well.

About six publishers, seeing announcement of my Guggenheim project, have written to ask a chance to bid on it. One thing this means: it may take me as long to get back to my unfinished novel as it has taken you to add volume II to the *Big Sea.* So now I'll start showing you more sympathy in that matter. . . . Have you seen the excellent revised version of Charlemae Rollins' *We Build Together?* Don't miss.

Best,
Arna

International House
1414 East Fifty-Ninth Street
Chicago
May 27, 1949

Dear Arna:

Did Dorothy Johnson ever write you that there is a youngster in her school whose first names are *Langston Arna?*

Also you might be interested in this paragraph from one of her recent letters:

> Have you read the article in Sat. Review of Lit on the anthology by Jean Untermeyer? I told Ivan that it is too bad that all of the majority group, before trying to express an opinion on what Negroes think and do are not required to pass at least one month as a Negro.

You are a lying dog! You know you do not remember Alexandria at the age of six. And you have forgotten all the Creole you ever knew. (By the way, is Alexander named after Alexandria?)

Today I got my money from the Lab School and am immediately retiring into public life again. Seven o'clock in the morning lower-school teaching is too much for me at my advanced age. Since I did not do it in my youth and was never on time for school myself when I was a pupil, I see no need to start straining my ego now just to improve race relations.

By the way, I met Allen Tate but it was in a crowd so I did not remind him of the party-to-have-been in Nashville. (They say on the campus here that Robert Lowell, while visiting the Tates recently, went completely out of his mind and had to be flown back to a sanitarium in Boston. Like Forrestal, I reckon he thought he saw the Russians coming—after what he tried to do to Elizabeth—from whom I recently had a very a sweet letter.)

Better write me next to New York. Since you will not co-edit *Voices* with me would you review the new Gwendolyn Brooks book therein for that issue which I have simply (mindedly) agreed to edit? Have you received page proofs of it? If not (and if you will) I can send them to you. (It's a very good book.)

To celebrate my release from academic duties, I went and heard all kinds of little-bar be-bop music last nite. Also, so that I can deduct the expenditure from my income tax, this might be termed preparation for imminent revision of my be-bop poems manuscript which I brought out to Chicago with me to revise— but haven't turned a page yet. Shall tomorrow.

I also have 40-11 cousins to see before I depart. It has been my good fortune to find these last few days a most reliable and helpful typist so I am also answering 40-11 letters before I return to New York to face the mountain of mail which must have piled up there while I have been helping the young idea to sprout.

Ask Charles S. Johnson if he has an ivory tower for me there at Fisk. I think I eventually would like to retire from both public and private life. (I have been showing the C.V.V. photograph of him to all my students as the man who practically single handedly propelled—or maybe snow-balled—the Negro Renaissance to its present inter-cultural proportions.)

I will now close this here letter as it is now past dinner time and I have not had dinner and the dining room is closed down stairs and I fear that I will have to—in fact prefer to—go way over to the Cullud Southside to dine.

I've used up my eight weeks of columns. But as a starter for the next issue have just invented a brand new character whose name is Old Ghost. (Being a ghost he can go anywhere and do *and do* anything—even live in Stuyvesant Town.) So watch out for him in next week's issue of the *Defender*.

May God watch between thee and me (my chief and leading collaborator) while we are absent one from another.

I saw your other chief and leading collaborator, Jack Conroy, at the party which Gwendolyn Brooks gave for me and he was cold-stone sober. But his son ably upheld the family honor and would not let his father go home until the last dead soldier was stacked against the wall. It was a swell party and you should been there. The next day I had my one and only hangover since I had been in Chicago. (Hangovers and inter-cultural teaching being incompatible one to the other.) (At least for the colored end of the see-saw.)

    Selah!

Sincerely,
Lang

8 June '49

Dear Lang,

Maybe this will overtake the note I sent to you and Nate yesterday re: the job for the library. I hope I made it clear therein that we can't spend more than $20 dollars on the operation. Maybe Nate will want to spend one day taking notes and one writing them up.

Me, I'm working like crazy down here, getting up at 5 o'clock in the morning and all like that. But I'm driving a fine, new, sky-blue Chrysler, and it will have to be paid for somehow or another. Also Joan is off to Atlanta this coming Saturday to begin her work in the School of Library Service, and something tells me that will cost money too. So you see why I have to get up at sunrise. I want to finish my teen-age novel for the *Land of the Free* series this summer and get on my Guggenheim book by fall. Incidentally, Maxim has just negotiated a good contract for the latter with Houghton Mifflin. Otherwise I'd have been satisfied with a used Ford.

When will we get a report on the Anthology—have you any idea? I'm scratching in every direction.

The old ghost didn't seem to me to have Simple's easy and disarming ways—in his first visit—but he shows possibilities. With more frequent appearances I'm sure he'll gain in naturalness and audacity. As I recall, Simple himself started off rather unpretentiously and slowly grew into his present majesty. The old ghost has a good chance. He can pry into secrets. . . . Have you been seeing *Story* in the *Afro?*

Those hexographed products of your work at the Lab School are both highly interesting. You must have done an excellent job.

I don't think I ever answered your request that I review G. Brooks' book in that special issue of the poetry mag. Perhaps the reason is that the spirit is willing but the flesh weak. Since I have on hand now books from the Herald Trib that I can get to, I think I ought to beg out. Don't you? Why not ask Dick Wright who is not only one of her original advocates but also connected with *Presence*

260

Africaine in which some of her work recently appeared? If you cabled him—or asked the mag to do so—I'm inclined to think he might just accidentally want to do this. Horace could give you his address—or Harpers (since they publish both Gwen and him). In fact that nice lady there in their publicity dept. who always sends me Harper books might even make the request, if you wanted her to. I believe her name is Ramona something.

Sorry about Lowell but not too surprised, if it's true. He has read and remembered more than he can synthesize. The whole T. S. Eliot coterie, including Ezra Pound and those who gave him that big award this year, is a sick lot.

Ralph Bunche was here for Commencement—also at about ten other colleges, I gather.

More anon.

Ever,
Arna

20 East 127th Street
New York 35, New York
June 22, 1949

Dear Arna,

The Literary and Theatrical Agency of the Syndicate of Czech Authors has just written for permission to see about putting our *Poetry of the Negro* into Czech, which request I turned over to Lieber. . . . . . . Did you notice in the *N.Y. Times* review of Frost's Collected Poems that we're both mentioned as in the great tradition of American poetry—I mean you and me?. . . . Nate has gone to Jersey this evening to work on the music collection which he says is very interesting. He spent all day Saturday over there, thinks maybe he'll get it all down on paper tonight. . . . . I'm busy on the musical and the *Simple* book, Simon and Schuster having sent a very good and complete chapter by chapter editorial comment to aid me in revisions. The *Voices* special issue is coming along fine, lots of poets having responded with good stuff, Tolson with his BEST poem yet, so I have almost enough for an issue already. Do you have a loose poem around, since you refuse to be included either as an editor or a book-reviewer? If so, send it on. . . . . . My *Montage* book is revised and being copied. Looks good. . . . . . Dorothy Johnson's brother showed up yesterday from the Merchant Marine. . . . . Carlo had a birthday. . . . . . And on the 30th of July *Street Scene* will be sung at the Stadium. . . . . . Do you know any nice gentle old Negro who could play the lead in *Cry the Beloved Country* which I've been trying to help Maxwell Anderson and Kurt Weill to cast. (Roland is the type but couldn't read lines.) They don't want a sonorous Lawd type but a frail sweet old minister who can sing some but act more. I phoned Benjamin Mays for them, but he's not interested. . . . . . I have a fall offer to be Poet in Residence at another college. Might go. Need dough. So don't know. Safer than a show, though, I trow. No? What ho?

Lang

Dear Lang,

A person you should have Mamoulian-Anderson-Weill consider for *Cry the Beloved Country* is none other than M. B. Tolson. His hair is gray, he has the gentleness, etc., and moreover he has been a director of little theatres and debating teams for years. He is at home on a stage. I think he would love it, that he could easily get a leave from Langston U. for this purpose, and that he would be a stomping success. And he is very much the Roland type! Tell Reuben I send this nomination with my warm regards and best wishes for the success of his new production. The novel on which it is based is very fine, and even YOU should not neglect to read it!

You are doing so many interesting things I think it is time you wrote another of those columns for the *Defender* in which you sort of check up on your activities as a writer in Harlem. Sometimes it was in the form of a sifting of a typical day's mail or appointments. But I advise you to dispose of the *Simple* revisions before that vague musical hits you on the head. Everything else will of course go blank when that happens. . . . . Happy to hear about the Czech inquiry about P of the N. Also the progress report on your *Montage* (on which I'm betting heavily) and the special issue of *Voices,* for which I'm grieved not to have a poem to my name to contribute. This Poet In Residence thing isn't bad. You might as well do the circuit.

Paul has just gone to St. Paul on the promise of a summer job as dining car waiter with the Great Northern. He had planned to go with the Fisk boys who annually work on the Canadian Pacific but didn't realize the need to be nimble this year—as a result of employment reduction—and let them get away without him. I am turning his cool basement quarters into a hot weather writing studio. If this makes it possible for me to finish my present job (the *Land of the Free* book) by July 25th, I might be tempted to drive Alberta up for the Stadium *Street Scene.* She missed the original. But this is a very iffy dream. The book in question moves rather slowly. If it should work out, I presume there would be no problem about a pair of tickets—or another pair for *South Pacific* and *Kiss Me, Kate* on the following Monday and Tuesday nights (August 1 and 2nd)? If you'll ask Nate to explore these possibilities, I'll try to come to a definite conclusion by the next letter. Maybe *Miss Liberty* for the Wednesday matinee, the 3rd.

Best,
Arna

Leslie Collins has gone to Norway for the summer. Other Fisk folk in Hawaii, Fontainebleau, Mexico City, etc. Also Jamaica, B. W. I, Sweden (John Hope) and possibly California.

20 East 127th Street,
New York 35, New York,
June 30, 1949.

Dear Arna,

The theatre situation being what it is for hit shows, I thought I'd better try for your tickets right away, whether you come or not. So I got you a pair for *Miss Liberty* on Tuesday, evening, August 2, and for *Kiss Me Kate* on Wednesday,

Matinee, August 3. Leaving Monday open for *South Pacific* if seats can be gotten through the Playwrights or your Leah, since the box office is out and speculators are charging $25.00 each for them. Fortunately, I had mine way before it opened for this week, saw it the other night, and found it the best yet since *Oklahoma*. Juanita is wonderful, ditto Mary Martin. And Juanita gets the curtain call right after the two stars—she and the leading comic.

I've writ a new beginning and a new end for *Simple* and a song for the show this week. If I could take ten straight days out on the book alone, could have it done shortly, in fact, in ten days. Just needs cutting, rearrangement, and a slight plot thread binding it together.

I missed Reuben today at *Cry* auditions, but told Eddie Brinkman, (your *St. Louis Woman* stage manager, by the way, who will be there, too) to tell him what you said. Kurt had already had me phone Tolson, who was thrilled at the idea, but didn't sound too sure about his singing abilities. They may bring him on, however, to audition next week if Clarence Muse (whom Mamoulian liked very much at a reading on the coast) is not liked by Weill and Anderson for whom he is flying East to read in a few days. As clever as Clarence is and as experienced, he probably will get by with them. But I want to be there when he opens up and hollers AS HIMSELF at rehearsals. It will be better than the show itself! . . . . . . Ruby Hill seems in the running as the night club girl. . . . . And they say they have found a wonderful new boy with a French Creole name I never heard for the son.

Where is Joan? I found her graduation invite among my stacks of letters (some of which I haven't read yet) just the other day and would love to send her a little present.

The *Defender* folks cut OLD GHOST down to a shadow of himself this week, evidently to allow for Mrs. Bethune's extra long column. She has crowded out ten or twelve lines of mine before, so I think I'll just write shorter columns from now on instead of my regular three pages. O.K. by me, busy as I be.

I hope you-all do get up this way. I'd love to see your new car—not to speak of you and Alberta. . . . . . . Glimpsed Alta today in a passing taxi long enough to yell, HY! She looked fine. I understand Doug is back down South painting somebody's portrait.

Amazing goings on that nobody would believe in a book are happening in and out of our house, wonderful anecdotal material, but too much to write down in a letter—for free—so will tell you some of them when you come—such as an old man on the corner (whose wife had broken up his glasses) mistaking Aunt Toy for his wife and knocking her flat down in the street. But that is only one of the minor happenings of the week! Getting like Chicago.

Lang

Frances just married a man who ("they say") has been married 4 times before!

20 East 127th Street,
New York, 35, N. Y.,
August 18, 1949.

Dear Arna,

Thanks for your card and the news that you-all arrived home safely. It was certainly nice having you both here with us, but the time was TOO short. Come back and stay longer next time.

Aaron and Alta spent that week in Wilmington with Grace. We finally reached them on the phone. And today I talked to Alta again as we wanted to have them for dinner on Sunday, but they are driving to Canada for ten days tomorrow in their new car. A new car is something! Look at you!

Let me know if you take the California trip. . . . . I have FINISHED my *Simple* book—50 chapters (short), 4 sections, 232 pages, so it can stand a half dozen chapters cut down to about 200 pages—which I will do after I get another editorial reading on it.

The show, too, is about up to schedule, a third of the lyrics done, just finished a very nice little waltz song production number and a ballad.

The rains have set in, though, and the chill of autumn, so I guess no beach for me again!

A friend of my Argentine translator has just arrived. Next week a Jamaican friend comes for a week with us on the way to London, Hugh Gloster, Earl Conrad and other out-of-towners have called this morning—so I am thinking best way is to invite them all in Sunday ALL AT ONCE. . . . . . The phone man came and toned ALL bells down to a mere whisper, also put my plug-in-and-outs in, so I can now detach my phone entirely as I wish!

Aunt Toy was 62 on Tuesday and we had a few friends in and a big white birthday cake and a very pleasant evening. Wish you-all had been here.

I'm putting the *Poetry* magazine issue together now. Have more than enough good poetry—a fine long O'Higgins poem on Bessie Smith, etc. But am really stuck for book reviewers. HELP! Who can you suggest of the race who will write a credible review that sounds literate and literary??????? PLEASE! (Since, you, our *leading* one, will not pen even a page!)

Jack Conroy came through on the way to Yaddo and phoned. Which seems to be about all the news. Except that John Howard who shared the room with Griff Davis has departed for home and his place is taken by a Haitian (a light one) here studying at Columbia for a year, just moved in today.

Sincerely,
Lang

20 Aug. '49

Dear Lang,

We're trying to get ready to make an early start tomorrow. If we make schedule, we should be somewhere in Oklahoma when you get this. So write me in California.

The Doubleday-O statement came. Looks like we'll be another six months catching up. Some of those folks really stuck us up for permissions—for example the E. B. Marks Music Corp. Evidently the publishers didn't question anybody's asking price or check with us to see if we wanted to go for all of them at any cost. But that's spilt milk. Nothing to do now but sit back and wait for sales to catch up—or rather hope for them to.

Main point here, however, is that Talemaque, the Trinidad poet, will be in N. Y. on September 8th. George I. Daniel, a graduate assistant in the social science department here and a fellow countryman and friend of Talemaque's, will go up there to meet and greet him. They'd like to meet and greet you too. I'm giving Daniel your address. Okey? Talemaque is returning from London, being sponsored on the tour by the British Government. He was on the BBC and everything over there. I take it he is being discovered by the Crown. He will be whisked about America now in the interest of culture. So offer him a leg of fried chicken. Maybe a column about him would interest your newspaper following.

Negro magazines might find him good for a story—saying in each case, of course, that the only place to read his poems is in our anthology.

So now on to California!

Best,
Arna

Your letter—very newsy, very interesting!

20 East 127th Street
New York 35, N.Y.
September 7, 1949

Dear Arna:

I had your letter advising of your trip west but have been so busy trying to get my *Simple* book in by September 1st as contracted that I haven't had a chance to write you. Also there have been a lot of other little jobs and summer visitors that have taken up what spare time I might have had. I trust that you have seen Dorothy and Ivan, Loren and Juanita, and other friends of ours by now. (Perhaps you are even on your way back by now.)

Thank you for advising me of Telemaque's impending arrival. I had just as leave be in Arizona. It seems to me we have had a house full of people for the last month of varying nationalities at all hours of the day and night, but I suppose one more won't make much difference. A Haitian family with two very charming little girls have been occupying Mrs. Harper's bedroom but have departed today. A Jamaican educator was here for ten days and has just sailed for London. A friend of my Argentine translator is due to phone at any moment. As though there weren't enough Americans in town! The only way one can achieve peace of mind would seem to be to leave town, but I've overdrawn my bank account $87.00 and this—of all weekends—is the one when I must entertain the Omegas who can consume at least $50.00 worth of liquor at one sitting.

Drop me a line and let me know how you all enjoyed the trip. Doug and Alta drove to Canada and have just gotten back. Best regards to the Troys, Alberta and the children.

Sincerely,
Langston

735 Winona Ave.
Pasadena 3, Calif.
9 Sept. '49

Dear Lang,

We're still here, but I expect to head toward Nashville about the 15th. Up to now I have looked up nobody and have only seen kinfolks and the close friends

265

of Ruby and Owen. But I have an appointment with Gross and Harold Arlen today and after that I'll try to see some of the bunch.

We spent the Labor Day weekend on the ranch in Mexico—thirty-five miles from Ensenada—the ranch on which you and I planned to write that Mexican juvenile many years ago. On Labor Day itself we went to Ensenada, then back up the coast to Tia Juana and got caught in the bull fight crowd returning to L. A. at night.

Since I started writing this letter, a wire has come in connection with my book in the *Land of the Free* Series. They are rushing me frightfully. I'll have to decide whether to try and finish it out here or put them off longer. If I decide to try and do it here, that will mean a longer stay. It will also mean my going into seclusion at my father's place at San Bernardino (705 Valley View Ave.). But I can't decide on the spot. Write me here first, anyhow.

Thanks for the *Book Review Digest* quotes on *The Poetry of the Negro*. And thanks to you for serving as official host for literary Afro-America in N. Y. No one could do it better. My greetings to the distinguished visitors.

Best ever,
Arna

20 East 127th Street
New York 35, N. Y.
October 24, 1949

Dear Arna:

It would delight me greatly were you trying to make tomorrow's deadline with the special Negro issue of *Voices,* which I took upon myself to edit while you were enjoying yourself in California. You will recall that the co-*honor* was bestowed upon you but you backed out, so I am now left with *both* honors, and only twenty-four hours remain to carry them off with honor. (No Arna, only honor). Also, I would be delighted were you announced to do a special article for the Fourth Quarter, special number, issue of *Phylon* on higher education among Negroes. I do not see why they did not choose you instead of me, because you have been moving in higher educational circles much longer than I and on a much higher level. And I have six other immediate deadlines to meet.

I, too, had a note from Mike Brown which I haven't had a chance to answer yet. In fact, I have not put pen to paper in two or three weeks, but tonight our mutual friend and most amiable and fluent writer of letters, Hugh, has kindly consented to neglect his own duties in order to help me. (Hugh Smythe who says, "Ha, ha, ha!") So between us this evening we'll probably turn out a great big pile of mail. I will tell Mr. Brown we will all await your impending arrival before coming to any decision about the project. Meanwhile, I have been approached by two other show-minded groups and seem on the verge of signing a new contract this week for another musical, in case the proper amount of cash is forthcoming at the same time. Also, there is a possible biography "as told to", like your W. C. Handy job, but I may not take this in case the show works out.

I have written about a thousand songs since I last saw you. It looks as though Burl Ives is going to do an album of some of them, two are being considered very favorably for the new Wiman review, and others seem in line for recordings. Last

Friday I worked from 2:00 P.M. to 2:00 A.M., with three different composers, one right after the other. So you see I shall have plenty of practice by the time I get around to doing our own show.

Did you or didn't you finish your Land of the Free story? And when do you expect to come to New York? Write soon.

Sincerely,
Lang

P.S. The opera version of *Mulatto* goes into rehearsal in about ten days. Ten performances at Columbia U beginning in January.

P.S. I have just received a book from Poland called, *Wielkie Morze*, which, on page 225, speaks of you as follows: "Arna Bontemps, poeta i poczatkujacy powiesciopisarz, spokojny erudyta." Emerson says you had better have this translated and find out what they are calling you!

26 October '49

Dear Lang,

I was concerned about you, thinking that perhaps you had embarked on that round-the-world trip mentioned in *Negro Digest,* if Broadway had not swallowed you up. But since poetry is the stuff that flows in your veins, perhaps your friends should not be alarmed when lyrics, special issues and the like account for your disappearance. Me—almost the only sensible thing I ever did was to beg out of that very tempting invitation to help with the special issue of *Voices*. My *Land of the Free* book is still not finished, and you can imagine where it would be if I were trying to do something else with my left hand at the same time. But I have my company of singers (the original Jubilees) in Oberlin now and all that remains is to work them East to Henry Ward Beecher's church in Brooklyn, up and down the Atlantic from D. C. (before the president) to Boston (before J. Strauss) and thence to the European triumphs. Perhaps I can put all that in 3 or 4 more chapters. The editors seem generally pleased with the story thus far, but they have pushed me to the point of distraction on it. Deadlines are a curse!

Joan is still enjoying Pasadena and USC, but winter has struck St. Paul and Paul may be ready to turn his face toward the South. . . . . Dorothy Peterson, CVV, etc. are all expected here next week for the opening of the new art gallery, you know. . . . . Bob Hayden is dreaming of going around the world with his wife who appears to be playing the piano for Talley Beatty's company, but how real the prospects are I don't know.

Let's hope I get a chance to hear *Mulatto* at C. U., as well as the new Wiman revue, but I'll sure catch the Burl Ives album when it comes along.

Those biographies are about as safe as anything as potboilers, but I doubt that you'll find a subject more profitable than your own second volume, if you're in the mood for life stories. What's happened to the Bethune job? Buck told me he thought Rackham had fallen down on it. That's about as promising as anything I know in the field.

I expect to leave here after Thanksgiving, stopping briefly in D. C. en route to N. Y. C.

Best,
Arna

267

29 November '49

Dear Lang,

I'm putting the N. Y. trip off till early February. At first I thought I'd do it in December, but it now develops that I can kill more birds the other way. For one thing, I'll be able to save money by hooking it up with a couple of talks—in Oak Park and *possibly* Boston. And I'll save energy and writing time by hitting the road once instead of twice. Moreover I'll be less rushed in February than I'd be in December, trying to get home for Xmas. So please pass the word to those who inquire, since I may have told one or two folks about the former plan. Where does this leave me vis-a-vis the performances of *The Barrier?* I've forgotten the dates. But I do want to hear it.

About a week ago I finished the *Land of the Free* book, *Chariot in the Sky*—a bigger job, as it turned out, than any of my adult novels. I believe it is actually longer than any too. Hope it is worth the candle. I assure you I worked and sweated. Now I'm worrying about my typist who is making poor headway with the copying. If the publishers are satisfied and put it into immediate production, so to speak, this will mark the first time I've had two titles headed for the trade marts at the same time. The other: *Sam Patch: The High, Wide and Handsome Jumper* (Houghton Mifflin). So here I go, after a few more days of rest and fooling around, on the magnum opus: Douglass-Washington-Du Bois. But I intend to play this one cool and to interrupt the work once in a while to keep from going stale. Might even work on the Jelly Roll Morton show for recreation, if you and Mike Brown are in the mood.

My father has just had some difficulty. Ran over an Oakie in his automobile, the fellow pushing a wheelbarrow load of wood on a dark road around midnight. Loren looking into it for me says my father not at fault. . . . Joan still enjoying USC. Paul doing research for me while waiting for second semester to begin in January. Alberta still tolerating Sanger's Circus.

Best ever,
Arna

20 East 127th Street
New York 35, New York
December 2, 1949

Dear Arna:

It was good to hear from you after such a long silence, and I am glad to know that you have gotten your book finished. Leah Salisbury called me up yesterday and wants me to come in to see her next week. She suggests that I call Brown and talk with him before seeing her, as it seems he is anxious to get to work on the show. Maybe, if you have time, before you come to town you could prepare a little dramatic outline of it and bring it along with you so that we would be ready for serious conferences while you are here.

The Barrier opens on January 18th for ten performances, so I imagine it will be over (at least as far as Columbia University is concerned) before you get here. But I will be able to tell you about it.

I am sorry to hear about your father's accident and I hope that he comes out all right. *Simple Speaks His Mind* goes to press tomorrow. They are featuring it as one of the few books of contemporary Negro humor. I recall that you said you would like to send a revised comment on it. Since I don't see the old one at the moment anywhere about, if you want to, why not just write a completely new one of about eight or ten lines. Or maybe you'd rather wait until you get here, since there is no immediate rush.

Give my best to Alberta and tell her that we all hope to see her again soon.

Did I tell you that we had a most wonderful Thanksgiving Day dinner with Nate [White] and Gerry. The turkey looked like a dream bird and Aunt Toy swears the dressing was the best she has ever eaten. They are in their apartment at last, have lots of room, and seem to be very happy. Nathaniel's efficiency continues at a high level, and Simon and Schuster says that they have never received a better looking manuscript. And, if they only knew it, some of the Simple touches may be laid at his door.

Sincerely,

Lang

12/8/49

Dear Arna,

Here's your original comments—lines underlined are the ones I particularly like. Revised or combined statement I'd be delighted to send on Simon and Schuster. As you know, already have them from Charles S., Archibald Carey, Ira de A. [Reid], etc. . . . . . . Was in bed all day practically deceased—but am O.K. tonight and doing publicity for "The Barrier" (*Mulatto*'s new name.)

Lang

> When Langston Hughes' "My Simple Minded Friend" columns began appearing in the *Chicago Defender* back in the early 1940's they produced a spontaneous effect among Negro readers that was almost electrical. They were talked about in all kinds of groups and were often reprinted for wider distribution. Here was a Harlem peasant, a Lenox Avenue ne'er-do-well, spouting the folk lore of the city streets. It was all so familiar, so true to the character, that it was recognizable immediately for its authenticity. I had the feeling that this was the freshest, most stimulating feature Negro journalism had produced in our generation. In the months that have followed, Simple has lost none of his wit, none of his drawl. I am delighted to hear that the best of these columns are available in book form.
>
> Arna Bontemps

Fisk Library
30 January 1945

Dear Lang:

Simple would go well in a comic strip but, as you say, not too young a one. I'd like to see it done, provided it doesn't get in the way of a little book such as everybody is urging. *Simple,* as I have said elsewhere this week, is the freshest thing to come out of Negro journalism in my time. He is the only new humorous creation in black flesh in a very long time. He catches

269

the wisdom of the Harlem folk character as no one else has done. And he is funny, man, downright funny. A well-balanced book of pieces about him should last a long time. Might even become a play like *Life with Father* and *My Sister Eileen*. *Simple* is the kind of funny man who will not make Negroes ashamed. He is the very hipped, race-conscious, fighting-back, city-bred great-grandson of Uncle Remus.

Arna Bontemps

20 East 127th Street
New York 35, New York
December 9, 1949

Dear Arna,

In talking on the phone today with Alan Lomax regarding a Negro folk musical idea based on Leadbelly's life and times, he said that he was exhausted and about to go away for a rest, having just sent his new book to press, *Mr. Jelly Roll,* about —you guessed it—our character! I am to have luncheon with him and Edward Gross on Tuesday and will tell him we thought of it FIRST in so far as a theatre idea goes.

Gross is interested in a non-Negro musical idea and had Leah Salisbury send for me to see if I had any. He said maybe a mixed cast—so I proposed Leadbelly's story involving the Lomaxes, and another idea, both of which seemed to excite him. . . . . . He told me they are thinking of doing *St. Louis Woman* in white-face in the movies—like *Anna Lucasta!*

Simple Speaks His Mind is announced in the press today for Spring. And the jacket design has just come to me—a beige and blue cover with a lovely sort of Paris-looking Harlem street etched across the bottom. The only thing indicating color is a bar sign; SUGAR RAY'S, over one of the buildings. They're checking all the blurb and advertising copy with me so as not to offend the race, and are most careful and cooperative about everything. A really fine office to deal with. And I haven't been in it yet—all by mail and phone so far!

With some of the major things out of the way: *The Barrier* (Mulatto), the Wiman song, *Simple,* and the Negro issue of *Voices,* Nate, Hugh and I have been attacking two drawers full of mail with some slight effect. Hugh just left at 1 A.M. but I am going on a bit longer—having run through two assistants today. I really need a staff for all this non-commercial "art" work. Nobody would think poetries and operas could take up weeks, months, and years of one's time!

A big can of pecan brittle from a fan in Texas arrived a short time ago from the Defender. In acknowledging it tonight, Hugh and I discovered it was mailed from Texas last January 6. The *Defender* had kept it sitting in their office almost a year to forward on to me! CULLUD! But the candy was still good.

IT IS C O L D here now!

Sincerely,
Lang

Please return this nice clipping about our Anthology.

270

2-27-50
1611 Meharry Blvd.
Nashville 8, Tenn.

Dear Lang:

This is the first of the post-N. Y.-visit letters; a few more will trickle along presently (in case you see Dorothy, L. Murphy, etc.). And this one is touched off by an idea: Why don't we call our musical show (tentatively) "Mayme Dupree" and offer it as a starring vehicle for Pearl Bailey? Pearl has stopped her last two shows *(St. Loo* and *Arms & the Girl)* and should be ready to consider an opus written specially for her. Leah knows her as do you, and if you okey the suggestion, an approach might be to interest Pearl herself first and then take it up with a producer who can be shown the timeliness of a musical tailored for her. She would make a good Mayme as we have projected the outline, and even though she appeared only in the first half, her influence would be central throughout and we might devise a reprise with her memory appearing later behind a scrim and doing her blues . . . that is with her as remembered by Pepper and her daughter.

You have seen Doubleday's statement on *The Poetry of the Negro,* I suppose. Well, we should be off the hook by the first of September, I reckon, the time of the next accounting.

One of the things I forgot to tell you in N. Y. was that I read with delight all your early articles in the *Brownie's Book* in Du Bois' office. . . . And this prompts an aside to Nate. I hope he and Lillian Murphy have no trouble arranging a suitable time for him to do that work for me, but I am in no special hurry, of course. At his own convenience.

Carlton Moss has completed a book called *In Person: Lena Horne* and is making a lecture tour of South talking about this and other Hollywood matters. . . . . My father can't drive his car for a year (a surprisingly light penalty, even though he was not too much at fault); it's time he quit driving anyhow, being 79. . . . I'm still revising *Chariot in the Sky,* doggone it. But Hello to Toy and Emerson, thanks for the party and more anon!

Best ever,
Arna

P.S. I left a little batch of paper, notebooks, etc. in your name at the Theresa desk when I left. They *may* be there still, but that was a long time ago.

21 March '50

Dear Lang,

Yes, I'm invited to the opening of the new library at Lincoln. See you there. Maybe I'll drive. Would you like to return home via Nashville? Either way I'll see that you make contact with my copy of *Simple* for signing. And I'll let you know when mine arrives. . . . Alta was here a week but has now returned to N. Y. C. Milton Wood & Co. passed through last night en route to L. A. by car & trailer to do engagement in Belasco theatre in L. A. Carlton Moss is expected hereabouts in April. He's touring the schools and lecturing on Hollywood personalities. . . . . Maybe we'd forget my suggestion about Pearl in view of her private wars. . . . . Never heard anything more about the Bethune book from either

Lieber or Doubleday. Don't know what happened. . . . . Have you heard how one N. White is getting along with the typing of Du Bois items?

Best ever,
Arna

Thanks for *Midwest Journal* poems.

May 1, 1950

Dear Arna,

Simple has sold 12,000 to date—⅔ paper—which is about the same ratio as their other paper books as compared to the cloth.

The editor of the *Oracle*, our Frat magazine, asked me what Q could review the book for them—short, a page or a page and half at the most. Said he would be delighted if you would—as he is trying hard to give the magazine some quality and real interest. I told him I would ask you. It needn't be in until mid-June. So let me know if you maybe could, please, sir, and I'll pass the word on to him, also send you his address which I haven't on my desk at the moment.

Had to do a new opening for *The Barrier*—which is trying my nerves now! Hope this is the END of revisions. It goes into rehearsal for summer theatres soon, Charles Weidman to direct the ballet, which is being redone, too.

Pearl Bailey is quite ill. Husband came and took her out of the hospital and off to nobody knows where without permission, so 'tis said. Dolores Martin is doing her role in the show for past ten days now.

THREE records out all at once! Juanita Hall [actress], Burl Ives, and The Striders! Never rains but it pours. And the Nellie Lutcher due at any moment. Hope one of them clicks. Burl's is real hill billy—"Got the World by the Tail" on Columbia.

WONDERFUL about Gwendolyn Brooks getting Pulitzer Prize! I've just sent her a wire. I got her first poem published in *Negro Quarterly* when Ralph was editor.

I'm to be interviewed on television for first time (for me) this week. Meyerberg is interested in *Simple* for a play. And Maurice Ellis for radio. And Leeds has the song, I "Might Look Simple Still I Ain't No Fool," hoping to interest King Cole. Do you reckon some one of these activities will bring forth a solvent statement—just once in life? I am near about weary with well-doing! And fain would rest.

Practically everybody is going to Rome or Paris these days but us.

Have not heard nary word further from those Lincoln U. Mo., folks. Maybe fee plus fare was too much for them. But can't take a week out of my life for "honor". Just can't!

When do you return this way? Hope soon.

Sincerely,
Langston

Just wrote a finale for the Savannah Club's new show—"There Goes A Pretty Girl". P.E.N. Club is having a cocktail party for its authors with new books Wednesday—me, Carl Carmer, etc. And we're trying to get Sugar Ray to have one for Simple who drinks at his bar. Mahalia Jackson is hearing my Gospel songs this week. She's in town. Still says, "The church will be here when the cabarets are closed." To which my song says, "LET THE CHURCH SAY AMEN!"

3 May '50

Dear Lang,

You putting a new beginning on *The Barrier* me trying to put a new ending on *Chariot in the Sky*. These revisions go against the grain with me; I've broken out with psychosomatic boils as a result. And the publisher flew down here this week to check on my progress. There seems to be quite a lot of pre-publication interest in the book despite my difficulties with the editor of the Series, so I continue to thrash the water with my oars. Because of this bottleneck I have not been handicapped for want of the Du Bois material which Nate is copying. You may tell him that any time this month (May) will do.

My last letter from Lincoln, dated April 14, says that you are expected—you and Sterling and Allison Davis and Hayakawa and me, so I don't think they have dropped the plan, and if you'd like to come here and drive up with us or return this way, we'd jump for joy.

You do seem to have hit the jackpot, and I can see why you would be dreaming of Rome and Paris. I aim to get all your records pronto, and I'm sure there is a rich career ahead for *Simple,* be it play, musical, radio, television or what. Sorry I can't get to the parties for him, but I'll do a short review for the *Oracle* if I'm asked. However, Ted's is so good I'm afraid I couldn't top it, and I believe he's a Q and maybe he could whip up an effective recast of his POST job for the purpose. So offer the editor that possibility too.

Carlton Moss was here till yesterday and says he looks forward to seeing you in N. Y. He has a bag full of new projects, including the biography of Lena Horne, completed and accepted. . . . And I have had at least one letter crediting me with Simple: another case of mistaken identity. From a grad-student at Wellesley. . . . Being at the end of my Guggenheim and still on half salary at Fisk and with Joan still in USC (till August), it may take me a little while to corner enough resources to make an N. Y. trip, but I'm thinking about it nevertheless. Sooner or later I must do a hitch in the LC in DC, and when I do of course I'll come up to N. Y. to catch my breath in an air-conditioned show.

After a week of cold rain spring landed today with both feet. I begin to get a picture of myself wrapped in sack cloth, covered with boils, sweating out the summer at this machine in the basement of a steaming house. You can bet I'll run away from it if I get a chance.

How's your ghost writing job going? That might make a movie aimed mainly at the 800 Negro houses. I've been trying to stir up interest in high quality pictures for this audience—high quality but modest budgets, comparable to the Italian things, *Shoe Shine, The Bicycle Thief,* etc. Your biographical book about the Cop would suit, I believe. I have others in mind that might interest this largely southern bunch of Negroes. Carlton was impressed with the possibilities, I believe. I've turned over to him an offer I had to write something to this effect for one of the movie magazines. He plans to talk to the editor in N. Y. What do you think?

Best ever,
Arna

273

20 East 127th Street
New York, N.Y.
5 A.M.
6/17/50

Arna,
 Carlo's birthday party tonight. (He's giving one for Dorothy next Friday, 23, but I won't be in town for that one). . . . . Nice time at Ann Arbor. Now (naturally) more revisions to do before another summer theatre date at Woodstock. . . . The other show opens July 31 at Algonquit, Maine—the little light musical. . . . Did you see the review of "Simple" in Sunday's Herald Trib—the same one as appeared in the Afro a month ago. 2nd or 3rd time I've noticed such repeats. How does he get away with it? Not even rewritten!!!! I didn't know the Herald Trib syndicated the Afro's material!
 Mail is mountain high. I guess it'll be sky-high by summer's end. Can't write 3 shows and answer letters, too. C'est *im*possible!
 See current *Defender* column re Lincoln Univ. and us.
                                                      Lang

18 June '50

Dear Lang,
 The enclosed explains itself. The county of Warren, N. C., wants the two of us for Book Week. I'd like to do it if you would. Miss Cooke asked me for your address, which explains why your letter may not have been received yet.
 Thanks for your card from Michigan. In the N. Y. Times Book Review section too *The Barrier* is hailed as a headline prospect for the coming season: the double-page spread of pictures, including you, Hemingway, Algren, etc. So I'm crossing my fingers for my own chances of getting to New York to hear it in the fall. Is there a tentative date?
 At the moment, in addition to melting away slowly in this heat, I'm teaching two summer school classes, as a means of turning a fast half grand, waiting for the publishers to comment on my latest revisions of *Chariot,* and trying to strike a lazy lick or two on the D-W-Du opus. But the heat is against all work. Wish I knew some place in upper Canada where I could go!
                                                      Best ever,
                                                      Arna

22 June '50

Dear Lang,
 Your *Defender* column re: us at Lincoln makes a good point. I hope each and every Negro institution will work on it in its own community. Fisk does somewhat better with such matters—though there is room for improvement (I believe CSJ is in the market for a good director of public relations). But the ofays will be sorry if they ignore Mose—what with the Supreme Court carrying on as it is and Congress letting fly occasionally, they will be jolted rudely.

Thanks for the program and throwaways from Ann Arbor on *The Barrier* for the G-Room. You'll also get a regulation acknowledgement.

Irita Van Doren once reproved me for reviewing a book in the Herald-Trib *and* a Chicago paper even though I wrote two entirely different pieces. She said it wasn't fair to the author who is entitled to as many reactions as there are publications carrying reviews. So I'd *think* the same would hold in the case of the *Simple* review which they reprinted, even though it is favorable to the book.

Tomorrow (Friday) I complete my second week of summer school teaching. Three to go, but I think I'll cut the last one short in order to get to Cleveland in time for the Newbery dinner and Knopf's pre-dinner cocktail party there. Otherwise it begins to look as if I'd be chained in my pit all summer. Have failed to land a house in the Cape May area of the Jersey coast.

Alta and Doug are here—he to paint a portrait, I believe—and Loren is expected Monday for the Race Relations Institute, he and many others. . . . . I know how you feel with all those shows incubating, and one of them, *at least,* such a good bet! So tell Nate I also understand how tied-up they must keep him and that anytime in July will be okey for the rest of that *Du Bois stuff.* Meanwhile,

Best ever,
Arna

9-7-'50

Dear Lang,

I think I was the most disappointed of all when we decided to turn south instead of north after crossing Delaware River. But Alberta wasn't feeling too well at the moment and everybody else was pretty exhausted by fifteen days of swimming in the sea, romping on the sands and riding bicycles on the board walk. Not to mention playing canasta with their new Philadelphia friends till all hours every night. Me, I worked mornings while the house was quiet and joined the others—the fish, the fowl and the folk—in the water at about 3 P.M. I also gawked on the board walk and played canasta, so I was a little tired too. Anyhow I'm counting on getting to N. Y. C. for *The Barrier.*

Ima was cheerfully featuring your photo on her table in Princess Ann. I hope Joan will enjoy her work there. The salary is good and the people seem friendly, but she turned down Florida A & M and Long Beach Public (Calif.) to go there and I hope she won't regret the choice.

At first I had asked Miss Cooke at Warrenton for $100 plus expenses from Nashville. To make it more definite—and more in line with yours—I have now written to suggest a flat fee of $150. I hope it works because I might then be able to continue to New York and see the shows.

In Philadelphia I worked three days in the offices of the Winston Company and *Chariot in the Sky* now seems about ready for the printers—my most drawn out job to date—but the illustrations are wonderful, especially the jacket. With *Sam Patch* scheduled for spring also, it seems that I will have two books coming out at about the same time—another new experience.

It was nice of Toy to expect the kids, but there'll be another time. Meanwhile

Best ever,
Arna

20 East 127th Street
New York 35, N. Y.
November 4, 1950

Dear Arna:

That worriation, *The Barrier,* has finally opened on Broadway to much razzing of the music by the critics and so is closing almost as soon as it opened. Tonight, Saturday, being the final performance. The complications are too numerous to mention here, but I will tell you about them when I see you. Everybody is just about worn to a frazzle except me. This time I didn't even get bursitis—nor my Washington money as yet.

Everything seems in order for our appearance at Warrenton, North Carolina on Thursday, November 16th. When they first wrote me they did not mention any morning engagements and so I booked a Wednesday evening at Livingstone College in Salisbury, which means that to get there by eleven o'clock in the morning, I shall have to take a seven o'clock plane. But if the weather is good, I can arrive. If not, you carry on until I make it by train.

I have ordered five *Poetry of the Negro* and a few *Popo*'s sent so that we might do some autographing as well as speaking.

Please let me know if you plan to wear a tux. I think it best if we don't since it just makes extra luggage to carry. I have an engagement at the teachers college in Bowie, Maryland on Friday, so shall have to take a late night train out of Raleigh. Do you maybe plan to come on up to New York? If so, come along with me. I am only stopping for Baltimore and Havre de Grace programs on the way, since I thought I might as well make a good week of it while being out of town.

I ran into Charles S., one night last week and he told me about the Atlanta Library situation. Otherwise, I have had no news of you lately. What's cooking? Best regards to Alberta and the family.

Sincerely,
Langston

8 November '50

Dear Lang,

No tux, *please.* Since no one has mentioned such a thing on the other end, I think we are safe in assuming it will not be expected. I hate to add an outfit like that to my normal luggage, and I won't unless YOU insist.

A couple of other engagements have come my way too since the Warrenton folks went to work. I expect to arrive in Raleigh the evening of the 14th for talks there and in Durham (the Library School) on the 15th. The morning of the 16th I'm to be driven by automobile, I imagine, up to Warrenton. If you could meet me in Raleigh we might go together and at the same time exchange notes on our joint performance for the teachers and their friends. I'll be available through Mollie Lee who is finding me a place to stay and fixing the schedule there. . . . Jay Saunders is to be at St. Augustine's the same afternoon, I've heard.

Following the evening program at Warrenton, at 10:12 o'clock, I must catch a bus for Norfolk. It is the only available transportation which will put me in Norfolk by the next morning. I'm to make high school and library appearances there too. I'll be free after Friday night, the 17th, but I don't think I'll go to New

York this time, *The Barrier* having closed. I'd be terribly rushed to get home if I did. Maybe I can arrange a theatre-going visit later.

Which reminds me, perhaps our solid Broadway success is waiting on *The Compromise,* the Booker-T theme, perhaps climaxed by the episode in which he was beat up in N. Y. C. by a janitor in an apartment house—or perhaps by someone else. So keep it in the back of your head; it will have to be written eventually. Meanwhile I'm glad you have stood up under the strain of *The Barrier,* but I know what you've been through and I share your feelings.

Best ever,
Arna

20 East 127th Street
New York 35, N. Y.
December 27, 1950

Dear Arna:

Just to let you know that I have had a letter from Miss Henninger confirming my engagement at the International Student Center on Thursday, February 15th, so I shall probably be arriving sometime that day and would be *delighted* to be a guest at your and your amiable wife's home, no doubt overnight, as I think I will be going down to Normal the next day, but might be back your way for the weekend.

Do you think it might be a nice idea to display Sally Alexander's recent acquisition of all of the various drafts of the *Freedom Train* and its musical setting as well in connection with my program at the center? I have sent Miss Henninger a copy of the song, along with some other songs of mine, in case they might like to have some of them sung at the program.

I expect to make New Orleans by February 5th in time for the two big Mardi Gras parades, lecturing my way on back northward, having almost filled up Negro History Week already. Why don't you come down to New Orleans to see King Rex arrive?

We are all busy recovering from Christmas, having taken the day off ENTIRELY yesterday. Nathaniel and his wife spent Christmas with us and Gerry cooked a wonderful goose stuffed with wild rice so we were all full and sleepy for 24 hours thereafter. I got an electric blanket for a Christmas present, and Mrs. Harper got an electric toaster, and from her husband, Geraldine got an Electric Mixmaster, so everybody is electrivised—and I hope I am not electrocuted.

I am a literary sharecropper, struggling with Mr. Battle's book and Mr. Siegmeister's play, and have just signed a contract for a Children's book—advance now, manuscript due next fall—but to tell the truth, I can't see my way clear beyond the Mardi Gras. However, it is my determination to see that *come what may.* I was just talking to Ralph Ellison on the phone and he has not finished his book YET. So if he can take that long, why can't I—and he has been several years. I do not understand why my people all want their work delivered within the year, contracts not withstanding. They must be simple, and do not seem to realize that creation needs to germinate.

I send you all my good wishes for a Happy New Year to you all!

Sincerely,
Lang

31 December '50

Dear Lang,

You are booked but definitely! We'll count on your staying overnight the 15th of February and possibly returning for the following weekend. Moreover, a familiar blue Chrysler will be waiting for you at the station or port if you will indicate whether you will arrive by land or air and at what hour. And in line with your suggestion there will be an exhibit in the Library's display cases. Staff members have already been assigned to prepare this. I'll suggest the *Freedom Train* material to them if they have not gone too far with their plans. It *is* a good idea.

I'll be home because I decided against taking lectures myself in view of the fact that I'll be around Chicago about a week beginning January 27th, and I wouldn't want to make two whirls so close together. The Chicago trip will probably eliminate Mardi Gras too, though we had toyed with the notion of driving down —Alberta having never seen my home state.

Joan is here for the holidays, which fact alone would make Xmas a success for the rest of us, but Paul is restless, knowing that the armed forces will claim him on May 28th. I wouldn't be surprised if he upped and volunteered to break the suspense. Lots of other Fisk faculty kids are home for the holidays too, the CSJ's, the Jno. Work's, the Creswell's, etc., but none of them show up at the functions at which their parents celebrate. Imagine *any*body passing up such sparkling company! I can't believe it's because they consider lilting forty-eight year old kids like us as has-beens. (I've read *The Disenchanted,* and now I'm going to re-read the stories of F. Scott Fitzgerald to see where I stand.)

Luck to you with your pending contracts. I have no doubt you'll do better with a handful of simultaneous commissions than most artist-writers, since you thrive on pressure. But I've had to turn down two offers this month. Of the four I had on my hands when 1950 began, only two have been completed. The big one is only a little better than half finished, and another juvenile has scarcely been touched. I think I'll coast a while before shouldering such a load again.

The difference between your situation and Ralph's [Ellison] is that Ralph is evidently making this one novel his life's work. That's one way to follow a literary career, but it requires a special kind of mentality. When one is producing such a book, the idea is not to finish it till one is tired of living. You, on the other hand, have formed the habit of finishing projects, and that is what keeps you going.

My best to all your electrified associates. Right now I must start making egg nog with which to drink to your health and theirs tonight at 12 o'clock. Happy New Year!

Best ever,
Arna

20 East 127th Street
New York 35, N. Y.
January 5, 1951

Dear Arna:

Under separate cover I am sending to you a copy of *I, Too, Sing America,* a song cycle composed by Serge Hovey. It contains my poems, "The Dream-

278

keeper", "Border Line", "Stars", "Silhouette", "Night: Four Songs", and "I, Too, Sing America". This is for the George Gershwin Memorial Collection. However, before you lay it to rest in the collection's archives, I wonder if you would be so kind as to show it to the head of Fisk's Music Department or to some singer or singers there who might be interested in singing it. Perhaps someone might even care to use some of the songs on my forthcoming Negro History Week program there.

It was certainly nice to have a good long newsy letter from you once more in life. With so many burdens on my head, it indeed helped to bear me up. My week of lectures is completely filled now, night after night, except for one day, but I hope to sell that one out soon.

The publication date for *Montage of a Dream Deferred* is now February 19th, but they promise to let me have advance copies to dispose of on the tour.

Did you know that Ridgely Torrence [playwright] died just before New Years? Also Monty Hawley and, so they tell me, Jackie Mabley. I AM STILL HERE!

Next time you come I can show you a picture of the original SIMPLE—the man who said, "Cranks, cranks!" I found it last night in going through a big box of pictures looking for my Haitian snapshots to show a young man who has just returned from a month in Haiti with a wonderful voodoo collection, recently on display at the Schomburg. He spent quite a lot of time with Piquion whom he says is very close to the new President (in fact, they were schoolmates together), and is in line for a big position, and is driving about in a brand-new car.

With all good wishes as ever,

Sincerely,
Langston

20 East 127th Street
New York 35, N. Y.
April 10, 1951
11:30 P. M.

Dear Arna,

I have been just about as busy as I ever hope to be in my natural life, since getting back from my Southern tour. And, to cap the climax, without any experienced help—for, during March, just about the time that Hugh Smythe departed for Japan (on whom I could depend in a pinch), Sonny entered night classes in college and got himself a full-time daytime job, and Nate decided to resign to devote himself to a possible warplant job and his own writing—so I was left with none of my old hands—*all* leaving more or less at once. Just like Negroes! . . . . . However, Sonny's full time job beat him down, so he has now returned to the calm and comfort of my studio on a half day basis, so at least I have someone who can find something in the files and address envelopes. And Griff Davis has been helping me out an hour now and then. Bob Lucas [radio writer] promised to come two or three times but didn't show up. A new boy didn't know B from Bull's Foot. Nate and Gerry have busted up for the moment and have been living apart for the last month. And, at last hearing, he hadn't found the kind of job that suits his needs, so phoned offering to do extra work for me if it doesn't come through this week. Maybe Hugh will not like Japan and come back, too. Meanwhile, I've been thinking of hiring a Japanese. Cullud ain't got no consideration.

Well, I thought I could jot you this note before the show guys came at midnight to finish a tune, but Griff tells me they are downstairs. So more in the wee A.M. We're auditioning *Just Around the Corner* again with a new book, so there are a few lyric changes to work out tonight. Always something in show biz that is never done. . . . . . . I just wrote a new waltz for the *Barrier* which Broude Brothers is publishing. . . . . And actually met the deadline for the Siegmeister show's audition in Philly day after tomorrow, having finished about a third of it—some really very beautiful songs on which the committee hopes to start raising money for a fall production.

4 A.M. It took the composer, the book writer, and I exactly four hours to find six lines to fit a counterpoint to another song! Only two more lyrics now remain to do on this "Corner" opus—as it now stands. It seems in line for another summer try-out with the new book.

Chariot came and looks wonderful! Unfortunately, I haven't had more than a moment to glance at it as yet. What with no help, Mrs. Harper was in bed ten days—so I had to answer phones and bells, too—so have gone up and down one thousand stairs. *Montage* has gotten several very good reviews, we had a FINE book party at Afro-Arts; and *Simple* in London is doing excellently. Two portions of it have been dramatized over BBC. I've posted you excerpts from some of the reviews.

I had a letter from Kitzmiller, too, and will look up our scripts for him very shortly, (just haven't had anybody to send to the basement to find the play box) as soon as I come back from Philly's audition, and Washington where I am going to see their local version of "Just A Little Simple" now playing there with John Tate (formerly of *Anna Lucasta* in the lead). . . . . . . Delighted to hear about Ira's talk, and relayed the news to S.&S. . . . . . . I found two of the old Jacques Roumaine books for the lady in Wisconsin. . . . . C.V.V [Van Vechten] and Fania just returned from a West Indian cruise. I saw them at the Haitian Festival which was pleasantly good but over-theatricalized a la [Katherine] Dunham but less expertly, so it sort of fell between the stools of folk art and the revue stage. Only the drummers, who were real, got an ovation. . . . . . Love to the family. . . . .

Sincerely,
Lang

15 April '51

Dear Lang,

Those British reviews of *Simple* certainly are ripping. For some reason, which surprises me, the English seem to catch the Harlem comedy better than American whites. Their reviews call to mind the bubbling response of Negroes over here. So now I'm wondering if those white critics who took the book more or less in stride were not putting on an act in some cases. In other words, *Simple* may be a greater embarrassment to American ofays than they let on.

I missed Horace's column in this week's *Courier*. Can you explain? But your piece on Simple's comments re: formals and funerals is one of that gent's very best performances. It should fit beautifully into that dramatization which you will someday make of the sketches. I see it as a stage musical and a TV serial, but you seem to have enough plays on your docket now to last several seasons.

Don Stewart's *The Kidders,* I note, is on the try-out trail. Here's luck to him.

We have secured a house at Wildwood, N. Jersey, for the first two weeks of August, so you must plan to visit us and soak up some sunshine. Also Toy and Emerson. Either on the way there or while returning home we'll try to give the younger kids their first glimpse of New York City. For the rest of the summer I expect to be chained to this machine I'm now operating. Looks now as if I'd be a full year late with the manuscript of the Douglass-Washington-Du Bois book. Of course I'm in no hurry, but it seems that Houghton Mifflin was born impatient.

See the second issue of the magazine *New Story* which contains stories by James Baldwin and William Demby, both featured on the cover. NS is edited by the son of WB and MF, founders of *Story.* I'm now reading Spender's *World Within World,* which I think you would enjoy too.

The turnover in secretarial help is well-known, but the reasons generally given have to do with the marriageability of the young women who dominate the guild. From your experience it would seem that men secretaries are just as inconstant, however.

More anon.

Best ever,
Arna

20 East 127th Street
New York 35, N.Y.
April (NO!) May 1, 1951

Dear Arna,

I, too, need to get some publicity photos made up, having only two or three left. So if you want to send your negatives up here to me, with the size and number you wish indicated, I'll have them made up for you when I order mine. Not having had any for a couple of years, I don't know what the prices are, but I imagine not more than a nickel each. In any case the Bass Photo Service is the cheapest I've found yet. It takes about ten days. . . . . . I spoke for the Phi Deltas in Camden Sunday and went to Father Divines Fifth Wedding Anniversary afterwards. Gave your new book a plug before the teachers. . . . . I've written Alvin Cooper a note inviting him to visit the Countee Cullen Workshop with me tomorrow night. . . . . Thanks a lot for the John Work program and clipping. Hope I can hear the group sing sometime. . . . . . Met William Gardner Smith in Philly who is covering Trenton Six trial for the *Courier.* . . . . . *Ebony*'s Louis White was here visiting Griff tonight, in state of shock, having just flown home to Washington on week-end to find *another* man in his wife's bed—and, in his own words, "a man who didn't even use good grammar!" Divorce story is, I believe, in current Afro. . . . . . . Nate and Gerry are still apart last I heard. He's typing envelopes at an address service downtown, he tells me. Sonny is working part time and is not bad as a copyist, slow but quite accurate, so I am making out O.K. at the moment, and putting the money I save into a couple of suits I NEEDED real bad. . . . . . Ralph Ellison was by today and has FINISHED his novel! It took as many years as *Knock on Any Door,* so I hope it'll be as good. . . . . . Mrs. Harper declares she intends to visit you-all in Jersey this summer (which I doubt when the time comes). She and Marion and Edith Wilson are downstairs playing canasta now. . . . . . Send the negatives. . . . .

Sincerely,
Lang

P.S. I told you I sent *When Jack Hollers* to the guy in Rome, didn't I?. . . . Thyra sent me a clipping of *Mulatto* from there. Maybe its production will help get other plays on. Hope so. . . . . . Frances has a job in Paris, being divorced, and is staying another year. . . . Jimmy Davis is doing pianologues there and air-mailed for some hair straightener. . . . . Ulysses Kay is in Venice. . . . . And where are we—literary sharecroppers that we be! I will NEVER take another advance—unless it is BIG enough!

L. H.

I pray
Each day
To get underway
But money ahead
Makes creation dead!

5-6-51

Dear Lang,

Let me first try to find out what the Winston Company of Philadelphia, publishers of *Chariot,* paid for the publicity photos they had made of me. Since I have no negative, that might be simpler if the price is right—their engravers, I mean. But more about this in a few days, so try to wait with yours.

It appears that you and I ran out of suits as well as publicity pictures at the same time. I've just bought *three* new ones. Previously the most I'd ever bought at once was two. But two of these are summer numbers and the third is to go into the bag for fall. It was a breath-taking outlay for me nevertheless. And since Poppy will graduate from high school at the end of this month and go to Bennett in September, it may be years before I do the same for myself again.

Keep me informed on publication plans for Ralph's [Ellison] novel. I'd like to review it, as I did Willard's and Yerby's firsts, and keep up my record of hailing the major Negroes on their initial bows. It's exciting to hear that he has actually finished it. Sometimes I wondered whether or not he ever would. It must be a solid item.

Looks like I'm doomed to go on and on revising *Chariot* forever. The Family Bookshelf, one of the second-string book clubs, seems to be interested and is asking eight additional pages plus a few changes. Can you beat that? The thing that amuses me about it is that they are considering distributing the book to adults, though it was written and published by Winston as a teen-ager.

Ida [Cullen], who has been here a week and a half, made up her mind to leave Countee's literary effects in our collection of Negroana: letters, manuscripts, the books of his library, everything that was still with him at his death. He had given much away previously, of course, but much remained. This can go beside the forthcoming Chesnutt collection.

And from one of the Foundations the Library has received the promise of $25,000 to be matched by another equal gift to make $50,000 for strengthening our book holdings in other areas which I specified. This to be spread over three years.

I join you in renouncing literary sharecropping. No more small, or even medium-sized, advances. Too many cullud have been bought too cheaply—in literature, in art, in education, and the rest. Confederate holiday, gentlemen; no more business on this front.

Best ever,
Arna

Tuesday morning
6-5-51

Dear Lang,

My ghosts, alas, have retired to their attic for the nonce, so I'm sending your column to Paul in the hope that he will have one he'd like to write about. Another reason for not disturbing mine right now is that I still hope to get around to a book on the subject or with such a background and nothing could be more bothersome than a ghost in one's study ahead of schedule. I'm engaged otherwise right now. It will be interesting to hear what your readers report. I'm sure that after you receive one or two publishable letters and run them in your column, other readers will be encouraged to tell their stories. But maybe you'll have to ghost one or two yourself to start them off.

Me, I'm living in the 19th century this summer and trying to find out what ghosts haunted the brothers back there.

Did I tell you that Percy Julian [scientist] quoted you most effectively in his commencement oration here—substituting for Mme Pandit? He's a spellbinder anyhow, but he also did a good turn for himself by calling upon your poetry and Countee's "Incident," which he did in German as well as English.

The campus gossip, which Doug will be able to detail for you, is that CSJ is being haunted by CVV and GO'K. No word from CSJ, but the whisper is that the ghosts in question are being difficult, very difficult. I believe you once wrote something pertinent about patrons, gifts, etc. No? Well. . . . Doug leaves for N. Y. today, having just completed a commission to do five portraits for Meharry. Quite a lot of folding green involved, I gather.

Best ever,
Arna

11 June '51

Dear Lang,

Don't talk about broke because that's me. All the money bags seem to be tied up or shy or something, and the publishers who ordinarily send me royalty the first of June haven't peeped yet, though this is the 11th. But here's a check for the pictures nevertheless, and thanks for handling the project. Will they send me the negative they made for me so that I'll have it next time I want prints?

PFC Paul Bontemps, U.S. 53047678, is with the 41st Trans. Trk. Co., 9th Highway Group, Fort Eustis, Virginia. Another person he would like to hear from, whose address I can't give him, is Murial Corin or Karen, now employed by Doubleday, the first colored girl to be hired by that firm. He used to date her here, and her handsome mother from East Orange, here yesterday to pick up another daughter, stopped by to report on Murial's progress. I told her that you and I, Doubleday authors, congratulate her. Paul is a hard man to get a letter from, but he may respond to you or Murial. Generally he would rather telephone home. I suppose it's easier.

The *Nashville Tennessean* has never run my review of *Montage,* so here is a copy for your files—or perhaps to be spotted in some magazine, if you think of one which has not yet reviewed the book. It is not unusual for poetry reviews to appear long after publication. Same with juveniles, as you know. The ones on *Chariot* are still coming in at about five or six a week and ranging from good to excellent—exciting. Both N.Y. Sunday book sections have reviewed it as a juvenile, which reviews you apparently missed. Others have treated it as general fiction. The *Library Journal* went to town for it, which is all to the good, I hope, since so many public libraries use it as a buying guide.

Your dedication to poetry, translated or written, even in periods of shortage, is something to commend. So luck to you with your three commitments. I'm under enough strain with my two (both booksize, Houghton and Messner) and have reached the same resolve as to the future—never no more! I'm already a year late on the big book (Douglass-Washington-Du Bois) and scarcely more than half finished. At least another year will be required—though I keep talking about 6 months to Maxim and H-M. The little thing for Messner—Lord knows.

Being broke and needing a change, I'm taking on summer school classes again beginning tomorrow (the 12th) but *may* play hookey long enough to attend Owen, Jr.'s wedding in D.C. on July 8th and the ALA meeting in Chicago the same week. If so, and if I were to route myself through N.Y.C. to Chi., could you and I see *Guys and Dolls* or *The King and I* on the 9th? Tickets possible?

Who is Ralph's publisher? Random House? His book will surely be a solid sender, after such sustained work. Gives me a notion to take 2 or 3 more years on the big one above and try to make it a s-s too, but I fear my gang here would come to the end of patience. They should learn a lesson from Fanny. So hello to her and Ralph and to the Harpers and all.

Best ever,
Arna

P.S. Beau Jack's story is a sad one for true—a theme for an opera or at least a short story or novella. I have a side-light. Some of his camp-crowd was in the room next to mine at the Theresa one night. I got a vivid impression of the vermin from the conversation that came through the wall. Beau, it seemed, was somewhere down the hall.

14 June '51

Dear Lang,

This is just a second thought on my suggestion that I might route myself through NYC on July 9th. Better not count on it. May be impossible. And the soldier whose address I gave was assigned to the wrong rank. He is Corporal. So much for corrections. I have two summer school classes, which means lectures by me from ten to twelve each day. Hope I can keep it up for six weeks.

Best,
Arna

31 August '51

Dear Lang,

The news about Maxim is shocking. Under the conditions, however, I think he is well-advised to put his health first and let the work go. I have sent an expression of this sort to Minna, but if you are going to be in conversation with her, I'd appreciate your suggesting that I had counted on royalties due Sept. 1st and hope they will not be delayed by this unhappy turn of events. *The Poetry of the Negro,* I believe, is among the titles due to report.

Hope you are getting along better with the country pests, now that you have castigated them all roundly. Your column on the subject has been read with much amusement hereabouts. I wonder what you would say about this 100 degree heat, however, after about a month of it, night and day. With humidity. Yesterday broke the Nashville record for August 30th and the weatherman promised that today would top that. Right now it feels like he knew what he was talking about.

Ask Alvin Cooper if he heard that Bill Demby is working with Roberto Rosollini (sp) as some kind of assistant director. That's what his brother is putting out. Actually it wouldn't surprise me if it were confirmed.

How far advanced is your musical? And the Battles book? Me, I'm still in the 19th century with my Negro leaders. Nearly a hundred years to go.

Best ever,
Arna

1611 Meharry Blvd.
Nashville 8, Tenn.
25 Sept. '51

Dear Lang,

Yes, the Doubleday check arrived finally and surprised me by being twice as big as I had expected. After some delay I also received my book club money which pleased me by being enough to cover all Poppy's expenses for her first year at Bennett. But another question has arisen—or perhaps two.

Minna asks (and makes it plain that it is just a request) if I would mind having the publishers continue to send Maxim [Lieber] a ten percent cut on the books he negotiated for me: the publishers to divide the income and send me the balance direct. Since this involves you on one of the books *(The Poetry of the Negro),* I need your view before I can answer. Off hand, I wonder. While I would be disposed to do something for Max out of gratitude, personally, I wonder if this is the best way. I wonder if it would not complicate my relations with publishers and possible future agents in a number of ways. I question the reasonableness of such an agreement in view of the fact that the services of Maxim's agency (literary advice, exploitation, etc.) will be terminated, the services which had been the basis of past fees. Thus my thought, off hand, would be to continue his percentage payment on the books he negotiated for a limited time (not more than a year) not out of a sense of obligation but out of friendly gratitude. I would be inclined to ask the publishers to stay out of it, to send me the full checks for royalty and let me send Maxim the ten percent cut from here. How do you feel? Would you be able to ask Arthur Spingarn's view? Could you contact someone at the Author's League? I'm telling Minna that I must consult with you because of our joint concern at one point.

I'll talk about lectures next time.

> Best ever,
> Arna

You may show this to Arthur if you have a chance to talk with him—if you wish.

> 20 East 127th Street
> New York 35, N.Y.
> October 11, 1951

Dear Arna,

Back in the city to stay a while before departing for N. C. for Book Week talks. De-lighted to see Harlem again!

I've talked to Arthur Spingarn, Minna Lieber, and Leah Salisbury (who's going to handle my plays, *Street Scene, Barrier,* etc. for me from now on). Spingarn and Salisbury both state ethical and legal thing to do is let Lieber continue to collect on books, etc. placed in the past and on which no further activity is required. (The way in which such percentages is sent him doesn't matter—your way being O.K.) Spingarn says, however, any new activity relating to old properties (for example should our *The Poetry of the Negro* be sold to Pocket Books, etc.) the agent handling the new deal would get the complete percentage on that new edition. Minna Lieber also said the same, and that Max would in no way want his going out of business to prevent his clients from getting someone to handle anything that might come up in relation to any of the properties he has handled for his authors, and full commissions would go to the new agents. In fact, Mrs. Lieber has released me to turn over to another agent some contracts (such as the Battle book, and the new Henry Holt collection of short stories) on which Max had already done some negotiating before his illness but, being unable to carry through, won't collect further. Same is true for TV contracts of *Street Scene* just received. . . . . . So what I'm doing is let Max continue to collect on *Simple, Montage* etc., in so far as the *books* go for the American, English, and Italian editions of *Simple,* but any future editions sold, etc., would go to whatever new agent I may get, who would handle those contracts. The contracts Max got for me are so much better than any I ever signed myself that I think he deserves this, especially since ALL other than book rights are retained by me, so these I can now turn over to another agent on ALL my Lieber placed books.

I haven't had a chance to think about a new literary agent yet. Who is good that you know of? Do you have anyone in mind for yourself? I really need someone right away with the Battle and Holt books to negotiate.

In a hurry today so more anon. Best regards,

Sincerely,
Lang

15 October '51

Dear Lang,

A letter came from Ingersoll and Brennan, the literary agents, as a result of Nelson Algren's mention of my name and Jack Conroy's to them, but there has been no follow up since I told them how my literary business is split up. I have heard that they are live-wire literary agents and have done well by Nelson as well as David Davidson whom they represent. If you care to talk to them, I'll be glad to know what you learn, but if I hear no more direct, I'll wait till I come to New York again and try to arrange a conference with them or some other agency. I had rather set my mind on I & B, but I don't want to push them. Moreover I'm resolved to handle my own juveniles from here on.

Max was never able to get any better terms for a juvenile than I was for the ones I negotiated. The terms are standard. Nor was he ever able to turn up any subsidiary business that did not come through the publishers themselves: no foreign editions, reprints, movie or radio sales, etc. All I've had came in unsolicited. My conclusion is that an agent can't help with juveniles. Also the publishers dislike dealing with them in this field, or so they (Macmillan and Houghton) have told me frankly.

But my present major work will need an agent soon, so I too am in the market for one. I have met a couple of writers (Engstrand, George Martin, Max Schulman, etc.) who swear by Harold Matson, and I have heard Ann Watkins and Harold Ober praised, but all that is hearsay. I don't know a thing.

Apparently no Book Week lectures for me. I had two letters but neither cared to buy at $150. I'll stay home and write about Booker-T and Du B instead. . . . A wonderful autumn has arrived. I went fishing in a small river day before yesterday and caught seven bass, perch and brim. Beginner's luck!

Best ever,
Arna

20 East 127th Street
New York 35, N. Y.
March 3, 1952

Mr. Arna Bontemps,
1611 Meharry Boulevard,
Nashville 8, Tennessee.

Dear Arna,

From both Japan and Germany have come requests to translate the poems in our anthology *The Poetry of the Negro*. I have replied, of course, that except for my own poems, neither you nor I have authority to grant permissions. But I am sending to each of the editors a list of the addresses of those poets I have so they can be contacted directly. I am also enclosing this list for you in case you have such requests, you can simply have your secretary send the writer a copy.

Maybe if Paul is nearby, he could drop in on the lady in Munich. She writes excellent English and I imagine could do a good translation. Apparently she is connected with a Hamburg publisher, Rowohlt, whom she says is considering translating various Negro novels into German.

Josh White and Sam Gary and Margaret Bonds have been here all afternoon rehearsing for the Garden N.A.A.C.P. rally Thursday night, with Sammy Heyward on my "Ballad of Harry Moore" to be performed there. Always something in New York to keep one from creating.

Advance copies of "Laughing To Keep From Crying" arrived. Shall send you one shortly, soon as I get out from under piled up mail, and acquire some string and wrapping paper. And get my sleep back from that tour.

So glad you got Limon for the Festival. . . . . . Juanita Hall goes into Cafe Society tomorrow night. . . . . Georgette Harvey died last week, Mercedes Gilbert yesterday. . . . . . Rosamond Johnson's wife very ill. . . . . . I haven't been out the door since I got back, so no more news.

ANOTHER crazy lady has started writing me l-o-n-g letters! The third! What is it about my work that attracts these folks?????? This one will get no parts of any kind of answer.

Aunt Toy is sending Alberta those things she thinks might be useful to the kids.

Lang

April 8, 1952

Dear Arna,

I had quite a long talk with Edward Dodd, Jr., this afternoon re the *Uncle Tom* intro I'm to do, a writer for an African Negro looks at Africa book they're thinking of (for which I suggested Ted Poston), and the Josephine biography which they are delighted that you're considering. Dodd says they've sent the contract up to von Auw and are hoping both you and Joe will sign. She's still in Mexico, but will be back after Easter for a Las Vegas engagement, then East, I believe they said, in late May. (I've got two of her rather superficial French biogs, I'll lend you if and when you need them.) And when I see you in July (or whenever it is) will give you my few memories of contacts with her. I hope you'll be doing it, as I'm sure you could do a swell job.

My big typewriter broke down today, so I'm working on the old 28 year old one for the moment. Having TWO secretaries now, the big one just wore down.

I told you Griff and Muriel got married in Africa, didn't I? Home in April.

Just got a copy of the new picture book, *Literary America,* Dodd gave me today. It has me and Dick Wright in it, only cullud. But considering it has only about twenty living writers in it at all, that is right good. Beautiful looking book!

288

What about ICE CREAM? (Maybe we can work out the outline when you come North next.)

RE-gards and Good Wishes,

Sincerely,

May 5, '52

Dear Lang,

If you had more money you wouldn't *ever* sleep, so maybe the lack of it is a blessing in disguise. I've also noticed that you seem to do your best work when you're booked solid with a full range of assignments. . . . . And right now I'm noticing that the cleaning fluid isn't dry on this typewriter and that your letter is getting spattered. I take it you do not insist that I remove it and begin again, hunh?

Tommy Dodd wanted to sign me for a song, but I had my mind set on money. What troubled me even more, however, was the discovery that he had not been in touch with J [Josephine] Baker re: the story of her life but planned to communicate *after* he handcuffed me. I didn't think that was realistic. Nor did I believe la Jo would bite. Now von Auw is trying to reach her by letter, and if she will let him make a package of the job, representing all concerned, it may be possible to sell it to a publisher who is willing to treat the project seriously. I am still full of hope, for I'm a Baker fan of long standing, and it would be a delightful interlude to work on her story after I've done with Booker T. and WEBD. As of now, nobody seems to know what the lady's attitude is toward the whole matter. Do you? And if you hear of her being in NYC, will you tip off von Auw pronto?

The festival wore me out. I should have had a vacation afterwards. Instead I'm trying to recuperate by doing other things and gradually picking up the threads of my writing. By school close, maybe, I'll be in swing again. And by then the sun, which is hot now, will be blistering. . . . Jan Carew is expected tonight for his reading day after tomorrow. He'll have plenty of chance to meet the folks, evidently. And I see that neither Alvin Cooper nor Vilma Howard got their Whitney Fellowships, though their friend and classmate Ben Johnson did. Also Martha Flowers of Fisk, same vintage. I sponsored Cooper and Johnson. Two throws; one winner. Ben, by the way, is trying to get someone in Rome to translate *The Poetry of the Negro.* I have written to Doubleday asking them to send him two copies, but they have not replied, so I don't know what they have done. I'm delaying my answer to him till I hear. Which reminds me that we should be due some royalty from that source. Did Mina arrange for the payments to come to us direct in the future? Nothing was said to me, and I'm afraid I've been sort of counting on you to nudge someone, if nudging is needed.

Your poem "Africa" is a successful sequel to "Danse Africaine" and "Afro-American Fragment." A sort of rounding out of your African series.

ALA in NYC is June 30–July 4 but I'll probably stick around a few more days in the hope of seeing *Guys and Dolls,* etc. Meanwhile,

Best ever,
Arna

Greenwood Lake,
June 21, 1952

Dear Arna,

Believe it or not, mon cher ami, I have only five chapters (as outlined) to go on the Battle book—and could do those over the weekend if I didn't have to stick to FACTS. No wonder you do only three pages a day. Last night in dealing with his lodges, I got only 2 done! Then, to make things worse, the family with grandchild and dog have come up for 10 days in this small cottage with Dodgers on ALL the time—so I'd better be home. That wasn't in the understanding when the place was loaned me. But having brought half my files, and big typewriter, can't get home until they go with the car. . . . . . My current assistant, Collier, has been a great deal of help, but is taking the summer off to go home to Chicago and help his parents out in their extension of business. Promises to come back to work with me in the fall. I hope so, since conscientious, capable, and tactful folks are VERY hard to find (in or out of the race, I've discovered, since I've had Rob—whom Aunt Toy says the Lord must have meant to make a Negro—with two g's and an i in her version). . . . . It seems there was only 1 matinee ticket for *King and I* left, so Rob got mine for the night before. Sorry it looks like won't be making any shows with you. . . . Have to go up to Yale on Monday, the 30, or shortly thereafter and would love to have you come along for an afternoon if you'd like. . . . Dorothy will be delighted, I know, that you can drop by for a drink. Me go, too! I won't be in town until late the 26th, it seems. But will see you by weekend, anyhow. . . . . Gloomy and cool up here again. Fireplace going this afternoon.

Sincerely,
Lang

20 East 127th Street
New York 35, N.Y.
July 16, 1952

Dear Arna,

Well, you left New York just in time to escape the hottest heat since the Lord knows when. Everybody is prostrated but me. I manage to hold up right well, and am heading toward the end of the Battle book. . . . . I reckon you got your Doubleday check all right. I did. I sent the Junior Debutantes of Bermuda a copy of our anthology and got two nice letters in reply, saying they're reading our poetries all over the island. I gather from that that we are a cultural force, and will probably have some effect on the future writings of that small island.

All the mail which came while I was up in the country which I did not want to read on my return, I put a rubber band around and hid. I just came across it today and am reading some of it by degrees tonight. I can tell from the looks of an envelope (after years of experience) when somebody wants something. I was not wrong in regard to most of these letters. So I think I will let the rest stay unread until August, when maybe I will have more time to attend to folks who want a parole, immediate cash help, lyrics for music, and such time-taking and thought consuming things.

I was in the Waldorf today for an ASCAP meeting—concerning where the 13 million will go that came in this year in performance royalties. Exciting, as usual, with Negro members doing more talking than ever I hear before. One called the Board "gangsters" and talked and stalked out. Later another made a most beautiful tribute to the value of the organization to creative song makers. And everybody was still taking the floor when I left. A new plan is up for consideration which is supposed to keep future Stephen Fosters from starving in their old age. With 13 million even those who can't write songs shouldn't starve. And when the juke boxes get taxed it'll be maybe 18 or 20 million a year coming in. And there are less than 3 thousand song writers in America, that is, professionals.

It was so nice and cool in the Waldorf I almost froze. I had on my new breeze-weight suit which I bought with the money I trust the new plan will bring me in the FUTURE.

I saw the *Miracle* and was most moved by it. Otherwise haven't seen anything else of late. Too busy making contracts for juveniles—four new ones to date.

Due to have my new Simple finished by mid-August. So got to go to work soon —a third done now. *Should he or shouldn't he get married at the end?*

Carpenters have driven me out of my studio. New shelves in the office, new windows, etc. Getting ready to sort and arrange Yale stuff.

Juanita Hall's about to record four of my blues. . . . . . And a second Deep South lecture has come in, so reckon I'll wire Margaret to affirm hers, if she's having it, and go that way in October, since it looks as if it'd now cover expenses anyhow, and sell a few books. After election cullud may not be able to travel.

Langston

18 July '52

Dear Lang,

If I missed the worst of the NY heat wave, I have not been so lucky on this end. Even this basement has finally been penetrated, and my creative drive has sagged accordingly. If we get the house we are now trying for at Wildwood, perhaps there will be relief there. Certainly there will be plenty of room for you to visit us the 2nd or 3rd week of August, and you may enjoy the best beach I've seen on the Atlantic coast, the summer theatre at Cape May and plenty of fine sea food. You may even go crabbing. I have sent a deposit on the house but have received no reply yet.

Yes, I think it will be just right to have Simple get married in the new book, but don't spill it in a column before hand. Let this be something of a surprise to readers of the column. It will give you an incident you can enlarge as the climax of the volume. Besides, I think he has held Joyce off long enough. You spoke of having more of a central theme running through this book. Well, that would certainly give it to you: the build up and the conclusion. I'm all for it.

I've checked on those *Famous* books and found that the series is a very solid one. Looks like you've landed another good backlog. If you include any living people, however, make sure you select those who stand the best chance to *stay* famous if you want the book to last a long time. Also it helps to select people about whom it is hard to find good biographical material, especially on the school level.

If you have four juveniles on the line, you're two up on me (Messner *Biography* and Winston *Adventure* Series), though I have a sort of verbal understanding with H-M about the Douglass junior biography. I've still a long ways to go on Booker and WEBDuB, and the heat won't let me hurry. The Jo Baker story and another adult job are still in the talking stage. I envy you that Carmel possibility, which seems to me a wonderful way to catch up on things, while at the same time getting a change of scene.

If you now have two Deep South lectures for fall, you'll probably be able to add a couple more and build the jaunt up to a profit. You might even let Mary Thompson of the International Student Center know your schedule, but don't tell her I put you up to it. If it fits in just right, she might not think it too soon for a repeat, considering the success of your last visit. . . . I've heard nothing from Margaret since her telegram arrived. Guess I'll have to write her too.

So more anon. Hello to Toy et al. Card from Doug and Alta in the Grand Canyon. Pearl Fisher here for Race Relations confab.

Best ever,
Arna

20 East 127th Street
New York 35, N.Y.
August 17, 1952

Dear Arna,

The Lord has no intention of permitting me to come down to see you-all this month. But at any rate, one way station in history has been made: I HAVE FINISHED THE BATTLE BOOK, all typed and everything, just waiting to go down to Von Auw [Ivan Von Auw, literary agent] when he returns from his vacation on the 26th. What prevents me from accepting your kind invitation to the seashore is that the 2nd *Simple* book was due August 15th, *day before yesterday.* Gracias a dios, however, my editor is in Europe and not due back until the 25th. I plan, though, to have it sitting on her desk that day—everything being in it now and ready for 2nd draft typing *but* the plot. That I intend to insert along with next week's final typing, having it all out-lined. Of course, after an editorial reading, I'll rework the whole into last draft form. Also Elie Siegmeister wants his show done by the time he gets back from the country right after Labor Day —so I'm still a literary sharecropper with deadlines from past larcenies to meet. Once I get out from under these, no more until April, 1953—when ALL three of my juvenile contracts come due. Bet I'll have 'em, too! However, you see why I can't leave town—at least, not that leisurely or that far. . . . . . I heard "Come Rain, Come Shine" on the air the other night, sounded like a beautiful new arrangement, but heard no credits. . . . . Now 11 P.M. I'm invited down to the Cartwrights to see Peggy Wyke en route from Port au Spain to Paris, so maybe will get dressed and try to make it by midnight. . . . . Japanese version of our *The Poetry of the Negro* (with such as subtitle) has arrived with you and me in it (names of authors in English, too) otherwise can't make head from tails— except I gather it is put out by the Left—with a photo of Dr. Du Bois when he was in Japan in it. . . . . . Let me know if and when you drive through N.Y. (Won't ask this time when?) Would love to see Alberta and the young ones.

Lang

19 August '52
c/o Faulkner
128 West Roberts Ave.
Wildwood, N. J.

Dear Lang,

Somehow or other I've let your new telephone number get away from me. Would you mind calling and entrusting it to Doug [Aaron Douglass] and Alta or better still shooting it back here by Thursday so that I can reach you if things do work out a little better this trip? Our time is up at Wildwood Friday morning, and we expect to pull out bright and early that day, but whether or not we get up that way still depends. I'd like to keep the way open, though Constance and Joan have irritated throats today as a result of too much sea water and sea wind.

Sorry you can't come down. We have the biggest and best house we've had here. Leslie visited over the week-end. Horace Scott [B. T. Washington's sec'y] (Emmett J's youngest, Clarissa's Brother) is across the street with his family. Arthur Fauset is expected today or tomorrow. Lots of others who mention you. And half the night spots have Negro talent: Louis Jordan, Sarah Vaughn, Billy Eckstein, etc. either here, just gone or coming. Many smaller fry.

I'm glad you've got Battle off your hands, however, and Simple 2nd so well advanced. Wish I could say the same for Booker et al, but at least I'm staying out of the water today and hoping to get in a lick or two after as many letters. Have reviewed Carl Rowan's *South of Freedom* since coming here. You're mentioned favorably. A thrilling book! DON'T MISS.

Saw Charles S. just before leaving Fisk. He was saddened by the condition of the Negro writers he saw in Paris. His words: "They're living off each other's entrails." The first rate writers in France, he gathered, were in small cities living almost incognito—the Americans, that is. In short, he thought the Negroes there were going to pot instead of flowering. He thought the atmosphere in England was healthier. He did not get to Rome.

Wish we could take these cool breezes back to Nashville. They're almost too good to be true. So more in a minute.

Best ever,
Arna

September 11, 1952

Dear Arna,

Hy! . . . . . . Look here, Moe Asch, Folkways Records, wants me to record two poems for his anthology of Negro Poetry on records, which he says you are the editor of, or the poem-selector. He wants to record next week, so let me know which two poems of mine you think best, by return mail. I'd suggest the best known: "Negro Speaks of Rivers" and "I, Too, Sing America"—or else, if we want one rhymed lyric one, in place of the latter, "Refugee in America."

Rushed like mad this week trying to finish up the *Simple* book in order to finish up Elie's show as he has gotten back from a summer in the country and I have to take a draft over to Brooklyn this week-end. These two are my LAST big dead-lines, thank the Lord! *Simple* I can rework after an editorial reading, so am turning it in next week for the moment. . . . . The *Uncle Tom* is out. The kid's book comes out October 18, big party for it (if you're in town) November 12 after my return from the South. Did you receive the Spanish *Poemas?* An anthology of Negro poetry in Chinese arrived the other day (not based on ours, but older collections) and in the same mail a possum from down South in dry ice, which we're cooking tomorrow. Both tributes to art! . . . . New recording of "Cool Saturday Night" by white Berenice Parks (whose folks own the Ruby Foo restaurants) is out. Disk jockeys now playing it. . . . . . .

REGARDS,
Lang

9-13-52

Dear Lang,

In the same mail with your letters was one from Ida saying that Countee's recording of "Heritage" is available for the album. It includes also some talk by Countee about the poem and about his teaching experiences. Ida also told me how I can reach Grace Johnson by mail re: a recording Jim made at N. Y. U., I believe (not the one Moe pressed). I'll go to work on that Monday. Meanwhile, I hasten to suggest that my preferences among your poems, for this purpose, would be "Negro Speaks of Rivers" and "I, Too, Sing America." They are the most widely known of your poems and most suitable for high schools, to which many of the albums should be sold. So pass all this along to Moe Asch when you see him this week and say that I will communicate with him as soon as I have made an effort to reach Mrs. J. W. Johnson. . . . Let's hope a way can be found to make the album help promote the anthology and viceversa.

The interest in Negro poetry shown by the Orientals is most encouraging. Bob Hayden is thrilled by the news. Which reminds me that he and I both wondered if it would be necessary for us to spend a whole week at Jackson and wrote Margaret to that effect. That is quite a long absence from work, and we asked if our events could somehow be scheduled so that we would not have to spend more than a couple of days on the campus. Naturally we have heard nothing more from Margaret, but I note that her letter says she will return from vacation September 8, so maybe she will write again soon.

The idea of meeting you in Memphis appeals to me. I'll keep it in mind and see if we can make everything fit together. That should be about Sunday, October 19th, shouldn't it?

Tonight we're staying up to put Poppy on the 1:20 A.M. train for Bennett. The house is jumping with Fisk, A. & I. and other college kids coming in to tell her good-by, which means there is a noisy background.

Your possum column very interesting. I always like those writer-at-home things you sometimes do. In your case they are good reading. Hope you will do them more frequently from the far West. I should think you would also clip copies of them for the basket or box or drawer in which you keep notes and random items for the next volume of *The Big Sea.*

Did you read about yourself in Rowan's *South of Freedom?* Don't miss it. Also read about Beverly Hills in the current *Holiday.*

That Carnegie concert should be a treat. Wish I were going to be there. Unfortunately I don't even see how I can get up for the *New York Times* book fair, to which I have been invited—November. If Jo Baker would only return and stay put long enough to talk shop, I might be able to tie the two things together, but as of now—no prospects.

Folks pouring back to the campus. And Emmet May rang our bell the other night. Driving through to Mexico, just pausing long enough to have a cup of coffee. Which reminds me, I'll have to go down and put the pot on if I'm going to stay up till two or three o'clock. So more anon.

Best ever,
Arna

20 East 127th Street
New York 35, N.Y.
September 27, 1952

Arna, mon cher ami,

Yesterday I turned in the "Simply Heavenly" book at luncheon with Maria Leiper, bound all the drafts (5) last night, and boxed them for Yale—about 20 pounds of manuscript, which, to combine with the 40 pounds of Battle, may cause Yale to have to build a few extra shelves in the JWJMC Room! I have begun to write by the pound. . . . . "Simple" is 315 pages at the moment, so can stand a bit of cutting after editorial comments are forthcoming. It's more of a story than before so I hope can safely be called "A Conversational Novel". About a third of it is brand new material, not used in columns, and the columns themselves have mostly been so cut and interwoven as to make it really a new book. Lots of intensive work this past month. White folks (and Ralph) would take at least two years on such. A past due deadline speeded me up a little. Fortunately my typist was on vacation from N.Y.U. and could give me extra time, too.

Next job is Elie's musical show which I hope to complete before leaving for Mississippi. Just put in for train reservations. Discovered that City of New Orleans goes through Memphis, not Nashville. Looks like a place called FULTON is nearest mainline stop to Nashville. It passes through there at 3:05 in the afternoon, through Memphis at 5:15, reaching Jackson at 8:55 P.M. I plan to leave Chicago on Saturday, October 18th to reach Jackson that night, otherwise no good train arriving before the opening Vespers on Sunday at which Sterling is speaking and whom I'd like to hear. I tell you all this in case it's feasible for you to join me on this train somewhere along the line.

In return what you can tell me is what is best way to get from Jackson to Nashville in case I'll be coming over there after my Tougaloo College date on October 31. I've written Miss Henninger Sunday, November 2nd is open. Also wrote LeMoyne same. Since I want to be home in time to vote, that's about the last day I could remain South.

I'll be in Chi for a radio program re "The First *Book of Negroes*" before coming to Jackson. They've got a whole slew of them lined up here starting October 8th with a TV show with me, Ben Carruthers (as a character in the book) and Juanita Hall doing a song of mine, probably. Watts is really doing some promotion on that little juvenile! And plan a big party November 12th to which you're invited.

Edith Wilson brought news of you-all this week. . . . . "Don't You Want To Be Free" opens in Newark tomorrow night, but I don't intend to see it until I return in November. Can't add another thing to my calendar between now and Southward departure—and expect to finish what's on my docket to get done by then re show and other little odds and ends, plus the kid's book interviews and shows. Times like these I miss a full time secretary. Badly need one! Wish I could pay one! Wish I had one! Ain't got none! (Echo: Cullud ain't suppose to have none!)

I believe I'll give a party in November for Jean-Louis Barrault when he gets here with his French troup to do "Hamlet", etc., I used to know him in Paris when he was reciting my poems around. . . . . . Jan Carew writes from London (remembering that last party of mine whence you caught your train).

Sincerely,
Lang

20 East 127th Street
New York 35, N.Y.
October 4, 1952

Arna Bontemps, Esq.,
Hotel Algonquin,
New York, N. Y.

Dear Arna,

You must be simple—expecting to get a seat to the Series! I tried several agencies, old man Battle, and Rudolp Thompmas at the Y who gets seats direct from Jackie. He'd sold his last pair to Hubert Delaney. Only way anybody knows to get in is to go up and stand in line early in the morning. Me, not that interested. 71,000 today and Sunday's crowd will try to be bigger. I'd suggest you go to see the Cinerama at the Broadway Theatre, which is said to be fascinating. . . . . . Just got your letter Saturday noon. Checked on your reservation which is O.K., as you know by now. . . . Rob does not work on Saturdays, but *Guys and Dolls* is sold out for next Saturday, however Algonquin agency at cigar stand in the lobby says try them on Monday. Called other agencies with no luck, sold out all next week, they say. Today being a matinee day, couldn't get Juanita or Benny by phone, so all I have for you is your check which I'm holding. You might be able to get *Guys and Dolls* yourself through Leah. Personally, I didn't like it much. Have seen MUCH better musicals, including *St. Louis Woman* and *Street Scene*. . . . . . I've got a deadline to meet Monday with a condensation (one act version) of Elie's show for those Penn. Music Society folks, so couldn't go to series anyhow Sunday even if it were humanly possible. But phone me in the afternoon, or come up. I'll be up by noon or so. Have been working all night for last month trying to clear things up before leaving for Mississippi. Be seeing you. Welcome to our city!

Lang

Dear Arna:

Hey, now! At the very end of this here program the lady librarian who was introducing authors in the audience pulled two beautiful "all-Negroes-look-alike-to-me" boners. She got ALL the white authors, illustrators, and editors *right*. Then she looked at Pearl Fisher and said, "And you are Ellen Tarry, aren't you?" Pearl said no, and identified herself, amidst laughter. (Ellen was not there, being on lecture tour in the South). Then the lady looked at me and said, "But you *are* Arna Bontemps." I would have taken a bow under your name but too many folks there knew me. So I had to rise and deny your name, too, as Pearl did Ellen's. Whereupon the lady gave up and did not introduce another living soul, but said, "We will now retire to the Children's Room for refreshments." I had to rush off to an interview at the Herald Trib so didn't get a chance to explain to her that we've often been mistaken for each other, which might have relieved her a bit.

Just talked to the Countee Cullen Writers Workshop at . . . the Library. Books sold: $13.00. At YW the other night: $70.00. So have had a good bookselling week. If I can sell that many in North Carolina Friday, day after tomorrow, I will give myself a bonus.

It is now 1 A.M. and I am supposed to finish Elie's show and take it to him before leaving tomorrow, but haven't started work on it yet, and am no further than when I saw you in Nashville. Do you reckon ever?

What happened about *St. Louis Woman?*

I saw the cullud-white *Aida.* Sleep-lulling mostly, but pretty Lem Ayres pastels to look at and one or two very good dance spots. Otherwise on the A-r-t (big A) side. Went unfortunately on a Monday when all the main leads were off, alternates singing. Barrault sleep-lulling, too, so believe I'll give up theatre for awhile. $4.80 is too much to pay for a nap.

L. Hughes, Litt. D.

17 November '52

Dear Lang,

If I can find a copy of this week's *Fisk Forum* (the undergrad newspaper), I'll enclose it herewith—since you were in the headline. The drama of your lecture-reading, followed by the thud of Stevenson's defeat, appear to have touched off a chain reaction hereabouts. Some of the events related, some unrelated and some uncertain. While those who came to criticize you remained to praise, a few die-hards continue to growl, and Charles S. discovered that they had tried to get the FBI as well as the local police to meddle, but were rebuffed by each. So it all turns out to be educational.

Doug has had an operation for a growth on his neck. He is back at work but not yet walking very fast. A freshman whom we all knew, having studied all hours in the Chemistry building, preparing for the mid-term, fell somehow into the elevator shaft this A. M. and is in a dangerous condition. In one of the Jefferson Street beer and eating places where Fisk and Meharry folk foregather evenings local detectives made an unpleasant scene Saturday night and tried to get white members of the party to leave. Blyden is named as one of those present, but I have not seen him to get details. (Not for publication, of course.)

But the campus pinwheel never stops. I'm booked solid for this week, including evenings. Have just dusted off my dinner jacket, in fact. . . . Meanwhile, Leah Salisbury is in Hollywood, and I hope something comes of it. . . . I'm trying to tell Shirley Graham and Dr. WEBD that Fisk is the place for his library and papers, that we can do a better job on them than this "foundation" they are trying to organize—have you seen how poorly the Douglass home in Anacostia is kept? The library there is of no use to scholars or writers, but people come from far and wide to use our AMA, Langston and Chesnutt papers. I'm negotiating with at least half a dozen *right now,* arranging time and hours, etc. All working on doctoral dissertations or books. Would appreciate if you could at some time have a phone conversation with Shirley about it, listening to the pro and con, and asking her opinion of the argument I tried to advance. Evidently Du Bois has left it up to her to decide.

Paul Williams of L. A. thought that Noel Sullivan (remembering his interest in several young singers) might be a person Charles should know, a person who might now and then be able to direct a promising student to Fisk's rather strong music school, the alma mater of Roland H., Eddie M., Cecil Cook, Warner Lawson, etc. That was behind my mention of the possible invitation, if it could be arranged, of CSJ to Carmel next time he goes out to call on the Ford Foundation in Pasadena. But use your own judgment. I have not indicated to Charles that you know Noel or that I am mentioning this.

Don't let the homecoming whirl wear you down. Save enough time to write a few more FIRST books and at least one FAMOUS one.

Best ever,
Arna

25 November '52

Dear Lang,

If you think Ulysses and Florence Prince would like to have copies of this program, here are two for them. I don't have the address of either. Both well received by a good audience. . . . . You could afford to lecture near to home for free when you can sell $70 worth of books per evening.

I'm still writing statements for MGM. First I had to answer references to me in the left-wing press. Then I denied that I am or was ever a communist, in a separate statement. Next I was asked for another statement denying that I had ever paid dues to the communist political association. All of which I have done. What will be asked next I can't imagine. I might have added (except that I feared it would not be believed) quite truthfully that until I learned it by reading about the recent investigations in the newspapers, I never knew that communists paid dues—any more than republicans and democrats. I suppose a person who has actually been hobnobbing with the left can more easily disclaim it than one whose activities have been so far removed he doesn't know what it's all about. This is all I hear about *St. Louis Woman.*

Best ever,
Arna

20 East 127th Street
New York 35, N.Y.
December 19, 1952

Dear Arna,

My writing arm is not paralyzed. But I've been waiting to send you a carbon of my note to Carmel re C.S.J.'s coming out, and just haven't gotten around to writing Sullivan yet. Have had nightly engagements every night for past week or more—Tonight just came from a P.T.A. group meeting at Riverton where I sold a dozen books. They're planning to buy 60 "First Book of Negroes" for school! libraries in the area—so I love those folks!

Last night I went to a reading of the play Helen Hayes is going to produce, *Take A Giant Step,* a really beautiful study of a Negro adolescent and his realization of color as his white neighborhood friends begin to grow up and the white parents object to him being around their girls. It's by Louis Peterson who was at Morehouse with Griff Davis, very talented young Negro. Judge and Mrs. Waring were there, also Mrs. (Rosenwald) Levy with more diamonds around her wrist watch than I've ever seen in a shop. She remembered that farewell dinner in Chicago, and is delighted with the progress the race is making. I said, "Yes, m'am." And rid the bus back to Harlem.

I'm sure Noel will be delighted to meet Charles S. and have him at the Farm. And will write him soon as the Christmas rush is over. Have only got my European cards off. Domestic ones still to do. And Rob was off all week with exams. So was snowed under. What with interviews and radio for the kid's book still taking up time. Watts are really promoting it.

Thanks for all the Fisk papers and the release you sent me. I see where some Senator has attacked the new translation of the Bible as being Red and is thinking of introducing a bill to prohibit its circulation. Mrs. Levy says they're also about to investigate the Rosenwald Fund, although she doesn't know why, since it's out of existence. Which is right simple!

When I was running for the subway last night on the way to that Park Avenue play reading, the cops on 125th Street seemed to be trying to arrest a VERY large colored lady of at least 300 pounds who seemed to be too large to get into the squad car. Being late, I was unable to stay to see the end. But I had already read the play, so didn't miss much. And the author reads like most composers sing.

The new Meyerowitz cantata for Christmas got razzed, but good! Although the audience liked it, and gave him about six bows. I do believe the critics want to do him in. Wait till they hear our Easter one! His publishers have asked us to do some more.

"Simple Takes A Wife" is scheduled for April. I'm doing final revisions now. It's listed in the Spring catalogue.

So MERRY CHRISTMAS to you-all!

Sincerely,
Lang

Thursday, 1-15-'53

Dear Lang,
I've been working like a beaver. With Paul free to help me for a couple of weeks, I have been getting a sample of what a literary factory is like. He stays here and types or does research when I have to go to the library or otherwise occupy myself on campus. So the chips are flying, even though the results may be remote.

Your line up of personalities for the *Famous* book is just right in my opinion. The few living people are fairly safe, and the dead ones make a good cross section. It would be easy to expand the list but rather hard to leave off any now on it. I think the latter is a good test.

The BBC transcriptions are good. I hope the business office will not delay putting through the check I warranted for you in the amount of $13.00.

I have also received several of the Moe Asch recordings of you and Sterling reading your poetry, for which I wrote an introduction—and was paid!

And I am asked for quick articles by the Sat. Review and by the Message on the most recent trend in handling Negroes in fiction and the new revised Bible respectively. Neither of which have I will power enough to turn down, what with the uses for ready cash being what they are.

Roland Hayes sings tonight in the Chapel. An elderly lady named Miss Adler arrived yesterday from New York for his concert. I showed her the library. That's the kind of fan to have. She is a retired Juilliard teacher as well as the sister-in-law of the late Julius Rosenwald.

Charles S. is expected back from the coast tonight in time for the concert, but I have had no direct word re: his meeting with Noel, if it happened. . . . Irwin Edman expected at the ISC tomorrow night (Friday). So more anon.
Best ever,
Arna

February 8, 1953

Dear Arna,
Mr. Wycliffe Bennett, c/o H.M. Customs, Kingston, Jamaica, B.W.I, the Secretary of the Poetry League there, co-editor with W. Adolphe Roberts of *The Poetry of the Caribbean* now almost ready, and a very amiable and interesting young man writes me that he would like to lecture in this country next season and suggests the following subjects:

    THE GROWTH OF NATIONALISM IN JAMAICA
    LIFE IN PRESENT DAY JAMAICA
    RACE RELATIONS IN JAMAICA TODAY
    THE POETRY OF THE CARIBBEAN
    THE POETRY OF JAMAICA
    THE POETRY OF THE BRITISH WEST INDIES

I have suggested he write our bigger colleges. But, if you would be so kind, you might turn over this information to your Lyceum Committee, in case they'd be interested in contacting him directly.

Carl Cowl asked me for suggestions for reviewers for Claude's new book. Naturally I suggested you for the *Times* or *Herald Trib* or *Saturday Review.* I haven't seen the book yet. But got an advance copy of James Baldwin's today from Knopf. It looks good.

The National Book Awards this year were midly interesting, papers *all* read, and John Mason Brown not chairman (as last time) to spark things up. I saw Ralph at the P.E.N. cocktails the other day (he's a new member so they gave a party for him at the Algonquin) and I told him not to read no two hour paper when he comes to Fisk, nor let anyone else do it either—recalling that 9 A.M. to 2 P.M. session I once attended. There must be some way of keeping academic things short and exciting. I think Jackson College did pretty well—only a week was too much!

Swiss radio man here yesterday to record an interview (in German partly) for their Basle station, says Eva Hesse is really a FINE translator, a true poet herself, and her translation WAY above those in *Afrika Singt* and others I showed him. I am sending her the Roumaine poem about the tom-toms, but never did have the French of the one on me. We got it from the Underwood translations, I think, in English. Will also find out for her about those permissions, if I can. Haven't had a moment to breathe this week (pre-Negro History Week engagements) with more coming during the Week itself—Ethical Culture Forum (with Fannie Hurst and Judge Waring), Brandeis University, etc. But no Deep South this time—although I had offers near enough to again attend the Mardi Gras, could I have gone that far. But with 3 kids books due in April, COULDN'T, to my regret! And King Zulu is rapidly turning into a mulatto, I fear! In a few more years they won't let him throw any more coconuts.

Did I ever tell you last Negro History Week at N.Y.U.'s program they had a sweet old ex-slave, Mrs. Maria Watkins, 92 Willoughby Street, Brooklyn, New York, who says she was in school with Booker T. Washington, and remembers a lot about him? I just came across her address in my files yesterday, so am sending it to you for your book. But I don't know if she can write, so you'd probably have to interview her when you come to town. She says she remembers a lot about Booker T. (as I've noted on her slip) and I wish I'd remembered to tell you about her before. . . . Both Margaret [Walker] and Gwendolyn [Brooks] never write a living word—and it would do no good for me to "prod" them. But I might try anyhow. . . . . What is your Signatures book? Best regards to Paul Bontemps and all,

Sincerely,
Langston

Simple is preaching Jim Crow's funeral in column to come.

Noel was sorry not to see Charles S. He tried to reach him, too, but missed. Says let him know ahead next time he'll be on Coast.

1611 Meharry Blvd.
Nashville 8, Tenn.
10 Feb. '53

Dear Lang,

You'll laugh: the Signature book is *The Story of George Washington Carver*. Finished and delivered. Of course it may bounce back for revisions. Seems that every publisher of juveniles wants at least one book on the wizard. Two more bids to do series books have come in, but I'm booked solid for this year. Either they will have to wait or get somebody else.

I'll give the name of Wycliffe Bennett to the ISC and other groups interested in literature or in the Caribbean area, but I doubt that any of them can say much till he offers a definite schedule, and I think he should plan his tour on the basis of relatively small fees. Only well-known names can consistently command stipends of $100 and over. Itinerant people about like Bennett, I've noticed, are ordinarily available at from $40 to $70. And some of them turn out to be fairly exciting. There are a couple of International Educational organizations in N. Y. C. which book such folk.

My Negro History Week stint will be done in Memphis. Two appearances at LeMoyne. . . . . Hope I can eventually talk to the old lady who knew Booker-T. I am also anxious to meet children, grandchildren, pals and others of some of the men close to Booker: Charles Anderson, T. Thomas Fortune, Fred Moore, etc. I am tentatively planning a week of research at the LC in Washington in March (not definite, of course) and would like to extend it to NYC for the purpose of meeting some such people—as well as seeing a few of those new shows. But that's all fantasy at this date.

Paul is back in school and apparently liking it. So I'm on my own again—and not making much headway. If anyone sends me Claude's book, I'll be glad to review it. Right now I have Dick's new novel and two others from the *Saturday Review*, however.

Best ever,
Arna

Nice card from Ulysses.
See the translations of French-Colonial Poetry in current (Winter, '52) issue of *New Mexico Quarterly*.

20 East 127th Street
New York 35, N. Y.
February 18, 1953

Dear Arna,

If you'll tell me what Dick Wright's book is like (since I haven't it) I'll tell you about James Baldwin's *Go Tell It on the Mountain* which I've just finished: If it were written by Zora Hurston with her feeling for the folk idiom, it would probably be a *quite* wonderful book. Baldwin over-writes and over-poeticizes in images way over the heads of the folks supposedly thinking them—often beautiful writing in itself—but frequently out of character—although it might be as the people *would* think if they *could* think that way. Which makes it seem like an "art" book about folks who aren't "art" folks. That and the too frequent use of flashbacks (a la Lillian Smith's "Strange Fruit") slows the book down to a sleepy pace each time the story seems to be about to start to go somewhere. And everyone is so fear-ridden and frustrated and "sorry" that they might as well have all died a-borning. Out of all that religion SOMEbody ought to triumph somewhere in it, but nary soul does. If it is meant to show the futility of religion, then it should be sharper and clearer and not so muddy and pretty and poetic and exalted without being exalting. It's a low-down story in a velvet bag—and a Knopf binding. Willard Motley-like writing without his heart-breaking characters fitting the poetry Motley weaves around them. As Motley's does, but Baldwin's don't. Has a feeling of writing-for-writing's-sake quality. I'd hoped it would be (and wish it were) a more cohesive whole with the words and the people belonging to each other. The words here belong more to the author. Although there are one or two VERY good sections, it is on the whole not unlike "John Brown's Body" (stage version, not the poem itself) which I saw last night and which nearly wore me down trying to bear up and look cultural in a hot crowded theatre 7th row orchestra with a party of folks who'd paid an ENORMOUS price for benefit tickets and had just et an enormous dinner starting with whole lobsters as just the first course, and running on down to demi tasses and brandy. With that and Baldwin's book, I've had my culture for the YEAR. When folks are dealing with God and John Brown there ought to be *fire* and FIREWORKS too, not just endlessly stretching taffy that lops over and pulls out again and declamation and taffy colored lights and heads held noble and all of it kind of sticky. If you've read it,* tell me what you think. Also about Dick's book.

Got your check for the London transcriptions, so will now pay that little bill. . . . . . . Read and returned the "Simple" proofs. . . . . . Saw the Blacks yesterday at a cocktail party (heads of Doubleday) and they're still remembering our FINE "Poetry of the Negro" party that you missed. Also saw Buck Moon at a PEN party (did I tell you) and he's with Collier's. . . . . And did I tell you some Reading Circle in Midwest is buying 1500 "First Book of Negroes"? . . . . . And waded through my first big snow of season at Brandeis U. the other day where there are 7 Negroes amidst all those of "the other persuasion". Had a pleasant half hour with Ludwig Lewisohn at his place there. I have now uttered my last public word for the season—in fact, the whole YEAR. Folks will just have to buy my records the rest of 1953. . . . . . Jane White and Bill Marshall are getting ready to do "readings" of plays and things, too,—just like white folks— which delights me. But I swear I do not believe I am going—that is, not until the "far-away voice" in poetry is strangled. *Go Tell It on the Mountain* should go swell done that way. (At $8.80 a seat). But it ain't my meat. I wish he had collaborated with Zora.

Sincerely yours truly,
Lang

*Theme: It's one-day (his birthday) in-the-life-of-a-14-year-old boy—plus all the lives of those around him—set in and seen largely through the religious estascy of an all-night store-front church meeting.

20 Feb. '53

Dear Lang,

Simple Takes a Wife arrived this morning bright and early. A beautiful book, beautifully made, beautifully inscribed and, judging by the first page, beautifully written. Alberta and Paul are also cheering it as I write. Thanks loads. My only disappointment is that none of the usual media sent it to me for review. (I refrain from asking for books for review nowadays, feeling that enough come in the normal course to take up all the time I can allot to reviewing at the present rates.) The unusual format S & S have used is most attractive and most appropriate. Here's to good sales and a warm reception generally!

Horace Bond's letter about Africa has finally arrived too. I am answering forthwith to the effect that I am in a good mood for a good proposition. Something roughly in line with your suggestion would be quite okey.

Houghton Mifflin is trying to find an illustrator for the little juvenile I've done for them about a little trumpet playing hep-cat. They are sounding out artists like Topolski, Benton and Groth to begin with. I hope it doesn't take them forever to settle on one. They claim to be very high on the story.

The Story of GWC is the manuscript that clutters this room at the moment, however, and next on the docket is the Winston Adventure Book, which will have to be postponed if the Nkrumah thing materializes. Either way, it seems that my big book of biographies for H-M is on the shelf for a few months. Wish I could meet deadlines as you do!

Best ever,
Arna

3-4-'53

Dear Lang,

We've had rain and clouds without sun for nearly a week, and the happenings hereabouts have been in harmony with the weather. If ever you have rain and clouds without sun, even for an hour, be informed, the mess can be general sometimes. Perhaps a good bit of it is mood, but the cares of parenthood do increase with time, the insistence and finickyness of editors certainly do, and the tea-pot tempests of campus life do grow more numerous when the weather is bad. So woe, woe, woe!

Your spirited reaction to Baldwin's novel was a pick-up, however. I have sent in my piece about Dick's *The Outsider* to the *Saturday Review,* and I am sure you will not find it thin or tame or much-ado-about-nothing, as I gather is the case with *Go Tell It on the Mountain.* Dick's new book is rougher, louder, bader, and probably more controversial than *Native Son.* It is certainly not dull. The spirit and outlook seem to be Existentialist, and the theme is not racial, though the characters and settings are. You will have to read it.

You will have to read also—in order to oppose—the short articles by Baldwin and Gibson in the 2nd issue of *Perspectives, USA.* Off on the wrong feet, I fear. Too bad the first attention given to Negroes by this periodical for foreign distribution of American ideas, etc. should be an attack on Negro writers by two aspiring new Negro writers. (Under influence of the New Critics mainly, I gather.) I would like to do a piece that might serve as a corrective but can't afford to do one for nothing at this moment. Hence I sha'n't volunteer.

Meanwhile watch for my essay-review of the the SAT. REV. I've got to get back to revising the Carver story now.

Best ever,
Arna

P. S. Owen due from Pasadena tonight, passing through.

20 East 127th Street
New York 35, N. Y.
March 7, 1953

Dear Arna,

Thanks a lot for calling my attention to the Gibson and Baldwin pieces in *Perspectives 2,* both provocative comments, I thought, with which, to tell the truth, I somewhatly agree—particularly after reading Baldwin's novel, which must be one of the books he is protesting against. At any rate, it would certainly be a bore if the young writers kept on writing like the old. And I think it is encouraging to see them trying to leap fences and get out of pens—even if they do fall into lily ponds. Baldwin's critical pieces are much better than his fiction, and I think he writes beautifully.

Amusingly enough, my new "Simple" has a passage about being washed whiter than snow very much like Baldwin's! (Advance comment in Virginia Kirkus Bulletin on book is quite good. And one of the proof readers (who seems to be cullud) wrote me a wonderful letter about it.)

The Barrier is being sung again tomorrow and Monday. May repeat on week-ends later. Sounded right good yesterday.

In arranging the Claude McKay book evening at the Schomburg in honor of his new poems, it seems his publishers find out that some folks are STILL mad at Claude, even though he is daid and gone! . . . . . I find about two dozen long letters in his own hand from him in basement (which I didn't know I had, at least not so many)—all before I ever met him in person while he was still in Europe. Also find 40-11 of yours which I trust I have your permission to put in a box with gold letters at Yale. Posterity can almost reconstruct the literary (cullud) history of our times from them. I found one too in Arthur Schomburg's hand. Bill Delany (Hubert's nephew) is sorting and dusting for me. The whole history of Zora has been unearthed! (I'm still in a mind to sell a few things to get the money to sort the rest of them!) (Yale money already long gone!)

Avec mes sentiments les plus sinceres,

Langston

11 March '53

Dear Lang,

Of course I have no objection to your giving my letters to the YALE Library, particularly in view of the beautiful blue box with gold lettering. What more could one ask?

Those letters from Claude sound most interesting. You should make copies of them before giving them to Yale. Either you or somebody else will have to write something objective about the controversial poet. It could be a book of widespread general interest if written quite frankly and with feeling. Claude moved among interesting people at an exciting time. He wrote poignant and sometimes stirring lines. He reacted violently. He had secret loves and open battles. What better subject could a biographer want? Yours may be one of the better collections of his letters.

You are very generous to the boys in *Perspectives USA*. They do have some talent, especially Baldwin, but in my opinion it remains to be seen whether or not the New Critics, under whose influence they have fallen, mean them any good. That group traces its geneology to the Fugitives of Nashville, the group which produced *I'll Take My Stand,* a very anti-Negro book. Not all have been reconstructed. Naturally they have their own reasons for opposing protest in fiction writing. They are ready enough to protest the things they don't like. They simply object to protesting the disabilities of the Negro in America. . . . Did you also read the interview with Robert Lowell in *Poetry,* two issues back, I believe?

I'm glad you are stimulatingly busy but regret you couldn't get away for that season in the sun of which you spoke last fall.

Best ever,
Arna

New York, New York
April 20, 1953

Dear Arna:
I have enjoyed your recent letters and am grateful to you for telling me about the Fisk Jubilee Singers on the Ed Sullivan program last night, even though they did not sing my song. I went from the annual Art Show at the Harlem Y.W.C.A. to a concert version of *Othello* with William Marshall and a white substitute for Jane White who failed to appear, to Bill Valentine's house to catch the TV show, so I had a full afternoon and evening of Sunday culture, and did not get home to dinner until almost midnight.

About twenty people have sent me the George Sokolsky column from all over the country, and one lady sent me a good answer to him which I am enclosing.

I think all of the colored actors in America were present at the *Othello* opening yesterday, and I got invited to all of their various shows that they are now appearing in. But the only one that I think I shall have time to accept—and really want to see—is *Camino Real* for which Frank Silvera is sending me tickets later in the week.

Has anything developed for you further on the African book? I have just put into writing some information which I gave Horace Bond on the telephone. Carbon is enclosed for you.

Continued good wishes ever,

Sincerely,
Langston

2 May '53

Dear Lang,

The new *Simple* is better, definitely. Sketch by sketch they are on a par, but something has been added this time: perspective in depth. That you have achieved by arrangement, organization. Simple does not change his ways as he goes along, but as we go along we see deeper into him and find traits that did not meet the eye at first: a hidden domestic instinct, pride in his young nephew, a kind of upward glance. We begin to almost admire the amusing scamp. He cries for an *Ebony* story.

When it comes to truck with the dentist, you have nothing on me. I share your woe. Also appointments. Two extractions this month already. More to follow. With partials, etc. in the offing. But I am cheered by memories of my wonderful grandma. On the day I enrolled in kindergarten she lost her last. The plates she acquired in the weeks following served her till last year—nearly 46 years—and she often suspected that they may have been responsible for her strength and endurance in the last half of her life. Perhaps my partials will teach me not to eat too much or too recklessly.

Thanks for the library items, which will get formal acknowledgements presently. That job you did on Lincoln should be a lesson to present day students who gripe without attempting anything constructive. If there's time, I may ask the *Forum* to review it. If not, next year.

Everybody liked Ralph and Fanny. We nearly wore them out, but according to Fanny's note they have forgiven us. Every copy of *Invisible Man* in Nashville was sold.

I have not gotten around to that eastern trip because I have not been able to finish off my Signature juvenile. Still revising. If I don't get to it before ALA (Los Angeles in June), it will have to be cancelled for this season. Do you reckon Noel Sullivan would be disposed to repeat an invitation he made to me in '34 to visit Hollow Hills Farm? ALA is roughly last week of June. . . . I have an invitation to cocktails with Mr. and Mrs. Arthur Hays Sulzberger (N.Y. *Times*) on May 21st. Naturally I'll go IF I'm in N. Y.

Best ever,
Arna

20 East 127th Street
New York 35, N.Y.
May 5, 1953

Dear Arna,

Programs and communications received with gratitude. And Fannie reports that they had a "wonderful" time at Fisk, and it has changed greatly for the better since her day there. Haven't talked to Ralph yet, but will probably see him tomorrow at the P.E.N. Club Cocktails at the Waldorf where me and Simple along with Dylan Thomas are to be guests of honor. . . . . . Thanks for telling me about Blyden's speech. (Tell him HY!) And I'm glad you got the book for the Herald Trib. Arthur Davis has written an excellent article on the character as displayed in the two books, but doesn't feel it is right for publication yet. I hope he'll complete it soon. . . . . . Evidently bookshops no longer pay any attention to publication dates, because a number of them are displaying "Simple" already and selling it. . . . . . Why didn't you tell me when your review of Dick's book came out in SRL? I missed it. I have the book but only got around to reading the blurb. . . . . My phone bill is so big this month I guess I'll never have time to read again! What, with my royalties statements nothing but book bills! I reckon I really do write for FUN. "Precious Lord, Take My Hand!". . . . . How is Africa coming out? I think it is good for an author to get away! I am contemplating going as far West as this Continent permits as soon as I can get downtown and get a ticket especially with summer visitors already starting to arrive with manuscripts. So I will tell Noel you're coming out in June—by which time, unfortunately, I'll have to be back, it looks like. But I'm sure he'll be glad to see you at the Farm. Dorothy Maynor and Shelby have recently returned from there. It's a charming place and you ought to see Carmel once in life—if only to recuperate from dentists. We've also had a plague of carpenters and electricians. They took days to put in a shaving mirror–medicine cabinet over my sink—started in March, I do believe, and aren't through yet! I wrote a book meanwhile! . . . . . . If we keep on writing juveniles, we'll never get an adult book done! Has anybody ever started with a juvenile and just kept on writing the same characters every year or so until they grew up and then turned into novels and grown up books—letting the books grow up as one's audience grew? Might be an idea for somebody. Maybe then one could turn one's large juvenile audience into a large adult audience of continuous readers. Do you get what I mean? If one should live so long.

Did I tell you my lady fan in the midwest sent me a beautiful brand new portable typewriter? And the one in Mississippi sent Joyce some drawers she made her ownself! No lie! Simon and Schuster did not see the possum, but I shall take this gift to a Simple character down there and show them.

> Who knows
> What the day will bring,
> Now that it is
> Spring?

> Lang

> Hollow Hills Farm,
> Route 2, Box 775,
> Carmel Valley Road,
> Carmel, California.

Dear Arna,

If you think there's peace and quiet in Carmel, you're wrong! I've been to more concerts, shows, and dinners in the three days I've been here than I attend in a month (sometimes) in New York. Sunday this very fine young colored singer gave a concert. She was here the whole weekend but nobody could see her Friday night or Saturday—being a devout Adventist—but she came out Sunday and sang like a bird. She knows your father and Troy quite well. Has she been at Fisk? Noel thinks she's the finest young talent to come along in years. . . . . . And he'd be delighted to have you here at the Farm when you come West. Proceedure: drop him a note first as to when (a week or so ahead, since he's in San Francisco on some days of the week for Board meetings). Or phone him a few days ahead: Eulah is here too and will be delighted to see you. Various guests always coming and a-going, so train or plane meeting is an everyday thing. Today for example a guest just left on 10 AM train for L.A. At noon another arrived from there by plane. And at six this afternoon, another flies down from San Francisco. So Noel should really have a station-airport bus. . . . . I'll be here just a week more, so if you airmail me a note soon, I'll get it before I head South and Eastward via New Orleans, my favorite Southern town, and maybe a summer school lecture in Georgia on the way home. "Simple" has a fine Book of Month News review and N.Y. Post. Not so New Yorker—which everybody but me seems to think is very bad. . . . . Extra copy of this program for your collection. . . . . . Regards to all.

Sincerely,
Lang

P.S. Reason I stopped short is cocktail guests have arrived—before heading for the airport to meet the dinner guest.

12 May '53

Dear Lang,

Could you give me a quick assist on this? Fisk has 10 full scholarships available for white students—through an outside source. But ordinarily white students do not include Negro schools in their college plans. What to do to round up some?

Well, they have offered to pay my way to N. Y. on the 20th if I will make an effort. But I'd hesitate to accept unless I felt that I could show some results. Perhaps the best approach is through well-placed individuals (since publicity will probably not help). I wonder if you could find a moment (if you have not left for the West) to telephone Dorothy Peterson and/or anyone else who pops into mind and beg a lead or two.

Fisk should appeal to white kids who a) plan to make careers in music, b) expect to major in sociology, c) are thinking of social work, Y-work or religious education, or d) look toward futures in dark countries. Others who can't quite make college in the East due to finances should find these scholarships quite ample. This represents a beginning in two-way integration as promoted by the outside source (backed by Ford Foundation).

If you are out of town or too rushed, could you just pass this letter along to Dorothy?

Best ever,
Arna

Rush! Telephone me at Library collect if you have lead.

9 July '53

Dear Lang,

As usual I failed to touch all points. At the last minute I was asked to meet and interview a scholarship applicant in S. F., and that took the time I had allotted to Carmel. To have extended the trip would have meant changing my ticket (or rather the reservations), and I didn't feel like starting all that over again. Nevertheless I had a fine trip. ALA was good, and I saw most of the old faces, including Jasmine Britton who talked about nothing but you. Loren and Juanita came out to see us in Pasadena, and had a look at Ruby & Owen's new mountainside house, for which they give thanks to Loren's fight against the covenants. S. F. was cool, and I loved it, walking down Market Street in a top coat on the evening of July 1st.

In Beverly Hills I was told that the contracts for the movie of *St. Louis Woman* had been drawn and put in the mail, but I have not seen one yet. If true, perhaps they are being checked by the Dramatist's Guild. Having waited half a life-time on the rewards from that property, one way or another, I should have learned patience by now, but apparently the end is not in sight. In any case, there is enough going on to require me to run up to New York from Wildwood next month, though I do not plan to bring the kids. Will you be in town toward the middle of the month? August, that is?

The Race Relations Institute closes today. I returned to the campus right in the middle of it, but I have attended only one meeting, what with catching up on mail and routine work and trying to keep cool. Bruce's pretty nurse wife introduced herself, and I wondered if I was dreaming. I always imagined him to be a confirmed bachelor. Of course, according to Handy, a brown-skinned gal will make a preacher etc. Ethel Rey (or Ray) of old Harlem and Opportunity days is here also. And Annabelle Sawyer (Alta's sister) and Prattis and Charlie Thompson (Howard) and nearly everybody else. I think Charles S. is going to try to keep Ethel here for his office.

A long and very nice letter from Billy Haygood was here on my return. His twins are both walking, and so is he, he says, being on the water wagon. He has a piece about the overseas libraries and the book burnings coming out soon in the Saturday Review. I have a review of Will Thomas's *The Seeking* (several interesting pages about Horace included) with them and am about to do Ann Petry's forthcoming *The Narrows* for them.

When 1953 began, I had five books hanging over my head. Two have been written. One approved, the other in the hands of the editors. If I can finish one more juvenile this year, I'll still be behind the game at year's end, but two is better than five in this case.

Moe Asch, whom I saw on the Coast, still hopes to bring out that anthology of Negro poets on records. Isn't there anything you can say to Margaret and Gwendolyn to bring them across? Margaret will soon be at Yale in connection with her Ford fellowship, and Gwendolyn has a forthcoming novel with Harpers, so both should hit New York one way or another. I'll write them too, of course, but I count on your letters more. I wish this could be finished up this summer.

You did not tell me about that robbery of which you speak, so more anon. All well here, and all but the very youngest quite busy at one thing or another.

Best ever,
Arna

P.S. I'm particularly glad to hear that you have contracted to do another volume of your autobiography. Yeats did about five volumes of his, Sean O'Casey about as many, Fred Douglass three (each covering the whole span of his life to date), and I have always thought that yours should be extended to four or five.

310

Next to your poetry it is the part of your writing which I expect to stand the longest. In fact I can't see how the two can be separated in the long run.

20 East 127th Street
New York 35, N. Y.
July 13, 1953

Um-huh!

Answering right back at you on the new typewriter one of my lady fans sent me! . . . . . I reckon you'll never get to Hollow Hills. . . . . Bruce [Nugent, poet artist] was down to see Dorothy fly off to Geneva and told me his wife was at Fisk. Marriage has improved him no end. . . . Thyra Edwards died last week. Cremated. No funeral. But a Memorial yesterday at St. Phillips. . . . Somebody told me it was in the papers here last week about Sinatra and *St. Louis Woman.* So glad at last! . . . . I am glad to hear Juanita's out and about. . . . . What a tall son Owen has. You, too! . . . . . Sure I'll be in town in August, except for a trip to Pittsburgh at the very end of the month for a *Street Scene* records evening. . . . . Speak at Columbia on July 21 in Summer Lecture Series. Hope I can get through in 29 minutes like Charles S. did last time I heard him there. . . . . I read Billy Haygood's piece in SRL. It were right good. Thomas book have not seen, no free copy. . . . Guess I told you you're in the Czechoslovak cullud poetry anthology. Also Waring's one immortal and ubiquitous "No Images". . . . . My suggestion is to PHONE Margaret and Gwen re recordings. Otherwise you'll never get a yea nor nea. They don't answer me, either. I wrote them once as you requested. Have I heard a word? No. . . . . Mary Elizabeth Vorhman is in town. Shall see her soon. . . . . Robbery: Me standing at hot dog stand in front of station on Saturday A.M. as bars let out reading my *NY Times,* street full of people, stand crowded, busses passing and lights ablaze. Next to me fat Jewish gentleman. Notice cullud boy pacing around behind us. Thinking he wants to get to counter I look at him. He smiles and motions for me to keep quiet. Thinking he meant to play joke on someone, I kept on reading. Next thing I know, he snatches Jewish guy's pocket-button off with one hand, seizes wallet with other, and flees. Not a pickpocket, just boldly and brazenly grabbed it openly. Man yelled bloody murder—such a scream you never heard. Gave chase. No results. Must of had a lot of money in it. Oh! So—

Lang

26-July '53

Dear Lang,

If you get a telephone call from a Mr. DeWilton Rogers within a week or two, blame me. Since he will be in NYC only a few days and knows almost nobody there, I thought you would not mind my giving him your number. I charged him not to give it to anyone else, and he promised. He is an earnest and talented fellow from Trinidad. He taught school down there and for the past two years has been studying at Fisk. He has had a novel published in the BWI's, and it shows promise. He is also musical and has a store of folk things which he can play and sing for you, if you can do with an hour's relaxation. He is a friend of the local writers, of course, Talemaque and the rest.

Blyden [Jackson] is not here. He is teaching summer school at N. C. College at Durham, so I have not been able to nudge him into the interesting literary debate you and Turner are currently carrying on in the *Defender.* Maybe he will put in an oar when he returns next month. At least, I'll suggest it. Meanwhile here is something of his that came out in this morning's *Tennessean,* though it was written some months ago.

My lectures at Peabody came off satisfactorily, I gather from the reactions. Of course, I read "Dream Variation," "The Negro Speaks of Rivers," "Havana Dreams," and "I, too, Sing America," and the like from their outdoor platform under the stars and traced the Negro ethos as a thread of our literature from Lucy Terry (whom they fell in love with) to the Harlem group (whose tunes they went away singing, I believe), and I have never been more warmly received. Either they are ripe for integration or they just like Negro poetry. I hope they will all go home (most of the students are school teachers in the smaller towns of the South) and put our Anthology in their courses. The fact that most of them know little about any of *us* seems less discouraging when you discover that they know little about the Fugitives or T. S. Eliot either. I'm not even convinced that most of them are well-informed about Faulkner. But the Negro in literature they are ready for.

Lest I forget it, please put this in your address book: at Wildwood we can be reached in care of W. J. Faulkner. We'll be living a block away, but mail sent to us there will reach us. The Faulkners also have a phone. We will not be leaving here till the 1st of August, however, and it seems definite that I'll need to run up to NYC for a day or two sometime during the month—perhaps around the middle. It'll probably be the Algonquin when I do.

Read Malcolm Cowley in this week's *Saturday Review.* Fine, fine, fine. And right in line with what you said about the James Baldwin book. Also read Nelson Algren on Hollywood in this week's *Nation.* Funny. I'm trying to get Ann Petry reviewed for the *Saturday Review,* but things are off-schedule as usual, and I am late. . . . I promise to try phoning Margaret and Gwen before leaving for vacation. . . . It has occured to me that Moe Asche might like to hear Dewilton Rogers' BWI songs.

Wish I had a lady fan who'd give me a brand new typewriter. I NEED one!

More anon &
Best ever,
Arna

20 East 127th Street
New York 35, N. Y.
September 22, 1953

Dear Arna,

Would you please ask Paul to send: Miss Eva Hesse the addresses of a few Negro soldiers* or officers? She feels they might be interested in our anthology. I wrote her I would turn said request over to you. Did you ever receive any copies of it, by the way? I didn't yet, altho she says it's for sale there. Everyone here

*in Germany.

says her translations are very good indeed. . . . . Did you get copies of the Negro issue of *United Asia.* I did. . . . . And did you ever hear from John Kitzmiller in Rome to whom I sent our *When the Jack Hollers* two years ago? I never did after his request came. At any rate, Meyerowitz is conducting there now, so I've asked him to look him up if he has time. . . . . Vilma Howard writes from Paris that she is singing blues in a night club there, and wants songs! . . . . And Jimmy Davis (author of "Lover Man") writes that Paris is so expensive he is moving to Spain. . . . And Nancy Cunard writes from the South of France wondering what's happening to the Negroes. . . . . And Ralph (right here) is thinking about taking a teaching job, which makes me wonder why anybody with a best seller would think about working. . . . . Alvin has finished his novel. . . . . And *Famous American Negroes* just about finished me. But they say they like it! . . . . . The Doubleday check hasn't come yet! . . . . But over a thousand dollars in book bills from S. & S., Holt, and Knopf have. Another year of starvation! My art costs me more than I make. . . . . . Precious Lord, take my hand! . . . . . . But, miracle before God to come from show business, Katherine Dunham sent me a CHECK for the ballet libretto I did for her! The only time a libretto ever paid off—a-tall! I mean, a-tall! The rest of them have cost me more than books. . . . . I love *Maude Martha,* maybe partly because it's ten times shorter than any other book this year. . . . . . I've sent pounds of manuscripts off to folks this week, returning with comments. Alvin helped me read some. And written my annual letter to the fellow in jail for life that NO, I CANNOT GET HIM OUT. And thanked the midwest lady for her umpteenth present. And sorted out dozens of the crazy lady's letters for Yale. So a writer's work never ends. I see now why Ralph wants to teach. And you rest in your office.

Lang

On the 9 millionenth word my typewriter broke down, so I had to rent this one. How much was the Doubleday check, by the way?

20 East 127th Street
New York 35, N. Y.
September 24, 1953

Dear Arna,

My copies of *Meine Dunkle Hande* and your letter both came at once. A charming looking book indeed! I wonder what it sells for? . . . . . Since they only sent me four copies and I want to give one to Meyerowitz and one to Carl for Yale, would you care to send Ivan von Auw one of yours, since he didn't get nary one, he says? Your poems read beautifully therein—and everybody's look so nice! When you write Eva Hesse, suggest that a copy go to not only *Jet,* but also to *Phylon* and *The Crisis.* These latter, I am sure, would review it, as they did my *Poemas* from the Argentine.

I've just come from the opening of *Take a Giant Step* where I saw Walter and Poppy, W. C. Handy, Wm. Warfield, Alain Locke, Ruth Ellington, etc., etc. Lots of cullud out. Play good and has some fine performances, but seems to be directed for comedy mostly, so some of the pathos and charm in the script as I read it has gotten lost. But it's probably more "commercial" this way, audience seemed to like it, but I'd hoped it would come over a bit more emotionally. Well, we'll see what the reviews do to it tomorrow. Right now I have to go to my sleep. 3 A.M.

Saw Juanita tonight, many pounds slimmer, and quite smartly dressed in a new gold coat. Chicago bound for a night club engagement.

Drum from South Africa has a spread on me with some quaint mistakes. Also see my picture in *Message,* one I never saw before in life.

How do you like *Maude Martha?* I do.

Sincerely,
Lang

9-30-53

Dear Lang,

No sooner said than done. The copy of *Meine Dunkle Hande* went to von Auw 48 hours ago, and 24 hours ago I dictated a letter to the *Defender* re: your interesting column on the need of a Negro monthly magazine. You'll get a carbon copy eventually. I have NOT yet written to Eva Hesse, but will do, will do. . . .

Right now I'm going around in a daze. The MGM contracts and related papers for *St. Loo* arrived, and the parcel weighs several pounds, I'd estimate. There are 9 separate sets of documents, containing from 5 to 7 copies each. I'll have to sign or initial over 100 times! Of these, 20 will have to be notarized. There are even two sets of documents to be signed by every member of my family. Alex will have to make his 8-year-old signature 12 times. These two sets, of course, had to be sent to Bennett College for Poppy and Camille to sign first. I am now waiting for their return. I gather Loews Inc. (MGM) wants to make sure it leaves no stone unturned. Have you ever seen the equal of this? It goes without saying that most of the wording is Greek to me.

And those two lines I've just written suggest to me that I'll need a new typewriter directly money crosses my palm.

I did not get an advance copy of *Maud Martha.* Nobody has asked me to review it, but I look forward to reading the library copy when it arrives. . . . We do get *United Asia* in the library, as I said, but we could use a copy of *Drum,* if you will tell me where one is available.

The review of *Take a Giant Step* which I read (Times) was very good. Let's hope audiences respond. I get the feeling that a fresh surge of interest in Negro themes is beginning. Both Harpers and the Atlantic have important articles in the October issues (one by James Baldwin and one about Howard Thurman). Others are scattered around. I never seem to have anything ready when the tide comes in, but if my typewriter holds up, I'll keep working on Booker-T and WEBDuB.

Best ever,
Arna

314

20 East 127th Street
New York 35, N.Y.
October 2, 1953

Dear Arna,

I am fascinated by all that goes into the making of a movie contract! Tell me more, and sign on! Sign on!

That's a fine letter re the magazine. Hope a few more folks write, too. Maybe Johnny Johnson would bring it out as a cultural by-product.

Thanks for telling me about the current Harper's. I met the editor at the P.E.N. cocktail party the other day, and he reminded me that he'd asked me (via Ivan) some time ago about doing some Simple pieces for them some time ago. But I couldn't think of any suitable subjects. Any suggestions? (To tell the truth, I forgot about it with all those book deadlines on. Now that they're turned in, I will give it a little thought.)

I don't know where you'd get Drum except directly from them: Drum, etc. (sub blank enclosed).

My typewriter broke down, too, and is in the shop. This rented one seems also about to give out.

Negro History Week engagements are coming in already. (We're getting more like white folks every day. Used to wait until the last minute, week or so before.)

I'm invited to see *Porgy and Bess* tomorrow, the alternates who do matinees, with Miss Leonardos who understudied Muriel in *The Barrier* doing Bess. Sunday Mahalia's annual Carnegie Hall Concert, with shouting in the boxes. Tuesday *Tea and Sympathy.* So looks like my show week coming up. When are you coming to town to open your theatrical season?

Sincerely,
Lang

10-8-'53

Dear Lang,

The piece on Howard Thurman is the lead article in the October *Atlantic Monthly.* It is the article by James Baldwin, as you saw, that appears in *Harpers.* I thought it was interesting that BOTH those magazines featured pieces by or about Negroes in the same month. And I think you should not miss an opportunity to let Simple make a bow before the fine Harper audience. Handled right, such an appearance could stimulate interest in both of the Simple books. (One of my new hobbies is promoting the backlog.)

Why don't you (as a suggestion) pick out a few of the *ideas* previously used, ideas which seemed to catch the fancy of ofays who read or reviewed the books, and work up new treatments or new situations in which to air them. For example, the idea of elevating one Negro (like Ralph) while neglecting or closing the eyes to the millions. Or the portrayals of Negroes on screen, stage or TV.

It now dawns on me that I have still more papers to sign in connection with this MGM business. There is a separate Harcourt negotiation for the rights to *God Sends Sunday.* I don't know how many more months all this will take. But I hanker to come to NY for some shows, so I hope it will not be forever. Besides, I must do some research at Columbia and N. Y. Public Library (42nd Street) and talk with Du Bois again. At Columbia there is a scrapbook on Douglass which I must see before I complete my revisions, and the 42nd St. Public has a file of *Voice of the Negro,* which carried much about Washington and Du Bois.

Sorry to hear about Dorothy's fall. I had just written her a note. Likewise Bruce's wife's accident.

Keep after Johnny Johnson about the magazine. He could deduct the loss from taxes while buying oodles of good-will from the more literate Negroes as well as the large inter-racial-minded audience of whites. Negro schools and colleges would pick up on it. Moreover, JJ owes this crowd something; it was they who put over *Negro Digest* and launched his empire. (You may quote me)

Best ever,
Arna

20 East 127th Street
New York 35, N.Y.
October 19, 1953

Dear Arna,

That is a fine outline for the anthology and I have sent it on to Ivan as is. Let's hope it works. I've had to get new flooring, etc. for my studio, so could use a small advance. . . . Just finished the revisions and Introduction for *Famous American Negroes* so that's off my hands until proofs. February publication. . . . Meyerowitz is back from Europe with another of our cantatas, *The Five Foolish Virgins,* under which the piano bent and swayed at first playing last night here. It's to be done at Town Hall in Fe. And now he wants me to do another opera with him! Some European opera houses are interested in *The Barrier* so he wants to have another one ready should that come off there. . . . Theatre interest in Simple has turned up again. Conference this week. But I'll believe when I see cash on line. The Broadway trend is certainly to comedies at the moment. *The Tea House of the August Moon* which I've just seen is about a lot of white (and lighter weight) Simples. It's amusing. But most delightful show I've caught is *World of Sholem Aleichem,* really different and human and though half fantasy, doesn't seem contrived and "theatrical," as so much current Broadway stuff does. . . . Incidentally, do you reckon we could get a picture of Mason Jordan Mason? Or definite proof that he is colored. Some say he might not be. Do you know anyone in Taos who could tell us truthfully? As editors, we can't afford to be hoaxed. I like him and think he's probably O.K., but want to be sure. Maybe Charles S. could find out from Georgia O'Keeffe for us. . . . My lecture season opens tomorrow—and I'm catching cold today! Depleted by carpenters, shows, and Famous NEGROES. . . . What?!X!*! At last the Stagecrafters* are going to do a colored play? Tell me again so I can believe it and start looking for one of them.

Langston

*The prize winning play of the Phillis Wheatley contest of which I was a judge might suit Dr. Voorhees. It's about PHILLIS.

316

22 Oct. '53

Dear Lang,

No word has come from Margaret yet. The Convocations committee will meet at lunch time next Wednesday (the 28th). It would be good if she would let me have some word as to the trio's availability and terms by then. I am trying a) to introduce new type convocation features and b) to influence a policy for paying rather than building the programs around representatives of organizations who are eager to provide us with speakers and entertainment at their own expense. (You'd be surprised at the number and power of the groups using this "good-will" device. During my year as chairman, however, I will pass them by.) And what about this Bill Marshall *Othello* reading?

I've passed the Phillis play data to Lillian Voorhees. Hope she will move on it.

Your introduction for *Famous American Negroes* is more than adequate; it is fine. Very fine. I hope they will use it as is, perhaps as a balance to the tendency to cut race problems from the stories of these folk. I know what you mean about that. Ran into it with Erick Berry on *Chariot*. Crazy! In *We Have Tomorrow*, however, I was not asked to pull punches. Perhaps because it was published during the war. One way or another, in the juvenile field, the author is less free. You have to accept a lot of silly stuff from adults in order to get the ears of little people. Sometimes the editors know what it takes to get the books on approved lists (absolutely essential), however, so I don't resist them over-much. The fact that a book like FAN can be included in a Famous series is quite an advance, and kids will catch a good many hints even though you don't dwell on Jim Crow.

I'll have to look up my letter from the editor of the Minnesota Quarterly in which, I believe, Mason Jordan Mason was completely identified. I seem to remember that it was because he is a Negro that his work was brought to my attention. So more anon.

> Best ever,
> Arna

P.S. If ever MGM crosses my palm, I'll bring Alberta to N. Y. C. for a few days of shows and shopping.

> 20 East 127th Street
> New York 35, N.Y.
> November 21, 1953

Dear Arna,

Simple says the gospel singers are making so much money these days that when they sing, "I Cannot Bear My Burden Alone", what they really mean is, "Help me get my cross into my Cadillac."

I am running a literary factory right now with three assembly lines going, and trying to read the proofs on *Famous American Negroes* in between. They gave up and didn't cut nary another racial word! . . . . But the Wattses cut out of *Rhythms* the fact that the rhythms of the moon make luny folks lunier each full moon.

I suggested to Macmillan that they have our *Popo* on exhibit where they're having a photo of me enlarged and lighted up with the story of my first poem written at grammar school for graduation in Lincoln, Illinois, repeating itself on tape at the Sherman in Chicago in December. Look at the hussy's reply! (And my answer). Kindly return it to me. Every other publisher was appreciative of my suggestion and said they'd send books.

Take a Giant Step is, unfortunately, closing. Also it's the *current* end of *Porgy and Bess*. It'll probably be crap-shooting again next year. Those of the other expression *love* it.

Yesterday was my Latin American day—a Brazilian in the afternoon came to call, and two Argentines at night. Brought me a beautiful Gaucho book.

Haven't seen nor heard hair nor hide of Margaret Bonds lately, but the singer tells me we've a Kansas engagement in February. (They're doing all the booking, NOT I). . . . . . Georgia Laster sings at Town Hall shortly. Also Adele Addison. And Matiwilda Dobbs in the Spring. . . . Mrs. Harper stepped off a ladder backwards and sprained her ankle so is immobilized (as the Dr. puts it) for Thanksgiving. We just can't keep her from climbing.

Sincerely,
Langston

20 East 127th Street
New York 35, N.Y.
December 9, 1953

Dear Arna,

The Macmillan people reversed their stand on *Popo* and wrote a nice note saying they're sending five copies for display at the Illinois Education Association. Return the note I sent you.

Almost simultaneously renewed interest in Simple for entertainment purposes turned up—radio, TV-films, and stage, the theatre folks being the only ones offering a contract and advance immediately which von Auw is studying now. Some things have to be fixed before we can sign, if we do. Anyhow, while negotiations were going on (and still are) I went ahead and wrote the play! So I'm *way* ahead of them, having a month to just write an outline after the advance is given. Play has more plot, naturally, than the books, but is, of course, over long in present draft. I think its good, though. Hope so. Will let you know what happens. Meanwhile keep it *secret,* or all the actors in town will be calling me up—nothing colored playing or being cast at the moment.

Page proofs for *Famous American Negroes* ready today. Due out February 1 in time for Negro History Week. Abbott chapter is in current issue of the *Defender.*

Alvin was by last night and gave the good news of Paul being an honor student. How are the rest of the family? And what's new with you? My mail piled sky high while I was recreating Simple. Didn't do another thing for two or three weeks but playwright, and Hugh has typed up a mountain of drafts—and money! Wonder will I ever come out ahead in the theatre? I have the Dutch opera tape of the *Barrier* with full orchestra. Sounds wonderful! Now Meyerowitz is planning to do a new one based on an old Gilpin Players comedy of mine—the bride

318

by mail one—making the characters white since the situation is not racial. Write soon. I've got a Cantata for your collection.

Sincerely,
Lang

10 December '53

Dear Lang,

That Macmillan thing is irritating, and I hope they realize it by now. Companies and institutions can do incomprehensible things—often beyond the understanding of most of the individuals connected with them. Especially the larger ones. Due to large staff and frequent turn-over of help, they run by a manual of operation or hand book. Newcomers never stop to reason but follow the book. Pretty soon—chaos.

I have just thumbed through the *Famous Humanitarians.* New format for the "Famous" line. I reckon yours will be its running mate. Good team. And I also calculate you and I will meet on the book pages come February. My Signature Series *Carver* should come out then. I have returned the page proofs. Negro illustrator for a change, Harper Johnson. The book reads better now than it did in the late summer, when I got so tired of it.

H-M have finally received preliminary sketches from Felix Topolski of England for my *Lonesome Boy.* This is the book I *enjoyed* writing, perhaps because I did it impulsively for myself, while editors hounded me for my misdeeds and threatened me if I did not deliver manuscripts I had contracted for. So I closed the door for two days and had myself a time. Now it's being illustrated by the artist in whose studio the daughter of Sir S. Cripps met her African prince! Remember him?

We had Carolyn H. Stewart at Convocation last week. Good show. Thurgood [Marshall] speaks next, the 17th. On Feb. 18, the Ryder-Frankel dance duo. (They have a special rate for college assemblies—$150.) Still some open dates in spring.

My chances of getting up to NY again in '53 have vanished. Perhaps late January. What shows should I see? . . . . MGM business reported signed & sealed, but *no check* yet! Don't know what's holding it. Anyhow,

Best ever,
Arna

9 Feb. '54

Dear Lang,

By now, I hope, young Peterson has received the letter I sent him in your care, but he has not replied. Are you able to reach him by phone? The Festival Committee would like to have him on a literary panel or seminar if they could find out *promptly* whether or not he is available. Maybe with Gwendolyn Brooks, who has never been here either.

Tolson is due Thursday. Negro History Week. Did you read Selden Rodman's N. Y. Times rave for his book last week? I think Rodman, who has written books

319

about Pippin and the Haitian painters, but excluded Negro American poets from his various anthologies, is trying to cover his deeds by overpraising Tolson and at the same time slapping all other Negro poets. Nasty boy! Folks here and in Chicago (I just returned from ALA) are burned up. They do not blame Tolson, however.

Famous American Negroes looks good beside *First Book of Negroes.* We'll save Camille's copy till she comes home from Bennett. What goes with you? Other than books and plays?

Best ever,
Arna

20 East 127th Street
New York 35, N.Y.
February 10, 1954

Dear Arna,

I'm back in town for a day, after two busy speaking days in Norfolk. Find a note from you about *Louis Peterson.* I forwarded your note to him before I left via a friend's address (as I did not then have his) so maybe he didn't get it as yet. However, I phoned him just now. Not in. But left word to call back. Meanwhile, you'd better write him yourself. It would be nice to have him and Gwendolyn both down to Fisk.

I sold four boxes of books in Norfolk! So that's what I call a successful trip. Negro professional folks are building 80 and 100 thousand dollar homes in suburbs, with landscape lawns and swimming pools. We's rising! And they have practically NO books to go with the rest of the furnishings. Let's get together you, me, and two or three more cullud authors, borrow Dick Campbell's station wagon, and go on a Negro Authors' Caravan to some of these well-to-do-Southern centers, selling our books and popularizing Negro writings, for a month sometime, huh? Want to? I bet we could sell up a breeze.

More power to tongue-in-cheek Tolson! He told me he was going to write with so many foreign words and footnotes that they would *have* to pay him some mind! Last year I sent Rodman a copy of my column about exclusion of Negro poets from the anthologies. Nary an answer. (Until his *Times* review, which I, like you, take to be one.)

How many of your children are at Bennett now? And when are you coming to New York? Did I tell you Margaret looks like she did that time she went a-lecturing. (She is pregnant again. Each time Yale turns up, it rhymes with— creation!). . . . If *Peter Abrahams* [African writer] comes over (Knopf is bringing out his new book and he says he hopes to come) you-all must have him at Fisk, too. Address: 37 Jessel Drive, Loughton, Essex, ENGLAND.

Sincerely,
Lang

P.S. Ralph is going to the Harvard Seminars at Salzburg this summer, he tells me. We's rising plus!

20 East 127th Street
New York 35, N. Y.
February 26, 1954

Dear Arna,

I love your book. Awfully good looking, too! And simply and beautifully written. I see you left the lynching out entirely, huh? I hear tell the artist is cullud. Good! We're trying to get E. Simms for my *First Book of Jazz*. . . . . . Contract and check for *Simple* play came, sight unseen. I've a month to turn in an outline. (But have the play done! At least a very adequate draft which I'm sending down in a few days). . . . . All major deadlines are now met. So I can go off lecturing next week with no hangovers. St. Louis, Florida, and Maryland on way back. Think I'll fly to Florida. . . . . Who's going from Fisk to Mrs. Bethune's college's 50th Anniversary? Ralphie will be speaking or giving a seminar there. I was to have, too, but they ask me to change the date till later as part of the regular lecture series. But since I'll be in Florida anyhow, I will stop by for [Ralph] Bunche and Ralph's talks. And it'll be a relief not to have to open my mouth myself. . . . .The Association for the Study of Negro Life and History is auctioning off the manuscript of *Famous American Negroes* at a fund raising affair Friday night. First review came from Canada—good! First "Simple" review also came from England today, good, too. And folks who heard the *Barrier* there on the Dutch broadcast say it sounded swell. Peter Abrahams understands Dutch being from South Africa, and it seems his wife is Dutch Javanese. He writes that it was very well translated. . . . . What a shame about Eddie Matthews. Funeral Friday, I hear, in Ossining, I believe. . . . . . Mrs. Harper is poorly again. . . . . . Weather rainy and warm here. . . . . McCarthy's newest, the cullud lady, says she doesn't belong to anything but the First Baptist Church!

Sincerely,
Lang

3-3-54

Dear Lang,

I'm suddenly summoned to Boston to look at a collection of books which Fisk will consider buying. My appointment with the owner is for Monday the 8th. I should be back in NYC the evening of the 9th or the morning of the 10th, Wednesday. Are you going to be home by then? I'll stay around two or three days, either at the Algonquin or the Theresa perhaps. I'm now trying to decide which in view of several errands in the City.

Thanks for the poems of Ray Durem. They are like Hughes, but they are *not* Hughes. Their main problem in gaining an audience is going to be that readers accustomed to the American Original may not be ready to settle for even a good imitation. Durem certainly has the poetic unction. But I don't quite feel that he is a natural. He will have to cultivate his talent and perhaps develop it slowly. That quality of new-born surprise which the gods gave the boy Hughes is no more his than it was Gwendolyn's or Tolson's. But maybe this does not differ too much from what you said. . . . . See you in New York?

Arna

20 East 127th Street
New York 35, N. Y.
March 30, 1954

Dear Arna,

Man, I didn't know anything about the Anisfield Award until I got home day before yesterday and found the check awaiting me. It's not announced officially yet, is it? How did you know? Anyhow, I can use that money to write my second *Big Sea* which I'm due to turn in this year.

Nassau was delightful. Met some nice folks, friends of Jerri Major's and Mrs. Bethune's, the last night before leaving, who alarmed the town and had visitors banging on my hotel door at eight o'clock in the A.M.—but by that time I was near about gone, and had already been everywhere at my unbothered leisure, so didn't mind too much. Three carloads of folks saw me off at the airport. It's only an hour from Miami, $36.00 a roundtrip. Fly over there sometime. It's a kind of West Indian-British Carmel—rather expensive, high as the mainline or higher for some things. And, while not as interesting as Cuba, Haiti, or Jamaica, has a much higher standard of living for all concerned, Negroes dressing just like Miami, no barefoot folks, and salaries (hotel workers mostly) on a par almost with States. It's chief charm is its beauty, the entire island is nothing but a winter resort, and even the poor folks live in flower gardens and palm tree yards, and are most friendly to visitors—with no hustlers or beggars in evidence as in most of the rest of the West Indies where I've been. Met their only cullud poet, who isn't exciting. But in Miami came across a kind of colored Francois Villon, in case we ever revise our anthology.

Found everybody O.K. on return to New York. Certainly sorry to have missed your visit. What shows did you see? Tell me what I ought to catch, having seen almost nothing this season. . . . Just phoned Peterson and he says he mailed you his subject, etc., Sunday. Cullud boy! I'm still not officially home, so haven't seen anyone. Getting caught up on my thank-you notes, etc. first, re lecture tour. I saw Cairo, at last, the one remaining city in U.S. that I've always wanted to see. That electric sign is still pointing at the NAACP's lawyer's house. Some folks drove me by to see it, and from another car a rock had just sailed through his window, so he came running out prepared to shoot US! I was introduced to him in the street under rather distraught circumstances! No lie! I'm telling you, something happens everywhere I go. But I'm still here!

Mrs. Bethune looked fine. I had dinner with her and Ralph Bunche, who flew in at six and out at eleven—New York to Florida and back within the day. Airplanes are really something.

Don't eat any Japanese tuna! I expect next time we go to California, everybody out there will be hydroactive. The Pacific must be full of atoms by now.

Simply and sincerely,
Lang

20 East 127th Street
New York 35, N. Y.
June 30, 1954

Dear Arna,

Delighted to have your note and news of the Race Relations doings. I've been trying to write you a letter all week to tell you of a couple of ideas discussed at luncheon with Edward Dodd, Jr., the other day. It seems the book business is looking up, so publishers are looking around for new books. (Watts tells me they did Ten Thousand Dollars more this June than in 1953, so they've advanced some new proposals for kids' books to me, too.) Anyhow, *Famous American Negroes* has about sold out its first edition—which usually in that series takes two or three years to exhaust—so Mr. Dodd wants me to do another one.

But the things that concern you are these:

1. In talking about various ideas for books on the race, I told Mr. Dodd that you and I had once had the idea of a *Harlem Anthology* comprising the best pieces about Harlem from both literary and journalistic sources. He seemed to immediately like the idea, and suggests that we submit a tentative outline of the possible material we might include. Does the idea appeal to you again? If so, I'd say send me *soon* your list of suggestions, or those you can have Joan or someone cull from your library resources. I'll add mine, have Hugh type it up, and send it down there. Maybe we can get a few hundred advance on it. I seem to recall we were going to include Bud Fisher, portion of your "They Seek A City", possibly parts of "Black Manhattan" and Claude McKay's "Harlem", maybe a few pages from "Nigger Heaven", a short story of mine—and Ann Petry's piece from "Holiday" comes to mind; also that wonderful *PM* interview with Billie Holiday which I've saved; one of Jimmy Cannon's *Post* pieces on Sugar Ray or Joe Louis, occur to me with no thinking at all. I think we could get 30 to 40 pieces of material outlined an hour. So put yours down this evening, and I'll gather mine over the week end, and we'll turn it in before all the editors go on vacations. That is, if you'd like to do it. If not, lemme know, and I'll make a stab at it.

2. The second idea is to be kept mum, and doesn't involve me, as I told the man I was no scholar, so it isn't exactly down my alley. But I think a part of it might be down yours, especially since you have a whole library right at hand to draw on, so I offered your name as one of the authors and Charles S. Johnson as the over-all editor, and Introduction writer. About 8 years from now, in honor of the 1963 Centennial of Emancipation, Dodd, Mead wants to bring out a series of books on Negro progress and achievement—at least three volumes planned at the moment: Arts, Business, and Political and Social progress. I told the man you could do a wonderful Arts one! They'd sort of like them correlated, so I said Charles S. was exactly the guy for that, and that the volumes might even be brought out under the sponsorship of Fisk University—which Mr. Dodd seemed to think was an excellent idea. So you might tell Charles S., so he'll be prepared, since Mr. Dodd said he would be writing him regarding it. (Him first to see if he likes the idea and would help in selection of the authors for the various volumes). But keep it quiet, as I guess they don't want other publishers to beat them to the draw on a Hundred Years of Freedom series.

Been up till dawn every night this week completing my jazz discography. Just about done. Answer soon concerning the Anthology. . . . . The record is out, but without your intro booklet as yet. I got an advance of the disc. It sounds good. And has a beautiful jacket with a couple of cullud Arabs or Mohammedans in robes on the cover! Or maybe bebop boys. Anyhow, it's pretty.

Langston

Read "Tell Freedom." It's beautiful! (Peter Abrahams—Knopf.)

323

Dear Lang,

Let's hope this turns out to be a red letter day for the Harlem Anthology too! Your revival of the project delights me. I'm all for it. So to start things rolling again, here's a copy of the pertinent part of my letter of 2-17-48 wherein I broached the idea originally. I still like most of the suggestions I offered then, but I can add a few at this time, in no particular order:

1. Ralph Ellison's story in New World Writing #5 "Did You Ever Dream Lucky?" (A knockout!)

2. Something on Garvey, the brightest and best we can find.

3. Earl Brown's piece on Joe Louis in Life maybe.

4. The editorial in the NYU student paper on Countee during his senior year, wherein he was handsomely hailed and called a greater credit to his U. than its undefeated football team.

5. A section called "Profiles" (distinguished from the longer essay-articles) to include shorter character sketches of a variety of Harlemites. To be gleaned from newspapers mostly.

6. A section which might be called "Events" which might include in addition to the piece on the Florence Mills funeral the article Du Bois did on the Countee-Yolande wedding, "The Girl Marries." Also others in this category. Maybe a good one on the Riot, for example.

7. Alex Woolcott on Paul Robeson maybe.

8. Possibly a section of outlandish things taken from the Negro papers.

9. Comb the Crisis and Opportunity for additions.

10. Time's cover piece on Walter perhaps. Or possibly Walter's unsigned piece in the Century, written in his early days and called White yet Black, I believe. We could call it, "Harlem Abroad."

11. Possibly something from Ovington's "Portraits in Color"—possibly.

12. Possibly P. M.'s profile of Randolph, if it reads well enough at this date.

13. Something from JWJ's Along this Way.

14. Look at Thurman's Bookman and New Republic pieces. See how they stand up.

15. Something from Zora perhaps.

16. The chapter from Big Sea about house rent parties.

17. The additions mentioned in your letter of June 30, '45.

18. Something on Thurgood.

I'll keep all this in a folder and let it constitute the new beginning. If Mr. Dodd will put a grand on the line, which we could divide, I could get started immediately on a good bit of the research and copying. We have complete runs of *Crisis* and *Opportunity* in the Library here, likewise a microfilm copy of the New York Age and one of the Amsterdam News. We have most of the magazines mentioned thus far, but I would have to depend on your able assistant to run through the files of P.M., which we do not have. Likewise the back numbers of Vanity Fair and Smart Set in the N.Y. Public (42nd St.)—we do not have these either. Neither do we keep a file of Esquire (we get it and throw it away because it is not indexed and hence of limited research value)—Hugh would have to dig up the pieces from this source.

Is this enough Harlem for a starter?

I'm equally interested in the other project (shall we call it the 100 year project?), but I'll go into it in more detail after CSJ returns to the campus and I have a chance to discuss it with him. As for me, the answer is *yes.* I'd enjoy doing a book about the Negro in the Arts for such a series. And I think the overall idea very timely and fitting.

Ever,
Arna

P.S. Couldn't we use something like this as a rough working pattern for the Harlem Anthology or Treasury: A. Short Stories, B. Essays and essay-length Articles and Profiles or Biographies, and C. a section of shorter things to include the newspaper or journalistic "profiles," the "events," and the colorful "gleanings" from the Negro Press. In short, three major sections. How would that look to you? Let me say it another way: A. Fiction, B. Literary Non-Fiction, C. Journalese.

8 July '54

Dear Lang,
Your outline of suggested material gives us a good start on the *Harlem Reader,* assuming Mr. Dodd's interest holds up. Other things will come to mind. In fact, I already think of a couple. There was the story by Kay Boyle, for example, of the colored ladies going to the sanctified church. It appeared first in the New Yorker. Real gone. Then there was my piece about the Schomburg Collection. It appeared first in the Library Quarterly but was reprinted in the *Negro Digest* as "Buried Treasures of Negro Art," I believe. All about Schomburg and the Negro digging up his past, the need to re-make the past before he could start making a future, about the interest in such matters in Harlem.
The O. Henry Prize Story, "No More Trouble for Judwick," is by Louis Paul. It appeared in the early or middle thirties, I believe.
Your outline omitted CSJ's good *Carolina Magazine* essay on "The Blues as Poetry." I think it was pretty good, as I recall. Maybe we could also find a good personality thing on Jake Lawrence [Jacob Lawrence, artist.]. And how about a folio of art reproductions? Say 8 to 10 pages? It could range from one of Doug's stylized Harlem things to one of Barthé's pieces, from a Bearden to a Campbell. Then maybe a place should be found for something by Locke. And just for fun I'd love to dig up a piece by Schuyler in the old *Messenger* in which he roasted Du Bois, JWJ and others for marrying women of light skin. *Maybe* he would have sense of humor enough to let us use it. Finally, there should be something by or about Handy, if available. Also possibly Canada Lee. But more anon.
Best ever,
Arna

20 East 127th Street
New York 35, N.Y.
July 17, 1954

Dear Arna,
Well, since my autobiography is due at the publishers the day after Labor Day and I haven't written a word of it yet, I thought this quiet Sunday afternoon I

would get started. So I sat down and wrote three chapters, some 30 pages. Between 4 P.M. and now, about 3 A.M. Which isn't bad. I hope it reads as easily as it writes. If I can keep this up, I'll have 330 pages in a month—which is with narrow margins, so that would be 400—which is just about a book.

I meant to sort out all the stuff in the basement, take notes, etc., and work from them. But if I wait to get around to doing that, it is liable to be Doomsday, and I'll never get a book done. So I think I will just write it from memory like I did *The Big Sea.* Then, if I have time, and it needs it, I can check through the basement stuff and see if I've forgotten anything important—in which case I can put it in Volume III, the next one. I can remember enough without notes to fill an enclycopedia.

If publishers want a really documented book, they ought to advance some documented money—enough to do nothing else for two or three years. I refuses to sharecrop long for short rations! Doubleday's royalty report was the ONLY one this year that had a check along with it. All the rest sent me BILLS with their reports asking ME to kindly remit to them—for books I had purchased. Share-cropper for true. Anyhow, I did get to the Bahamas for a few days. Don't reckon I'll ever get anywhere else. Kindly remember me in your prayers. (I wish somebody would remember me in a will.)

Hope your book is about done. You've been writing as long as Ralph!

Sincerely yours truly,
Lang

20 East 127th Street
New York 35, N. Y.
August 8, 1954

Dear Arna,

Here is hoping I'll see your new house in due time. I hope you-all like it. . . . . . . Did I tell you I ran into C.S.J. in Brentano's? Haven't heard any more about the Dodd, Mead 100th Anniversary proposals—vacation time, things are quiet downtown. But will mention it again next time I'm in that office. . . . . Didn't keep up the pace on the autobiography. Stopped to write another children's book —*The First Book of The Caribbean*—since I was broke. Hugh just finished the typing of it before leaving for his Atlanta vacation yesterday, so I am turning it in tomorrow, Monday. It came out quite colorful and nice—from pirates to parrots, calypsos to carnivals, Toussaint to turtles. But I will not do any more of these until next year now.

Better send me your Wildwood address again. I've got to go to the Jazz Roundtable in Lenox, Mass., weekend of August 21, and again Sept. 2–4, for talks. It runs three weeks this season, but I can't stay up there all through, although I'd like to with such folks as Willis James, Pearl Primus, Rudi Blesh, and Hayakawa on the programs. Sept. 4th is Gospel Song Night, which I'm to introduce.

Well, I have a conference on the Simple play tomorrow, so I am struggling with it today.

Hope you-all get to New York and that I will see you. Take note of above dates I'll be away. Otherwise right here—with ice cream and watermelon on tap.

Dorothy's sister-in-law and children will be visiting her for a month while Sidney is in India. They're flying over from Geneva. Colored do get about these days! Did you know that there were quite a few colored pirates in the Spanish Main? I bet they were B-A-D #*&%#!!!, too!

Sincerely,
Lang

9-23-54

Dear Lang,

Your letter cheers me no end. I made sure I had written you not once but several times since Wildwood. Maybe I've been dreaming. Anyhow, we've got cool weather too now, though not cool enough for heat, and I feel like a natural man again—cool weather creature that I am. I've even written my stint for this morning and have time left over for this before running to the library. A little energy makes a world of difference. Next summer, if I'm in Nashville, I've promised the Lord that I'll buy some air conditioning.

I have not yet read the piece in the *London Times* but plan to do so within an hour. Charles S. told me had had luncheon with Dodd and that so much is cooking he will have to take an evening to tell me all about it. Hope we can find one free before he leaves the campus next week. . . . Charles is having trouble with the left-wing elements on his faculty. He has given them more breaks than any college prexy I know, but you can probably guess how they are reacting to that. Lorch, who has been before an Un-American Activities Committee in Ohio, where he declined to talk, will have to talk to the Fisk Trustees on October 28, no doubt. . . . Quite a tempest. (Practically all, if not all, the colored faculty sympathize with Charles wholly, of course.) Some dust is being thrown in the eyes of some students, as you would expect from your old Lincoln study.

Seems I'll be lecturing a heap this year. Atlanta, Greensboro, Milwaukee, Los Angeles and Redlands already scheduled. All came in unbid. Well, I hope I can somehow get to NYC for some shows. . . . More presently.

Best ever,
Arna

Chicago
November 1, 1954

Dear Arna,

Your letter to Dodd (which Hugh [Smythe] forwarded on to me out here) seems an excellent one. Not having been in Chicago for a long time, I've been kept so busy I haven't had a chance to write him myself. But will probably see him on my return to New York shortly, so can talk to him further about it. I should think he would be most amenable to the ideas your letter sets forth— which seemed originally to have been his train of thought anyhow.

This time in Chicago, starting out as guests of the Brownell's, I've been caught in the train of Southside society and entertained from the Truman Gibson's up and down! And offered the use of the Sengstacke's Eldorado with chauffeur (in which Tubman rode while he was here) but I couldn't think of anywhere to go in it, except down to the *Esquire* office. Lots of folks ask of you. And I've seen almost everybody we know except Gwendolyn Brooks, who's said to be deep in a new novel, so I haven't seen her about. But may phone her tomorrow, Era Bell, Roi [Ottley], and all are O.K., ditto Charlemae and Miss Harsh.

But Chicago itself (as one of the actors in the Eartha Kitt show said—the show itself, by the way, being real FINE I think) seems like a city about to explode, or a wire about to snap. Everybody going like mad, a million things happening—but as many untoward as pleasant happenings. And almost everybody seems in deep trouble, husbands, wives, parents, children, nobody doing right, so the others say. I never heard so many tales of woe. And all of Southside society seems to be being psychoanalyzed—but nowhere near as sane as they used to be back in the WPA days when many lived a month on what they now pay for a session with the analyst per week. It really seems to me quite different from Harlem, which I would say is quite calm by comparison. This always did seem to me a mad town. It seems madder than ever now. With everybody just about real gone!

Paul was fine when I left, going to classes, working at Countess Mara's fine tie place, and playing scrabble with Mrs. Harper's of evenings. Another Fiskite, Bertram Doyle, is staying there, too. And a Chinese named Zepplin Wong, my assistant of summer before last, who came for 3 days but had been there a month when I left, so Aunt Toy was about to put a double-decker in the dinette. Wong's brother recently married Howard Thurman's daughter in California. Paul dines with us ever so often, and has a GOOD appetite. Aunt Toy loves him because he helps wash dishes. Real nice boy! Tell Alberta we're glad to have him around.

I am currently behind a three-way dead-line 8-ball. But would probably be DEAD if I stayed in Chicago, so shall return to New York shortly and face fate. None of my fall commitments are anywhere near finished. But I got a FINE "Story of Jazz" record done for kids—which I enjoy playing my own self. . . . By the way, the new June Christy LP album, *Something Cool* has my song "Lonely House" on it from *Street Scene*. Sung real *cool*—which means you might not hardly know it.

My cousins want to *give* me my namesake—16 before he finished the 8th grade so automatically got put out! Should I take him????? Huh?

Lang

P.S. Did I tell you there's a lot about me in Koestler's auto *The Invisible Writing?* Haven't read it all myself yet. Can't in Chicago!

20 East 127th Street
New York 35, N. Y.
Friday, Jan. 28, 1955

Dear Arna,

I was out all afternoon, just got in and opened your letter, 7 P.M. Friday (as it only came today—and after I'd left the house at noon) so I imagine it's too late to call you collect at the Library, therefore this note. The information's scant, anyhow.

Margaret Walker I have not heard from since she left New York, but I presume she got back to Jackson College where she was contracted to teach. I suggest you try phoning her there, person to person, (and let me know if she is there, too, please). She said NO more babies. So I imagine she's in lecturable condition.

There was only two little snatches of Booker's speech on the tape they sent me. So we didn't use it, nor Carver. The record is now being mastered and should be ready for release in a few days. Nobody noticed until the very end that I'd said, "John Brown was *hung,* " and it took no end of doing to insert a new reading of that line and try to match up the voice levels. In the end, it didn't work, so the sentence had to be cut out. But I guess it won't be missed. . . . . The *Jazz* record seems to be going very well, is being played at the New School Jazz class tonight, and the book's reviewed in Sunday's *Times.* . . . . . Saw Albert Hague's *Plain and Fancy* last night and went to his party afterwards. Show's a BIG hit, and really very enjoyable—sort of lighter *Oklahoma* and first play I've seen built around the Penna. Dutch. MGM already signing up Hague, and sent a car and chauffeur for his use opening night. See what happens to white! In US about as long as Meyerowitz. Cullud here all their days and—! . . . . . Anyhow, re the First 100 years, did I tell you Mr. Dodd said he'd love to see you when you're next in town?

Sincerely,
Langston

10 Feb. '55

Dear Lang,

My trip to Southern U. for a Negro History lecture turned out to be a sort of official welcome to the state of my birth. There were more than 2,500 in the auditorium-gymnasium, with a couple of hundred standing for want of seats. The whole talk was recorded on tape, and I was told that parts of it would be radio-ed on half a dozen stations throughout the state. I was surprised and cheered from Monday morning till past midnight. The events ended with an entertainment by the Fisk Club of Baton Rouge that evening in the home of a local family of distinction (Fiskites). So I got up the next morning (Tuesday) very weary at 6 A.M. and headed home. Now I'll write letters for an hour or two and try to calm down enough to find my place on the ms. I'm writing.

We are trying to round up practically all the known Negro writers who have thus far missed Fisk in making their lecture rounds. Margaret telephoned from Jackson last night and Roi Ottley from Chicago this morning. Neither seemed to have time for letters, but both are available they said. If we can get Gwendolyn Brooks, we'll be able to announce a slate. We have written to Carl Rowan also. He's supposed to be back from India about now, I hear.

Did I tell you the copy of *First Book of Jazz* arrived before I left. Excellent. I predict a good bit of adult interest in it. . . . There is also a note from Marion Palfi here. . . . . And one from Leah which says work on *Blues Opera* is moving ahead, but there is doubt that an April opening can be made. A bit later, perhaps. Paris Opera House. . . . The Woman's club of Pasadena which is booking me sends a back-breaking schedule, ending with Dorothy's club on March 13th (Sunday). So more in a minute.

Best,
Arna

P.S. Tell Paul I'm anxious to have a letter from him for a change, not to mention a report on those photos.

20 East 127th Street
New York 35, N. Y.
February 16, 1955

Dear Arna,

Enjoyed your letter. That Southern U. I always did like. Wonderful audiences, and wonderful gumbo, etc., in Baton Rouge. And I hear from Dot they're all looking forward to your coming to the Coast. Will you have a chance to visit Carmel this time? If so, let me know, and I'll alert them.

Ralph Ellison tells me he hears there's a kid at Fisk claiming to be his son—of whom he's never heard tell before. Do you know the joker?

I saw Jerry Arlen, Harold's brother, at Juanita's party Sunday. Tells me Harold is still writing additional music for the Blues Opera.

I thought your estimable son had long since sent your pictures. He asked me about the place (Moss) weeks ago, and I gave him the address. His checks didn't come through till just the other day, so he's been broke. (Maybe he is also cullud). But he looked fine for the Urban League Ball, all dressed like a shiek of the desert, and his girl an Elmer Campbell haremite. Came home at 4 A.M. with a big can of spagetti—starved—which I helped eat! There has been an epidemic of broken-ness hereabouts. And I owe ALL my publishers—instead of them owing me—according to THEIR statments. Can't figure it out!

Now, after a third draft of Simple as a comedy, they want to turn it into a musical, and start all over again! SHOW BUSINESS! After this one, I retire. (If not before).

Best to Alberta.

Sincerely,
Lang

20 East 127th Street
New York 35, N. Y.
February NAY March 2, 1955,

Dear Arna,

Lonesome Boy is a perfectly charming and unusual book. I read it right off it came in the mail today. I LOVE books that short and easy and pretty to read. It ought to make a wonderful gift book. I must tell Frances Reckling's Gift Shop about it.

When I went to the bank up the street today I saw your son, Pablo, in a restaurant ordering a great big (albeit chopped) steak—so I asked him what he was in training for!

Did I tell you I had dinner with Elton Fax, the artist who's been living in Mexico? He's going next week to five South American countries lecturing on his art as a cultural mission for the State Dept. (All expenses and 700 bucks per month!) Why don't you get Charles S. to get you such a trip—like Redding and several others have had? You look cultural.

When do you leave for California? Train or plane? Why not fly back via New York and relax yourself after all that speaking?

Man, I have almost 50 stories now selected for my African anthology! Been dreaming Nigeria in my sleep. (The Nigerians write the most vividly, the South Africans the most poetically. The Liberians *not at all*—inhibited by being part American, I reckon. Griff Davis says there's not a writer in the whole Republic! He's been here on leave and about to return.

I'm glad your new book is dedicated to that adorable Constance! We had Chinese food for dinner tonight. 汰 廾 乑 牪

Lan Sin Hews

Sunday, March 20, '55

Dear Lang,

I left here by train but completed the return journey by air, thanks to a strike on the L & N, which is still going on. Now I must send in my return ticket and try to collect a rebate. Work is piled a mile on my desk, so I may have to come to NYC to rest up yet. (If I should be that lucky—which is by no means sure —it should be in early or mid-April, perhaps).

My voice almost gave out in California, I spoke so much. Hosts of your friends wanted to be remembered, of course.

Thanks for the several items which arrived during my absence. I particularly like the reserve column for the *Defender* which recommends basic books for all Negro homes. Let's hope your circle of readers will heed. I will alert the Fisk music department to the cantata performance on April 17th, and I'm delighted by the good play your *Jazz* record is getting. We are buying all of you on records for the library.

I'm also glad you like *Lonesome Boy*. No clippings have come in yet, but HMCo. writes that they are getting some good ones, and I have seen the fine one by Augusta Baker in the current *Saturday Review* and the excellent plug in the March *Vogue* under "People are Talking About—in New York". *Vogue* called my attention to it. Virginia Kirkus gave the book high praise, I hear, and a star. So let's hope some sales come through. I'd especially admire to have you mention it to Frances Reckling as a gift item suggestion, if you get a chance.

I wrote a lot of notes and a poem (!) on the train. Now if I can pull myself together, I'll try to make the typewriter talk. So back again to Booker-T and WEBD. More presently, and best ever.

Arna

20 East 127th Street
New York 35, N. Y.
April 23, 1955

Dear Arna,

Milton Meltzer came by today and showed me that absolutely thrilling pictorial history of his—and I don't see how you can bear to give it up. But since you did, I'm looking forward most happily to working on it, starting in July. And we are to hold more conferences before then. Thanks no end, old man! I love the idea —and having just done the Folkways record, and *Famous Negro Music Makers,* I'm not too far behind on our history, so it's not like starting from scratch. Besides my granduncle is in it. And maybe my grandma will be—that charming picture of her *Ebony* published as the first cullud lady at Oberlin some months ago. (Only thing is, I don't think she ever graduated, as *Ebony* said. She got wild, and up and married Sheridan Leary, who went off to Harper's Ferry—and all that came back was his shawl which I gave to the Ohio State Historical Museum at Oberlin's suggestion).

Thanks, too, no end for all your trouble in finding the Jubilee Singers' photo for me. It'll be credited to Fisk University Library in the book, which is now down at the publishers being rushed to press. White folks sure like to hurry! (Meltzer was here AHEAD of time today—and I were hardly out of my bed! And Mrs. Harper—who was awe-struck by his pictures—said, "Now, why didn't some Negro do that?" But my feeling is, why be selfish about culture.)

Anyhow, I have written 9000 letters today, and don't seem to have made a dent in the pile that has been neglected during the writing of *Music Makers* to the extent that I now believe it is undentable! So this is the end for a Saturday night. I now hie myself excitement-ward to see who has fit and who is fighting.

With sincere gratitude ever,

Langston

P.S. I'm telling you, I'm almost as excited about that *Pictorial* as I will be when (and if ever) we get around to writing our Booker T. Washington play. . . . . Clayton Corbin is the boy to play it. He looks lots like the young Washington, too. DON'T forget that play!

Monday (4-25-55)

Dear Lang,

Here is a ticket to the affair which I addressed the other night. Now that the last of these speaking chores is out of the way, I hope I can catch up with some reading as well as writing. I have the Ira Aldridge article on my bedtable, and I'll look up the New Yorker piece today. Meanwhile, as I noted in my last letter, we have found the original of the picture you requested for your book, and we are having the glossy print made. I hope to find it on my desk in the library when I go over in about an hour.

Our Festival planning brought to light a hidden feud which had been unknown to me: Roi and Era Bell. As you see, we had them bracketed for the same seminar, but Era Bell telephoned to say that would not be possible. She then filled in the details. Now I'm trying to put her on with Margaret in the afternoon and bringing O'Hara into the morning session with Roi [Ottley]. I hope we can keep the belligerents safely apart. . . . The first of the Festival guests has arrived: Vivian Harsh came in last night (or was supposed to).

CSJ [Chas. S. Johnson] tells me he was on a panel in DC on last Friday night (while I was in Chattanooga) and that the subject was the Harlem Renaissance. Sterling, [Brown] he said, was the most vocal heckler from the floor, denying that there *was* any such movement. But young Negroes are increasingly intrigued by that era and the people who created it, and a little argument, I find, is all to the good.

You must read and own a copy of "The Distinguished Negro in America, 1770–1936." It is a key article by Richard Bardolph of Woman's College of the

University of North Carolina and is published in the current issue, April, 1955, of *The American Historical Review,* the leading U. S. historical journal for scholars.

My Chattanooga speech will eventually be published in the *Tennessee Librarian,* I suppose. If so, I'll see that you get a copy. I called it "Three Visitors to Tennessee." I've never had anything so warmly received. . . . The Lookout Mountain Hotel reminds one of something in the Alps, I was told by those who could speak with authority. Certainly it is one of those de luxe things Negroes have never even *seen* before, unless they belonged to the service crew, and it is located on a high point of the ridge to which sightseers are not ordinarily brought. The banquet was a sell-out, with some being turned away. Dozens of the major publishers, etc. represented, along with prominent librarians (U. of Virginia, Library of Congress, etc.) and leading Chattanoogans (a state senator, wealthy "Friends of the Library," et al).

So now to write something again.

Best ever,
Arna

P. S. If you talk to Mr. Dodd again, tell him I'd like to make that definite about seeing him in June. I hope to be in NYC for a few days beginning on June 6th. And I hope also that this time we succeed in seeing a couple of shows.

Wednesday A.M. (4-27-55)

Dear Lang,

I'm glad you are excited—as I was—about the pictorial history. It took a real struggle for me to tear myself away from it. But I knew I could not deliver the manuscript this year without getting into deeper hot water with Houghton Mifflin on the book I owe them. Besides, the family has me booked up for a good part of the summer and the show threatens to draw on my time also. When you expressed a willingness to take the assignment with Crown and Meltzer over, I immediately felt better. The book will be done and I should at least have a chance to read and own and recommend it.

Nice article about Aldridge in the *Crisis.* I wish someone would do a similar job on Edmonia Lewis, the sculptress. I'd love to write a short piece about her, but I'd hate to have to start the research from scratch. Maybe I'll ask Meltzer if he'll research it for me sometime. . . . You'll like him, incidentally. Excellent person and most capable and helpful as a researcher—at which he has big time experience.

I'm thinking always about the Booker T. play. *Directly* the trio-bio is completed, I'll be ready to work on it with you. And it added stimulation to know there is a suitable young actor ready for the role. I find Clayton Corbin a hard stage name to remember, but maybe audiences will not. *Clayton* is okey, but *Corbin* fades in the mind, like a chord of music.

Best ever,

5-26-55

ARNA—
I wrote you a little memo re this piece just now and lost it somewhere. Anyhow, it's two chapters combined from *Famous Negro Music Makers* for possible magazine use. Note yourself therein. . . . . . Please show it to Bob Hayden if you find it convenient, as I've written him for permission to use his poem therein.

A note from Germany today from the editor of a new book there on spirituals and gospel songs tells me he refers to your *Rock, Church, Rock.* (I expect leans on it for his commentary—as I don't know what else they'd have over there). Anyway, I've asked him to send me the book, since I sent him $1.50 worth of gospel songs last year, some of which he uses in the book, he says.

Just saw a one-night semi-concert reading, but with a set and mostly acted, of *Moby Dick* at the Phoenix Theatre's Monday only shows. It was very good indeed. Clayton Corbin, my Negro History Week record boy, played Quege, or whatever his name is, very well. Frank Wilson and a colored Cabin Boy were also in it. I'd never read the book, so enjoyed it a lot.

That FINE picture of the Jubilee Singers came today. Gracias!

Sincerely,
Langston

6-25-'55

Dear Lang,
Your idea for a book about Negro Heroes is good, especially as you hold to the traditional conception of the hero as warrior or adventurer. For this reason I would leave Joe Louis out. Kids will not be so apt to make symbolical extensions of the term hero, even though they admire old Joe greatly for what he was. I would rather suggest adding the names of Robert Smalls who, single-handed, I believe, delivered the Confederate warship to the Union—he later became a Congressman from S. C.; Jean Baptiste Point Du Sable of whom the Indians said, "The first white man in Chicago was a Negro;" and Jim Beckwith (see *They Seek a City*) who fought the Indians coming and going and helped to open up the West. All involved in deeds of physical daring which had a bearing on the nation's history. A second reason for including Smalls is that you could stand another figure involved in the Civil War fighting. The other two would fill out their respective periods also.

I expect to leave here Tuesday (28), making a couple of stops before reaching the Ben Franklin in Philly on the 2nd. I'll call you from there soon thereafter, and I will probably come up to NYC the morning of the 9th, Saturday.

A letter from Winstons (they did *Chariot in the Sky*) reminds me that I owe them another book and says they will be ready to pounce on me in Philadelphia.

Oh, yes. Young Col. Davis is now young Gen. Davis, remember.
See you soon.

Best ever,
Arna

Dear Arna,

You being more experienced in these matters, since you're a Curator and Librarian yourself, kindly give me your opinion on this: I've finally gotten around to sorting and filing by name or category some several hundred letters for Yale of persons in public life mostly: writers, artists, actors, NAACP personalities, etc., most of them still living. None of them contain anything which I myself would object to anyone seeing. But since no one wrote with a Library collection repository in mind:

1. Do you think these letters should be restricted in any way? (They can be locked away for any number of years I, as donor, wish)?

2. Do you think perhaps any publication of them or any parts of them should be prohibited without the writer's permission, although they would otherwise be open to researchers?

3. In the case of your own letters (at the moment I've come across a hundred or more from the '30s to now) which carry a thread of the history and personalities of our times—nothing that I see objectionable to anyone's eyes. Would you wish them restricted in any way? Or would you rather they be not given at all now? (With hurricanes, leaking roofs, bursting pipes, they ought to be somewhere safe for posterity's delectation and enlightenment)? I've boxes more to sort in the basement. But would value your opinion as to propriety in regard to museums and other people's mail, before sending the present boxes off. So when you get rested from your vacation, let me know, please.

Georgia Douglass Johnson, I hear, is not well.

Sincerely,

Langston

PS: Having sent thousands of ordinary folks' letters to Yale already, now I get concerned about "name" personalities—Zora for example!X&%$! Claude, Walter, Wallie, Mrs. Bethune have gone to Glory so could hardly object. Maybe hant!

29 August '55

Dear Lang,

We have been home just long enough for me to catch up a little sleep, read the accumulated mail and dust off the typewriter. We drove more than 5,000 miles, saw Yosemite and the big trees as well as other wonders, visited a half dozen or so relatives and stopped in motels every night en route. Returning, we grew anxious to be home again so stepped up the speed and covered more than 700 miles the last day. It was all strenuously relaxing. Which means I probably won't be fully rested for a week.

Your letter picked me up. I had almost forgotten *Boy of the Border,* but I recall now that I liked it while we were doing it, and I can't imagine why it was not published. Perhaps the Depression was to blame. I also seem to recall that I thought of it as a companion piece to *Popo and Fifina.* Whether Macmillan would take it as such is a question, but I would be pleased to have Ivan von Auw try to place it—now that times are better for books and both of us have strengthened our positions in the juvenile field. I have dug out my copy of the ms., and the second paragraph convinces me that certain revisions will be in order. For example, "twenty-five years ago" would have to be changed to at least "forty years ago" if not more.

Mecca was located between the present location of Palm Springs and the Selten Sea. It was the place just beyond Indio. This was on the old unpaved road to Blythe. The new paved road by-passes it, and cuts across the desert right out of Indio. On the present shining ribbon of road one skims across the desert in no more than four or five hours, with comfort and gas stops in between. When I crossed the old wagon path made by prospectors and desert rats, it was during my high school days. We traveled in an old Overland automobile, and it took us nearly 20 hours. On that trip I heard about the herds of wild horses they used to bring across those wastes for sale at the Plaza in L.A. And I had earlier seen some of those sales, at one of which my Uncle Ward bought a lovely looking little filly with stars in her eyes and a devil in her heart. She promptly broke his leg when he tried to put a saddle on her. So do try to get a belated publisher for our *Boy of the Border*. It might have a good sale now. I'll look over the ms. more completely within a day or two. Also *Bon Bon Buddy*.

Meanwhile, I'll speak to our ISC director about John Aker as soon as the former shows on the campus. Nobody here yet. I think there is no doubt Aker will be wanted if a suitable date can be arranged.

Mr. F. A. Moore sent me a copy of his anthology published in Japan. Also a small check. I'm delighted.

As to the letters for Yale, speaking as a librarian, Curator, etc. as well as letter-writer and author, I would say that the letters of Claude, Wallie, Walter and Mrs. Bethune could immediately be made available to the public without restriction, unless some of them concern (rather intimately) other persons who are still living. Of course these letters may not be published without the written permission of the proper heirs, of any. As a whole, I would say, it would be safest and best to restrict the use of letters written by living persons till they have passed on. In any case, the writers of the letters would have to be consulted before any scholarly or literary use could be made of them. Under these circumstances there is not too much point in encouraging the curious to browse. Just the same, I think you are right in putting this correspondence in good order and sending it along for safe keeping in the library at Yale.

In the case of my own letters, specifically, the same principle would apply— though I can think of nothing in any of them that anybody could not see. Yours will no doubt go to Fisk.

Thanks for the copy of Saunders Redding's review of *Lonesome Boy*. I may have told you that I missed it when it came out.

There is quite an assortment of other mail here, which I hope to get to eventually. Knopf wants new material for the forthcoming 6th edition of *Story of the Negro*. Winston wants a substitute for a series book I took on and begged out of. Houghton Mifflin wants me to appear at the Cleveland Book Fair. The International Press Agency of Cape Town hopes to do something with my novels in South Africa. I want to get going on Booker T. et al again. So more anon.

Best ever,
Arna

P.S. Paul and Sonia drove up (or should I say down) in their station wagon Saturday. We were surprised. We had no more than taken our hats off, so to speak, from our own travels when they arrived. Now they are catching up the night of sleep they missed. They'll be in NYC soon after Labor Day.

8 October '55

Dear Lang,

Did I tell you how elated we are about the inscription in *Famous Negro Music Makers?* But the book itself is a delight too, so we'll try to keep it in the public eye hereabouts.

Janet Collins wrote Byler a nice long letter in her own hand, but alas she was not accepting bookings this year or season. She's working on completely new things and wants to develop them further. So that keeps us hoping and looking ahead.

Charles S. and Dodd are getting together on a November 14 meeting in NYC to launch the 100 Year project. If it works out, I hope to attend. Charles should be flying home from Europe about the 19th or 20th of this month, and I suppose the date will be confirmed then.

Some excitement was caused here when it was discovered that Fisk had booked a concert by Leontyne Price on the same night that State had booked Wm. Warfield. Imagine an agent doing a thing like that with a husband and wife! Well, Fisk demanded another date, so they will be in town a week apart.

Bill Demby writes from Rome to say he has finished a new novel and that he will be in the U. S. on a visit around November. Ben Johnson, his good friend and classmate at Fisk, is written up in a picture story in the October *Hue*. Peter Abrahams is down for a lecture here on Dec. 7th. I hope he knows about it. Could you pass the word to him or give me his present address? Nice notice about both our records in SAY. I'm having some publisher trouble about my big H-M book, but it's too long and complicated to write about. So more about that anon.

Best ever,
Arna

20 East 127th Street
New York 35, N. Y.
October 29, 1955

Dear Arna:

I've been head over heels lately trying to complete my autobiography so I can move on again to the PHOTO HISTORY. Just got it done, *I hope,* the autobiography, 789 pages, weighs in manuscript 7½ pounds. Do Jesus! Now goes through the Spanish Civil War and Paris in 1937–38. You are in it several times, including Watts, and the day that lady came out to get me to give thirty thousand to a foundation for Afro-American Cultural Relations. Remember? And ended up taking a dollar to get back to Pasadena.

Purpose of this note is re the Centennial Project for which Charles S. has just written me setting a conference date in New York for Monday, November 14th,

at which I'm taking for granted you'll be present. Therefore, so that we might present a united front, give me beforehand your ideas, and specifically your reactions to these ideas of mine, some of which we discussed last time I saw you:
1. Find out what Charles S. would like to write himself, so we can plug for it.
2. Let me know what you'd like to write, so I can plug for it.
3. Here are some other ideas:
   a. A CENTENNIAL POEM: Margaret Walker
   b. CENTENNIAL PHOTOGRAPHS: Roy DeCarava, editor. (Possibly with Simon and Schuster as they have fine photographic department).
   c. NEGRO HUMOR: An Anthology of prose, poetry, and cartoons. Bontemps & Hughes, editors.
   d. THE NEGRO IN THE ARTS: Bontemps. (Or if you don't want to tackle it all by yourself, me and you).
   e. THE FIRST ONE HUNDRED YEARS: History. Bontemps.
   f. EQUAL RIGHTS FOR ALL AMERICAS: The history of the struggle for civil rights, etc., possibly by Thurgood Marshall

If you like some of these ideas and think it wise, you might buzz Charles S. on them, so they won't take him entirely by surprise. If an over-all editorial board is set up, you certainly should be on it.

Any other ideas? If so, let me know shortly.

Flypaper publication date delayed again—November 22nd now. But I've just seen the first advance copy. Looks fine. You're on publisher's list, but if you don't get one in week or so, lemme know. Mine due, soon.

Lang

P.S. I found an old clipping in my father's papers re Booker T. rather interesting, I'll send you soon as I make copy.

20 East 127th Street
New York 35, N. Y.
November 2, 1955

Dear Arna,

Can't seem to find time to read these clippings now about Booker T. to extract what I might use for a column. (They were in my father's stuff, only one dated, but by looking at news items on back, etc. one can figure out approximately their time—from 1904 to Woodrow Wilson, it seems). If there's anything in them useful to you and your book, copy it out, and please *return* the clippings to me. There are four of them. That 1904 editorial is *something*—about shipping burned Negroes to Roosevelt. Did you ever hear of it? Mrs. Stowe received a Negro ear in the mail after "Cabin" came out.

Just saw an Equity Library production of the old Paul Green play, "House of Connelly" tonight. Negro parts so toned down (by NAACP advice, they tell me) that the point of play is almost lost. *Everybody* (Negroes and whites) was evil in the original production, as I remember it, and the two Negro women—Rose McClendon being one—were like the witches out of Macbeth. Toned down they're just giggling morons. My feeling is, either leave art alone, as created, or don't do it at all. What's the point of blurring everything?

I do believe cullud liberals and white liberals both are related to ostriches. Or am I prejudiced?

I wants some Foundation money to collect versions of "Shine, Shine, save poor me."

Sincerely,
Langston

20 East 127th Street
New York 35, N. Y.
December 6, 1955

Dear Arna,

Hastily, because I'm due at the annual Y dinner right now—if I want to eat for my $5.00. . . . . Anyhow, I checked on Peter Arahams soon as your letter came. Bill Cole at Knopf says they wired him re change of dates and think it is O.K. now. So I presume you will see him by Thursday. Tell him to get himself here by Saturday night at 8, otherwise I will be left with two or three dozen assorted writers on my hands and nothing but licker to entertain them with. Knopf tells me Peter is to speak for Afro-Arts group at the Harlem YMCA on Sunday night, so since I've never heard him in public, I shall go. Ida Cullen Cooper, tell him, will be there, so he can name a time to her to get the information he wants about Countee. I've also contacted Harold Jackman for him.

Charles S. sent me the working papers of the others that came in to him, including one from J. Saunders. I LOATHE the title "The Glory Road" as it reminds me of Clemment Wood and that synthetic spiritual of his that George Dewey Washington used to bawl from L. A. to Paris, in rags and with the loudest voice of the century. Sure John Hope is fine. I just put Ira because "he were there" looking us in the face, also because he's done some papers on the store front church—*Phylon* used one once, I believe.

I will now go eat and see the baseball players get awards—since I never see them play.

Sincerely,
Langston

Programs and clippings indicate *Street Scene* is a hit in Germany. Will send you copies for the Gershwin Collection. Phoenix Library now has a De Carava exhibit, and from there it goes to Allied Arts in L.A. On way back east, why not have it shipped to Fisk in February?

20 East 127th Street
New York 35, N. Y.
February 15, 1956

Dear Arna,

I'm dying! After two weeks of sunshine I get back back to Harlem from California to find two years of unfinished commitments clouding the Eastern skies with gloom—ranging from books to operas for which nobody has given enough

339

to cover working time adequately—and dreaming time and creative time NOT AT ALL. (Colored are supposed to do in two months what white folks take 2 years for, or more.) . . . . . Anyhow, and historically speaking (in case you give this letter to Yale or keep it for the Fisk archives) Stevenson has *LOST* beyond retrieve the Negro vote in San Francisco by his "gradualism", and if any Negroes in Harlem were on the Spingarn Medal Committee this year (judging from my one brief hour up and down the streets tonight) that noble disc (or whatever it is hangs on the Spingarn ribbon) would go to the two cullud boys who beat up the white boy in Tuscaloosa yesterday "just to get even for Miss Lucy". Which means, I reckon, that the Civil War has started all over again, but the Union troops this time are lonely cullud kids who "just want to get even".

Airplanes are amazing! I left San Francisco after dinner and got to Harlem way before my usual breakfast time, so went to bed at home before I even had coffee, or read your two letters I found gratefully awaiting me. The *Humor* anthology: can be pure folk, or not, as one chooses. I incline to including Ted Poston and Zora and *Simple* from the in-between field, also Dan Burley—or including them as only slightly diluted folk transcriptions. . . . . Roy Wilkins was diplomatic (and bad) on Tex and Jinx last night, Thurgood forthright and good on Bill Leonard tonight, and neither saying what the guys in the corner bars are saying, which is why, I suppose, so few leaders ever catch up with the people.

Sincerely,
Lang

I stayed in the Booker T. Hotel in San Francisco on my return trip and the first chair in my room that I sat in sunk *right* to the floor—so cullud hotels under integration haven't yet changed much. On the way out I stayed at the Fairmount where the chairs are quite solid. The difference comes in joie de vivre: the Booker T. is much more amusing.

Everybody at Hollow Hills was sorry they missed your call.

Evidently Noel S. had not yet heard from Charles S. re the project, as he didn't mention it. Nor did I, since I thought it best it come from official source first.

20 East 127th Street
New York 35, N. Y.
February 25, 1956

Dear Arna,

Thanks for your carbon of that very nice note to the Award folks. But it might be more effective a year from now after my autobiography comes out, and the *Pictorial History*. Right through now I think it would be good if the Award went to Dr. Howard or someone like that from the Deep South who risks life and limb for the race, not just words that are lynch proof, and quite beyond the reach of Citizens Councils. Anyhow, gracias!

Almost verbatim I got a Simple column out of a visit to the barber shop on Seventh Avenue last night preparatory to going to Bucknell College today for an NAACP program. IT'S ALL ACCORDING TO WHOSE OX, OXEN, OR ASS IS BEING GORED. Enclosed. Next week I go to Alfred University, which concludes my speaking season, these two being hangovers from last year promises, since this season I didn't take any engagements, and wish I didn't have these. Both are in

340

out of the way places that take practically a day to go and a day to return. Tain't worth it!

Today is the Feast of Purim with whose origin my new Meyerowitz opera, *Esther,* is concerned. I believe I WON'T dedicate it to my old Jewish slave-trading great-grandfather, but reserve the one we may do on HITLER for that.

Did I tell you about the fellow in the cafeteria in San Francisco, large and colored, sitting all by himself, who suddenly yelled out, "I'm a great dane dog!" Then added softly, "No, I'm not. If I was the world wouldn't treat me so bad." . . . . . Verbatim.

Lang

Leap Year day, '56

Dear Lang,

The TV is downstairs, so I just ran down to hear the announcement from D. C. that Eisenhower will run again. Which reminds me of Simple on Adlai. The only trouble with disqualifying a "liberal" candidate on absolute grounds is that the alternative is backing a third, fourth or fifth party chap who is clean out of the running from the start. It amounts, in most cases, to abandoning the field. That appears to have been Frederick Douglass' position. He therefore rejected all affiliation with thirds, fourths or fifths in favor of the Republicans of his day. He was what you might call a "practical" politician. If he were active today, he would not spend much time in search of the ideal candidate but would try to make a cool choice between the likely possibilities. But this takes nothing from the cogency of Simple's reasoning. It certainly depends partly on whose ox, ass, etc., but it depends in some measure certainly on how said goring will affect the election returns too. A philosophical politician like T. V. Smith would say this is all to the good. In a democracy of any kind the politician is a sort of a-moral entity who absorbs all influences in his person and reacts to the assortment, perhaps in the direction of the strongest. Well, I sort of get the idea, but I'm no authority on that.

Tell me about the Bucknell engagement because I have also been invited by them in the past at a time when I could not accept. Good crowd? Good pay?

I think this would be a good year for the Spingarn Award committee to bestow their blessing on an obvious choice, even though a poet. I do not lean toward these "men of the moment" who are needed and all that but sink into oblivion soon afterwards. I think the committee should believe their selection has done something that will stand. Did you notice that Robert M. Lovett died at 85, while you were in the West?

Best ever,
Arna

7 March '56

Dear Lang,

I get the Bucknell picture. Brotherhood seems to be a good gimmick for getting professional lecturers and writers to work at cut rates. I'm lined up for two such

341

myself: one for the Deltas in March and one at Vanderbilt in April. We will never learn, I fear.

T. V. Smith blazed the trail for Paul Douglas from the U. of Chicago to Congress. Smith, a philosophy prof., reached the conclusion that the thinker should enter the affairs of men. Nudged, no doubt, by Lovett and others he first ran for the state legislature from the area around the University. Then it was the state senate and then the Congress of the U. S., where he served several terms. He did not go back to Chicago after that but accepted one of those fancy special chairs at the U. of Syracuse, which he still holds, I believe. Something like the so and so chair of Political Science. He first attracted wide attention because his radio voice was almost indistinguishable from Alexander Wollcott's. He has lectured at Fisk, and his theme often touches on the philosophical overtones of democracy.

The library is checking on our copies of your Knopf books to make sure we are stocked. If this going out of print is a prelude to a collected volume of your poems, I don't think that is bad. I notice that Sandburg and all the others who are collected are generally out of print in the separate smaller volumes. Next time you are in the library take a look at the latest volume of *Books in Print.* So cheers and chin up and silver lining and all that. I have also written to Horace M. Bond for the copies of his speech. More anon.

Best ever,
Arna

26 March '56

Dear Lang,

Being snowbound must have been fun. I saw the pictures on TV. And last night I saw Louis Peterson's moving play "Joey" on the Goodyear Theatre hour. This makes the 2nd full length drama of his I have caught on that series, and I think this represents the wave of the future for young writers, Negro and white. Especially, I would say, where fiction is concerned. TV has already killed the pulps, or at least reduced them to insignificance, and I suspect it is punishing the other fiction outlets. Of course there will always be justification for stories that can be *adapted* to the newer media, and perhaps some of them can actually be sold as stories or novels, but if I were a beginning writer, I wouldn't waste too much time on them.

It seems that I'll be in New York on the 12th of April (Roosevelt), and chances are I'll get there a day early and stay at least a day after. Only one poet has come up for consideration for a Whitney Fellowship. Have they all gone underground? If they were discouraged by the fact that William Carlos Williams turned down all he judged in the three years he served, word might be passed to the ones you know at least that such is not now the case. Of course it may be that the talent is running to something else at present. Certainly the most gifted young people at Fisk are working in other fields. The teachers may be partly to blame. Having themselves soaked up some of the bad features of the "new criticism", they have at times made poetry seem alien and meaningless, if not distasteful to the young.

Charles S. has been on campus so little I have not had a chance to ask what goes with the centennial project. So more anon,

Best ever,
Arna

20 East 127th Street
New York 35, N. Y.
5 A. M.
April 26, 1956

Dear Arna,

I've been out nightclubbing with Jack Robbins & Yvonne Bouvier—Inez Cavanaugh at the Valentine, and Mabel Mercer at the Byline—and came back to cut a dozen more pages from my *Life*. From 783 pages I've got it down to about 500 and am working on the last sequence now from which I hope to extract 20 or so more pages. Unfortunately, in the cutting our Alabama Christmas and the meatless roasts got cut out. But the tale of Watts and the white lady who came a-begging remains—when we wrote *Boy of the Border* which I wish you'd add to while I'm cutting this, please! Let there be a stampede or a chase or something kicking up lots of dust.

My *No. 2 Life* is going to be good. I never really read it before until this week. I've now cut out all the impersonal stuff, down to a running narrative with *me* in the middle on every page, extraneous background and statistics and stories not my own gone by the board. The kind of intense condensation that, of course, keeps an autobiography from being entirely true, in that nobody's life is pure essence without pulp, waste matter, and rind—which art, of course, throws in the trash can. No wonder folks read such books and say, "How intensely you've lived!" (The three hundred duller months have just been thrown away, that's all, in this case; as in *The Big Sea*, too. And nobody will know I ever lived through them. They'll think I galloped around the world at top speed). Well, anyhow, I remain,

Sincerely,
Langston

9 June '56

Dear Lang,

The notes I have made on the manuscript in red pencil are only suggestions, of course. As a whole, the script is excellent. You have recaptured the mood as well as the essential details of the Harlem Renaissance. I am proud to have "been there" when it happened. . . . I wondered a little about the rather slight reference to Charles S. Is he mentioned elsewhere in the book? I'd think he rates a good sentence somewhere, if not indeed a short paragraph, as director of Urban League research, or founder of *Opportunity*, or A-1 sociologist, or most influential Negro behind the scenes (foundations, etc.) since Booker T. Six honorary degrees, including Harvard, Columbia, U. of Glasgow, Howard, Virginia Union and one

I've forgotten, scores of major U.S., ... I can scarcely wait for my copy of the full book. You've got it well in hand.

Boy of the Border is also coming along, but slowly. As I feared, there was no way I could get around rewriting the whole story, I began by doing chapters one and two over again and then pulled out the "Story Beneath the Stars" to make place for some action and excitement experienced first hand by Miguel and the rest of the outfit. Obviously this will take time, but I like it more and more, so I might as well dig in and try for the Newbery Award! (The Oscar of the juvenile book field). This version may be a bit shorter than the first, but I gather Macmillan will not mind.

So more anon.

> Best ever,
> Arna

July 26, 1956

Dear Arna,

How was the wedding? I airmailed a little gift. Hope it got there in time.

Do you want to read another play, after *Godot?* (By the way, did you like it?)

If you're in a play reading mood, I'll send you a carbon of my new one just finished, *Tambourines to Glory.* It's short, mostly gospel songs, with a minimum of melodramatic script. If Mahalia Jackson won't go into the theatre, I'd like to have Juanita Hall and Sister Tharpe for the two leads, and pretty little Reri Grist (who was in *The Barrier*) for the daughter, Dots Johnson the handsome villain, and the rest is up to the Tambourine Chorus and a little old lady drummer who turns the tables for the Lord, that would be played by Alberta Hunter. It's a singing, shouting, wailing drama of the old conflict between blatant Evil and quiet Good, with the Devil driving a Cadillac.

What kind of car have you got? (Present company excepted.)

Ask Charles S. how 1963 is coming? Tell him it will be here before we can turn around.

I stopped answering letters (after about 6) to write the play. Now I have a ton to attend to before taking off for Ann Arbor around the 4th. Might stop a few places on the way back, to get to Harlem about the 12th—in case you-all pass this way. Bring *Boy of the Border.*

> Sincerely & hopefully,
> L.H.

P.S. Did you see Horace Gregory's FINE preview of Graves' book with FINE remarks on poetry and colleges in the current SRL?

29 July '56

Dear Lang,

The wedding was a happy occasion indeed, but it has had a sad sequel. Camille, who participated and looked very well at the time, suffered an appendicitis attack the following day, and before she could be operated on the appendix had rup-

344

tured. She is very, very ill at Riverside Sanitarium (800 Young's Lane, Nashville).

If she pulls through in time, we will make the annual summer trek, this time to New York and points east, and we will certainly not get there before you return to town on the 12th of August. I'll let you know what works out.

Your new play seems to be the outgrowth of an idea that's been turning in your mind a long time—something making dramatic use of the gospel music. Maybe that's why you could do it so quickly once you decided to actually get it on paper. The idea, as you mention it, sounds like a modern day morality play, and your cast suggestions sound like solid senders. I hope you can get a producer with a proper feeling for the material. (I drive a Chrysler, thank you.)

Ruby and Owen Jr. were here for the wedding, along with a good many other out-of-towners, and I have just returned from the airport, where I put Ruby on the plane. Owen Jr. had left with the car for some eastern stops before returning. . . . . Camille's married name is Mrs. Jerrod Graves, in case you want to send her a card.

Your wedding gift arrived in plenty of time (Saturday afternoon), and your distinguished autograph was one of the sensations of the festivities. Joan's note about the gift will come along in time, I'm sure, but I can assure you it was warmly received by both her and Avon (he is a cousin of Thurgood, if I haven't told you, and the young law partner of Z. Alexander Looby). . . . . I hope I can get down to writing again someday. Till then,

Best ever,
Arna

More about *Waiting for Godot* anon. And I'll look up the Horace Gregory piece in the SRL. I'm woefully behind. Thanks for the programs of your summer appearances!

20 East 127th Street
New York 35, N.Y.
September 6, 1956

Dear Arna,

Since it is a Jewish holiday and everything is closed, I might as well write a letter.

Most shocking news: Instead of a check from Simon and Schuster, out falls an itemized bill of $1079.00 for books I've bought. I sent them $50 on account, which only leaves $1029 to go! My lovely editor down there brought me a piece of edelweiss back from her mountain climbing in Switzerland.

Dorothy Peterson brought Aunt Toy back a real scarab from Egypt.

Milton sailed. My cat is spending his last day at 20 East. He went in the potato bin under the frigidaire and mistook it for his box.

Juanita Hall is back in town and reading *Tambourines to Glory* which is all typed up at Obers in red leather covers with gold letters and looks wonderful. Second draft of the novel is done tonight and Adele took half of it home to type —will be about 160 pages—and is funnier than the play—another Harlem folk piece.

Today Watts called up and wanted to know when they'd have the *First Book of Africa* and I said in six weeks, so reckon I have to explore that continent directly. Had intended to do *Heroes* first for Dodd. But I might do both at Thanksgiving, since I just didn't have to read! . . . . Enjoyed that game—Yankees-KC! Thanks to you and Alex.

Lang

P.S. Looks like I'll have another musical play to do shortly. I'm a literary jobber.

You didn't tell me what you thought of "Waiting for Godot."

You-all got good white folks in Tenn. and BRAVE cullud kids!

20 East 127th Street
New York 35, N. Y.
September Seventeenth 1956

Dear Arna:

Did I remember to show you Max's letter when you were here? He said concerning your Douglas, Washington, Du Bois book, that:

> That is a book I feel confident would go over big in Europe and earn him a pile of money. And I'd be happy to lend a hand out of friendship for Arna. Could you tell him that for me?

It was very nice to have both of your recent letters and to know that the Fisk Jubilee Singers are going to Europe this fall. It is also comforting to learn that someone else has debts besides myself and it is interesting to have your views on the eternal mysteries. I told Leslie to send me a copy of your statement for his class.

I have put you on my list of prominent persons to receive a copy of both *A Pictorial History of the Negro in America* and my autobiography, *I Wonder as I Wander*. A new bill of $700 from Watts for books purchased gave me pause to such an extent that I fear I better not order another book myself *in life* from another publisher. However, if you don't get copies of these books from Crown and Rinehart, let me know and I will bring pressure to bear.

Bert moved but left no forwarding address so his mail is piling up here, including a card from his Draft Board. Maybe the Army can do more for him than matrimony. Or do you reckon?

When I got back from visiting Marian Palfi and her husband in their new home on Long Island this weekend, a wire shortly thereafter came, and a telephone call from Eulah, informing me that Noel died of a heart attack on Saturday evening in San Francisco, the second within a few days. It seems that the first one overtook him on the way to the theatre, so he was active and intent on enjoying the things he liked right up to the end.

All good wishes to you, as ever,

Sincerely yours,
Lang

346

20 September '56

Dear Lang,

Your "Danse Africaine" is apparently in the touring program of the Jubilee Singers. I saw their chartered bus stop at the Music Building while one of the boys went in and got the drums and cymbals they use for that number. They had a concert in Evansville last night and should be rolling across Pennsylvania right now.

I will write Maxim [Lieber] as soon as I dig up the slip of paper on which you wrote his address for me. Things got jumbled as usual in the trunk of the car. The status of the book Max mentions is suspended animation. I am at liberty to either finish the present version and peddle it elsewhere, repaying Houghton Mifflin 1,000 dollars, or do a new version for them, about a third of the length of the present one. H-M gave as their reason for declining to bring out such a large work of this kind a) the increased cost of plates and b) a certain decline in the market for Negroana since I began the job. I don't question either, so I decided to give myself a few months in which to think it over. If I can knock out a few short things now, I'll try to get back to it after Thanksgiving.

I always thought the Army would have been good for Bert. Let's hope it's not too late.

Though I actually saw Noel Sullivan only once, it did me some good to know that writers and artists had a friend like that in Carmel Valley. Now I'm sorrier than ever that we missed seeing him when we drove by last year.

I'll start watching the mails for the *Pictorial* and for *Wander*. . . . I'm back on my writing schedule, despite wholesale campus activities,

Best ever,
Arna

20 East 127th Street
New York 35, N. Y.
September 22, 1956

Dear Arna:

If I were you I think I would finish the big book as you planned it. Certainly some University press would publish it, maybe Oxford Press, because I think it is too important a study to be unnecessarily cut down.

That poor boy who just got married had to go to the police station and take out a peace warrant against the other woman to keep her from interfering with his domestic life.

The Educational Radio and TV Center, Ann Arbor, made six TV films last spring, each devoted to a separate writer and including Archibald MacLeish and myself. Perhaps this might be of interest to Fisk and you might want to inform whomever is in charge of such things there to contact the Center, as I understand they are ready for fall and winter showings in college classrooms as well as on whatever TV networks will use them.

I just had to cut the index and bibliography of *A Pictorial History of the Negro in America* exactly in half in each case—so your name went out along with mine and all other writers who are not deceased. I thought those who are no longer in this world deserved indexing in case someone wants to look them up quickly.

Also, all book, play and magazine titles had to come out as they had no pages left to accommodate such a long listing.

I see you are mentioned three times in the *Negro in American Culture* which I have just gotten. You can be grateful you are not mentioned in Billy Holiday's book, but I am looking forward to Eartha Kitt's to see if she remembers that I attempted to introduce an African to her in the face of the ferocious cat she had on her shoulder. All the women seem to be publishing their memoirs this season, including Pauli Murray.

All my good wishes to you, as ever,

Sincerely yours,
Lang

26 September '56

Dear Lang,

I'm glad to have your reaction to the publication problem of my trio-bio. Next time I pick it up (probably after the November lectures and book fair appearances) I hope to get it off my shoulders, physically at least, by giving it no rest till the manuscript is finished. Oxford was one of several University Presses that expressed interest in it at one time or another, but only time will tell whether or not their interest has continued. H–M has asked for some of their money back in case I do place it elsewhere, but I'm not sure they have a just claim under the circumstances. That too I'm sleeping on as I divert myself by writing (at least in first draft) several shorter and more relaxing things I've been saving for just such an hiatus as this: a ghost story, a parable and whatnot.

I'll report to our folks pronto on the Ann Arbor TV films of writers. They should find a ready user here. Just what Fisk is looking for—and intending to do itself in some cases.

Billy Holiday's book made me mad, as I'm sure la Anderson's will also, mainly because of the inclination of certain lady celebrities to confine themselves to just one certain kind of ghost writers as well as accompanists. Prejudice in reverse. Or perhaps the outgrowth of prejudice. And I won't feel good again until I hear of Bill Demby, for example, doing an "as told to" story of Lollabrigida. Or Marilyn Monroe. I hear that Eartha wrote her own. Let's hope. Also Pauli. Poor Billie didn't even get a best seller out of her naked exposure. My guess: it lacked the pathos a writer like Frank Harriott might have given it. No tears with the gut-bucket. None of the overtones we hear in her singing. Her jazz band never sobbed.

Best ever,
Arna

20 East 127th Street
New York 35, New York
September 29, 1956

Dear Arna:

At any rate, Marian [Anderson] cannot be included among the "Great Low-raters," even if accompanist and biographers (both past and present) are among "the other persuasion." I certainly agree with you. If only Frank Harriott could have done Billie's book, his *PM* piece about her, being one of the great interviews of our day. (Harriott died last year, by the way.) As to Demby writing Marilyn's "as told to," Waring who just left says he doesn't think we will live so long. He borrowed my Butcher book to read and just brought it back. Glancing through it, I wish it were more of a really critical commentary, rather than just mainly another listing of achievements. We need a Van Wyck Brooks. It's time somebody did a truly critical evaluation of Negro writing, an analysis rather than simply who-did-what. Don't you think? I'd suggest you do it, only you'd be too kind to everyone. Me. I'm too lazy to figure out why things are good or bad, I just like them or don't. But maybe Arthur P. Davis could approximate such a book, or the [Henry] Winslow fellow who does the excellent reviews sometimes for the *Crisis*. But someone ought to evaluate, not just inventory, interpret not just describe. What a bore!

Current off-Broadway production of *Take a Giant Step* is largely a bore, too. Except that Rosetta LeNoire as the MAID in her one scene runs away with the show, and gets the biggest hand at final curtain.

Did I tell you some 200 were turned away at my JAZZ talk the other night with Dave Martin at the new modern Donnell Library across from the Modern Museum? And the next morning we got a PAID date for a Long Island Art and Music Society this winter, with maybe more coming up. (And what I really know about Jazz would fill a thimble!) I'm going to MC a Mahalia Jackson program at Hunter College in February, so I shall read your piece over again. Why don't you-all have Mahalia on the Fisk Series this Spring—Arts Festival? I'll MC that, too, if you wish. Or you could.

Meyersberg expresses an interest in *Tambourines to Glory.* And the novel is now being read by Rinehart. Zell has done some BEAU-ti-ful line drawings for headpieces I hope I can persuade them to use if they publish the book, very simple strong rhythmical black and whites.

I am going to hear a Steel Band Clash tonight. And tomorrow I want to catch Jackie Mabley at the Apollo—anything to keep from attacking the 716 letters unanswered which I have hauled out for attention from various nooks and corners. I just answered the Mississippi lady who has written 103 letters since I wrote her last, now boxed in order of dates for Yale by my junior helper—who's about to leave me for a $65 a week welding job, since he graduated from trade school last June. How is a poor writer to keep assistants in the face of such junior beginners salaries? "I Need Some Rock on Which to Stand," some ground that is not literary sand.

Guess who I ran into at *Giant Step?* Theophilus Lewis, whom I hadn't seen for years. He's dramatic critic for *America* and works with the Catholic Interracial Council. Round as he is tall.

Lang

P.S. You better also during *hiatus* finish "Boy of The Border" since we could probably get some $ on that. And it might be a movie.

October 24, 1956

Dear Arna,

Sure, I'll be in town on Nov. 20th, and will struggle out of my bed at any hour whatsoever to see you get that book award—so let me know where and when. . . . Last night I had supper with Arthur Spingarn—quite mellow and witty and delightful he is, and full of anecdotes about Du Bois, Poppy [Cannon], Walter [White], etc. He says he has a copy of a rare Arabic book that you once said you'd like to have for the library which he will give you, and hopes you can come by or have supper with him when you're in town, as he can't go out—except next door to dine—as his wife is now really bedridden. I went down to take them the first copy of *I Wonder*. . . . He always gives me lots of books. Among others this time the Chester Himes paperback *The Primitive*, a really sickening interracial passion tale, that I read most of on the subway home. (Have you read it?) Chester goes out of his way to paint another friend of Henry and Mollie's horrifically— the rich Southerner who used to give the champagne parties for the Urban League Guild, etc., and with such detail of house locations and all that nobody could fail to recognize him. I admit I didn't like him myself, but I'd hardly do him in so in a book, and with such putrid detail. At the end the cullud hero knocks the white heroine all up against the television, then apparently happily phones the police, "I'm a nigger and I just killed a white woman." Do they reckon our literrati are now out to ruin the Race? ? ? ? ? ? ? ? ? . . . . Anyhow, the Eartha Kitt, Pauli Murray, Henry Armstrong, me autographing party is Nov. 8, the day *Wonder* comes out. . . . Monday, incidentally, Modern Museum is giving me a private screening of *Birth of a Nation* which I've never seen. Did you? . . . . And what you'd enjoy when you come to town is *Me, Candido* at the Mews about a Puerto Rican kid and adoption red tape in New York. Quite funny, warm and charming—and a hit. . . . Read Baldwin on Faulkner in *Partisan Review*, Capote's two pieces on the *Porgy* trip to Moscow in last two *New Yorkers*. . . . And finish your 3-way biog, and bring *Boy of The Border* with you when you come. A little kid in our block heard it read in school the other day, he said. So—you see? Words get around. Put some more down.

Sincerely,
Lang

P.S. Hey, you had my house number wrong on your letter—*20* not *2*.
Planned Parenthood wants us to do a booklet a la "Flypaper" for them.

20 East 127th Street
New York 35, New York
October 27, 1956

Dear Arna,

I was certainly shocked tonight to learn from Mollie Moon of the loss of Charles S., from whom less than a week ago, I'd received a very nice note in response to my congratulations on his *Times* article. I phoned you at once, as I guess Alex told you; and have just sent a wire to Marie.

I phoned various friends to tell them about it; and in talking to Alvin Cooper, learned that he is newly married. Paul had not heard it, either. He and Sonia are well, and promise to have us up to the new house soon.

Saturday night and I'm beat from a week of running downtown for appointments regarding the new books, and trying to entertain foreigners in between times—a Haitian architect, Claude McKay's former son-in-law from Jamaica, and a lady fan from Bermuda all choose this time to have "only a few days" in New York. Next week, after I see a private showing of *The Birth of a Nation* Monday which the Modern Museum arranged for me—and to which they said I might invite a dozen other interested folks—I think I'll go into seclusion. I'm real tired.

Mollie's doing promotion on the *Pictorial* for Crown re Negro contacts. Bound copies will be ready in about a week and you're down to get one. *Wonder* you should have even sooner. I've just gotten my copies, and it's a big nice looking book. And reads better than I'd hoped, I think. Let me know how it stacks up beside *The Big Sea*. . . . . The new Marshall Stearns *The Story of Jazz* (Oxford) is a must for your library—a simple straightforward history of the music, readable and giving the Negro full credit, but elucidating other influences as well. Gilbert Seldes and Meade Lux Lewis were at Marshall's dinner last night in honor of publication. Thursday's Poppy's book party at her house, to which I just got an invite. Busy literary autumn!

Langston

Most kind of you to phone. It rang while I was writing my name.

December 4, 1956

Mr. Edward H. Dodd, Jr.,
Dodd, Mead & Company,
432 Fourth Avenue
New York 16, N. Y.

Dear Mr. Dodd,

Your letter of November 30th reached me just as I was completing the Sectional Outline and Sample Selections for our *The Book of American Negro Folklore* which I have just forwarded to your office. Your quite frank reactions, and any suggestions concerning it, would be welcome. Only the fact that I have only a part-time assistant (working evenings) prevented our typing up even more samples to show you—but I think there is enough to give you the flavor of each section. Once I started looking through my files and on my bookshelves, I was surprised at how much folk material I have at hand immediately, and how large my own personal collection has become over the years—some of which I've used in my Simple books, but most of which is unpublished, like that very old Negro entertainer, in Paris in 1924, which I've included in the manuscript sent down to you, or the "Duprees Blues" which Delancy Anderson sang for me in Cleveland in 1936. (He later got life in the pen for hitting a man and killing him dead with a billard cue, but I got letters from him in jail all the time, and probably can get him to send us some prison folklore or prison songs).

There would be, Bontemps and I feel, a general INTRODUCTION to the book, and a brief Commentary for each Section, putting the material into historical and social perspective.

About half of the book would consist of selections from other folk collections and published sources, such as Odum and Johnson, Zora Neale Hurston, Botkin, Handy, and Talley's *Negro Folk Rhymes,* the latter, like a number of other volumes, long out of print, and some probably in open domain. But there would be some permission fees to pay. . . . . About half the material would be fresh unpublished material gathered or so acted by ourselves, some like the urban and contemporary stuff, *completely new;* some hitherto unpublished variants, like the Palmer Jones version of "Rakkie Baker," the variant of "Frankie and Johnnie," and the Blues verses I've collected, the Harlem jive, and the Race Relations satirical contemporary anecdotes and jokes that are numerous in Negro communities today throughout the country in varying versions. I plan to gather more later to supplement the Industrial Folklore by spending a little time with the steel mill workers in Pittsburgh and the stockyard workers in Chicago. Arna wants to explore the folk files at Tuskegee. And one or the other of us would like to spend a week or so listening to Library of Congress recordings and tapes in Washington—so an advance would come in handy to help us complete the gathering of new material. Would you take up the matter with Ivan von Auw who represents us both?

Langston Hughes

P.S. If you'd like to publish this book for Fall, 1957, we feel we could send you the completed manuscript no later than June 1, possibly a bit before.

Arna—Just so you'll know what I told the man.

L.

5 December '56

Dear Lang,

Your two cards and the carbon of the column nominating Mrs. Roosevelt were in my mail when I returned yesterday, but I have not yet found the "list" referred to on one of the cards. Since you tell me to "ignore" the list, however, I suppose it is immaterial now. Still I am never comfortable when I have the feeling that perhaps a piece of mail has been lost.

I've been thinking more about the folklore book than anything else since leaving New York, and I have piled my desk with collections to be gone through. I have also been jotting things down. This can surely be an exciting volume—and possibly a big selling one. So let's shoot the works and put out something that will last as long as *Uncle Remus.*

The grape vine has it that somebody at Dodd, Mead had written our Comptroller, following up the suggestion we made in Mr. Bond's office, so the wheels have begun to turn. I have some additional ideas for the series as a whole as well as an outline for the book I will propose for myself on the public individuals whose personalities have shaped the image America has of the Negro (Douglass, Booker T., Du Bois and half a dozen others). More about all that in about a week.

The trip was good, but it left me tired. Changing plans late in the game left me with awkward schedules and rushed me by bus, train and whatnot, and in each place I was booked much too heavily: 3 speeches, two group meals, one radio interview and one TV appearance in Winston Salem, for example. About the same in Norfolk. Hampton was fun, and I welcomed the chance to talk folklore with Roscoe Lewis *(The Negro in Virginia).* Also ran into Lewis Gannett down there. His daughter is married to the Art teacher, and Lewis was there to visit her and see his author (J. Saunders). So more soon.

Best,
Arna

10 December '56

Dear Lang,

Yesterday I had the long sleep I've been craving for nearly a month, and it did a world of good. I'm on the pace again today. Meanwhile, I've given the *Pictorial History* the close reading it deserves, and I agree with the fine recommendation it receives in the *Library Journal.* It is certainly a job well done. Despite a few minor slips, like using one of Douglass' early pictures twice (also Gwen Brooks), it is over all something of which we can all be proud. It should be active a long time—saleswise, that is. In our living room on the table it attracts immediate attention, and even the nonbookish say: 'That's something I must get.'

The prospectus for our prize book, *The Book of Negro Folklore,* arrived Saturday (8) and gave me another spin. This should work into a really big item in every sense. The stuff from our Humor job reads awfully good after this lapse of time, and I think the sections you have indicated are fine. Maybe the wording could be changed in a few cases (would *Recollections* sound more folklorish than *Remembrances,* for example?), but there will be time for such fine points. The others I'm thinking about in this connection are "Past-time Rymes", "Race Relations", and "Humorous Anecdotes", but none *need* be changed unless we think up better wordings.

I'm collecting like a weaver. I have something in just about all the categories, and in some quite a bit. There is good stuff here in the Source Documents of the Social Science Department (none published), and I'm having myself a time while reading it. The book resources of the library are just about complete, and I'm digging in that too. John Work is expected back from Europe with the Jubilees toward the end of this week, and I expect to get some leads from him. I also expect to start playing recordings made by him and others on folklore sorties into Mississippi and elsewhere. All told, a thrilling operation! It's easy to get folks to help on this because it's so much fun.

The idea of paragraphs or pages by us to introduce each section also appeals to me—for several reasons. A Fisk thesis I've found on the Folk Sermon will help me do a good statement on "Sermons, Prayers, Testimonials." I'm also primed for several others. Maybe we could divide these up and initial the ones we do. This would simplify the matter of possible quotation, etc. Also we might get going and want to do a short article on one or another. You would obviously want to do the little piece on "Blues" and "Rhymed Jive, Etc." While I am rather up for "Ghost Stories" and "Recollections," for example. Your introduction to "Party Cards and Advertisements" could easily touch off an article that you could sell.

By the way, I favor leaving *American* out of the title. People will probably understand or guess that it's American, coming from us, and by opening the book they'll soon find out for sure. But more important, James Weldon Johnson used that adjective so conspicuously in his several "Books" (American Negro Poetry, American Negro Spirituals) ours might get mixed up with his—or at least seem to lean a bit too heavily on his titles. Besides, the title is shorter without it and probably better for promotion.

Alberta re-arranged and improved my working room while I was away. The only trouble is that it may take me a few months to find everything. But I'm certainly set up better now. I wish I had more hours to spend in it.

The lectures helped out a lot on the budget this month. One more windfall (will it be the *Folklore?*) and I should be up even again.

Best ever,
Arna

Jan. 9, 1957

Arna, Esq.,

Well, I finished putting my new Simple book together just now, *Simple Stakes a Claim,* and am off to Chicago tonight by air to utter a few simple words at the Press Club banquet in honor of Rev. (Montgomery) King. . . . . Edith Wilson came in for the past weekend and had an old time theatrical party here at our house Sunday night with Leigh Whipper tale telling, Adelaide Hall, Timme Rogers, and others singing and dancing down till all hours. (And I had not recovered from New Years yet, when I went to 3 white parties downtown and 2 cullud uptown and the Baby Grand at 6 A.M.) So I am ready to retire to an ivory tower, but have never yet spotted one in Harlem. . . . . Milton is down with a virus, which he says left him too weak to go to work this second week out. Everybody hereabouts has been taking turns getting sick (I have about bought out the GET-WELL cards at my stationery store) but I reckon that is the only way to get any rest in New York—just collapse. . . . . The Watts [Publisher of Hughes's first book series] came to the party and brought me the most beautiful spinning colorama top I ever saw, along with a quart of Scotch. She is having a "controlled nervous breakdown"—one you catch before it breaks, she says—so is going West to the desert for a month, and maybe Carmel. If I were only well-off and white, would do same! (Or just well-off would be enough).

How are you? And where is the Centennial outline? DON't break yourself down now before the HUNDREDRETH cometh!

Wait till you see Simple's Acrostic on M-i-s-s-i-s-s-i-p-p-i, one version for the *Defender* but a better one for the book, making a double entendre out of P-P over Mississippi, which Simple will do when he gets to be an angel, hoping the Dixiecrats don't have time to get their umbrellas up as he wets all over Mississippi, which is now so dusty and dry.

The MAN come—so I had to hand back that $213.05 song check! Broke again!
Lang

14 January '57

Dear Lang,

I did the Centennial outline—a brief description of each of the proposed books as well as a note on the series as a whole—together with a prospectus for the

354

over-all book I'm suggesting for myself as soon as I returned home after Thanksgiving. Both are here on my desk, but I have not bothered to have copies made while waiting for the Dodd, Mead decision on *The Book of Negro Folklore.* Two things were on my mind in this connection: 1) a question as to whether it would be best to have the two things before Dodd at once and 2) the possibility that the reaction to the Folklore book might suggest revisions in the outline. If you think otherwise, however, I can have these things typed up this week.

I'm delighted to know that another installment of the *Simple* saga is in the works. You had not mentioned it earlier. I like the title too: *Simple Stakes a Claim.* . . . Did you finish up the new *Famous* book that you were working on when I was in NY? . . . . The paragraph review of *I Wonder* in the current *New Yorker* is good. It would be nice if Rinehart would do for that book some of the things Crown did for the *Pictorial History.* The circulars, for example. That montage on the jacket would be great for a mailing to the alumni of the Negro schools where you lectured during the '30's and '40's. Most of them have alumni secretaries with such lists, and many of the students who heard you are now teaching or doing other things in places where they could at least talk about the book. And this operation does not cost much!

I'm still putting things aside for the *Folklore* collection. I suggest you get *Tone the Bell Easy,* edited by J. Frank Dobie (Texas Folk-Lore Society, 1932), mainly for the section *Juneteenth* by J. Mason Brewer. It contains an earlier and different version of your talking alligator story, though not so good, as well as versions of many others that I heard as a kid and then forgot. We should probably go through everything Brewer has collected. He is a Texas Negro, you know, and you may have met him at Houston-Tillotson, where he teaches.

Mrs. Watts' "controlled breakdown" sounds rather smart. I'm trying to contrive a California trip too, but on a much simpler level. If you're going to be there in March, we might meet. My father seems a little nervous about his age (though his health is good)—he is 85—and keeps urging me not to make my visits so infrequent. My stepmother, who has been blind for more than a year now, has taught herself to typewrite. I believe I told you how well-read she has become through books on records as well as braille.

Man, that lie-throwing is the latest thing! Simple ought to take note of it. So

Best ever,
Arna

20 East 127th Street
New York 35, N. Y.
January 18, 1957

Dear Arna:

If Fisk is interested in securing the *Writers of Today* film prints, they may be secured from the address at the top of the enclosed letterhead.

Mr. Dodd has asked me to come down and talk to him regarding the Folklore outline and he has some further suggestions for making it the kind of book they visualize.

Yesterday we held the first audition of the music for the *Simple* show for the Greenwich Mews people and it seemed to have gone quite well. The director they have settled upon is Michael Howard, whom I did not know before but who seems quite intelligent and has done some successful little theatre and summer theatre productions. *Simple* is now scheduled for April so it may be on the boards by the time you get here—since I see by the papers where you are receiving another Award, this time with some cash attached. More Power To You!

Best wishes as ever,

Sincerely yours,
Lang

20 East 127th Street
New York 35, N. Y.
January 25, 1957

Dear Arna:

Man, I read that newspaper notice wrong. I thought you were *receiving* $5000, instead of giving it away! Cullud! Still and yet, yours is the greatest privilege and honor! (I-reckon).

Well, it looks like King Zulu is dead and gone in New Orleans. I just wish the NAACP would put something equally folksy and amusing in its place. Do you think they will?

We better hurry up and get that folk anthology out before the folk are all integrated and liquidated. I'm to see Mr. Dodd on Thursday.

Meanwhile, I see no harm in sending on to me that Centennial Outline, or submitting it, either—since the Folk Book can, or need not, be a part of it, in any case. The Centennial is not tied up hard and fast with it, is it?

Meltzer has come up with a sort of Centennial photo book idea (quite apart from us, as I never mentioned our project) and has already drawn up a BIG outline to see if I wish to work on it with him. Not yet submitted to a publisher, however, as we're awaiting Crown's reaction to the *Photo History of Negro Entertainment* first, which they've promised to give us soon. But once an idea is in the air—you know!

I've turned down at least 20 Negro History Week engagements—only to be accused by one white lady of not being willing to "sacrifice" as she herself is working night and day to put over our cause in her PTA—and I won't even come and speak! (In spite of fact my week was already full.) I've 4, all I can contemplate doing, that week. And after this year, am thinking of cutting out ALL speaking —what with the advance letter writing, and the follow-ups, it is just *too* time taking. (And I AIN'T honored!)

If the NNPA Banquet at Fisk was as good-tasting as the Chicago Press Club chicken, it was good indeed. (Or maybe I was just hungry.) I trust the speech making was as brief as ours, too. (Hope you didn't pull a Jefferson City! Ask Alberta.)

Did I sleep (almost) at the cullud *Godot!* Good, but just as talky as last year's. But a white man behind me snored so loud I thought he was a part of the show! It's closing this weekend—stage hand trouble, they say. (I rather imagine no business). What Broadway needs is a real good old-time colored singing and dancing HAPPY show, instead of all these sleepy white-orientated problems and half integrated watered down white-scored musicals—like frozen string beans, or canned phalarops. Pearl Bailey or somebody will probably come up with one before the Centennial. Let's hope. . . . . Judy Garland certainly sings your "Come Rain, Come Shine" beautifully—at the Palace and on LP.

I will now close, hoping you are the same,

Sincerely,
Lang

PS: Hear tell a colored actress got cut off TV the other day as she was saying a white man raped her mama, so she didn't like white folks! (Nope, wasn't Billie.) (Neither Ethel.)

PS 2—My secretary is flying to the Virgin Islands for her winter vacation, and I can't even get to a movie! (For mine).

20 East 127th Street
New York 35, N. Y.
January 28, 1957

Dear Arna,

Sensing doom coming (with so many unfinished deadlines on my hands) a Thoreau like spirit of simplifying life has overtaken me again, so I am engaged in throwing out, Yale-giving, sorting and eliminating (hoping to get more space for working papers).

I have two or three dozen settings of poems of mine in manuscript by various composers (including Roland Hayes). Would your Gershwin Collection like to have them—on condition that if I should ever need a copy of one, it could be photostated for me at Fisk? (This eventuality is hardly likely, however—since I neither sing, play—nor care much for—concert music).

I'll also send you reproductions of the songs for my *Simple* show we're having made up for rehearsals.

Josh White's new album, *The Josh White Stories,* has some of Waring Cuney's blues therein—"Jim Crow Train," etc., reissued. Quite good.

Are all the juke boxes in cullud Nashville playing La Verne Baker's "Jim Daddy To the Rescue," too? It's the moment's MOST. And Georgia Gibbs hasn't taken it over yet—so far only the reverse side, exactly a la La Verne—who signed over her air insurance to her the other day (as you probably read) saying if the plane fell, Georgia would still be taken care of—even if she (Miss Baker) didn't make any more records. A pleasingly catty publicity stunt!

Langston

HARLEM BAR
by Langston Hughes

Weaving
Between assorted terrors
Is the Jew
Who owns the place:
One Jew,
Fifty Negroes—
Unintegrated lace—

357

Embroidery of the evening
In this historic place

Historic?
A bar historic?

I'd say so—
Even heroic!
Not to speak of
Stoic.

(In the mood of "Montage"—
Lang)

20 East 127th Street
New York 35, N. Y.
January 31, 1957

Dear Arna:

The Book of Negro Folklore seems now in the bag. Mr. Dodd made a memo to start drawing up contracts while I was there. We had an hour's conference with Mr. Bond and Allen Klots (Dodd's Editorial Assistant) also present.

Mr. Bond (with whom we talked when you were here) is Vice President and seemingly head sales advisor, and he did most of the talking. I was interested in what he came up with. Although not stated in so many words, it amounted to a *socially slanted* book of folk lore—a sort of "people want to know what the Negro is thinking, and has thought in the past, about life in this country—not so many animal verses and things like that." He liked the integration jokes, etc., and the urban stuff, house rent party cards and ads. And thinks the book should be—in his own words now, "One that an Englishman could pick up and find in it something of how the Negro lives, thinks, and reacts to life in the U. S. A."

Mr. Dodd agreed to this, but added that, of course, the book should contain *some* examples of all the various categories of folklore we had outlined, and certainly the famous songs like "John Henry," etc., and a representative group of spirituals, including the well known ones like "Swing Low" that teachers and students might be looking up. But he approves the general social slant, too, and feels in this age of interest in race problems, it gives the book more vitality than merely a collection of folklore per se.

I found their viewpoint amenable—thinking to myself all the while that if I had proposed it, they would have thought me a leftist! I assured them there was certainly enough such material available to make an exciting book, mentioning the Fisk plantation material, the Jack Conroy industrial material, chain gang songs, boll weavil verses, etc., plus the current racially slanted jokes like the drunks and the bus. I read them your bit about mama never reaching California which they liked. And we all parted happy. Suggested length for the book—300–350 manuscript pages. Deadline November 15, which would give us the summer to assemble it, and probably you'd be North for a week or two when we could complete the details, section intros, etc., long about August. Meanwhile, we can be selecting, gathering, and typing up material. Is that date O.K. by you to put in the contract? If you've any contractual suggestions, better airmail them to me and/or Ivan.

The only mention of the Centennial project was that they said they'd written Cresswell some time ago, but had no answer as yet. And I said we were still preparing the outline, but would have it soon. So was glad to find your note when I came home saying it's on the way. . . . Nice clipping from the Birmingham paper! . . . . . Oddly, Mrs. S. Barr was up to see Aunt Toy today. Rain kept Dorothy home. . . . It *was* Miss Waters. First rumor was another Ethel. Seems she's cut several hogs (verbally) lately. Too bad!

Lang

Carlo and Fania sent me two big boxes of champagne jelly for my birthday!

20 East 127th Street
New York 35, N. Y.
June 2, 1957

Dear Arna:

I saw Paul and his house on the holiday when I went up to Fleetwood to Adam Powell's barbecue lawn party. All's well with your No. 1 son. . . . . Wonderful write-ups continue to come in about the show—the *Christian Science Monitor, Cue, Show Business,* etc., plus this week's *Chicago Defender* and the front page on today's (Sunday's) *Times* by Atkinson, who came back to see the play again a few nights ago. Curiously enough, WHITE folks seem to love it as much, if not more than the RACE! There've been a number of repeaters already, and one man has reserved three front row seats several times. Carlo is coming on Tuesday. . . . . We're having union musician trouble, Local 802—which may be all for the best in that now the producers will probably *have* to get bang-up good piano and guitar players, instead of just passable actors who can only play at playing, although they're excellent looking types. . . . . Also hot weather has come early this spring and the theatre is not air-cooled! Always something, as Simple says, when a man is colored! But business is good, and the weekends capacity so far. . . . We're still smoothing out rough spots, so I've been BUSY! Still rehearsing, putting in another song, and reading understudies, so haven't been home a minute lately to write you. But will write more shortly. . . . . . Come HERE in August! I got the new folk stuff, but haven't had a chance to read it yet. Proofs for the new *Simple* book have come today, too. So have to attend to those on the weekend. WOW! What a Spring! Plus a new batch of radio appearances for the show's publicity! I'm heading West!

(I mean, I'd *like* to!) (Got to get a breather). . . . . .

Sincerely,
Lang

And with all this, I've seen several accidents and fights lately, just in passing!

20 East 127th Street
New York 35, N. Y.
June 16, 1957

Dear Arna:

The poetics pieces are FINE! Only thing I miss is a mention of Sterling Brown somewhere, either with the poets, or with Cuney [Waring Cuney, poet] and me in the Blues. . . . . . We're having a HEAT wave here that won't don't! It's so hot in the theatre that 3 folks have fainted in the audience. One man passed out last week in the 1st act, was revived, and came back for the 2nd! (He must've liked the show!) But Jack Benny, Gracie Allen and George Burns came, left after Act I, but sent a wire saying they would be back for the 2nd Act when it got cooler! Eartha will be there tonight. Meanwhile, it takes 3 to 6 weeks to install air-conditioning. The poor actors are melting away now, and I'm afraid audiences will do likewise! Always something—when an author is cullud!

The Blues from the show is scheduled to be done (as it is in the show by Claudia McNeil and John Bowie) on the early morning Dave Garroway TV show on June 28th, they tell me. It's a hookup show, so I guess you can see it in Nashville.

W.C. Handy stopped by to see us yesterday. But I was auditioning understudies, so didn't see him.

After this week, I'm forced to put that show down, and try to catch up on other things. It has taken ALL my waking hours for the past six weeks. But now most of the problems seemed solved—except the heat—and last week it made over the quota, so all the actors got a bonus—which is customary in off-Broadway theatres when the box-office reaches a certain point.

Carlo's [Van Vechten] 77th birthday is Monday. He had a pre-party last night, Dorothy and I and a few more for dinner. But says his next BIG party won't be until he is 80.

Sincerely,
Langston

20 East 127th Street
New York 35, N.Y.
July 5, 1957

Dear Arna:

Yep, I've got a royalty arrangement on Mistral, 5% to me, 5% to her estate.

Simple now scheduled to open August 1 at the Playhouse in 48th Street, provided slated contracts are signed next week as promised. Did I tell you Sam Goldwyn (his *own* self) called me up from Hollywood Friday and asked for a script. Said he had only heard of me as a writer, but not a play writer. I started to tell him that I once wrote a play *(Mulatto)* that would make the hair *curl on his haid.* But didn't.

It seems *A Part of the Blues* based on my life stories and poems is now scheduled for 16 weekend performances in Hollywood. Folks write that it is very entertaining.

I'd say just before you start North, send me ALL the folk material you've copied, including Fauset, and I'll go over it all at once, before you get to Harlem in person.

Dave and my *Simple* party was an overflow—a mob, a madhouse meant to celebrate the 50th performance that never came off (due to Fire Dept., etc.) but we celebrated anyhow, and the producer announced the pending Broadway opening—to champagne and cheers. And me and Dave have discovered a new starlet —Anne English—who broke it up with two songs. Very striking, very stylish, with the kind of personality that radiates in waves. Peach colored. She looks like a younger Josephine Baker—and lives at the YWCA!!!!

Well, anyhow—

Langston

P.S. Just got the most wonderfully perceptive letter about jazz from a Kansas farm woman (I never met) who borrows records from the library—but really digs them. Remind me to show you her letter—the part particularly about Duke's descent to "A Woman is a Drum."

20 East 127th Street
New York 35, N. Y.
July 20, 1957

Dear Arna:

Would it be safe to set aside 4 opening night seats for you-all and Paul and Sonia for Tuesday, August 20, when *Simply Heavenly* takes to the Broadway boards at the Playhouse on West 48th Street? If so, *let me know,* and you are invited to the opening.

Understudy cast is all completed, except for Simple, and I'm hoping they'll sign Nipsey Russell as his alternate or standby. Brownie McGhee got back from his *Cat* tour just in time to sign as Gitfiddle, and Danny Barker will be his understudy and also play in the off stage combo—so we'll have two bang-up good folk guitarists, and a new Zarita. Otherwise just the same as before, keeping its off-Broadway simplicity—I hope! The Playhouse manager is an old showman, was with *Porgy and Bess* during its New York run, and knows what he is doing. Incidentally, the Playhouse is just across the street from the Court (once the Vanderbilt) where *Mulatto* ran, and that theatre then belonged to the current manager of the Playhouse, then, so he remembers well my former show in the same street.

Just got done with Mistral, gracias a dios! Although it was a real pleasure to work on such lovely poetry. I've sent you some spare carbons you can discard when looked over. Now I GOT to do some mail! It's piled up like mad. Carlo had a New Mexican cullud poet send some things he wants you and I to look at, as he thinks the boy is very good, and wants him to apply for a Fellowship. I'll send on to you soon as I've read them.

Langston

20 East 127th Street
New York 35, N. Y.
October 16, 1957

Dear Arna:

I was in the Dodd Mead office yesterday and learned that Mr. Dodd is away on an extended vacation until mid-November. I told them that our book was coming along fine.

The John Jasper sermon, I think, might well be included in its entirety and I like the poetry selections which have just arrived. I agree with you that this is enough for the poetry section along with what I have here. I see no reason why we should not assemble the whole thing about the first of November. Adele has been so busy with other things that we have not done any copying so far, so we are hardly likely to copy anything you have done there.

I see in the papers where Cab Calloway is in Los Angeles for the filming of the Handy story. You may have noticed on the front page of last Sunday's Times where the Ford Foundation has given a grant to the New York City Center for the production of operas. Among the possibilities listed is your Blues Opera, as well as my Troubled Island and Street Scene. Because none of the Meyerowitz operas were listed, he called me up seven times that Sunday urging me to do something about it, so I was finally forced to write a letter to City Center calling their attention to The Barrier and Esther.

Simply Heavenly closed last Saturday since it had been running under the necessary twelve thousand weekly to keep it on Braodway. However, plans are now on foot to reopen again off Broadway. Meanwhile Columbia Records' album has now come out and is available in the shops at $5.95. In case you want to order one for Fisk it sounds fine and has pictures of the show on the cover.

That's about all the news at the moment, so with all good wishes to you, as ever

Sincerely yours,
Langston

20 East 127th Street
New York 35, N. Y.
October 26, 1957

Dear Arna:

De Sun Do Move being copied at this moment. Adele is back in the West Indies, but Ramona Lowe is helping me evenings, and Raoul [Abdul, musician, assistant to Hughes.] returns from a concert trip Monday. (Everybody always leaves at once!). . . . . I'm determined to finish up *Famous Negro Heroes* next week, so will be hibernating. Too many folks from every-which-a-where are always turning up, dropping by or phoning for appointments, so HAVE to hide out. Think I will go up to Zell's in the Bronx, as he has a whole empty wing in his house.

Meanwhile, I'm engaged in trying to help my name-sake cousin who's visiting me realize that 24 hours is too long to stay away from home, even if he is "carried away" by a teen-age Zarita—whom I must say myself is real cute. I wish you were here to advise since you've brought many a Bontemps through that late adolescent period. He's a basically nice kid, but with some WILD Chicago ways. Fortunately, he is the confiding type, and can tell you some things about contemporary teenage life that would make my hair stand on end if I were a parent. I can write another *Corner Boy*, I expect, when he leaves. That, incidentally, starts out like a very interesting book—just sent me yesterday. I also like *The Hit*, as I guess I told you. The young writers are coming on! But young ones who can't make art out of their derelictions, where are they going? "Montage of a dream deferred

—daddy, ain't you heard?. . . . Lenox Avenue headed toward the Park—faster, faster, faster after dark. . . . ."

It's the first cold day today.

Lang

20 East 127th Street
New York 35, N. Y.
November 6, 1957

Dear Arna:

I'm head over my black heels at the moment trying to finish *Heroes*—and Adele is in the West Indies, Raoul has the flu, and Ramona's little boy is sick —so no help a-tall! God love me!

Also the usual commotion with *Simply Heavenly* in rehearsal *again* to reopen Friday at the very charming little Renata Theatre in the Village—where the management is hoping it run awhile this time. Me, I'm somewhat weary of it— and show biz in general.

I agree with you, it would be nice to get the *Folklore* in by end of month, although I saw Mr. Bond yesterday and he says April 1 is their deadline. However, the sooner, the better on my part. So will give it some attention in a week or so. But they want *Heroes* right NOW! So have to stick to it until done. Push done come to shove!

Did you hear the show album yet? It's getting nice display in all the downtown record shop windows, and Claudia is on the Robert Q. Lewis show this week, and is slated for the *Winesburg, Ohio* drama coming up, in a good role. She's not in our Village company—replaced by Miriam Burton, who's good.

Cordial regards,

Langston

P.S. My good-natured namesake cousin is going joyously to the dogs—which seems to be the Lord's will.

20 East 127th Street
New York 35, N.Y.
December 3, 1957

Arna:

Send me a list RIGHT NOW of ALL the things you've chosen and had copied for the *Folk Lore Book,* in their proper categories, so I can tell where to fill in, and what else may be needed—or what you think we're short on—from the BIG lot of stuff I have filling all the left bottom shelf of my bookcase (as you'll recall) and the shelf above. . . . Did you choose anything from Botkin's *Lay My Burden Down?* From *Congree Sketches,* Dr. Adam's—wonderful stuff, sermons, bits of prayers, ghost stories, etc.? ? ? ? From *Gumbo Ya-Ya????* *Folk Beliefs of the Southern Negro? ? ? ? Mister Jelly Roll? ? ? ?* Botkin's *Southern Folklore? ? ? ?*

And have you got any contemporary race-relations jokes???? These things I'd like to know specifically, please, sir.

Adele is copying some stuff tonight I've picked out, also the further revised (dialect-wise) *Sun Do Move* which was TOO hard to read as those white folks had transcribed it—even spelling messed up words which come out *exactly* the same as good English so far as pronunciation goes. (Just wanted to make Jasper seem more ignorant that he could possibly have been). Which he warn't.

Here's an extra copy of Ted's [Poston] interview. Maybe you can get it microfilmed to keep for posterity. (By 3¢ post.)

I've got 5 chapters to go on *Heroes*. Won't be long now. Thanksgiving out-of-towners cut in on it real bad. I should've LEFT town. (But these were cullud. ALL foreigners I've had to omit seeing—except Dioup—as there've been 50–11 dozen in town this fall from everywhich awhere. And *all* want to SEE Harlem—which is what now?) The State Department and the P.E.N. Club must think I'm a professional guide to uptown New York. (They ought to give me an allowance for entertaining them.)

Sincerely yours truly,
Langston

20 East 127th Street
New York 35, N.Y.
December 28, 1957

Dear Arna,

Could I have your personal permission to quote the enclosed marked paragraphs from your chapter "Wings On His Shoulders" concerning Col. Ben Davis, Jr., from *We Have Tomorrow* in my forthcoming *Famous Negro Heroes?* Nobody could write that sequence any better, and if I were to write it, I would just be *re-*writing you—so you might as well get paid for it. If it is O.K. by you to use it, I will have Dodd, Mead write Houghton Mifflin for the official permission and fee. Merci beaucoup!

I've finally gotten *Heroes* off my hands, and will now turn my attention to *Folk Lore* and have it ready in a jiffy. . . . . So, if you've any more stuff on hand, shoot it this way tout de suite, please.

The *Simply Heavenly* feudin' and fightin' is due to make the papers this week. Charges and counter charges of which I can't make head nor tail, and am not trying since, besides being busy, I've got a stiff neck, too, plus holidayitis! Show may close this week, since Equity made them put the WHOLE cast back on the Broadway salary scale—since it does not like the Off-Broadway Association's proposed contract draft. It would *have* to be a cullud show the first to get caught in the squeeze play! Meanwhile, the Equity deputy (cullud) has accused Stella Holt of being anti-Negro, plus other crimes. Result, she's had two heart attacks. So, between doctors, lawyers, Negroes and unions—Happy New Year!

Lang

364

20 East 127th Street
New York 35, N.Y.
January 21, 1958

Arna—

Man, I fooled around and let my aftermath of Buffalo's 15° below day in the University Library land me with a cold in Mt. Morris Hospital for the last five days. Real nice! And I would've rested even better if I hadn't been *so* tired when I came in. But cold's all gone—and I'll be out in time for Eartha Kitt's house-warming tomorrow night—which it is my determination to attend. Then back to our Folklore which ought to be fully assembled by the end of the week—and I'll airmail you a *Table of Contents* as it finally lines up. . . . This little hospital is so friendly and nice—and mostly West Indian—and very cullud—that I'm already looking forward to a return visit. And we eat around the clock—sort of like Father's.

By the way, do you approve the selections from "The New Day" for our book? It's a folk paper, if there ever was one.

Langston

20 East 127th Street
New York 35, N. Y.
Thursday, Jan. 30, 1958

Dear Arna:

The Book of Negro Folklore was delivered in person today—a foot and a half of manuscript, all 12 pounds of it—and looking very nice as Adele and Raoul typed up the contents and covers, etc. . . . . . Mr. Bond and Mr. Klots seemed duly impressed, and Mr. Bond went then and there into the accounting office and requested that they send out our check to Ober's. So you ought to get it early in the week. I'll phone Ivan and tell him to rush it through channels. . . . . . We discussed a few details:

1. FOREWORD: They would like to have one; to contain possibly comments on the origin of some of the material, African roots of animal stories, etc; creative continuity of folklore right up to today.
2. Perhaps where sections have no lead article a half page note or so might precede each.

(My suggestion is that *YOU do the Introduction,* and between us, we'll knock out the notes—for example, I could do right now in no time one on "Songs in the Folks Manner," and "Harlem Jive." One of Zora's short items already included on nature of magic, might be moved up to serve as an introductory note to "Black Magic."

3. They'd like soon a list of *all* sources, particularly those for which we might have to pay permissions fees. We're allotted $750, as you know. Anything beyond is deducted from our royalties.

Most sources are annotated on bottom of each piece. So Monday I'll have Raoul start listing them. Any I don't have, or know, I'll appeal to you. So hold off until then, unless you think of information I ought to have that you know I don't already have.

Your carbon was posted off today—mail, not express—since they wouldn't pick up until Monday. Maybe now you'll have it by Monday. Many sets are incomplete, as you have your own third carbon, so finish the assembling yourself, please. In a few cases, I had only two copies, but Index will indicate what is missing of things you don't have.

You never did tell me who or whence that dialect verse on "Good Manners" came from, or do you know?. . . . I found "The Rock" amongst your items, previously reported missing. . . . . It was SOME job putting all those carbons together, and weeding out duplicate versions, etc. But it did NOT drive us crazy this time—like it did Nathaniel when he and I were assembling *Poetry of the Negro.* The next time, I want *you* to be in on these nerve wracking proceedings. There's always a lost page, or a missing carbon of some item, or something all mixed up with the wrong material, that refuses to turn up until a section is all indexed and bound. Then it has to be inserted! Adele and I worked all night several times this past week getting it all straight, and trying to have 3 copies in *same* order. The one I sent you suffers with things missing here and there, since I thought I'd better keep the really *complete* carbon here for working and editorial purposes. . . . . How do you like the "Songs" section, with the old Bert Williams, etc., in it? . . . . The Dodd Mead folks were intrigued by it, and it started calling up old memories—as almost everybody down there is right agreeable.

I saw the wonderful collection of Ollie Harrington cartoons finally assembled. *(My idea, you recall).* Probably will be called *The Best of Bootsie* and other cartoons—of which there are many other good ones—integration, etc.

Sincerely.

Langston

20 East 127th Street
New York 35, N. Y.
February 2, 1958

Dear Arna:

This weekend I've been going through the manuscript of *The Book of Negro Folklore* listing sources of material for Permissions, and just about have them straight for *every* piece of material—your listings being, of course, of great help. . . . . However, in future, I'd suggest that you have your typists always list the ORIGINAL source of material taken from anthologies, NOT the *Negro Caravan* or Botkin, etc., when the original source is also listed in the anthology, as it is in most cases. Fortunately, I have most of the anthologies here, so could look up the basic source from which the permissions must come.

Now, a few queries:

1. What about the numerous verses we've used from Talley's *Negro Folk Rhymes?* Do we need permission, or what? Since some of the Talley family are at Fisk, would you want to discuss it with them or not? For *Golden Slippers,* did you get permissions for the Talley things used therein? Let me know the dope on this to relay to Dodd, Mead. . . . . Incidentally, I discovered that "Teaching Table Manners" is from Talley, so I'll have to switch it from "Poetry of the Folk Manner" to "Pastime Rhymes." However, it seems pretty formal to me to be a folk poem. I don't have a copy of Talley, so could you look it up and see if it is anonymous, please.

2. Aunt Toy and Adele are of the opinion that "Just a Closer Walk with Thee" is a hymn, although now used as a gospel song. Can you get any information about it from your Music Collection. If composed, are its authors Negro? If not, we should leave it out. Let me know.

3. Also "I Do, Don't You," which you mention in your gospel song piece. On the record I have of it by the Pace Choir, authorship is credited to E. O. Excell, (Or is this a hymbook name?) NOT to C. A. Tindley. But certainly it is used by Negro gospel choirs a great deal. Can you help straighten this out. If Excell is author, is he cullud? Or could it be that what he really gets on record is arranger's credit? This on many folk records is confusing. (For example many of Harry Belafonte's folksongs on records are copyrighted by the arrangers— but the credits make it look as if they *composed* the song and OWN it outright). In our "Blues" section on page 22, change the title of "Southern Blues" to "Gypsy Blues" and scratch off Rainey and record credits, as *every* verse of it is traditional, so no reason for us to have to track down copyrights.

4. Although texts of a number of the SPIRITUALS you sent are copied from *Caravan,* etc., since these are traditionals, is there any reason to credit any source? At any rate, on my Permissions list, I did not do so. Certainly, we *don't* want to have to pay for these songs.

Several of the Pickens stories, as you probably noticed, I omitted—since some really had little or nothing to do with The "Problem" and others would not, I am sure, sit well with Negroes. When he used to tell them to an all-colored audience, they were funny, but not so much so in print, and seem a little "Uncle Tommish" now, some of them, I fear. We have more than enough material, anyhow.

5. Since the Pickens book is probably long out of print, do you reckon we should apply to the family for permissions, or what?

Allen Klots at Dodd Mead is going to be our Editor on this book, so any information you ever feel the need to send him can go direct to him, or to us both, with (or via) carbons. Since he wants to start on permissions as soon as possible, I'm having my lists typed up tomorrow and they'll go down to him Tuesday. So your information or clarification on above mentioned little problems will be welcome any time it comes along SOON.

I cut some of the "niggers" out, but didn't have time to comb the manuscript thoroughly for them, and tonight notice some I missed in my carbons. I will get them all out eventually, or if you spot them, send me the page numbers. One in "Jazz, Folks" at end of a story where it is effective for the Jim Crow point, I'm leaving in. Can't recall the story right now. But all the others can be changed to black, blacks, colored, Negra, Negro or just *man,* without spoiling the flavor of the tales.

Yesterday was my birthday, and a few folks dropped in, had a nice evening. Today a BIG birthday cake arrived from the woman who makes and sends one every year—the present-giver of the many handkerchiefs and cigarettes.

Eulah is still here from California, and my name-sake cousin is back from Chicago and starting job hunting tomorrow. But up to this point has been balling, is spending the weekend with my brother's kids in the Bronx, was due home tonight (Sunday) but just phoned (midnight) that "la fete continue. . . . . . Do you know that wonderful Jacques Prevert song in the Germaine Montero album? (Vanguard). . . . . . I met Marcel Marceau, the mime, and Claude, the French actor in current movie hit, and Brigitte Bardot's director and Lilo and whole gang of French artistes at a party Friday given by the man who is translating *Simply Heavenly* into French. Hadn't heard so much French all at once since Paris. . . . . What's this I hear about you going to Brussells? To the World's Fair or what? The Newport Jazz Festival (on whose Board I now am) are sending a jazz contigent, if the State Department collaborates.

I've turned down at least 99 Negro History Week engagements. I'm already long booked up, and have the excuse of recent flu NOT to take any more before or after—or ever! Have to cut out something, and public appearances are the most worrisome. Especially in COLD weather.

Kindly AIR MAIL back your replies to above queries, as I'm closing up this here *Folklore* box, so I can get on my LONG overdue *First Book of Africa* for Watts —before they demand their money back, which they've already hinted at. Precious Lord, take my hand! . . . . . I wish a few of my laurels would turn into greenbacks—I'd give EVERYBODY their money back!

Proofs of *Famous Negro Heroes* are here, and those of the *Langston Hughes Reader* arrive tomorrow. So I'm proof-ridden!

Cordial regards to the family, and thanks for that Chicago card!

Sincerely,
Langston

9 March 1958 (Sunday)

Dear Lang,

Our automatic reactions were apparently the same in re the permissions requested from Associated Publishers. As I recall, we are not using anything from Faulkner, but check me if I am wrong, and I will undertake to secure the permission. I telephoned Sonoma Talley about the selections from her father's book, and she said she would grant the permissions if she receives a letter listing the items. I passed this information along to Allen Klots. If he gets no response, ask him to let me know and I will call her again. I don't believe the things in the Fisk Social Science Archives are copyrighted, but I will verify tomorrow and get any needed release. Finally, I think maybe we should wait for Dodd, Mead's report on the permissions as a whole before deciding how many substitutions are needed. But meanwhile I'll be earmarking some things, just in case.

Thanks for the Christmas Spirituals. You should hear from the chairman of the Festival committee presently. I am following with interest your jazz poetry programs at the Vanguard. I think something of the same sort would be just dandy here, and I will go into the details this week, including the question of the combo. So more about that anon.

About Lloyd Addison's poetry there is one main problem at this point in his career: he will have to prove himself as a comprehensible artist before serious critics or judges will stick their necks out for his incomprehensible efforts. Remember Joyce had written his Dublin stories and his Portrait of an Artist as a Young Man before asking serious attention for his experimental work. Likewise Gertrude Stein. A second problem for him in re the Whitney Fellowships is that a couple of obviously better poets are also applying. One in particular seems worth watching, and I doubt that the Committee will give more than one grant in poetry—if that. So I'd advise Addison (and you may quote me to him—after

368

mid-April) to consider the careers of Joyce and Stein *as a whole* if he intends to make them his examples. Right now his warmest references seem rather patronizing, and I suspect the reason behind it to be about as I have indicated.

Thanks to Adele for the news about the NBS. I favor the selection of the Forthcoming Martin Luther King book for Spring. While I don't know what the book is about, I believe our folks will want to know what he has to say and that the book will therefore have appeal. Incidentally, I have lost my copy of Rowan's *South of Freedom* and would like another at your best discount. And here is an idea: What about a travelling exhibit for libraries? Libraries welcome these if they are attractive and easily put up, and one by the NBS would certainly attract attention. Throwaways to be distributed at the circulation desks could go along with the exhibit. But I know it will take a little time to prepare and then to put such an exhibit on the road. I will discuss it further when I'm in New York if the idea still seems promising after a month of thought.

You may assure Mr. Klots, if you talk to him, that I will try to get in touch when I'm in NY and do my best with any loose ends of "The Book of Negro Folklore."

So

Best ever,
Arna

20 East 127th Street
New York 35, N. Y.
March 27, 1958

Dear Arna:

Well, we toasted the new *L. H Reader* with champagne down at the publisher's yesterday, and 8,000 copies have gone out already as a bonus book to members of the BOOK FIND CLUB, so there'll be a second printing soon, they say. All who want 1st editions better buy soon. . . . . I wrote Banks, and will be sending him poetry scripts before I leave, and to YOU a dub of the MGM recording which you may play first, then lend to him, with the stipulations that it *NOT* be played for anyone other than the musicians working on the project, so they can see the general moods used, which they themselves need not in any sense duplicate, as they'll probably have ideas of their own, and pieces in their repertoire they can background me with. But I think hearing the disc might help them. (I got this dub so quickly BY THE HARDEST and it *MUSTN'T be played publicly*). . . . . . On Monday I'm to spend the afternoon at Dodd Mead going over our *Folklore* manuscript in the light of what might be cut to reduce permission fees, but especially since cutting HAS to be done, anyhow, as the production department feels it is about 200 pages too long to sell for a reasonable price. They think it's about 700 pages now, and would like to get it down to app. 500. . . . Such little old things keep delaying me setting a date for Coastal departure, but I've promised the Hollywood folks I'd be no later getting there than April 8, so hope to get off in time to stop by Chi next week for a day or two to see relatives for information Uncle Johnny wants. *Got* to do that. . . . . Meyerowitz and I have just finished a new One Act Opera that is BEAU-ti-FUL! And our *Esther* is being performed in Boston May 7 and 8, so reckon I'll go up for it. . . . . Sorry to be missing you when you are in N.Y. but I'll be seeing you at Fisk for early morning jazz! . . . . . .

Cordial regards,
Langston

BRAZILLER wondered if our *Poetry of Negro* was out-of-print. If so they'd like to take it over and enlarge by bringing up to date with new poets. I said it wasn't. But we'd like to do a new edition with new poems if Doubleday so agreed sometime.

4-10-58

Dear Arna—
I've ordered some books (L.H. Reader) sent.
Re the Omegas, very good of them—but unless they are having something, *anyhow,* in honor of the Inauguration visitors—I'd not be the least slighted if they did nothing special for me. (You know!) At any rate, I'd like nothing *at all* scheduled before my Convocation talk. I'll get to your house the evening (or so) before—but I've such a heavy schedule all preceding days in L.A. and Hollywood, I'll probably reach Nashville (by air) beat to my sox. So need that first night for rest, contemplation, unpacking, pressing, seeing you-all, etc. *Don't* want to go out *a-tall.* Or even come downstairs. (I'm getting right agreeable, unsocial, and like Dr. Du Bois.) But, no kidding, between the Jazz dates, and the book dates, and *3* radio, *1* TV show here, I'll need my first night in Nashville to just catch my breath. (Else I'll die!)

Lang

20 East 127th Street
New York 35, N. Y.
May 24, 1958

Dear Arna:
Thanks for your note enclosing the Guthrie version of "Stagolee." I like Onah's better, and would rather keep it, if possible.
Re O'Banion, I'll surely see him. In fact, intended to hear the Tuskegee Choir at Radio City anyhow.
Allen Klots tells me the production department says the book will have to sell for $6.95. To make it $5.00 we'd have to cut at least a hundred pages, which would mean pulling out two or three sections in their entirety, Klots feels. So I am inclined to say, let it stand and charge the higher price. Book prices keep going up anyway, and if it came out at $5, next year they'd probably raise it to $6 (like *Poetry of the Negro*) so we might as well start out with the higher price, and make that extra change from the beginning. Besides, it would be a shame to cut so well rounded a book down any more.
Enclosed is a good poem from Dorothy Rosenberg, but too late to include, even if had room, so let's file it away in case of revisions and additions to *Poetry of*

370

the Negro, for which I've quite a file of stuff already—Patterson, Vesey, and other new Negro poets.

Do you see the George Norford NBC TV show, "The Subject Is Jazz," in Nashville? I was on it Wednesday—live to some 40 cities—but show on film in various others during the next two weeks. It is a weekly show, on different days in different towns. In New York it's on film Saturday, May 31, so I can sit home and see myself—reading jazz poetry to Billy Taylor's music, and talking with Gilbert Seldes and Harold Taylor about jazz. Discussion came off not so good, I felt. But the music was good.

Looks like I'll be doing a transcontinental lecture tour again next fall. Requests for dates keep coming in, including two state library association meetings, Kansas and California, both in October. Helpful to promote the *Selected Poems* out in September.

I promised Camille a *Reader,* so sent it to your address, since I didn't have hers nor recall her married name. Hope she got it O.K. I phoned Paul and told him what a nice time I had with you-all. Oh, by the way, ask the football player Omega man who taped my Poetry-Jazz program, if the tape he promised me is ready? I'd like to have it, and will pay costs if he'll send it. I'm going to do an afternoon of it in Harlem with Ram Ramirez, so it would be helpful to play for the new jazzers to get an idea of what to do. We tested a few poems at Bowman's on the hill one night, and a colored lady walked out, stating, "What are you reading about Negroes for and there are white folks present?" Integration can no further go! She looked real brownskin, too, so I started to say, "How dare you be so dark in the midst of a white culture?" Only I thought of it too late!

Best ever,
Langston

28 May '58

Dear Lang,

I must confess I like Onah's "Stagolee" better myself, partly because I helped him fix it up in the first place, but Onah has now acquired illusions of grandeur about it, so I thought of Guthrie's version as insurance against any difficulties Onah might offer. But you will know better whether or not his permission has come through. I also wonder about the permissions from John Work's book and for Sterling's blues piece. Any news?

$6.95 is an impressive price for a book, but I suspect that anyone who was aiming to pay $5 for it will not be put off by the extra $1.95. So I say, Let's not fight it. Indeed, the higher price might have a certain snob appeal, and I certainly do not want to have to slash out some of our treasures. Keeping the collection big and rich and juicy is bound to pay off.

Fisk went all out for Du Bois. Wright read a fine—and lengthy—citation at Commencement. The Phi Beta Kappas gave him a key. The Class of '35 announced the endowment of an annual lecture in his honor—himself to give the first one this coming fall. It was like the return of a king from exile. We had him and Shirley to dinner once and we attended a luncheon Wright gave. Then I was selected to drive them to the airport. Du Bois was in fine fettle throughout, jolly, humorous and energetic. He marched in the academic processions, sang with the oldtimers in the choir, joked with everybody and generally had fun. . . . Shirley whispered to me that while he has made no public statement, he has felt in recent years that he was losing contact with his own folk—which he wished to reestablish. So I read a good bit into that statement.

The *Reader* came, and I have delivered it to Camille. . . . We do not see "The Subject Is Jazz" down here—at least I haven't found it. . . . Nothing is better than library association meetings to plug a book. And your Selected Poems should lend themselves in many ways. Especially on the heels of this jazz tie-in. Something about it (you as the original jazz poet in U. S.—or anywhere) should be said clearly on the jacket. . . . Moorehead, the Omega footballer (and honor student) who taped your reading here, got away just ahead of your letter, but I'll try to find someone who can tell me about the tape. Moorehead is probably in NYC now, with a carload of Fisk fellows looking for summer work. So more about that anon.

Dorothy Rosenberg's "Bim Bam" is real good!

Camille's married name is Mrs. Jerrod Graves.

Best ever,
Arna

20 East 127th Street
New York 35, N. Y.
June 4, 1958

Arna—

The INTRODUCTION is FINE! Glad you dealt with that derivation question so adequately—so the who-claims-what argument by possible critics is forestalled. You are a scholar. Erudite! No jive.

Du Bois has been moving in triumph across country. So glad to hear of his Fisk reception. He's about the most!

Bus strike is giving *Simply Heavenly* a hard time in London. Something is always happening to cullud! Bertice Redding as Mamie stole the show—one critic calling her another Ethel Merman or Pearl Bailey. She's a brownskin platinum blonde, stout as Juanita Hall—who, by the way, just phoned me from the airport that she's flying to England for the opening of *South Pacific* to be gone ten days. The Race does get about.

I've added another publisher to my list. John Day liked the teenage integration outline, so is publishing *Tambourines to Glory,* on next winter's list.

And I've done ⅛ of the *First Book of Africa* this week—a year and a half overdue. But everything gets done in time.

Unsolicited lectures are coming in like mad for next season. Why is it depression times seem to be the best for lectures? When headed for the pit, I guess folks seek knowledge—or at least poetry. Have you any other explanation? (Just when I had sworn NEVER to open my mouth in public again! Even doubling fees doesn't seem to deter sponsors).

Life is photographing me tomorrow for some new series it's doing on Negroes —the new Niggeratti, I reckon.

Langston

6 June 1958

Dear Lang,

I'm glad to have your reaction to the INTRODUCTION, which I do hope serves the purpose. Have you heard whether or not anything is still outstanding in the way of permissions?

Sometime ago you asked about Jan Carew's novel. It is announced for fall publication by Coward-McCann (August) under the title of *A Touch of Midas*. You remember Jan—tall, handsome, here in a minor role with the Old Vic Company. A mulatto from British Guiana.

Which causes me to ask whether or not you know Anatole Broyard. His picture in *Time* this week makes him look Negroid. If so, he is the only spade among the Beat Generation. His story "Sunday Dinner," I gather, is included in the new anthology, *The Beat Generation and the Angry Young Men*.

You are, as the expression used to be, *smoking!* Books, lectures and all. But I can well understand how this new Poetry with Jazz thing, plus the show and so many solid new publications would boom your box office attraction as a lecturer. It all figures. So make hay!

I'm trying to get a gang of small things done this month, including one small book. All way overdue. So I appreciate that rushed feeling you describe. The trip to San Mateo is scheduled to begin July 1st.

By the way, don't be afraid to set your lecture fees *high*. Clifton Fadiman charges $1,250 flat, and his only agent is his brother. Some relatively minor ones (without agents to cut in) think nothing of making $275 plus round trip air fare (Carl Rowan, for example), but he does have an agent). Others more. I suppose this cuts down on the number of engagements they get, of course.

Best ever,
Arna

20 East 127th Street
New York 35, N.Y.
June 13, 1958

Dear Arna:

Klots says *Folklore* is coming along O.K. and he loved your Introduction. Now they're pushing me for my Intro to the Ollie Harrington cartoons. Always something one is behind on—not to speak of behind the 8-ball. . . . . *Simply Heavenly* closed in London. Very mixed reviews ranging from two very good to some VERY bad, most on negative side except for praising Bertice Redding who apparently clowned down, in most "downhome" style. The *Manchester Guardian*'s London critic gave show a good analysis, blaming the direction for spoiling its qualities. Evidently it was turned into a sort of musical minstrel from all I can gather from Rosey Pool and Ella Winter's letters about it. And Delores Martin's single phrase: "Shades of Shuffle Along"— meaning that last bad revival of "Shuffle" a few years ago. At any rate, McRae's wife flew over just in time to find it closing—and lost her mind, now confined to a resthome there. . . . . Incidentally, I just hear today that same thing happened to Horace Cayton a couple of months ago, and he's in

Rockland State Hospital for the Insane. Alta says she knew it when we saw her at Fisk, but I don't recall her mentioning it. Did she tell you? . . . . . And Angelina Grimke died this week, funeral in Washington Saturday. No relatives, and Harold Jackman is her executor. . . . . The lady who wants me to do Poetry-Jazz for the California Librarians in the fall wrote me they're all looking forward to your coming. When do you take off, and for how long? . . . . Dot writes that Norman Hopkins died. You probably knew him and Irma in L. A. . . . . Lots of dying news this week (Harcourt Tynes, Evelyn Ellis, too!), etc. . . . . Well, anyhow, as a *Crisis* story writer (Anita Coleman) once wrote, "You can stand anybody dying but *yourself.*"

> Comme toujours,
> Langston

Just got a long letter from Katherine Dunham in Tokyo, lamenting fact that 20 year struggle to keep her company together hasn't yet resulted in any subsidies, backing, or State Department aid—only her own hard work. Now it seems taxes on foreign earnings by U.S. has out run income. Always problems for cullud! Me tired, too! White folks always getting $20,000 grants and things. Editor of my *L. H. Reader* writes he's expecting some such. Me still struggling for subway fare!

> 20 East 127th Street
> New York 35, N. Y.
> July 9, 1958

Dear Arna:

Found your card of the Great Stone Faces on my return from Newport. The Roosevelt that ought to be up there is F.D.R.

The Newport Jazz Festival was lots of fun, the Jazz Dance seminar being one of the hits with two cullud dancers. Also Hayakawa's Blues lecture was FINE with Jimmy Rushing demonstrating. Ralph Ellison and James Baldwin and me were there. Also Rose Morgan, Mahalia, and Jerri Major, plus half of cullud Harlem. Gate: $160,000 dollars! Cullud ought to be in on some of this jazz PROMOTING instead of just the playing.

Proofs of *Folklore* will not be ready until the first week in August. Printers are all on vacation (all at once) this month. So I told Allen to send yours to Fisk to greet you on your return.

Ralphie is getting real baldheaded—further proof that he is an intellectual. . . . . Mahalia with Duke not good. Duke not very good either. It must be hard to keep from falling between so many stools.

By the time you get this, I reckon I will be in Canada. That leisurely drive of yours westward sounds wonderful. John Wakeman, English exchange librarian, maybe you met in San Francisco. Nice guy. I told him to look you up.

> Sincerely, comme toujours,
> Langston

20 East 127th Street
New York 35, N. Y.
August 3, 1958

Dear Arna:

Well, I am back from my travels, somewhat weary with welldoing. Stratford was nice, pleasant place and cool to vacation sometime with family. Try it. Jazz and other divertissements if you get too much Shakespeare. All quite prejudice free and unhectic, not like Newport's busy jamsessions. . . . In Chi I found (with most patient help of long distance operator, the missing relatives whose names I only knew half and addresses not at all) in Joliet and Gary, so did not have to visit those cities, instead the never-before-seen cousins drove up to Chicago to see me, and very nice folks they are, too, a brother and sister, both married with kids, homes, and cars—real solid citizens—as Uncle John thought they would be—yet fun loving and took me night-clubbing; and next day the Gary fellow came back and drove me around to see our Chicago relatives whom he had never met—their various kids range from one year to a boy of twenty—and one is a star basketball player in Gary highschool. So we all liked each other and I am glad I located them for my Uncle—and myself. They had lots of old family pictures I'd never seen before, even old tin types. The kind of folks who *don't* lose their history in basements. . . . . Far from the SUBTERRANEANS of Jack Kerouac's novel—which I read on the planes—an interracial love affair of the Frisco bars and bohemians. Have you read it? Did Redding review it? I'd be curious to see Negro critical reactions—which shouldn't be harsh since everybody is equally drunk and half-mad. Tell me what you think of it. . . . Also have Motley's new one, but guess I'll have to save its reading for another trip. . . . . Nobody told me my *Mother to Son* is in front of *Willie Mae!* . . . . Dig that real different de Carava photo on my MGM poetry-jazz album! . . . . Also dig those nude photos of Rev. Harten in current *Amsterdam News.* The *most* I ever saw in the public prints! And he without his nose glasses and ribbon! Unfrocked indeed! But still got his church! TAMBOURINES TO GLORY!

L. H.

20 East 127th Street
New York 35, N. Y.
August 30, 1958

Dear Arna:

The New York Omegas, who last year awarded me their Manhattan MAN OF THE YEAR plaque, now wish to nominate me for the National Award at the coming conclave. In getting together information for them (as you can see from the enclosed cartoon) I recalled that last year you were kind enough to suggest nominating me for the Spingarn Award, and I asked you to hold off until my *Selected Poems* were published. Now that they will be coming out in January, and I think it is in late January or February that the NAACP Awards Committee begin their deliberations (as I recall from once being a member of the Committee myself) if you would like to make the nomination within the next few months, I'd say go to it. And (if you want to work at it that hard) get a few other folks around the country to also send in nominations: maybe Ivan Johnson in California, Truman Gibson (who's a great Simple fan) in Chicago, and C. V. V. in New York, or others if you think of them.

I suppose the categories of achievement to consider would be, among others:

POETRY: 9 books, and almost 40 years of magazine publication, beginning with *The Crisis* in 1921.

PROSE: 15 books of my own, not counting collaborations, such as our *Poetry* or *Folk Lore*.

TRANSLATIONS by myself of other writers: 3 books—*Gabriella Mistral, Jacques Roumaine,* and *Nicolas Guillen* and numerous poems and stories from the Spanish and French.

LECTURES: This season will be my 8th Cross Country tour, not counting hundreds of other engagements covering practically all the major American colleges, and a great many high, grammar, and even kindergarten schools, reform schools, penitentiaries, and hospitals. Most Negro U.S.O. Clubs during the war and many Army Camps.

PLAYS, MUSICALS, AND OPERAS: 12 from the Karamu Theatre to Broadway— *Mulatto, Street Scene, Troubled Island, The Barrier, Simply Heavenly. Mulatto* has been performed in Italy, the Argentine, Brazil, and currently in Japan. *The Barrier* is being given a major production on the Rome radio in November for which Meyerowitz is flying over.

TEACHER OF CREATIVE WRITING: The Laboratory School of the University of Chicago; Atlanta University.

BOOKS PUBLISHED ABROAD: in every major language, including Japanese, Chinese, Bengali, and Hindi.

UTILIZATION OF NEGRO FOLK MATERIAL: In poetry, prose *(Simple)* and song. Our *Book of Negro Folk Lore.*

Enough! . . . . . Gracias! . . . . .

> Sincerely yours,
> Lang
> Litt.D. (Um-huh!)

SPECIAL AWARD: P.S. Have lived longer than any other known Negro *solely* on writing—from 1925 to now without a regular job!!!!! (Besides fighting the Race Problem)!!!!

23 October '58

Dear Lang,

Here is the original version of "Go Tell It On the Mountain," which I sent to Allen K. to replace the one you took from the record. John Work assures me he and the Presser Company have a copyright on the middle 8 lines (so noted on the published song) of the version you recorded. This one is just as good, and I hope it will avoid even minor complications. Meanwhile, John requests the name of the record in question and the label. You gave me this data, but I can't lay hands on it at this minute. Bayard Rustin, I believe. *Please repeat.*

I was interested last night in the TV readings by Carl Sandburg on the Milton Berle show. Poetry with Jazz. Even he has gone for it. He gave 1919 as the date of his first jazz poem: "Jazz Fantasia." He also talked of the first N. O. and Memphis jazzmen to hit Chicago, at a time when he was a young newspaperman and very alert to such arrivals. Point: something of this sort for you would seem to be a natural. It would be a terrific way to boom your *Selected Poems,* if the publishers would go out of their way to set it up. I'm thinking of one of the big commercial shows at one of the prime hours. Or maybe the new Omnibus series could be sold on such a feature.

Tell Maxim the trio-bio is on the shelf for the nonce while I do my Dodd, Mead book of the first 100 years of freedom. If he thinks *that* could be translated, it will be at his disposal.

I saw my song in the *Meine Dunkle Hande,* and thanks for calling my attention to it. . . . I'm now trying to get Knopf and Harpers to let me keep about a dozen or so lines from you and Countee each in my San Mateo speech when it is published, but not a peep this far. . . . That book shop sounds like a Harlem Renaissance dream come true—almost on the very spot.

Best ever,
Arna

18 November '58

Dear Lang,

While I have not been out of Nashville in weeks, these last few have been as full of activity as if I had been barnstorming. But I did eventually write the review of *Tambourines,* which I enjoyed loudly, and enclose the carbon herewith. Your publishers are right, I think, in presenting it as a humorous novel, despite the serious note and the stark climax. For the most part it runs along like a tale told in a bar, accompanied by bursts of laughter, and I like it that way.

The card they are using for the autographing at the Market Place Gallery & Bookshop looks good. I'm glad there will be copies of *Folklore* for the occasion and regret I can't attend. My copies of *Folklore* have not yet arrived, and I have not heard what publication date was finally set. I suppose I will soon.

I see where May Sarton had a poem in the *Nation* addressed to J. Saunders Redding . . . and that young fellow named Gibson has a novel announced . . . and Harper & Brothers have accepted L. D. Reddick's biography of Martin Luther King for publication . . . and Ann Petry had a story in the *New Yorker* two weeks ago . . . and that the Yale University Press has a new book out on the Negro novel . . . and that Augie Meier (who was here at Fisk for several years) has a piece in the current *Crisis* on race relations on campuses which have integrated faculties in the South (shades of your undergraduate study at Lincoln) . . . and that Poag at A. & I., who has a good production of *Inherit The Wind* going now (lends itself well to a Negro cast), plans to do something of yours— No?

So best ever,
Arna

12 December '58

Dear Lang,

That article about you in the January 1959 issue of the *American Mercury* seems, on the surface, to be an attack. On second thought, however, it strikes me

377

as a sly plug. Indeed, it ought to sell hundreds of books! Certainly the author manages to work in some very, very complimentary remarks and implications. There is nothing like a weak or baseless attack to promote a literary (or perhaps any other kind of) reputation. Certainly, too, it is too late to wave that old red flag with any real conviction.

The same mail that brought the Library that issue brought from Allen Klots a copy of Dr. Poling's rave about *Folklore*. I just hope his words have wings. All this book needs is a good start, and a few more assists like this might do it. At any rate, I have fingers crossed and am trying all the other good luck devices.

Did you miss the big New York snow, or are you back in town?

The Herald Tribune gave good space and position to my review of *Tambourines*, and the N. Y. Times carried my review of Lorenz Graham's *South Town* on the same Sunday. . . . Ivan says Knopf reports my new *Story of Frederick Douglass* as editorially satisfactory now, following a few revisions by me. A new edition of *We Have Tomorrow* is in preparation, without the halftone photographs. I'm glad for that, since the pictures were getting dated, I thought. Houghton Mifflin is ready to start talking about my next book for them, but there's not much I can do about it till I finish my 100 Years item for Dodd.

Meanwhile speaking bids are showing up again. But none very attractive.

Best ever,
Arna

20 East 127th Street
New York 35, N. Y.
January 31, 1959
(Day before I was born)

Dear Arna:

Kindly please look in Botkin's new *Illustrated Book of Folklore* and see if the illustrations compliment our Race. I have not glimpsed it.

To add to your already over-burdened schedule, I send you under separate cover Knopf's Spring Catalogue marking my *Selected Poems* so you might send it on to the Spingarn Award Selection Committee if you deem it now the moment to make that nomination. (It is about the month, I believe). Maybe you could get Mrs. Ivan Johnson III, 697 East Vernon Avenue, Los Angeles 11, California, to make such a proposal, and perhaps one other person in the East or somewhere, so it would not all come from one source. And I'll get an Omega man from Long Island to do so, too.

Anyhow, I went to the opening of Faulkner's *Requiem for a Nun* last night. And the best critic there was a member of the Race who sat just behind me and snored real loud for *long* stretches at a time. The newspaper critics treated it all most respectfully this morning, and LOVED Bertice Redding as the cullud dope-taking servant-whore, who is called a "nigger whore" throughout the play. Curtain rises on her in the dock saying "Yas, Lawd! I believes, Lawd! I do, Lawd." Only she says *Ah do*. And somewhere along about Act 2, questioning her fervent belief, somebody asks her what she would do in heaven, and she says, "Ah kin work." (Which is about the LAST thing any Negro expects to do in heaven). So I have put Faulkner down. C. V. V. was in the first row center. Most cullud were upstairs, including me. Wish you were there.

Which gave me added material for this speech I have writ out for the African Society of Culture Writers Symposium which I see you are slated to attend in New York Feb. 28–March 1. Is that true? You're listed for another panel simultaneous with the one I am on, so I can't hear you and you can't hear me, therefore I send you my speech now. DRAFT, so gimme your suggestions and criticisms. (Adele don't like it, but doesn't dig the irony—which I really reckon I ought to let alone after *Goodbye, Lawd*—it being hard to make irony clear to most earnest people. Do you reckon?) Clarify me, please.

Looks like I am going to crown my career with a big long-playing blues record of a dozen or so of my blues from Handy to Kurt Weill, which I am looking forward to playing everyday—United Artists Records.

Dodd, Mead wants MY book, too! I said I thought they ought to schedule yours first—that mine demanded long research, deep study, and a grant.

SIN-cere-ly yours VERY truly,
Langston

2 February 1959

Dear Lang,

Your speech "On Selling Writing" is fine, fine. I don't see any serious danger of having the irony misunderstood. Besides, it will cause sparks, and that's better than causing snores. But the most remarkable thing about it, from my point of view, is that you have it down on paper one whole month ahead of time! Now that's professional, Jack. And just another reason why Dodd, Mead is absolutely right in asking for your Harlem book ahead of my 100 year opus. I strongly approve. You're a full-time writer and will get the job done on schedule. I will nag and fret and arrive at the finish like the turtle. Also, the subject matter of yours makes it a better middle book than finale. Mine is more sweeping, cover-like. In time as well as in space. So pass this along to Dodd, Mead, along with the sad fact that I will need all of next summer to finish my assignment. Fisk is just working me harder than ever before.

As soon as the spring Knopf catalog arrives, I will use it as a basis for my letter to the Spingarn Award committee. I will again call attention to the earlier and better tendency of the Committee to give the Award for a career of service rather than just a season.

Are you going to read those blues on the United Artists Record or are they going to be played and sung? In either case, I look forward to making good use of it myself. Let me know when it's to be released.

The AMSAC has asked me to participate in a panel, and I am available, but I have not yet received a letter of confirmation. I'll have to go straight to Oklahoma from there. . . . Have not ordered *Illustrated Book of Folklore* for the library yet, but will look for it next time I'm in a bookstore. . . . Happy birthday. 57 is a prime age!

Best ever,
Arna

New York—Just back
Feb. 16, 1959

Arna—
The African folks say they will write you an *official* letter re fare, etc. (I phoned as soon as I opened your note.) *Where* does their money come from? . . . . Flew back over that watery runway into LaGuardia today—which the papers now say is "a death trap." Had an all sold-out, seats-on-stage, 3 performance Poetry-Jazz deal at Karamu in Cleveland. Fine reviews! And between Chi and Cleveland did a half dozen T.V. and radio shows, mentioning our "Folklore" each time. (Sold well at Karamu House—and they are keeping it in stock for their Gift Shop.) Weather bad—4–5 hours late via plane or train—*all same* this rough winter. And me, no good on Chi program—due mostly to hospitalization of lead folk singer, and Mahalia backing out of appearing in 1st half. (After hearing the trio, I don't blame her.) So I was left stranded on that great big Orchestra Hall stage with an *integrated* (God help us) threesome that one critic said "must have been lent by the Salvation Army." But at midnight Mahalia, Sidney Poitier, Linda Darnell, Johnah Jones, Barbara Dane and I did a fine TV show that was an exciting combination of blues, gospels, and jazz.

Lang

P.S. I am afraid I am not only anti-white, but anti-Negro.

20 East 127th Street
New York 35, N.Y.
March 17, 1959,
Day of St. Patrick.

Dear Arna,
Peter Abrahams is coming to town to do a piece on Harlem for *Holiday.*
And Simple has dreamed up a new way to put Dixiecrats in the dozens—without anybody knowing he is slipping them. In fact, he has already declared that in his youth he was raised by a dear old white mammy named Mammy Faubus.

He has also discovered new words to an old Spiritual:

SWING LOW,
SWEET INTEGRATED CHARIOT,
COMING FOR TO INTEGRATE MY HOME.
 I LOOKED OVER GEORGIA
 AND WHAT DID I SEE
 COMING FOR TO INTEGRATE MY HOME?
 A BAND OF THE N.
 DOUBLE A. C. P.
 COMING FOR TO INTEGRATE MY HOME.
SWING LOW,
SWEET, SWEET, SWEET CHARIOT,
COMING FOR TO INTEGRATE MY HOME, etc.

Everybody was at the *Raisin* opening. And Charlene was at St. Philip's when Margaret Bond's *Mass in D Minor* was sung—a beautiful composition. And Charlene comme to dit.

380

Did I tell you I'm invited to Bermuda to read my poetries? And that Simple, like Mrs. Roosevelt, is doing commercials—except for free: Negro College Fund radio spot appeal, and Search for Peace, using the prayer from the first book. . . . Get Rome radio April 6th and hear *Il Mulato,* with Magda Lazlo, Rome Philharmonic, etc.

L.H.

April 29, 1959
Harlem, U.S.A.

Mon cher ami:

Mildred Stock, co-author of *Ira Aldridge,* writes wanting a collaborator on a kids' book about Blind Tom. So I've suggested that it might just maybe interest you. NOT me—I don't even want to collaborate with myself right now. . . . . . And the "folks of the other persuasion" are already preparing for our Emancipation Centennial, as various letters recently indicate, re books and TV, etc., so YOU'd better get your book done. ME, TOO! Else they'll beat us to the punch. Lawd, have mercy! How come they are always ahead? Maybe the wise thing to do is just let them run themselves out. Then we'll be all nice and rested and ready to go from there when they drop dead. Or get atomized, or Africanized.

Sincerely,
Langston

22 May 1959

Dear Lang,

Thank Raul for me for sending the Frank Horne NY address. Have passed it along. . . . And that Bermuda card was enticing to the stay-at-home traveler. I'd mighty much admire to set foot there once in life.

Meanwhile: Mildred Stock showed me her Blind Tom material a couple of years ago, but I couldn't see it as a juvenile. Rather an ugly and sordid story of shameless exploitation of Tom by shameless managers and owners. Nor did I see it as an adult collaboration for me. So I sent it back. However Miss Stock is another of those energetic people, not basically a writer, who manage to get things published somehow.

My editor at Houghton Mifflin is switching to Pantheon. Can't imagine who will take her place. It seems to be my destiny to work with *many* editors and quite a few publishers. A representative from Little, Brown was here. He also picked up on the Mahalia idea, which I vaguely mentioned in passing, and fired a letter back offering to buy it. With this third expression of definite interest by a publisher (Harper and John Day previously), I wrote Mahalia. The William Morris agency, Chicago branch, answered. They already had a writer for Mahalia's story, thanks. They also had sold it to the *Saturday Evening Post,* with book publication to follow. So once more a lady of color will be ghosted by one of the other persuasion! I can't make out for sure whether this is something they rushed around and did (there was time) *after* receiving my letter or before. Possibly I made a mistake by telling Mahalia that #3 different publishers were interested. Certainly I didn't know she was now the property of the Morris agency.

Did you miss the newspaper items about Sammy Davis, Jr. being signed up by Chase and Breen for *Free and Easy?* I hope this means we are now in business. Best story was in the Herald Trib. May 18.

Owen has apparently recovered. So all is not gloom.

I found in the attic a small part of a novel I started when I was at Oakwood in Alabama! I like it, and I'm tempted to dust it off and show it.

And I see now that Robert W. Hill has now gotten around to writing Mahalia and sent me a copy of his letter. I hadn't told him that I had written her—and heard. Brace yourself for another *His Eye Is on The Sparrow* or a *I Always Wanted to Be Somebody.*

So welcome home. Did you ever receive my *Douglass* book?

Best ever,
Arna

20 East 127th Street
New York 35, N. Y.
May 28, 1959

Mon cher ami:

Just back from Bermuda and (not for quoting, but *just* between ourselves) hardly a place to give your eye teeth to visit. Carmelish weather, English seashore type, 62° when I left this morning; sort of greenish like North Carolina, and almost as segregated, full of British crackers; also they pull in the sidewalks after 10 at night, dark and quiet as can be; bars close at 12 mostly, and only two cullud places open after midnight in the whole island where one can get a hamburger; everything imported, food from the States, music watered-down Caribbean, nothing indigenous of interest but the Gombey Dancers to be seen (other than Christmas) *only* in white night clubs where cullud can't go. The coloured 400 charming people, but selfsame faces at EVERY party. Their theme song should be, "I Grow Accustomed To Your Face." Cullud guests houses about the same as Greenwood Lake or Idlewild, prices same as in states on about everything. White and coloured rather on homely side, run-through-wringer but not rinsed complexions, sort of pug faces; no amusing dialects as in West Indies. Living standards about as here (maybe generally better) for most coloured, with great big houses for well-to-do, dully furnished, but often nice gardens, and always everywhere a view of the sea—which is blue and beautiful, but the tradewinds not very warm to me! Folks treated me so nice and gave me such cordial audiences, I reckon I ought to love their Island, too—but NOT I. Nay! Anyhow, I told them they should invite *you* down—in which case you can see for your cullud self! . . . . Do, Jesus! So Mahalia goes the way of most of the rest. Which is why I write my own autobiogs my own self! . . . . Your *Douglass* begins charmingly. Merci! And now that I'm through with lectures, I'll read it all real soon. . . . . Bermuda has the most persistent verse-writers and manuscript displayers I have *ever* encountered anywhere, and they all use the English term "scribbling" in relation to work they INSIST on showing you, one even wanting to come at 7 in the morning as I was rushing to the airport! How BEAUTIFUL Idlewild Airport this afternoon!!!! How nice this New York heat in nice noisy Harlem! BUT DON'T TELL NOBODY what I said.

Langston

Quite a few Bermudians have our *Poetry of the Negro.*

20 East 127th Street
New York 35, N. Y.
May 29, 1959

Dear Arna:

I get constant inquires from my foreign readers and translators about the *dozens,* too, and have been meaning for several years now to look up that article about the dozens which I have been told appeared about 10 years ago now (nearly as I can gather) in *The American Scholar,* by the sociologist, Dollar or Dollard, whom I am sure you know who I mean.

If you can trace it, or locate it in your library and photostat it, please send me a copy; or let me know the date and I'll look it up here; or have George Bass do so when he arrives. Seems to me Horace Cayton first told me about the piece, but didn't recall what date or issue.

Carlton Calmer, Port-au-Spain librarian, tells me the intellectuals give Charles S. Johnson's lectures there credit for bringing to power the current crop of political intellectuals now in power in Trinidad, such as Eric Williams. They claim they plan to invite me down next season. I am sure it is artistically much livelier than Bermuda, where the dampness makes even the cigarettes almost unlightable, let alone the creative flair.

I have got a $400 piece to write between now and Monday (this being Friday night) as it is due June 1 at the latest. So I got to get to work. Officially, I am not back home yet, and the phone is still unplugged.

Barthé, I hear, is in town on a brief visit. They say he lives like a feudal lord in Jamaica. (Servants are very cheap there, so can't say I blame him).

Langston

P.S. The typing of my plays for microfilming was begun during my absence, and a note from Mr. Vosper indicates that so far Fisk and Yale will participate, and very likely the Schomburg—making the cost about $50.00 per institution, I believe. Incidentally, I thought for historical purposes, it would be interesting to include that commissioned Federal Theatre adaptation of your and Countee's *St. Louis Woman* which Clarence Muse had me do for his unit in Los Angeles, although it was never produced, as Federal Theatre ended before his long-running *Run Little, Chillun* completed its record run—and which *St. Louis Woman,* as you probably recall, was to have followed.

Yes, Aunt Toy has saved for me the notices about Sammy Davis and *Free and Easy.* Let's hope it really is about to roll this time.

Things look hopeful for a major producer for *Tambourines to Glory,* too, and I am to resume talks concerning it this week. But you know, "many a slip. . . . . . ."

It is as hot here as Bermuda was chilly, so I am getting thawed out at last. Or

383

melted down, one. . . . . Raoul has gone to Cleveland, and my Puerto Rican boy to the army this week end. Everybody always leaves just when needed most; Adele conspicuous by her absence. So if and when Bass arrives, I think I will chain him to the third floor staircase permanently.

6 June 1959

Dear Lang,
I guess I never told you that Larry Lipton was on the Illinois Writers' Project. He was eager, ambitious. . . . A bit later, when he met and married Craig Rice, the successful mystery story writer, there was an outlandish story of how each had tried to hoodwink the other and how. . . . they wound up with each other just as they were. . . . Back there on Erie street in Chicago he had been a great admirer of Dick Wright. After Dick's *Black Boy,* Larry had written and talked about a parallel work of his own which he was calling *Jew Boy.* I don't think it got published—at least not under that title. Eventually, I believe, he did get a novel published, but it was not widely noticed. Now comes this Beatnik thing and a poem in the Atlantic. I've seen the latter, May issue, I believe, and it's quite good. Apparently the Beat thing is taken seriously too. So maybe old Larry is a late bloomer! As I recall, he and I used to talk about your poetry back on the project. He also knew Nelson Algren, Jack Conroy and Lou (Gig) Gilbert. Also Studs Terkel. I used to see Craig occasionally too. She may have been older than Larry. At least she had some children, nearly grown, by an earlier marriage, and I had the impression that Larry had been a bachelor up to then. But to get finally to the point: the beatnik vocabulary is obviously right out of Negroana. They have scarcely added an inflection. They are *not* a very talented group as a whole, in my opinion. Bohemians without the creative ability that is the traditional and classical justification for bohemianism.
I'm writing Horace about the "dozens." Did not find in the mags. Hope he replies. Thanks again for the low down on Bermuda. I'll pine no longer.
Best ever,
Arna

20 East 127th Street
New York 35, N. Y.
June 23, 1959

Dear Arna:
Allen Klots phoned today to discuss a possible *Famous Negro Athletes* for their young folks *Famous* series. That subject is not down my alley, but I told him of your long interest in sports from the jockeys at the turn of the century through the boxers of the twenties up to current baseball. So if Dodd Mead should approach you, and it is something you want to do, when the time comes I will lend you a couple of files I have of sports clippings right up to the current Patterson fight.
Incidentally, Allen tells me they are about to print up a second edition of our
384

Folklore. So if you have any corrections to make in it, they should be sent him soon as possible. The credit for Dorothy Rosenberg's poem and a few other little things will be straightened out.

Aunt Toy has departed for California, driving with Kid Thompson (Florence Mills' brother).

I reckon I will go to Newport for the JAZZ FESTIVAL July 2–5.

Saw Ralph Ellison at P.E.N. Exec Board meeting the other day. He's to be P.E.N. delegate to the Frankfurt Conference in Germany in August, returning to continue teaching at Bard next fall. Looks fat, fine, and worried (about the Hungarians and such) as usual.

I'm to review *Trumbull Park* for the Herald Trib, having already read it when I reviewed it for *Jet* which Irita Van Doren says that (being special circulation) won't matter to her.

Carlo, by the way, was 79 on June 17th.

Hello to Alberta. . . . . .

Sincerely,
Langston

20 East 127th Street
New York 35, N. Y.
July 21, 1959

Arna:

I was wondering if you got home O.K., so it was good to have your letter today from Nashville. It's HOT and HUMID here, too, but I must say I like it better than the somewhat chilly and damp climate at Newport. Tonight Azikewi had a party of his own just for friends at the Waldorf's Empire Room, with an after-party in his suite, which was lots of fun, mostly Lincoln fellows and Eartha there—whom it was my pleasure to escort home. Saw Bunche at the downstairs party, also Donald Wyatt and Tyus whom I told of your Colorado sojourn. He in turn told me about your speech on RATS when you first went to Fisk—a tale I had never heard before. George has also been telling me some amusing Fisk tales. Two of his fraternity brothers are rooming here with us while working in New York for the summer: Richard Jones and Ted Smith from Fisk. And last night Alvin Cooper called up. He now has three children—in three years—so isn't writing any more.

I talked to Allen Klots on the phone today and gave him the name of the fellow whom you quote: Stanley Hyman, who is on the *New Yorker* and whom I saw at Newport. Allen will make the insertion. If you have any more, airmail them to him. Seems I spotted a few typos, but can't find them now.

Did you get a Doubleday check this week? Nice! And did you hear any more about the Dodd sports book? I think you could write a nice one.

Having closed my social season tonight, I will now get down to work for real tomorrow—except I've got to finally go have a couple of teeth pulled out I've put off all winter. Always something!

Hope to see you-all in August.

Langston

20 East 127th Street
New York 35, N.Y.
August 17, 1959

Dear Arna,

No chance to get to Wildwood—usual busy summer, trying to catch up on last winter's left-overs, plus new little odds and ends like an Odetta TV script, a Belafonte album blurb, a Trib book review, etc., and on Thursday I have to go to Boston for the Newport Festival there and Board meeting. Big Miller, the blues singer who made my album, is due to sing a couple of my songs on the Festival. . . . Meanwhile, I've finished rewriting the play-with-music version of *Tambourines to Glory* and got it off to the downtown typist this morning, since the contract is now in the works, with advance due and payable. . . . . *Shakespeare in Harlem,* the Dallas little theatre version of my poems is now in rehearsal here (with a very cullud cast) for two showcase performances at the White Barn Theatre in Westport on August 29–30, preceded by Butterfly McQueen and others doing monologues, etc., since mine is only a one-acter. . . . I'm on *"Harlem: A Self-Portrait"* Tuesday 7:30 CBS Channel 2, filmed here in my studio. Hope they don't edit out all they recorded for 3 hours to get 10 minutes for use, if that, in the end. . . . . Hey, you better come on up to New York and see what is happening to your show. How can you be so near—and not get here? Everytime I turn around I hear something new about *Free and Easy,* auditions, etc., and just now I was talking to Melbe Liston on the phone (the trombone girl who's wonderful) and she says she is opening with it in October in Amsterdam with Quincy Jones (wonderful, too) Orchestra—new big band he's just organizing. Looks like you are going to have a great production. . . . . When do you leave Wildwood?. . . . . I'm invited to Trinidad for lectures in the fall. That ought to be fun! Best regards to the family,

Langston

Afro-American Committee for
Gifts of Art and Literature to
Ghana
555 Edgecombe Avenue
New York 32, N. Y.
October 10, 1959

DORIS M. DUBISSETTE
Chairman
LAWRENCE ALLEN
CHARLES ALSTON
IDA CULLEN COOPER
ROBERT COOPER
AARON DOUGLAS
ADELE GLASGOW
LANGSTON HUGHES
JEAN BLACKWELL HUDSON
ZELL INGRAM
ESTELLE M. OSBORNE
LOUISE T. PATTERSON

Dear Arna:

Being a writer myself, I know how many requests come in daily. But this is something I and the other members of this Committee feel (and very much hope)

that you might wish to be a part of by contributing an autographed copy of one (or more if you wish) of your books, and especially a page (or pages) of a hand corrected manuscript of a portion of your work, for the guidance and inspiration of the young writers of Ghana.

In recognition of Ghana's leadership toward African freedom and the advancement of culture there, this Committee was formed to assemble a representative collection of paintings, books and manuscripts by outstanding American artists and writers of color to send as a collective gift on the occasion of the celebration of Ghana's second independence year in 1960. We believe that such a contribution by leading Afro-American artists and writers will be greatly valued by our African brothers.

The Ambassador of Ghana to the United States had officially assured us that his government will welcome our gift and will facilitate its shipment and proper exhibition in Ghana, as well as careful housing and permanent cataloguing for scholarly use there. Our Committee plans to assemble the books, manuscripts, and paintings by early December of this year in time for a New York showing prior to its shipment to Ghana.

It is our sincere hope that you will join with us to make this project successful. Since we are writing only to a limited number, we will welcome your early and we hope favorable response. Books and manuscripts from writers may be sent directly to me: Langston Hughes, 20 East 127th Street, New York 35, New York, as soon as you wish.

With cordial regards,

> Sincerely yours,
> Langston

My 57th Birthday, '59

Dear Lang,

The sun do move! Anyhow, thanks for your card and I'm going to send you some books for Ghana right soon now. Maybe tomorrow. Thanks too for the sports items, all most interesting and all going instantly into my new box of lore on great Negro athletes. Incidentally, Allen Klots has sent me copies of their *Women of Modern Science* and *Modern American Career Women,* indicating that these represent the level and type of book they have in mind for my job.

I celebrated my birthday by cancelling three lecture engagements: Tugaloo, Vicksburg and New Orleans. All for the week before Thanksgiving. Can't afford the time, now that the literary pot is boiling again. But I do plan to fill the engagement in Philadelphia on the 27th of this month, and I hope to get up to NYC right after, if not before. *Free and Easy* is calling rehearsals on the 26th.

The acquiring of *Tambourines* by the Theatre Guild is most exciting. And that this news should tie-in with the excellent reviews of the book in England is right as rain. It's all a perfect outcome, and should compensate adequately for your having to return that Hollywood money.

I'm reading Chester Himes' *The Real Cool Killers,* offered here as "An Avon Original 35¢". It is the book that won the French prize and made Chester the toast of Jean Cocteau, Jean Giono, etc. It really is a good performance by Chester, real good. For sheer narrative drive Chester takes nobody's dust. But what the

N. Y. Times mystery reviewer took as a distorted view of the U. S., I take as a kind of non-representational art—and effective as employed in this story.
So more anon.

Best ever,
Arna

November 6, 1959

Dear Arna:
Dorothy sailed today on a freighter, quite a few folks down to see her off, including me. Her address from here on in (since she says she intends to reside there) is:

Miss Dorothy Peterson,
Hotel Madrid
San Pablo 1,
Seville, SPAIN.

And noon tomorrow I am off to Trinidad—if I can make it up in time. Got a week's work to do yet tonight before I can leave. And Adele hasn't come yet to take final letters. And it is raining. But I've half packed anyhow.
Looks like Sugar Ray might play BUDDY in my show. He phoned yesterday for the book to read. And seemed interested and excited.
I'll be back Thanksgiving eve. So drop me a line. Ida says why didn't you let her know you were in town? Leah told her. She hasn't seen a rehearsal yet, but I told her it is going to be real GOOD.
First Guild show, *Tallest Tree,* is a flop—7 bad reviews. And the Kitt show is not faring too well out of town. If mine is the 3rd, as it now so seems, maybe that will be the charm! Langner had a cocktail party for his new book yesterday at the Guild—*The Importance of Wearing Clothes.* I met Paulette Goddard there, beautiful as ever.

Sincerely,
Langston

9 November '59

Dear Lang,
I aimed to write you before you took off, but I never did catch up with myself after returning home last week. And it was all I could do to keep the University from sending me to Atlanta to visit high schools for THREE whole days as part of the annual search for talent. I enjoy the high school kids, but this is no way to get a manuscript out!
So greetings on your return from the Indies. As a lover of islands and palm trees and tropical skies and pirates and pieces-of-eight, I can only envy you. I hope you bring with you a parrot and a bottle of rum, not to mention the latest literary lore from down there.
I also hope that by now Sugar Ray Robinson has been signed up for *Tambou-*
388

rines to Glory. He'll be just right for *Buddy.* And he's bound to be a draw in his first play. Have you considered Juanita Hall as one of your lady evangelists? If she still has her vocal chords, she ought to be able to do a good job in one of the roles. Sugar Ray will have to have seasoned actors around him.

Thanks for the Dan Burley column on athletes. It makes several points I can use. So I'm setting it aside carefully.

Georgia Douglas Johnson came through handsomely on the Pinchback questions I asked. A most fascinating character Pinchback. I'd give anything if I could get Jean Toomer to say something about his grand parents, but I don't suppose there is any hope. I suspect I know *some* things about them that he does not know. I have found a file of Pinchback's newspaper for 1870 to 1882. Wonderful coverage of the Reconstruction! Gives me many ideas.

More presently.

Best ever,
Arna

18 November 1959

Dear Lang,

Welcome to winter! It's freezing down here, and I don't imagine it's much warmer in New York. So I hope you've soaked up enough sun to last a few months.

I've been reading almost everywhere about your TV program with Odetta, but I did not catch it. Too early Sunday morning, I gather, and besides I was not alerted in advance.

The *Free & Easy* company flew to Amsterdam, leaving midnight Sunday, on a chartered Belgian plane. Final contract agreements for this production did not reach me till the following Tuesday. However, by then everyone else had signed, so I added my name and initials here and there and returned the copies other than mine just yesterday. Leah and Ida and others saw a run through just before departure and say they were most favorably impressed. So yesterday I dug out my old passport and set it aside in a convenient place, just in case. But I won't make any plans to travel till I hear something positive from abroad!

I'm fascinated by what I'm learning about Pinchback, and I'm giving much more space than planned in the 100 Year book. He deserves it. He is important to the story. Besides, exciting things happened to him, and he had a lively youth and early manhood. He may have grandchildren (other than Jean Toomer) who are passing for white, and this may explain the silence and the mystery that surround his memory. The one thing Georgia Douglas Johnson has not told me is whether or not his two sons have or had children (Jean's mother was his daughter). Pinchback is buried in a white cemetery in New Orleans, as were many colored of his era and earlier, and the record keepers are close-mouthed about giving information on family connections down there—as you might expect. But Pinch himself was a race man heart and soul, though he looked sort of Spanish or Italian.

Best ever,
Arna

20 East 127th Street
New York 35, N. Y.
November 27, 1959

Arna:

I got back in time for Thanksgiving Dinner at home, chilly here after a SWELTERING 36 hours in San Juan spent mostly drinking rum on the rocks in an amusing water-front club frequented by colored seamen from the sailing ships that ply the Caribbean and speak all sorts of quaint English dialects and are wonderful friendly fellows all of whom seem to have brothers or sisters in Harlem. I failed to see the University or anything but the distant wall of the Fortaleza. But in Martinique I drove to Mount Pele and saw the town it burnt out in 1902 and ate lobster by the sea there. But couldn't get up the energy to go call on Aimee Cesaire (who's now mayor of Fort-de-France) and whose son runs the Bamboo Club night spot for tourists which is the only place on the island open late. But I bought a half dozen books by Martinique authors of color. . . . I learn on my return that Langner's gone to the hospital for a rest so the Guild's made no progress on *Tambourines.* But *Simply Heavenly* has been bought for the Christmas week "Play-of-the-Week" on TV's Channel 13, David Susskind production, and is already in rehearsal to be filmed with most of the original Broadway cast except for Fred O'Neal who is Boyd. (And as you see from enclosures, it is now running in Prague). . . . . Glad Mrs. Johnson helped on Pinchback. It occurs to me that maybe this fellow who worked on the WPA Federal Writers histories and guides and was Lyle Saxon's right hand man might have information, too: whom you know, don't you? If not, you should. Very interesting guy. Write him, or run down and see him, since you're not far. . . . . Man, I am beat. The Trinidadians kept me on the go, ending with a dinner to meet the Premier and the Manley's there for opening of Parliment.

Langston

20 East 127th Street
New York 35, N. Y.
December 13, 1959

Dear Arna:

Ida Cullen tells me she is going to Paris in January for the opening there of *Free and Easy,* and she wonders if you are going, too? Are you? If so, take a couple of sweaters along, as they don't have much heat there indoors in the winter time.

Leah wrote me a very nice note about the TV showing of *Simply Heavenly* that has been going on all week.

Just came from a prospective investors' cocktail party for the proposed off-Broadway production of *Shakespeare in Harlem* that they're hoping to bring to the boards in late January. Party was in Harlem, and out of it came a few promised investors. Budget is only $15,000. They plan to use "God's Trombones" as a frontispiece.

Tambourines is awaiting Pearl Bailey's doctor's decision as to when she's had enough rest to resume work—or to make up her mind if she wishes to do a Broadway play. Meanwhile, they're contemplating a lesser name.

390

I think I'll flee the struggle right after Christmas and take a jet to California and see my Uncle Johnny for a change. Might even settle there amidst the smog —for a week at least. . . . . Eartha's play closed last night. Papers say Josephine Baker is making a N.Y. return in February. Her Paris show is a BIG hit, really teriffic, everybody says.

Sincerely yours truly,
Langston

16 December '59

Dear Lang,

Era Bell's Christmas card is just about the most: Been nowhere, done nothing, sending Christmas cards to nobody! It certainly expresses *me*.

[Some producers] are carrying on worse than Negroes, fussing and fighting and damning one another to hell. Leah and Abe Berman (Harold & Johnny's agent) are firing cables at them and trying to make them act like folks and stop disgracing the (*not* colored) race. Anyhow, I'm not venturing overseas just yet. I hope it's just try-out nerves and that it will blow over, and on that wish I'm keeping my fingers crossed. However I'm writing Ida today.

It will certainly be nice if *Shakespeare in Harlem* can go on off-Broadway pending developments on *Tambourines.* And above all, I hope it will stay on till I can get to NYC again! Pearl would be great for your lady evangelist. So would Juanita Hall, if she has enough of her singing voice left.

I think your "Poem for a Man" will be effective when it is read in Carnegie Hall. It also sizes up Phil Randolph just about as history will, I believe.

But did you read Karl Shapiro's fine, hard-hitting front-page essay in last Sunday's New York Times *Book Review?* A terrific call to arms of all whose poetry-hunger has become an unsatisfied craving and have been fed straw by the cohorts of Eliot and Pound and the "new critics". I am writing him (Shapiro) a letter today too. It would be good to have him say such things as he has been writing lately right here within shouting distance of the bailiwick of the Fugitives. I wish you (as if you didn't already have enough letters to write) would encourage him to accept our invitation. . . . . And speaking of invitations, I have not heard from Stearns. . . . So more anon.

Best Ever,
Arna

20 East 127th Street
New York 35, N. Y.
December 17, 1959

Dear Arna:

An African Treasury; articles, essays, stories, and poems by black Africans, is what I've got spread all over the room now, as your letter arrives, and on the table is the Poetry Section which I'm putting into sequence. In the newspaper pile on the floor is the Shapiro piece in last Sunday's *Times* which I haven't had a chance to read yet. But such-like opinions as you say he expresses must be in the air these days. In the current *Indian P.E.N.* recently arrived I read a quote from Earl Wavell: "Poetry should dance in the mind, and blow one a kiss; or gallop to adventure with a cheer; or whisper gently of sad things past; not shuffle or slouch past with dark incomprehensible mutterings." Which I think is charmingly said.

But lemme get back to my work! The phone has been ringing constantly all day, fact, all week. TV "exposure" (as they say in the trade) brings 50-11 more letters and phone calls than books do. So for the weekend I'm cutting my phone off and posting notices all over the house "OUT OF TOWN" as I GOT to get this anthology all in by Christmas so I can go see my Uncle Johnny for New Years—on a jet, Window Seat No. 14. (But it *just now* occurred to me, I'll be sitting NEXT to *13!¡%ı?!*)

Lord have mercy! I hope *Free and Easy* don't become a free-for-all battle royal way over there where the LAW is different.

Era Bell just phoned me from Chicago and I told her how amusing her card is. But be of good cheer—the New Year is here!

All *but* 4 writers (3 of whom are abroad) sent Gifts for Ghana. Even Baldwin from Paris. Our greatest one here didn't. Maybe might will yet. (Guess who?)

Langston

LETTERS
1960-1967

20 East 127th Street
New York 35, N. Y.
January 21, 1960

Dear Arna:

Was way over in Brooklyn tonight for rehearsal of the Poetry-Choir program. Back at 1:30 and revised part of *Shakespeare in Harlem* for which I hear they've got the money and go into rehearsal next week for off-Broadway opening mid-February. Then on my way to bed I started to read the *Cool World,* novel version, and just finished it now at 8:30 in the A. M. so am *really* on my way to bed. (Someone at rehearsal lent it to me.)

Play script is much *more* repellent than novel, although it uses most of the dialogue. But, lacking the asides and overtones, it comes out (in my opinion) a holy horror with nobody at all sympathetic or likable—just a script full of unpleasant kids, each one depicting a vice of one sort or another—a kind of colored juvenile *Beggars Opera* without that play's sardonic humor and social commentary. (Or am I becoming oversensitive racially, and NAACP-ish? I just hate to see a whole stage full of Harlem kids at a big Broadway theatre—in front of white folks—depicted that way—without a single decent one in the bunch). None are *that* bad.

Oh, well, set back 50 years again! The Race! But the last setback—when it comes—will be the boomerang that will set back the setter-backers! Some old slingshot somewhere in the world is going to throw the rock that slays Goliath. Selah! A 14 year old strumpet and a 15 year old pimp and a 16 year old junkie whose brother goes to Fisk is just *un peu trop!* Didn't Lillian Smith's loose young lady go to Fisk, too? Why do they pick on *you-all* so much—suppose to be our most polished college? (It turned out Du Bois, but nobody puts him in a play). I think they're out to do us in, myself. I know you have a more protective feeling than I toward liberals. Didn't somebody say, "I can take care of my enemies, but God protect me from my friends."

And I hear it's got a movie sale, already!

You're colleged. If I'm over-sensitive, tell me. I tries to be objective.

But, honest, I never saw or read a white play about so many assorted bad people *so young* on any stage. Even in *The Bad Seed* and *Tea and Sympathy* and *Hatful of Rain* and *Black Orpheus* and *The Respectful Prostitute,* somebody is trying to do right.

Respectfully yours,
James L. Hughes
(My full and legal name)

Hy, now—

Bomb scare at the program in Grand Rapids yesterday (Sunday) afternoon! Anonymous phone call a few minutes before starting time to the church—an *interracial* very old, very rich, Baptist church. But the minister said the same thing happened when they presented Robert Frost—so we figure somebody in town just doesn't like poets. Anyhow, we started on time, audience never knew, although half the police force turned out to search the halls and basement while I was speaking. Never tell what you can run into on a lecture tour. Here in Buffalo there's *tons* of new snow. No taxis, no red caps at station. This is my *last* season (as Du Bois has also just announced). Like Pearl Bailey, "Ah'm taired." Hey, now! Of course, if Fisk invited me—

Lang

20 East 127th Street
New York 35, N. Y.
March 7, 1960

Dear Arna:

Growing out of the *Spirituals Spectacular* which I did in Brooklyn a few weeks ago, Gary Kramer of Atlantic Records has conceived the idea of doing an LP with my poetry combined with songs by the student Fisk Jubilee Singers, and will probably be writing their director, Matthew Kennedy, about it, and the possibility of recording the singers this Spring at Fisk. I have suggested to Mr. Kramer that you do the liner notes for the album, and have told him about your beautiful book on the original Singers. So I am simply alerting you, in case you hear tell of it further.

Been rushed and harrassed with show business details for the past week, so haven't had time to work out details of album with Kramer, (and can't now until I come back from Atlanta and my Spelman program for which I'm now packing to depart). *Shakespeare in Harlem* closed with one of the lady backers (a Mrs. Cohen) seizing the box office door and refusing to be kept out, creating quite a scene in the lobby. Says she is going to sue producers for inaccurate accounts. . . . . Meanwhile the pending Coffee Concerts concert version of *The Barrier* blew up at its first rehearsal with Muriel Rahn and Meyerowitz exploding at each other, Charlotte Holloman weeping, others pacing the floor in Mrs. Harper's living room. (I were not present—and have shut off my phone to keep from being bothered with either them or Mrs. Cohen for the past two days). . . . In midst of all this, a sudden spurt of reading *Tambourines to Glory* for summer production up with a long conference at the Guild today again. . . . . So I really don't mind heading for the troubled South tomorrow for a breather.

I hear tell Ida Cooper's husband is quite ill again. . . . . Also that another one of those cullud shows in Europe has folded. . . . . This is a hard year for shows, both at home and abroad. . . . . . But I have lately been sent a novel, a foreign play, and a musical to consider working on for production next season. I think

I will turn them ALL down—and write myself a nice quiet prose book all my own.

How are you-all making out with the sit-downs? The papers here make it sound most exciting. One North Carolina college on my coming itinerary has written in advance asking me not to stir the troubled waters further when I come to read my poetries—and it wasn't Chapel Hill—but one of the cullud ones. I writ back I am just reading my same old "deep like the rivers."

Sincerely,
Langston

11 March '60

Dear Lang,

Snow is half a foot deep. It's been like this a couple of weeks. Just one snow after another. We have had eight, I believe, this winter, and the total snowfall is a record for Tennessee. So every flake that falls from now on—and it's falling now —breaks a record. The weather has been such a big thing here, with cars stuck in the snow everywhichaway, schools (public) not being able to hold, help not getting to work, it has competed with the sit-in demonstrations and the arrests and all. Boy, have we had it!

One whole wall of the new Student Union is covered with telegrams the kids have received from all over, including long ones from other student bodies like Harvard, U. of Chicago, Oberlin, Rutgers, UCLA, and the rest. Reading them almost moves to tears. And the adult Negroes of the town are showing their support in scores of ways. For example, the Meharry doctors quickly raised several thousand dollars and put it at Fisk's disposal for bonds, bales, fines, etc. A Pomona faculty member called me by phone (I'm faculty adviser to the exchange students) to offer the same for the Pomona kids who went to jail along with ours. Just drama all over the place. Meanwhile, here, the trials have been continued for a few weeks to await the results of the efforts by the Mayor's committee (our prexy and the prexy of A & I are the Negroes on it). So hold your hat.

Leah's letter last week said that Stanley Chase had not yet returned from Europe and she had been unable to get more information, but his lawyer expects him soon. The latter indicated that while Chase is said to have lost the whole financing of the *Free & Easy* production abroad, some *300 Grand,* he still says he intends to go on with plans for the production in the U.S. Of course, I don't know what to believe. But I believe I told you the first check was *good,* and I understand the French Society has collected the royalty for us on the later performances. We shall see.

Sorry to hear about Bob Cooper's illness. I'll send a card. Also about the feudin' and fightin' in or near the box office of *Shakespeare in Harlem.* And at the *Barrier's* rehearsal. Folks must be frustrated. They're even snapping at each other in faculty meetings and around the campus (the older ones, that is). I have been saying it was due to all this snow, but since it's happening elsewhere, maybe it's something else. I wish they'd let me get some writing done.

That record featuring you with the JUBILEE SINGERS should be a winner. I'm always available, should Kramer want me to write the notes for the album. And

397

I have a lecture in Dallas coming up the 28th of this month, I believe. Let's hope the weather clears up a little by then.

Meanwhile, I hope you're back from your swing South.

> Best ever,
> Arna

Friday the 25th of March '60

Dear Lang,

Police cars are circling around the campus at this moment and rumors are flying. I have heard nothing from the horse's mouth, but the drifting word is that our prexy, who's away attending something in Denver, I believe, has resigned from the Mayor's committee on the sit-in demonstrations with a statement to the effect that the Committee wasn't getting anywhere. The further word is that the kids are getting ready to demonstrate again and possibly "fill up the jails." If true, it's all pretty rough. Especially so in the wake of what happened in South Africa. Many of us had hoped that Nashville just might sober up and decide to set a good example. Obviously that is not going to happen right away.

The hassle among the *Free & Easy* parties is almost as perplexing. Conferences are still underway. Breen and Chase refuse to even meet, much less settle their quarrel. Leah and Harold Arlen and Abe Berman, I understand, are all in there punching from their shoestrings. Imagine, if you can, the obscure, half-forgotten author of the original story picking this time to assert that from now on he wants a say in what is to be done with his property! But that's what I have just written. Maybe it will help them get their minds off themselves. Maybe they'll join up and turn on me. This is my Mou Mou blood coming out.

I'm flying to Dallas Sunday, but I'm thinking of taking a roomette to NY in April to see if I can get some creative thinking done en route, if not indeed some writing. A dry land version of a freighter trip! I believe I told you that ALA meets in Montreal in June and that I plan to take Alberta. But prior to that Constance has a graduation and a wedding scheduled. I'll be needing a short vacation, no doubt.

> Best ever,
> Arna

Sunday, 7-17-60

Dear Lang,

I treasure my copy of the *Treasury,* and I hope it will get the sale it deserves. The *First Book of Africa* has not come yet, but I look forward to it.

Which brings me promptly to an important item. Can you give me the *present* address of Peter Abrahams or tell me how he can most quickly be reached by mail? I'd like to ask a few questions of him before I go to Africa.

That piece about Harlem by Jimmy Baldwin in the July *Esquire* (not *Holiday,* as I believe you-all said in commenting on it at your house) is quite a piece of writing, despite the reactions from the Riverton. What he says cannot help but disturb up-town and down-town alike. I'm glad he wrote it. One of his strongest

398

efforts, in my opinion. . . . In the same issue there is an unusual short story by Truman Capote. Don't miss it. And in the August issue I have just read the piece about David Susskind, which mentions the *Raisin in the Sun* production. Has your work with it been completed?

Meanwhile, Countee's flirtation with party politics in 1932 does indeed give food for thought, considering what went ahead as well as what followed. Obviously his convictions were sound, but I still think the poet, who cannot so easily switch gears or reverse his field with changing scenes, might serve his cause better by highlighting long-range rather than short-range objectives. Let the journalists and stump speakers hammer away on short-term business like elections. Their words are written on the wind and will not come back to haunt them, and if so they can explain them away.

Alberta is nursing and being treated for a painful bite by our cat, who previously had always been gentleness itself. Connie is trying to get a job in San Diego during this lean year of her husband's internship in the General Hospital there. My father is in the sanitarium near his home in San Bernardino and losing ground steadily. He was 89 on the 9th of July. Alex has a little summer job, and I have a BIG one, as you might guess.

Did you by any chance clip and save the *Post* series on THURGOOD a couple of weeks ago? And if so, would you mind letting me copy it? I would like to put him and Adam C. P. in my *100 Year* book and am looking for vivid new stuff on them. Sharp angles. Intimate details.

So more anon.

Best ever,
Arna

20 East 127th Street
New York 35, N. Y.
August 2, 1960

Dear Arna:

4 A.M. and I've just waded through a big box of URGENT mail—answered about 15 letters—and it still looks as if it were untouched. So I now give up and write to YOU. Tomorrow I go to Tanglewood for the premier of my Meyerowitz opus, *Port Town*—was supposed to be there tonight for dress rehearsal, but couldn't make it; had an appointment with Denis Mitchell from London about doing a Harlem film for BBC-TV. And last night a music conference with my *Tambourines* folks—as auditions for singers start next week, and rehearsals August 15th. With all that, about a third of my mail seems to be summer school folks, researchers in cullud lit., etc, in town now who want appoints *right away quick*—and how am I going to see all these folks? Tell me? You're colleged. Not to speak of all the foreigners who are doing papers on us cullud these days, and need reams of material! I think I'll begin doing like Covarrubias did, or Marian Anderson does, and just not answer NOBODY. . . . . I've got the beautiful de Carava photos of *Raisin* in Chicago spread out on my mantle piece to do captions for, too, and nary one done yet. And right beside my typewriter a swell musical script by Ben Hecht wanting lyrics that I'm turning down—since they wish a RUSH, rush, job. Anyhow, I can do my own scripts and lyrics. And Andy Razaf's manuscript that has

399

been with me to Trinidad, Puerto Rico, Chicago, and California and back—and is still not even opened. And he's calling up from L. A. every other week about it! ! ! ! ! Do, Jesus! I think I'd better go to Africa, too! Man, I envy you.

Saw Doug. He looks fine. I hope to have him to dinner or something before he leaves.

Tambourines going *too* smoothly, so far. Hope I don't get one of those psychosomatic knees like you did during *St. Louis Woman.* I've just been playing the records again tonight. Such lovely songs. That show deserves a beautiful revival.

Did I tell you I might be on the Jack Paar Show—maybe with Olga James for whom I've written a new song for the show, we might preview there on TV. Decision still pending..... Will you, by any chance, be up this way around Labor Day, so you can see *Tambourines* at Westport? .... And how did Alberta come out from the cat bite? .... Leslie wrote she was ill, when he advised me he'd be coming through town and would phone. I never got the call. ... And your father?..... About Thurgood in the *Post,* I missed it, being out of town, so don't have it. Wish I did, as I gave the guy my Lincoln memories of him..... WHEN do you go to Africa? And where? Let me give you my writers' addresses in whichever countries you go, before you leave. Hugh Smythe will probably be back soon, and can be helpful, too.

Bed time! So, till next time—

Lang

P.S. You are so wise re Countee.

5 August 1960

Dear Lang,

I expect to be working right up to leaving time (Sep. 18 or thereabouts) on the Dodd, Mead book, so the stop-over in NYC will probably not be long on the out-bound trip. Still, if your show is near enough at that time, we would certainly do our best to get an initial look at it. Meanwhile, thanks for Peter Abrahams' Kingston address. I'll drop him a note right away.

Our base in Africa is to be Makerere College, Kampala, Uganda (roughly October 2 or 3 to Nov. 27 or 28), followed by a fortnight in Kenya—address to be determined. I will be grateful for leads to writers, etc. thereabouts as well as a few good names in London, Paris and Rome, the first two of which we hope to touch going and the latter on the return. Also anything from Hugh.

Alberta's unusual cat bite gave her a lot of pain, but it seems about well now ... Leslie flew to Florence, Italy, for a month of seminars of some kind. You may hear from him when he comes back. I believe he intends to spend about a month around New York. He is beginning a sabbatical semester which lasts till February. ... My father is still in the hospital, growing weaker. Ruby and Owen have visited him and are now driving back to Washington. Connie and her husband are standing near-by in San Diego, where he is interning and she is looking for a job.

Seems that *St. Louis Woman* is on the shelf till the Breen-Chase rights revert (2 years), their differences being past conciliation, but we are looking ahead.

Meanwhile, I'm looking around for some quick contracts I can sign to give me a few extra dollars for the trip. Which means I'll probably return to the U. S. as a slave.

You should send a copy of the "Simple and the Congo" to Ralph Bunche. He'd like it, I'm sure, as I do. I'm also glad the *African Treasury* is getting attention. It's solid, as well as timely, reading.

What is *Port Town,* a cantata, an opera or what? Good title, in any case.

Not to add to your list of callers, but because I think you will find him interesting and unobtrusive, I'd like to mention George Gardiner. He is a very literary former Fisk student who has been keeping the Negro collection room in the library for us this year—and handling your manuscripts and other items— and who is a stranger to New York (though he originated in Boston). George is headed that way by bus and hopes to shake hands with you, Braithwaite, Jean Blackwell Hudson and possibly others during a week's vacation in the city. I believe George Bass knows him. I believe you will quickly see why George Gardiner has been so helpful to us. He loves the lore that he handles. He has done much work on the CSJ papers.

So more anon.

Best ever,
Arna

P. S. I can't believe that Africa is any hotter or more humid than is Nashville at this moment.

20 East 127th Street
New York 35, N. Y.
August 20, 1960

Dear Arna:

Will you and Alberta be in this neck of the woods the week of September 5–10? *Tambourines* opens at Westport (about 40 minutes from Mount Vernon) on Monday, September 5, playing the week. I'd like to invite you-all and Paul and Sonia (the latter in any case) any night you can come. The opening if you can make it. So let me know soon so I can reserve seats.

First week of rehearsals have gone very well—no blowups at all—yet! And I think Hazel Scott is going to be very, VERY good. All, in fact. And Clara Ward should floor them sitting way up high singing and playing drums. Only principals this week, the choral rehearsals begin next week under Eva Jessye's direction.

Let me know when you'll be in New York—even aside from the show—I want to know.

Hope your book is going well. *Tambourines* has kept me so busy I've been missing my *Defender* deadline. Well, one can't do everything! Getting too age-able.

LeRoi Jones and Richard Gibson both lost their jobs for going to Cuba! Probably not job-safe to go to the CONGO either right now. "*The* problem of the 20th Century. . . ." said old Doc 50 years ago. He sho did!

Lang

20 East 127th Street
New York 35, N. Y.
August 26, 1960
4 A.M.

Hey, Arna!

Rehearsals going FINE! And until yesterday I thought the cast *not* actors but ladies and gentlemen. But in one day, three blow-ups and threatened kickings of mutual so-and-so's! However, this morning all calm. And this afternoon came the first complete run-through of the show without stopping—which I hear tell was thrilling. (I was home meeting an urgent deadline on a promised record liner of the Abyssinian Gospel Choir of Newark John Hammond recently recorded.) At the moment, it looks as if Clara Ward might steal the show in her character-comedy role of the little old drum playing lady, Birdie Lee. Everytime she opens her mouth to sing or speak SOMETHING happens. She seems a "natural" and is certainly authentic. The show is really a musical, 23 tunes, some old spirituals, but most my own gospel songs, plus two ballads and a scat song. But we are calling it a play "with music" so don't tell nobody. . . . . . Hazel Scott is creating a warm and very human portrayal—not as funny, of course, as Pearl Bailey's might have been—nor as earthy, but most believable and HUMAN and sort of lovable. Show seems so good to the Guild folks that they are talking about not touring first, but bringing it to New York in October as an early season opener. But this is not definite, nor is anything else beyond Westport. But here's hoping you'll see it some how or another. Sorry you and Alberta can't be here for the Labor Day Westport opening. I've written Paul and Sonia a note, but no answer as yet. Maybe they're away. . . . . Anyhow, I WANT to see you-all when you come through town. I know you'll be rushed, so lemme know where, and I'll drop around. . . . . AFRICA! I'm envious and jealous!

Best ever—
Lang

20 East 127th Street
New York 35, N.Y.
September 29, 1960

Mon cher Arna:

So nice to get a communication directly from the Cafe de la Paix even without the cinzano or cafe noir . . . Castro really shook Harlem—and the U.S.—up. Papers report the government preparing a White Paper to answer his U.N. charges. *Post* and *Times* reported me at the Castro dinner at Theresa—which I were not, didn't even get an invite. So today's *Post* (Leonard Lyons) carries a correction. Claim they took my name from his guest list. During his stay everybody and his brother milled around that corner. Folks I hadn't seen in years in the crowd. Barricades up every whichway, and groups of cops on every corner in Harlem. When Nasser came for a visit, the BUY BLACKS had a guard of honor across the street. Nothing so exciting since the riots! But nobody trampled to death. Just cheering and hollering. . . . Send me Dick Wright's current and correct address, please. Someone is always writing me for it. . . . Arthur Spingarn, John Hope Franklin, and others got off to Nigeria this week. . . . I got *Tambourines to Glory* off to the typist for the 10th copying. . . . Mrs. Harper has painted herself into bed again, really quite ill today. . . . Have you seen Josephine Baker's show? . . . . If you visit HAYES AND GABBY'S, 7 rue Manuel, Paris 9ᵉ—same arrondissement as your hotel—so should be near, the cullud restaurant of Paris, tell them I got their menu-greeting via Ida and Bob, who recommend it as a good eating place. . . . I'm going to see the *Ballets Africaine* tonight, and a few other shows this weekend. Saw the *Connection* and got a "contact high" from it—the junkies on stage are so real. They are planning Genet's *The Blacks* next—a Paris sensation of last season, I believe—a kind of shocker on the race problem. *Deep Are the Roots* is being revived, and *Taste of Honey* opens next week. Looks like another RACE season in theatre, maybe. *Tambourines* is the only one on tap NOT about the PROBLEM of intermarriage, etc., which methinks is made into TOO much of a problem—it being such a minor one. Vive les noirs! Hello to Alberta!

Langston

P.S. Did you get my note of a few days ago to GRAND HOTEL? I didn't have the street address then.

It cost me $3.75 to send you "African Treasury" by air to Uganda! So the other books are coming by boat, man! Uganda is a *long* ways. Even a letter costs a quarter.

Makerere College
The University College of East
Africa
P. O. Box 262
Kampala Uganda
13 Oct. '60
(My Birthday, 58)

Dear Lang,

If I can make this strange typewriter (Imperial 60) work, I will hasten to say that the copy of *Treasury* was here when I picked up mail the first of this week, and I'll be talking about it at length and will then present it to the library. I regret, however, that the copies (2) I requested Doubleday to send of *Poetry of the Negro* have NOT arrived, and I'm booked to lecture on the subject. I wrote Doubleday TWICE about this. Would you mind telephoning and asking if they would mind, under the circumstances, and if they have not done so, sending me a copy (my expense) via air immediately? I find NO literature, poetry or prose, by Negro Americans hereabouts. Correcting this will be my first objective in this otherwise glorious setting. I did see in a bookstore in town a paperback (British) of *Strange Fruit,* and the German engineer who seems to be in charge of buildings and grounds told me he is a Frank Yerby fan. These are the nearest things I've found to us. But the student body impresses me tremendously. More serious than in the states and probably of higher average ability, being more highly selected. About 8 out of 10 are African men (representing many tribes and ranging in color from brown to black), about 1 out of ten are women and the final 1 out of ten are Indians. But a fair percentage of the women seem to be Indian. On the negative side, the Indians and the Africans appear to stand off from each other. I don't know what efforts if any are being made to correct this.

403

Alberta and I are delightfully situated in a very, very modern apartment. The building was given to the college by the Ford Foundation mainly to house such as us, I gather. It is known locally as the Ford Flats, and we are the first to occupy ours. We are on the top floor overlooking an indescribably beautiful view. I've been taking pictures from the window, and I hope some of them come out.

I can't begin to tell you about London, Paris, Strasbourg and the flight down here, but I hope to anon. Nancy Cunard's [address], if I failed to make it clear, is c/o The Virgin Water Hospital, Surrey, England. You may judge from this. We spent pleasant hours with Dick, Ollie Stewart and Jean Wagner and saw Ollie Harrington and his lady once. Rudy Aggrey was also a delightful host with his new Mercedes Benz car. And the homecooking at Hayes and Gabby's tasted good after so much of the other kind. Everybody asked to be remembered to you.

You have at least one and maybe two books *(Famous Negro Music Makers)* in the USIS libraries, but on the whole the Negro is POORLY represented. *The Poetry of the Negro* and *Folklore* certainly should be included, not to mention the *L. H. Reader* and the *Selected Poems.* I believe my *Story of the Negro* would also fill a need . . . *Please ask George to clip the football scores from a Negro paper and send them to me.* No such news here. Scarcely know Negro Americans exist. Was asked today if there are more whites or Negroes in the U. S. and in what part of U. S. is Tennessee (this by members of non-professional library staff). We have work to do. Johnson pubs., Defender et al should send *free* copies to this really grand (and intensively used) library. USIS gives them *Sewanee Review* etc. Somebody should also send them the *NY Times.* They get the *Christian Science Monitor* free, and it is read. Please pass the word. Mr. H. Holdsworth is the head librarian. Z. N. B. Kanaiya is the only African on the professional staff. He was trained at Denver University.

Best ever,
Arna

New Stanley Hotel
Nairobi
Dec. 1, '60

Dear Lang—

We saw the snows of Kilimanjaro this morning. We were flying 35,000 feet in a *Comet* and the view was excellent above the clouds. We also saw Mount Kenya about which Jomo Kenyatta wrote.

This hotel is tops and Africans are employed to good advantage—*now.* Nairobi is as beautiful a city as you will ever see. It would make a wonderful capitol for an independent *Federation* of East Africa. As I write, Alberta is listening to radio —the first we have had the use of since we left the states.

We are scheduled to leave Rome by Pan American about 10:30 the morning of the *14th* and should be in New York (Idlewild) same evening. I'll be telling you about Uganda and Kenya a *long* time if you don't stop me. Read about *Zik* and Nigeria in European *Times* this morning. Glad to hear that *Simple* will be in paperback soon. Hello to *Ivan,* Allen Klots, and Larry Hill. Hope to talk to each of them in N.Y. Also Leah Salisbury. On your advice,

I'm not writing too many letters. Just notes and stuff . . . Next stop Anglo-American Hotel, Rome.

Best Ever,
Arna

20 East 127th Street
New York 35, N. Y.
January 20, 1961

Arna:

Nice to have your letter. . . . . We've got a BIG snow here again. . . . And my TV is on the blink again, so haven't yet seen the current Play-Of-The-Week which is cullud, about the sit-ins. . . . Haven't had time for TV looking, anyway, as push finally came to shove on the Columbia Pictures *Raisin* de Carava photographs of last July for which I was to do captions and articles. Wires and phone calls caused me to work all night till noon next day to get three sequences downtown on Friday. Three to go over the weekend—as prints of the film are almost ready and its release is scheduled for March. . . . . The play was a sold out hit in Hollywood—result, very few cullud got in so Dorothy writes—but it's scheduled for a return date after San Francisco. . . . . Add these LINER NOTES to your manuscript of *Ask Your Mama* which I am trying out to Randy Weston's music at Adele's before I leave for the Coast where I'll read it with Buddy Collette's Band at a Poetry-Jazz program for the NAACP in Santa Monica on February 18th. . . . . Just got my ticket reservation in today—round trip by train this time so I can get my sleep back—and maybe read a book. . . . . I've turned down about 20 lectures for the rest of this season including Wayne, Syracuse U., Yale NAACP, NYU, and am taking NONE at all for next season—which I vowed before, but this time I MEAN it. Just the art of writing from here on in. . . . Did I tell you I got a Permanent Pass to the Apollo to go in and out (with guests) any and all the time? Let's go next time you come. . . . . I hope you will be up for the Whitney. . . . . Meanwhile, you-all take care of you-all's selves.

Sincerely,
Langston

26 January '61

Dear Lang,

The Nashville snow is up to here, and more is promised for tonight. Examinations (semester) ended today, so the kids have been having snowball fights. They made the mistake of throwing a few at Pearl high tigers, and I believe the college boys got the worst of it. At least that's Alex's opinion.

A letter from my white folks (one of the white Bontemps who sometimes write me) tells me they are spitting mad about the behavior of those "white trash" in New Orleans and that they (the Bontemps, of course) are coming through Nashville next month and would like to visit us. They have a daughter at Emory in Atlanta, it seems, and a son who recently graduated from Villanova. It should be fun to meet them and try to figure out just how we are connected. Nothing like a weird name to bring folks together.

Ask Your Mama is undoubtedly a milestone in your writing career. It indicates, for one thing, that you are not yet ready to play it safe, but prefer to try new rhythms and styles for new effects. It compares with your first jazz poetry about as the new progressive jazz compares with the folk blues. Moreover, it challenges the current trends in beat poetry with something more subtle and at the same time more solid. I'll have to read it off and on over a period of time before I'll be satisfied with my estimate of it, but I don't have to wait to know that there's a sturdy beat here—something strong to reckon with. I hope it can be published properly, but it's highly original, and you know what that means.

I see in *College & Research Libraries* that someone has been given a grant of $500 to complete a bibliography of your writings. And I enclose herewith Leslie's review of *Treasury* from last Sunday's *Tennessean*.

Wasn't it nice that Carl Rowan got that fine post in the State Department? Just hope Bob Weaver gets confirmed in his now.

Jimmy Baldwin couldn't write badly if he tried. His piece on Dick seems deeply felt and has the ring of truth, but the account Dick gave me of their encounters was quite different—showing how the same episodes can make different impressions on different people all equally involved. . . . I hope to write a chapter on Dick in my African book (reflections upon getting the news of his death while we were still in Kampala). My recollections of him begin when you and I were trying to find him in a Chicago telephone book, then calling a number and asking for a writer named Wright only to have the party think you were talking about a numbers writer. Then the meeting at Tony Hill's place the following week-end at a party. Then Dick meeting me later in the Loop and borrowing 2¢ to complete his car fare, rejecting more and then walking to our apartment several days later (a distance of a couple of miles) to repay the money. And he had already written, though not published, the stories that later went into *Uncle Tom's Children!* What a man!

Best ever,
Arna

January 27, 1961

Dear Arna:

Your letter just came with the sad news of Owen's death. I am so sorry to hear about this.

I don't see why a poet would quarrel with press delays. Better late than never seems to me better than no publication at all.

Black Nativity has stirred the Theatre Guild into action again on *Tambourines to Glory*—which they now want to produce "in the same simple manner." . . . . . Lo, the poor Negro—always reduced to simplicity. . . . . . My feeling is that someday we are going to reduce a considerable segment of this globe to gravy. (How unfortunate).

The big record hit in Lagos (blaring away on all the jukeboxes) is a high-life dance-song praising Lumumba in Ibo.

NAACP book about ready for press. I am having dinner with Arthur tonight to discuss his Introduction. Norton is bringing out the hard cover edition in June.

Zell is getting ready to go to Mexico to get a Mexican divorce from Garnett who sliced up a few of his paintings before he departed for the Lenox Terrace. He has just been made Executive Director of the Childrens Aid Center he's been at so long. (Even without a degree in Social Work—or anything else. He has a real talent with kids.)

I am looking for somewhere to flee: the world being too much with me!

Langston

20 East 127th Street
New York 35, N.Y.
January 28, 1961

Dear Arna:

Don't think you have to sit down and write right back, just because I reply to your welcome letters with promptitude occasionally. I know you are BUSY. Me, too. But get tired of being BUSY about 4–5 A.M. as now, so take pen in hand . . . Been wrestling with the preliminaries to income tax tonight. . . . Also trying to figure out if I have LOST my mind. Just signed contracts for TWO new books today, and haven't even started the last TWO I've spent the advances on. But I've heard tell the Lord DOES help children and authors—and I DO need the money paid on signing. (I got back from Africa with less than a hundred dollars in the bank—after 52 years of what Mrs. Bethune called "SERVICE." But then she also said, "The reward for service is MORE service." Do you reckon that is ALL?) Anyhow, I am nothing but a literary share cropper. Swing low, sweet chariot and rescue me!

The King of Ragtime called up from Florida (he's white) and says Missouri is giving a big thing March 15th in honor of Blind Boone and his music, and wanted me to do some new lyrics for some of Boone's outmoded "darkie" lines. (Which I've been thinking ought to be done to some of the old but good stuff written in the minstrel tradition—maybe once mentioned it to you). Unfortunately, as I'm about to go on tour, can't do this particular job in time for the big Missouri concert which is having the Lincoln U. Choir, a big symphony, and this ragtime man, Bob Dorch, as soloist. Wish I could.

Thanks for the comments on *Mama*. The first time, to my knowledge, the Dozens have been used in poetry. I'm reading it for the NAACP with Buddy Collette's combo in California. That ought to be fun!

See Jimmy Baldwin's piece on King in current Harper's. Some wonderful sentences on Negro leaders. I sent C.V. his Memoirs of Dick, and C.V.V. writes that his version and Chester Himes are quite different as to why they all fell out, which jives with what you say. Also Worthy on Muslims in "Esquire;" Peter A. on Puerto Rico in "Holiday." How come we never fall out with NOBODY. Or do you? I don't believe I ever did. Maybe it's about time. My most vivid memory of Dick is relative to Margaret and his fleeing from her in New York and she running after the 5th Avenue bus and never caught up with him again. He went to Paris. But she's in HIS Mississippi.

Hope C.R. stays sober in his State Department job. Tipsy tales about him come from all around the world. . . . Nice about Leontyne busting the wall of the Metropolitan wide open last night. Negroes and Italians do sing the most! . . .

My Selected Poems (of a sort) just came out in Italy: *Io Sono Un Negro* (Il Gall, collana omnibus 58, Edizione Avanti, Milano—in case the Library would like to order it. They only sent me one copy, so can't present you with one). . . . I've recently gotten another letter from Germany from a researcher who can't find hardly anything by cullud authors in Amerika Haus. I hope Mr. Rowan takes up this dilemma on our cultural front.

Langston

1 February '61

Dear Lang,

Now that Dodd, Mead have announced *One Hundred Years of Negro Freedom* for the 22nd of May, it might be a good idea for you to make your Harlem book the *first* on your docket so they could start talking about it in connection with the promotion of *100 Years*. In any case, I think I know how you feel with *four* book contracts looking at you. . . . Like a giant when you're fit and rested, like a sharecropper when you're tired. . . . . But all things considered, I think perhaps it's better that way. Me, I've just got the two I signed in Africa (one a juvenile, one to be a simultaneous paperback and hardcover adult), but two others are being talked about and either or both could come to the point of signing if I'm not careful. In addition there's the opus Dick and I planned to collaborate on. I don't know how that will work out now, though he had completed his part: the first draft. So don't mention this latter item yet.

In re: literary falling-outs. Sometimes I think they are sort of ritualistic. The young writer makes a pilgrimage, meets the great-name writer, lingers till the spell wears off, then as the final act disagrees or quarrels with his diety and turns away on his own. There were no literary dieties among Negroes in the Harlem days. Just pilgrims. Since then you and I have always been too busy to go through the ritual: you with the many facets of your writing, me with my two full-time jobs. It may be a necessary spiritual experience for those like Dick, Ralph, Chester [Himes] and Jimmy, like conversion, but I find I can get off all my aggressions on people in the *educational world* and don't have to use other writers who bug me somewhat less.

As soon as Carl Rowan is settled down in his new job I will definitely take up with him the question of Negro authors in USIA libraries, etc. I'm sure he will be sensitive to the fact that his books were just as *absent* as yours or mine. So more anon.

Best ever,
Arna

20 East 127th Street
New York 35, N. Y.
February 7, 1961

Dear Arna:

Enclosed my new biog sheet and current book list for your Library.

Last night's reading of *Ask Your Mama* to two standing-room-only sessions at the Market Place was lots of fun. And lots of folks there you know. Margaret Bonds played behind the poem. And I've a tape of it all—amusing discussion afterwards, too—that you can hear when you come to town.

I'm trying to answer all VISIBLE mail and pack at the same time to catch an early train tomorrow for Kentucky. Hope I make it. Thence S. F. and L. A. where I trust it is warm. We've MOUNTAINS of snow here. I think only for their MAMA would folks come out last night. You should have seen the PILE of rubbers and galoshes in Adele's foyer!

Me always dead tired starting out on tour—and no prepared speech for that Carter Woodson Memorial Lecture I'm to give at Berea. (My intentions are always good, though—I MEANT to prepare one).

My address until the end of February: CLARK HOTEL, Washington & Central, Los Angeles 28, California. Drop me a line of encouragement. "The struggle staggers" me. Margaret Walker—Who also said (of the late lamented) "He's low! He's low! He's lower than a snake's belly!"

Sincerely,
Langston

17 February '61

Dear Lang,

Heard from you simultaneously from NYC and Berea, so I assume that by now you are expanding (if that's the word) in the LA sunshine etc. Here we don't have anything but WEATHER—which is *not* the same thing.

As usual during one of my extended absences from the Library (it happened first when I was on the Guggenheim, '49–'50), something happened to make Carlo FURIOUS. Actually, however, my staff was more innocent this time than before. One of his shipments of material to the Gershwin Collection arrived with about a dozen or so breakable records cracked or chipped. My secretary rushed to acknowlege the parcels upon receipt, as she had been taught to do, but somewhat later, when there was time to check more closely, discovered the damage. She reported this to the "acting librarian," and together they decided to set the damaged items aside for *me* to report to Carlo upon my return from the other side of the planet. This I did, but by then Carlo had thrown away his insurance slip, having concluded from my secretary's note that all was in order. So he went into a spin. However, Gayle (the secretary) had preserved the insurance slip from the package, and this she has now photographed and sent to Carlo. I'm not sure it will calm him, but I hope for the best, and I will write him again when the air is clearer.

Frustrating things happen to me too, and I know the feeling, only in my case they happen so often, what with an administrative job, the academic rat race, and a huge family, not to mention the literary life, I would be blythely (?) spinning all the time if I reacted normally. So when you see me laughing, etc.

Thanks for the "Biographical Information." We have made some copies in the Library to distribute to those who inquire. We also wrote for and received a small supply of the Negro History Week publication of the N. Y. Teachers Union, which you sent me and which contains the review of *Folklore,* for distribution. The copies went in a hurry.

I like the jacket and format of the new edition of *We Have Tomorrow,* which H-M have brought out with my new introduction. The pictures, all dated now, have been left out. . . . It's also nice to hear about the translations of *Popo & Fifina,* after all these years. And it's amusing to me, just beginning to crack the translation barrier, that several foreign editions of my *unwritten* paperback have already been agreed on, according to the editor, at least.

Since you left New York, I have received, read and returned the proofs of *One Hundred Years of Negro Freedom.* Now I am making a bibliography, which will free ME from this particular slavery for a time, I hope.

Speaking of the MAMA in Negro writing, another publisher has asked me to read and comment on a manuscript titled *The Trouble with Being a Mama.* It reads well. An autobiography. Seems like you will touch off another vogue. The vogue of the Negro *mama.* And yesterday at the Library somebody asked if we could help them find a poem called "The Negro Mother."

So tell them about it when you give your readings.

Best ever,
Arna

Sunday, March 19, 1961
At the midnight hour.

Dear Arna:

George did the continuity for this [See program following letter], and it was really very nice. The program is being repeated on Friday for the New Brunswick Urban League and next Sunday for the Jamaica (L.I.) NAACP. Tuesday I've got a Spanish Teachers dinner to address on the art of translating—reading things in both Spanish and English—so my first week back in town is a BUSY one speaking-wise (I could have lingered a while longer in the Cal. sunshine had it not been for these dates)—but 'tis the end—after this Spring, no more public appearances. PROOF: I've written turning down a half dozen colleges and Writers Conferences from California to Maine yesterday—letters that were here awaiting my return. Some pay real good fees, too! . . . . I flew back home on the bumpiest jet yet—seatbelts fastened most of the time—it rocked and rolled—which I thought jets didn't do! . . . . . California was delightful weather wise all during my stay—just sunshine and no smog and only rained once—the very day I left. . . . Your "nephew" is a personable young man, quite Chinese looking with, I believe, gray-green eyes; looks about 25, married, expecting (I believe) an increase in family. Poetry no worse than most folks bring to show me. Nothing like yours when you were his age, however. . . . . I found a BEAUTIFUL Haitian painting here on my return. But the painter who brought it by didn't leave his name and has gone back to Haiti. Quel betoise! . . . . And my Guinea Sorbonne student (who gave me the idea for the Paris section in *Ask Your Mama*) writes from a Paris jail that somebody called him a "salle nègre" and he broke the man's three ribs! And it's cold in jail, so he needs a sweater. . . . . And my Uncle Johnny in L. A. is getting older by the minute. But I persuaded him to go for a week to the hospital to have a check up and get a rest from washing his own clothes in the bathtub. (He could BUY the hospital, if he wanted to). . . . . . The Fisk Spring Festival looks fine. But somebody better tell Dr. Italiaander to take off his

410

publicity about "fighting the Mau Mau" or *not only* the Muslims will run him ragged if he ever shows up in Harlem. And nary a drop of my gin will he get to drink. . . . . Did Jean Wagner send you a copy of his article about me in French in the USIS mag? If not, let me know, as I've a few extra copies. He's mad because they cut the punch lines off most of the poems. (My wonder is they published the piece at all.) . . . . . Karamu is doing *Shakespeare in Harlem* in April, Hunter College the mine-and-Meyerowitz opera, *Esther*. And Indiana University has decided to publish a collection of my plays. But still haven't made up its mind on the *New Negro Poetry*. I guess they write too much like white folks, which is Eva Hesse's complaint in Germany, too, in trying to put together a contemporary cullud anthology. . . . . At her Beverly Hills reception last week, Mahalia introduced her arranger—who is now white. (For gospel songs, can integration any farther go?????) Otto Huiswood just died in Holland. He's the guy who first published *Goodbye Christ* in Holland—without my knowledge or permission and where copyright laws prevail not—so started all the hullabaloo that continued right up to Mills College now. Hey, hey! . . . . I'm still here!

Lang

Germaine Montero's Vanguard LP in Spanish of Lorca's poems is about the most beautiful ever. Perfect enunciation! So clear! Get it for your Library.

There is no carbon of this letter—so if you do not give it to Yale—who will?

LANGSTON HUGHES

Reads His Works

in a

SPIRITUAL SPECTACULAR

with

Westminster Choir

Church of the Master, N. Y.

VOICES INC.

acapella octet

At

CHURCH OF THE MASTER

Morningside Avenue at 122nd Street

Sunday evening, March 19, 1961

at 8 P.M.

Admission Free (Free will offering)

AN EVENING WITH LANGSTON HUGHES

PART I

"Voice of His People"

This is a musical narrative, written by George Bass, based on the life of Mr. Hughes.

It is performed by Voices, Inc., acapella octet. Musical effects are written and scored by Inez Kerr. Voices, Inc., now in its 11th month of organization, specializes in spirituals, as does the Westminster Choir.

Singing personnel include:

ALTOS:
Josephine Jackson
Sylvia Jackson

SOPRANOS:
Anne Smith
Inez Kerr

TENORS:
William Barron
George Bass

BARITONE:
Henry Doswell

BASS:
Jesse DeVore

Mr. Bernard Moore is the narrator.

PART II
Included in this section are the poems:
"Ma Lord"
"Spiritual"
"Testimonial"

Also the spirituals:
"Jesus Walked this Lonesome Valley"
"Little David Play on Your Harp"
"Live-A-Humble"

OFFERTORY

PART III
Included in this section are the poems:
"Mystery"
"Fire"
"Feet O' Jesus"
"Mother to Son"
"Merry-Go-Round"

Among the spirituals heard are:
"Keep Me from Sinking Down"
"Scandalize My Name"
"Ain't Got Time to Die"

FINALE
"Battle Hymn of the Republic"

22 March '61

Dear Lang,

Sometime I'll tell you about the family tree, but my hunch is that John Bontemps is my second cousin rather than nephew. However, I have never met his immediate branch and would be glad to know them. I suspect we all come from Hippolite Bontemps of Marksville (Avoyelles Parish) but that John's family is the issue of Hippolite's second wife, we of the first (a Laurent). Mrs. Emma DeLavellade [dancer] (Carmen and Janet's grandma) could have told you the details had you visited her in L. A.

I don't believe I ever commented on George's poetry, which I received in Kampala, but I was pleasantly surprised by it and turned the copies over to our Negro collection here. I hope I may have a chance to read more. I'm glad he got the chance to do the continuity for the "Spiritual Spectacular."

Rolf Italiaander drank all the gin here too! But I believe I told you that. By all means send a couple of copies (if you can spare them) of the Jean Wagner article from the USIS magazine. I have not seen it, but he may have read it to me when we visited in their home. I am pulling for him to complete and publish his dissertation because I believe it will have real significance in academic circles. He is that kind of old world scholar, and he is leaving no stone unturned. That's mighty nice news about Indiana U. and your plays, and I suspect you-all are right about the *newest* Negro poets writing too much like white folks—and not always the best white folks. In other words, the beat ones.

This morning I spoke to Leslie's large class on the Negro in American Lit. In the mail came a copy of *African Voices* for me to review in *The American Scholar* and a check from Abingdon Press for my comments on *Trouble with Being a Mama* (These Mama things are multiplying). Also a contract to write 20 short pieces for the *Americana* Encyclopedia.

Nice piece by Saunders Redding on Dick Wright in the AMSAC newsletter. Nasty articles by S. Alsop on Africa in the *Post* (S. E. P.). The *Urbanite* looks pretty good. Eric Lincoln's *Black Muslims* starts off well, but I don't think I'm going to like Rudwick's *Du Bois* as well as Broderick's. He appears to have been miffed because Du Bois wouldn't let him use his (WEBD's) papers. As a result he (Rudwick) lost his cool.

What do you think of my introduction to JWJ's *Autobiography of an Ex-*you know what? I tried to plug the Renaissance good.

Oh, yes, the trouble with Carlo: he gets mad and falls out about NOTHING! Nevertheless I'm saving your letters and many, MANY more for Yale!

I'm glad to hear that your Uncle Johnny is still in good fettle as well as chips.

My lectures come up in April. I'm going to have to start thinking about them.

So Mahalia has fallen into the hands of the commercializers too. I'm sorry, but I can't say I'm surprised.

Best ever,
Arna

Dear Arna:

I thought I told you A LONG TIME AGO I liked your Intro to JWJ's *Ex*. It is real good—to be so short. If your pieces for the Encyclopedia are any briefer, I'd say you'd be earning your money on brains alone. . . . . What is this *Trouble with Being a Mama?* I've heard of it only through you. (Maybe you could send me a carbon of your comments). Did I tell you Knopf took my *Mama?* In the light of reading it to jazz on the Coast, I've smoothed it up quite a bit here and there, and added thereunto in places. . . . . So many Bontemps! But that Carmen De is the PRETTIEST one—almost—outside of your charming daughters. . . . Incidentally, my brother's Help Needed figure has gone up—in line with price rises, I suppose. (Thinking of one of your tales). . . . . Did you know Oscar Brown, Jr., when you lived in Chi? He's coming UP in the pop song world. Real clever! He was my first SIMPLE years ago in Chicago—made little sketches from the columns and played them himself with a couple of other folks, very amusingly. I tried to find him when we were casting the play. He, Carmen, and another favorite of mine, Nina [Simone, concert artist], are opening up in a revue April 1, currently trying out in Toronto, but without Oscar who is at the Apollo this week where I just caught his act. Uses "social" material, too, which seems to be coming back —like in the '30's. Maybe I should revive *Don't You Want to Be Free?* only with a Sit-In ending—instead of union-organizing as formerly. . . . . Karamu, I might have told you, is doing *Shakespeare in Harlem* in April. . . . They took up a right good collection when I got through reading my poems from Rev. Robinson's pulpit last Sunday night. A few more years, I may take to preaching. All my friends of the cloth look fat and fine, brows unfurrowed, unwrinkled by care— whilst I can hardly make ends meet. I need a bigger place. Between the Ph.D. researcher and the bibliographer (who comes every day) my bedroom looks like the Schomburg's spread-out department—so much material has been hauled out and unshelved for them. The biblio man's grant only allows him two weeks in New York, but he could spend two months on my top floor alone, not to speak of the basement. And he has still got to go to Yale. (Being white, however, I expect he can get another grant without too much trouble. The poor colored fellow is doing his research with nary grant a-tall. But maybe in due time—.)

And if I do not go to bed, it will be time to go to New Brunswick for my Urban League program, before I get up. 4:30 now, A. M.

Oh, before I sign off, are you interested in being on staff of any summer writer's conferences in woods, on campuses, etc.? I suggested you for one—I've forgotten which one now—trying to clear up via hurried notes lots of mail at once. But I turned down three, and think there's still another unanswered round about. Must be due to the Nat. Inst. Arts & Letters thing, I reckon—the academicians think I've suddenly become an authority or something on how to write. Sterling Brown would be good at that sort of thing, too. I wonder if Redding would? Me, I think I'd rather be taught by you or Sterling in the summers. Maybe Jay for winter time.

Avec mes compliments les plus sinceres,

Langston

P.S. An African who's been admitted to the University of Colorado, he says, writes me for $1800 to help him get there! I'm flattered, indeed. Never saw that much money in my WHOLE life, let alone possessed it ALL AT ONCE. (Except the few *Street Scene* weeks.) Every time I go to L. A. or anywhere and come back, I hardly have $18 left. Remember that white lady who came begging to Watts? ? ? ? ? A dear soul!

20 East 127th Street
New York 35, N.Y.
April 12, 1961

Arna,

I've really been SNOWED UNDER, and every day something on my date pad to cause me to have to go out! Last night was the National Institute of Arts and Letters welcoming dinner to new members—and I, being the only cullud present, was seated at the first table with Robert Frost who recited several poems from memory, which is more than I can do at my young age. After the dinner I rode down to the Plaza with Carlo (I had to go to an Eartha Kitt rehearsal) and on the way heard all his grievances against Fisk—which are numerous along with those of Georgia O'Keeffe. Seems like she is on the verge of taking her paintings away from you-all, since they got leaked on, and she's sent the money for certain repairs which nobody will make anent the museum, etc., and nobody will answer letters. At all of which, I expressed my amazement—and just listened. . . . Tonight I'm going to dinner at Dorothy Maynor's—so I know the eating will be good . . . and the next night I've got to show an Italian movie star Harlem. . . . Thus the week goes. So yesterday I made a big red ink signed [NO] so as to remember to say No to everything for the rest of the month, except what I already have on my calendar, which is ENOUGH. And in May three or four more lectures in Philly and round about, ending in early June with the Boston Arts Festival in the Common itself. After that nothing else, ABSOLUTELY, for the rest of 1961. All future lecture requests are being answered with regrets—even those for next Negro History Week—for which a couple have already come in. Dates may seem far off, but before you know it, here they are cutting into one's creativity. So for me from here on in concerning public appearances—*NO!* . . . . Knopf has interesting plans for *Ask Your Mama* for Fall in a bright gift book style aiming at Christmas sales. *An African Treasury* has just come out in paper (Pyramid) at 50¢. And from Sweden today comes an attractive edition of *Not Without Laughter.* I could only send you one copy of the USIS Jean Wagner piece, but I am sure you can get more by writing for them. Tuskegee has just performed *Simply Heavenly.* And Karamu is doing both *Shakespeare in Harlem* and *Street Scene* this Spring. Guess I'll have to fly out to see them. The opera (me and Meyerowitz) *Esther* is due to holler at Hunter College on the 27–28 of this month. And he sails for France the next day to conduct one of his ballet scores there. He's a-rising! And who started him out? Did I tell you Oscar Brown, Jr. . . . ? Yes, I did, I remember now. If the *Simply* play is ever revived, I hope maybe he'll play it. He was real good in his own early adaptations. . . . Are you coming up here for the Whitney? Hope so. Sunday I had a little gathering for Andrew Salkey of Jamaica here on a Guggenheim. Arthur Spingarn came. He sails for England today until end of May. Julia Fields I invited, too. She's really quite pretty, most talkative, and to

415

me not a very interesting poet. Maybe because she says she writes 85 poems a week! . . . . Anyhow, hasta luego—

Langston

P.S. Awful weather here still. Biting rain and chilly wind tonight. . . . Bravo, yuro! And more space to him!

The more I see of Eartha the more I admire her. 20 white folks run and jump whenever she lifts a finger! Out of all the entourage, I was the only cullud at her Plaza dress rehearsal.

Tell Alberta, HELLO!

20 East 127th Street
New York 35, N. Y.
Sunday, April 30, 1961

Mon cher Arna:

Uncle Johnny on the West Coast, and Aunt Toy on the East are driving their respective relatives slowly crazy—enjoying their agebility to the full—and paying nobody no mind.

I'll be crazy myself if I go to see any more "art" shows. I thought *The Blacks* tonight (preview) a 33rd degree bore—more far out than *Godot* and even less amusing. Genet's *The Balcony* I loved, but not this one. Maybe the translation is at fault, or the direction (this, I think, sadly so) and miscasting of some otherwise excellent actors—all cullud cast—who go about it tooth and nails—whereas what the play needs, I'd think, is lightness and a humorous approach to its fantasy—which is extreme, grotesque, and long-winded. What seemingly is meant to be humorous satire gets only a few sort of embarrassed laughs—like jokes told by somebody who can't tell them. But who knows? Maybe critics and white folks will like it. Hope so—to keep a dozen or so actors working a while. . . . . Real Sunday night theatre audience—Eartha, Claudia, Lorraine, Earl Jones (whose son has a lead) etc. . . . . But the first act seemd so long to me, I couldn't wait for the second—and I wasn't alone in leaving. Went to Village Gate for a sandwich, drink, and Nina Simone. And home to do a bit of work—like writing a column, or something. And a cool gin and tonic. NO MORE ART SHOWS this, or any other, season. NO! With Jackie Mabley, Pigmeat, and Pearl Bailey *The Blacks* might come off, or superb direction, or real style. Perhaps done with midgets and very tall people—or gospel singers.

Such ills the flesh is heir to—

Langston

23 May '61

Dear Lang,

Well, the excitement is on again. As you will see from the current *Time,* not to mention *The NY Times* and other newspapers, the Fisk kids have signed on for the "Freedom Ride," among them exchange students like Jim Zwerg (I'm his adviser) and Sue Herman and veterans of the sit-in and stand-in campaigns in

416

Nashville like Matthew Walker Jr. (his dad is head surgeon at Meharry) et al. I heard Alex telling one of his Pearl High buddies, "They've been talking about what a rough ride they had in Alabama. They haven't had any rough ride yet. Wait till they hit Mississippi!"

Benjamin Mkapa, whom I met at Makerere College, where he's an honors student in English and the most promising of the young writers in East Africa, came through Nashville with a team of three representatives (here to report on INTEGRATION in education!) of the international organization of student councils (he from Africa, one other from Europe—Norway—and one from Asia—Singapore). He spent Sunday with us and promised to get me the address and more data for you on James D. Rubadiri, author of "Stanley Meets Mutesa." Mkapa and Rubadiri are friends, having met at Makerere before Rubadiri left. Rubadiri is an African, of course, a native of Nyasaland. He has been politically active and as a result "detained" officially, I gather, but he is now somewhere in England. I have just one poem by Mkapa. Do you want to see it? He has also written short stories and short plays. I think his prose is better than his verse.

Ruby now tells us that it will take a miracle to bring Owen through. The doctors found a malignancy near his spine. They are treating it by X-ray, the only method possible in this case. A somber thought indeed.

Evidently my publication date on *100 Years* was moved ahead a week, according to the Book Note in the *NY Times*, 5-23-61. I had expected it last Monday rather than next.

Has your copy arrived? I gave your name to the publishers as a columnist who might possibly find occasion to speak about the book.

If you don't have enough will power to resist the personal appearance circuit, you can't blame me if I don't! In any case, I find myself booked for two as far apart as Hot Springs, Arkansas, and Detroit for the first week of November. Nice way to start the fall season!

How was your Uncle Johnny? And did you see Connie and Tommy?

And did I send you a program of Dickie Jones' senior art show? It was well received. I suppose he will be heading for more study in the East now.

Best ever,
Arna

May 25, 1961

Dear Arna,

100 Years of Negro Freedom arrived today in its handsome blue and gold binding, and it starts off with a wonderful bang-up good Introduction—which is as far as I've gotten during the day's interruptions, except to glance at the early days of Du Bois at Fisk—which reads delightfully. I am anxious to get at the rest of the book. Can't say I'm too fond of that literal minded artist who does so many Dodd, Mead jackets. If I ever get *Harlem* down, I shall veto him. I think the back of the jacket with your photo should have been the front. Anyhow, that cabin looks just like the South I've just seen from the train window last week. . . . ARTS AND LETTERS yesterday was long and dull as usual. (There ought to be a law against people reading speeches and citation.) Elmer Rice and one other speaking off the cuff were good. Most of the rest went on and on about their devotion to

417

the "higher things" and so forth. I was the only cullud alone on the platform amidst a sea of white folks—including both Van Dorens—but could look out in the audience and see several non-whites dozing—including Fania. But Carlo and I both got scrolls—with a gold seal thereon. . . . *Mandingo* got a terrific panning —seems it is more *Tobacco Road*ish than *Tobacco Road.* Maya Angelou (of *The Blacks*) is said to have arisen during the 2nd act at a preview and stalked out flinging back curses at the cullud actors on stage for being such "Uncle Toms" —in a real loud voice. How *Mandingo* outdoes *The Blacks,* I have yet to see. White folks are claiming it is GREAT—*The Blacks.* Come see for yourself. They also love the current *Porgy and Bess* which has a sex scene that out does all the other productions put together, I hear. Maybe all 3 companies should be sent South on a free FREEDOM RIDE. . . . Love that photo of Du Bois and Spingarn in your book. Arthur is back from England this week.

Sincerely,
Langston

20 East 127th Street
New York 35, N.Y.
June 27, 1961

Dear Arna:

Surely its O.K. by me that *Presence Africaine* use our anthology as a basis for a French one. But contract wise, I think we had from living poets only English language permissions (as I had on *African Treasury*) so foreign publishers have to make their own arrangements with the authors, their heirs, or agents. If Doubleday would handle the whole matter, it would be easier for you, in case a bit of royalty is to be paid. If not, I'd say let *Presence* worry with it themselves. I recall that it took WEEKS and a *couple of hundred* letters on both my and Doubleday's part to clear up permissions when we put the book together. If the French wish to tackle it now, more power to them. NOT I! In any case, they'd have to get from Doubleday—if it's still there—a list of poets' addresses, etc.). But we as editors cannot give *carte blanche.*

My SPORTS material now being posted to you. And I think I have more in the basement—which will require a bit of looking—so, in due time. . . . .

Dickie, [Jones, actor] tried out for *Kicks & Co.,* no dice, so is still job hunting. Was staying here at our house until today.

*Me, I'm looking for a summer hideaway—so I can write my NAACP paper back—which just got a hard cover publisher, too, this week. It is due in August. Then I want to tackle my Harlem book in earnest, having finally sort of formulated in my mind how I wish to approach it. Eartha backed out of *Tambourines* to do instead a musical she told me she likes about Marie Laveau. So, stymied again! Archie Moore's new *Jazz Day* intends to print a part of *Ask Your Mama* in initial issue, they say. Knopf galley proofs came yesterday; and *The Best of Simple* proofs are due any moment now.

RE-gards—
Lang

I saw Doug Sunday.

418

P.S. *Everybody comes to town in the summer. In spite of best intentions to keep this *whole* week clear, it is now ALL booked up with mostly out-of-towners —started Sunday with German Pardo Garcia (famous Colombian poet only here 3 days and HAD to see me) and yesterday an editor from Philadelphia; and today, just left, two fellows from Paris working in theatre there; tonight the Director of the Wisconsin Theatre Research Center; tomorrow Peter Abrahams up for 2 days from Jamaica on a *Holiday* assignment—etc. right through next weekend. So I've added to my big NO sign (that doesn't seem to work) OUT OF TOWN TILL LABOR DAY, which I'm now telling everyone. And which I guess, if any work is to be done, I'll have to try to be. Can't seem to achieve any protection at home—my will being weak anyhow. Last night, all set to work, the Chinese painter who married Howard Thurman's daughter in Frisco showed up after dinner, brother of Zep, my former secretary, which made the third outside visitor for the day! And when I woke up for breakfast, he was still here, as the Harper's put him up for the night. My nerves! Got to flee. But still promised to see one more African before I go—a nice chap sent over to find out how Americans run magazines. After him, nary one.

P.S.-2: If your Library doesn't get the *New York Post,* I'd say subscribe to it until your SPORTS book is done, as it has the best coverage of any papers of the Negro in sports—good feature pieces almost daily.

Congratulations on F.I.A.L., and the nice reviews. The K.C. Star is best paper in midwest.

L.

Fourth of July 1961

Dear Lang,

I'll write Diop presently, making clear the problem of permissions as mentioned by you but offering to do anything I can personally to facilitate it. I suppose if he were to begin by listing or indicating the poems he would like to include in the French collection, I could tell him offhand which of them (if any) are in public domain and say which of these I could attempt to secure from the poets themselves and which might better be undertaken (Jean Toomer, for example) by the publishers of the American edition. Anyhow, I'll speak encouragingly. (Maybe not)

The only trouble with the Athletes book is the September deadline. I'll need good weather, good health and good luck to make it. Another difficulty, however, is the high level of the other books in the *Famous* series, which I have been reexamining. You all have put the curve way up, but I suppose that is why the books are in demand—and in stock here in town.

Sorry about Dickie and *Kicks & Co.* I thought sure he'd make it, if dancing's what they need, but maybe he can't tap. I believe I heard somebody in Philly was trying to reach him with an interesting job offer. Dr. Voorhees says she gave the inquirer his Cincinnati address.

Those three pieces by George Bass in take-off of the Alby (how do you spell it?) approach are neatly done. George Gardiner let me see them. There's nothing like being a writer's secretary to bring out buried talent: Barnaby Conrad (Sinclair Lewis), John Hersey, et al. At the moment George looks more promising as a writer than any of the kids who were studying Creative Writing here while he was studying Business Administration!

Sorry about Eartha—bewitched by Marie Laveau. Well, she's not the first.

We're off to ALA Friday morning. We'll be at the Sheraton-Cleveland Hotel 8–14. Possibly a day longer.

Meanwhile,

> Best ever,
> Arna

P.S. Jack Conroy writes that he is en route to Mexico City to be the house guest of Willard Motley.

P.S.S. (7-5) The packet of SPORTS material arrived. Thanks loads. All very useful.

P.S.S.S. That Boston Festival must have been a *Wampus!* .... Herbert Hill was here, talking about his projected Knopf anthology. . . . I'm looking forward to *both* your forthcoming paperbacks: *NAACP* and *Best of Simple*. Be sure to keep me posted. . . . One of the larger Universities has decided that *Lonesome Boy* has not received the attention it deserves. Can you imagine that?

> July 14, 1961
> Bastille Day!

Dear Arna,

There are other interesting observations in Kitamura's paper. He writes and evidently speaks English well, having been graduated from a college in Texas a few years ago, I believe Baylor. (I may have sent you a charming little sketch he wrote about the Negro janitor there). He is currently teaching English at the High School of the University above [Chuo University, Japan], and it must be a good school, as 3 of students are coming in the fall to top New England prep schools for their U.S. college preparation—Choate, etc., and he has asked me to see them when they come through New York.

At any rate, when he gets his M.A. from I.C.U. in Tokyo in a few months, Kitamura wishes to return to the United States for further study in the field of Negro culture, and it seems that Dr. Hotchkiss of the Congregational Churches in New York has suggested Atlanta to him. He has also been talking with Dr. John Lovell, Jr., (Negro prof. whom you may know teaching in Japan). I personally think Fisk would be better for this young Japanese than A.U. might. What do you think? At any rate, I suggest, if you will that you ask your Registrar to send him to the above address catalogues and any relevant information concerning graduate courses at Fisk specifically related to Negro life and literature, which is what he wishes to pursue. (I think and Leslie and others at Fisk would be more helpful to him, were he to study there, than anybody I know at A.U.—but don't TELL anyone—since Dr. Tilman is in semi-retirement and Mozell Hill is in Africa Negroizing Nigerians.)

I gather Kitamura is seeking scholarship aid, but am not sure of this. Maybe the Congregationalists are helping, since he writes of being in contact with them. At any rate, from his many letters to me in the course of writing his thesis (I must have spent $50 or $75 bucks on books and airmail postage to him) he is certainly a serious and thorough student who has worked hard on his current paper. And

420

seems deeply and sympathetically (and intelligently) interested in the Negro. So, should he get back here to study further in the U.S. I'd like to see him in good academic company. So, please, at least see that he is informed about Fisk.

Merci a vous,

Sincerely,
Langston

1 August 1961

Dear Lang,

Here is the new picture. I'd like about a hundred glossies for publicity. The old ones are not only way out of date but also exhausted. However I don't remember the name of the studio, the prices charged, etc. I do know the negative will have to be made by them and that that will be extra. I'll be much obliged to George Bass for this, and if he will advise me, the check will be there by return carrier pigeon.

I missed the George Schuyler pan of my book in the *Courier,* and since you warned me, I will not look it up. Maybe he resented what I said about him. Or perhaps what I quoted from Randolph about the *Courier.* One never knows what will become controversial. I didn't expect the fuss about *St. Louis Woman,* and I sure didn't see how anybody could take offense at *100 Years.* Most of those who are hot think I should have written more about Africa (I don't myself know how I could have wedged that in), but a goodly number think I should have forgotten about Douglass—Washington—Du Bois and concentrated on the young lions. So you can bear this in mind as you project the final book of the series. Nevertheless, each week seems to bring in something on the positive side also.

We are suffering from heat and humidity here. The typewriter doesn't like to budge under the circumstances.

So more anon.

Best ever,
Arna

August 16, 1961

Dear Lang,

Tell George [Bass, H's secretary] he should be a reference librarian at a starting salary of about $5,000 a year! I'm gladder than you'd guess to get the data on Dozens (Elton and Dollard). We have been asked several times to search for these pieces, and we were just about to write Dollard and [Ira] Reid for help. One of the people who inquired, I believe, was Cedric Dover. Anyhow, we'll look for Ira's piece and write him if there's no other way. I should think these would make most provocative publicity in connection with *Ask Your Mama.* Might start an exchange (a *conversation,* as we used to say at the U. of Chicago) between poets and sociologists. They need to start speaking again—as they used to in 1927 and 1928 when Charles S. Johnson wrote on "Blues as Poetry" and "The Negro Enters Literature" for the *Carolina Magazine.* Louis Jones (Dr.), a former pro- tege of CSJ now at Tuskegee but here this summer on a special assignment of some kind, seems to have some fascinating sidelights on the Dozens as he picked them up when he was in the army. He is here connected with the Race Relations Department of Fisk.

Well, sir, they will bring you out of seclusion if they have to die to do it: Harold, Muriel. Seedtime and Harvest. The sun do move. Which reminds me, I came across a *picture* of the Rev. John Jasper. Owen is still strolling in the halls and looking out of his window at the National Institute of Health in Washington: multiple myloba, I think it's called: cancer of the bone marrow.

Paul Bremen tells me he will publish Fenton Johnson's WPA poems in his forthcoming series, edited with an introduction by me. . . . . Did I comment on "Blessed Assurance?" I think I spotted the reason for the many versions. But there is now just one little thing the story lacks, as I see it. Delmar, the organist, the little sister—all come to light. But the father remains at the end exactly where he started out. I should think that understanding, as it comes to him at the end, should either give him something to do (provoke him to do something unexpected) or somehow change his outlook. His reaction at that point should be more positive. I suspect that what has kept you revising is that, despite its liveliness and interest, the story somehow seems unfinished. For example, the father might either accept Delmar as a "girl" after the disclosure, and decide to orient his feelings accordingly, or he might reject him as a human being—give him the boot. But as long as he is simply dismayed, well that's where he started.

By the way, George Gardiner dug up a story by Jean Toomer in the old *Dial* about a man whom Toomer described as a "gelding." I don't know why "Blessed Assurance" reminded me of it.

Nice of Dodd, Mead, don't you think, to prepare the enclosed and mail them around. So hurry up and get started on the Harlem volume and don't leave out or slight any of the current headline figures if you don't want to get lambasted. Fortunately for the book they all came to Harlem. . And Martin Luther King came near meeting his Maker there—after the stabbing. But *I* will defend you if you also keep in a *plenty* about early Harlem, Marcus Garvey, etc. Not to mention the golden days of the Renaissance.

Interesting card from Jack Conroy and Willard Motley in Mexico, where they appeared to be celebrating and having what they call "a high old time." Jack's name is quite legible. Willard's less so. Before he left for his vacation, Jack seemed on the verge of getting a settlement from Putnams, I believe, on account of one of their authors plagiarizing Jack's original version of *The Fast Sooner Hound*— which is not really a folk item. I hope it came through and that it added a cup of joy to the Mexico jaunt.

Best ever,
Arna

20 East 127th Street
New York 35, N. Y.
August 25, 1961

Dear Arna:

Since you won't do your own publicity, I thought I'd do a bit for you. There would be no harm in publishing this column in the *Defender,* would there?

Meanwhile, when you get time (no hurry and off the top-of-your-head) send me a few names of sociologists-psychologists who might engage in "conversations" such as you mentioned regarding the Dozens and *Ask Your Mama*. I'll drop each a note with a book when it comes out. Who's the top man at Fisk, for example? And the one you named from Tuskegee?

I've listed Valient, Drake, Cayton, Bond, Kenneth Clarke, Ira Reid, Hayakawa already as folks who'd probably be interested in this first use of the Dozens in formal poetry. Of course, Dan Burley [folklorist]! And Franklin Frazier [sociologist]. If a little hoopla could be started, it might be fun—and informative to white folks.

It's been raining here for two days. But the Elk's Parade was held in the clear yesterday—and wonderful it was indeed—for hours down Seventh and up Lenox. It included three Chinese lodges with dragons and gongs and firecrackers. . . . Adele is out of the hospital, home and doing well. Slight heart attack, I guess I told you. Maybe the stars are uncrossed again. Last month everybody I knew was ailing, almost, or worse. . . . . I sure would like to have a little $$$$$$ before I die. Do you reckon???????????? I now have citations, scrolls, plaques and doctorates a plenty. Just turned down invite to Chi from Nat. Negro Musicians to receive another; also one from some Poets Society. Costs too much to go get them.
. . . .

Cheers,
Lang

P.S. You probably saw the little review of *Ex-Colored Man* under PAPERBACKS in Sunday *Herald Tribune Books.* Mentions your Intro.

Sent to Bontemps
August 28, 1961

CHICAGO DEFENDER

by
LANGSTON HUGHES

AN HONOR TO HONOR

It is about time some learned institution made Mr. Arna Bontemps a Doctor. (Take note Yale, Fisk, Harvard, Lincoln, Howard, Princeton, Wilberforce, the University of Chicago and other repositories of honorary doctorates). The distinguished author and Librarian of Fisk University has long been an outstanding contributor to the American literary scene as well as to the field of national scholarship. He is an authority on Negro life, literature and folk lore. He was co-editor of "The Book of Negro Folk Lore" and "The Poetry of the Negro" and has written for encyclopedias and academic journals on such subjects. He has built the Fisk University Library into one of the best libraries in the South.

But it is as a creative writer and popular historian that Arna Bontemps has made his greatest contribution to American letters. In the days of the Negro Renaissance in Harlem, his poetry attracted wide attention. His moving "Nocturne at Bethesda" and "A Black Man Talks of Reaping" have been used in innumerable commencement speeches and included in various anthologies. His first novel, "God Sends Sunday" became the Broadway musical, "St. Louis Woman" from which came "Come Rain or Come Shine," the standard popular song now heard so often on radio and television. His second novel, "Black Thunder" was a brilliant use of historical material in its recreation of the great Gabriel Prosser slave rebellion of 1800. If Hollywood were not blind when it comes to Negro history and Negro heroism, it would long ago have made a motion picture from this stirring novel so suitable for great film material.

Some twenty years ago in collaboration with Jack Conroy, Arna Bontemps wrote "They Seek A City" which is the only factual study of all the great Negro migrations from pioneer days to World War I and later when streams of Southern Negroes poured into the North. It ranges from the brown DuSable who founded Chicago through the runaway slave days of Harriet Tubman and the followers of the North Star to freedom, to the "Chicago Defender" appeals of the twenties, "Come North, Negroes, come North." The Bontemps-Conroy book vividly portrays in moving prose the trials and tribulations, achievements and triumphs of the millions of black men and women over the years who sought a city where their children might grow up in greater freedom, go to better schools, and find as grown-ups decent jobs.

About a smaller band of very famous travellers, Arna Bontemps wrote in "Chariot in the Sky," the story of the Fisk Jubilee Singers who first carried the Spirituals to foreign shores. Their singing of these songs in public in far-flung places from Oberlin to Oslo almost a hundred years ago, helped to make Negro music known around the world. This book is another effective use by Bontemps of the historical and folk material of the race. In "We Have Tomorrow" published in 1945 and recently reissued, he catches up with today in the series of contemporary biographical sketches which compose the book. It concerns the contributions of younger Negroes to the various forms of American culture, and tells the stories of such outstanding examples as Brigadier General Benjamin Davis, Jr., in military aviation; the cartoonist of international fame, E. Simms Campbell; the symphonic conductor, Dean Dixon.

Bontemps' charmingly written account of Negro history from the great days of Benin and the African kings to Ralph Bunche at the United Nations, "The Story of the Negro," deservedly received the Jane Addams Children's Book Award. But the book is as valuable for adults as it is for young people. Of all the histories of the Negro, Arthur B. Spingarn termed this one "by all odds the best written, the most interesting, accurate, and concise work for the general reader." Currently continuing his explorations into the Negro's past and present, Arna Bontemps' recently published 100 *Years of Negro Freedom* is a most valuable contribution to the pending centennial celebrations of Emancipation. It is primarily a dramatic study of Negro leadership from Douglass and Pinchback to A. Philip Randolph and Dr. Du Bois. It contains new and fascinating highlights of American Negro history and adventure. Besides all these volumes there are the delightful Bontemps books for children on library shelves across the country. An excellent writer, a thorough historian, a distinguished librarian, a charming platform speaker, and a scholar who for well over a quarter of a century has contributed in many varied ways to American culture, it is about time Arna Bontemps became Dr. Bontemps, Litt.D., for any institution honoring him would honor itself.

20 East 127th Street
New York 35, N. Y.
September 19, 1961

Arna:

On Labor Day there was an old race track man here after Saratoga ended, and knows all the living old jockeys. Says about the most famous colored one is Samuel J. Bush, whom he phoned to see if he was in town. It seems he goes back and forth to Europe a lot, keeping a little stable of his own in France, friend of Aga Kahn, etc. Bush won the Grand National, 1917 and 1918—only *jockey* to repeat, says John Ewing, our informant. So I relay this to you in case its of value. .... And I found in my basement files a BIG Sports File full of old clippings. If you think you need it, I'll box it up and send you.

George got his deferment and is back in grad school, this time at NYU. His Voices, Inc., did an excellent series of song-documentary programs on CBS "Protestant Heritage," closing this Sunday with Thurgood Marshall as guest. (Me, Spaulding, Carol Brice were the others—Literature, Business, Music).

I'm on the last 50 pages of my NAACP book—but about beat down. Eyes wore out from reading so much, and typing all night. So had to lay off a day yesterday. Besides a namesake I had not seen in 20 years woke me up after only two hours sleep, arriving in town with lots of song lyrics he hoped to place! About the same time a Dutchman showed up, but I couldn't see him, too. Couldn't hardly see anyhow!

Both *Simple* and *Mama* look fine, sample copy of each has arrived. Others due next week. *Mama* is stunning, in fact, should win a Graphic Arts prize for format and unique design.

Lang

20 East 127th Street
New York 35, N.Y.
October 22, 1961

Dear Arna:

Nice to have your note, and hope all your speeches came out O. K. Me, retired from the lecture platform, thank God! But am invited to AMSAC arts festival in Lagos for 3 days in December, so might do that since it should be fun—with Nina Simone, K. Dunham, a jazz band, Willis James on folk songs, etc. Looks like at last I'm about to get caught up with the most urgent deadlines, and by Dec., all of them ought to be done, I hope. And I'll need a change of pace. Been at typewriter so long my hair is down to my shoulders and have grown a beard which is two-toned.

Sports Illustrated wants me to do a piece which might bring me to Tennessee State after Christmas. I tried to turn it over to you (since you're there, and doing a book, too) but seems they want my "Simple" touch, and have been after me for two months, but just yesterday did I have a chance to talk with them in detail and in person. I've still to say YES definitely, since what I know about sports could be put in a teaspoon.

Reason for this note is, the Japanese doing his masters on my poetry (and it is good) sending it to me in parts to read and correct, says he has NOT heard from

Dr. Masuoka at Fisk at all. So perhaps you could have the President's Office (or somebody there) send him graduate study information and catalogues, etc., *right away,* please:

Mr. Takao Kitamura,
Suginami High School,
Chuo University,
Tokyo, JAPAN.

He has a real interest in Negro lit., problems, etc., and lots of Negro contacts in Tokyo—army, Billy Banks, etc. I'd think Fisk good for him and vice-versa.

Thanks! . . . Regards,
Langston

25 October '61

Dear Lang,

That Lagos jaunt is certainly a terrific way to change the pace after long weeks and months at the typewriter. I envy you both the deadlines made and the festival in warm December. . . . Incidentally, by that time I may be trying to line up some African writers for a project Larry Hill has just broached, and I'd like, if you don't mind, to give you a message for Chinua Achebe, should you meet him in Lagos. And I would like to get leads from you, if this is agreeable, to such other writers as you would recommend, as a result of your experience with the *Treasury,* in other African countries. But more about this anon.

I suppose Poag has told you (as he did me) about their plan to do *Simply Heavenly* at A & I sometime during this school year and their hope of having you come down for it. What I'm thinking is that you might contrive to make this coincide with your trip here for *Sports Illustrated* and thus enhance the profit. I would hope that your assignment might also help me set up my own meeting with Wilma Rudolph for my *Athletes* book. Up to now I've been too busy to try to arrange it, and President Davis has been too involved with court action by some of his students who were expelled for participating in the freedom rides (Carl Rowan had also turned down an honorary degree from A. & I. last summer because of this action by the school vs the students) seeking reinstatement (Avon and Looby are the lawyers for the students vs the college) and other details of college administration to help me. In any case, it will be wonderful to have you in Nashville after Xmas, and I hope you will not be in too much of a hurry. Will you be staying at A & I or shall we have the pleasure? Guest cottage, hotel, our home—you name it.

I'll contact the president's office about Kitamura TODAY. I can't imagine why Masuoka has been dragging his feet (if that's what it is), but I hope to find out pronto.

Best ever,
Arna

P. S. Nice occasion at U. of Wisconsin. I had hoped to see *Kicks & Co.* in Chi. en route, but nothing cooking as I passed through. Instead I saw *The Best Man.*

20 East 127th Street
New York 35, N.Y.
October 30, 1961

Dear Arna:

Would it be worth while to send an *Ask Your Mama* to Herman Long at Fisk for comment on the Dozens aspects of the poem? . . . . . I've ordered copies sent to Don Hayakawa, Dan Burley, Ira de A. Reid (who never wrote a piece on the Dozens, he tells me), also to E. Franklin Frazier, Mozell Hill, Louis Jones (as you suggested) and Dr. Horace Mann Bond. Would be nice if we could start some "conversations."

Did I tell you Charles Jones, Program Secretary of the Whitney Foundation, spent a couple of hours here at my studio discussing ways to improve their Fellowships deal, and to get more applicants in the creative fields? (Between us —his ignorance of things Negro seemed to me abysmal).

Pres. Sédar-Sénghor (the poet-politician) of Senegal is in town and has asked the State Department to arrange for him to meet me. So we're trying to work it out for this week.

Both Hugh Smythe and Zep Wong (my former secretaries) seem to be in line for big government jobs. (The Man has been here investigating them). All my secretaries eventually get more secretaries than me! Zep, it seems is to be U. S. Attorney-General of the California area—a Kennedy appointment—and I reckon the highest such post a Chinese-American has had. And Adam Powell has put Hughie's name up for something, so George saw in the papers. Meanwhile, he's with a United Nations U. S. bureau. Oh, well, maybe I'll get there someday, too, and have enough secretaries to catch up with my mail!

I've done already given away my book royalties for the next five years—in books.

Langston

20 East 127th Street
New York 35, N.Y.
November 7, 1961

Mon cher ami:

The menu at the White House was all in French (in honor, no doubt, of Senghor; and last night at the Arts and Letters dinner for Sir and Lady C. P. Snow, in French also. (Why, I don't know). But when it came to talking for or against to whom the 1962 Gold Medal for Lit is to go, I was forced to rise and state in plain English why I wouldn't give it to the leading Southern cracker novelist if it were left to me, great "writer" though he may be. I was sitting next to Carson McCullers and we had fun translating the French menu into jive English for her cullud cook to try some of the dishes. Carlo was there. . . . . . Mrs. Estelle Massey Riddle Osborne had cocktails for Zelma Watson George on Sunday; and the Lincolnites had same for our new president, at the Waldorf. So my social season started off in a big way—so big I've about had enough already —at least till I come back from Africa—if I get gone. . . . . . Mrs. Harper is still in California. . . . . Spite of all I've finished another deadline. Now only have one more really urgent one to go—a promised magazine piece. So I hope to see a few shows, and a few friends, and take a breather in a week or so. But I don't believe I'll go to Hot Springs—I were there once and found it real simple. . . . . Zelma is on a lecture trek—Omaha preceding N.,Y., now to Beloit, Wisconsin —she being with Colston Leigh, which is the way they jump folks around—and take 35%. She says they have one other cullud lecturer on their list this season, but I forgot to find out who it is. Anyhow, I'm glad it's not me! Two more African parties coming up this week—Alioune Diop of *Presence* and Mphalele, the good writer. (His I think I'll go, but can't make them both—not and make my deadline and get my sleep, too—with two radio interviews and a book party for *Mama* this weekend) Too much! . . . .

L.H.

P.S. Emanuel's Ph. D. thesis on my short stories (see excerpt in *Phylon*) runs to over 300 pages. I'm to read it this weekend before he turns it in.!!!!
Your DIGEST piece is real good.
J. Saunders Redding's father died.
Channing Tobias, too, I see in tonight's paper.
Rosey Pool is also invited to Nigeria.

11–15–'61

Dear Lang,
Simple was excellent in his fallout dream. I also thought of him last night at a dinner meeting of the Fine Arts Club. The wife of a Meharry official was saying how upsetting her day had been. The wife of a Med. student (who happens to be a Lincoln grad.), who dropped out of school herself and worked to put him through college and is now off somewhere working to keep him in Meharry, arrived in Nashville suddenly. She went to the officials of the Med. school and told her story. She was broke, of course, having spent every cent she had left on a one-way ticket. But her purpose was to find and kill the young husband-student. She had learned, she said, that he was not just going to Med. school on her earnings but also living it up with other women, at least two of whom, she understood, were Fisk students, one colored and one white. This had produced conferences and tensions all day. The colored girl in question had quickly come forward, surprised to learn that the fellow was married, and promptly bowed out. The white girl was still unidentified at nightfall, but this did not prevent the disturbed wife from taking action. She got in touch, I am told, with the local White Citizens' Council and reported to *them* that her husband was going out with a white girl in Nashville. I don't know what has happened since, if anything.
No, I had not written Knopf anything specifically about *Ask Your Mama,* but I have jotted down a note, I will incorporate it in a letter presently. Meanwhile, I have about a dozen other important letters to write also. The unimportant ones I always bat out immediately, but the important ones I tend to hold till I can give them more thought—and you know where that leads. Whoops. . . . (hold the phone). . . . Herbert Hill just telephoned: what about my article for his anthology? Next week, I promised.

Best ever,
Arna

20 East 127th Street
New York 35, N. Y.
November 21, 1961

Dear Arna:

Did Macmillan send you a copy of the Czech *Popo and Fifina?* I've asked them to send one to E. Simms in Switzerland, too. . . . . . You remember the white lady who called on me in Watts wanting a large sum of money? Well, the same thing happened a few days ago, only this time it was a white man (who sat on the steps all night one night, came back several times, and finally got in on the heels of a visitor who had an appointment). He said he'd given away $100,000 helping others. Now, being down and out and having a book to finish, he thought I might advance a few thousand! He finally came down to a few hundred, then $50, then $25. I gave him $3.00 since he said he was down to his last penny. The other visitor had brought a tape of a play he had written—which he played in full—poetic and highflown, but almost put me to sleep. So my day was shot! Took me 24 hours to get my nerves together again. At the moment, neither white folks nor Negroes get past the front door. . . . . A more amusing visitor was the Nigerian poet and playwright, Wole Soyinka, whom George helped to teach the Twist and Soyinka in turn taught him the JuJu. He's about to have a play done in London. Bright boy. . . . . Diop of *Presence* [*Presence Africaine*] is here, too. But I just can't see everybody. Africans are a whole career in themselves nowadays once one gets started. Mphalele was just here last week. Senghor the week before. There's got to be a limit—unless one is endowed with both time and money—as I told the State Department lady last year—if I'm to be the official host of Harlem.

Quand meme,
Langston

My Xmas show goes in rehearsal next week. I'm standing in need of prayer!

P.S. 2nd SPORTS file posted you today.

12–13–61

Dear Lang,

If you have not taken off for Lagos yet, I hope the reception which *Black Nativity* receives will brighten the journey. I'm anxiously awaiting word. Meanwhile, Simple's remark that Negroes being just one tenth of the population raise nine tenths of the hell is positively wonderful. It should last a long time. Moreover it hints at something profound: the Negro's vitality. Let those who say the Negro is retarded, prone to crime, etc. brush *that* aside! We may have all the faults they list, but we sure are powerfully alive. I think it was a cracker who predicted that the negras and the mules would ultimately survive all else in the South.

The Detroit Book Fair was a wampus. Biggest I ever performed in. I had four overflow crowds in the new Wayne University auditorium and another out at a school in suburban Oak Park. During one of the merriest of the Wayne events, somebody stole my new Italian overcoat. I was sick for a couple of hours, but the Free Press (co-sponsor of the Fair with the Board of Education) sent a man to take me to a good shop and buy me another. I se-

429

lected the best I could find and felt better afterwards, but the new one is not like the one from Italy.

I saw your picture in Publisher's Weekly, taken at affair by Negro Book Club. Is that club actually doing as well as PW indicates? If so, that is just about the best news yet. If 10,000 Negroes are now buying books, we are entering the era we started crying for back in the Harlem days. This would mean final emancipation for the Negro writer. Read James Weldon Johnson on the subject in "Negro Americans, What Now" and remember that you and I have helped to bring it about!

So remember me to the Nigerian writers and send a card.

Best ever,
Arna

20 East 127th Street
New York 35, N. Y.
January 18, 1962

Dear Arna:

Just back day before yesterday, to pull your letters out of TONS of mail. . . . I had a wonderful trip, went to Ibadan and Benin; Paris on the way home, lovely even in the rain, rain, rain, and the old Grand Hotel is getting to be like home. Ollie Stewart and his charming girl friend send regards, Jackie especially to Alberta; Ollie, Jimmy Davis, and Inez Cavanaugh were the only folks I let know I was in town. Nigeria kept me so busy, I did not want another round of "must" engagements in Paris; so only had fun, saw shows, and those 3 friends. Marpessa Dawn is so BEAUTIFUL in her little comedy, *Cherie Noire,* now in its 700th performance. I left Paris at 1 PM and was in New York by dinner time. Jets are something! Really just big transAtlantic busses about a block long. . . . . *Black Nativity* still rocking the theatre; better even than when I left—at last night's show. (I brought all the women tiny bottles of Paris perfume). . . . . Well, I've got 3 or 4 hundred letters here to look at so this is to say if you're going to edit an African series, if you don't get Peter for South Africa, Ezekiel Mphalele should be good. For Sierra Leone, Abidoseh Nicol; for Ghana perhaps the poet-journalist, Francis Kobina Parkes, who is on his way to New York soon. I saw him in Lagos—delightful young fellow—currently of the Ghana opposition—so can't go back right now. . . . Saw Julian Mayfield and wife at the airport as I came through Accra. They'd just seen Dr. [Du Bois] and Shirley [Graham] that afternoon, say they're fine. . . . Lagos is HOT, crowded, Chicago-like, most interesting, boom town, sky-high prices, snakes in the gardens and alligators paying calls a bit too frequent for me in the "St. Albans" areas; and everybody arguing politics. Marguerite Cartwright [sociologist] there as usual every other week. Valients had a FINE dinner party for me. Send regards to you-all.

Lang

Be sure to get for your Library *Jazz Street* (Doubleday) beautiful photo book. I've decided not to do the Ralph Boston piece. No time.

Dear Lang,

The Slovak edition of *Popo* is as cute as it can be, and I hope the folks at Macmillan have sent a copy to Elmer Simms too. Meanwhile, I have referred a Ginn & Co. editor to you for permission to use your little poem "City" from *Golden Slippers.*

As for the scaling down of plans for the production of *Tambourines to Glory,* all I can say is that we are left without alternatives in these cases, but if we can't win in a rush, sometimes we can win as the tortoise wins. I think I would go along with the plans and hope for bigger things to follow.

I'm glad to hear that the NAACP book is about ready to move, and I trust *you* are about ready to move on the Harlem book in our series. What with Jan. 1, 1963 being the very Centennial date, I believe much would be gained if your book could be on the way by then. I believe it would benefit from quite some tumult and shouting if it were.

I've been missing your column in the Defender but note that you are on vacation and will be back in your accustomed place soon!

Reviews of *100 Years of Negro Freedom* keep showing up in out-of-the-way places, but I appreciate them all and especially the fact that general approbation for it seems to have increased as the slow and thoughtful readers finally got around to it. I'm now on pins to find out what this indicates saleswise. An old Yaddo-ite has just written to say she saw a copy in the window of a leading bookshop in Zurich.

Sorry about Zell and Garnett. So more anon.

Best ever,
Arna

Dear Lang,

Your letter today re: the Du Bois papers fits in with one from the Ghanaian Permanent Mission to the U. N. asking whether or not the collection contains correspondence between Du Bois and Nkrumah. So I am having a search made forthwith, and I will report to you about the 2nd Amenia Conference in a *few* days. Right now I can tell you the papers are in great disorder. They have been rifled and robbed, I suspect. Also, I suspect, the bales of letters removed by Aptheker for the purpose of possibly editing and publishing may not have been returned, and I am now about to inquire into that. If he still has them, I would hazard the guess that the correspondence you ask about is included. If you could contact him and inquire, you would also be doing us a great favor. His daughter helped pack the Du Bois library when it was sent to us. Du Bois assured me in person that everything went with the collection we acquired *except* his Africana, which he was taking with him to be given to the University College in Accra. So I would say that Fisk rightfully owns any papers that may have been removed from the main body of the collection.

Tell Arthur Spingarn, when you talk with him again, that we are working on the books now and will have a list of the duplicates it contains before summer, I hope. He will be the first to see this list. Then we will tackle the pamphlets, leaving the manuscript material and correspondence for the last. He may also wish to know that our American Missionary Archives (1839–1879) is being cataloged this year and will be in applepie order by fall for any and all researchers. It will fill more than 20 legal size filing cases (4 drawers each), a treasure trove indeed. And this still leaves us the Charles S. library and literary effects to process.

Best ever,
Arna

20 East 127th Street
New York 35, N.Y.
February 16, 1962

Dear Arna:

In getting ready to do another script for the producers of *Black Nativity* (who now have all kinds of plans, and think *they* discovered the format of dramatizing the gospel songs *themselves*) I was looking through our *Book of Negro Folklore* (which I haven't done for a long time, and so with an objective eye) and it is a GREAT book, and if we were white we would be recognized as doctors and authorities and professors and *such* because of having assembled and put it together. All of which helps me to understand and appreciate Dr. W. E. B. who went off to Africa and said, "Kiss my so-and-so!" For which I do not blame him.

You've probably read where white gospel singing groups are beginning to appear on the scene. In another six months, they will claim to have originated the idiom—and maybe get away with it in the public prints. As Eva Tanguay tried to do with the Charleston, and Gilda Gray did with the shimmy.

"They've taken my blues and gone. . . . . ."

George tells me he has an offer of a $200 a week job. Do you have at Fisk anyone else looking for a New York apprenticeship?

There's a wonderful book by a white lady coming out called *Her Name Was Sojourner Truth.* (Hertha Pauli, Appleton Century).

Lang

20 East 127th Street
New York 35, N.Y.
March 4, 1962

Dear Arna,

Explain this to me, if you can—after all these years, now, *all within a month,* I get word from 5 separate people that each intends to do a *book* about ME, or on some aspect of my work. What's happening, this sudden and simultaneous interest bookwise?????? Maybe I told you, but James Emanuel (cullud) has a contract from Twain Publishers for one on me as a part of their American Authors Series; a white woman in California I've never met has begun interviewing folks out there who knew me for her biography—which I am writing her I cannot authorize or in any way help on; another in Florida who has Harper's interested in a series of biographies for children on Negroes, past and present, wishes to do, or have one done, (and wants others writers to do biogs) so I've given her your name, Ellen Tarry's, Gwen Brooks—since her setup seems feasible; the fellow in Japan is turning his masters thesis into a book there; and the bibliographer, Dickinson, writes that he has some funds for research into a history of my relations with publishers—as an extension of his bibliographical study—for a book growing out of it, and how my various books managed to get published. Do you reckon they all think I'm dead? And me still intending to write my third autobiography??????? One or two books, I can see, maybe—but 5 and all getting underway at once!!! Coincidence, or what???????. . . . Nate and Dee White are separating. . . . Zell hopes to get a Mexican divorce this month. . . . Juanita Hall is quite ill, collapsed on stage in Las Vegas, left limb paralyzed. She's at Harkness Pavilion, New York, in case you'd like to send her a card. Josh White is in Flower Hospital, Fifth Avenue, N.Y. . . . . Two of my Chicago cousins are hospitalized. . , and another one's grandson (9) killed by a car last week. . . . What a year!. . . . Me, still here!. . . . And hope to live to write a couple more lives. . . . One *Black Nativity* producer collapsed again. Also Stella Holt (my *Simply Heavenly* producer) having had two off-Broadway hits this season (Troubles she had with one of them are fantastic.). . . . Lemme know if Alex received his record O.K. . . . . 50–11 people have served notice they are in New York or coming. Loren is in town. And before day this morning (about noon actually George says) a Japanese came bearing gifts from Tokyo. I didn't see him, but he left 3 lovely fans with my poems thereon in Japanese and English, an enameled box, and a beautiful woven mat. . . . I'm off to Philly tomorrow to see *Black Nativity* there—a special performance. . . . Being in process of simplifying my life, did I tell you I turned down my biggest fee yet for a banquet speech for National Council of English in Miami next fall? Also a nomination to the Authors Guild Board, and two other committee things. I am not taking NOTHING more at all, not *AT ALL,* NOTHING A-TALL until I get out from under things already promised. And am not seeing any more thesis people—other than those I've already agreed to (and have been) helping. Can't—as a new one turns up now almost every week. I'm referring them ALL to Yale, Schomburg, etc.,—but NOT HERE. . . . George is pretty good at politely getting rid of unknowns, and Mrs. Harper even better, if not so politic. Most interesting caller lately (by invitation) has been young William Melvin Kelley (cullud) whose novel (for June) Doubleday is keen on. Bright boy. Did you ever know his father back in the 20s when he was editor of *Amsterdam News.* Seems like I have vague memory of him, Kelley, Sr. . . . . The son was educated in prep schools and Harvard and is just now "discovering" Harlem—with excitement. . . . Zelma George's lecture, I thought, was brilliant—so the series got off to a good start—although Adele's salary for the next two months will go toward paying for it. Culture really needs patrons. Like Harlem little theatres, nobody ever seems to think of promotion—only the "art" side—not realizing printers, hall rentals, etc., must be paid. Oh, well—I've been through it all before!

Langston

P.S. Thanks for the info about the boy at Fisk. I've heard no more from George lately about his possible new job. He's been so involved in the Lecture Series, Voice, Inc., and Benin Arts, plus his college work, haven't seen him much. I hope my next secretary is not interested in culture a-tall.

L.H.

433

6 March '62

Dear Lang,

The indications are that you have reached a point vis-a-vis your public comparable to that which some years ago drove Hemingway to Cuba and which this week caused Thornton Wilder to announce that he is moving to Arizona (halfway between Nogales and Tucson) for the next two years. There, without tie or shoestrings or even cultivated conversation, he hopes however to remain within reach of the bars of each of the above cities. So that seems to be the price one pays for becoming an institution, a part of the culture, a classic in his own time. One thing is sure: there's no turning back. This has been in the cards ever since you wrote "The Negro Speaks of Rivers." Since you did not pause at that moment to count the cost, you are now in this fix: biographers, bibliographers, researchers and all such as that sitting on your steps!

Incidentally I have heard from the fellow in Japan, and I hope his plans to study at Fisk work out. I also had a note from the U. of Michigan bibliographer. We want to make sure we get a copy of his opus when it is finished.

Half a dozen reviews of *100 Years* have appeared since Negro History Week, and I have passed along some ideas to Allen Klots for trying to give the book a push in connection with Jan. 1, 1963, which is *The day of the 100 Years.* Will your Harlem book be ready by then? Could it not at least be announced at that time? A very psychological moment, I'd say. If you get a chance to emphasize it to Allen over the telephone, I hope you will do so.

I'll be looking forward to the novel by William Melvin Kelley, whose story in "The Urbanite" I saw. He is obviously one to watch. I don't remember his father, though I must have met him.

No word yet from the Whitney Foundation re the Opportunity fellowships, so I may go in the hole when I make my trip up for the lecture—unless they call on me as in the past. But they never waited this long before.

There is snow today here, but it is no worse than the rains of the past weeks. So out now to breast the storm!

Best ever,
Arna

(Next day)

P. S. You'll like, I think, "A Problem of Poetry," the first letter to the Editor, p. 44, New York Times Book Review, March 4. I did. Also "Poetry in English: 1945–62" in *Time,* p. 92 and on, March 9. Compare the point of view of the former especially with mine in my San Mateo Poetry Festival talk a few years ago. I used it recently for a talk at the ISC and got into an argument with Bob and a Vanderbilt prof. But the worm is turning our way, I suspect.

PP. S. Incidentally, Bob made up with Paul Breman by mail and promptly received the proofs for the book of his poetry Paul is publishing. What is this book of Waring Cuney's poetry Arthur Spingarn lists in the *Crisis?* I have not seen it but need a copy for the Library.

P. SS. I hope I made no mistake by giving your phone number to George's fine young brother Freeman. He asked for it; and I just couldn't decline to give it under the circumstances, but I asked him not to give it to anyone else, and I'm sure he must have had a reason for wanting to get in touch with George in a hurry.

PP. SS. Will notify you when the record comes.

A.

March 6, 1962

Dear Arna:

I'm just back (rather shook up) from Philadelphia where *Black Nativity* was done last night, and got rave notices today—so much so that the management is thinking of presenting it there for a possible run before it goes to Spoleto—as this was just one-night stand in honor of the star's anniversary, Marion Williams, in her home town, done at an enormous place, the Met, but to quite a crowd.

My Lincoln classmate, whose house guest I was, had just come back from a Puerto Rican vacation with Rev. Gardner Taylor, Rev. Marshall Shepherd, and Martin Luther King, to find his mother slightly ill but up and around—88 years old. While I was there, she slept away in the night and was gone when we woke up. (Rev. Frank Mitchell's mother). So I've been spending the last several hours since I got home phoning Thurgood and other classmates the sad news, for she was a sort of "college mother" to many of the Lincoln boys of our day. Friday I'm going back for the funeral, and on to Washington, I think, to see Gordon Heath in Owen's production of *Dr. Faustus* for which he came over from Paris to do. I'm anxious to see Howard's new theatre, which I hear is the last word in college playhouses. . . . . George has gone to see *Night of the Iguana* tonight, which I had to miss on account of today's events. Will also have to miss *Fly, Blackbird* on Friday—charming little integration revue I saw on the Coast, but it has been rewritten for New York, and folks are liking it here, too. I'm glad for, for one thing, it has brought Avon Long to the New York theatre.

Found in the mail on my return today that another old friend died in Montana —Bernard Powers whom I write about in *"I Wonder"* of Howard and Tashkent. . . . . If you up and die, I will kill you!

Langston

8 March '62

Dear Lang,

Your post-Philly letter is here today, and last night, after I had written you, Alex received the record "Best of Simple," which I look forward to playing a time or two come this weekend. Meanwhile thanks from both of us.

This afternoon the dentist is repairing one of my movable dentures, so I am using this as an excuse to stay at the typewriter in my study and, incidentally, to miss a routine and tedious committee meeting on campus.

Your experiences in Philly remind me that I have within the week heard from two Quaker friends and sometime associates of Jean Toomer, both of whom indicate that he is less than well and "lonely." If you're down that way again, why not call him and see what he says? Of course he was not lonely enough to answer a letter I wrote him sometime ago, but it may be possible he was not well enough either. These friends seemed to be vaguely encouraging me to telephone him or ask someone else who knew him to do so. (I didn't really know him.)

I have also received an interesting letter from one Ch.-Aug. Bontemps, publisher of *Les Cahiers Francs,* who says, among other things, "I am a vice-president of 'the International League against Racism and Antisemitism' and the author of several books, articles and, for one thing, of the two essays: 'Man and Race," 'Man and Freedom.' " He says further: "It is a remarkable fact that we have the

435

same name and the same way of looking at the struggle for advance of racial questions." Can you beat that? He had seen my *100 Years of Negro Freedom* and suggests that we exchange books. So next time you're in Paris I'll give you a letter to this most remote kinsman, if that's what he is. . . . Will you be passing through en route to Spoleto? It will be grand if *Black Nativity* can have a Philadelphia run in the meantime. . . . What is the status of that book of your plays you mentioned once? Will this one be included?

Best ever,
Arna

16 March '62

Dear Lang,

I am happy to hear that George has decided to stay in the fold, and I will pass the word along to John Baker next time I pass him on campus.

Wasn't that a nice piece Saunders Redding wrote in the *Afro* this week: "Nigerian Art Reminds Redding of Harlem, 1920"? I am especially grateful to him for bringing back to mind your statement, which I would call the Manifesto of the New Negro Renaissance. As I recall, I first read it in the *Nation* away back when, but I'll try to quote it in my Renaissance talk next month. It would be interesting if the New Africa were to pick it up and make it a touchstone.

All those people dying brings to mind one of the first of your poems I ever read, "I am waiting for my mother/ She is Death/ etc." Incidentally, I think changing that *mother* to *mammy* spoiled the tone. But I was much impressed when I first read the poem in the *Crisis* in 1924.

Have Bill Branch get in touch with our Prexy right away! Our Dr. Voorhees in Speech and Drama is near retirement. Either this year or next will be her last. Also, we have been looking for a publicity director. He might start there with a view to stepping into the Little Theatre when she leaves. He would be a fine person to add to the Fisk Family and having a white wife would not be a problem now: we have another mixed couple on the faculty now. Wright will be here over this weekend, he tells me, but then will be off somewhere. Maybe New York. So have Bill call or wire him and make an appointment. He may use my name if he wishes.

"Misty" is my top favorite among the popular songs. I hope you will write that lyric for Garner.

Alex just started working as an afternoon page in the downtown library (public), which is now integrated. Connie is due here Sunday to visit us till her husband completes his indoctrination as a Captain in the Med. Corps of the Army. He has been drafted and their present orders call for them to go to Japan in a month or so. My 82 year old aunt (my mother's sister) was here for a few days, after visiting Ruby in D. C. but has now continued on to L. A. She is close to some of the Delavellades, but she had left when your word on the passing of Adele Young (whom I liked very much and who visited us last time I was in Pasadena) arrived.

Seems like folks are just beginning to read *100 Years of Negro Freedom*. My books take the cake when it comes to slow starts. Seems to take at least a full year for any of them to get off the ground. I have had no report from Dodd, Mead since last year, but letters and late reviews have started to flow, and I hope that means something. So in the midst of all your other activities please save a little time to work on the Harlem book, and let's round out the series by the 100th year!

Best ever,
Arna

20 East 127th Street
New York 35, N.Y.
March 17, 1962

Dear Arna:

I am sending you, addressed to the Library, a packet of material that may be of interest to your L. H. files. Included in it is the final script of *The Gospel Glory, A Passion Play* to be enacted to the Spirituals (the *first* Negro Passion Play, so far as I know). Has there been a previous one authored by the Race????? The Library copy is autographed to Fisk.

I have, however, enclosed an *unsigned* copy of this song-play which I would like you to *give* to whomever at Fisk might be interested in staging it there—if only in a concert version—perhaps the head of the Jubilee Singers. I would send it direct, except that I don't know to whom it might best be addressed. I think the Music Department would probably find it of more interest than the Drama folks—since the Crucifixion story is told largely in and through songs.

Re Jean Toomer—I don't feel I ever knew him well enough, either, to intrude upon his privacy by writing or phoning him at this late date in life—especially since he never answered any of my notes in the days when we were preparing *Poetry of the Negro*—and I was told he'd gone over entirely into the white (and Quaker) world. Not even Georgia Douglas Johnson, of whom he used to be quite fond, and she of him, had had any contact for years. . . . . Waring Cuney has also disappeared from sight. Nobody's seen him for more than a year. I've written him —no answer. I hope he's not ill. I'll try asking Breman in London if he's in touch with him.

Langston

Georgia has a new little booklet of poems out. Get it.

P.S. Are you making any headway on your SPORTS book?. . . . I saw Jackie Robinson and his quite charming wife riding down Broadway the other night in a great *long* car. . . . Duke has moved out of Harlem! Who's left? Just me—and Ralph (if you include Riverside Drive in Harlem). Hall is back in Cal.

March 25, 1962

Dear Arna:

Good to see your letter to the *Times* re Jimmy Baldwin, which is certainly *Touchez!* Of course, Braithwaite did manage to do some general criticism, didn't he? But only by having all but his left heel over the white fence—and that had on a white sock (sox).

Books by and about (or about) cullud keep coming in so fast these days, I can't even open some of them. But the most interesting I've glanced at this week is

The African Image, Ezekiel Mphalele (Faber and Faber, London) in which he takes most of the wind out of the sails of *negritude,* and explores with objectivity the relations of Afro-Americans to Africana, humanly and literarily speaking. I'm anxious to read the whole book carefully. And I hope it will be published in the U.S.A.

I'm grateful to you for more than once reminding me that my Harlem book ought to be getting under way. IT IS: I've just written the opening paragraph this 3 A.M. of the above date, after having observed the late night streets as I went for the Sunday papers. Once I get started, a book sort of rolls on in spite of all else in the way. I hope it doesn't keep me from finishing up a couple of immediately urgent deadlines, however, that bear no relation to the Centennial.

If you were to write a book about me, it would be the BEST. But if you are going to wait until you retire, I might be retired also (in the other world) and not be here to read it—or to help you on it—with some tales I wouldn't tell anybody else.

Quand meme—
Langston

I'll relay what you say to John Akar—whom I haven't seen myself this trip.

Broussard's sister is married to Franklin Williams (former California NAACP executive, now Asst., Attorney-General of State, I believe) and they are light Louisiana stock, I think she told me. He's a Brooklynite. . . . . That handsome German *Jazzlife* is by Joachim-Ernst Berendt. Bruda Druck Und Verlag, Offenburg-Baden.

20 East 127th Street
New York 35, N.Y.
April 1, 1962

Dear Arna:

Bill Branch just phoned me. Said he had a long and pleasant talk with Dr. Wright and that he promised him a letter setting forth details on his return to Fisk. But so far, nary a word.

Takao Kitamura also writes from Japan (for about the 4th time) that he's gotten no response from Fisk regarding his application.

So I reckon you-all must be short handed down there. (Like the *Defender* that couldn't find time to write a note for *six* months—then come calling me up last week: "Where's the column?" And suddenly sent 6 weeks checks—when they owe me 6 months!)

I told you, did I not, that Rosey Pool is invited to Livingston College for a term in the fall. And that John Aker is already at Tuskegee and may be addressed there. And Augusta Savage's funeral was Friday. And Lawrence Langner is flat on his back in the hospital but holding conferences from his bed and spent two hours with me today going over plans for *Tambourines* which he says now tops the Guild list for fall, *Passage to India* and the other shows ahead of mine finally having had their innings. (He would go *down* just when *Tambourines* comes *up!*) Ay, the theatre!

I've done nothing but mail this week—answered at least 200 letters and acknowledged dozens of books, proofs, manuscripts and things. Doesn't seem to have made any visable dent in the pile still before me—so reckon I'll give up for the nounce-nonce—or whatever—and return to creation. . . . . . .

                                             Sincerely,
                                             Langston

P.S. George has written some quite charming fables for children, several performance scripts for Voices, Inc., and will soon have to hire a secretary for himself. For me, maybe the Lord will send "one angel down."

                                             20 East 127th Street
                                             New York 35, N.Y.
                                             May 6, 1962

Dear Arna,

Well, send me Connie and husband's Japanese address as soon as they get settled there, so I can advise my half-dozen amiable translators in Tokyo of their presence, also Billy Banks who is a radio-TV star there now. And Dr. Kojima, currently here at N.Y. Hospital, a charming fellow, brain surgeon, and my translator's younger brother.

Re a *Renaissance Anthology,* I have lots of letters of the period still in my basement, I think—a considerable batch having gone last year to Yale—but more to sort out, I'm sure, which might contain amusing extracts. And we could put House Rent Party cards and other entertaining michelanei—as we did in *Folklore.* I hope Doubleday or somebody likes the idea. Try to sell it.

Hill and Wang are going to do the Short Stories, so I'm now in process of making a sequence, and weeding out a few. There'll be 36 left—11 never in book form before, and of those four or five never published at all.

My "Waldorf" poem is definitely dated now—since it was in the format of the Waldorf ads at the time of the opening—so today none would get that satirical touch. But I'll send you a copy anyhow when I come across it in the current basement sorting.

William Melvin Kelley (whose *Different Drummer* has an excellent advance review in the current *Publishers Weekly*) sorted and sorted while I was away. But stopped to read so often that I am afraid he didn't get much done. Had stuff strewed all over the basement when I got back home. Anyhow, a couple of big boxes of Latin American books, mostly autographed to me by the authors, are ready to go to Yale. And the major thing—all my income tax records, bank books and statements and cancelled checks for twenty years—if any future researcher wants to see how *little* a cullud author made—all in files by years, except for the checks, which fill a box of their own. (Not as many as Booker T. Washington left, though, nor for such sizable amounts).

Donald Dickinson writes me that his Phd. dissertation project has been O.Ked —the publishing aspects and bibliography of my work—so he'll be here again shortly to delve in the basement, too, and/or at Yale. If he gets here before the now-ready boxes and files go off, he can see the publishers' statements over the years—and my own book bills which almost never equaled royalties. Usually the publishers wrote *me to remit to them*—rather than the other way around!

Teachers Union News just came with your picture and speech in it. But was it THAT short?

I find no word on my return from the Mbari-Makarere conference folks. And am sort of thinking of not going, anyhow. Don't see how I can possibly catch up on urgent undone things by June 4th in time to get away. So if I don't have confirmation Monday, think I'll write them to that effect—although I would like to see Lake Victoria and a few rhinos. But one cannot wait till last minute to get inoculations and things. Spoleto will be enough for this Spring, if I get there. Gospel singers are more fun than most writers, anyhow.

Langston

P.S. Did you see A. & I "Simply Heavenly"—or Alex? Thanks for slips.

Noel Sullivan's favorite niece's husband, Bill Mahoney of Phoenix, is to be U.S. Ambassador to Ghana. He'd be delighted. They're going with all 8 children.

Only Ethel Bell in L.A. dared to say she didn't like *The Blacks* (a hit out there, too). All the others said, "It's interesting." Ethel, like me, spent the 2nd act in a bar.

8 May '62

Dear Lang,

By now, I take it, you are in London and trying to adjust your sleeping habit to the new time. This should follow you to Kampala. I have just written some names for a Meharry Med student who plans to spend the summer with some sort of study at Makerere. He will miss you, he says, because he is scheduled to arrive about the 19th of June, I believe. Anyhow, you might tell Matthias Mosha and Zechariah Kanaiya I have directed him to them, and I hope their meeting with him will be mutually agreeable. His name is Otis T. Hammonds.

If I neglected to mention it earlier, I might say now that luncheon or dinner at the Lake Victoria Hotel (where Hemingway stayed) is quite delightful, should you want to repay courtesies or anything of the sort. You can visit the Botanical Gardens en route (where Tarzan scenes have sometimes been filmed, I believe). For mellow occasions in East African watering places the Pim's Cup is an excellent drink—it has a gin base. Have one on Alberta and me in honor of our earlier trip!

Also, meet and greet for me, Mr. and Mrs. Maxwell Jackson and ask him what about that planned production of *St. Louis Woman* by his theatre. He is the director of the National Theatre in Kampala. You will want to see this. It also occurs to me that his might be a good theatre to premier *When the Jack Hollers*, considering the folk quality of the play and the East African closeness to wild life, etc. They would also dig the KKK.

Also, if you get a chance, you will enjoy meeting (and remembering us to):

John Kazzora, lawyer, P. O. Box 3260, Kampala. If he invites you to dine, go. He serves *very* well.

E. M. K. Mulira, who was once *detained* for political reasons. Has been at Columbia U. where he met Charles S. J. Good scholarly family.

The Binaisa family.

John Bikangaga, principal of the Makerere high school department. His wife is a Watusi but not very tall.

Dr. & Mrs. Martin J. Aliker, P. O. Box 249, Kampala. He was educated in

U. S. at Northwestern Dental school. His wife is an American Negro. Charming home.

Mr. B. K. M. Kiwanuka, President General of Democratic Party, first head of government but now removed, I believe. Fine person.

Balam Mukasa, educated at Atlanta University (Morehouse) and Yale. Friend of John Hope.

Mr. & Mrs. Leonard D. Matovu (Ruth), P. O. Box 3136, Kampala, Ministry of Social Development.

Mrs. Barbara Kimenye, Librarian and Stenographer for the Kabaka's Council of Ministers (telephone 64331), Library Memgo, Box 91, Kampala. Charming. Has European *mother,* African husband, whom we did not meet. Mentioned by Era Bell in her book, I believe. Knows everybody.

Don't miss anything!

> Best ever,
> Arna

9 May '62

Dear Lang,

The short story collection was mentioned to me by Larry Hill and Arthur Wang, and I'm glad it is now definitely in the works. *Something in Common* strikes me as a very good title. I wish the book might have contained the rest of the stories from "Ways of White Folks" as well as the 36 listed, but I believe Larry said Knopf has plans to reissue that book and hence limited the number. If that is the case, it is understandable, of course. Even so, *Something* will be appreciated.

I thought it was you who told me Charles Harris had spoken to you at your party for me that Doubleday was interested in a Harlem Renaissance book or anthology by you and me. If so, he has only to say the word on paper, so far as I am concerned. The ideas are all ready to spring.

Meanwhile, Hill and Wang has asked me to compile a poetry anthology (Negro) which can be issued in both hardcover and paperback at the same time. I am working on the outline now. May I count on using at least a dozen of your finest? Actually my plan is to use some of the "standard" ones plus some that I think should *become* standard. And if *The Poetry of the Negro* is going to ever be updated, I will make a point not to duplicate more than is absolutely necessary.

The royalty report from Dodd, Mead on *100 Years* is quietly encouraging.

That was just an extract from the Waldorf speech in the *Teachers Union News.*

Horace Cayton writes that he tried to see you in California and still hopes to get in touch. He is writing his autobiography.

Connie and Tommy (Captain Ernest M. Thomas, Jr. 05707262) now have an address:

> Box 3084
> Kuma Station USAG
> APO 181
> San Francisco,
> California

I missed the A & I production of *Simply Heavenly,* but they are repeating the big scene this week at Fisk, and I hope to see it here. Talked to Poag last night, however.

So more presently.

> Best ever,
> Arna

> 20 East 127th Street
> New York 35, N.Y.
> May 9, 1962

Dear Arna:

Thanks a lot for that handsome program of the Fisk Festival. I am delighted my *Conga Se Va* was done. Did you see it? How was it? And with what music? (I love that program making ME seem like a composer). . . . . George is perturbed that the Jubilee Singers have so many non-Negro numbers. He thinks they should preserve the Negro heritage, and let the Choir do the standard things. I'm inclined to agree with him. Anybody can sing J. S. Bach or Gerald Strang. . . . . Or do *J.B.*

The confirmation came, so guess I will go to Uganda. But they sent no details at all about route or anything. (Cullud!). . . . . How did you go? What special inoculations did you have to have? (I've got smallpox and yellow fever). Anything you think I ought to know, please tell me. . . . . And if you've folks in mind I should meet at Makerere, give me their names. I should leave by June 3rd, I reckon, to be there until the 19th. Then, I hope, Cairo for a day or two, and Spoleto by June 24th when *Black Nativity* opens there. Back home I think by mid-July. But USIS wants me to go to Ghana.

Takao Kitamura writes me that he's admitted to Howard next fall and, in various ways, all tuition and expenses are covered. He'll come through New York at end of August. He asked me to thank you for your interest in him and Fisk, and says he will be writing you. . . . . Columbia accepted Emanuel's thesis on my stories, and he successfully defended it. As a result, he becomes a *DR.,* I reckon.

Will you-all be coming to Cape May this summer? Or New York? Would love to see Alberta, and how big Alex is getting. . . . .

> Cordial regards,
> Langston

> 11 May 1962

Dear Lang,

I'm delighted to hear the confirmation on your Makerere trip has come through. In the early literature Uganda was described as the El Dorado of East Africa. We found the weather and the greenness delightful after a Nashville summer, and the wild life and the rain forests we got a chance to explore were just what the Tarzan books (some of which were filmed there) had led us to expect. The longer we stayed at Makerere the better we liked it. I suggest that if you can make weekend safaris to Murchison falls and other interesting parts,

442

you try to do so. If not, rent a taxi, fill it with friends and drive to the Lake Victoria Hotel (Hemingway used to stay there) for Sunday dinner. Explore the Botanical Gardens there (at Entebbe). At some other time drive to Jinja to see the place where the Nile pours out of the Lake (the fabled source). This will take you through the stretch of original rain forest and let you see how the Heart of Darkness was before any of it had been cleared. In a few days I will send you a list of people we found delightful, as you will also, I hope, and to whom I'd like you to remember us.

The best way to get to Entebbe (where the airport is located) is by B.O.A.C. from London. You can get a jet direct. We did not go the best way. We stopped first in Paris and then Rome. But the plane we took in Rome could have been boarded in London, and that would have been an advantage travel-wise. Ours was not a jet on this leg and put down briefly at Khartoum. Returning, you can make a longer stop at Khartoum, if you wish, and make a side trip to Cairo. I suspect there is also service from Khartoum and Cairo to Ghana. There is none (or there was none in '60) direct from Entebbe or Nairobi to Ghana. From any of these points to Rome is easy via Alitalia, but we liked the Air France service best of those we used. The B.O.A.C. next. But this may have been because of the particular personnel we had on our Alitalia flight (Nairobi to Rome).

You will need a visa for East Africa (Uganda and Kenya), but the only inoculations, as I recall, were smallpox and yellow fever. We were told by Pan-Am that we would not need a visa, and we would have been in trouble had not our friends at Makerere fixed things for us.

There is a college bookstore at Makerere, and you will find it interesting, but the one to see is the Uganda Bookstore in the heart of Kampala. A fine place to get cards and souvenirs, etc. also. Like Brentanos. Also papers from all over. And don't forget to check the USIS library in Kampala—and Nairobi if you get there. Be sure to have someone show you the Ford Flats at Makerere where we lived and to drive you up on Kolola Hill at night for the view. You will want to see the new Bahai temple and the two Cathedrals (Catholic and Church of England), the new national theatre and the government buildings, but the folks there will take care of that, no doubt.

I am ashamed to say I missed seeing the Fisk dancers do *Conga Se Va*. I had a conflict, but would have gone anyway had I known they were going to do your piece. However, from all I hear, it was well done indeed. We have a number of excellent student dancers. Almost like pros. I agree with you and George about all that Bach and Strang and J. B. while many good things by Negro composers and dramatists continue to be neglected, but I don't know how to get this across. Incidentally, another area of Fisk excellence is indicated by the *two* recent Fisk graduates among *Ebony*'s "Best Dressed Negro Women." They are Mrs. John S. Stone, p. 109, and Mrs. L. Morris Jones, p. 118. The former was Gertrude Holiday when she graduated. The other was Adrien Lash. George might know them.

Finally for now, we ARE hoping we can vacation at our favorite spot at Wildwood, N. J. this summer. That would have to be the first two weeks of August, perhaps. Hope to see you then. So more anon.

Best ever,
Arna

20 East 127th Street
New York 35, N.Y.
6 A.M. May 12, 1962
(Still up and at it)

Mon cher ami:

I am getting ready to go abroad. (Doesn't that sound comme il faut?). So won't be writing you as often because I have to get ready to go abroad. Looks like I'll be going to Ghana, too, after Spoleto, where Noel Sullivan's nephew-in-law is about to be the new Ambassador, and I'm going to do a ceremonial. Alors? I don't dare come back home to all the undone work I'm leaving behind.

Thanks for sending me Connie's mailing address. But instead of asking Billy Banks and my Japanese friends in Tokyo to look them up, I'll send them Japanese addresses.

I'm glad you like *Something in Common* as a title—it means *both* racially and humanely—like the *Blacks* with masks on—all same white-black, front-back—a la Genet.

Delighted to know where Horace is. I've sent him already *Ask Your Mama* and *Best of Simple* to spur him on his way. Just heard from Irma in Detroit. Reckon they're sailing their boat on the lake now. Did you see it? They had it in the garage (instead of the car) when I was there.

Our *Renaissance* anthology no sooner said than done. I've selected some stuff already, and am making a tentative outline for YOU to fill in before we send it to Doubleday. It was Harris spoke to me, and I told him to talk to you. Thought he had. As I said you are the one with the critical and objective mind and balanced judgement.

(Besides, you have a whole library to copy stuff out of).

Re your poetry anthology, sure, use whatever of mine you wish. When you're ready, I'll send you some unpublished manuscript poems, in case you'd like one or two not in book form. Also, you know I've a whole lot of younger poets gathered for my proposed Indiana U. book, any of whom you can have, if you don't gather them fresh yourself. I've sent them to Rosey Pool in London, Eva Hesse in Germany, etc., so they'll be coming out every-which-a-where before Indiana makes up its so-and-so mind!X%#*!

I'm going to have sukiyaki dinner with Dr. Kojima tomorrow night. He's heading home shortly. (My translator's brother).

We had a dog-fight such as you never saw, three dogs, in the next door backyard today. Alarmed the neighborhood. And in the midst of it, Melvin Kelley's book arrived, bound in simple dignity, with a blurb by McLeish on the front. Melvin has been sorting Yale stuff in my basement. And we got all the lecture programs of mine over the years sorted out, so I'm sending your library a batch on Monday. I think it includes my first poetry reading in Washington in 1926 with Locke as chairman. A long time ago!

Quand meme,
Langston

Wednesday (5-16-62)

Dear Lang,

The heat has us going here already. Hottest May since 1944. We are also head-over-heels in other ways. Visitors: Ruby is here for a week, for example, and John Killens paused en route to west Tennessee and says he will stop a day or two on his return, not to mention the usual Fiskites, etc. So I can appreciate your going away excitement. Meanwhile, however,

1. May I request you to make a note about my series of books on the new nations of Africa and keep your eyes open for possible authors? Gerald Moore will be a good person to discuss it with in Kampala. I will add details later, but I would like you to get the notation in your folder, if you don't mind.

2. Please do send me the manuscript of your younger poets. This will help me a great deal as I work on the prospectus for the Hill & Wang job.

3. You might ask George to check at the NY Public Library (42nd Street, Theatre collection) and see whether or not a copy of Wally's [Wallace Thurman] play *Harlem* is available. If it stands up okey, we might consider it for the *Renaissance* anthology. If not, maybe Toomer's *Kabnis* as done at Howard. But we'll need a play from the period. What we need FIRST, of course, is a go-ahead from Doubleday.

4. For the record, I think you gave a reading of your poems at a tearoom or something over near Columbia *before* the 1926 reading in D. C. I took my then girl friend Charlotte, and that had to be 1925, because Alberta and I were married the summer of '26. I remember that Charlotte and Jessie Fauset struck up a conversation and we met Wytter Bynner (sp), and this was the only time I ever saw him. I also remember that this followed rather soon after you read to the group at Ethel Ray and Regina's apartment—which was so soon after your return to NY that you told me you did not have an overcoat yet (though it was December '24 or Jan. '25). Then you went on to D. C., early '25, and we exchanged our first letters. In the summer of '25 I was in Washington for a few days, visited you at the YMCA, was introduced by you to Bruce and Whatshisname Lewis Alexander and was taken by you to Georgia Douglas Johnson's house on Saturday night. Once when we were walking you pointed to a kid on a skatecoaster and said, "There goes my brother." It was the first I knew you had a brother. You were working for Carter Woodson at the time.

So more anon.

Best ever,
Arna

20 East 127th Street
New York 35, N.Y.
May 18, 1962

Arna:

I got my ticket N.Y.-London-Entebbe via BOAC today. Inoculations O.K. so now need only the visas. . . . . What is Ben Johnson's address in Rome? Ellison, who was invited, isn't going to Uganda, but says I should see Ben in Rome. . . . . I'll discuss your project with Gerald Moore. . . . Wally's play in the Broadway version was more Rapp's than his (so Wally said) and unless we had the original

445

manuscript, don't think we should use it. I prefer Toomer's, or *Plumes* by Georgia Douglas which came along about then. . . . . You certainly have a good memory. You're right about that first reading, presented by Harry Block of Knopf's at that tearoom near Columbia. I guess there was no printed program. . . . . Re *New Negro Poets,* my file box shows notations on the two sets of manuscripts, that on 5/2/60 and 5/3/60 complete carbons were sent you. Not too much more has come in since then, and what I have is not sorted or copied yet. Best of the ones lately (if she's not in stuff I sent you) is Miss Mari Evans. Hill is using some her poems in his Knopf anthology and likes her very much. She'll send you oodles at the drop of a hat—much not too impressive, but when she is good, she's very good, I think—a lyric poet. So write her. Phil Petrie and George both have poems, too—at this address. Some pretty good. . . . . T. Guild conference on *Tambourines* again next week! Sure can talk a lot in the THEATRE. . . . . First paper copy of *Fight for Freedom* (NAACP) came. Some NAACP cuts and an addition on why Du Bois finally departed. But no really deleterious revisions far as I can tell at a quick glance. But done without a by-your-leave! (Cullud!)

Langston

5–23–62

Dear Lang,

Just deposited in the Negro Collection your latest sheaf of material. Most interesting. Like Kelley, I had to stop and read much. That long letter from Maye Grant to AMSAC was *quite* an item! . . . . . John Killens was here for 24 hours. We had a long session over literary matters. . . . As for my proposed Hill & Wang poetry anthology, I think I'll confine selections to published work, especially where the younger group is concerned. Otherwise I'd be reading mss. forever. Of course, I'll stretch this to include things *accepted* for publication, like the contents of your anthology or Rosey's, and I won't hesitate to use unpublished items by the established poets, if I can get suitable ones. But thanks for Mari Evans' address just the same, and be sure to let me see the manuscript of the anthology some time this summer. I also hope something by George and Petrie is included or has been accepted for publication elsewhere, such as in Herb Hill's book. . . . On the other side of this sheet I will list addresses for you, including Ben Johnson, Bill Demby and some of the folk at Makerere. . . . I was glad to see the cover for *Fight for Freedom* in your sheaf mentioned above, and I can hardly wait to read the book. As a prelude to that, no doubt, the *Saturday Review* has sent me the uncorrected proofs of Louis Lomax' *The Negro Revolt,* which I'll try to get to this coming weekend. . . . That letter from Randolph Edmonds is exciting. I'm sure they'll make *Simple* jump on their USO tour. With this touring in one direction, *Black Nativity* in another, and *Tambourines* under discussion by the Guild, it looks like you've got a dramatic summer ahead. Might it not be a good time for that collection of your plays that was mentioned earlier? . . . . I'll try to get *Literatura Negro* for the Library. . . . Alex just came in to say he received his football letter today in school and was chosen one of the players who had *done the most for the team.* So he's feeling good. More presently.

Best ever,
Arna

20 East 127th Street
New York 35, N. Y.
May 26, 1962

Arna:

CONGRATULATIONS to Alex!

Thanks for the Rome and African names and addresses.

Mari Evans poetry is to be included in Herbert Hill's Knopf anthology. In fact, he thinks she is the best of the new ones.

Those who've published in magazines or booklets include LeRoi Jones, Ted Joans, O. G. Oden (Gloria), Mance Williams.

In Westport yesterday the Guild heads decided to get on to *Tambourines* at once, choose a casting director and production mangager this week, and sign up Nikos Psachoparoulous (Greek director of Yale Drama School) and beginning tying preliminary threads together for a fall production. We'll see.

Did you see where Jane White married white?

What if the man in the moon is a coon, coon, coon? Wasn't that an old turn-of-the-century song?

Seems like I remember it from my childhood.

Ernestine Washington's temple in Brooklyn is going to do my Passion Play in the fall with its enormously big hand-clapping gospel choir; Abyssinian Baptist reviving *Don't You Want To Be Free;* and the Negro actors in Rome, *Shakespeare in Harlem:* all of which should be fun, especially "The Gospel Glory" in a gospel church. The walls will probably be completely rent.

Sincerely yours truly,
Lang

This you won't believe, but you can see for yourself when you come to town: our block has its first gospel church (very small) called *GOD'S BATHTUB.*

20 East 127th Street
New York 35, N.Y.
May 28, 1962

Dear Arna:

Thanks for that fine quote you gave me to use in Uganda. I'd also very much like to have a copy of your *full* Harlem Renaissance talk, if one should be typed up before I leave next Tuesday, or if it could be airmailed to me:

c/o Writers Conference,
Makerere College,
Kampala, Uganda.

An announcement of some of those participating in the Conference came today: your Robie Macauley is one. But who is J. T. Ngugi of Uganda, and Grace Ogot of Kenya—if you know from your visit there? Also today USIS confirmed my trip to Ghana and also wish me to go to Nigeria, as does Mbari that is celebrating, right after the Kampala gathering, its First Anniversary at Ibadan—so with two invites now to Nigeria, reckon I'll fly on down there, too. It is less than an hour from Accra. Sam Allen tells me he is also going to Ghana and Nigeria for USIS at the same time. *Negritude,* in that case, will be amply represented. . . . . George

447

is reading the Baldwin novel now. (It's for sale here for the past two weeks) A hasty look on my part—seems like he is trying to out-Henry Henry Miller in the use of bad BAD *bad* words, or run *The Carpetbaggers* one better on sex in bed and out, left and right, plus a description of a latrine with all the little-boy words reproduced in the telling. (Opinion seems to be, he's aiming for a best-seller). With John Williams turning down an Institute of Arts and Letters grant, cullud is doing everything white folks are doing these days! Even getting their hair cut in white barber shops, and being buried by Campbell's on Park Avenue—latest vogue in Negro funerals with all-white undertakers and pallbearers. (Integration is going to RUIN Negro business. With the *Defender* able to get Leonard Lyons and Bennett Cerf's syndicated columns for $5 a week, why pay me my former fee for mine, is just about what Sengstacke said.) Oh, well—

Lang

19 August 1962

Dear Lang,

The London news on *Black Nativity* is most exciting! And your Simple column reprinted in *Jet* is socko. I was also pleased to hear "I've Known Rivers" on the CBS program of American Poetry, even though the young Negro actor who read it did stumble and seem to forget his lines once. But at least we are beginning to be included. And that's a giant step.

Which reminds me, I've been working on my new Hill and Wang anthology this morning, and I wonder if you can give me Sam Allen's address. If you see or talk to him again in passing, please let him know I'm counting on including something of his and would like his permission. I have his Denmark Vesey book, and I have a manuscript of your *New Negro Poets* from which to select about three poems of his I should say.

Things were piled up here, as expected, but the only bad news we met was the discovery that Alex' blood pressure was unaccountably up. The team physician noted it and accordingly sidelined him for this season. A real disappointment to him, even worse than the low sodium diet on which he has been placed till it comes down. So it looks like he'll have to get his kicks this year in other ways —perhaps from WRITING, of all things.

Sorry we missed you in NYC after the delights of Monday afternoon and evening at Patricia Murphy's and at your house, but we shopped and went to shows (*Camelot* and Radio City) on Tuesday and on Wednesday went down to Highland Beach for the rest of the week. Alex and Paul went out in Dr. Simmons' boat and caught fishes' mammy, and I upset my stomach by eating too many. . . . Alberta and I also visited the Arthur Davises while the kids fished. He told me the new *Negro Caravan* is on the way again. What about Herb Hill's book and your *New Negro Poets*? I'm about ready to start pulling the threads of my Anthology together. Have you a real fine *unpublished* poem (in any book, that is) I might include? Would you mind my using that suicide poem so many people used to like (especially Countee, now that MM is so widely discussed), Oh, the sea is deep// The knife is sharp// And the poison acid burns, etc. Have you a copy of it handy? I also want to be sure to include the Raisin in the Sun passage and the I Dream a World. These are hard for the lay reader to find, but he keeps thinking about them. All told, I would like to use about 15 poems of yours.

I wish we could have helped to celebrate Toy's birthday. It's powerfully encouraging to see folks carrying on so beautifully against the years. What do you hear from Dorothy Peterson?

So more anon.

Best ever,
Arna

7 November '62

Dear Lang,

Now I can scarcely wait for Christmas Eve to see and hear *Black Nativity* on ABC–TV. The Lincoln Center's booking is another exciting landmark! Nothing thrills me quite so much as seeing original Negroana make its way in the world outside the usual channels. The usual channels so often hinder rather than help.

I liked your piece in the *Afro* this week on the heavy financial demands made on the Negro writer by those who take him to be wealthy. Why don't you have reprints made so that you can include them with letters to future applicants?

Alberta went with me to Washington, and the bus ride was a joy, what with autumn hanging so heavily on the trees in Virginia and Eastern Tennessee. I did the Richmond job while she visited with Ruby and Lucille (Sonya's mother) in D. C. While we were there, Paul and Sonia came down for the weekend.

Thanks for the Ted Joans poems, one or two of which I can use. However I found my secretary ill on my return, and this is a handicap to work on the anthology. Nevertheless I hope to get to the letters soon. As for my new poem, well I thought of it as an air exploration of the tropical regions within and without. I hope this can be considered native ground, if not necessarily *negritude*.

I have just written a note to *The Book of Knowledge* saying, since you nominated me, I'll do my best to provide an article on the Negro Spiritual. I'm sure I can include something about the likes of *Black Nativity, Chariot in the Sky,* and *The Book of Negro Folklore.* So I think it's worth doing.

Connie's son Eric was born while we were away (November 1), and the cable was here when we returned. Mom and Pop and 7½ pound youngster all said to be doing well.

Florence Crannell Means and her husband Carl were here this morning. Someone called me at 8:30 A. M. to say visitors were waiting for me in my office. And me not rested yet from my trip. She wrote *Shuttered Windows* and *Reach for a Star,* among other things, *(Great Day in the Morning)* and she and he were driving down to the Carolinas via the Smokies and stopping along the way. So you see it's hard to catch up on sleep even down here.

That NAACP flyer for *Fight for Freedom* reminds me that I have promised to review the book for the *Crisis* and hope to get at it this coming weekend. Nice flyer—outstanding book! I see copies every where I turn. I'm sure it will be in steady demand at least as long as there is an NAACP.

Looby was re-elected last night, along with several other local Negroes and no doubt many others across the country. I have this against all of them: they kept me up past midnight listening to election returns on TV, when I was aiming to read and perhaps start writing my introduction to the Anthology.

Now that *Negro Digest* has started its own list of Best Sellers, I wouldn't be surprised if my prediction re: Negro writers and predominantly white vs predominantly black audiences were beginning to be realized. Publishers ought to find this worth watching.

So more anon.

Best ever,
Arna

December 16, 1962

Dear Arna:

I am not in Lagos, but sometimes I wish I were. My stars are somewhat cross-eyed. . . . . The new play starring Claudia McNeil is somewhat cock-eyed, doing nobody connected with it much good except Dianna Sands and Cicely Tyson who, in minor roles, prove themselves brilliant young actresses headed somewhere in the theatre. . . . . Juanita Hall is having a chitterling supper tonight which I forgot about. It being now 3 A.M., I guess I won't go. . . . . . But I did FINALLY get off just now to Indiana University Press my Foreword to the *Poetry of Black Africa*—the last of my pressing deadlines—due since July and one of the things I meant to do in Africa. Shades of good intentions!. . . . . Just when I have a show coming into Lincoln Center, *Black Nativity,* the newspaper strike starts here, so nobody knows when anything is playing where, or if openings are off or on! As Simple says, "Something is always happening to cullud."

Tonight I finally got hold of Adele to take dictation for me and we found under shoals of mail your letter of a month ago regarding permissions for my poems, poets addresses, etc., lost in the shuffle due to my California trip and George's Nashville one and Westport and all the other comings and goings and shows and stuff. Sorry this delayed answer. But I am sure you know you can use any poems of mine you choose in your anthology. (What is it to be called?). . . . . . "Lenox Avenue Mural," should be credited to *Montage of a Dream Deferred* used by permission of the author; "I Dream a World" from the opera *Troubled Island,* music by William Grant Still, used by permission of the author; "Without Benefit of Declaration" and "Pennsylvania Station" used by permission of the author. (These two are in no book). . . . . . "We, Too" is a title I do not recognize, but use it anyhow if it is mine. (You don't mean, "I, Too, Sing America," do you?) George says it might be the one about the Congo—"We have no tribal marks, etc."—which is now called "Congo Brother." (He has just looked it up, and it is)—so change the title on it. Not in any book, so used by permission of author.) . . . . . George has sent you the poets' addresses you asked for—except that we do not know who William Browne is. Can you give me a clue? . . . . . . When is your anthology due out?. . . . . . Mabel Smythe is just back from Africa and Hugh Smythe has just gone to Africa, and cullud are crisscrossing all the time. Me, I want to go to Brazil; and probably "I shall go, I will go—to see what the end will be."

White reindeers and black Santas to you,

Sincerely,
James Mercer Langston Hughes
(Ha! Ha! You didn't know I
have *four* names.)

450

Dear Arna:

I am sending Pauli Murray's letter on to Garrison's law firm. If she is not still on the staff there, I am sure they will forward it. Everybody is moving these days to the new housing projects 'private' which are already beginning to crumble and tumble down, and the self-service elevators are worth your life to ride in alone. (But might be nice for maiden ladies who've never been raped). . . . . As for Margaret Walker and Helen Johnson, I'd say go ahead and use their poems, and pay if and when contacted. In Margaret's case, only way to get a YEA or NAY is by telephone—as I advised Herbert Hill (I believe it was) who finally phoned her. She's like Marian Anderson, Sterling Brown, Miguel Covarrubias (was) NEVER answer a word to anybody, not even wires. . . . . I'll see if Helene Johnson can be reached by phone, as I believe it was Adele who gave us her address, but I cannot locate it just now, and George (staging 6 TV shows for his class at NYU) is sight unseen. Next time you send me a secretary DON'T send one intrigued by the arts, or with any talents of their own. . . . . . Lawrence Langner dropped dead only a few hours after I'd had a long conversation with him on the phone about Eartha Kitt and *Tambourines,* and he was to have seen *Black Nativity* that night as the Guild is considering it for their cross-country subscription series next season. Again, as Simple says, "Something always happening to cullud." His funeral: 11 A.M. tomorrow. I must struggle up and try to make it. . . . . End of week *Nativity* began to sell out in that ENORMOUS Lincoln Center. Last-night-Sunday-seats all gone, and there's no standing room. Did Nashville see the TV showing? L. A. did. . . . . I am snowed under with mail up to the ceiling! Rosey Pool is in town, plus 50–11 other out-of-towners, and folks think I'm the *Nativity* box office, so I've unplugged the phone. HAPPY NEW YEAR!

Langston

WHEN is your anthology due out? WHAT are you calling it? Paper covers, too?

January 2 1963

Dear Lang,

Today's mail brought, in addition to yours, letters from Gwen Bennett, Helene Johnson and Mose Holman, thus substantially reducing the list of the unheard-from's. Gwen asks for your address and wants to hear from *you.* So you don't need to wait for me to tell her, in case you have a card or something you wish to send her (same old address). Meanwhile, I'll follow your advice re: Margaret Walker and the few other silent ones. My letters to Waring Cuney have NOT been returned, as I expected, but they have NOT been answered either. The one to Frank Marshall Davis was returned, however. Nevertheless the anthology is moving toward a conclusion. A number of women poets practically threaten me if I give their ages, and even some *men* whose ages can be found in print elsewhere ask me to list them as much younger than their real ages. I am trying to contrive a way out of this difficulty. Needless to say, I will not print lies to please their vanity, even if it means leaving out the biographical notes. Of what value would fictitious notes be?

The contract gives the title of the book as *American Negro Poetry,* and I suppose that's what it will be, but we haven't talked about it. It includes only the USA poets of this century, the first two being JWJ and Dunbar. A paperback edition is planned, but H & W are still debating whether to bring out both at once or publish the hardback first and the paper later. I believe I incline a little toward the former, but I suggested they flip a coin. Publication is supposed to be in May or June.

The paper edition of your *Famous American Negroes* looks good. I am all in favor. I hope such editions will perk up the Negro audience, here and in Africa!

We did not get the *Black Nativity* broadcast here. However we have had several more European scholars studying Negro American writers and researching them here. Two of them working under the same professor at the Sorbonne who guided the dissertation of Jean Wagner. This professor appears to have done his own graduate study at Harvard and to have written one of the major books on Walt Whitman. He is certainly doing right by the Negro American writers of today.

Let's hope 1963 will be good for *Nativity, Tambourines, Prodigal* and your other productions. Luck is the main factor in show business, I sometimes think. I'll keep my eyes open for the kind of amanuensis you describe, but they are far apart. In fact, I've had a hard winter for a similar reason. Mine hasn't functioned either—or not much. Between illness, marriage and other causes of absenteeism I have seldom seen her.

The Haydens' dog named Saki had thirteen pups the other night, and I understand eleven are doing well. No wonder he has asked for a sabbatical leave next year. Even one dog can demand a lot of attention.

Best ever,
Arna

8 January '63

Dear Lang,

After talking to you on the phone I called Mike Lunine, and I assume that by now you have heard from him again. He said he would write, but first he wanted to explore possibilities for presenting you at a later date, perhaps during the spring. I have not seen or talked to him since.

Meanwhile, the big thing here continues to be weather. Since the two big snows, we have had two steady rains, and the promise is for more of the same—one or the other. Up here on the hill and this distance from the Campus and with all our doors and windows designed to take advantage of the views—well, you might say we are more involved with outdoor conditions than we had ever been before.

If I may judge by the publishers' catalogs, you would seem to have another active season ahead, bookwise, what with the anthology from Indiana U. and the reissue of *I Wonder* by Hill and Wang. The latter is especially gratifying, I think, because it is one of those books that got less attention than it deserved back in the days when nobody was paying too much attention to Negroes or caring very much. Also, because I hope it means that volume III is just ahead!

You are also the ideal person to do the Josephine Baker book. I hope you waste no time getting to it. Her differences with the U. S. press (or a section of it) may hurt her personal appearances here, but I can't imagine this harming the book; it should help. The warm element of controversy combined with the warm element of sex and no strings and the French flavor! This could be your first best seller as well as a solid possibility for serialization, etc. So I urge again, let no grass grow etc . . .

Me, plodding as usual, an updating of the chronology for *Story of the Negro* (which still sells surprisingly well), an essay on Du Bois requested by AMSAC, the section on Literature for Johnny Davis' (and Phelps-Stokes') Negro Reference Book, and gentle nudges from both Knopf and Houghton Mifflin to ask how "that" new juvenile is coming on.

I also had an odd letter from Ted Joans requesting two crisp five dollar bills —which I promptly sent. He said he and family are stranded in Greece, living in a cave and reduced to begging. Address c/o American Express in Athens. I also sent him a copy of a review of *American Negro Poetry* in which one of his poems was singled out for quotation. . . . since man does not live by bread alone.

Could you or a member of your staff get me a copy of the program of *In White America?* I'm anxious to see what selections from American history they are using. I am also curious as to which J. W. Johnson poems are used in *that* show, if any of you know.

Meanwhile, power to *Jerico-Jim Crow!* May the wall fall, y'all.

> Best ever,
> Arna

January 14, 1963

Dear Arna:

After the reception at Wayne in Detroit the other day, there was a big midnight party of authors and writers at which I saw Margaret Danner and others who spoke of you.

Ronald Milner, as you no doubt know, is completing a novel, currently on a Whitney Fellowship. Detroiters seem to think very highly of him as a writer and from what I heard, the first portions of his novel have excited definite interest at Harpers as well as Little, Brown. In talking with him, he seems to be a most sensitive and intelligent young man, and I have the feeling that he might very well be a good creative writer. He has a wife and two little children, is 24 years old, and has taken a year off from work to complete his novel, but now feels under pressure he might not get it quite done before his fellowship runs out this spring, but feels that if he could work throughout the summer, without taking a job, he could have it entirely completed by August. Would you know if the Whitney might consider giving an additional partial grant for this purpose? And do you think that he might graciously request this? Did you meet him when you were in Detroit, or have you read any of his material? He tells me that the *Negro Digest* has accepted one of his short stories.

When I got home, I found the Paris reviews of *Black Nativity* awaiting me. All absolute RAVES with one on center FRONT PAGE with BIG photos *(Paris-Presse)* headed: "A Dozen Black Angels Invade Paris"—"their wings rustling with gentleness and love—causing the opening night audience to explode with joy."

Another refers to Marion Williams as a "mystical Josephine Baker. Alex and Princess Stewert get their share, but it is Marion hailed as a new star in Paris— "Probably one of the most extraordinary personalities ever seen on the stage." (*Arts*).

With cordial regards,

Sincerely,
Langston

20 East 127th Street
New York 35, N.Y.
March 7, 1963

Dear Arna:

Allen Klots tells me you have NOT turned in your book either. I thought it was to have been a Centennial Edition!?#?! Is or ain't we ready?

Bloke Modisane spent the weekend with us. (We have a guest room now on the first floor where you can stay anytime you wish). Bloke gave a very amusing and informative talk at AMSAC, then headed for Virginia. According to his schedule, Fisk is his last lecture stop, March 26, 27, 28. He is likable and lively, so look out for him, and give him a beer.

Sunday I gave a cocktail party just for folks he knew in London or Africa— Rosey Pool, Vinnette Carroll, a couple of Johannesburg jazz boys who play for Miriam Makeba, etc. We had fun. Rosey Pool departs tomorrow for a Caribbean Islands hop until end of March. Flu has had so many folks down here—me half down all last week—that I wish I could hie me to warmer climes, too.

Black Nativity is back in London at the Picadilly in the very heart of the theatre district. In April it goes to Rome.

I saw the jacket of Herbert Hill's anthology. It looks good. Herbert is carrying the jacket around as if it were the book already!

Mari Evans' little boy ran away from home . . . Raoul got robbed . . . Alice Childress is quite ill. Also Marvel Cooke not well . . . Waring Cuney is on a religious kick and won't see sinners, Rosey Pool reports, therefore his seclusion . . . I am making my will next week. Anything you want to be left? Chappell wants to inherit my *Street Scene* and *Tambourines* copyrights, so I have to make it for them. . . . . . Hi-o-de-derry-O!

Langston

8 March '63

Dear Lang,

Your letter would have gladdened this grim Nashville winter like a breath of spring had you not gotten off on wills and flu and runaways and the like. But since you mention it, and since we have both marched across the frontiers of sixty, I might say that, God willing, and should you wish it, I'd be mighty proud to edit and properly introduce your *Complete Poems,* and I would hope the copyright picture would be clear enough so that no one publisher could monkey-wrench such a project. I have also in mind, as you know, a biography, and it would help if this could be properly authorized.

Does the Chappell interest in *Tambourines* mean they are about to publish it? I don't see how else they would be entitled. . . . I'm glad *Black Nativity* keeps rolling. We have ordered three copies of the *Five Plays* as a starter. Likewise the *Poems from Black Africa* and *Something in Common*. Also new copies of *Pictorial History*.

American Negro Poetry has gone to press WITHOUT the birth years of *James Emanuel* or *James Vaughn*. Could you or one of your elusive aids telephone the two for me and ask if they would pass this information by phone to Mr. William Hoffman at Hill and Wang? I am writing notes to both, but knowing poets and knowing how rushed they are at H & W, I am trying both approaches.

My manuscript for Allen Klots is indeed late. However, my desk is now clear of poetry, and I promise not to touch anything else till I have delivered *Athletes* to Dodd, Mead.

Meanwhile, I'll put something in the ice box for Bloke Modisane. I'm glad to know about your *fourth* name. It definitely goes in the Biography!

Best ever,

Arna

P. S. We're building a house of our own. Did I tell you? I don't expect we'll ever get it paid for, but we hope to move into it this coming summer, perhaps July. It seemed like a good idea to do something like this before we reached the retirement age at Fisk (65). Have you got a picture I can put on the wall of my new study?

20 East 127th Street
New York 35, N.Y.
March 11, 1963

Dear Arna:

Since you have known me nigh on to forty years, and since you have, in my numerous letters to you, information possessed by no one else, this grants you permission to write whenever you may choose my oficially authorized biography, as you state in your letter to me of March 8, 1963, that you might like to do.

Regarding a volume of my *Collected Poems,* this note also grants you access to all of my poetry to be found at any time in manuscript or unpublished in my files or in the James Weldon Johnson Memorial Collection at the Yale University Library. Donald Dickinson at Bemidji College in Minnesotta should eventually have a complete bibliography of my published work in magazines, newspapers, and elsewhere. The rights to all the poems included in my three volumes of poetry now in print as of this date, namely, *The Dream Keeper, Selected Poems,* and *Ask Your Mama,* belong to Alfred A. Knopf, Inc., but *all* other poems including those in previous Knopf books but *not* in the three above mentioned, are my property, and may be used without Knopf permission in case there is a *Collected Poems.* All my previous books of poems published by Knopf are now out of print and the rights have reverted to me. These matters may be cleared with my literary representatives, Harold Ober Associates, whom you know.

Since a *Collected Poems* need not include bad poems, or specially written occasional verse, etc., I am willing to trust your literary judgement to exclude all manuscript or magazine verse you may judge to be not up to par. Such poems should be destroyed to prevent their being used elsewhere or, if given to Yale or any other collection, marked: NOT FOR PUBLICATION AT ANY TIME OR IN ANY FORM ANYWHERE.

As you know, James Emanuel is doing a brief biography of me in his study of my work for the American Authors series, with my permission. Constance Maxon, whom I do not know, declares herself to be doing an unauthorized biography of me, and I have written her that it is unauthorized by myself, and was begun without my knowledge or consent.

I myself plan to do perhaps a third autobiographical volume in due time; maybe even a fourth. You may, of course, make use of any of my published books for your proposed biography. Much unpublished manuscript material omitted from *I Wonder As I Wander* may be found at Yale, since that book originaly was much too long and had to be cut considerably.

Langston

P.S.OSOS: S.O.S.: Between George's [Bass] TV and radio NYU shows and Raoul's Coffee Concerts and Adele redecorating the Market Place Gallery for its Spring reopening, I can't hardly get hold of a soul to type a page. I trust the next assistants I get will not have an ounce of artistic interest anywhere in *any* field at all.

You probably did not know I have a fourth name: James *Mercer* Langston Hughes.

Again sincerely yours truly,

Lang

13 March '63

Dear Lang,

Your letter of Monday (11) covers the matter of the *Collected Poems* and the *Authorized Biography* of L. H. with your usual thoroughness and feeling for essentials. I propose to do both, and I regard my authorization as a sacred trust. Meanwhile, I'll keep an eye peeled for the Emanuel and Maxon biogs, as well as your third and fourth installments of the autobiography, all of which will contribute, I'm sure, in some measure to the work I plan.

The journey in time always fills me with wonder, but we have no choice but to keep cool till we see what the end will be.

But back to earth, I'm proud to be "nominated" as you mention in yours of the 8th, but I've learned not to pin hopes, as they say. I have also heard from the MacDowell Colony, and I think I might like to spend June there, if it can be arranged at this end and that, since July promises to be our moving month. I could then promise Allen Klots to have his manuscript by that time for sure, if I don't make it by May as I now aim.

The new house, incidentally, is at 3506 Geneva Circle, Nashville 8, Tenn. It is on a hill from which we can see A & I, the river and most of the north-west part of Nashville, and I hope you can arrange to come and inspect it SOON.

I have now heard from Emanuel, and I trust Hoffman has made contact with Vaughn. Invitations to speak in Shreveport, Raleigh, Greensboro and Milwaukee

456

have come in. My first thought was to decline them all (all for Library Week in April), but I may change my mind and go to Milwaukee.

So more presently.

Best ever,
Arna

20 East 127th Street
New York 35, N.Y.
Sleepy—5:30 A.M.
March 11, 1963

Arna—

After its lying around unread for a week (we're all so BUSY it seems) I've just opened the February "Crisis" and find your charming review of "Fight For Freedom." It's FINE! Thanks a lot! I'll almost forgive you for not getting your Dodd Mead book done since I realize it's such "little" things that always keep one from major writing. (Well, to my woe, do I know!) So *double* thanks for such a nice review.

Lang

P.S. Can't hardly make it to my bed. I wrote a requested poem (for the Jelliffe's Testimonial) and a month *over-due* "Sat. Review" fried today. "Little things— that take one's *life*. The getting *to* them is worse than the doing!

20 East 127th Street
New York 35, N.Y.
Weekend epistle,
March 16, 1963

Dear Arna:

Your new house on the hill sounds as if it will be charming. Lemme know when's the housewarming. . . . . . Last night I went to see *The Milk Train,* but started out too late so saw the film, *Sundays and Cybele,* quite beautiful; and tonight *The Milk Train,* big comedy melodrama with a bravura performance by Miss Baddeley of London, but weakest of T. W.'s plays to date, seemed to me in terms of depth of characterizations and warmth. Some great individual scenes, though, and loud enough to keep one awake. Seems it had TOO much changing and cutting and adding in rehearsals, and could have ended twice before it did. . . . . My African godson (the grown one) asked me for a name for his first son, so since he is Catholic, I suggested *Martin,* after Blessed Martin, and he so named him. . . . . . My New York godson, now 15 and at the want-to-quit-school-age, came by today. He is, as Simple says, about the darkest *young* boy I ever saw. His papa lately went and snatched him by main force from what probably was a den of iniquity, a week or so after I went and got him out of a hospital at 3 A.M. because his

457

papa has no phone so couldn't be reached after he busted his knuckles fighting off (so he said) junkies who attacked unawares. He goes (?) to Jane Fisher's school where I also know others on the staff, but he is so dark none of the teachers could see him in classes (or else he wasn't there, I don't know which). Anyhow, I told him that if did not make himself visible or audible, I would give him back to God. The very next day, one of the teachers told me he saw him in his room! So? (He's the one has my (almost) whole name: Langston Hughes Mickens. My favorite godchild! *Regardless.* Today I bought him some work clothes (blue jeans) and had his hair cut so short he *can't* conk it. (Until Easter). At which time I am in favor of eggs being colored and haids conked. . . . . Would you not be?

Lang

20 East 127th Street
New York 35, N.Y.
March 29, 1963

Dear Arna:

The Jelliffe's Testimonial in Cleveland was quite something—over a thousand diners; Sissle and Blake and others for entertainment; and a moving program— a bit too long, of course, but not a soul left. Besides the dinner, I did two TV shows and a radio program in 24 hours. Got back exhausted. Nobel, Eubie, and I did TV history of jazz filmed for $$$$$. Seemed to have come off good. . . . . . . Bloke Modisane got back a few hours after I did. Reports splendid tour, but a little perturbed that *only* place nobody met him at Fisk, and nobody knew he was there for 24 hours or so, or even took him to the International Student Center. But he was pleased to meet you and Doug. And came back fatter than when he went away. . . . . I hear tell Rosey Pool is due there soon. Tell her HELLO for me. . . . I have one more testimonial dinner to do—which will POSITIVELY be my LAST public appearance of the century. The wear and tear and autographing are too much. Each time I swear off, looks like something comes up one HAS to do. But this next one is the LAST. I started out to be a writer, not a public speaker, and a writer I intends to be! I started a new novel on the train to Cleveland. . . . . *Street Scene* back in the City Center Opera lineup for this Spring. *Mulatto* opens in Madrid April 5. *Black Nativity* played its 3rd return engagement in Brussel's largest theatre, then Geneva, now in Rome this coming week. . . . . My namesake (darker than Canada Lee and Clarence Muse *combined*) just came by at 2 A.M., was looking for his father in the vastness of Harlem but couldn't find him, so came here, feeling rejected. I played him Billie Holiday's "God Bless the Child That's Got His Own" and we discussed the strange ways of parents, me having been rejected, too. Then went and ate 2 big bowls of spaghetti. . . .

Lang

P.S. I told everybody in New York I was going to California until after Easter, so hope to have a little peace next week to maybe see a movie, or go to the dentist, or cut my toenails, and just let the phone ring. . . . .

458

20 East 127th Street
New York 35, N.Y.
April 5, 1963

Your Honery:

Thanks no end for bring me *au courant* on the title *Honorable*. Mr. Measures does not include Judge Pigmeat, who is always addressed as Your Honery.

Are you coming up for the Whitneys? Just had a long letter from the Detroit novelist in embryo, Ronald Milburn. Mr. Jones saw him out there recently. We both have a strong feeling he is WORTH encouraging. Milburn's own suggestion is that we find his WIFE a job! (Another Ralph Ellison—in more ways than one, as he says he doesn't want an advance if the publishers keep wanting to tell him how to write and revise his novel while it is still in progress. Sensible, I think. I told him he is, no doubt, a DEEP writer. He says he wants time to think out his novel's resolution. I told him I let my characters resolve themselves. At which point, I put down:

THE END

But I told him not to try to write like me. We need a few writers who also think.

Bloke is just back from a lecture in Wilmington; and has gone to see the white man kiss Ruby Dee's foot in *The Balcony*—which scene they will probably cut out down South. . . . . The new edition of *Pictorial History of the Negro* looks fine. Tell Looby his bombed house is therein. Your *Story of the Negro* is listed as recommended reading. . . . . Bob Cooper reports your son Paul as being a *top notch* youth worker. . . .

Sincerely,
James Mercer Langston Hughes

P.S. I am going to enroll my namesake in a jiu-jitsu school, so he won't get any more busted knuckles fighting. He can just throw his adversaries over his left shoulder by one thumb.

20 East 127th Street
New York 35, N.Y.
April 13, 1963
Easter Sunday

Dear Arna:

The first night, naturally, in *Les Poètes Nègres Des Etats-Unis* I read about *myself*. Last night I got around to scanning some of the others. I had not heard all those varying stories of Cullen's birth as related in the first section of the chapter on him, *Une enfance mystérieuse* (1903–1918) in which you are quoted. And I imagine if anybody of the reputed trio of "notoriété publique" were living, somebody might sue Jean Wagner over his "faits. . . . jamais fait l'objet de declarations écrites." Don't you reckon? Wagner certainly did a lot of research —but he seems to have missed that wonderful *Afro* headline: "Groom Sails with Best Man."

Wagner seems not to grasp Negro humor too well, anyhow—which I think weakens his discussion of the blues in my chapter. He's also a bit off the track relative to religion and myself—which I indicated to him in my note congratulating him on his "monumental work" and thanking him for the first really compre-

459

hensive critique of my poetry as yet in print, done with great sympathy and over-all understanding on the whole. But I wish I had had (for the sake of his book, not mine) a chance to clarify him a bit more on the two areas mentioned above. Re humor, he takes dead serious some of the things that we would take as jive. And sometimes confuses the universal or racial "I" as personal. Is he Catholic, by the way? And have you had a chance to read (at) the book this Easter?

Langston

20 East 127th Street
New York 35, N.Y.
5:45 A.M.
April 23, 1963

Dear Arna,

CONGRATULATES on your Milwaukee haircut! I am glad it were not your haid! .... I sat next to Emily Kimbrough and across from Marc Connelly at the Lloyd Garrison Dinner (though we being "surprise guests" dined privately and "intime" with beaucoup cocktails and wine and hilarity) and we got to talking about lecture tour adventures. Emily said once she went out to take a walk in the cool of the evening before her lecture, but neglected to remark the name of her hotel, got lost, panicked, and could not even remember the name of the town she was in or for whom she was speaking, so stopped to buy a paper, thinking she would at least learn the name of the town and her sponsor therefrom, but it turned out to be an OUT OF TOWN NEWS STAND and the paper she bought was Indianapolis or someplace she wasn't so when she asked passersby for the name of the biggest hotel in Indianapolis, they thought she was crazy! She was almost due on the stage before she got straightened out. . . . Then they got to talking about Texas. I asked if anybody there had met Billy Sol Estes. None had, but said "Let's talk about somebody else we haven't met." I suggested Elizabeth Taylor. It turned out half the table had met her, and she was a schoolmate of Emily Kimbrough's twin daughters. So there followed many a tale about her, Mike Todd, and all, as our table host was the head of MGM or whatever company made *Around the World in 80 Days*. By the time we did our surprise appearance at the main dinner, there wasn't much fun left to be had. But since we "topped the bill" and I was the last speaker, it was O.K. Except for Adlai Stevenson and Garrison himself—who quoted about half my *Big Sea* in his speech!

George, me and the sorting student have been up all night preparing for the Yale truck to come tomorrow—which, I think, is getting its most precious haul yet: several hundred letters of the Harlem Renaissance period. I came across an enormous big dusty box full of 1920–30 letters, that must have been boxed up before I went to Russia and unopened until now: *everybody* in it—you, Zora, Wallie, Du Bois, Aaron, Bruce, even Jean Toomer, a hundred or so C.V.V. cards and letters including the whole Zora-MULE BONE episode from both sides with him as an arbitrator who finally washed his hands and declared he wanted no further parts of it; Alain Locke, and a real treasure trove of Jessie Fauset letters, from the one accepting my first poem to 10 or 12 years thereafter; lots of James Weldon Johnson and Walter. I guess I never threw anything away ever. Wonderful letters from you! You will HAVE to go to Yale to ever write a book about me

—or about yourself, either. (These make up 39 separate manila folders in a BIG transfer file. Plus various small boxes of categories too large to fit into single folders. I don't know how I ever read so many letters. It will take posterity quite awhile! . . . . I also found some letters I *never* had opened or read. Some, I just left that way and sent on to Yale. I am sure I told you I have a bad habit of *not* opening letters I feel at the time I do not want to read—worriation letters and such. Usually I get around to opening them eventually—unless they get buried in piles, as some of these of the 20s and 30s evidently did. . . . I have a half dozen unopened from March-April of this year, *right now* 1963, until I feel better toward the projects, persons, or causes they represent, or can maybe cope with what I am sure some of them want, or am less pressured by deadlines. . . . Once I opened one some years ago months late—and found a check—fortunately still good. . . . . My namesake godson brought me his junior high graduation photo today. I am proud of that boy, getting through school and cannot read a lick. But, being most amiable, teachers all like him. Also seems like he plays good basketball. . . .

Sincerely,
Langston

20 East 127th Street
New York 35, N.Y.
April 25, 1963

Dear Arna:

This must be good luck and $ week for the writers-in-residence at 20 East 127th Street!

GEORGE received word he has been awarded a Whitney Fellowship—on the day after his 25th Birthday.

The same day BLOKE MODISANE (who is still our guest) was taken to the Four Seasons for a drink by his editor from Dutton's who, on that day and date, accepted his autobiography for American publication, with a nice advance.

And today Yale sent me a check for almost $1000 to cover what I have paid out in sorting and filing and listing and boxing fees to William Melvin Kelley, Raoul Abdul, and others working in the basement preparing my material for shipment to the James Weldon Johnson Memorial Collection. They had agreed to pay up to $300, but generous, assumed the amounts expended to date in 1962–63 in full. (My dentist, who in all these years never sent a bill, will get half of it as a token payment. The remainder I will use to clear up the rest of my stuff in the basement, as there is still a lot of tedious sorting to be done. Did I tell you I found a letter from Henry Miller in his own hand? And several more from Ezra Pound.)

Eros is pulled out of downtown bookshops, editors indicated on obsenity charges—which I predicted as soon as I saw the black-white nude spread. So I don't know if we can find you-all one or not. Will try.

L. H.

Marion Palfi is here with her 200 photos of Greenwood, Mississippi, and tales of hiding in church toilets, etc. to save her films. If you think Fisk is a site of X#!*X!# and all, visit 20 East 127th!

May 10, 1963

Dear Lang,

Say $$$, and I jump. What with moving day (July 1st) bearing down, and all that that will mean, I will not willingly miss any promising $$$ opportunities in the next three years. So I quickly posted the lists you mentioned, though the week here has been so mad with interruptions I have not till today (Friday) been able to take my seat at this machine.

Joan's new baby was a week old yesterday (May 2 was her birthday. Wendy's, that is.). While she was in the hospital, her firstborn (Avon) spent the days here. In his three-year-old majesty he had things his own way, with even Alex retreating as he bowed.

Yesterday I reread, slowly and thoughtfully, your charming piece "My Early Days in Harlem." I would not like to see a word of it changed, and I look forward to its appearance in print. Where? I only wish I could recall for sure the name of the librarian you ask about (Mrs. Lattimer). I knew her too and generally saw her in the Schomburg collection when I returned to visit NYC after moving away. Regina Andrews could tell you, as could Jean Blackwell Hudson, no doubt.

I also gave a close reading to Elaine Elinson's very good paper. With a little more work, I would say, it would be publishable. If she has this in mind, I would think she might strengthen the piece by confining it to poetry. Where she digresses to prose, she might *instead* consider some of the other poems in *The Weary Blues, Fine Clothes to the Jew, The Dream Keeper,* which books she apparently did not use. Maybe she thought the *Selected Poems* adequately covered these. In any case, her application of the criteria of the New Criticism (more or less) to your poems is interesting, like the belated decision of music critics to give jazz serious consideration as art. More often than not, I make light of the academicians when they get pious about the techniques used by spontaneous, natural-born, creative folk, but I don't suppose we can do anything about it, and in this case I think the writer starts with her own personal response to the poetry and works her way outward—which I think is proper.

What about this European jaunt I hear talk about?

I'm glad Bloke saw the folks at Hill & Wang, and I hope he does the book. A *general* book on South Africa by one of the blacks seems to me an excellent idea. Imagine a general book on Alabama or Mississippi by one of us? Imagine *Holiday,* for example, asking me to write a piece on New Orleans. South Africa seen whole, but through black eyes!

So more presently.

Best ever,
Arna

462

20 East 127th Street
New York 35, N.Y.
May 26, 1963

Dear Arna,

I've got a half dozen letters around I am scared to open. Still behind the 8-ball on contracts and things—at the moment *Prodigal Son*'s got in the way. Producer of *The Blacks* seems raring to go, hopes to clinch a theatre this week, so naturally wants new songs and revisions right away—which I've been working at the last few days to neglect of all else.

Peace reigneth! Bloke flew back to London yesterday; George has gone to Cleveland this weekend to see his mother; and my other assistant, Raoul Abdul, to Vienna for 3 days to sing a Birmingham concert way over there. Left Friday, too, and says he'll be back tomorrow. (Just like Harold [Jackman] in the Renaissance days going to Cannes for a weekend on Princess Murat's yacht). Such a quiet weekend, with nobody to work with—or for—I have not had for a long time. Phone rang all day. Nobody answered. Guests came and went below. Me no see! Three Latin Americans dropped by without appointment. Me, not home. Peace!!!!!! (See P.S.)

Do you reckon Father has gone to Glory? Nobody has seen him in quite a while. He doesn't come to his 128th Street Kingdom any more.

Peace. . . . .
Lang

P.S. I really would like to know if Father has gone to Glory. Can't any of your researchers find out?????????????????????????

Emerson went to Hartford to play in the Elk's parade band. Our photographer roomer went to Washington, Lou Draper. Sort of mass exodus from 20 East. How coincidental can things be?

I want to know about these coincidences—totally unrelated. You are colleged; also, I guess psycoanowledged.

Lots of folks seem to have read my *Post* "Simple's President" on suggestions to Kennedy: "I reads the line." Today's papers report Jimmy Baldwin suggesting same procedure—via the Attorney General—to lead the Alabama students in.

6-25-63

Dear Lang,

Speaking of objets d'art, the Harmon Foundation sent an exhibit of African art down here for the Festival. From it we bought for our new house a watercolor by a Congo artist. The price was $80, which makes it just a little more expensive than the photo by the Whitney photographer. We now have East and Central Africa represented, with the West and North yet to be heard from. . . . also South.

Ted Joans was not one of the poets who had asked or been promised fees for their poems, but on your suggestion I am asking Hill & Wang if they will now consider doing same in his case. On the whole, they are nothing like as open-handed with their money as was Doubleday, being less wealthy, no doubt. I don't know whether they have even sent notices to the included poets, much less books, though I supplied them with a list of addresses. One or two poets have written

463

to ME for copies, and now my 10 are gone. And I didn't receive enough money in advance to pay for typing and postage. I am hoping, of course, that eventually royalties will earn it.

So I can at least appreciate your feelings as hands reach out from everywhichaway to put the touch on one they believe to be loaded. Your sojourn abroad ought to turn their thoughts in other directions for a while. So in Europe, stay hid at least long enough to break off some of that communication. By the time you return, I'll try to have a replacement copy of *American Negro Poetry* for your library.

Gwendolyn Brooks appears to have gone way-out, but it's nice to have a poem about you in her forthcoming book, and I'll keep digging till I get the meaning. . . . Thanks for the excellent snapshots.

Congrats to George on his songs. Alex is writing a *play!* He is relieved to receive a scholarship from Fisk, since he didn't want to leave home anyhow. Says he is too fond of home cooking. So U. of Louisville, Colorado, Virginia Union and others who seemed to want his 250 lbs. on their football line are now out. He also likes his little evening job in the downtown public library (Main), which he hopes to hold. First Negro employed at a desk (periodicals room) and serving the public. Just two or three years ago cullud couldn't enter the door. . . . A group of Negro ministers went down to make a test. Since this didn't seem the place to pray or to sing "We Shall Overcome", they strode to the desk. The lady there asked, "What do you gentlemen want?" The one with the loudest voice said, "We want to borrow a book." The librarian smiled pleasantly and asked, "What book, sir?" Not one of the Negroes in the group could think of the name of a book, so they backed away shamefaced and left. They decided thereafter to confine their non-violent protests to stores and movies and YMCAs and the like. So the library quietly desegregated, and Alex is the one who hands them (the Negroes as well as whites) the magazines they ask for when they come in on certain nights—and I am a member of the NASHVILLE PUBLIC LIBRARY BOARD, which meets this afternoon, incidentally. Well, maybe I used a little influence to get him the job, but several members (white) of the City Council have done the same—and they were not even trying to break down segregation.

So more anon.

Best ever,
Arna

Hotel Westminster
Rue de la Paix
August 25, 1963

Dear Arna:

Paris has been rainy and cold (50 and such) but still as lovely as ever, and I've had a week or so of complete peace, nobody knowing I'm in town, except Eunice Carter, Louise Logan, Lucille Armistead, Babs Gonzalez I ran into on the Boulevards—Americans passing through. And Mollie Moon and daughter arrive to today, so I'll probably see them, as I did in Rome. . . . . Last night was the Fetes de Liberation de Paris from the Nazis, and Josephine Baker in her French army uniform was the star, sang "Mon Paris" and "J'ai Deux Amours" before what looked like a half million people in the square of the Hotel de Ville (City Hall). She had all her medals on and without makeup—quite thrilling. And the crowd was made up of all the races of this now very cosmopolitan (more than ever) city —Many, many Africans, Algerians, Indo-Chinese, Moroccans, Americans—and I ran into three colored stateside friends there, and we managed to get right under the stand where Josephine and Yves Montand appeared—since I had cased the site in the afternoon, and dined practically on the spot. . . . . . George is learning French at the rate of two words a day, and I am leaving him here for a few weeks before he comes back to classes. I've gotten a half dozen cables to come home tout de suite: *Tambourines* finally going into rehearsals Sept. 15, a TV show pending, and a film to be made in Nigeria in December. So looks like I will have a BUSY fall. In preparation, I have been catching up on sleep here. . . . . Had a pleasant three days in London last week with *Black Nativity,* Bloke, Rosey, Richard Rive, and others. The whole trip has been delightful. I only wish I could stay longer. In London Paul Breman gave me proofs of your poems. The Intro-duction of yours is BEAUTIFUL, the poems FINE. It's about time! . . . . . As usual, I brought some URGENT work to do. Haven't done a lick! But anyhow, you are getting a note on the typewriter we lugged from Israel to St. Michel where we are staying (after the de luxe above) in a real French hotel full of African students —run by a wonderful massive lady named Madame Tina who mothers everybody and shouts all over the place when they get too loud. (At Lorca's BODAS DE SANGRE a big section of African students must have thought they were at the Apollo in Harlem—they laughed so loud in the (to the French) wrong places). Same off-beat sense of humor Harlemites have. When the lover touched the girl, they fell out! It added a new dimension to the play. . . . . Paris is very expensive this year and getting more and more so. No wonder lots of tourists are by-passing it for Rome and Madrid. . . . . Drop me a line at home. . . . . Hello to the family.

Langston

20 East 127th Street
New York 35, N.Y.
Labor Day, 1963

Dear Arna-
Nice to find your letter awaiting my return last night. I had *delightful* flight back—jolly vacationers all around and charming seat companions. Found all O.K. at home—tons of mail still be read—Mrs. H. giving a yard party for the block kids—Zepplin Wong in residence, having flown from Frisco for the March —Emanuel in basement *still* (after a year or two) going through my (inexhaust-ible) files—for his book on me—"Tambourines" for the umpteenth time audition-ing *same* (everybody cullud) actors over and over. . . . How big is your new house? Send me a snapshot of Alberta in the garden. . . . Sure good to see the Toomers. . . . Sidney Peterson fell down a glacier, so Dorothy was in Geneva. . . . George is in Zurich. Me, home, gracias adios!

Langston

P.S. Karl Priebe sent me a big beautiful painting in a BIG box—and I don't even know him.

465

Adele's uncle died in West Indies. Ramona's mother here, so both came into their own $! Adele has bought a car, Ramona a house! $$$ lovely

6 September '63

Dear Lang,

With your letter today came a copy of the letter you received from Harper & Row asking to include the short things from *Golden Slippers* in one of their forthcoming readers. Meanwhile, I'm cheered to see your intro to *Poems from Black Africa* reprinted in the *Authors Guild Bulletin* and a selection of these poems spread out in *Time* this week.

If you can't read the enclosed, you might want to pick up a copy of the current *Library Journal* or ask for it at the Library. Another piece I wrote this summer has been circulated by USIS to papers in Africa. It is a piece about American Negro poetry, but I haven't heard yet whether or not any papers have picked it up and used it.

Give my greeting and encouragement to Emanuel. I look forward to reading the book he is writing.

At the moment I'm writing the story of Willie Mays for the ATHLETES book. I still have Althea Gibson, Wilt the Stilt and Wilma Rudolph to finish. Hope I can make it. If you find yourself talking to Allen at Dodd-Mead, you might say the end of the opus is finally in sight, but the work on the new house set my work back *months*. In any case, I'll not make travel plans (to NYC) till I complete the job.

We don't have much in the way of a garden yet, but Alberta is working hard. Anyhow, I'll send you a picture as soon as I can get one developed.

I liked your column answering the letter-writer who didn't like Simple. The anti-folk element is becoming vocal again. They are ashamed of Mahalia and Ray Charles. Down with them!

Best ever,
Arna

20 East 127th Street
New York 35, N.Y.
October 28, 1963
4 A. M. after a
long production
conference.

Dear Arna:

Thanks a lot for those schoolboard clippings you sent me. But the bit of excitement down there is as nothing to the current goings on at the Little Theatre —near knock-down-and-drag-out in the aisle after dress rehearsal between producers and the young and most cocky 27-year-old theatre owner (who, by the way, made his million in buying marsh land in Nigeria then selling it to the government there at 10 times its purchase price, I hear). "Hold him!". . . . No, let him go, I'll knock his teeth out! . . . "Call the police" in this lovely old bandbox

466

of a playhouse. . . . . The next night at the first preview *between the acts,* the same thing, only this time on the sidewalk in full view of the public. All parties forcibly restrained by others. Then the theatre owner called for his bouncer-manager who barred two of the three producers from the Little Theatre forever and would not let them re-enter to see the second act. (They haven't been back yet. A million dollar lawsuit threatened, also "We'll move the show to a Schubert house". . . . . "You can't because you have a contract with me and I dare you to move." (Owner). . . . . "Don't threaten us—or you'll find yourself with all the fire-violations in the book on your theatre before opening night!" Etc., Etc. . . . . Anyhow, we're still there and performing—and things on stage look pretty good. Cullud behaving (on the whole) beautifully. But the white folks!!!!! . . . . . Incidentally the backer's millions come mainly from housing for Negroes (projects, etc.) in Texas which began with a Negro partner in construction, since dead—so a project is named after him in Dallas!!!!! Do, Jesus! . . . . . Me, still "smiling through" and taking a nice comfortable orchestra seat every night to watch the real-life dramatics in the aisles—which are more exciting than even my own on-stage creations. "No biz like . . . etc.

Lang

Added to this—a 2 day stagehands strike against our theatre only.

P.S. All this show news, of course, *confidential.* . . . And to top an incredible day (and night) find on my return home just now an urgent note to get in touch with my godson's (the dark one's) mother, with a Bail Bondsman's card attached —so I guess the kid must be in jail. Anyhow, they have no phone, so can't find out at 4:30 A.M., and hardly enough energy to do so, anyhow, right now. Only 4 hours sleep last night. GOT to go to bed!

A bientot,
L.H.

In the midst of all the strife and turmoil, the money man from Dallas announced to the cast that he is making a profit-sharing setup for the show, a sizable share of the profits (if any) to be prorated among all the members of the company —so they will have a bit of extra money to further their acting studies, musical careers, or what ever they want to do. Sort of nice, no?

21 January 1964

Dear Lang:

Well dog if you-all DIDN'T pass a miracle around *Jerico!* It's tremendous. Such reviews I haven't seen in I-don't-know-when. Long may the banners wave. I look forward to adding a full dossier on it to the collection here—and to reading it too. I suppose it is too much to hope that the play will still be running in Mid-May, when I hope to get up that way, but I do.

Meanwhile, thanks for the clippings. Thanks too for speaking to Allen Klots re ATHLETES. He has now written me, and it seems I'll have to go ahead and put Althea and Wilt the Stilt back in the book. Maybe also Wilma, but she remains optional. Will try to do in next month or two, but boy am I bogged down! Everything always happens at once, and I find myself with four or five deadlines near the same date. Of course I'm an old hand at NOT making them.

467

My copies of Paul Breman's limited edition of *Personals* just arrived. Are you on his list of subscribers (or comps) for the series, or should I set one of my copies aside for you? I don't suppose they'll last long.

Another good report from *Story of the Negro,* which is being updated again. It's nice to have a few titles like this that rock with a steady roll.

Did you let Lunine book you for a later date at Fisk?

So trumpets and drums to you and your marchers, and may you not leave one stone upon another in the whole of Jerico!

Best ever,
Arna

January 25, 1964

Dear Arna:

"Life for me ain't been no crystal stair." Almost everybody is behaving like varmints. Eccept Stella Holt, the sweetest, nicest, most honest producer in the business. Jerico is her 31st show. We did capacity tonight. She's off for Honolulu next week on a grant to set up a theatre there. (See article in today's (24th) *Times* about her. (Blind, so never sees her own shows.)

George graduates in June. Talented boy who has done some excellent radio and TV scripts, and will eventually probably make more money than you and I put together. I'll be needing someone else like him (but preferably *NOT* interested in the arts—although not a requirement). Look around and see if another coming Fisk graduate fits the bill. Please—for June–July on.

You know the old saying, "Hard times will make a monkey eat red pepper." *Tambourines* losses forces me to return to the public platform: Hampton to open the new 2 million dollar communications building. Detroit for a week end of Negro History Week festivities. (I dread such a long period), University of Pittsburgh, University of Buffalo, etc. My bank account was down to hardly stamp money last week, so I started answering 50–11 unanswered requests for speaking dates, picking out the better fees. *Black Nativity* is some $7000 behind, VIP syndicate several hundred on my column. Both contracts being abrogated —Bob Ming in Chi my lawyer. Not even statements yet from *Tambourines.* So in the red for 1964.

4 A.M. now. My full-name godson just this minute phoned. 16—but a nightowl like me. His boon buddy, barely 16, is the proud father of a bouncing baby girl by a 15-year-old white girl. Present at the birthing, when the nurses asked, "Who's the father," and this little 4 foot colored boy stepped forward, they like to fainted. (Life is at least amusing.) My godson was looking at my TV LATE-LATE-LATE Show in the front room last week. I went in and didn't see anything but the screen. In the dark I couldn't see him at all. He is THAT dark! He quit school to go to work. Home problems. He claims nobody likes him. I used to feel that way myself, so I understand. "Lonely house, lonely me. . . ." Lotte Lenya, Martha Schlamme have recorded.

Langston

July 19, '64

Dear Lang,

If you missed the exciting book review in *Life* July 3, '64, *do look it up.* By Albert Murray, the most vigorous and perhaps most capable new Negro writer to appear recently! Move over, Jimmy B. . . . I assume you caught the first installment in the current *Holiday* of the crosscountry trip by the Negro novelist who wrote *Sissy.* Both of these the kind of assignments we never could have gotten in years gone by. We is rising!

The copy of *God Sends Sunday* arrived yesterday. Thanks. I'll be proud to have you use a passage from it as you indicate, and if you have occasion to mention the book to Hill & Wang, I'll admire that too.

Johnny Davis called about my revisions on the Phelps-Stokes essay and told me *you* had finally promised your piece this coming week. With so many little things breaking, it becomes harder and harder to deliver. Not to mention the secretary problem you describe so vividly. I'm employing my daughter Poppy during her vacation months to help me with the work here at home. No longer possible to find anybody around Fisk to take on extra work. Anyone who can type can get good pay.

Was Hugh Fisher the son of Bud? Otherwise I probably didn't know him. And who is Dee White? Your godsons—boy!

Please forward my congratulations to George on the Rosenthal award. . . . Julius Lester, another Fiskite gone Village-ite, was here to talk about Zora. He plans an article and possibly a book. Will try to interview you, Carlo, Fannie Hurst, etc. He has lots of ability. May make it.

Best ever,
Arna

20 East 127th Street
New York 35, N. Y.
December 9, 1964

Dear Arna:

I don't recall ever having any autobiography of Mrs. Bass and have looked on my biography shelf and don't find one. But just the other day I had an announcement of the opening of her reading room.

No, I didn't get nary copy of your *Famous Negro Athletes* and would surely like to see it. *Black Thunder* I love, as always, and wish it would be reprinted here, too, as well as *God Sends Sunday.*

Thanks for Darryl's information. Perhaps if he is coming home to Cinci for the holidays, he could stop by h e after Christmas, he could see the set-up, get acquainted, and we could see if something might be worked out for later in the winter. Tell him, please, and ask him to phone me collect after 4 P.M. most any day and I'll talk to him about it: LE. 4-7739

My flu's about over and I'm getting out again—tonight to see Harry Belafonte and his African benefit show at Philharmonic with a fine troup, they say, from Guinea, plus my Zulu folks from the Fair that Lucille Lortel and I got extensions for, so ten are still here. And my own little protegee, Philamon, who is 24 but looks 14, is going to the American Academy of Dramatic Arts. The oldest one is at U. of Illinois on a Fellowship that came via the prof who edited my PLAYS out there.

I told you about being offered a WRITER-IN-RESIDENCE at the University of Grenoble, via Jean Wagner, didn't I? Another such offer has just come from the University of Colorado. And there's still the one from the University of Nigeria. Regrets, in all cases. No can do.

Lemme hurry up or I'll be late to the show. It's 8 P.M. now.

Sincerely,
Lang

20 East 127th Street
New York 35, N. Y.
January 28, 1965

Dear Arna:

This afternoon I had a conference with Charles Harris, editor at Doubleday's, regarding the proposed updating of our *The Poetry of the Negro,* which it seems the publishers are at last of a mind to do, thinking the new edition might be brought out in both hard covers and paper, keeping the book in size and format about as it is now, so that the price would not have to be too much more.

To keep to approximately the same number of pages, but at the same time adding twenty or so new Negro poets, and adding samples of those white poets who have written significantly about the Negro since 1950, I proposed dropping in its entirety the "Caribbean" section, and placing Claude McKay in the U. S. A. group, our first section. We keep all the poets presently therein, and add the new ones to it. This would call for additional "Biographies," of course, and the lengthening by perhaps a page or so of the "Introduction." Permissions, as before, are to be negotiated and paid for by the publishers, plus (as a tentative proposal) $1000 advance to us. Think over these things, and perhaps save an hour when you come to town next week to discuss them with Charles Harris, and to see (if you haven't already) Doubleday's beautiful new Park Avenue offices.

Harris is chairman of the Book Committee for the Dakar Festival to be held in Senegal in April, 1966, the date having been pushed back. I'm a member of the general committee and the book one, too. Both of us hope that you can take part in this Festival. And Harris is proposing an anthology of the papers the various writers might prepare for seminars in Dakar. Seems like to me you ought to do the one on Poetry, which I have so said. So when you come to town, this could be discussed, too.

My what-I-hoped would be a hideway (but ain't) is just across the street from the Park-Sheraton, so look me up in Room 625, Hotel Wellington. And don't tell anyone. Cicely Tyson, I hear, lives on the same floor, saw me, and found out from the bellmen (cullud) I was registered, so has already spread the word. Oh, well! It's my DETERMINATION to get the *First Book of Negroes* revised! Meanwhile we can have a sandwich at the Stage nearby. So I'll be seeing you when you reach Manhattan.

Best ever,
Langston

20 East 127th Street
New York 35, N. Y.
February 23, 1965
(As Malcolm X lies
in threatened state)

Dear Arna:

Thanks for the Lowell poem which I haven't had a chance to read yet, what with all the excitement going on in Harlem, sirens wailing and fire engines screeching by...... Anent our anthology, can't seem to catch Harris in by phone as yet. But I will.... In the meantime I have Raoul, Lindsay, and George on the trail of new poems by whites, and have also pulled down all my white poetry volumes and anthologies since 1950 to see what I might have on my own shelves. Meanwhile, you keep up the search down your way, too..... Of contemporary cullud poetry, I have plenty here. And have already begun having some copied for our mutual consideration—having two receiving folders, one COLORED, one WHITE, at hand for storing until you come this way and we can make final selections together.

CONSIDER THIS PROBLEM: Much of Mason Jordan Mason's poetry is *really* good; some poems I like enormously. If he is colored, he should be in our book. If he is white, he should be in our book—either way, one or the other; else in a mystery section all by himself. How can we find out his ethnic background? In the light of rumors, would it do any harm to write Judson Crews and ask him point blank if Mason is him or somebody else, explaining the situation and that we would like to use three or four poems in our book? Would you like to do this: Judson Crews, Ranchos de Taos, New Mexico. I have a half dozen of Mason's books here when we get ready to make a selection, when and if we can decide how to do it. Let me know what you think.

You'll shortly be getting a permissions sheet on your poems chosen for the French anthology. . . . 4 A.M., signing off. . . . .

Sincerely,
Lang

P.S. The first section DO of Tolson's LIBRETTO is not bad. I think we well might use it. Maybe also FA. And something from the new book, short.

March 2, 1965

Dear Lang,

I'm still trying to catch up with the flow of routine trivia that backed up here while I was in Boston and New York. A big part of my problem traces to secretarial weakness at the Library and in the new office (I'm holding—or trying to hold—down both jobs), where we have two greenhorns stumbling over each other. So the fact that Charles Harris has been elusive has not yet been a hardship. Today I sent some poems out to be Xeroxed, and these you will get presently. I think your suggestion to reduce Claude McKay's number of selections ties-in with what his present publisher (Bookman Associates) will demand. They would not let me have more than 10, I believe, for my *American Negro Poetry.* We can easily solve the Fenton Johnson thing, since I have all his later poems here and

471

can eventually make more copies, I hope. As for added poems from my PERSON-
ALS, they are at our disposal. Have you any suggestions? If not, I will offer some.
And I agree we should look over Melvin Tolson's two new books with a view to
finding something we can include.

I've read the LeRoi Jones poems you sent. I find a sameness about his poetry.
However we must represent him adequately, without using anything that will
knock us out of the high schools of the nation. This is where the battle for Negro
poetry vs the New Criticism is going to be won, and I don't think we should be
lured into playing the latter's game. In fact, I think we are more than holding
our own now. Thanks to you and Jean and Claude and Countee and JWJ and
all! So more presently.

Best ever,
Arna

March 20, 1965

Arna:

I'm catching up on a few minor deadlines, at least, holed away in a downtown
hotel across the street from where you're due to be again soon, aren't you? Lemme
know. Right now I'm listening to Odetta records (on Cicely Tyson's borrowed
machine from across the hall) to try to select some songs for an Easter TV show
for her on the Coast. . . . . Phoned today to see how Dorothy came out of her
operation. O. K. . . . . Juanita Miller told me Mrs. Lester Granger was buried
recently. And today was Dupree White's funeral here—Nate's former wife. And
I read where Nancy Cunard died in Paris. This is the DYING season. I hope I get
back to Paris one more time once. Seminars there are now scheduled for May.
Dakar for next April and Harris and I have put your name on the proposed list
—which seems like will be limited to five writers. The music, jazz bands, and
dancers are getting the big budgets. We ought to *also* play a trumpet. . . . Wm.
Melvin Kelley's new novel just came, also proofs of Tolson's book, who will be
in New York Monday. This volume has no footnotes, but a lot of BIG words: (says
Tolson)—O Cleobulus / Othales, Solon, Periander, Bias, Chilo, / O Pittacus, /
unriddle the phoenix riddle of this?. . . . . I say, MORE POWER TO YOU, MELVIN
B., GO, JACK, GO! That Negro not only reads, but *has read!.* . . . . .

Sincerely,
Langston

With all I've got to do, looks like my *Prodigal Son* will up and go into rehearsal
next week, too, as companion to a Brecht one-acter at the Mews. They want to
start casting tomorrow. So much to do, NO time!

Dakar
April 27, 1966

Dear Arna—

It was something! Almost everybody you ever knew was here—from New
York, Chicago, Cleveland, Alabama, Mississippi—even California—and Bill

472

Demby from Rome, Josephine Baker from Paris, Rosey Pool. Never saw the like. Too much to tell now, as I'm off to the Sudan in an hour. Congratulations to Hayden on top Dakar Poetry Prize. Rosey Pool and I "went to town" in his favor!! Final vote was unanimous.

Langston

P.S. Write USIA, Wash. for French edition of *Topic* with you in it.

Khartoum Continuation:
May 1, 1966

Didn't get a chance to address this in Dakar—was kept on the go right up to plane time. . . . Changed planes in Lagos and had luncheon there with the Joe Hills. Arminta Adams and Godfrey Amacree with me on plane to Khartoum. Seem to run into folks I know EVERYWHERE. Etta Moten looking like a million dollars in Dakar. Margaret Danner, Sidney Williams. Zelma Watson George renting a car and driving all over Daker just as if she'd lived there forever. . . . Lagos is more like the old Chicago of gangster days then ever. Held up and robbed two folks on the main street in their car, made them get out, and the bandits drove away the day I was there. Folks are buying automatic locks for cars that refuse to budge for anybody but the owners. . . . Here in Khartoum *all* Sudanese dress alike in white turbans and nightgowns. At a garden party last night for me, I mistook the Speaker of the Assembly for the head waiter, and asked him for a plate! Khartoum looks like a Texas-Mexican border town, blazing sun, dust, and the Nile here about the size of the Rio Grande. One blessing, no snakes—it is TOO hot!. . . . About a dozen Negroes from States here in gov posts, etc. Population 80% black—but not as dark, DARK, DARK as the Senegalese who are the absolute blackest in the world. Most exotically clothed of all Africa— Dakar is colorful no end. Nigeria, too, and West Africa in general much more eye-catching in color than Sudan and East Coast, everybody here agrees. French African cities are gay, British ones gray. And given to rather stiff garden parties —Sudanese writers are giving another one for me today—most speak English, have been to Oxford. Have had a fine trip so far, and will arrive in Addis on May 5, Liberation Day, big fete! USIA asked me to write a poem for the Emperor. Write me to Dar-es-Salaam.

Langston

The Kilimanjaro
Dar Es Salaam
Tanzania
July 7, Paris, 1966

Arna—
I'll be home about the 18th, ready to work on any of our projects, if and when you're in New York. . . . Ted Joans and I gave a reading at Shakespeare & Co., and had fun. Paris seems to be full of young cullud writers and artists and actors from the States. . . . Nice weather here these days—

Langston

3506 Geneva Circle
Nashville, Tennessee 37209
September 1, 1966

Dear Lang,

What is the name of that fellow who wrote and compiled your BIO-BIBLIOGRA-PHY? He is at this moment lost in my alphabetical file. This sometimes happens when so much water is passing under the bridge. Just the same, I wrote and sent to the Shoe String Press for ARCHON BOOKS the long delayed "Introduction," and I wonder if it is Okay by you.

All signs point to Chicago these days, and our preparations are beginning to take more definite shape. Alberta and I went up a week ago and (by the hardest) secured an apartment, not too far from the old Rosenwald Fund offices. We are now trying to coordinate packing, hauling and other arrangements. In the midst of it all I have a long and urgent book review to write, but I'll try to keep my cool.

Meanwhile, I'm standing by for further word from you and the publishers re: the updated *Poetry of the Negro* and the proposed Dodd, Mead college textbook. Steve Wright [pres. of Fisk] suggests Hugh Gloster (a dean at Hampton) as a sub for Chas. Davis if the latter is not available to work with us. You know Hugh's *Negro Voices in American Fiction*.

Have you heard that Eric Walrond [author of *Tropic Death*] died in England a couple of weeks ago and that Melvin B. Tolson passed last Sunday and that his funeral will be at Langston, Oklahoma Sat., Sept. 37 (27?) Eric's was a heart attack (about his 5th) on a street in London. M.B.'s followed his 3rd or 4th cancer operation. So "let the choir sing a stormy song."

Best ever,
Arna

20 East 127th Street
New York 35, N. Y.
October 22, [1966?]

Dear Arna:

ONE real discovery in the BIG box of manuscripts and stuff for our anthology that accumulated here during the summer and the bottom of which I HOPE I'm nearing, having devoted the past two days to nothing but it. (I wish you were here for reading and *weeding*,* too.). . . . . The discovery is Len Chandler, a folk singing lad who's been in Mississippi with the Song Caravan, and lives way down by the Battery in New York, and sings in Village clubs. Just tonight I came across his envelope sent while I was away. The best of all the younger ones (to my mind) that I've come across since Mari Evans. Monday, soon as Raoul comes to work, I'll have him copy the things we might use, and send you carbons.

If you've anything more, or any suggestions, please post them to me *now*, as I'd like to be able to give our new editor a sort of rundown when I see her for luncheon.

Margaret Danner has written that she has some new poems. I've asked her to send a set to both you and myself at the same time, to save time, giving her your

*So much is bad—and must be returned.

474

address. She is living in Chicago now, as I guess you know.

I'm thinking of begging out of the Virginia theatre conference this coming weekend, especially since Edmunds come writing here for me to send *in advance* a *paper.* Nobody told me it was going to be that academic, and Ah has no no paper—and won't.

Sincerely,
Langston

20 East 127th Street
New York 35, N. Y.
4:30 A.M.
Saturday Morning,
October 29, 1966

Bon Jour:

I just weighed on my scales the new and freshly typed material for our *Poetry of the Negro* and it comes to 5½ pounds. If I remember correctly *Folklore* at this stage of preparation weighed 7½. . . . The box of rejects and manuscripts still to be returned (all in a big carton in the corner) must weigh about 10 pounds. . . . . I have really been immersed in poetry all week. . . . I've come across some interesting additions for our NON-NEGRO section: Jack Kerouac, Norman McLeod, Alfred Kreymborg, Hodding Carter, and the kid who wanted to be in my *New Negro Poets* the worst way because he is born and raised in Harlem—but happens to be white Mexican-American, although he swears he is colored (environmentally speaking, true, I guess) *Frank Lima,* youngest of all, but good. . . . . Raoul has been typing all week, and Lindsay Patterson came in for a couple of evenings—so the typing so far, library research, photostating, postage to return several big old manuscripts, etc., has come to around $120.00 this past week. And there's still a few days work to do—getting biog dates and writing those who haven't sent in any such material, sorting and putting poets in proper sequence, etc., but everybody being off over weekend, Monday will have to do. . . . I wired Virginia I couldn't make the theatre seminars—otherwise I'd never be ready to meet our lady editor—whom Ivan tells me is tops, and senior editor of Anchor Books. She sounds delightful on the phone, and sent me a fresh copy of P. of N. by messenger today, that I can mark and cut up in making insertions, etc. Such a good-looking book I hate to mark it up, but that's the simplest way to do portions of the updating. . . . I'll be sending you some things shortly. Sleepy now.
. . . . .

L. H.

20 East 127th Street
New York 35, N. Y.
5:45 A.M. Monday
Morning, Oct. 31, 1966

Dear Arna:

In looking for the poetry of Jack Micheline (a Village beatnik poet published in the little magazines and who has been sending me manuscripts off and on for several years, and who may have something worthy of our book) I suddenly remembered I had a *BIG* box of poetry in a closet somewhere I'd forgotten about. I hauled it out—and found not only Micheline, but an overflowing folder of *old* Negro poetry and manuscripts (some by hand and many signed) including dozens of Waring Cuney poems sent me to keep for him when he was in the South Pacific in the Army, letters and poems from Richard Wright—some I'm sure unpublished—dozens of Frank Gorne's—and a whole sheaf of YOUR poems from *way back* all signed by you and some I'm sure you've probably forgotten you ever wrote! (Maybe you gave them to me when you were living in Watts. Unfortunately, they're not dated). Also found a large folder of poems written about (or to) me; the Fenton Johnson poems you once sent me; Georgia Douglas Johnson's poems on cards she used to send friends; and various other poetics, including some Jessie Fauset verses she had long ago sent, too. All of which has taken me ALL NIGHT to sort out and put in some semblance of order in manila folders— in the process finding a few items which I'd put in that box a year or two ago especially for our *P. of Negro* and forgotten about—but which seem good on rereading. Micheline has *too* much to look into before going to bed, so I've put him aside until waking up a-fresh. Lloyd Addison manuscripts I also found, too difficult to read when sleepy, sent when he was at University of New Mexico. He's on order of Russell Atkins, strange typography, etc., but some folks think he is good. Notation on corner of one of his typscripts says I send *"And Some—"* to *you* once. What did you think of it?????

> Anyhow, cheerio,
> Langston

4939 S. Dorchester Ave. 3-E
Chicago, Ill., 60615
November 6, '66

Dear Lang,

Check these off. Braithwaite died in 1962. Angelina Grimke in 1958. Fenton Johnson in 1958 also. I will now go to the telephone and try to call Donald Jeffrey Hayes in Atlantic City, where he lived, and where I once visited him. So wait a minute. Now I can tell you that a D. J. Hayes has an unlisted telephone and Information would not complete my call to him. The address I have for him is *1004 North Ohio Avenue,* Atlantic City, N. J. I will write Fisk re: Vilma Howard, pronto.

Effie Lee Newsome was doing poorly this past summer, I was told by a lady from Wilberforce, but she was still alive. Her address has been Box 291, Wilberforce, Ohio.

Nanina Alba's address is 303 Fonville Street, Tuskegee, Alabama. Shall I write her for bio-notes, or would you like to? I like the two of her poems that I sent you: "Be Daedalus" and "Prophecy." Particularly the first.

The best way I know to get some data on Margaret Danner is to call Mrs. Dixon at the John Hay Whitney Opportunity Fellowships office. Mrs. Dixon knows your name well and will cooperate, if you telephone. Or ask for Miss Rosenberg (?). I doubt that I can reach the poet here, but I will try.

There is a Charles E. Wheeler, Jr. listed in the Chicago telephone directory, but I can't get an answer there—yet. Will try again. I am not sure (in fact, I doubt) this is the poet. The last address I had for Charles Enoch Wheeler was 6327 Ingleside Avenue, Chicago 60637.

Catherine Cater was at 203 Seventh Street, South, Morehead, Minnesota, when last I heard ('63). Probably still there. Not Olivet, but another college.

You and Bruce introduced me to Alexander in D. C. in the twenties, but I never saw him again or heard tell of him since. I did not bring a copy of an address list I made for Hill & Wang on the poets in *American Negro Poetry,* but maybe Mrs. Wang will make a photocopy for you, since they have a machine in the office, and she is in charge of permissions, etc.

The new address I have for Danner is 8822 Wabash Avenue, Chicago, Illinois 60619.

Jean Toomer is still in a nursing home in Doylestown, Pa. His wife Marjorie Toomer can be reached at their home, "The Barn", R. D. 2, Doylestown. *She will answer letters promptly!* I have visited her twice. She is active for civil rights. Jean's literary disappointments after *Cane* were shattering. He tried desperately to repeat that artistic achievement (but not as a Negro) and failed. . . . I persuaded her and him to give his papers and literary effects to Fisk. A large collection. There is now a chance that *Cane* may be reprinted along with some of Jean's unpublished writings. At least it is being considered. If so, I am to write an introduction, perhaps. Arthur Pell at Liveright Publishing Corp., 386 Park Ave. South, New York 16, N. Y. may be the one to grant the permissions from *Cane,* however. I believe that is the way Doubleday secured them before. . . . There is nothing new on Fenton Johnson, except that he died as indicated. See my note in ANP.

November 10, '66

Dear Lang,

The sonnet by Allen Tate is perfect for *The Poetry of the Negro.* His background as a Fugitive and a redhot I'LL TAKE MY STANDer adds to its effectiveness. As Countee said about himself, Allen's "conversion came high-priced," no doubt. I served with him on an ALA committee, you know, and there are letters from him in the Toomer Collection. Hart Crane was trying to arrange for the two (Toomer and Tate) to meet. In any case, we can now see that the early anti-Negro expressions of the Fugitives probably reflected guilt feelings, as this "Sonnet at Christmas" makes clear in Tate's case.

You asked about Danner and Brooks. Gwen was at a party given for Alberta and me by a U of I prof and his wife a few weeks ago. She was with her husband and looked well, and she said her son is out at the U, though he is not in either of my classes and has not identified himself yet. The children of people I know seldom do at Fisk either—or not till the last week of the school year. Then they come in and wave so they can go home and tell their parents they met me, as they had been told to do.

Danner wrote me at length at Fisk to say she recently discovered that she is diabetic but that it is under control, thanks to insulin. She gave this condition as a cause of her failure to go to Africa on her Whitney grant. Picked up the travel check and all but didn't leave Detroit. She recalled all this when writing about her trip to the Senegal Festival, feeling that she had thus paid off her earlier obligation. I had been responsible for getting her the Whitney, and she surmised (correctly) that I may have been a bit embarrassed by her being so prompt to pick up the passage money and so slow to catch the boat. Charles Jones was the Opportunity Fellowship director then, but he is not there now.

By the way, I also sponsored Frank Lima for his Opportunity. We should let him pass for colored, if he wishes. I thought he was Puerto Rican at the time. Nobody would object to a Mexican identifying as a Negro. Not even a black muslim or a black panther. And I will not object to a couple or so poems by Mason Jordan Mason so long as we make it plain in the biographical note that at least we are not sure. He certainly writes in Negro, as Karl Shapiro says of Tolson. And he's good.

I don't expect us to find anything from the Allen Ginsberg cabal that meets our criteria. So why don't we close the door now.

Listen: THE CARVER BANK IN NEW YORK (for which you did a calendar) has a new one this year on NEGRO INVENTORS, and I need it for my class. Will you ask them to send me a few PRONTO? I'll gladly pay what they cost. One will help, but I could use more.

Thanks for those income tax exemption ideas! Also, hope I get to meet Alice Walker. I'm looking forward to reading her poems! This new collection of ours is going to SWING!

> Best ever,
> Arna

> 20 East 127th Street
> New York 35, N. Y.
> November 17, 1966

ARNA:

Here's the 3rd Section of POTNegro, including my selection re yourself, to be augmented by your self as you may choose. These are, of course, really additions to SECTION ONE (1) bringing up to date those poets who have had significant work since 1948. . . . . To make room for *their* new poems, also, to increase space for the large number of additions we have in this section of brand *new* poets, and in case of JW Johnson and McKay's increased permissions fees, I suggest deleting about a dozen or so old poems as follows:

p.	30	THE GLORY OF THE DAY	Johnson
	49	THE BLACK FINGER	Grimke
	99	LITTLE GREEN TREE	Hughes
	102	AFRO-AMERICAN FRAGMENT	"
	103	CROSS	"
	103	SONG FOR A DARK GIRL	"
	191	MENTORS	Brooks
	192	PIANO AFTER ME	Brooks
		Transferred from Carib	McKay
		HERITAGE	McKay
		TO O. E. A	McKay
		RUSSIAN CATHEDRAL	McKay

478

Also TRANSLATORS NOTE, as there's none now. In case you see other possible omissions, let me know. .

New biog material is coming in every day in response to my recent letters.

Enclosed also herein *A Baltimore Poet Speaks* by Sam Cornish, who's had a rather attractive booklet published by New Era Bookshop in Baltimore. His work is not bad, I think. Got left out of material sent you yesterday, by mistake. So insert in *1, Negro Poets,* please. . . . . . *Negro Short Stories* comes out officially February 20. I imagine you can have copies ahead, if needed. . . . . . Sincerely yours truly,

> Ph. D. Squared,
> Lang

> Langston Hughes
> 20 East 127th Street
> New York 35, N. Y.
> November 18, 1966

Dear Arna:

Tonight I've been returning unusable manuscripts, some so beautifully typed I hated to send them back—particularly Norman Pritchard's (who sounds better than he reads in type—on a recording with Calvin Hernton and others, called DESTINATIONS, they sent me). He'd enclosed an envelope for return. . . . . Those poets who haven't called up 90 times to see what's happening, or who didn't specifically request their work back, I am not returning. . . . But how about Darwin T. Turner, the bulk of whose poetry I think *you* have (sonnets, as I recall)? I find here only the long poem on Kennedy, ONE LAST WORD. Do you think he wants it back? I did not like any of his things myself. Did you? So chose nothing. . . . . I'm also sending back the poems of Ray Grist, (Reri's brother—the charming little singer who began her operatic career in my *The Barrier,* and went on to the Met). . . . . . *
One white poet send a BIG sheaf of poems here, $1.60 postage, but I think I'll return it EDUCATIONAL MATTER. And why they write two page single-spaced letters too long to read, I'll never know. . . . . The big carton box of poetry you saw when you were here, is now about down to *half.* Somehow it seems like more TIME and more WORK assembling this updated material, than it did to put the *whole* anthology together originally—with Nathaniel's help. I wonder why? I've read enough poetry this month to last me for *YEARS!* And almost everybody that sends a biog this week, sent pages of *NEW* poetry they've written—like Jay Wright, who has completely revised most of his poems—some for the worse—and is engaged on a curious creative process —variations on themes from other poets, but rather good. Too late for us, though, and would (like Tolson) require footnotes—or top notes. . . . . Have you finished your FOREWORD yet? (Smile) (As they say)

> Comme toujours, quand meme,
> L.H.

Mrs. Harper real poorly—Emerson tried but failed to get a doctor in the middle of night last night. The old family practitioner is passé in cities.

*Everybody keeps telling everybody else about the anthology—now that it is in action. Better *not* mention it in Chicago—or you'll be flooded with things from Margaret Goss Burroughs!X! *Don't* send them to me! Like Pilate, I now wash ma hands.

Selah!

4939 S. Dorchester Ave.
11-22-66

Dear Lang,

I returned to the post office this morning and picked up the PON manuscript that had been bouncing around since last Thursday. It is long indeed, and I look forward to giving it a close reading during the rest of this week. Maybe the publisher's editor will tell us whether or not the new inclusions should be reduced in length for the sake of the book as a whole, but one of my first impressions is that some poets should be trimmed for the sake of *balance*. That is to say, minor or fledgling poets being given too much more space than the more established ones. I'll examine closely with this in mind.

About DARWIN TURNER. I promised him that we would make a selection from his published poems (Wesley University Press—I thought I sent it to you). So I feel committed to look at his work closely and see if there isn't something there at least as good as some of the unpublished poets from whom we have made selections. I would not select one of his longer pieces.

As for the revision of the INTRODUCTION, I would like to make that the last act in the project, both for the sake of giving me the maximum time and for letting me see the finished book as a whole. The use of this book in schools and colleges is what will keep the updated book alive, and I think the introduction should relate to the inclusions and indirectly direct the attention of teachers, etc. I am learning something of how this works in my Negro in American Literature sequence at the U. of I. this quarter.

I glanced at the Ted Joans poem you selected and see that he has in one line knocked us out of all the Catholic schools and colleges. Could you either get his permission to take out the rather unnecessary disrespect for nuns or else make a substitute selection? Even at best, I think his comments on living and active TV and movie personalities will date "It is Time" long before the book as a whole is dated. Likewise Madison Ave. slogans like Mr. Clean. So I lean toward a more timeless selection, if possible.

Are you acquainted with Ray Durem? We had a person by that name at Fisk once upon a time, and it was a woman and Jewish, not Negro. Because of this circumstance, I looked at the poems under that name and found them strongly imitative of the mood and manner of one LH. I have glanced at *New Negro Poets* and see that you have a note on him. On his own, however, I don't think he is a strong contender. Just so-so.

Another first impression is that you have scratched Claude McKay's "Russian Cathedral." Don't you like it? I always thought it interesting that such a poem should come out of his Communist phase. It sort of plants the seed for his conversion to the church about twenty years later and makes a discussion topic in classes. But I have nothing to urge. It was one of the poems in the *Survey Graphic* issue that became *The New Negro.* At that time Claude was writing to lambast the *Crisis* and Du Bois for *not* joining the red revolution! I came across the exchange in old issues of the *Crisis.*

So the sun do move, and I have your letter of 11–18 before me as I plunge into the manuscript. Also earlier correspondence.

Best ever,
Arna

P. S. Sorry to hear about Toy's miseries. I reckon we're all getting on, boats against the tide. Alberta's out shopping for Thanksgiving. Some of my students are writing beautifully (better than anyone before them) on the Renaissance, etc. They perk me up. And my classes for next quarter are already FULL. You should drop in on them at least once while I'm here.

20 East 127th Street
New York 35, N. Y.
December 20, 1966

Dear Arna:

I love your piece on the "3 Pennies for luck." Also the Christmas card information about your ancestors. Merci!

So glad you like Alice Walker. Everybody thinks she is an up-and-comer. And Ishmael Reed's forthcoming humorous novel is, so they tell me, a humdinger. Also last night at the Soviet U.N. Embassy party for Yevtushenko, Bill Cole (used to be with Knopf) was raving about A. B. Spellman's poetry —thinks he's the best of the newer ones. . . . All of whom we've got in our book.

I'd say make me a list of the poems you consider dispensable while you're loafing and inviting deadlines to conquer during the holidays—and I'll compare it with the one Anne Freedgood will make—and do the eliminating here. . . . I have biog material for almost all the new people, only a matter of writing them up—which I can do here, too. . . . So I reckon all *you* have to do is the INTRO. Then we can get the second half of our money during the New Year's early quarter—and buy some Easter clothes or something.

A half dozen WHITE birth dates remain to be gotten—Norman Macleod, Marie Welch, etc.; but almost every day one comes in.—Today Dorothy Rosenberg, San Francisco, 1906 (but raised in India, she says).

Best Short Stories will be in paper eventually, but not right away. . . . . Dig the current hard cover price—$7.95—whew!!!! Culture is being priced out of the market.

Lang

P. S. If I can get Jessie's birth date, I'm sure you can get Vilma's. Don't let cranky old ladies defeat you.

Dear Lang,

I have the Ken McLaren poems, and I look forward to receiving those by Lucille Clifton. I have left the others that I am to re-read and weed (if that is the word) in Chicago, it appears, but I will do them all directly I return. Don't send anything there before the 2nd of January, because I know the small mailbox is stuffed. But it is all right to send it to me at the University, History Dept.

Putting Danner, LaMarre and their ilk back with Dunbar is what they deserve! I'm all for it.

Your photo with Carlo interests me for a reason that would have pleased him, I'm sure. Lyle Saxon *(Fabulous New Orleans)* once told me that he collected paintings and pictures of well-to-do white creoles with their mulatto sons. He described the poses and the beaming pride on the faces of the papas. I have tried without success to find out what became of the pictures after Lyle's death, and I suppose I would have to go to his summer house at Melrose (you have read about it) on Cane River to be sure. He said once that he feared what the Daughters of the Confederacy would do with them if they searched his house after his death. Well, I have no doubt they would mistake this picture of Carlo and you as one of them, if they saw it. It wouldn't surprise me to find Noel and Hyppolite among the paintings at the Melrose house. Hyppolite's oldest son, Louis Fenelon, married one of the daughters of Aloysius Metoyer, whose family of homes de couleur built the famous Melrose mansion for themselves. So it could have happened.

Carlo in his declining months looked like a man who had been everywhere and seen everything . . . I intend to check him out in N. O. to see whether or not he stopped down there prior to settling in Mansura. I'll try to get Father Yves Robitaille to inquire for me through church records.

I enclose herewith two short poems by Darwin Turner, as I promised, that I would like to recommend for inclusion in *The Poetry of The Negro*.

Tell Toy my Connie just received from her husband (he is a physician, you know) a Lincoln for Xmas. Truly the sun do move.

Best ever,
Arna

Dear Lang,

Commenting on your Section 2 ("Tributary Poems by Non-Negroes") list, here is the information I can give without research: Fletcher, Torrence, Patchen, Bodenheim, Hervey Allen, Benét are all dead and dates should be easy to find from either the sources you suggest or from the *N. Y. Times* index. If Rodman, West, Porter or McKelway (two people?) have passed, I did not hear about it. Write Josephine Jacobson c/o the Baltimore *Sun* literary page. Randall Jarrell died in 1965 or early this year, I believe. Robert Lowell's publisher is Farrar, Straus, Giroux. Doubleday publishes Hodding Carter, who is alive and kicking. Allan Tate is at the University of Minnesota. Nearly all the others have publishers who would at least supply birth dates (and/or deaths) by telephone, which might be time-saving. If Raoul goes to the Library, I would suggest he consult the latest volume of *Books in Print* and then call the publishers shown there for up-to-date information on their authors (where questions remain).

My students here are so full of zing they keep me jumping. I'll be glad when the Quarter ends (the first week in December) so I can go to Nashville and rest up till the 2nd of January, when the 2nd Quarter begins.

Dorris Saunders who used to be in charge of the book publishing at JOHNSON Pub. Co., but now writes a column for the Defender, tells me it is true about the Defender and Courier merging most of their papers, if I didn't tell you.

I went to the Avant-Garde bookstore around the corner and saw that Kenneth Patchen is published mostly (his poetry) by the City Lights group in San Francisco. The blurbs say he is from the Mid-West but now living in California.

I went through Ginsberg's "Howl" and found nothing there suitable for *The Poetry of the Negro*.

There was a copy of the 5th edition of *The Best of Simple* on the shelves.

Little-Brown told the English office at U of I that copies of your anthology of Negro short stories would be available in late January, '66. I had told them to find out if I could assign it. Larry Hill at H & W says that Clarke's is selling briskly, "almost as well as *American Negro Poetry.*" One thing I have learned is that these somewhat parallel books help each other. Like the way *The Poetry of the Negro* perked up following publication of ANP and your *New Negro Poets*. Libraries and schools that have one seem to feel they must get the others.

Did you read in the *N. Y. Times* (Saturday, 12) about Negro poetry almost starting a rumble at East Orange High School? Wow! They said that "The Creation" was by Countee Cullen, so I don't trust the reporter. But it is good to know that kids react explosively to you-all's poetry. The story is on page 31.

So more presently.

> Best ever,
> Arna

> 20 East 127th Street
> New York 35, N. Y.
> January 5, 1966-7-7-7
> (Got to get used to it)

Dear Arna:

I reckon you're back up North in God's (?) country by now. How're things in the deep dark Southland?..... Do you ever see *ETC.*? Don Hayakawa's magazine. He just sent me the September issue with a provocative article of his on WATTS. I always think of him and Horace and the wild Rosenwald gang in Chi in one breath—Vandy Haygood, etc.—and somehow Karamu—maybe wilder in some ways, if the truth be known. Shades of DOLCE VITA, U. S. A...... Somebody ought to (NO!) write a book on the good-time side of *do-gooding*. (Or am I out of my mind?)

Did I tell you that the night after Aunt Toy was rushed back to the hospital in an ambulance, her oldest friend, our house guest for the holidays (for the past twenty years)—(Will Vodery's widow, Rosana from Saratoga) went to the clinic at Harlem for a headache at 9 A.M. and by 5 hadn't come home so we got worried

483

about her and went looking—and she had been LOST in Harlem Hospital! They'd *kept* her, but nobody could find her for 24 hours (and she weighs 250). Mignon Richmond from Salt Lake, who was going home the next day, was allowed to go all through the wards looking for her. No luck, no records. *Absolutely LOST.* New York hospitals are so crowded they'd put her and lots of other patients on cots in a corridor until beds were available, but nobody knew in *what* corridor *where?* What with Aunt Toy being gravely ill, and Emerson's nephew-in-law dropping dead just around the corner, we've had quite a holiday week between Christmas and New Years. . . . And now up comes a community committee INSISTING on giving me a testimonial for my Birthday—and me saying now *(of all times)* is *not* the time.

I do NOT *now* want *NO* testimonial—although they claim I will not have to be involved AT ALL. (But, having gone through them *before*—). Help! Wait a little while, till I'm 75 anyhow, and the days are less hectic. I haven't recovered from the Detroit and Brooklyn ones yet—and have enough scrolls and plaques to last me a life time. . . . Anyhow, HAPPY NEW YEAR to you-all!

Lang

30 January 1967

Dear Lang,

The first mail in five or six days was delivered today, but we are still snow-bound. The University was closed Friday, and today (Monday) I decided not to fight the elements. I am staying at home. I trust your flu has abated. What may turn out to be the first reaction to your magnanimous suggestion (in the Introduction to *The Best Short Stories by Negro Writers*) has arrived by carrier pigeon, and I'll let you know if it turns out to be for real. Even as fantasy, however, I deeply appreciate the thought.

It would be nice to meet the sheik-poet of the Sudan and his wife, should they come this way. We should be able to arrange some hospitality in the English department, given reasonable notice, and we might invite representatives of *Poetry*, etc. Maybe also someone from the U. of Chicago press, etc. But reasonable lead-time is important.

The Ambassador from Sudan to Paris entertained Dick, Rudy Aggrey, Alberta and me, together with a bevy of beauties from Senegal and other French-African countries at cocktails in his plush Paris diggings when we were there in September '60. I regret that I did not write his name down and have forgotten it. Maybe Sheriff would know. But the Ambassador was about your color or mine, with hair similar, and not "very Cullud" as you say of Sheriff. I'm glad to learn about the range of Sudan types.

Dodd, Mead has forwarded Lindsay Patterson's request to reprint my "Rock, Church, Rock" in the book he is editing for the Association for the Study of Negro Life and History. With foundation support they should be able to pay more than they are offering, but naturally I'll cooperate.

So something more on *The Poetry of the Negro* coming up pronto.

Best ever,
Arna

March 28, 1967

Dear Lang,

I always figured you were at least part psychic and part Negro, not to mention the other things, but your sending me "Langston Hughes: Poet of the People" at this time sort of bears it out. I find here on my return from Soulville (including Nashville and Tuskegee) a letter from the *Encyclopedia Britannica* asking me to write the piece for your inclusion in that great reference source (your first appearance there, I reckon), and the "springboards" piece will help. Do you have anything else like it ready at hand? I am asked for 400 words. At the end of these entries they sometimes publish a note on sources. Can you give me the titles of Emanuel's (exact) and the Shoe String bio-bibliography books for listing? I will, of course, mention *The Big Sea* and *I Wonder As I Wander*.

The *Britannica* also asks me for suggestions of writers to do Chesnutt, Locke, McKay and Dick Wright. Who is that lady at North Carolina College doing the Chesnutt book for Twayne—Sylvia Lyons something or ruther?

Tuskegee was beautiful and deep into spring, but the problem of finding and setting up another house down there is more than we want to take on. Besides, I would be more chained to the campus than here and more available to Tom, Dick and Harry. So I came back and told the folks at the Circle Campus of U. of I. we would stay. They are going to reduce my teaching to ONE class—the same as Tuskegee requires.

I have been re-reading the poems in our manuscript, but I can't make snap judgments, and it is taking longer than expected. However, I am nearly ready to send you my report. This week for sure.

So more presently.
Best ever,
Arna

April 19, 1967

Dear Arna:

I've just spent a couple of hours with Anne Freedgood and the Permissions budget lady at Doubleday's. If more than a third of the material in the book is new, it becomes not the *same* book reissued, but another book, a NEW book, and all old permissions must be renewed and permissions paid again on old poets as well as new ones; and if a paper back is published, it must in any case then be done. It seems Charles Harris and the Japanese boy failed to take these facts into consideration. So the whole thing seemingly will have to be taken up by the Board at its next meeting and re-budgeted again. Anyhow, in the excitement and the shuffle, I said anyhow give us OUR remaining money *now,* or very soon, even though the BIOGS are not yet written up on the new poets we are adding. Of this request Mrs. Freedgood made a memo. So I reckon we'll get our half-and-half soon.

Secretarial troubles again—Lindsay has returned to the MacDowell Colony for the third time to complete his novel; and Raoul all last week was doing his *Negro Speaks of Rivers* trio program in a little Off-Off-Broadway Theatre, and this week has had the flu. There is about a week's more work to do on our book, so tonight I phoned Gloria Oden (who recently lost her very good long-time editorial job and is looking for another one) to see if she can help me by the hour arranging our material chronologically, writing up the remaining biogs and bringing the old ones up to date, preparing a complete address list for the permissions department (all from materials and data I have but which must be assembled) and making a TABLE OF CONTENTS for the book in final form. These things, as you know, take TIME's mammy. G.C. Oden promised to let me know this week if she can help. (I wish your white boy were here). In any case, I'll let you know how much this will cost, and you can send me half. I guess I told you we've put almost $7,000 in the house upgrading lately, and Aunt Toy's extra blood transfusions have added to Emerson's burdens to the extent he's had to make a bank loan. So right now money is of the essence—$$$$$$—and as you once told me, even the poorest white folks usually have somebody to turn to—but, poor cullud. . . . .

And it has happened AGAIN! When I asked about our old editor, Clara Classen and Anne Freedgood said, "Why, she's just down the hall from us," and took me in to see her, Miss Classen cried, "Oh, *Arna,* how wonderful to see you!"

Thanks to yours and Mrs. Freedgood's list of suggested exclusions, the manuscript is now reduced by 10 white poems and 60 black poems—in all, *70 poems have come out.* Both lists were most helpful, and if I had time myself, or secretarial help, I'd type up an omissions list for you. You and our editor *agreed* on 14 poems (on both lists) liked least. Otherwise, individual differences. A few you didn't like, *she* likes very much—for example Ishmael Reed. And a few neither of you like, *I like.* So I've tried to balance the compromises, keeping in some of each—particularly those with humor—which kids and ordinary readers like, I know from past experience. The substitutions you suggest, I have made.

Just had a happy time in Philadelphia last night on Jack McKenny's midnight talk-athon radio show, "Night Talk," which I think reaches far as Chicago on tape. New York heard it this morning, I believe. . . . Selah!

At buffet for Loren Miller at the Montero's night before last (did I write you?) Roy Wilkins, Best Granger, etc. all so *mad* with Martin Luther's they could Klux him. Me, no! I love him.

Did I tell you Ted Poston got clouted in the head in Bedford-Stuyvesant—in his own yard? Six stitches. And Emerson refuses to go outside the house after dark.

Langston

Hotel Wellington
Seventh Avenue
At Fifty-Fifth Street
New York N. Y. 10019
April 22, 1967

Dear Arna:

I believe I asked Raoul to drop you a card requesting that you revise, as you like, your own biography, and add to it what you wish, to bring it up to date for the *Poetry of the Negro* and send it to me post haste as I'm now ready to type those sheets up for Doubleday, having all the material—but Lewis Alexander's birth date—which I intend to find if it KILLS *me.* Ran into Kurtz Myers of the Hackley Collection in Detroit, who says he thinks he can get it for me through a library researcher who finds things for him in Washington.

The house is still ALL torn up, and Emerson is going around in circles, not being good at "law and order" and quite lost without Aunt Toy, who is wasting away by the hour to wisp of her former self, now too weak to sit up, but wants to come home—which really would put an end to her if she saw the house as it is now —and full of paint fumes, dust and debris. You never saw the like.

With such confusion there, I shall stay here at the hotel until I go to Europe (maybe not till July now). So you may best *write me here,* ROOM 41, at the above address. Impossible to work at home.

Meltzer's second draft of his book: *Langston Hughes,* is good. And I've just added a little chapter for him about my African trip. But this is the *LAST* book or thesis I can take time out to help *anybody* with. Enough, anyhow—four—with Emanuel and the two in France-Belgium. . . . . *Simple* got off to good start in Paris, so they write me, and still urge me to fly over *right now* for interviews. Wish I could. But not for just a week, not for just a year. . . . . as the song says . . . but—

> Toujours,
> Langston

April 22, 1967

Dear Lang,

What do you think of this Chicago weather, first the big snow and now the big wind! It roared and whistled so last night I scarcely slept a wink. I may fall asleep tonight when I sit at the speaker's table for the annual feast of the Friends of Literature. But I'm not going to call any of those white folks Negro as *Time* said you did Marianne Moore. Anyhow, I've been saying for years that it's no disgrace to be the greatest Negro anything—ball player, prize fighter, football star, writer, you name it. One has to be a hell to be the best Negro. Or even a good one!

I hope you were able to have the outstanding work on *The Poetry of the Negro* done, and if you will let me know the cost, I'll fire my check right at you. Haven't those 70 poems left out reduced the size of the book enough to bring it under the ⅔ rule? I have no strong feelings about Reed's "Cowboy," and no protest. Nor do I object to humor—unless it's dated, likely to soon become dated, or dirty. Some of it goes better in public entertainment and oral reading than in book reading, but I trust your judgment.

There is an explosion of interest in Negro poetry, as you must have felt. *American Negro Poetry* is in its 7th edition, and when I spoke to The Catholic Adult Education Center the other night, a big stack of them disappeared like leaves in a hurricane. I wrote my name till I could scarcely hold the ball-point pen. So tell Mrs. Freedgood to hurry up with the new edition, especially the Anchor book edition.

I'm off to Cambridge Tuesday (25) and will miss my first lectures on Wednesday the 26th. I'll be *consulting* on schoolbook projects. A Ford Foundation operation. Then back here on the 27th to attend a Palmer House reception for Historians and greet a visitor (State Department) from India. He is comparing King's nonviolence with Gandi's. I can't imagine what he will think of Stokeley's black only, fist in the air, peace march!

Had dinner last night with the James Bonds. He teaches Biology at the Chicago Circle and is the cousin of Horace Mann. His white wife also teaches Biology but at another college. That's where I was during the storm.

Alberta still in Nashville. Due back after I return.

Best ever,
Arna

May 1, 1967

Dear Lang,

If you go to Paris for always, as you say, we will visit you there every now and then. Suddenly I feel footloose. Maybe we're approaching that age. In any case, I think one whose career in writing has reached the point of warm reflection and the reading of biographies of himself has earned residence in Paris, prior to residence in glory. It would be the ideal place in which to write volume III of your *autobiography*, for instance. Moreover, Harlem's problems appear to have reached a plateau and can probably be viewed just as well from a certain distance.

I saw Larry Hill last night. He came out for the presentation of the Society of Midland Authors awards to Jack and me. They are beautiful, and I now have something more to hang on the wall. A Doubleday man was present also (at the North Shore Club) and I kidded him in front of Larry for not publishing the updated *They Seek a City*, which we therefore had to take to Hill and Wang. However the Doubleday representative needled Larry by boasting of the updated *The Poetry of the Negro* and telling how they expect big sales.

Listen, I believe you have an address for the individual who can give permissions for reprinting poems of Georgia Douglas Johnson. I thought the permissions department at Doubleday could be of help, but the man I put in touch tells me they could find no record. Would you mind advising him?

This past week I was at the Sheraton Commander in Cambridge, Mass., consulting with an educational services outfit working on Afro-American materials for junior high schools. They offered me a job, but I'm not looking for more work. Besides, I think I gave them all the ideas I have on the subject in the couple of days I was there. My big problem now is to finish up this Quarter (June 9) and try to get in shape to do some writing during the summer.

My biog in *The Poetry of the Negro* does indeed need updating, and I will fix it for you in the next day or two. Quite a lot has happened, including new books, since 1949! So hold everything.

I remember Kurtz Myers of the Hackley Collection. Maybe he will come to my talk in Detroit on May 13, hunh?

Toy's wish to return home at this stage recalls to me my father's lingering, when he was restlessly, impatiently back and forth from the sanitarium. Unfortunately, there comes a time when you cannot completely respect their wishes. As the doctors say, all you can do is try to make them comfortable when it comes to that.

So stand by for the revised biog.

Best ever,
Arna

EPILOGUE:
The Summing Up

"The Ripeness is all."

We expect a writer to sharpen our awareness of the conscience and the consciousness of the age. Langston Hughes was the most widely read, the most prolific black author in American literary history. Arna Bontemps, author of more than 25 books, his closest friend and collaborator, heightened, too, our sense of the range, the peril, the promise of American life in our pluralistic society. Their association was fruitful and mutually satisfying. And their work is clearly related to a number of significant developments in our recent literature. The letters they exchanged constitute, therefore, a precious legacy for posterity. For if literature is the memory of a culture, the private correspondence of literary men is a repository which often reveals what lay behind their public personalities. These letters are indispensable sources for several kinds of readers and scholars. They provide valuable insights into the genesis and reception of their imaginative works and revealing glimpses of their relationships with their contemporaries. The letters enlarge our grasp of the literary history of their times, their view of the dominant concerns and artistic achievement of the twentieth century in America. They bring alive vividly the Negro's struggle for fulfillment, for freedom and for recognition. They expose the psychological and social forces behind the Afro-American experience as it relates to our culture, our artistic life and our sense of community.

These sources will augment any significant study of such authors as Countee Cullen, Claude McKay, Sterling Brown, Wallace Thurman, Jean Toomer, Zora Neale Hurston, Eric Walrond and Richard Wright. The life of the southern Negro before and after World War II is seen in his distinctive life-style, in the indignities he suffers, and the institutions and organizations which embody his hopes and strivings. Blacks are revealed here, too, in urban ghettoes, in clubs and fraternities, in schools and colleges, and strikingly, backstage in the theater. Important, too, is Hughes's and Bontemps's confrontation with the public— through the mass media, through lectures, newspapers, radio, television and film. In the study of the two men too little attention has been given to their relations to the black African nations. Their correspondence shows how deeply involved they both were in the life and culture of non-white peoples around the world.

The availability of these letters will provide important details for those now preparing studies of Langston Hughes and Arna Bontemps—as well as the whole group whom we associate with the "Harlem Renaissance." As early as 1962 Langston Hughes wrote to Arna Bontemps, "All within a month I get word from

5 separate people that each intends to do a book about ME, or some aspect of my work!"[1] Foreign readers complain repeatedly to the directors of the United States Information Service and its libraries that books by and about Afro-Americans are not to be found in American overseas libraries. It would not be difficult to prove the influence of a writer like Langston Hughes in Haiti, Cuba, Jamaica, Trinidad, Europe, Japan and other parts of Asia and Africa.

The permanent legacy of both men is not only in their fervent advancement of the central tradition of American writing—the tradition of Whitman, Twain, Howells, Chesnutt, Dunbar and William Carlos Williams. It is that many-colored glass which diffuses the bright light of the common man's striving for a just and humane community. Specifically, what both Hughes and Bontemps bequeathed us is their capacity to experiment with a variety of literary forms, their use of the common rhythms and speech of Afro-Americans, their use of the spirituals, blues and jazz in complex and original forms. To be sure the black idiom may be seen and heard in American writers like Mark Twain, Joel Chandler Harris, Du Bose Haywood and Eugene O'Neill. But it is especially in the "Beat Generation" poets —Kerouac, Ginsberg, Gregory Corso, Norman Mailer and (of course) Le Roi Jones that the daring search for new forms took shape, achieving widespread public attention. Among younger black writers of the 1960s there was also a conscious revival of a "Black aesthetic"—vaguely defined and artistically unsure, but stoutly defended.

The "Beat" writers owed even more than they acknowledged to writers like Hughes and Bontemps. For "beat" is a word derived from the language of lower-class Negroes meaning "poor, down-and-out, dead-beat, on the bum, sad, sleeping in subways." But as Gregory Corso wrote, "To be beat is to be 'hip.' Hip means love, means indifference, means not wanting to be bugged or to bug. Hip means metropolitan cosmopolitan solitude, hip means being on the street corner bombed out of your mind . . . if he is true to his soul, if his message is stripped to the nuts of love, and proceeds from his archetypical essence, selfless selfhood, him, simple poor tones, he is beat."[2] The Beat writers represent in a dramatic way the sensibility of modern man who, as he confronts the massive power of the state, the grinding force of the economy, the threat of atomic annihilation, the crass and isolating indifference of the modern city, is thrown back wholly on his own spiritual resources. The sensibility of the Beats is the raw desperation of the self-conscious victim who refuses to keep step with the march of the complacent, the powerful, the smug, the avaricious. As Norman Mailer has pointed out, when "the juvenile delinquent came face to face with the Negro the hipster was a fact of American life." The Negro brought the "cultural dowry." For the source of hip, Mailer maintains is the Negro who "living on the margin between totalitarianism and democracy for two centuries had the simplest of alternatives, a life of constant humility or ever-threatening danger."

This mood, this language, this psychological transformation of desperation into transcendence was in the rhythm and sound of the black man's life. It had found its poetic expression in authors like Langston Hughes. In seeming indifference the "hipster" is "cool." He can give new force to words like "go," "put down," "swing," "flip," "crazy." Le Roi Jones (Baraka), Larry Neal and Ishmael Reed created a new sensibility, a revolutionary attack on the aestheticism, the elitism,

1. Letter, 3/4/62.
2. *Variations*, pp. 47–51.

the materialism of a nation which was stockpiling atomic bombs and fire-bombing Asian peasants.

There was work for the writer to do. Hughes had little patience with those whose excuse for not writing was expressed in terms of the familiar tale of discrimination and prejudice. If you are a writer, you must write, he said "until you get white, *write!*" Le Roi Jones was even more explicit:

> The Negro [he writes] could not ever become white and that was his strength; at some point, always, he could not participate in the dominant tenor of the white man's culture, yet he came to understand that culture as well as the white man. It was at this juncture that he had to make use of other resources, whether African, subcultural, or hermetic. And it was this boundary, this no man's land, that provided the logic and beauty of his music. And this is the only way for the Negro artist to provide his version of America—from that no man's land outside the mainstream.[3]

There is no doubt that the Beat writers and the assertive black writers and "New Poets" (some of them whom Hughes himself launched in a fine volume in 1964) routed the aestheticism and academic poetry of the 1940s and 1950s. The New Criticism found itself on the defensive, but losing so much ground even in the universities that the folklorist and Marxist critics are today more in evidence. Hughes and Bontemps were well aware of the racism and the antidemocratic attitudes of Pound, Eliot and the Fugitives. At Yaddo Robert Lowell patronized Langston Hughes by saying, "You're not a bad poet." Referring to a reported nervous breakdown of Robert Lowell on one of his visits with Allen Tate in 1949, Bontemps wrote that "the whole T. S. Eliot coterie, including Ezra Pound, is a sick lot." This commentator will not deny that the Beats and the Black Nationalists had problems of their own as well. The best of both groups have come to reflect increasingly the sanity of that humanism which Hughes and Bontemps (not to mention Lowell) represented. They welcomed Tate's introduction to Melvin Tolson's *Libretto for the Republic of Liberia* and anthologized one of Tate's poems in *The Poetry of the Negro*.

The wide influence of Langston Hughes on writers since the 1940s is yet to be fully explored. The folk elements which inform the work of Sterling Brown, Gwendolyn Brooks and Margaret Walker owe much to Hughes's early poetry. James A. Emanuel has called our attention to the numerous experimental techniques that add interest to Hughes's poems. His use of folk diction, urban slang, the modernity of his spontaneity and emotional intensity anticipates the poetry of the Beats and of the Black aesthetic of the 1960s. The originality and use of folk images in Hughes and Bontemps is no less obvious in their short stories and dramatic writings. For *St. Louis Woman* is no mere imitation of the music and dance acts associated with the Negro in the theater in the early years of this century. And when we consider Hughes's *Black Nativity, Jerico-Jim Crow* and *Gospel Glow* the freshness of his artistic imagination was recognized by the large audiences who witnessed them. *The Panther and the Lash* (1967) and *The Prodigal Son* (1965) of Langston Hughes and the revival of Bontemps's powerful stories of the deep South he had known in the 1930s, *The Old South,* (1973) as well as their several efforts to bring to light and publish the poems and stories of young (and often unknown) authors *are* testaments to their extraordinary

---

3. Jones, *Home,* p. 114.

vitality. There is no decline in their vigorous support of the literary life. Both men wrote until a few days before their deaths and left behind enough projects to engage several active men of letters.

It is not too much to say that the careers of Langston Hughes and Arna Bontemps affected the total American consciousness. For not only did they produce a body of literature which interprets and ennobles the Afro-American experience, they infused a sense of unity, pride and richness into the culture. They created a myth, a spiritual heritage for their posterity. Both men are at last attracting some of the critical attention they deserve. This is especially true of Langston Hughes about whom several important works have been or are being written. Scholars like Arthur P. Davis and Saunders Redding led the way. They have been followed by James Emanuel, Richard Barksdale, Faith Berry, Darwin Turner, Ronald Baxter Miller and others.

These letters exchanged between friends and fellow artists are a valuable gift. Their lives—with all their varied works in every genre—we shall cherish more steadfastly with each passing day. For in everything they left us they echoed that other early patriarch, Alexander Crummell: "Our song, our toil, our cheer and warning have been given to this nation in blood-brotherhood."[4]

4. Quoted in Du Bois, *Souls,* p. XI.

CHRONOLOGY
for Arna Bontemps and Langston Hughes

1902   February 1, born: James Mercer Langston Hughes in Joplin, Missouri
       October 13, born: Arna Wendell Bontemps in Alexandria, Louisiana
1921   "The Negro Speaks of Rivers" by Hughes appears in *Crisis*
1924   Hughes and Bontemps meet in August in New York (Bontemps A.B., Pacific
       Union College, 1924)
1925   Hughes wins the *Opportunity* Poetry Prize
1926   Langston Hughes's *The Weary Blues;* Arna Bontemps marries Alberta Johnson;
       Alexander Pushkin Poetry prize to Bontemps
1927   Hughes, *Fine Clothes to the Jew;* Intercollegiate Poetry Award to Hughes
1928   Claude McKay, *Home to Harlem*
1929   Langston Hughes: A.B. Lincoln University, Pa.
1930   Hughes, *Not Without Laughter* (novel, Knopf)
1931   Hughes, *Dear Lovely Death, The Negro Mother* (poems); Arna Bontemps, *God
       Sends Sunday* (novel, Harcourt Brace)
1932   Hughes and Bontemps, *Popo and Fifina: Children of Haiti* (juvenile)
       Hughes, *Scottsboro Limited* (a play and four poems)
       Hughes, *The Dream Keeper* (poems, Knopf)
1933   First Scottsboro Trials
1934   Hughes, *Ways of White Folks* (stories, Knopf); Bontemps, *You Can't Pet a Possum*
1935   Hughes, *Mulatto* (first play, produced at Vanderbilt Theater, N.Y.);
       Hughes's Guggenheim Fellowship Award; Bontemps returns to Chicago
1936   Arna Bontemps's Fellowship Award; Bontemps studies at Graduate Library
       School, University of Chicago
       Bontemps, *Black Thunder* (novel, Macmillan)
1937   Bontemps, *Sad-Faced Boy* (juvenile)
1938   Bontemps: Rosenwald Fellowship for creative writing and travel in Caribbean
1939   Bontemps, *Drums at Dusk* (novel)
1940   Hughes, *The Big Sea* (autobiography, Hill and Wang)
1941   Bontemps, *Chariot in the Sky* (juvenile, Winston); Bontemps, *W.C. Handy Father
       of the Blues*
1941   Hughes: Rosenwald Fund Fellowship; Bontemps, *Golden Slippers* (poems, Harper)
1942   Hughes, *Shakespeare in Harlem* (poem)
1942   Bontemps (with Jack Conroy), *Fast Sooner Hound* (juvenile, Houghton, Mifflin)
       Bontemps (with Jack Conroy), *The Wonderful Sign Painter* (juvenile)
       Bontemps (with Jack Conroy), *Sam Patch, The High, Wide and Handsome Jumper*
       (juvenile)
1943   Hughes, *Freedom's Plow;* Hughes, *Jim Crow's Last Stand*
1943   Bontemps becomes Librarian at Fisk
1944   Hughes, *Lament for Dark Peoples* (Holland)
1945   Bontemps (with Jack Conroy), *They Seek a City* (history, Doubleday)
1945   Bontemps, *We Have Tomorrow* (history, Houghton, Mifflin)
1946   Bontemps (with Countee Cullen), *St. Louis Woman* (play, musical); *Slappy Hooper*
       (with Conroy)

1947	Hughes Visiting Professor in Creative Writing, Atlanta University
	Hughes, *Fields of Wonder* (Knopf)
	Hughes: American Academy of Arts and Letters Grant
1948	Bontemps, *Story of the Negro* (history, Knopf)
1949	Hughes, *One Way Ticket* (poems, Knopf); Bontemps, *Free and Easy* (play)
	Hughes and Bontemps, *Poetry of the Negro* (anthology, Doubleday)
1950	Hughes, *Simple Speaks His Mind* (novel, Simon and Schuster); Bontemps gets Guggenheim Foundation Award
1951	Hughes, *Montage of a Dream Deferred* (poems, Holt)
1952	Hughes, *Laughing to Keep From Crying* (stories, Holt)
1953	Hughes, *Simple Takes a Wife* (novel, Simon and Schuster)
1954	Bontemps, *Story of George Washington Carver* (biog. juvenile, Grosset)
	Hughes, *Famous American Negroes* (juvenile, Dodd, Mead)
1955	Hughes, *Famous Negro Music Makers* (juvenile, Dodd, Mead)
1955	Bontemps, *Lonesome Boy* (juvenile, Houghton Mifflin)
1956	Hughes, *I Wonder As I Wander* (autobiography, Rinehart)
	Hughes (with Milton Meltzer), *A Pictorial History of the Negro in America* (Crown)
1957	Hughes, *Simple Stakes a Claim* (novel, Rinehart)
1958	Hughes, *Tambourines to Glory* (novel, John Day)
	Hughes and Bontemps, *Book of Negro Folklore* (anthology, Dodd, Mead)
	Hughes, *Famous Negro Heroes of America* (juvenile, Dodd, Mead)
	Hughes, *Langston Hughes Reader* (George Braziller)
1959	Hughes, *Selected Poems of Langston Hughes* (Knopf)
	Bontemps, *Frederick Douglass: Slave, Fighter, Freeman* (Knopf)
1960	Bontemps at Makerere College, Uganda, Africa
1961	Hughes, *Ask Your Mama: 12 Moods for Jazz* (poems, Knopf); Bontemps, *100 Years of Negro Freedom* (history, Dodd, Mead)
1962	Hughes, *Fight for Freedom: The Story of the NAACP* (history, W.W. Norton)
1963	Hughes, *Five Plays* by Langston Hughes (ed. by W. Smalley, Indiana University Press)
	Hughes (ed.), *Poems from Black Africa* (anthology, Indiana University Press)
	Hughes, *Something in Common and Other Stories* (Hill and Wang)
1963	Bontemps, *American Negro Poetry* (anthology); Bontemps, *Personals* (poems, London: Breman)
1964	Hughes (ed.), *New Negro Poets: U.S.A.* (anthology, Indiana University Press)
	Hughes at writers conference in Europe
	Bontemps, *Famous Negro Athletes* (juvenile, Dodd, Mead)
1965	Hughes, *Simple's Uncle Sam* (novel, Hill and Wang)
1966	Bontemps Professor of English, University of Illinois
	Bontemps (with Jack Conroy), *Anyplace But Here* (updating of *They Seek a City*)
	Hughes (ed.), *Book of Negro Humor,* Dodd, Mead
1967	Hughes, *The Panther and the Lash: Poems for Our Times* (Knopf)
	Hughes (with Milton Meltzer), *Black Magic: A Pictorial History of the Negro in America* (Prentice-Hall)
	Hughes (ed.), *The Best Short Stories by Negro Writers* (anthology, Little, Brown)
	Death of Langston Hughes
1969	Bontemps (ed.), *Hold Fast to Dreams: Poems Old and New* (anthology, Follett)
	Bontemps (ed.), *Great Slave Narratives;* Bontemps at Yale: Professor and Curator JWJ Collection
1971	Bontemps, *Free at Last: Life of Frederick Douglass* (biography, Dodd, Mead)
1972	Bontemps (ed.), *The Harlem Renaissance Remembered: Essays* (Dodd, Mead)
1973	Bontemps, *The Old South: Stories* (Dodd, Mead)
	Death of Arna Bontemps

CHRONOLOGICAL TABLE
of Afro-American Affairs

1900   Du Bois's London Conference of African and New World Intellectuals; Negro Population: 8,833,994 (11.6%); Chesnutt, *The House Behind the Cedars;* Dunbar, *The Love of Landry, The Strength of Gideon;* Washington, *Up from Slavery,* begins in the *Outlook; The Chicago Defender* founded; first meeting of the National Negro Business League, Boston.

1901   Monroe Trotter founds the *Boston Guardian;* Whitman, "The Octoroon"; Chesnutt, *The Marrow of Tradition;* Dunbar, *The Fanatics.*

1902   Dunbar, Cook, Shipp and Rogers, *In Dahomey;* Dunbar, *The Sport of the Gods;* Virginia adopts "Grandfather Clause."

1903   Du Bois, *The Souls of Black Folk;* Dunbar, *Lyrics of Love and Laughter, In Old Plantation Days;* Countee Cullen born.

1904   Braithwaite, *Lyrics of Life and Love;* Dunbar, *The Heart of Hollow.*

1905   Niagara movement.

1906   James Weldon Johnson consul in Venezuela; Williams and Walker in *Abyssinia;* Allen, *Rhymes, Tales and Rhymed Tales;* Cotter, *Caleb, the Degenerate;* Du Bois, "Litany of Atlanta"; Atlanta riots.

1907   Locke graduates from Harvard, Rhodes scholar for Pennsylvania; Braithwaite, *The House of Falling Leaves;* Williams and Walker in *Bandanna Land.*

1908   Cole and Johnson write and play in *Red Moon.*

1909   Miller, *Race Adjustment;* Founding of the National Association for the Advancement of Colored People.

1910   Negro Population: 9,827,763 (10.7%); Du Bois made director of publicity, editor of *The Crisis* for the N.A.A.C.P.; first edition of Brawley, *The Negro in Literature and Art in the United States.*

1911   National Urban League organized: Du Bois, *The Quest of the Silver Fleece;* Marcus Garvey forms Universal Negro Improvement Ass'n.

1912   McKay comes to America to study at Tuskegee; James Weldon Johnson, *The Autobiography of an Ex-Coloured Man.*

1913   Harriet Tubman dies, Auburn, New York; Dunbar, *Complete Poems.*

1914   N.A.A.C.P. exposes and blocks anti-intermarriage, segregation laws in the District of Columbia, and bill to exclude Negroes from the army and the navy; Cromwell, *The Negro in American History;* W.C. Handy, "St. Louis Blues"; Mamie Smith makes the first blues recording.

1915   Booker T. Washington dies; first Spingarn Medal for achievement presented to E.E. Just; Association for the Study of Negro Life and History founded; J.W. Work, *Folk Songs of the American Negro;* Supreme Court outlaws "Grandfather Clause."

1916   James Weldon Johnson becomes secretary of the N.A.A.C.P.; first issue of the *Journal of Negro History,* Woodson as editor; Locke, *Race Contacts and Interracial Relations.*

1916–1919   Great migration of southern Negroes to northern industrial centers.

1917–1918   367,710 Negroes inducted into the military service; 1400 officers commissioned.

1918   Walter White joins N.A.A.C.P. staff; Miller, *The Appeal to Conscience.*

1919   Washington, Chicago race riots; Pan-African Congress, Paris; Claude McKay's "If We Must Die," in *The Liberator;* Fletcher Henderson's first Roseland Orchestra, first large Negro band to play Broadway.

1920   Negro Population: 10,463,131 (9.9%); "King" Oliver organizes his Creole Jazz Band; Du Bois, *Darkwater.*

1921   C.S. Johnson becomes director of research and publicity for the National Urban League; McKay goes to Russia; Handy, *Loveless Love;* Sissle and Blake, *Shuffle Along;* Gilpin plays *The Emperor Jones;* Benjamin Brawley, *A Social History of the American Negro.*

1922   Garvey's Universal Negro Improvement Association reaching height of its influence; *Shuffle Along* reaches Broadway, first of a series of popular musicals; first edition of Woodson, *The Negro in Our History;* McKay, *Harlem Shadows;* G.D. Johnson, *Bronze.*

1923   *Opportunity: Journal of Negro Life* begins publication, Charles S. Johnson, editor; Toomer, *Cane.*

1924   *Crisis* and *Opportunity* prizes for creative expression announced; Miller, *The Everlasting Stain;* Fauset, *There is Confusion;* Miller and Lyles in *Runnin' Wild;* Du Bois, *The Gift of Black Folk;* Immigration Act excludes blacks of African descent.

1925   Garvey imprisoned; Locke edits Harlem number of the *Survey Graphic, The New Negro;* Johnson and Johnson, *The Book of American Negro Spirituals;* Cullen, *Color;* White, *Fire in the Flint;* Louis Armstrong's "Hot Five" recording.

1926   Florence Mills in *Blackbirds;* Handy and Niles, *Blues;* Jessye, *My Spirituals;* Hughes, *The Weary Blues;* Walrond, *Tropic Death;* C. Van Vechten, *Nigger Heaven.*

1927   Garvey deported; James Weldon Johnson, *God's Trombones;* Hughes, *Fine Clothes to the Jew;* Charles S. Johnson (ed.), *Ebony and Topaz;* Wesley, *Negro Labor in the United States;* Louis Armstrong organizes own band, playing at the Sunset, Chicago; Duke Ellington opens at the Cotton Club, Harlem.

1928   Fisher, *The Walls of Jericho;* McKay, *Home to Harlem;* Du Bois, *Dark Princess;* Fauset, *Plum Bun;* Larsen, *Quicksand.*

1929   Cullen, *The Black Christ;* McKay, *Banjo;* Thurman, *The Blacker the Berry.*

1930   Negro Population: 11,891,143 (7%); James Weldon Johnson, *Saint Peter Relates an Incident* and *Black Manhattan;* Hughes, *Not Without Laughter;* Charles S. Johnson, *The Negro in American Civilization.*

1931   Fauset, *The Chinaberry Tree;* Bontemps, *God Sends Sunday; The Journal of Negro Education* founded; Spero and Harris, *The Black Worker;* first Scottsboro trial.

1932   Defection from the Republican party in the Hoover-Roosevelt campaign; Brown, *Southern Road;* McKay, *Gingertown;* Fisher, *The Conjure Man Dies;* first Negro detective novel.

1933   James Weldon Johnson, *Along This Way;* McKay, *Banana Bottom;* Fauset, *Comedy, American Style.*

1934   Hughes, *The Ways of White Folks;* Charles S. Johnson, *The Shadow of the Plantation;* James Weldon Johnson, *Negro Americans, What Now?.*

1935   Harlem race riots; beginning of the "swing" fad; Davis, *Black Man's Verse;* Hurston, *Mules and Men;* Henderson, *Ollie Miss;* Bontemps, *Black Thunder;* Hughes's *Mulatto* begins longest run enjoyed by play by a Negro.

1936   Brawley, *Paul Laurence Dunbar;* Harris, *The Negro as Capitalist;* Lee, *River George.*

1937   Hurston, *Their Eyes Were Watching God;* Turpin, *These Low Grounds.*

1938   Gaines vs. University of Missouri provides for equal educational facilities; Brawley, *Negro Builders and Heroes;* Wright, *Uncle Tom's Children.*

1939   Turpin, *O Canaan!;* Frazier, *The Negro Family in the United States;* Du Bois, *Black Folk, Then and Now.*

496

1940   *Phylon* established with Du Bois as editor; American Youth Commission volumes; *The Negro in Virginia;* Wright, *Native Son;* Du Bois, *Dusk of Dawn;* Hughes, *The Big Sea;* McKay, *Harlem; Negro Metropolis.*

1941   Mitchell vs. Interstate Commerce Commission, Illinois Central Railroad, Chicago, Rock Island and Pacific Railway Company; Locke, *The Negro in Art;* Richard Wright, *Twelve Million Black Voices;* Attaway, *Blood on the Forge;* Davis and Gardiner, *Deep South;* A. Philip Randolph's March on Washington Movement vs. Discrimination in Defense Industries and the Armed Forces; Roosevelt's Executive Order No. 8802 on Fair Employment Practices, June 25, 1941; Dorie Miller mans machine gun at Pearl Harbor.

1942   Justice Department threatens suit vs. black newspapers for sedition; founding of CORE.

1943–45   Abolition of Jim Crow in Armed Forces.

1945   End of World War II.

1947   Jackie Robinson enters Major League baseball.

1950   Gwendolyn Brooks's *Annie Allen,* a book of poems, receives The Pulitzer Prize; Edith Sampson alternate delegate to U.N.

1952   Ralph Ellison's *Invisible Man* receives National Book Award.

1954   Brown vs. The Board of Education, The Supreme Court rules school segregation unconstitutional.

1955–56   The Montgomery, Alabama, Bus Boycott led by Martin Luther King, Jr.

1957   Martin Luther King establishes The Southern Christian Leadership Conference; Eisenhower sends troops to Little Rock, Ark. to enforce desegregation.

1960   Founding of the American Society of African Cultures; sit-ins against segregation by students in Greensboro, North Carolina.

1961   The Congress of Racial Equality (CORE) challenges Jim Crow in travel.

1961–64   The Students' Nonviolent Coordinating Committee active.

1962   Robert F. Williams of Monroe, North Carolina publishes *Negroes with Guns* advocating self-defense by Negroes.

1963   The March on Washington; murder of Medgar Evers in Mississippi; rise of Black Muslims to over 50,000 members; Rise of Black Power Movement.

1964   Martin Luther King, Jr. awarded Nobel Peace Prize; Congressional action on civil rights legislation; stepped-up voter registration in the South; Jones, *The Dead Lecturer;* riot in Harlem.

1965   Murder of Malcolm X; 3 civil rights volunteers murdered in Mississippi; rise of The Black Panthers; King marches from Selma, Ala.

1966   James Meredith shot on voting rights pilgrimage.

1967   Widespread race riots in American cities.

1968   Assassination of Martin Luther King, Jr. in Memphis, Tennessee; Eldridge Cleaver publishes *Soul on Ice;* Riot Commission Report; Nixon elected; Black studies in universities.

1970   Black Panther Trial in New Haven, Conn.; arrest of H. Rap Brown; Huey Newton's conviction overturned; Kenneth Gibson elected mayor of Newark.

1971   Census reports black urban population increases by 3 million; white urban population decreases by 2.5 million; 1,860 blacks in political office; Attica prison riot.

1972   National Black Political Convention in Gary, Indiana; Angela Davis trial; Frank Wills, black security guard detects Watergate plot; McGovern gets Democratic nomination; Shirley Chisholm runs for president.

1973   Paul Robeson honored on 75th birthday at Rutgers; A.T.&T. settles suit to pay back wages to women and minority members; number of black elected officials rises to 2,991.

FACSIMILE LETTERS
of Arna Bontemps and Langston Hughes

Dec. 1, '60

Dear Tom —

[handwritten letter, largely illegible]

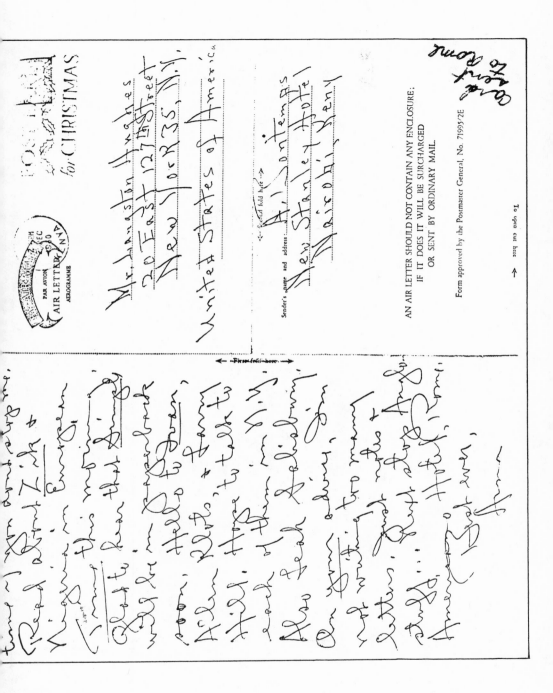

POSTED for CHRISTMAS

AIR LETTER
PAR AVION
AEROGRAMME

Mr. Langston Hughes
20 East 127th Street
New York 35, N.Y.
United States of America

← Second fold here →

Sender's name and address.... Al Montemas
New Stanley Hotel
Nairobi, Kenya

AN AIR LETTER SHOULD NOT CONTAIN ANY ENCLOSURE:
IF IT DOES IT WILL BE SURCHARGED
OR SENT BY ORDINARY MAIL.

Form approved by the Postmaster General. No. 71995/2E

To open cut here ↑

← First fold here →

Yaddo, 7/30/43.

Dear Arna,

I seem to have my mind set on being a song writer. It must be my fate. There is no sense in it otherwise — with not a record being made in the land!

"For This We Fight," the Garden pageant, was produced with great eclát at Bennett College — outdoors before 2000 people. (It's paid better so far than _both_ those shows we did for the Chicago Exposition.)

Did I tell you Jimmy Davis graduated as a Warrant Officer from the Army Music School? And now

from the colored sailors on a Pacific battleship.

has a band of his own in Virginia. Three colored. He was top of cullud list — 98. They even segregate the grades — so he doesn't know how he stood in reference to the whole class. (WAACS and colored last.)

Next week all we Yaddoites are going over to Katherine Ann Porter's farm for a weiner roast. The refugees here are overjoyed at the fall of Mussolini. Me joyed, too! (But not over.)

Say, you promised to send me a final script of "POPO." Where is it?

I'm booked for Detroit again in the spring. Columbia U and Montreal Forum this winter.

Lang

Claude McKay is ill in Harlem Hospital. Stroke. Won't see him till I'm thru.

De-lighted your play is done and good!

INDEX

510

511

512

513

514

515

517